INTERCULTURAL COMMUNICATION IN CONTEXTS

THIRD EDITION

Judith N. Martin

Thomas K. Nakayama

Arizona State University

McGraw Hill

Boston   Burr Ridge, IL   Dubuque, IA   Madison, WI   New York
San Francisco   St. Louis   Bangkok   Bogotá   Caracas   Kuala Lumpur
Lisbon   London   Madrid   Mexico City   Milan   Montreal   New Delhi
Santiago   Seoul   Singapore   Sydney   Taipei   Toronto

The McGraw·Hill Companies

Mc Graw Hill Higher Education

INTERCULTURAL COMMUNICATION IN CONTEXTS, THIRD EDITION
Published by McGraw-Hill, a business unit of The McGraw-Hill Companies, Inc., 1221 Avenue of
the Americas, New York, NY 10020. Copyright © 2004 by The McGraw-Hill Companies, Inc. All
rights reserved. Previous editions © 2000, 1997 by Mayfield Publishing Company. No part of this
publication may be reproduced or distributed in any form or by any means, or stored in a database
or retrieval system, without the prior written consent of The McGraw-Hill Companies, Inc., including, but not limited to, any network or other electronic storage or transmission, or broadcast
for distance learning.

Some ancillaries, including electronic and print components, may not be available to customers
outside the United States.

2 3 4 5 6 7 8 9 0 DOC/DOC 0 9 8 7 6 5 4

Vice president and editor-in-chief: *Thalia Dorwick*
Publisher: *Phillip Butcher*
Sponsoring editor: *Nanette Kauffman Giles*
Development editors: *Gabrielle Goodman, Nancy Lubars*
Marketing manager: *Sally Constable*
Production services manager: *Jennifer Mills*
Production service: *Publishing Support Services*
Manuscript editor: *Tom Briggs*
Art director: *Jeanne M. Schreiber*
Design manager: *Violeta Diaz*
Cover designer: *Yvo Riezebos*
Interior designer: *Susan Breitbard*
Art manager: *Robin Mouat*
Photo researcher: *Stephen Forsling*
Illustrator: *Lotus Art*
Production supervisor: *Rich DeVitto*

The text was set in 10/12 Janson Text by G & S Typesetters and printed on acid-free 45# New Era
Matte by RR Donnelly, Crawfordsville.

The credits for this book begin on page C-1, a continuation of the copyright page.

Library of Congress Cataloging-in-Publication Data
Martin, Judith N.
    Intercultural communication in contexts / Judith N. Martin, Thomas K. Nakayama.—3rd ed.
        p. cm.
    Previous eds. published by Mountain View, Calif. : Mayfield.
    Includes bibliographical references and index.
    ISBN 0-7674-3013-1
    1. Intercultural communication.   I. Nakayama, Thomas K.   II. Title.

HM1211.M373 2003
303.48′2—dc21
                                                                                2003046374

www.mhhe.com

About the Authors

The two authors of this book come to intercultural communication from very different backgrounds and very different research traditions. Yet we believe that these differences offer a unique approach to thinking about intercultural communication. We briefly introduce ourselves here, but we hope that by the end of the book you will have a much more complete understanding of who we are.

Judith Martin grew up in Mennonite communities, primarily in Delaware and Pennsylvania. She has studied at the Université de Grenoble in France and has taught in Algeria. She received her doctorate at the Pennsylvania State University. By background and training, she is a social scientist who has focused on intercultural communication on an interpersonal level and has studied how people's communication is affected as they move or sojourn between international locations. She has taught at the State University of New York at Oswego, the University of Minnesota, the University of New Mexico, and Arizona State University. She enjoys gardening, going to Mexico, and hosting annual Academy Awards parties, and she does not miss the harsh Midwestern winters.

Tom Nakayama grew up mainly in Georgia, at a time when the Asian American presence was much less than it is now. He has studied at the Université de Paris and various universities in the United States. He received his doctorate from the University of Iowa. By background and training, he is a critical rhetorician who views intercultural communication in a social context. He has taught at the California State University at San Bernardino and Arizona State University. He is a voracious reader and owns more books than any other faculty member in his department. He watches TV—especially baseball games—and lifts weights. Living in the West now, he misses springtime in the South.

The authors' very different life stories and research programs came together at Arizona State University. We have each learned much about intercultural communication through our own experiences, as well as through our intellectual pursuits. Judith has a well-established record of social science approaches to intercultural communication. Tom, in contrast, has taken a nontraditional approach to understanding intercultural communication by emphasizing critical perspectives. We believe that these differences in our lives and in our research offer complementary ways of understanding intercultural communication.

Since the early 1990s, we have engaged in many different dialogues about intercultural communication—focusing on our experiences, thoughts, ideas, and analyses—which led us to think about writing this textbook. But our interest was not primarily sparked by these dialogues; rather, it was our overall interest in improving intercultural relations that motivated us. We believe that communication is an important arena for improving those relations. By helping people become more aware as intercultural communicators, we hope to make this a better world for all of us.

Brief Contents

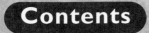

Contents

Preface

THE IMPORTANCE OF INTERCULTURAL COMMUNICATION IN A CHANGING WORLD

With the September 11, 2001, attacks on the World Trade Center and the Pentagon, the face of intercultural relations radically changed for most Americans. Intercultural conflicts that may once have seemed distant or peripheral to our lives now confront us with undeniable immediacy. In this climate, the study of intercultural communication takes on special significance, offering tools to help us grapple with questions about racial profiling, hate crimes, religious differences, and other, related issues that have intensified since September 11. Recognizing that these circumstances call for more advances in the field, intercultural communication scholars are turning their attention to these questions and conflicts.

> The study of intercultural communication offers tools to help us grapple with questions about racial profiling, hate crimes, religious differences, and other, related issues that have intensified since September 11, 2001.

Since we wrote the second edition of this book, the field of intercultural communication has grown and changed at a rapid pace, almost as quickly as our world has been changing. Those who study, teach, and conduct research in intercultural communication are faced with an increasing number of challenges and difficult questions to address: Is it enough to identify differences among people? Are we actually reinforcing stereotypes in emphasizing differences? Is there a way to understand the dynamics of intercultural communication without resorting to lists of instructions? Don't we have to talk about the broader social, political, and historical contexts when we teach intercultural communication?

Such questions are driven by rapidly changing cultural dynamics—both within the United States and abroad. On the one hand, the continued expansion of the European Union, NATO, and the African Union (formerly the Organization of African States) reflects movement toward unity. Also, technological advances have increased our ability to communicate with diverse cultural groups. On the other hand, events such as the continuing conflicts between India and Pakistan over Kashmir, disputes between Northern Ireland and Great Britain, and the war with Iraq illustrate ongoing intergroup conflict. These extremes demonstrate the dynamic nature of culture and communication.

We wrote this book in part to address questions and issues such as these. Although the foundation of intercultural communication theory and research has

In this third edition, we have further extended a dialectical approach that encourages students to think critically about intercultural phenomena as seen from three perspectives: the traditional social-psychological approach, the interpretive approach, and the more recent critical approach.

always been interdisciplinary, the field is now informed by three identifiable and competing *paradigms*, or ways of thinking. In this book, we attempt to integrate three different research approaches: (1) the traditional social-psychological approach, which emphasizes cultural differences and the ways in which these differences influence communication, (2) the interpretive approach, which focuses on communication in context, and (3) the more recent critical approach, which underscores the importance of power and historical context in understanding intercultural communication.

We believe that each of these approaches has important contributions to make to the understanding of intercultural communication and that they operate in interconnected and sometimes contradictory ways. In this third edition, we have further extended a *dialectical* approach that encourages students to think critically about intercultural phenomena as seen from these three perspectives.

Throughout this book, we acknowledge that there are no easy solutions to the difficult challenges of intercultural communication. Sometimes our discussions raise more questions than they answer—which we believe is perfectly reasonable at this point in time. Not only is the field of intercultural communication changing, but the relationship between culture and communication is—and probably always will be—complex and dynamic. We live in a rapidly changing world in which intercultural contact will continue to increase, creating a heightened potential for both conflict and cooperation. This book provides the tools needed to think about intercultural communication as a way of understanding the challenges and recognizing the benefits of living in a multicultural world.

We acknowledge that there are no easy solutions to the difficult challenges of intercultural communication.

SIGNATURE FEATURES OF THE BOOK

Students usually come to the field of intercultural communication with some knowledge about many different cultural groups, including their own. Their understanding is often based on observations via television, movies, the Internet, books, personal experiences, news media, and more. But many students have a difficult time assimilating information that does not readily fit into their preexisting knowledge base. In this book, we move students gradually to the notion of a *dialectical framework* for thinking about cultural issues. That is, we show that knowledge can be acquired in many different ways—through social scientific studies, personal experience, media reports, and so on—but these differing forms of knowledge need to be seen dynamically and in relation to each

This book provides the tools needed to think about intercultural communication as a way of understanding the challenges and recognizing the benefits of living in a multicultural world.

other. We offer students a number of ways to begin thinking critically about intercultural communication in a dialectical manner. These include:

- An explicit discussion of differing research approaches to intercultural communication, focusing on both strengths and limitations of each

- Ongoing attention to history, popular culture, and identity as important factors in understanding intercultural communication

- "Student Voices" boxes in which students relate their own experiences and share their thoughts about various intercultural communication issues

- "Point of View" boxes in which diverse viewpoints from news media, research studies, and other public forums are presented

- Incorporation of the authors' own personal experiences to highlight particular aspects of intercultural communication

> We offer students a number of ways to begin thinking critically about intercultural communication in a dialectical manner.

NEW TO THE THIRD EDITION

To reflect the increasing influence of modern technology in our multicultural world, we have **expanded our coverage of technology and intercultural communication.** For example, in Chapter 1, we discuss how increased mediated contact with people who are similar and different can provide communities of support. We also discuss the cultural issues surrounding "identity tourism" whereby people take on false identities in communicating on the Internet.

Our **increased discussion of the implications of religious identity** in Chapters 5 and 11 is prompted by awareness of the important role religion plays in intercultural communication. For example, in Chapter 5, we note that religion often is conflated with ethnicity and/or race, making it difficult to view religious identity simply in terms of belonging to a particular religion. In Chapter 11, we explore the role religion can play in exacerbating and/or resolving intercultural conflicts.

The **addition of new content concerning the September 11, 2001, terrorist attacks** acknowledges the importance of these events in intercultural communication. For example, in Chapter 2, we use the attacks of 9/11 as a case study to show how this one intercultural event can be viewed and analyzed from three very different paradigmatic perspectives. And in Chapter 5, we explore examples of stereotyping in the aftermath of the attacks.

We have also **increased coverage of the important topics of stereotyping and prejudice.** For example, in Chapter 5, we note that prejudices arise from normal cognitive functioning, and we identify and describe ways in which prejudices serve us in everyday life—not to excuse prejudice but to explain why it is so widespread.

Reflecting recent global demographics, we have **expanded our discussion of migration and intercultural communication.** For example, in Chapter 8, we explore the impact and trends concerning worldwide migration and discuss how tensions between old and newly arrived immigrants can lead to intercultural challenges both in the United States and abroad. In Chapter 5, we note the impact of migration in light of the increasing numbers of multicultural families and relationships.

Acknowledging the increasing interest in understanding and resolving intercultural conflict, we have added **new material on mediation and intercultural communication.** For example, in Chapter 11, we identify and describe alternative approaches to resolving conflict used by indigenous peoples in many societies and what these strategies have to offer in helping us understand and resolve contemporary conflicts. In Chapter 12, we continue the focus on resolving intercultural conflicts and developing productive relationships, even in the face of very difficult cross-cultural situations, such as war, oppression, and genocide. We note the potential power of dialogue, forgiveness, and transformation as strategies for meeting these incredible challenges.

We have also added **new content on cross-cultural notions of conflict.** For example, in Chapter 11, we identify characteristics that distinguish high- and low-conflict societies and explore reasons some societies have high levels of intercultural conflict and others do not.

Finally, we have provided **updated references and examples.** For instance, our explorations of intercultural communication take into consideration recent developments in the former Yugoslovia and the former Soviet Union, as well as the events surrounding the 9/11 attacks and the subsequent wars in Afghanistan and Iraq.

SUPPLEMENTAL RESOURCES

The Online Learning Center, at www.mhhe.com/martinnakayama, provides interactive resources to address the needs of a variety of teaching and learning styles. For every chapter, students and instructors can access chapter outlines, sample quizzes with feedback, crossword puzzles using key terms, and Internet activities. For instructors specifically, the Online Learning Center offers an online *Instructor's Resource Manual* with sample syllabi, discussion questions, and pedagogical tips designed to help teach the course in general and to help meet the special challenges arising from the controversial nature of much of the material.

In addition, a computerized *Test Bank* that allows instructors to edit and add their own questions is available in both Windows and Macintosh formats.

CHAPTER-BY-CHAPTER OVERVIEW OF THE BOOK

Intercultural Communication in Contexts is organized into three parts: Part I, "Foundations of Intercultural Communication"; Part II, "Intercultural Communication Processes"; and Part III, "Intercultural Communication Applications."

Part I establishes the history of the field and presents various approaches to this area of study, including our own. We begin Chapter 1 with a focus on the dynamics of social life and global conditions as a rationale for the study of intercultural communication. We introduce ethics in this chapter to illustrate its centrality to any discussion of intercultural interaction. **In this edition, we have expanded our discussion of the impact of technology on intercultural communication.**

In Chapter 2, we introduce the history of intercultural communication as an area of study and present the three paradigms that inform our knowledge about intercultural interactions. We also introduce the notion of a dialectical approach so that students can begin to make connections and form relationships among the paradigms. **We utilize the example of the 9/11 attacks to help explicate the three paradigms.**

In Chapter 3, we focus on four basic intercultural communication components: culture, communication, context, and power. **In this edition, we have extended our discussion of conceptualizations of culture and our critique of Hofstede's value framework as a caution against generalizing and stereotyping cultural groups based on their value orientations.**

Chapter 4 focuses on the importance of historical forces in shaping contemporary intercultural interaction. **We have expanded our discussion of the United States internment camps for Japanese Americans during World War II and placed more emphasis on history textbooks as an important arena for cultural identity.**

Part II establishes the factors that contribute to the dynamics of intercultural communication: identity, language, and nonverbal codes. Chapter 5 on identity is enhanced by **a new section on cross-cultural notions of identity.** We also have **extended the coverage of religious identity and multicultural identity, as well as the concepts of prejudice, stereotyping, and "isms."**

Chapter 6 addresses language issues and **includes new sections on code switching and globalization and expanded coverage of interlanguage.**

Chapter 7 focuses on nonverbal codes and cultural spaces **and includes new examples of postmodern cultural spaces.**

Part III helps students apply the material on intercultural communication presented in the first two parts. Chapter 8 addresses intercultural transitions. **We have extended our discussions of the role of religion in adaptation and "living on the border." We have also further developed our discussion of the tensions between old and new migrants and added more information on international migration and its effects on intercultural communication.**

In Chapter 9, we focus on popular and folk cultures and their impact on intercultural communication. **We have added new, more recent examples of popular culture resistance and English language dominance, and we present Stuart Hall's encoding/decoding model to help students conceptualize the consumption of popular culture.**

Chapter 10 explores intercultural relationships. **We have added a new section on cross-cultural differences in notions of friendship and have expanded our discussions of intercultural dating and marriage, as well as gay** and lesbian permanent relationships. We have also extended our discussion of intercultural relationship dialectics.

In Chapter 11, we focus on intercultural conflicts. **We have added a section on cross-cultural differences in conflict orientations as well as new material on mediation. We have also revised the section on gender, ethnicity, and conflict.**

Finally, in Chapter 12, we turn to the outlook for intercultural communication. We have developed our discussion on motivation and the difficulties in achieving effective intercultural communication. **We have also added new notions of dialogue, forgiveness, and transformation as key parts of "Applying Intercultural Knowledge."**

ACKNOWLEDGMENTS

The random convergence of the two authors in time and place led to the creation of this textbook. We both found ourselves at Arizona State University in the early 1990s. Over the course of several years, we discussed and analyzed the multiple approaches to intercultural communication. Much of this discussion was facilitated by the ASU Department of Communication's "culture and communication" theme. Department faculty met to discuss research and pedagogical issues relevant to the study of communication and culture; we also reflected on our own notions of what constitutes intercultural communication. This often meant reliving many of our intercultural experiences and sharing them with our colleagues.

Above all, we must recognize the patience and insights of senior sponsoring editor Nanette Kauffman Giles, who helped us in the transition from Mayfield to McGraw-Hill. Thanks also to developmental editors Nancy Lubars and Gabrielle Goodman, who skillfully guided us through the often complex and challenging tasks of publishing a new edition. And we want to acknowledge the fine work of media producers Christie Ling and Jessica Bodie, marketing manager Sally Constable, project managers Jen Mills and Vicki Moran, designer Susan Breitbard, photo researcher Stephen Forsling, and supplement producer Marc Mattson. In addition, we want to thank all the reviewers of this and previous editions of *Intercultural Communication in Contexts*, whose comments and careful readings were enormously helpful. They are:

First Edition Reviewers

Rosita D. Albert, *University of Minnesota*

Carlos G. Aleman, *University of Illinois, Chicago*

Deborah Cai, *University of Maryland*

Gail Campbell, *University of Colorado, Denver*

Ling Chen, *University of Oklahoma*

Alberto Gonzalez, *Bowling Green State University*

Bradford 'J' Hall, *University of New Mexico*

Mark Lawrence McPhail, *University of Utah*

Richard Morris, *Northern Illinois University*

Catherine T. Motoyama, *College of San Mateo*

Gordon Nakagawa, *California State University, Northridge*

Joyce M. Ngoh, *Marist College*

Nancy L. Street, *Bridgewater State College*

Erika Vora, *St. Cloud State University*

Lee B. Winet, *State University of New York, Oswego*

Gust A. Yep, *San Francisco State University*

Second Edition Reviewers

Eric Akoi, *Colorado State University*

Jeanne Barone, *Indiana/Purdue University at Fort Wayne*

Wendy Chung, *Rider University*

Ellen Shide Crannell, *West Valley College*

Patricia Holmes, *University of Missouri*

Madeline Keaveney, *California State University, Chico*

Mark Neumann, *University of South Florida*

Margaret Pryately, *St. Cloud State University*

Kara Shultz, *Bloomsberg University*

Third Edition Reviewers

Marguerite Arai, *University of Colorado at Colorado Springs*

Rona Halualani, *San José State University*

Piper McNulty, *De Anza College*

Karla Scott, *St. Louis University*

Candace Thomas-Maddox, *Ohio University, Lancaster*

Susan Walsh, *Southern Oregon University*

Jennifer Willis-Rivera, *Southern Illinois State University*

Our colleagues and students provided invaluable assistance. Thanks to our colleagues for their ongoing moral support and intellectual challenges to our thinking. Thanks to graduate student Tamie Kanata for her tireless foraging for interesting examples to make our writing come alive and for collecting material for the "Student Voices." Thanks also to graduate student Hsueh-hua Chen for her very patient and competent tracking of copyright permissions and help with the Glossary. And thanks to Sara DeTurk and Hsueh-hua Chen for developing terrific material and activities in writing the online *Instructor's Resource Manual* and *Test Bank*. And, of course, we owe thanks to our undergraduate students, who continue to challenge us to think about intercultural communication in ways that make sense to their lives.

We thank our families and friends for allowing us long absences and silences as we directed our energies toward the completion of this book. We want to acknowledge both Ronald Chaldu and David L. Karbonski, who did not "go nuclear" despite being saddled with more than their share of redirected burdens.

Our international experiences have enriched our understanding of intercultural communication theories and concepts. We thank all of the following people for helping us with these experiences: Tommy and Kazuko Nakayama; Michel Dion and Eliana Sampaïo of Strasbourg, France; Jean-Louis Sauvage and Pol Thiry of the Université de Mons-Hainaut, Belgium; Christina Kalinowska and the Café "Le Ropieur" in Mons, Belgium; Jerzy, Alicja, Marek, and Jolanta Drzewieccy of Bedzin, Poland; and Margaret Nicholson of the Commission for Educational Exchange between Belgium, Luxembourg, and the United States. Some research in this book was made possible by a scholarship from the Fulbright Commission. We would also like to thank Barbara Lafford and the ASU International Programs Office; the staff and instructors at El Centro Bilingue in Cuernevaca, Mexico; and a wonderful host family—*la familia* Perez-Franzoni (Carmen, Chucho, Victor, Laura, Concha, and Lola). In addition, we thank the countless others we have met in cafés, train stations, bars, and conference rooms, if only for a moment of international intercultural interaction.

Other people helped us understand intercultural communication closer to home, especially the staff and students at the Guadalupe Learning Center at South Mountain Community College, and also Dr. Amalia Villegas, Laura Laguna, Felipa Montiel, Cruzita Mori, and Lucia Madril.

In spirit and conceptualization, our book spans the centuries and crosses many continents. It has been shaped by the many people we have read about and encountered. It is to these guiding and inspiring individuals—some of whom we had the good fortune to meet and some of whom we will never encounter—that we dedicate this book. It is our hope that their spirit of curiosity, openness, and understanding will be reflected in the pages that follow.

To the Student

Many textbooks emphasize in their introductions how you should use the text. In contrast, we begin this book by introducing ourselves and our interests in intercultural communication. There are many ways to think about intercultural interactions. One way to learn more about intercultural experiences is to engage in dialogue with others on this topic. Ideally, we would like to begin a dialogue with you about some of the ways to think about intercultural communication. Learning about intercultural communication is not about learning a finite set of skills, terms, and theories. It is about learning to think about cultural realities in multiple ways. Unfortunately, it is not possible for us to engage in dialogues with our readers.

Instead, we strive to lay out a number of issues to think about regarding intercultural communication. In reflecting on these issues in your own interactions and talking about them with others, you will be well on your way to becoming both a better intercultural communicator and a better analyst of intercultural interactions. There is no endpoint from which we can say that we have learned all there is to know. Learning about communication is a lifelong process that involves experiences and analysis. We hope this book will generate many dialogues that will help you come to a greater understanding of different cultures and peoples and a greater appreciation for the complexity of intercultural communication.

COMMUNICATING IN A DYNAMIC, MULTICULTURAL WORLD

We live in rapidly changing times. Although no one can foresee the future, we believe that changes are increasing the imperative for intercultural learning. In Chapter 1, you will learn more about some of these changes and their influence on intercultural communication.

You stand at the beginning of a textbook journey into intercultural communication. At this point, you might take stock of who you are, what your intercultural communication experiences have been, how you responded in those situations, and how you tend to think about those experiences. Some people respond to intercultural situations with amusement, curiosity, or interest; others may respond with hostility, anger, or fear. It is important to reflect on your experiences and to identify how you respond and what those reactions mean.

We also think it is helpful to recognize that in many instances people do not want to communicate interculturally. Sometimes people see those who are culturally different as threatening, as forcing them to change. They may believe that such people require more assistance and patience, or they may simply think of them as "different." People bring to intercultural interactions a variety of emotional states and attitudes; further, not everyone wants to communicate interculturally. Because of this dynamic, many people have had negative intercultural experiences that influence subsequent intercultural interactions. Negative experiences can range from simple misunderstandings to physical violence. Although it may be unpleasant to discuss such situations, we believe that it is necessary to do so if we are to understand and improve intercultural interaction.

Intercultural conflict can occur even when the participants do not intentionally provoke it. When we use our own cultural frames in intercultural settings, those hidden assumptions can cause trouble. For example, when renting a small apartment in a private home in Grenoble, France, coauthor Judith Martin invited a number of her U.S. friends who were traveling in Europe to stop by and stay with her. The angry and frustrated response that this drew from her landlady came as a surprise. She told Judith that she would have to pay extra for all of the water they were using, that the apartment was not a motel, and that Judith would have to move out if the practice of having overnight guests continued. Differing notions of privacy and appropriate renter behavior contributed to the conflict. Intercultural experiences are not always fun. Sometimes they are frustrating, confusing, and distressing.

On a more serious level, we might look at "Operation Iraqi Freedom" in the spring of 2003 as yet another example of intercultural communication. The subsequent interpretations of and reactions to that televised event by different communities of people reflect important differences in our society and in the world at large. Although some people in the United States and abroad saw this effort as an attempt to liberate an oppressed people, others viewed it as imperialist aggression on the part of the United States. These differing views highlight the complexity of intercultural communication. We do not come to intercultural interactions as blank slates; instead, we bring our identities and our cultures.

IMPROVING YOUR INTERCULTURAL COMMUNICATION

Although the journey to developing awareness in intercultural communication is an individual one, it is important to recognize the connections we all have to many different aspects of social life. You are, of course, an individual. But you have been influenced by culture. The ways that others regard you and communicate with you are influenced largely by whom they perceive you to be. By enacting cultural characteristics of masculinity or femininity, for example, you may elicit particular reactions from others. Reflect on your social and individual characteristics; consider how these characteristics communicate something about you.

Finally, there is no list of things to do in an intercultural setting. Although prescribed reactions might help you avoid serious faux pas in one setting or culture, such lists are generally too simplistic to get you very far in any culture and may cause serious problems in other cultures. The study of communication is both a science and an art. In this book, we attempt to pull the best of both kinds of knowledge together for you. Because communication does not happen in a vacuum but is integral to the many dynamics that make it possible—economics, politics, technology—the ever-changing character of our world means that it is essential to develop sensitivity and flexibility to change. It also means that you can never stop learning about intercultural communication.

PART I

Foundations of Intercultural Communication

WHY STUDY INTERCULTURAL COMMUNICATION?

THE TECHNOLOGICAL IMPERATIVE
Technology and Human Communication
Mobility and Its Effect on Communication

THE DEMOGRAPHIC IMPERATIVE
Changing U.S. Demographics
Changing Immigration Patterns

THE ECONOMIC IMPERATIVE

THE PEACE IMPERATIVE

THE SELF-AWARENESS IMPERATIVE

THE ETHICAL IMPERATIVE
Relativity Versus Universality
Being Ethical Students of Culture
Changing Through Intercultural Contact

SUMMARY
DISCUSSION QUESTIONS
ACTIVITIES
KEY WORDS
REFERENCES

When I was back home [Kuwait], before I came to the United States to go to college, I knew all about my culture and about my religion. However, I did not really know what other people from the other world [United States] think of Middle Eastern people or Muslims in general. So, what I have witnessed is a lot of discrimination in this country, not only against my race but against other groups. . . . Yet I understand that not all Americans hate us, I met a lot of Americans who are cooperative with me and show me love and are interested to know about my country and culture.

—Mohamad

I have been transformed by intercultural experience every day. I am from a small town in the Midwest. There was little to no diversity. The experience I had that has stood out the most in my life was meeting my boyfriend, Josh. Josh is Jewish; I am a Christian. I did not know very much about Judaism. By getting to know my boyfriend and his family, I have learned a tremendous amount about their culture and their religion. I have learned what Hanukkah is about and have experienced it, just as he has experienced my religion.

—Angela

Both Mohamad's and Angela's experiences point to the benefits and challenges of **intercultural communication.** Through intercultural relationships, we can learn a tremendous amount about other people and their cultures, and about ourselves and our own cultural background. At the same time, there are many challenges. Intercultural communication can also involve barriers like stereotyping and discrimination. And these relationships take place in complex historical and political contexts. Mohamad's experience in the United States is probably more challenging today than it would have been several years ago due to recent political events. An important goal in this book is how to increase your understanding of the dynamics at work in intercultural interaction.

This book will expose you to the variety of approaches we use to study intercultural communication. We also weave into the text our personal stories to make theory come alive. By linking theory and practice, we hope to give a fuller picture of intercultural communication than either one alone could offer.

We bring many intercultural communication experiences to the text. As you read, you will learn not only about both of us as individuals but also about our views of intercultural communication. Don't be overwhelmed by the seeming complexity of intercultural communication. Not knowing everything that you would like to know is very much a part of this process.

Why is it important to focus on intercultural communication and to strive to become better at this complex pattern of interaction? We can think of at least six reasons; perhaps you can add more.

THE TECHNOLOGICAL IMPERATIVE

Today, with the explosion of computers and other communication technologies, we truly live in the **global village** envisioned by media guru Marshal McLuhan (1967). Communication technology links us to events from the most remote parts of the world and connects us to persons we may never meet face-to-face from around the world. Perhaps the most revolutionary advancement has been the Internet.

Technology and Human Communication

In past centuries, social relationships were limited by physical factors such as geographical distance and lack of mobility, but they evolved with each techno-logical advance, such as the railroad, the automobile, the telephone, the radio, TV, and movies. These relationships have now multiplied exponentially. The ex-tent to which the Internet has expanded our interpersonal networks is revealed in a story told by *New York Times* political writer Thomas Friedman (1999). His 79-year-old mother called him up one day, sounding upset. When he asked what was wrong, she said, "Well, I've been playing bridge on the Internet with three Frenchmen and they keep speaking French to each other and I can't understand." When Friedman chuckled a little at the thought of his mother playing bridge with three Frenchmen on the Net, she said, "Don't laugh, I was playing bridge with someone in Siberia the other day" (p. xvi).

By the end of 2001, there were more than 3 billion public Web sites and more than half of all Americans and Japanese had Internet access (Informa-tion Superhighways Newsletter, 2001). The same is true for most western Euro-pean countries (Asmussen & Arend, 2002). And the projections are that by 2003 about three-fourths of people in these countries will have Internet access (www.businessweek.com/ebiz/0005/dm0530.htm).

Consider these trends:

- As of February 2002, there are approximately 445.9 million Internet users worldwide, including 33.7 million users in China and 16.7 million in South Korea (*Business Asia*, February 2002, www.findarticles.com/cf_0/m0BJT/1_10/83759249/print.jhtml).

- Internet access is available in all 54 countries and territories of Africa, mostly in the capital cities. The number of dial-up Internet subscribers there now stands at over 1.3 million (February 2002, www3.sn.apc.org/africa/afstat.htm).

- In just seven Latin American countries (Argentina, Brazil, Chile, Co-lombia, Mexico, Peru, and Venezuela), an estimated 16 million people have Internet access ("TGI Latina Study," 2000, www.zonalatina.com/Zldata133.htm).

- In Scandinavia, 63% of Norwegians use the Internet, as do 62% of Danes. Norwegians use the Web primarily to gather product information (*Internet Business News*, July 9, 2001, www.findarticles.com/cf_0/m0BNG/2001_July_9/76405358/p1/article.jhtml?term-inte).

- Women spend less time on the Internet than men. They use the Internet for shopping, travel, banking, and sending e–greeting cards, whereas men use it for browsing, reading content, and downloading software (*Internet*

Business News, March 22, 2002, www.findarticles.com/cf/_0/m0BNG/
2002_March_22/84104315/p1/article.jhtml?term=).

- In the United States, 66.9% of Americans use the Internet, 54.6% use
  e-mail, 51.7% of Internet users purchase products online, 78.7% of adults
  say that children in their household spend an appropriate amount of time
  online, 70% of adults say that the grades of children who use the Internet
  stay the same, and 75% of adults say that they do not feel ignored by relatives and friends as a result of chat room activity (*Camping Magazine,* January 2001, www.findarticles.com/cf_0/m1249/1_74/69279024/p1/article
  .jhtml?term = internet%2B).

The advent of the Internet and other communication technologies has
tremendous implications for intercultural communication. We will focus on five
aspects of culture and technology: (1) increased information about peoples and
cultures, (2) increased contact with people who are different from us, (3) increased contact with people who are similar to us who can provide communities
of support, (4) identity, culture, and technology, and (5) differential access to
communication technology.

Increase in Information   The Internet provides access to information about
other cultures and other peoples. We can now instantaneously find out almost
anything about any group in the world simply by searching the Internet. This
should give us a better understanding of our global neighbors, and perhaps
some motivation to coexist peacefully in our global village; however, the evidence seems to be to the contrary. For example, there were more incidents of
ethnic strife in 2001 than almost any other year on record (National Defense
Council Foundation, www.ndcf.org/Conflict_List/World2001/NDCFWorld
ConflictCount2001.htm). Apparently, knowledge about others does not necessarily lead to better communication or heightened understanding. We will tackle
issues like this in later chapters.

Through communication technologies like the World Wide Web, people
also have access to increasing amounts of information about what is happening
in their own and other countries. This is especially important in countries where
media are government controlled. For example, people in Pakistan and Afghanistan learn more about military actions in their countries by accessing CNN.com
than through their local newspapers. In some ways, the Internet has democra-
tized information, in that more people control and disseminate information than
ever before. Friedman (1999) tells the story of meeting a prominent Quatari
journalist in Kuwait in 1998. Friedman suggested that she file for *The New York
Times* as a stringer during the upcoming Middle East economic summit. She responded, "To tell you the truth, I write for a Gulf news Web site, and my government doesn't know about it" (p. 208).

Increased Contact With People Who Differ   Communication technology brings
us in contact with people we might never have the opportunity to know otherwise. And many of these people are from different cultural backgrounds, as was

the case with Friedman's mother's bridge partners. The Internet/e-mail allows us to have "pen pals" from different cultures and to carry on discussions with these people in virtual chat rooms and on discussion boards.

However, such mediated communication across cultures does present unique challenges. Unlike face-to-face communication, mediated communication filters out important nonverbal cues. One of our students, Val, described the challenges of intercultural e-mails:

> *I met a girl from Korea my junior year of college, and we became good friends. When it came time for her to go back to Korea we decided we would stay friends and become pen pals via e-mail. I found it much more difficult to communicate with her because she didn't always understand what I was writing and I couldn't repeat my sentences like I could if I were speaking to her, and the same applied to her. It definitely puts a strain on our relationship.*

When we are talking to individuals face-to-face, we use nonverbal information to help us interpret what they are *really* saying—tone of voice, facial expressions, gestures, and so on. The absence of these cues in mediated contexts (e.g., e-mail, chat rooms) makes communication more difficult and can lead to misunderstandings. And these misunderstandings can be compounded when communicating across cultures. For example, a U.S. colleague reports that she was offended when the e-mails she received from colleagues overseas seemed too brief and to the point. She has since discovered that her colleagues overseas are charged computer time by the minute and so have learned to be very concise in their e-mail messages. What she interpreted as rudeness had more to do with the economic context in which the interaction took place than with the communicators themselves. If she had been able to observe their nonverbal cues while communicating, she probably would have known that they were not being rude.

Also, language may be a factor. The people we talk to on e-mail networks may speak languages different from our own. An interesting situation arose recently for one of the authors of this book. Tom was using an electronic bulletin board when someone posted a message in Dutch. It was met with a flurry of hostile responses from people protesting the use of an exclusionary language, one most people couldn't read. A discussion ensued about which languages might be acceptable on the network.

The decision reached was that subscribers could post messages in any language as long as there was an English translation. In a subsequent posting, someone from a university in South Africa recommended a book "for those of you who can read Dutch (heh-heh, all four of us)"—an apparent reaction to the exclusionary sentiments of other subscribers. The use of some languages is given even more privilege in the high-tech communication world, where we are likely to encounter many more people. Although many experts think that the Internet is dominated by English, there are indications that Chinese is becoming a formible linguistic player in the Internet world. According to one source, the first day that registration opened for Chinese language domain names, 360,000 applications were filed (english1.e21times.com/asp/sacd.asp?r=880&p=0).

Increased Contact With People Who Are Similar   Communication technology also allows us to have more contact with people who are very similar to ourselves. There are chat rooms and discussion boards for people with similar interests, such as those stemming from membership in the same ethnic or cultural groups. For example, international students can stay in touch with their local communities, keep up with what's going on at home, and receive emotional support during difficult times of cultural adaptation at a foreign university. Similarly, discussion boards can provide virtual communities of support for cultural minorities (e.g., Planetout.com, a discussion board for gays and lesbians). However, the Internet can also provide a venue for like-minded people to promote prejudice and hatred. According to one source, by the year 2000, worldwide, there were more than 2,100 racist and anti-Semitic Web sites (news.bbc.co.uk/go/em/fr// hi/english/world/americas/newsid_1516000/1516271.stm). It is important to remember that communication technologies are neither good nor bad in themselves; what matters is *how* people use them.

Identity, Culture, and Technology   Advances in communication technology lead us to think differently about ourselves and our **identity management.** In *The Saturated Self,* psychologist Kenneth Gergen describes the changes that occur as technology alters our patterns of communication. Gergen suggests that with the removal of traditional barriers to forming relationships—time and space—these technological advancements lead to **multiphrenia,** a splitting of the individual into many different selves. We are available for communication, via answering machine, fax, and e-mail, even when we're not physically present. Gergen (1991) writes:

> *The relatively coherent and unified sense of self inherent in a traditional culture gives way to manifold and competing potentials. A multiphrenic condition emerges in which one swims in ever-shifting, concatenating, and contentious currents of being. One bears the burden of an increasing array of oughts, of self-doubts and irrationalities. (p. 80)*

Identity on the Internet not only is potentially fragmented but also involves more choice and management issues than in face-to-face interaction. As noted previously, many of the identity cues individuals use to figure out how to communicate with others—such as age, gender, and ethnicity—are filtered out on the Internet. For instance, when you send an e-mail, you can choose whether to reveal certain aspects of your identity. The recipients won't know if you are male or female, young or old, and so on—unless you tell them. The same is true for chat room participation. You can choose which aspects, if any, of your identity you want to reveal. In fact, you can even give false information about your identity.

This capability has resulted in the opportunity for **identity tourism**—taking on the identities of other races, gender, classes, or sexual orientations for recreational purposes. And some online contexts (e.g., virtual games like Dungeons and Dragons) *require* users to take on new identities. How is this related to intercultural communication? One of the oft-touted skills of intercultural communication is empathy, the ability to understand what it's like to "walk in someone's shoes." Communication technology now affords an opportunity to do this— virtually. Thus, for instance, by taking on the virtual identity of a male, by participating in male-only online discussions, females might come to understand better what it feels like to be a male (Danet, 1999). The same might be true for other identities as well.

Although identity tourism provides intriguing possibilities for improving intercultural understanding, it also raises some important ethical questions. In one celebrated example, a male psychiatrist participated in online discussions as a disabled female. Ostensibly, he did so because he wanted to understand something of what it felt like to be a woman and to be disabled. The project backfired, however, as other chat room participants responded to him as a woman and, over time, even fell in love with him. Ultimately, many of the women suffered severe psychological problems as a result of their experiences with him (Turkle, 1995).

The idea of identity tourism may seem somewhat scary, but the same lack of nonverbal cues can result in less prejudice and stereotyping in mediated intercultural interaction. Some of these same nonverbal cues that are filtered out (indicators of age, gender, ethnicity, race) are often the basis for stereotyping and prejudice in initial interactions. When these cues are absent, communication may be more open, because people cannot use the information to form impressions that often negatively impact communication.

Access to Communication Technology As we've seen, technology plays a huge role in our everyday lives and often has a lot to do with our success as students and professionals. Friedman (1999) notes that, whereas a country's success used to be related to control of territory, the key now relates to how it amasses, shares, and harvests knowledge; perhaps the same is true of individuals. Access to technology is essential. What, then, are the implications for people who do not have easy access to the Internet and to other forms of communication technology? There may be an increasing class gap in technology access, and one that is often related to ethnicity.

According to a study by the National Telecommunications and Information Administration (NTIA), urban households with incomes of $75,000 and higher are over 20 times more likely to have access to the Internet as rural households at the lowest income levels and more than 9 times as likely to have a computer at home. Whites are more likely to have access to the Internet at home than are Blacks or Hispanics at any location. Black and Hispanic households are approximately one-third as likely to have home Internet access as households of Asian/ Pacific Islander descent, and roughly two-fifths as likely as White households. Regardless of income level, Americans living in rural areas are lagging behind in Internet access. Indeed, at the lowest income levels, those in urban areas are more than twice as likely to have Internet access as those in rural areas (*Falling Through the Net II*, 1998). And this rural–urban disparity in Internet access exists in most countries.

The implications for intercultural communication are enormous. How do people relate to each other when one is information–technology rich and the other is not? When there is increasing use of English on the Internet, what happens to those who don't speak English? Can this lead to resentment? Will the increase in communication technology lead to increasing gaps between haves and have-nots? To more misunderstandings?

Recent communication technology has impacted our lives in ways our grandparents could not have imagined and requires that we reexamine even our most basic conceptions of self, others, and culture. As Sherry Turkle (1995) observes, once we take virtuality seriously as a way of life, we need a new language for talking about the simplest things. Each individual must ask: What is the nature of my relationships? What are the limits of my responsibilities? And even more importantly: Who and what am I? What is the connection between my physical and virtual bodies? And is it different in different cyberspaces? . . . What kind of society or societies are we creating, "both on and off the screen" (p. 231)? We might also examine our own technological use: Who are we in contact with? People who are like ourselves? People who are different? Do we use technology to increase our contact with and understanding of other cultures or merely to hang out with people who are like us? What does this say about us and our identities?

Mobility and Its Effect on Communication

We come in contact with more people these days not only electronically but also physically. In Chapter 8, we'll provide data showing that more people than ever are on the move around the world. U.S. families move on the average of five times in the lifetime of the family. Of course, there are still communities in which people are born, live, and die in the same small area, but this scenario is less common than ever.

Mobility changes the nature of our society and affects the individuals involved. One of the authors of this book, Judith, remembers moving every few years while she was growing up. She was always facing a new group of classmates at a new school. One year, just before starting at yet another school, she wrote in her diary:

> *I know that the worst will be over soon. Always changing schools should make me more at ease. It doesn't. I like to meet strangers and make friends. Once I get to know people, it'll be easier. But I always dread the first day, wondering if I'll fit in, wondering if the other kids'll be nice to me.*

Although some families, like Judith's, move while the children are growing up, most moves are made by young adults, and some generations move more than others. According to the U.S. Population Reference Bureau (PRB), Gen Xers (Americans ages 20–29) currently are the most mobile. In 1998–1999, close to a third of all Gen Xers moved to a different residence. In contrast, older Americans (e.g., Baby Boomers, born between 1946 and 1964) tended to follow more traditional patterns and to be more stable. The PRB predicts that Gen Xers will live longer periods of their lives as housemates and put off marriage much longer than their parents did: "These newly mobile individuals and households will be the primary movers in the U.S. over the next decade and will shape new patterns of population growth and distribution" (www.prb.org/AmeristatTemplate .cfm?Section=Migration1&Templates=ContentManage).

Many families move because of divorce. Only about half of American teenagers live with both birth mother and birth father. The rest live with single parents or in stepfamilies or extended families (such as grandparents) or are shuttled back and forth between their parents' houses. Some children even commute between different geographical regions of the United States. For example, they might spend the summer with the father in New Jersey and the rest of the year with the mother and stepfather in Arizona.

Families also relocate for economic reasons. A U.S. company might relocate to Mexico and transfer the corporate personnel with the company. Many Mexican workers, for their part, cross the border to look for work in the United States. Similarly, Germans from the eastern part of the country move to the western sections seeking improved social and economic opportunities. Increasing technology and mobility mean that we can no longer be culturally illiterate in this shrinking world.

THE DEMOGRAPHIC IMPERATIVE

The U.S. population has changed radically in recent decades and will continue to do so in the future. The workforce that today's college graduates enter will differ significantly from the one their parents entered. These changes stem from two sources: (1) changing **demographics** within the United States and (2) changing immigration patterns. (See Figure 1-1.)

Changing U.S. Demographics

The changing demographic characteristics of the United States are dramatically revealed in the 2000 census. In the year 2000, Hispanics were the largest minority, accounting for 12.5% of the population. Some 12.3% of persons classified themselves as African American, 3.8% as Asian or Pacific Islander, and less than 1% as American Indian or Alaska Native (Brewer & Suchan, 2001). Over the next 25 years, minority concentrations are projected to increase, with Hispanics accounting for 18% of the population and African Americans for 13%. Over the same period, the percentages of Whites will decline by 10%. (See Table 1-1).

Another interesting demographic fact is the increase in multicultural people. The 2000 census was the first that allowed persons to categorize themselves as "two or more races," and 2.4% of respondents did just that. Of the "two or more races" population, 40% live in the West, 27% in the South, 18% in the Northeast, and 15% in the Midwest (Brewer & Suchan, 2001, p. 45). We'll explore the implications of the increasing numbers of multicultural individuals in Chapters 5 and 8.

FIGURE 1-1   Rapid changes in technology, demographics, and economic forces mean that you are likely to come into contact with many people with diverse backgrounds and experiences. Although many of these communication experiences will be in professional and work situations, many other interactions will be in public and social settings. (© *Esbin-Anderson / The Image Works*)

What is also interesting is the racial distribution in the various geographical regions. The Population Reference Bureau (PRB) computed a "diversity index" showing that the highest ethnic diversity is concentrated in the southeastern and southwestern regions of the United States. Minority concentrations are projected to increase especially in the South, Southwest, and West. The PRB estimates that, by 2025, minority groups will account for over 50% of the population in four states (Hawaii, California, New Mexico, Texas) (www.prb.org/Ameristat Template.cfm?Section=Estimates).

There is increasing diversity in the U.S. workforce as well. The workforce is expected to continue to get older, and there will also be proportionately more

TABLE 1-1   RACIAL AND ETHNIC COMPOSITION OF THE UNITED STATES, 2000 AND 2025

	2000	2025
Asian/Other	4.6%	7.0%
African American	12.3	12.9
Hispanic	12.5	18.2
White	75.1	62.0

Source: From *Mapping Census 2000*, by Brewer and Suchan, 2001, www.prb.org/Ameristat
Template.cfm?Section=Estimates.

women working. What accounts for these changes? The workforce will be older because the Baby Boomers are aging. More women are in the workforce for several reasons. First, economic pressures have come to bear; more women are single parents, and even in two-parent families, it often takes two incomes to meet family expenses. Second, the women's movement of the 1960s and 1970s resulted in more women seeking careers and jobs outside the home. In addition, the workforce is more ethnically and racially diverse—in part, simply because there are more minorities now than before, but also because of civil rights efforts, which led to more opportunities for minorities in business and industry.

Changing Immigration Patterns

The second source of demographic change is different immigration patterns. Although the United States has often been thought of as a nation of immigrants, it is also a nation that established itself by subjugating the original inhabitants and that prospered to some extent as a result of slave labor. These aspects of national identity are important in understanding contemporary society.

Today, immigration has changed the social landscape significantly. One in five Americans either was born abroad or born of parents who were born abroad ("Now a Nation," 2002). Prior to the 1970s, most of the immigrants to the United States came from Europe, but this changed in the 1980s and 1990s. As of 1999, over half (51%) the foreign-born population came from Latin America, 27% from Asia, and only 16% from Europe. Of the one million immigrants who now enter the United States every year, 90% are from Latin America or Asia. These shifts in patterns of immigration have resulted in a much more racially and ethnically diverse population. In 1890, only 1.4% of the foreign-born population was non-White; by 1970, 27% were non-White, and by 1999, 75% were non-White (www.prb.org/AmeristatTemplate.cfm?Section=Migration1& template=ContentManage). It's not hard to see that the United States is becoming more heterogeneous. We address the issue of Whites losing majority status in Chapter 5.

Here is one view of affirmative action that emphasizes the need to consider the contradictory character of this issue. Note how the author, Bernardo Ferdman, resists a simplistic position on the issue. His views are also very helpful in understanding current issues like racial profiling and the Racial Privacy Initiative (government should not be allowed to collect any data about people's race/ethnicity). All these issues seem to call for a balance between recognizing differences and yet remaining "color-blind."

> *It may be much more fruitful to see the debate as one over what constitutes fairness in dealing with ethnic differences. When we look at it this way, we can see that American society seems to be caught in a bind.*
>
> *On the one hand, to assess the presence and the extent of racial and ethnic discrimination, and to ensure group-level equity, we must take people's group memberships into account. Thus, to ignore people's race or ethnicity can be seen as patently unfair. On the other hand, recognition and consideration of racial and ethnic group membership can be experienced as discriminatory, and even as calling into question, for example, the qualifications of individuals whose group memberships are highlighted. Thus, to notice people's race or ethnicity can also be seen as unfair. . . .*
>
> *These views represent the elements of a paradox. In the individualistic view, we emphasize the commonalities among us and thus the importance of treating everyone alike, and we believe it is only when we let group labels get in the way that we discriminate.*

This **heterogeneity** presents many opportunities and challenges for students of intercultural communication. The tensions among heterogeneous groups, as well as fears on the part of the politically dominant groups, must be acknowledged. California's Proposition 187, which passed in the November 1994 election, excludes nondocumented immigrants from receiving public health and social services. This proposition has remained highly controversial and has led to protests and court challenges. The subsequent California Civil Rights Initiative (Proposition 209), which passed in November 1996, further extended the challenges to diversity by eliminating many affirmative action programs. And in 1997, Californians passed Proposition 227, which will eliminate bilingual education in schools, pending court rulings.

We should also note the potential opportunities in a culturally diverse society. **Diversity** can expand our conceptions of what is possible—linguistically, politically, socially—as various lifestyles and ways of thinking converge.

To get a better sense of the situation in the United States today, let's take a look at our history. As mentioned previously, the United States has often been referred to as a nation of **immigrants,** but this is only partly true. When Europeans began arriving on the shores of the New World, an estimated 8 to 10 mil-

In the group view, we emphasize the difference among ethnic and racial groups and thus the importance of being sensitive to these in dealing with others. We believe that expecting the same behavior and values from everyone is discriminatory.

How can these seemingly contradictory values be reconciled? The solution to the paradox does not lie in convincing the advocates of whatever perspective we more strongly disagree with that they are wrong. It is more likely to lie in giving up the type of thinking that says that one side must "win." Both perspectives are integral to American thinking and practice regarding civil rights and in their various versions find proponents among all parties to the issue. . . . When looked at this way, we can see that the individual must be valued and group rights must be protected. . . .

We must be more conscious of this tension inherent in the nature of an ethnically and racially diverse society and learn to better live with it. We could do so by acknowledging that ethnicity and culture are not extraneous to what makes individuals unique. Rather, they are important aspects of the person— all persons. . . .

There is no middle ground between these paradoxical visions of fairness, yet we must live according to both of them if we are to uphold the values of individual and group freedom. . . . I hope that we can give up the battle mentality and find mutually acceptable ways to maintain civil rights.

Source: From Bernardo M. Ferdman, "Supreme Court Shows Pitfalls in Doing Right Thing," *Albany Sunday Times Union*, September 17, 1989, p. D3.

lion Native Americans were already living here. Their ancestors probably began to arrive via the Bering Strait at least 40,000 years earlier. The outcome of the encounters between these groups—the colonizing Europeans and the native peoples—is well known. By 1940, the Native American population of the United States had been reduced to an estimated 250,000. Today, there are about 1.9 million Native Americans (from 542 recognized tribes) living in the United States (Brewer & Suchan, 2001).

African American Immigrants African Americans represent a special case in the history of U.S. immigration. African Americans did not choose to emigrate but were brought here involuntarily, mainly as slave labor. Many Europeans also emigrated as indentured servants. However, the system of contract servitude was gradually replaced by perpetual servitude, or slavery, almost wholly of Africans. Many landowners wanted captive workers who could not escape and who could not become competitors. They turned to slave labor.

The slave trade, developed by European and African merchants, lasted about 350 years, although slavery was outlawed in Europe long before it was outlawed in the United States. Roughly 10 million Africans reached the Americas, although most died in the brutal overseas passage (Curtin, 1969). Slavery is an important aspect of U.S. immigration history. As James Baldwin (1955) suggested, the legacy of slavery makes contemporary interracial relations in the United States very different from interracial relations in Europe and other regions of the world.

Slavery presents a moral dilemma for many Whites even today. A common response is simply to ignore history. Many people assert that because not all Whites owned slaves we should forget the past and move on. For others, forgetting the past is not acceptable. In fact, some historians, like James Loewen, maintain that acknowledging and understanding the past is the only viable alternative in moving forward. In his book *Lies My Teacher Told Me*, Loewen (1995) analyzes the content in contemporary high school history books and acknowledges that they do present the horrors of slavery. What is missing, however, is the connection of slavery to the current racial tensions in the United States:

> *Perhaps telling realistically what slavery was like for slaves is the easy part. After all, slavery as an institution is dead. We have progressed beyond it, so we can acknowledge its evils. . . . Without explaining its relevance to the present, however, extensive coverage of slavery is like extensive coverage of the Hawley-Smoot Tariff—just more facts for hapless eleventh graders to memorize. Slavery's twin legacies to the present are the social and economic inferiority it conferred upon blacks and the cultural racism it instilled in whites. Both continue to haunt our society. Therefore, treating slavery's enduring legacy is necessarily controversial. Unlike slavery, racism is not over yet. To function adequately in civic life in our troubled times, students must learn what causes racism. (p. 143)*

Scholar and theologian Cornell West (1993) agrees that we should begin by acknowledging the historical flaws of U.S. society and recognizing the historical consequences of slavery. For instance, the United States has several Holocaust museums but no organized, official recognition of the horrors of slavery. Perhaps it is easier for us to focus on the negative events of another nation's history than on those of our own. In Chapter 4, we explore the importance of history in understanding the dynamics of intercultural communication.

Relationships With New Immigrants   Relationships between residents and immigrants—between oldtimers and newcomers—have often been filled with tension and conflict. In the 19th century, Native Americans sometimes were caught in the middle of European rivalries. During the War of 1812, for example, Indian allies of the British were severely punished by the United States when the war ended. In 1832, the U.S. Congress recognized the Indian nations' right to self-government, but in 1871, a congressional act prohibited treaties between the U.S. government and Indian tribes. In 1887, Congress passed the Dawes Severalty Act, terminating Native Americans' special relationship with the U.S. government and paving the way for their removal from their homelands.

As waves of immigrants continued to roll in from Europe, the more firmly established European—mainly British—immigrants tried to protect their way of life, language, and culture. As one citizen lamented in 1856,

Four-fifths of the beggary and three-fifths of the crime spring from our foreign population; more than half the public charities, more than half the prisons and almshouses, more than half the police and the cost of administering criminal justice are for foreigners. (quoted in Cole, 1998, p. 126)

The foreigners to which this citizen was referring were mostly from Ireland, devastated by the potato famines, and from Germany, which had fallen on hard economic and political times. Historian James Banks (1991) identifies other anti-immigrant events throughout the nation's history. As early as 1729, an English mob prevented a group of Irish immigrants from landing in Boston. A few years later, another mob destroyed a new Scots-Irish Presbyterian church in Worcester, Massachusetts. In these acts, we can see the **Anglocentrism** that characterized early U.S. history. Later, northern and western European (e.g., German and Dutch) characteristics were added to this model of American culture. Immigrants from southern, central, and eastern Europe (e.g., Italy and Poland) were expected to assimilate into the so-called mainstream culture—to jump into the **"melting pot"** and come out "American."

In the late 19th and early 20th centuries, a **nativistic** (anti-immigrant) movement propagated violence against newer immigrants. In 1885, 28 Chinese were killed in an anti-Chinese riot in Wyoming; in 1891, a White mob attacked a Chinese community in Los Angeles and killed 19 people; also in 1891, 11 Italian Americans were lynched in New Orleans.

Nativistic sentiment was well supported at the government level. In 1882, Congress passed the Chinese Exclusion Act, officially prohibiting anyone who lived in China from immigrating to this country. In 1924, the Johnson-Read Act and the Oriental Exclusion Act established extreme quotas on immigration, virtually precluding the legal immigration of Asians. According to Ronald Takaki (1989), these two laws "provided for immigration based on nationality quotas: the number of immigrants to be admitted annually was limited to 2 percent of the foreign-born individuals of each nationality residing in the United States in 1890" (p. 209). The nativistic sentiment increasingly was manifested in arguments that economic and political opportunities should be reserved solely for Whites, and not just for native-born Americans.

By the 1930s, southern and eastern European groups were considered "assimilatable," and the concept of race assumed new meaning. All of the so-called White races were now considered one, so racial hostilities could focus on ethnic (non-White) groups, such as Asian Americans, Native Americans, and Mexican Americans (Banks, 1991). Sociologist David Roediger (1991) traces how devastating this racialization was, particularly for African Americans. In the growing, but sometimes fragile, economy of the first half of the 20th century, White workers had an advantage. Although White immigrants received low wages, they had access to better schools and to public facilities, and they were accorded greater public acceptance. People of color often were considered less fit to receive economic benefits and, to some extent, to be not truly American (Foner, 1998).

Economic conditions make a big difference in attitudes toward foreign workers and immigration policies. During the Depression of the 1930s, Mexi-

In this article, Craig Ray, an entrepreneur, describes the advantages of integrating immigrants into the U.S. workforce and gives some suggestions for businesses that have immigrant employees.

When my partner and I purchased Tommaso's Fresh Pasta *three years ago, our idea of a melting pot was what you use to make sauce.*

Today, however, it is our company's workplace that is a melting pot of cultures and languages, thanks to a core work force of immigrants.

[We] didn't set out to hire immigrants, just good employees. When a dramatic sales increase created an immediate need for workers and our state Employment Commission's matching system began identifying people who met our needs, many potential candidates were immigrants. Our employee diversity increased as we grew. Today, just 12 of our 33 employees are native-born Americans.

Hiring immigrant workers can create challenges but also can have rewards, such as employee loyalty and dedication. Here are some suggestions to consider in integrating such workers into your company:

- Know the law. Familiarize yourself with Immigration and Naturalization Service regulations and make sure proper employment forms are completed and filed. The INS will help you learn the law.

- Recognize, too, that you may want to get involved as an employee's advocate if you believe his or her work status or eligibility to stay in the U.S. has been questioned wrongly.

- Limit the number of languages spoken. Each language you bring into the workplace carries with it communication barriers. While your firm ultimately might resemble the United Nations, don't go in that direction too fast. Adding workers who speak the same language as your current workers allows you to limit the number of employee interpreters needed and the amount of miscommunication.

- Create a culturally tolerant and supportive environment. You and your workers must be as tolerant of the ways of immigrants as you are of the

cans and Mexican Americans were forced to return to Mexico to free up jobs for White Americans. When prosperity returned in the 1940s, Mexicans were welcomed back as a source of cheap labor. This type of situation is not limited to the United States but occurs all over the world. For example, Algerian workers are alternately welcomed and rejected in France, depending on the state of the French economy and the demand for imported labor. Guestworkers from Turkey have been subjected to similar uncertainties in Germany. Indian workers in Kenya, Chinese immigrants in Malaysia, and many other workers toiling outside their native lands have suffered the vagaries of fluctuating economies and

ways of Americans. We had one employee, for example, who kept her country's custom of fasting, wearing black, and not cutting her hair for more than a month after the death of her father. Largely because our company promotes tolerance, this behavior elicited no negative comment from her co-workers.

- Offer classes in English as a second language. Encourage employees to take English classes. If possible, offer classes on-site and at no cost before shifts or during lunch, for example. For us, these classes are a win–win proposition. Our employees learn skills that make communication easier, and we get a venue for covering training and procedures. Also, the opportunity for education helps attract workers.

- Don't have separate staff meetings. Initially, we organized employee meetings according to the linguistic backgrounds of our workers. We quickly found that employees wanted to meet as a group so that issues raised by one person could be discussed by everyone. Now that we have switched to general meetings, everyone hears the same information and moves forward together.

- Look at the potential beyond the language. Don't bypass an immigrant employee's capabilities simply because he or she hasn't mastered English. For instance, we have a Vietnamese employee with little mastery of English but great learning retention and math abilities. We have taught him to handle all of our computerized production planning, and we expect him to handle additional responsibilities as his English skills improve. He, in turn, knows how we see his future, and that has made him work harder toward achieving his potential.

A good worker is a good worker—if given the chance to do the job. Don't let someone's origin or language limit their potential, or your company's.

Source: From C. Ray, "The Potential of Immigrants," *Nation's Business*, August 1998, www.findarticles.com/cf_dls/m1154/n8_v86/20934415/print.jhtml.

immigration policies. In Chapter 8, we discuss the implications of these migration patterns for intercultural communication.

The tradition of tension and conflict between cultures continues to this day. The conflicts that arise in Southern California exemplify many aspects of the demographic changes in the United States. We can examine on a variety of levels the tensions in Los Angeles among Latinos/as, African Americans, Korean Americans, and European Americans. Some of the conflict is due to different languages, values, and lifestyles. Some African Americans resent the economic success of recent Korean immigrants—a reaction that reflects a typical historical pattern.

The conflict may also be due to the pattern of settlement that results in cultural **enclaves**: Blacks in South Central Los Angeles, Latinos/as in Inglewood and east Los Angeles, Koreans in the "Miracle Mile," and Whites on the west side of the city. As in other parts of the country, the majority of White suburban Americans live in neighborhoods that are overwhelmingly White (Schmitt, 2001).

Immigration and Economic Classes   Some of the conflict may be due to the economic disparity that exists among these different groups. To understand this disparity, we need to look at issues of economic class. Most Americans are reluctant to admit that a class structure exists and even more reluctant to admit how difficult it is to move up in this structure. Indeed, most people live their lives in the same economic class into which they were born. And there are distinct class differences in clothing, housing, recreation, conversation, and other aspects of everyday life (Fussell, 1992). For example, the driveways to the homes of the very rich are usually obscured, whereas those of upper-class homes usually are long and curved and quite visible. Driveways leading to middle-class homes, in contrast, tend to go straight into garages.

The myth of a classless society is hardly benign. It not only reinforces middle- and upper-class beliefs in their own superior abilities but also promotes a false hope among the working class and the poor that they can get ahead. Whereas real-life success stories of upward mobility are rare, fictitious ones abound in literature, film, and television. But all such accounts perpetuate the myth. The reality is that the income gap between rich and poor in the United States is more extreme than in most industrialized countries. The ratio between rich and poor (measured as the percentage of total income held by the wealthiest 20% versus the poorest 20%) is approximately 11:1, one of the highest ratios in the industrialized world. The ratio in Germany and Japan, in contrast, is 4:1 (Mantsios, 2001). And the gap seems to be getting wider.

Since the mid-1970s, the rich have fared much better economically than the middle class or the poor. Sociologist Andrew Hacker (1997) reports that the top fifth of the U.S. population did 24 times better than the bottom fifth and that all segments other than the top 20% lost ground (p. 10). The widening gap is due partly to the loss of stable industrial jobs, as companies move to cheaper labor markets within the United States and abroad. Class and demographic issues also play a role, with racial and ethnic minorities typically hardest hit by economic downturns.

Religious Diversity   Immigration also contributes to religious diversity, bringing increasing numbers of Muslims, Buddhists, Confucians, Catholics, and others to the United States. Religious beliefs and practices often play an important role in everyday cultural life. One example is the very different views on abortion, described by our student Tanya:

> *Pro-choice and pro-lifers have incredibly different worldview lenses. These different lenses they see through are most of the time influenced by religion and social upbringing. The values are different, yet no side is wrong and cannot see through the same worldview lens as their opponents.*

Our gender, class, and race all influence our position in society and also influence us to have a different understanding of social life. We all have different social realities based on what we were taught, and this fact makes communication between people very challenging. I believe that nowadays we come into contact with people of all types of backgrounds and nationalities more often than we did years ago. We find people of different standpoints at the workplace, at social events, at the grocery store, and so on. With all of these diverse people suddenly brought into contact with each other every day of their lives, it is extremely hard to take the time to treat everyone as individuals. Instead, we make categories based on our past experiences and from our different standpoints. This makes our lives simpler, but it also breeds stereotyping and prejudice. The categories that we make are based not only on our past experiences and our different standpoints, but also on what we hear from other sources and from the examples that the media give us.

—Tara

These different worldviews can sometimes lead to prejudices and stereotypes. For example, stereotypes about Islam are widespread in U.S. popular culture. Political scientist Ali Muzrui (2001) describes Islam as the "ultimate negative 'Other' to the Christian tradition" and laments the rising tide of "Islamophobia" (fear of Islam and the hostility toward it). He lists the contrasting stereotypes:

Whereas Christianity is supposed to be peace loving, Islam is portrayed as fostering holy war (Jihad). Whereas Christianity liberates women, Islam enslaves them. Whereas Christianity is modern, Islam is medieval. Whereas Christianity is forward looking, Islam is backward looking. Whereas Christians prefer nonviolence, Muslims easily resort to terrorism. (p. 110)

Muzrui goes on to present evidence to debunk each of these stereotypes. Religious diversity is part of the demographic imperative that challenges us to learn more about intercultural communication.

These increasingly diverse ethnic, racial, economic, and religious groups come into contact mostly during the day in schools, businesses, and other settings, bringing to the encounters different languages, histories, and economic statuses. This presents great challenges for us as a society and as individuals. The main challenge is to look beyond the stereotypes and biases, to recognize the disparities and differences, and to try to apply what we know about intercultural communication. Perhaps the first step is to realize that the melting pot metaphor probably was never viable, that it was not realistic to expect everyone to assimilate into the United States in the same way. Today we need a different metaphor, one that reflects the racial, ethnic, and cultural diversity that truly exists in our country. Perhaps we should think of the United States as a "salad," in which each group retains its own flavor and yet contributes to the whole. Or we might think of it as a "tapestry," with many different strands contributing to a unified pattern.

In any case, the United States is hardly a model of diversity; many countries are far more diverse ethnically. For example, Nigeria has some 200 ethnic groups, and Indonesia has a similar number. Nigeria was colonized by the British, and artificially drawn boundaries forced many different groups into one nation-state, which caused many conflicts. The diverse groups in Indonesia, in contrast, have largely coexisted amiably for many years. Diversity, therefore, does not necessarily lead to intercultural conflicts.

Fortunately, most individuals are able to negotiate day-to-day activities in spite of cultural differences. Diversity can even be a positive force. Demographic diversity in the United States has given us tremendous linguistic richness and culinary variety, and varied resources to meet new social challenges, as well as domestic and international business opportunities.

THE ECONOMIC IMPERATIVE

The recent trend toward globalization has resulted, essentially, in one world market. This means that the U.S. economy is increasingly connected to the economies of other countries. This was dramatically shown in the global financial downturn of the late 1990s. Daniel Yergin and Joseph Stanislaw (1998) describe how, in a pattern of "contagion," the downturn started with a weakening economy in Thailand that was ignored by most of the world's financial leaders. They soon realized their mistake as the crisis spread first to Malaysia, Indonesia, and Korea, and eventually to Russia and South America, at which point the International Monetary Fund (part of the United Nations) finally stepped in and took measures to stabilize Brazil's economy. The U.S. and other countries' economies are still recovering from what Yergin and Stanislaw term "the first crisis of the globalization era." As this example shows, the close ties between economies around the world mean that weakness in one can quickly spread to others, including the United States.

The point is that, to compete effectively in this new global market, Americans must understand how business is conducted in other countries. U.S. businesspeople should be able to negotiate deals that are advantageous to the U.S. economy. However, they are not always willing to take the time and effort to do this. For example, most U.S. automobile manufacturers do not produce automobiles that have right-hand drive, which prevents them from penetrating markets in nations like Japan. Stories abound of U.S. marketing slogans that were inaccurately translated, like Pepsi's "Come alive with the Pepsi Generation," which was translated into Chinese as "Pepsi brings your ancestors back from the grave" ("Ten Great Global Marketing Mistakes," 1998).

Cross-cultural trainers in the United States report that Japanese and other business personnel often spend years in the United States studying English and

Americans, including myself, sometimes have this belief that what we do here in the United States is the best and only way to do things. We put these "cultural blinders" on and are oblivious to any other cultures and/or values. Although American tradition has been and can be a big influence on other markets and business sectors, we are failing to realize that the way we do business is not the basis for all businesses. Most of our international business ventures are failing due to our stubbornness. In the past we felt that we could send someone to Mexico or Japan without any intercultural training and still show them how to do business. How wrong were we?

Today we realize it takes an understanding of others and their beliefs and values to truly gain respect and further our business and personal relationships. Businesses are taking the time and money to train their employees about the new culture that they will be submerged in. People in the past failed because we did not take into account that companies' attitudes and beliefs differed from ours. Good relations with other international businesses can produce a life-long bond that can create great economic wealth for each country. The companies are not only training their employees for this culture shock but are training their families as well, because they know that without family support, this venture will surely fail. The United States has taken strides to correct their errors of the past and are continuing their efforts to produce intercultural employees, and I hope this trend continues.

—Luis

learning about the country before they decide to establish operations here or invest money. In contrast, many American companies provide little or no training before sending their workers overseas and expect to close business deals quickly, with little regard for cultural idiosyncrasies.

Many management experts have examined other countries' practices for ways to increase U.S. productivity. One such idea was "quality circles," borrowed from the Japanese and now popular in the United States. Another Japanese strength is the belief in effort for its own sake. Japanese employees work longer hours and sometimes produce better products simply as a result of persistence. This trait also pays off in schools: Japanese students score higher on standardized exams than do American students.

It will also behoove Americans to research how to do business in the huge emerging market that is 21st-century China. As two experienced businesspeople describe it,

China is the largest and most difficult market a business can enter. . . . The last two decades are full of tales of firms that thought they had a lucrative business deal in China sewn up, only for the whole thing to evaporate almost before the wheels of their planes had touched the ground back home. (Ambler & Witzel, 2000, p. 28)

In the corporate world in Bangkok, the new year beginning on January 1 (as opposed to the Thai New Year or the Chinese New Year) is a time of giving gifts to valued customers. The company I worked for was real big on ethics, which was nice; they wanted to treat everyone equally and be fair in their business dealings, which was good, but they took it too far. During New Year's, companies usually give gifts to their customers as a way of saying thanks for their patronage. The gift you give depends on the customers' place in society and the amount of business they do with your company. What I hated is that this company (an American company) viewed that as unethical, as some form of a bribe. We could only go out and buy one item in bulk, and we'd have to give the same gift to all of the customers. I was so embarrassed to give those gifts. I hope the customers knew that I worked for an American company that just didn't understand the way things were done in Thailand.
—Chris

Why do so many businesspeople have difficulty succeeding in Chinese and other Asian markets? The reasons involve both differences in business practices and cultural differences between East and West. Ambler and Witzel (2000) explain that business dealings in China, as in many Eastern countries, are relationship-oriented, that businesses cannot succeed without respect and harmony. Specifically, in China, three concepts are crucial:

- *Qingmian* (human feelings), which involves respect for the feelings of others
- *He* (harmony), which emphasizes the smooth functioning of a group or society
- *Quanxi* (relationship or connection), which underscores the importance of relationships in Chinese business

The high value placed on these concepts highlights other differences as well. For example, contract law is practiced very differently in China. Whereas in the West the law is the essential set of rules of conduct, the "rules of conduct" in China are the ethics and standards of behavior required in a Confucian society. This means that social pressures rather than legal instruments are used to ensure compliance. Thus, what we might conceptualize as a legal issue may be seen in China as a relationship issue.

Sometimes there are cultural differences in work ethics. One of our students, Vincent, describes a difference he observed while working as an intern in a manufacturing company:

When looking back at this internship I can easily see that Mexican workers were more loyal to the company. I constantly noticed that American workers at this company would be walking around talking or smoking while they were supposed

to be at their work stations, but the Mexican workers would never leave their sta-
tions until it was time for break. This sometimes created problems between Mexi-
cans and other employees because of the differences in work ethics.

We discuss the implications of these types of cultural differences for relationships (Chapter 10) and conflicts (Chapter 11).

Cultural differences in business practices have implications not only when people from different companies do business with each other but also when people from different cultures work on the same team. One effect of globalization is increasing numbers of international teams—sometimes working as virtual teams and rarely meeting face-to-face. These teams present large challenges in intercultural communication. Elizabeth Marx (1999) recently analyzed the difficulties of a British–American team and found that problems stemmed from (1) excessive stereotyping, (2) lack of openness and communication, and (3) the "culture factor" as an overused excuse for not getting things done. As she worked with the two cultural groups, she found that the Americans were viewed by the British as "too directive, too aggressive, too fast and as thinking on the possible and not thinking about obstacles." The British, in contrast, were viewed by the Americans as "too consensus driven, too defensive, quality rather than quantity oriented, negative-thinking, bureaucratic and taking too many holidays" (p. 101). In her subsequent training, Marx tried to help the team understand and respect cultural differences, and also develop a common working language, set agreed-upon goals, and choose the best leader.

International teams are sometimes the result of mergers, like the Daimler Benz–Chryler merger announced in 1998. One of the differences between these two organizations and cultures (U.S. and German) concerns their attitudes toward pay and benefits for their chief executives. Germans are more concerned with equality in pay than the more individualistic Americans (Marx, 1999). In later chapters, we'll explore other communication implications for the differences between individualists and collectivists.

Globalization presents many new issues. Increasingly, ***multinational corporations*** are moving operations to new locations, often overseas, due to lower labor costs. These business moves have far-reaching implications, including the loss of jobs at closed facilities. Many U.S.-owned companies have established production facilities, known as ***maquiladoras,*** along the U.S.–Mexican border, where workers produce goods bound mainly for U.S. markets. These companies benefit from lower labor costs, tax breaks, and relaxed environmental regulations. Although Mexican laborers profit from the jobs, there is a cost in terms of environmental hazards. *Maquiladoras* thus present intercultural challenges for Mexicans and U.S. Americans.

Domestic diversity also requires businesses to be attentive to cultural differences. As the workforce becomes more diverse, many businesses are interested in capitalizing on these differences for economic gain. As trainers Bernardo M. Ferdman and Sara Einy Brody (1996) suggest, "Once organizations learn to adopt an inclusive orientation in dealing with their members, this will also have a positive impact on how they look at their customer base, how they develop

The following excerpt is from an article in a Thai newspaper by journalist Jennifer Sharples. Note that "modernization" does not mean "westernization." Thailand is becoming increasingly industrialized, which may give the landscape a Western appearance. But we should not ignore the cultural differences that reside within the landscape.

> *The apparent westernization that many foreigners see occurring in Thailand can be very misleading because, despite modern, well-equipped offices that equal—if not surpass—anything found in New York or London, this doesn't mean that the staff necessarily see things from the western perspective.*
>
> *Come to that, there are also many value differences between the various countries of Asia; Thailand, Singapore, and Japan, for example, all have very different ways of operating in the workplace, which means cross-cultural sensitivity is the name of the game.*
>
> *Dr. Viboonpon Poonprasit of Thammasat University's Faculty of Political Science, who has been involved in cross-cultural training for many years, says: "Because Thailand is developing well economically, many foreigners believe that western ways prevail. Little do they realize that they are faced with deep-rooted traditional values. Expatriates often believe they can work the way they would back home and believe among other things that Thais are nonassertive and noncompetitive.*
>
> *"Thais, on the other hand, expect foreigners to know some of their basic cultural values such as* kreng jai *(showing consideration for others) and* jai yen *(keeping calm or cool), but foreigners frequently make the mistake of ignoring these niceties, since they don't expect these things to create a big issue in the workplace.*
>
> *"Thailand having remained independent was never exposed to western values. But many Thais realize the need to compete globally and we have to adapt to international trade and business practices.*
>
> *"This means having to be assertive and decisive, while retaining some Thai characteristics such as* kreng jai. *In cross-cultural training courses, we tell Thais to be more flexible and to learn the western system as well as the Thai; much depends on how Thai-oriented the boss is, of course."*

Source: From Jennifer Sharples, "A Cross-Cultural Conundrum," *Bangkok Post Sunday Magazine*, May 28–June 3, 1995, pp. 10–11.

products and assess business opportunities, and how they relate to their communities" (p. 289).

Understanding cultural differences involves not only working with diverse employees but also recognizing new business markets, developing new products, and so on. From this perspective, diversity is a potentially powerful economic resource if organizations view the challenge as an opportunity. In this sense, then, business can capitalize on diversity.

THE PEACE IMPERATIVE

The bottom line seems to be this: Can individuals of different genders, ages, ethnicities, races, languages, socioeconomic statuses, and cultural backgrounds coexist on this planet? (See Figure 1-2.) Both the history of humankind and recent world events lead us not to be very optimistic on this point. And this imperative is even more evident after the events of September 11, 2001. Contact among different cultural groups—from the earliest civilizations until today—often has led to disharmony. For example, consider the ethnic/religious strife between Muslims and the Western world; the ethnic struggles in Bosnia and the former Soviet Union; the war between Hutus and Tutsis in Rwanda (Africa); the continued unrest in the Middle East; and the racial and ethnic struggles and tensions in neighborhoods in Boston, Los Angeles, and other U.S. cities.

Some of these conflicts are tied to histories of **colonialism** around the world, whereby European powers lumped diverse groups—differing in language, culture, religion, or identity—together as one state. For example, the division of Pakistan and India was imposed by the British; eventually, East Pakistan declared its independence to become Bangladesh. Nevertheless, ethnic and religious differences in some areas of India and Pakistan continue to cause unrest. And the acquisition of nuclear weapons by both India and Pakistan makes these antagonisms of increasing concern. The tremendous diversity—and accompanying antagonisms—within many former colonies must be understood in the context of histories of colonialism.

Some of the conflicts are also tied to economic disparities and influenced by U.S. technology and media. Many people in the United States see these influences as beneficial, but they also stimulate resistance. Communication scholar Fernando Delgado (2002) explains:

> *Such cultural dominance, though celebrated at home, can spark intercultural conflicts because it inhibits the development of other nations' indigenous popular culture products, stunts their economic development and foists U.S. values and perspectives on other cultures. These effects, in turn, often lead to resentment and conflict. (p. 353)*

For example, according to many Canadians, a Canadian cultural identity is almost impossible due to the dominance of U.S. media. This type of cultural domination is very complex. Delgado recalls that he noticed anti-American sentiments in graffiti, newspapers, and TV programs during a recent trip to Europe but that he also saw U.S. influence everywhere—in music, television, film, cars, fast food, and fashion. He notes that "resentment, frustration, and disdain among the locals coexisted with an amazement at the penetration of U.S. popular culture" (p. 355).

Some of the conflicts have roots in past foreign policies. For example, the attacks in September 2001 were partly due to the confusing and shifting alliances among the United States, Afghanistan, and Arab and Muslim countries. In Afghanistan in the early 1990s, the Taliban seized power in response to the

FIGURE 1-2   Many influences shape intercultural communication interactions. In this photo of Jews in an Arab section of Jerusalem, notice the Israeli soldier with the gun, the father's glance, and the child. Given the many forces that structure our world, it is often difficult to overcome barriers to intercultural communication. Larger social and cultural conflicts are often a part of intercultural interaction. (© *George Mars Cassidy/Getty Images*)

destructive rule of the Northern Alliance, a loose coalition of warlords. The United States had supported the Taliban in the fight against Soviet aggression in the late 1980s and had promised aid in rebuilding their country after the hostilities were over. However, with the withdrawal of Soviet forces and the fall of the Soviet Union, the United States wasn't as concerned about fulfilling its promises to the Afghan nation, leaving the Afghan people at the mercy of the Taliban. In addition, U.S. foreign policies toward many Arab countries in the last half century, coupled with open support for Israel, have caused widespread resentment (Friedman, 2002). Although there is no simple explanation for why terrorists attacked the United States, the attacks clearly did not happen in a vacuum. They need to be understood in historical, political, religious, and economic contexts.

It would be naive to assume that simply understanding the issues of intercultural communication would end war and intercultural conflict, but these problems do underscore the need for individuals to learn more about social groups other than their own. Ultimately, people, and not countries, negotiate and sign peace treaties. An example of how individual communication styles may influence political outcomes can be seen in the negotiations between Iraqi president Saddam Hussein and representatives of the United States and the United Nations. For example, just prior to the Gulf War, in 1990, many Middle East experts assumed that Hussein was not ready to fight, that he was merely bluffing, using an Arabic style of communication. This style emphasizes the importance of animation, exaggeration, and conversational form over content (Feghali, 1997). Communication specialists note that in conflict situations Arab speakers may threaten the life and property of their opponents but have no intention of actually carrying out the threats. Rather, Arab speakers use threats to buy time and intimidate their opponents. Thus, declaratory statements by U.S. leaders, such as "We will find the cancer and cut it out," seemed mundane and unintimidating to Arab listeners. Verbal exchanges, regardless of the different speech styles, often take the place of physical violence (Griefat & Katriel, 1989).

However, we always need to consider the relationship between individual and societal forces in studying intercultural communication. Although communication on the interpersonal level is important, we must remember that individuals often are born into and are caught up in conflicts that they neither started nor chose.

THE SELF-AWARENESS IMPERATIVE

One of the most important reasons for studying intercultural communication is the awareness it raises of our own cultural identity and background. This is also one of the least obvious reasons. Peter Adler (1975), a noted social psychologist, observes that the study of intercultural communication begins as a journey into another culture and reality and ends as a journey into one's own culture.

Examples from the authors' own lives come to mind. Judith's earliest experiences in public school made her realize that not everyone wore "coverings" and "bonnets" and "cape dresses," the clothing worn by her Amish/Mennonite family. She realized that her family was different from most of the other people she came in contact with. When Tom, who is of Japanese descent, first started elementary school, he attended a White school in the segregated U.S. South. By the time he reached fourth grade, schools were integrated, and some African American students were intrigued by his very straight black hair. At that point, he recognized a connection between himself and the Black students, and he developed a kernel of self-awareness about his identity.

We gain similar insights in intercultural experiences overseas. When Judith was teaching high school in Algeria, a Muslim country in North Africa, she realized something about her religious identity as a Protestant. December 25 came and went, and she taught classes with no mention of Christmas. Judith had never thought about how special the celebration of Christmas was or how important

This writer decries a certain kind of intercultural learning—the learning that some study-abroad students pursue—whereby people in other countries are objectified and viewed as exotic and strange. The real problem arises when these students are hired to write television commercials and to present ideas about other cultures.

One type of commercial model shows us exotic humans in all their tribal finery, but, in a multicultural twist, they—Masai warriors, Sicilian matrons, Tibetan monks, Irish fishermen—are revealed as strangely prescient consumers with a quirky knowledge of luxury cars or Internet stock trading. In one commercial, we witness an Inuit elder teaching his grandson about tracking by identifying marks in the snow. "That," he says, "is a caribou." Then, after a pause, during which the wise man stares at the snow, he reverentially intones the single word "Audi." From ads like those, astute students learn that foreigners are obsessed with us—our commodities and displays. What we may learn from them pales in comparison with the glories that they see in our consumer lifestyle.

Other commercials reduce distant lands to images of animals or nature and imply that nature can be thoroughly dominated by SUV's or swaggering, extreme-sports youths. Athletes and Nissan Pathfinders fight bulls in a ring, giant outdoorsmen tap the miniaturized Rockies, a hiker butts heads with a bighorn sheep. And, of course, sophisticated viewers know that all those animals are the creation of technology.

In one commercial, a driver—insulated in his fully self-sufficient cocoon—is able to program both the road and the various beautiful and exotic settings it passes through. Not only is the technologically empowered American greater than nature, we create nature to suit our whims. There is no outside world anymore, no dark places of mystery, yet to be seen. Our SUV's do not travel to an unknown world so much as create different options from a well-known list. Television's emphasis is on how the actor—whether a contestant on a reality-TV show or the driver in a car ad—is seen and manipulates how she is seen. Even when outsiders exist, everyone is looking at us.

When a promotional piece for the reality-TV show The Amazing Race *shows an American woman in a clearly foreign space—perhaps India— she is not troubled, confused or interested in her environment. Instead she*

the holiday was to her. She then recognized on a personal level the uniqueness of this particular cultural practice. Erla, a graduate student from Iceland, notes the increased knowledge and appreciation she's gained concerning her home country:

Living in another country widens your horizon. It makes you appreciate the things you have, and it strengthens the family unit. You look at your country from a different point of view. We have learned not to expect everything to be the same as "at home," but if we happen to find something that reminds us of home, we really

strips down to a bikini emblazoned with a U.S. flag to get directions to the next challenge from a bug-eyed and eager native. "Will I wear this if it helps me get home?" she says. "Hell, yeah!" The young woman clearly did not travel to broaden her horizons. For her, India becomes, as much as Salt Lake City or Kandahar, a place for aggressive performance of her American identity—unwrapping herself in the flag, so to speak.

We now are the world, to be looked at, admired, or despised; what is important about the activity of others is their response to our display. . . . [Study-abroad students] talk about interactions with outsiders only in vague abstractions, while expostulating brilliantly about the nuances of American students' interactions with one another. The few individuals who left their peers to engage the outside world explained that move as an individual rejection of the group and still found it easier to discuss their fellow students than the generically defined "friends" they met at bars.

One young American who traveled to Guatemala bragged that "I have a surprising ability to relate to almost everyone," but "everyone" turned out to mean members of preconceived categories of human-rights workers, Indians, and children, whom she described as objects of more first-person sentences. She specifically excluded less exotic, fast-talking city folk who were "just different" and not worth mentioning.

Students return from study-abroad programs having seen the world, but the world they return to tell tales about is more often than not the world they already knew, the imaginary world of globalized, postmodern capitalism where everything is already known, everyone speaks the same language, and the outside world keeps its eyes on those of us who come from the center.

. . . we should avoid pre- and post-travel orientation sessions that focus on group dynamics and individual growth. Instead, those sessions could be used as opportunities for students to learn how to question the way that we tell stories about our travels, and to discover for themselves how those stories share features with commercials about men who play football with lions and reality shows where contestants dare each other to swallow centipedes.

Source: From B. Feinberg, "What Students Don't Learn Abroad," *The Chronicle Review,* May 2, 2000, p. B20.

appreciate it and it makes us very happy. Ultimately we are all very thankful that we had the opportunity to live in another country.

However, it is also important to realize that intercultural journeys are not simply about personal growth and personal insights. They're also about learning about the amazing peoples on the planet we inhabit. One U.S. student who spent 10 weeks working on a college project in Zimbabwe, Lesotho, and South Africa said, "I learned that I'm a risk-taker, that I don't put up with people's bull . . . that I can do anything that I put my mind to. I can do anything I want. You know, it's just—life is what you make it" (quoted in Feinberg, 2002, p. B20). However, what this young man perhaps did not learn was that many Zimbabweans live difficult lives, that 25% of the population is HIV-positive, and that these people cannot do anything they put their minds to. As one faculty member lamented, "Like so many other traveling young people, he claimed to have learned about himself, and talked about group dynamics, students' transgressive behavior, like drinking too much and bungee jumping at Victoria Falls—rather than southern Africa's cultures or social problems" (p. B20).

Living in an increasingly diverse world, we can take the opportunity to learn more about our own cultural backgrounds and identities and about our similarities to and differences from the people with whom we interact.

THE ETHICAL IMPERATIVE

Living in an intercultural world presents ethical challenges as well. **Ethics** may be thought of as principles of conduct that help govern the behavior of individuals and groups. These principles often arise from communities' consensus on what is good and bad behavior. Cultural values tell us what is "good" and what "ought" to be good. Ethical judgments focus more on the degrees of rightness and wrongness in human behavior than do cultural values (Johannesen, 1990).

Some judgments are stated very explicitly. For example, the Ten Commandments teach that it is wrong to steal, tell a lie, commit murder, and so on. Many other identifiable principles of conduct that arise from our cultural experience may be less explicit—for instance, that people should be treated equally and should work hard. Several issues come to mind in a discussion of ethics in intercultural communication. For example, what happens when two ethical systems collide? Although an individual may want to "do the right thing" to contribute to a better society, it is not always easy to know what is "right" in specific situations. Ethical principles are often culture bound, and intercultural conflicts arise from various notions of what is ethical behavior.

One common cross-cultural ethical dilemma involves standards of conducting business in multinational corporations. The U.S. Congress and the Securities and Exchange Commission consider it unethical to make payments to government officials of other countries to promote trade. (Essentially, such payments smack of bribery.) However, in many countries, like China, government officials are paid in this informal way instead of being supported by taxes (Ambler & Witzel, 2000). What, then, is ethical behavior for personnel in multinational subsidiaries?

Relativity Versus Universality

In this book, we stress the relativity of cultural behavior—that no cultural pattern is inherently right or wrong. So, is there any universality in ethics? Are any cultural behaviors always right or always wrong? The answers depend on one's perspective. A universalist might try, for example, to identify acts and conditions that most societies think of as wrong, such as murder, theft, or treason. Someone who takes an extreme universalist position would insist that cultural differences are only superficial, that fundamental notions of right and wrong are universal. Some religions take universal positions—for example, that the Ten Commandments are a universal code of behavior. But Christian groups often disagree about the universality of the Bible. For example, are the teachings of the New Testament mainly guidelines for the Christians of Jesus' time, or can they be applied to Christians in the 21st century? These are difficult issues for many people searching for ethical guidelines (Johannesen, 1990). The philosopher Immanuel Kant (1949) believed in the universality of moral laws. His well-known "categorical imperative" states that people should act only on maxims that apply universally, to *all* individuals.

The extreme relativist position holds that any cultural behavior can be judged only within the cultural context in which it occurs. This means that only those members of a community can truly judge the ethics of their own members. According to communication scholar William S. Howell (1982),

> *The environment, the situation, the timing of an interaction, human relationships all affect the way ethical standards are applied. . . . The concept of universal ethics, standards of goodness that apply to everyone, everywhere, and at all times, is the sort of myth people struggle to hold onto. (pp. 182, 187)*

And yet, to accept a completely relativistic position seems to tacitly accept the horrors of Nazi Germany, South African apartheid, or U.S. slavery. In each case, the larger community developed cultural beliefs that supported persecution and discrimination in such extreme forms that worldwide condemnation ultimately resulted (Hall, 1997, p. 23).

Philosophers and anthropologists have struggled to develop ethical guidelines that seem universally applicable but that also recognize the tremendous cultural variability in the world. And many ethical relativists appeal to more natural, humanitarian principles. This more moderate position assumes that people can evaluate cultures without succumbing to **ethnocentrism,** that all individuals and cultural groups share a fundamental humanistic belief in the sanctity of the human spirit and the goodness of peace, and that people should respect the well-being of others (Kale, 1994).

Communication scholar Bradford J. Hall (1997) reminds us that relativistic and universalistic approaches to ethics should be viewed not as a dichotomy but rather as a compound of universalism and relativism. All ethics systems involve a tension between the universal and the relative. So, although we recognize some universal will toward ethical principles, we may have to live with the tension of not being able to impose our "universal" ethic on others.

A recent suggestion for meeting the ethical imperative is to employ a **dialogical approach.** The dialogical approach emphasizes the importance of relationships and dialogues between individuals and communities in wrestling with ethical dilemmas. Communication scholars Stanley Deetz, Deborah Cohen, and Paige P. Edley (1997) suggest that, even in international business contexts, a dialogical approach can work. As an example, they cite the ethical challenges that arise when a corporation relocates its operations overseas. Although this relocation may make good business sense, the move often has difficult personal and social (and therefore ethical) ramifications. The move may cause a wave of unemployment in the old location and raise issues of exploitation of the workforce and harm to the environment in the new location (especially where poverty is a problem).

Deetz and colleagues (1997) suggest that moving from an owner/manager model to a dialogical stakeholder model can help clarify some of the ethical issues. The dialogical approach emphasizes the importance of the relationship and dialogue between the company and the various communities and stakeholders. They propose forums for discussion even while acknowledging that sometimes discussions and forums are used by management to suppress or diffuse conflict rather than to promote genuine debate for the sake of company improvement. In this case, a dialogical approach

> *does not rest in agreement or consensus but in the avoidance of the suppression of alternative conceptions and possibilities . . . the heterogeneity of the international community and the creative possibilities residing in intercultural communication provide possibilities that may have been overlooked in national cultures. (Deetz, Cohen, & Edley, 1997, pp. 222–223)*

The study of intercultural communication not only provides insights into cultural patterns but also helps us address the ethical issues involved in intercultural interaction. Specifically we should be able to (1) judge what is ethical and unethical behavior given variations in cultural priorities, (2) identify guidelines for ethical behavior in intercultural contexts in which ethics clash.

Being Ethical Students of Culture

Related to the issue of judging cultural patterns as ethical or unethical are the issues surrounding the study of culture. Part of learning about intercultural communication is learning about cultural patterns and cultural identities—our own and others. There are two issues to address here: developing self-reflexivity and learning about others.

Developing Self-Reflexivity   In studying intercultural communication, it is vital to develop **self-reflexivity**—to understand ourselves and our position in society. In learning about other cultures and cultural practices, we often learn much about ourselves. Immigrants often comment that they never felt so much like someone of their own nationality until they left their homeland.

Think about it: Many cultural attitudes and ideas are instilled in you, but these can be difficult to unravel and identify. Knowing who you are is never simple; rather, it is an ongoing process that can never fully capture the ever-emerging person. Not only will you grow older, but your intercultural experiences change who you are and who you think you are. It is also important to reflect on your place in society. By recognizing the social categories to which you belong, and the implications of those categories, you will be in a better position to understand how to communicate. For example, being an undergraduate student positions you to communicate your ideas on specific subjects and in particular ways to various members of the faculty or staff at your school. You might want to communicate to the registrar your desire to change majors—this would be an appropriate topic to address to that person. But you would not be well positioned during an exam to communicate to your chemistry professor your problems with your girl- or boyfriend.

Learning About Others   It is important to remember that the study of cultures is actually the study of other people. Never lose sight of the humanity at the core of the topic. Try not to observe people as if they are zoo animals. Communication scholar Bradford Hall (1997) cautions against using the "zoo approach" to studying culture:

> *When using such an approach we view the study of culture as if we were walking through a zoo admiring, gasping and chuckling at the various exotic animals we observe. One may discover amazing, interesting and valuable information by using such a perspective and even develop a real fondness for these exotic people, but miss the point that we are as culturally "caged" as others and that they are culturally as "free" as we are. (p. 14)*

Remember that you are studying real people who have real lives, and your conclusions about them may have very real consequences for them and for you. Cultural studies scholar Linda Alcoff (1991/1992) acknowledges the ethical issues involved when students of culture try to describe the cultural patterns of others; she recognizes the difficulty of speaking "for" and "about" others who have different lives. Instead, she suggests, students of culture should try to speak "with" and "to" others. Rather than merely describe others from a distance, it's better to engage others in a dialogue about their cultural realities.

Learn to listen to the voices of others, to cultivate experiential knowledge. Hearing about the experiences of people who are different from you can broaden your ways of viewing the world. Many differences—based on race, gender, sexual orientation, nationality, ethnicity, age, and so on—deeply affect people's everyday lives. Listening carefully as people relate their experiences and their ways of knowing will help you learn about the many aspects of intercultural communication.

Changing Through Intercultural Contact

Sometimes communities lose their cultural uniqueness because of intercultural contact. While visiting the Navajo Nation, Judith heard an older Navajo woman lamenting the fact that many of the young people no longer followed Navajo traditions. In contrast, one reason the Amish have remained culturally intact is that they have resisted contact with outside communities. But not all communities are able to resist such contact. In many cases, it is forced on them. Sometimes, though, intercultural contact is welcome. International students who decide to

I have spent three years in the United States seeking an education. I am from Singapore, and I believe that in many ways both countries are similar. They are both multicultural. They both have a dominant culture. In the United States the dominant culture is White, and in Singapore it is Chinese.

Coming to the United States has taught me to be more aware of diversity. Even though in Singapore we are diverse, because I was part of the majority there, I didn't feel the need to increase my level of intercultural awareness. In the United States I became a minority, and that has made me feel the need to become more culturally competent.

—Jacqueline

stay in their host country rather than return home experience the transformative power of intercultural contact.

Everett Kleinjans (1975), an international educator, stresses that intercultural education differs from some other kinds of education: Although all education may be potentially transformative, learning as a result of intercultural contact is particularly so in that it deals with fundamental aspects of human behavior. Learning about intercultural communication sometimes calls into question the core of our basic assumptions about ourselves, our culture, and our worldviews, and challenges existing and preferred beliefs, values, and patterns of behavior. Liliana, a Colombian student, describes such a transformation:

When I first came to the States to study and live I was surprised with all the diversity and different cultures I encountered. I realized I came from a country, society, school and group of friends with little diversity. During all the years I lived in Colombia I did not meet more than five people from other countries. Even at my school, there was little diversity—only two students of color among three thousand students. I realized that big difference when I was suddenly sharing a college classroom with students from all over the world, people of all colors and cultures. At the beginning it was difficult getting used to it because of the wide diversity, but I like and enjoy it now and I wish my family and friends could experience and learn as much as I have.

What constitutes ethical and unethical applications of intercultural communication knowledge? One questionable practice involves people who study intercultural communication in order to proselytize others without their consent. (Some religious organizations conduct Bible study on college campuses for international students under the guise of English language lessons.) Another questionable practice is the behavior of cross-cultural consultants who misrepresent or exaggerate their ability to deal with complex issues of prejudice and racism in brief, one-shot training sessions (Paige & Martin, 1996).

A final questionable practice concerns research on the intercultural communication of U.S. minority groups. A common approach in the United States is for a White, tenured faculty member to conduct such research employing graduate and undergraduate students from the minority groups being studied:

> *Minority students are sometimes used as a way to gain immediate access to the community of interest. These students go into communities and the (usually white) professors are spared the intense, time-consuming work of establishing relationships in the community. (Martin & Butler, 2001, p. 291)*

These students are then asked to report their findings to and interpret their community for the faculty member. Unfortunately, doing so can jeopardize their relationship to their community, which may be suspicious of the academic community. The faculty member publishes articles and reaps the tangible rewards of others' hard work—promotions, pay raises, and professional visibility. Meanwhile, the community and the students may receive little for their valuable contributions to this academic work.

SUMMARY

In this chapter, we identified six reasons, or imperatives, for studying intercultural communication: the technological, the demographic, the economic, the peace, the self-awareness, and the ethical. Perhaps you can think of some other reasons. We stressed that the situations in which intercultural communication takes place are complex and challenging. Unfortunately, there are no easy answers.

We also raised some issues that will be addressed in the following chapters as we continue our study of communication and culture. What is the next step? Now that we have identified some of the reasons to study intercultural communication, we can look at how scholars and professionals have tackled the topic. In Chapter 2, we describe three approaches to the study of intercultural communication and give examples of what each approach contributes. We also present our dialectical approach, the framework for this textbook.

DISCUSSION QUESTIONS

1. How do electronic means of communication (e-mail, the Internet, fax, and so on) differ from face-to-face interactions?
2. How does the increased mobility of our society affect us as individuals? How does it affect the way we form relationships?
3. What are some of the potential challenges organizations face as they become more diverse?
4. How might organizations benefit from increased diversity in the workplace? How might individuals benefit?
5. How do economic situations affect intergroup relations?

 Go to the self-quizzes on the Online Learning Center at www.mhhe.com/martinnakayama to further test your knowledge.

ACTIVITIES

1. *Family Tree.* Interview the oldest member of your family whom you can contact. Then answer the following questions:

   a. When did your ancestors come to the United States?
   b. Where did they come from?
   c. What were the reasons for their move? Did they come voluntarily?
   d. What language(s) did they speak?
   e. What difficulties did they encounter?
   f. Did they change their names? For what reasons?
   g. What were their occupations before they came, and what jobs did they take on their arrival?
   h. How has your family status changed through the generations?

   Compare your family experience with those of your classmates. Did most immigrants come for the same reasons? What are the differences in the various stories?

2. *Intercultural Encounter.* Describe and analyze a recent intercultural encounter. This may mean talking with someone of a different age, ethnicity, race, religion, and so on.

   a. Describe the encounter. What made it "intercultural"?
   b. Explain how you initially felt about the communication.
   c. Describe how you felt after the encounter, and explain why you think you felt as you did.
   d. Describe any challenges in trying to communicate. If there were no challenges, explain why you think it was so easy.
   e. Based on this experience, identify some characteristics that may be important for successful intercultural communication.

KEY WORDS

Anglocentrism
colonialism
demographics
dialogical approach
diversity
enclaves
ethics
ethnocentrism
global village
heterogeneity
identity management

identity tourism
immigrants
intercultural communication
maquiladoras
melting pot
mobility
multinational corporations
multiphrenia
nativistic
self-reflexivity

 The Online Learning Center at www.mhhe.com/martinnakayama features flashcards and crossword puzzles based on these terms and concepts.

REFERENCES

Adler, P. S. (1975). The transition experience: An alternative view of culture shock. *Journal of Humanistic Psychology, 15,* 13–23.

Alcoff, L. (1991/1992). The problem of speaking for others. *Cultural Critique, 20,* 5–32.

Ambler, T., & Witzel, M. (2000). *Doing business in China.* New York: Routledge.

Asmussen, C. G., & Arend, C. (2002). *Internet usage and commerce in Western Europe 2001–2006.* www.idc.com/getdoc.jhtml?containerId=fr2002_04_19_115126.

Baldwin, J. (1955). *Notes of a native son.* Boston: Beacon Press.

Banks, J. (1991). *Teaching strategies for ethnic studies.* Needham, MA: Allyn & Bacon.

Brewer, C. A., & Suchan, T. A. (2001). *Mapping Census 2000: The geography of U.S. diversity.* (U.S. Census Bureau, Census Special Reports, Series CENSR/01–1.) Washington, DC: U.S. Government Printing Office.

Cole, D. (1998). Five myths about immigration. In P. S. Rothenberg (Ed.), *Race, class, and gender in the United States: An integrated study* (4th ed., pp. 125–129). New York: St. Martin's Press.

Curtin, P. D. (1969). *The Atlantic slave trade: A census.* Madison: University of Wisconsin Press.

Danet, B. (1999). Text as mask: Gender, play and performance on the Internet. In S. G. Jones (Ed.), *Cybersociety 2.0: Revisiting computer-mediated communication and community* (pp. 129–159). Thousand Oaks, CA: Sage.

Deetz, S., Cohen, D., & Edley, P. P. (1997). Toward a dialogic ethic in the context of international business organization. In F. L. Casmir (Ed.), *Ethics in intercultural and international communication* (pp. 183–226). Mahwah, NJ: Lawrence Erlbaum.

Delgado, F. (2002). Mass-mediated communication and intercultural conflict. In J. N. Martin, T. K. Nakayama, & L. A. Flores (Eds.), *Readings in intercultural communication* (pp. 351–359). Boston: McGraw-Hill.

Falling through the net II: New data on the digital divide. (1998, July). Washington, DC: U.S. Department of Commerce, National Telecommunications and Information Administration (NTIA).

Fallows, J. (1989). *More like us: Putting America's native strengths and traditional values to work to overcome the Asian challenge.* Boston: Houghton Mifflin.

Feghali, E. (1997). Arab cultural communication patterns. *International Journal of Intercultural Relations, 21,* 345–379.

Feinberg, B. (2002, May 2). What students don't learn abroad. *The Chronicle Review,* p. B20.

Ferdman, B. M., & Brody, S. E. (1996). Models of diversity training. In D. Landis & R. Bhagat (Eds.), *Handbook of intercultural training* (2nd ed., pp. 282–303). Thousand Oaks, CA: Sage.

Foner, E. (1998). Who is an American? In P. S. Rothenberg (Ed.), *Race, class, and gender in the United States: An integrated study* (4th ed., pp. 84–92). New York: St. Martin's Press.

Friedman, T. L. (1999). *The Lexus and the olive tree.* New York: Farrar, Straus & Giroux.

———. (2002, March 6). The core of Muslim rage. *The New York Times* www.nytimes.com/2002/03/06/opinion/06FRIE.html?ei=1&en=%20bd6293bb96564.

Fussell, P. (1992). *Class: A guide through the American status system.* New York: Touchstone Books.

Gergen, K. (1991). *The saturated self: Dilemmas of identity in contemporary life.* New York: HarperCollins/Basic Books.

Griefat, Y., & Katriel, T. (1989). Life demands *musayara:* Communication and culture among Arabs in Israel. In S. Ting-Toomey & F. Korzenny (Eds.), *Language, communication and culture: International and intercultural communication annual* (Vol. 13, pp. 121–138). Newbury Park, CA: Sage.

Hacker, A. (1997). *Money: Who has how much and why.* New York: Scribner.

Hall, B. J. (1997). Culture, ethics and communication. In F. L. Casmir (Ed.), *Ethics in intercultural and international communication* (pp. 11–41). Mahwah, NJ: Lawrence Erlbaum.

Howell, W. S. (1982). *The empathic communicator.* Belmont, CA: Wadsworth.

Johannesen, R. L. (1990). *Ethics in human communication* (3rd ed.). Prospect Heights, IL: Waveland Press.

Kale, D. W. (1994). Peace as an ethic for intercultural communication. In L. Samovar & R. E. Porter (Eds.), *Intercultural communication: A reader* (7th ed., pp. 435–441). Belmont, CA: Wadsworth.

Kant, I. (1949). *Fundamental principles of the metaphysics of morals* (T. Abbott, Trans.). Indianapolis, IN: Library of Liberal Arts/Bobbs-Merrill.

Kleinjans, E. (1975). A question of ethics. *International Education and Cultural Exchange, 10,* 20–25.

Kraybill, D. B. (1989). *The riddle of Amish culture.* Baltimore: Johns Hopkins University Press.

Loewen, J. W. (1995). *Lies my teacher told me.* New York: Simon & Schuster.

Mantsios, G. (2001). Class in America: Myths and realities. In P. S. Rothenberg (Ed.), *Race, class, and gender in the United States: An integrated study* (5th ed., pp. 168–182). New York: Worth.

Martin, J. N., & Butler, R. L. W. (2001). Toward an ethic of intercultural communication research. In V. H. Milhouse, M. K. Asante, & P. O. Nwosu (Eds.), *Transcultural realities: Interdisciplinary perspectives on cross-cultural relations* (pp. 283–298). Thousand Oaks, CA: Sage.

Marx, E. (1999). *Breaking through culture shock: What you need to succeed in international business.* London: Nicholas Brealy.

McLuhan, M. (1967). *The medium is the message.* New York: Bantam Books.

Muzrui, A. (2001). Historical struggles between Islamic and Christian worldviews: An interpretation. In V. H. Milhouse, M. K. Asante, & P. O. Nwosu (Eds.), *Transcultural realities: Interdisciplinary perspectives on cross-cultural relations* (pp. 109–120). Thousand Oaks, CA: Sage.

Now a nation of more immigrants than every. (2002, February 7). *Christian Science Monitor,* p. 1.

Paige, R. M., & Martin, J. N. (1996). Ethics in intercultural training. In D. Landis & R. Bhagat (Eds.), *Handbook of intercultural training.* Newbury Park, CA: Sage.

Roediger, D. (1991). *The wages of whiteness: Race and the making of the American working class.* New York: Verso.

Schmitt, E. (2001, April 3). Analysis of census finds segregation along with diversity www.nytimes.com/2001/04/04/national/04CENS.html?ex=987410510&ei=1&en =a2cf77e31f7952.

Takaki, R. (1989). *Strangers from a different shore.* New York: Penguin Books.

Ten great global marketing mistakes. (1998, January 19). *Sarasota Herald-Tribune.*

Turkle, S. (1995). *Life on the screen: Identity in the age of the Internet.* New York: Simon & Schuster.

West, C. (1993). *Race matters.* Boston: Beacon Press.

Yergin, D., & Stanislaw, J. A. (1998). *The commanding heights: The battle between government and marketplace that is remaking the modern world.* New York: Simon & Schuster.

THE HISTORY OF THE STUDY OF INTERCULTURAL COMMUNICATION

Now that we've described a rationale for studying intercultural communication, we turn to ways in which the study of intercultural communication is conducted. To understand the contemporary approaches to this discipline, it's important to examine its historical and philosophical foundations. Why should you study how the field of intercultural communication got started? Before answering this question, let us pose a few others: Whom do you think should be regarded as an expert in intercultural communication? Someone who has actually lived in a variety of cultures? Or someone who has conducted scientific studies on how cultural groups differ in values and attitudes? Or someone who analyzes what popular culture (movies, television, magazines, and so on) has to say about a particular group of people?

Consider a related question: What is the best way to study intercultural communication behavior? By observing how people communicate in various cultures? By asking people to describe their own communication patterns? By distributing questionnaires to various cultural groups? Or by analyzing books, videos, movies, and other cultural performances of various groups?

The answers to these questions help determine what kind of material goes into a textbook on intercultural communication. And intercultural communication scholars do not agree on what are the "right" answers to these questions. Thus, these questions and answers have implications for what you will be exposed to in this book and this course. By choosing some types of research (questionnaire, observation data), we may neglect other types (interviews, travel journal, media analysis).

To help you understand why we chose to include the material we did, we describe the origins of the discipline in the United States and the philosophical worldviews that inform the current study and practices of intercultural communication. We then outline three contemporary perspectives that recognize contributions from other disciplines. Finally, we outline our dialectical approach, which integrates the strengths from all three contemporary perspectives.

THE EARLY DEVELOPMENT OF THE DISCIPLINE

The current study of intercultural communication is influenced in part by how it developed in the United States and in part by the **worldviews,** or research philosophies, of the scholars who pursue it. The roots of the study of intercultural communication can be traced to the post–World War II era, when the United States increasingly came to dominate the world stage. However, government and business personnel working overseas often found that they were ill equipped to work among people from different cultures. The language training they received, for example, did little to prepare them for the complex challenges of working abroad.

In response, the U.S. government in 1946 passed the Foreign Service Act and established the Foreign Service Institute (FSI). The FSI, in turn, hired Edward T. Hall and other prominent anthropologists and linguists (including Ray Birdwhistell and George Trager) to develop "predeparture" courses for overseas workers. Because intercultural training materials were scarce, they developed their own. In so doing, FSI theorists formed new ways of looking at culture and communication. Thus, the field of intercultural communication was born.

Nonverbal Communication

The FSI emphasized the importance of nonverbal communication and applied linguistic frameworks to investigate nonverbal aspects of communication. These researchers concluded that, just like language, nonverbal communication varies from culture to culture. E. T. Hall pioneered this systematic study of culture and communication with *The Silent Language* (1959) and *The Hidden Dimension* (1966), which influenced the new discipline. In *The Silent Language*, for example, Hall introduced the notion of **proxemics,** the study of how people use personal space to communicate. In *The Hidden Dimension*, in elaborating on the concept of proxemics, he identified four **distance zones**—intimate, personal, social, and public—at which people interact and suggested that people know which distance to use depending on the situation. He noted that each cultural group has its own set of rules for personal space and that respecting these cultural differences is critical to smooth communication.

Application of Theory

The staff at the FSI found that government workers were not interested in theories of culture and communication; rather, they wanted specific guidelines for getting along in the countries they were visiting. Hall's initial strategy in developing materials for these predeparture training sessions was to observe variations in cultural behavior. At the FSI, he was surrounded by people who spoke many languages and who were from many cultures, so it was a great place to observe and test his theories about cultural differences. For example, he might have observed that Italians tend to stand close to each other when conversing, or that Greeks use lots of hand gestures when interacting, or that Chinese use few hand gestures in conversations. He could then have confirmed his observations by consulting members of different cultural groups. Today, most textbooks in the discipline retain this focus on practical guidelines and barriers to communication.

This emphasis on the application of theory spawned a parallel "discipline" of **cross-cultural training,** which began with the FSI staff and was expanded in the 1960s to include training for students and business personnel. More recently, it has come to include **diversity training,** which facilitates intercultural communication among members of various gender, ethnic, and racial groups, mostly in the corporate or government workplace (Landis & Bhagat, 1996).

An Emphasis on International Settings

Early scholars and trainers in intercultural communication defined *culture* narrowly, primarily in terms of "nationality." Usually, scholars mistakenly compared middle-class U.S. citizens with all residents of other nations, and trainers tended to focus on helping middle-class professionals become successful overseas.

One might ask why so few scholars focused on domestic contexts, particularly in the 1960s and 1970s when the United States was fraught with civil unrest. One reason may be the early emphasis of the FSI on helping overseas personnel. Another reason may be that most scholars who studied intercultural communication gained their intercultural experience in international contexts such as the Peace Corps, the military, or the transnational corporation.

An Interdisciplinary Focus

The scholars at the FSI came from various disciplines, including linguistics, anthropology, and psychology. Not surprisingly, in their work related to communication, they drew from theories pertinent to their specific disciplines. Contributions from these fields of study blended to form an integrated approach that remains useful to this day.

Linguists help us understand the importance of language and its role in intercultural interaction. They describe how languages vary in "surface" structure and are similar in "deep" structure. They also shed light on the relationship between language and reality. For example, the **Sapir-Whorf hypothesis,** developed by linguists Edward Sapir and Benjamin Whorf, explores phenomena such as the use of formal and informal pronouns. French and Spanish, for instance, have both formal and informal forms of the pronoun *you.* (In French, the formal is *vous* and the informal is *tu;* in Spanish, the formal is *usted* and the informal is *tu.*) In contrast, English makes no distinction between formal and informal usage; one word, *you,* suffices in both situations. Such language distinctions affect our culture's notion of formality. Linguists also point out that learning a second or third language can enhance our **intercultural competence** by providing insights into other cultures and expanding our communication repertoire.

Anthropologists help us understand the role that culture plays in our lives and the importance of nonverbal communication. Anthropologist Renate Rosaldo (1989) encouraged scholars to consider the appropriateness of cultural study methods, and other anthropologists have followed Rosaldo's lead. They point out that many U.S. and European studies reveal more about the researchers than about their subjects. Further, many anthropological studies of the past, particularly of non-Europeans, concluded that the people studied were inferior. To understand this phenomenon, science writer Stephen Jay Gould (1993) argues that "we must first recognize the cultural milieu of a society whose leaders and intellectuals did not doubt the propriety of racial thinking, with Indians below whites, and blacks below everyone else" (p. 85).

The so-called scientific study of other peoples is never entirely separate from the culture in which the researchers are immersed. In his study of the Victorian era, for example, Patrick Brantlinger (1986) notes that "evolutionary anthropology often suggested that Africans, if not nonhuman or a different species, were such an inferior 'breed' that they might be impervious to 'higher influences'" (p. 201). Consider this famous case, which dates back to the early 19th century:

The young African woman was lured to Europe with false promises of fame and fortune. She was paraded naked before jeering mobs. She was exhibited in a metal cage and sold to an animal trainer. When she died in Paris in 1816, she was penniless and friendless among people who derided her as a circus freak.

White scientists intent on proving the inferiority of blacks dissected her body, bottled her brain and genitals, wired her skeleton and displayed them in a French museum. That might have been the end of Saartjie Baartman, the young African woman derisively labeled the "Hottentot Venus."

[However,] 192 years after she last looked on these rugged cliffs and roaring sea [of South Africa], her remains returned to the land of her birth. In an agreement negotiated after years of wrangling between South Africa and France, her remains were finally removed from the Musée de l'Homme in Paris and flown back home. (Swarns, 2002, p. A28)

This return of Baartman's remains is part of a larger movement away from a scientific "era when indigenous people were deemed worthy of scientific study, but unworthy of the consideration commonly accorded to whites" (Swarns, 2002, p. A28). Indeed, the conclusions from such studies reveal more about the cultural attitudes of the researchers (e.g., ethnocentrism, racism, sexism) than they do about the people studied. An **interdisciplinary focus** can help us acquire and interpret information in a more comprehensive manner—in ways relevant to bettering the intercultural communication process, as well as producing knowledge.

Psychologists such as Gordon Allport help us understand notions of stereotyping and the ways in which prejudice functions in our lives and in intercultural interaction. In his classic study *The Nature of Prejudice* (1979), he describes how prejudice can develop from "normal" human cognitive activities such as categorization and generalization. Other psychologists, such as Richard Brislin (1999) and Dan Landis (Landis & Wasilewski, 1999), reveal how variables like nationality, ethnicity, personality, and gender influence our communication.

Whereas the early study of intercultural communication was characterized as interdisciplinary, over time, it became increasingly centered in the discipline of communication. Nevertheless, the field continues to be influenced by interdisciplinary contributions, including ideas from cultural studies, critical theory, and the more traditional disciplines of psychology and anthropology (Hart, 1999).

PERCEPTION AND WORLDVIEW OF THE RESEARCHER

A second influence on the current study of intercultural communication is the research **paradigm,** or worldview, of the scholars involved. People understand and learn about the world through filtering lenses; they select, evaluate, and organize information (stimuli) from the external environment through **perception.** As Marshal Singer (1987) explains:

We experience everything in the world not "as it is"—because there is no way that we can know the world "as it is"—but only as the world comes to us through our sensory receptors. From there, these stimuli go instantly into the "data-storage banks" of our brains, where they have to pass through the filters of our censor screen, our decoding mechanism, and the collectivity of everything we have learned from the day we were born. (p. 9)

As a child, I did not consciously think of myself as a German or as a Norwegian. Since I never viewed myself in terms of my culture, cultural heritage was something with which I never used to identify others. When I communicated with others, the cultural background of the person I was talking with never crossed my mind. To someone who constantly sees racism and prejudice, this situation may seem ideal, but ignoring a person's culture can cause as much harm as judging someone based upon that culture. Knowledge of someone's historical background is necessary when communicating on anything other than a superficial level. Not being aware of someone's culture can make a communicator appear ignorant. I tend to treat everyone the same, even in situations where I shouldn't. On more than one occasion, I went to a foreign friend's house and talked to his parents as I would to "American" parents. By not recognizing that their culture has much more formal communication between elders and children, I seemed rude. Being aware that someone may not recognize how your culture affects your communication skills can help you avoid judging others for their treatment of you. If I had condemned my friend's parents for thinking I was rude, I would have made an equally rash judgment.

—Andrew

In this sense, all of the information we have already stored in our brains (learning) affects how we interpret new information. Some of our learning and perception is group related. That is, we see the world in particular ways because of the cultural groups (based on ethnicity, age, gender, and so on) to which we belong. These group-related perceptions (worldviews or value orientations) are so fundamental that we rarely question them (Singer, 1998). They involve our assumptions about human nature, the physical and spiritual world, and the ways in which humans should relate to one another. For example, most U.S. Americans perceive human beings as separate from nature and believe that there is a fundamental difference between, say, a human and a rock. However, other cultural groups (Japanese, Chinese, traditional Native Americans) see humans and human reality as part of a larger physical reality. For them, the difference between a human and a rock is not so pronounced.

The key point here is that academic research is also cultural behavior, because research traditions require particular worldviews about the nature of reality and knowledge and particular beliefs about how research should be conducted. And these research paradigms are often held as strongly as cultural or spiritual beliefs (Burrell & Morgan, 1988; Kuhn, 1970). There are even examples of intercultural conflicts in which scholars strongly disagree. For example, Galileo was excommunicated from the Catholic Church in the 17th century because he took issue with theologians' belief that the earth was the center of the universe.

46

More recent examples of the relation between academic research and cultural behavior can be seen in the social sciences. Some communication scholars believe there is an external reality that can be measured and studied, whereas others believe that reality can be understood only as lived and experienced by individuals (Casmir, 1994). In short, beliefs and assumptions about reality influence research methods and findings, and so also influence what we currently know about intercultural communication.

At present, we can identify three broad approaches, or worldviews, that characterize the study of culture and communication (Gudykunst, 2002a, 2002b; Gudykunst & Nishida, 1989; Hall, 1992). All three approaches involve a blend of disciplines and reflect different worldviews and assumptions about reality, human behavior, and ways to study culture and communication.

THREE APPROACHES TO STUDYING INTERCULTURAL COMMUNICATION

Three contemporary approaches to studying intercultural communication are (1) the social science (or functionalist) approach, (2) the interpretive approach, and (3) the critical approach. (See Table 2-1.) These approaches are based on different fundamental assumptions about human nature, human behavior, and the nature of knowledge (Burrell & Morgan, 1988). Each one contributes in a unique way to our understanding of the relationship between culture and communication, but each also has limitations. These approaches vary in their assumptions about human behavior, their research goals, their conceptualization of culture and communication, and their preferred methodologies.

To examine these three approaches, let us start with a situation that illustrates a communication dilemma. You probably remember where you were on September 11, 2001, when you heard about the terrorist attacks on the United States, as two jets were flown into the World Trade Center, a third jet smashed into the Pentagon, and a fourth crashed in rural Pennsylvania. (See Figure 2-1.) As Paul Levinson (2001), a professor of communication and media studies at Fordham University, observes, "The televised images of the World Trade Center destruction and the Pentagon attack are surely the most searing in media history" (p. B15). In the shock that followed, people around the world scrambled to get more information about what was happening: They watched television news, and went on the Internet, and burned up phone lines. Communication became central to our understanding of what was happening in the days and weeks that followed. We talked and talked to our family and friends, read newspapers and Web pages, and left our televisions and radios on.

The events associated with 9/11 are another example of intercultural communication interaction that offers useful insights into how we might think about intercultural encounters. In analyzing 9/11, we will also outline the characteristics of the three approaches to studying intercultural communication—both contributions and limitations.

TABLE 2-1   THREE APPROACHES TO INTERCULTURAL COMMUNICATION

	Social science (or functionalist)	Interpretive	Critical
Discipline on which approach is founded	Psychology	Anthropology, sociolinguistics	Various
Research goal	Describe and predict behavior	Describe behavior	Change behavior
Assumption of reality	External and describable	Subjective	Subjective and material
Assumptions of human behavior	Predictable	Creative and voluntary	Changeable
Method of study	Survey, observation	Participant observation, field study	Textual analysis of media
Relationship of culture and communication	Communication influenced by culture	Culture created and maintained through communication	Culture a site of power struggles
Contribution of the approach	Identifies cultural variations; recognizes cultural differences in many aspects of communication, but often does not consider context	Emphasizes that communication and culture and cultural differences should be studied in context	Recognizes the economic and political forces in culture and communication; asserts that all intercultural interactions are characterized by power.

The Social Science Approach

The **social science approach** (also called the **functionalist approach**), popular in the 1980s, is based on research in psychology and sociology. This approach assumes a describable external reality. It also assumes that human behavior is predictable and that the researcher's goal is to describe and predict behavior. Researchers who take this approach often use **quantitative methods,** gathering data by administering questionnaires or observing subjects firsthand.

Social science researchers assume that culture is a **variable** that can be measured. This suggests that culture influences communication in much the same way that personality traits do. The goal of this research, then, is to predict specifically how culture influences communication.

FIGURE 2-1   The many meanings of the attacks on the World Trade Center on September 11, 2001, can be difficult to study. In this photo, people are running from the World Trade Center as the towers collapse. How would you study this event? What kinds of questions can you ask from each paradigm? What kinds of questions can't you ask from that paradigm? (© AFP/Corbis)

Applications   Other social scientists might investigate perceived reasons for the terrorist attacks and then frame appropriate responses to them. For instance, they might measure differences in perception among various cultural groups to try to understand how different cultures perceive the reasons for the attacks and what they view as appropriate and inappropriate responses by the United States. In this type of study, social scientists would be using culture as a variable to measure these differences while focusing on the perceptions that are widely held in a particular culture. To understand the aftermath of the 9/11 tragedy, social science researchers might try to measure attitudes toward Muslims and Middle

Easterners by tracking the increasing rate of hate crimes against those perceived to be Middle Eastern. One study in Los Angeles noted that, "in the three months since the terrorist attacks, there [were] seven times more reports of hate crimes directed against Middle Easterners in Los Angeles County than in all [the previous] year" (Winton, 2002, p. B1). Based on these attitude changes, social scientists might then try to predict future hate crimes and ethnic conflicts, and suggest ways to work to avoid conflict based on these attitudes.

Or social scientists might study what kinds of communication media people used after the attacks and how they used them. In one such study, by the Princeton Survey Research Associates, based on telephone interviews with 1,226 adults, the researchers found that, immediately after the attacks, the number of people online declined. Still, "there were conspicuously more Internet users getting news online after September 11 than in previous periods." And "the most significant development online after the attack has been the outpouring of grief, prayerful communication, information dissemination through email, and political commentary." But this study also reported that "there was a heavy reliance on TV and the telephone even among the most committed and active Internet users" (www.pewinternet.org/reports/reports.asp?Report=45&Section=ReportLevel1 &Field=Le). This type of study attempts to quantify the trends in communication media use and the primary motives in using communication.

Other contemporary research programs illustrate the social science approach. One such program was headed by William Gudykunst, a leading communication researcher. Gudykunst was interested in whether people from different cultures varied in their strategies for reducing uncertainty on first encounter. He found that strategies varied depending on whether people were from **individualist** or **collectivist** cultures (Gudykunst, 1998). For example, many people in the United States, which has an individualistic orientation, ask direct questions when interacting with acquaintances. In cultures with a more collectivistic orientation, such as Japan or China, people are more likely to use an indirect approach.

The **communication accommodation theory** is the result of another social science program in which researchers attempted to identify how and when individuals accommodate their speech and nonverbal behavior to others during an interaction. The researchers posited that in some situations individuals will change their communication patterns to accommodate others (Gallois, Giles, Jones, Cargile, & Ota, 1995). Specifically, individuals are likely to adapt during low-threat interactions or situations in which they see little difference between themselves and others. The underlying assumption is that we accommodate when we feel positive toward the other person. For example, when we talk to international students, we may speak more slowly, enunciate more clearly, use less jargon, and mirror their communication. We also may adapt to regional speech. For example, when Tom talks with someone from the South, he sometimes starts to drawl and use words like "y'all." Of course, it is possible to over-accommodate. For example, if a White American speaks Black English to an African American, this may be perceived as overaccommodation.

This essay is a good example of a social science approach to understanding the impact of the 9/11 tragedy on the attitudes and behaviors of various cultural groups. Unlike interpretive or critical studies, this study does not explore historical or political reasons for these attitude changes. However, it does provide a nice snapshot of how women, young people, African Americans, and people in the Northeast have changed their attitudes toward their families, strangers, and traveling. What are the implications for intercultural communication among these various groups in the aftermath of 9/11?

Six months after the attack on the World Trade Center, it is becoming increasingly clear that some groups have been disproportionately affected by the tragedy and are more likely to have changed their behaviors and attitudes as a result. Women, young adults, and African-Americans are among the groups most severely affected. Additionally, there are dramatic differences in the effects experienced by those living in different parts of the country. Among the major differences are:

- Women, young adults, and African-Americans are far more likely to say that the events of September 11th have changed their lives than other groups. Women are twice as likely as men, younger adults are 50% more likely than their older counterparts, and blacks are 44% more likely than whites to make this assertion.

- These three groups are less optimistic about the future of our country than others, and are more likely to say they are afraid to fly.

- Women and African-Americans have become more suspicious of strangers to a greater extent than other groups.

- Young adults and African-Americans are the most likely to have increased the time they spend at home and with family. In light of this finding, it's not surprising that they are the ones most likely to report increased cooking and home entertaining, as well.

In the weeks immediately following the attacks, those living in the Northeast were more affected than those living in other parts of the country. In November, they were the most likely to say they would travel less, were more suspicious of strangers, favored tighter immigration restrictions, welcomed tighter security in public places, and were willing to tolerate loss of privacy to make this country safe. Now they are no more likely to espouse these points of view than those living in other parts of the country, and are less likely than those in the rest of the country to support tighter immigration, or to say that they are more suspicious of strangers or that they will travel less. Southerners are most likely to report increased suspicion of strangers, patriotism, concerns regarding mail, fear of flying and reduced travel.

Source: From McPheters & Company/Beta Research, "Six Months After September 11th: Women, Young Adults, and African-Americans Most Affected by Tragedy," April 2, 2002, www1.internetwire.com/iwire/iwprj?id=40104&cat=bu.

Many social science studies explain how communication styles vary from culture to culture. Dean Barnlund (Barnlund & Yoshioka, 1990), a well-known intercultural communication scholar, compared Japanese and U.S. communication styles. He identified many differences, including how members of the two groups give compliments and offer apologies. Although people in both countries seem to prefer a simple apology, U.S. Americans tend to apologize (and compliment) more often; further, Japanese prefer to *do* something whereas Americans tend to *explain* as a way to apologize.

Another group of social science studies investigated how travelers adapted overseas. In trying to predict which travelers would be the most successful, the researchers found that a variety of factors—including age, gender, language, preparation level, and personality characteristics—played a role (Kim, 2001).

Strengths and Limitations Many of these social science studies have been useful in identifying variations in communication from group to group and specifying psychological and sociological variables in the communication process. However, this approach is limited. Many scholars now realize that human communication is often more creative than predictable and that reality is not just external but also internally constructed. We cannot identify all of the variables that affect our communication. Nor can we predict exactly why one intercultural interaction seems to succeed and another does not.

Scholars also recognize that some methods in this approach are not culturally sensitive and that researchers may be too distant from the phenomena or people they are researching. In other words, researchers may not really understand the cultural groups they are studying. For example, suppose we conducted a study that compared self-disclosure in the United States and Algeria using the social science perspective. We might distribute Jourard's self-disclosure measure (a common instrument used in U.S. research) to students in both countries. However, we might not realize that the concept of self-disclosure does not translate exactly between the United States and Algeria, and that Algerians and U.S. Americans have different notions of this concept.

To overcome these kinds of problems, social scientists have developed strategies for achieving equivalence of measures. A leading cross-cultural psychologist, Richard Brislin (1999), has written extensively on guidelines for cross-cultural researchers. He has identified several types of equivalencies that researchers should establish, including **translation equivalence** and **conceptual equivalence.** For example, in cross-cultural studies, literal translations are inadequate. To establish translation equivalence, research materials should be translated several times, using different translators. Materials that proceed smoothly through these multiple steps are considered translation equivalent.

Researchers can establish conceptual equivalence by ensuring that the notions they are investigating are similar at various levels. For example, problem solving is one aspect of intelligence that may be conceptually equivalent in many cultures. Once this equivalence is established, researchers can identify culture-specific ways in which problem solving is achieved. In the United States and western Europe, good problem solving might mean quick cognitive reasoning; in other cultures, it might involve slow and careful thought (Serpell, 1982). Establishing these equivalencies allows researchers to isolate and describe what distinguishes one culture from another.

The Interpretive Approach

The **interpretive approach** gained prominence in the late 1980s among communication scholars. One interpretive approach, rooted in sociolinguistics, is the **ethnography** of communication (Hymes, 1974). Ethnographers of communication are devoted to descriptive studies of communication patterns within specific cultural groups. Interpretive researchers assume not only that reality is external to humans but also that humans construct reality. They believe that human experience, including communication, is subjective and that human behavior is neither predetermined nor easily predicted.

The goal of interpretive research is to understand and describe human behavior. (Predicting behavior is not a goal.) Whereas the social scientist tends to see communication as influenced by culture, the interpretivist sees culture as created and maintained through communication (Carbaugh, 1996). This type of research uses **qualitative methods** derived from anthropology and linguistics such as field studies, observations, and participant observations. (A researcher engaging in **participant observation** contributes actively to the communication processes being observed and studied. The researcher thus is intimately involved in the research and may become good friends with members of the communities he or she is studying.)

Another example of interpretive research is the **rhetorical approach,** perhaps the oldest communication scholarship, dating back to the ancient Greeks. Rhetoricians typically examine and analyze texts or public speeches in the contexts in which they occur.

Cross-cultural psychologists use the terms **etic** and **emic** to distinguish the social science and interpretive approaches (Berry, 1997). These terms were borrowed from linguistics—*etic* from *phonetic* and *emic* from *phonemic*. Social science research usually searches for universal generalizations and studies cultures objectively, with an "outsider's" view; in this way, it is "etic." In contrast, interpretive research usually focuses on understanding phenomena subjectively, from within a particular cultural community or context; in this way, it is "emic." These researchers try to describe patterns or rules that individuals follow in specific contexts. They tend to be more interested in describing cultural behavior in one community than in making cross-cultural comparisons.

Applications   How might an interpretive researcher investigate the events of 9/11? One possible approach would be to interview both U.S. Americans and Arabs, and perhaps others around the world. From these interviews, as well as conversations with others, the researcher might gain insight into a variety of potential responses. For example, in the weeks after 9/11, communication scholar

September 11 was caused by the intercultural issue of globalization, or more specifically, Americans' tendency to be unaware and inactive in government and international politics. The U.S. government has done some very careless things, and the world assumes that our government does/does not do what it does with the full consent of its democratic people. That puts the entire U.S. into a negative light in the eyes of those who see this.
—Aleasha

Nola Heidlebaugh (2002) analyzed conversations on a Listserv where communication professionals were debating whether the attacks were an act of war or a crime. She argues that this rhetorical approach to understanding attitudes is preferable to the social science survey/polling approach because it focuses on conversations of those who are *engaged* with the topic. Attitude polls survey anyone, even those who haven't thought about the topic. (See Figure 2-2.)

Scholars in other disciplines have also explored the implications of a "military" versus a "crime" rhetorical response. Alan Dershowitz (2001), law professor at Harvard University, expresses concern about the loss of civil liberties in the aftermath of 9/11:

> *There will inevitably be some changes in our approach to civil liberties following the mass terrorism. The key issue is how the changes will be brought about. Will they be imposed upon us unilaterally by government officials and agencies? Or will appropriate accommodations be worked out with the advice and cooperation of civil libertarians? (p. B9)*

Catherine Lutz (2001), anthropology professor at the University of North Carolina, points to her own research to contextualize recent war rhetoric:

> *My research has shown me that many American soldiers and veterans are not nearly so sure [that a larger military increases our safety]. Some have been among war's most ardent critics. . . . Their experiences will never match the rhetoric and safety of the elites now planning a conflagration. As Bush talks about hunting the terrorists from their holes, and begins to elide terrorists and whole populations, I am reminded of the racial hatred that has preceded, stoked, and been inflamed by nearly every one of the 20th century's wars. (p. B14)*

But Jeane Kirkpatrick (2001), professor of government at Georgetown University and former ambassador to the UN, feels quite differently: "I believe that it's a military problem. It would be a very serious mistake for the United States not to respond with force" (p. B16). Perceptions of what the appropriate response might be reflect differences in what these attacks mean to different people. Have your family and friends discussed what appropriate responses might be?

Interpretivists might also study the cultural and communication phenomena that occurred immediately after 9/11 when many U.S. Americans felt compelled

FIGURE 2-2   One way to study and learn about cultural patterns is to interview other people, which is this woman's approach as she talks to a member of the Old Order Brethren in Manheim, Pennsylvania. What are the strengths and weaknesses of interviewing as a research strategy? (© Jeff Greenberg/PhotoEdit, Inc.)

to fly the American flag in their homes, cars, and businesses. In the social scientific study mentioned earlier, the Princeton Survey Research Associates found that 32% of U.S. Americans displayed the flag in their homes or elsewhere. By interviewing people who participated in this phenomenon, interpretivists might better understand what these people were trying to communicate and how displaying the flag functioned to do that. For example, why didn't people fly the New York City flag instead? How would that have created a different meaning?

Interpretivists might report some of the same findings as social scientists even though they approach the issue in a unique way. They would not assume that, because Arabic and U.S. cultures differ, they would elicit different responses. Instead, they would simply begin the project with a general research question and attempt to understand the cultural experience from the point of

POINT OF VIEW

In the aftermath of 9/11, many U.S. Americans displayed the flag on cars, homes, and clothing. In this essay, the authors give us a new perspective on the various meanings of flag display.

FIVE PROPOSED NEW LAWS FOR THIS CRISIS:

1. To display an American flag in any form, you must present proof of voter registration.

2. To wave an American flag in public, you must be able to name at least one of the following: A. Your Senator B. Your Representative C. Your President ("George Bush" does not count; ambiguous.)

3. To be permitted to scream "Arabs go home," you must list and correctly locate ten Arab homelands.

4. Priority for purchase of American flags will be given to those whose ancestors lived on American soil the longest. When all American Indians who wish to display the red, white and blue are satisfied, other applicants will be accepted.

5. A call for war on any radio talk-show will be construed as a public declaration of willingness to enlist in the U.S. Army; callers will have 24 hours to complete the paperwork.

Source: From J. Kim et al., *Another World Is Possible/New World Disorder: Conversations in a Time of Terror*, 2001, p. 50.

view of members of different cultures around the world. Yet, interpretivists might also discover disagreement about how to respond to the attacks within the same culture. For example, Amber Amundson (2001), who lost her 28-year-old husband at the Pentagon on 9/11, does not condone a strong military response:

> *I have heard angry rhetoric by some Americans, including many of our nation's leaders, who advise a heavy dose of revenge and punishment. To those leaders, I would like to make clear that my family and I take no comfort in your words of rage. If you choose to respond to this incomprehensible brutality by perpetuating violence against other innocent human beings, you may not do so in the name of justice for my husband. (pp. 37–38)*

Interpretivists would take care to reveal the complexity of the responses and meanings constructed both within cultures and between cultures.

Some interpretive studies investigate the language patterns in many different groups—from the Burundi in Africa, to the Athabascan in northern Canada, to various groups within the United States, such as urban Blacks or Cajuns. Other interpretive studies investigate the different communication patterns of one cultural group. For example, communication scholar Gerry Philipsen (1990) studied communication patterns in a White, working-class neighborhood of Chicago called Teamsterville. Philipsen discovered that men in this community consider speaking to be important only in some situations. For example, Teamsterville males speak when expressing male solidarity but not when asserting power and influence in interpersonal situations. That is, they are more likely to talk when they are with their equals—their buddies—than when they are with their children or with authority figures. With superiors or subordinates, other forms of communication are appropriate. With children, for example, they are more likely to use gestures or disciplinary action than speech. When they are with someone of higher status, such as a school principal, they may seek out a mediator (e.g., the neighborhood priest) rather than speak directly to the principal.

Molefi Asante's (1987, 2001) notion of **Afrocentricity** provides another example of the interpretive approach. Asante emphasizes that descriptions of the communication rules of a given people must be grounded in their beliefs and values. Most scholarly studies of communication are rooted in a European American perspective, and Asante suggests that this frame of reference is not applicable to African American communication. In this context Afrocentricity involves certain beliefs and attitudes that people of African descent share:

- A common origin and experience of struggle
- An element of resistance to European legal procedures, medical practices, and political processes
- Traditional values of humaneness and harmony with nature
- A fundamentally African way of knowing and interpreting the world
- An orientation toward communalism

Communication scholars have used this framework to understand various aspects of contemporary African American communication. For example, Thurmon Garner (1994) stresses the strong oral tradition of African Americans and identifies rhetorical patterns such as indirection, improvisation and inventiveness, and playfully toned behavior. These patterns underlay communication in many African American contexts, including rapping, playing the dozens (an aggressive verbal contest, often involving obscene language), and signifying (the verbal art of insult, in which a speaker jokingly talks about, needles, and puts down the listener).

Janice Hamlet (2000) explains the unique qualities of African American preaching in similar terms. She emphasizes the strong participative nature of the call and response and ties this style of preaching to the cultural values of emotionalism, interaction, spiritualism, and the power of the spoken word. In this way, the Bible is interpreted by Black preachers in the contexts of African American culture and experiences. Both Garner's and Hamlet's studies are descriptive of particular communication patterns of one cultural group. And both scholars use emic methods in describing communication that reflects and captures the cultural experience and lives of African Americans.

Strengths and Limitations   The utility of the interpretivist approach is that it provides an in-depth understanding of communication patterns in particular communities because it emphasizes investigating communication in context. Thus, for example, we learn more about African American communication in religious contexts and more about popular U.S. communication in talk show contexts than we would by distributing questionnaires with general questions on African American or European American communication.

The main limitation of this approach is that there are few interpretivist studies of *intercultural* communication. Interpretive scholars typically have not studied what happens when two groups come in contact with each other. However, there are some comparative studies, including Charles Braithwaite's (1990), which compares rules for silence in 15 different communities.

A second limitation is that the researchers often are outsiders to the communities under investigation, which means that they may not represent accurately the communication patterns of members of that community. For example, consider Renate Rosaldo's (1989) study of the cultural practices of the Ilongot in the Philippines, particularly their practice of headhunting. Reflecting on his own research, Rosaldo describes how his earlier limited understanding changed when his wife fell to her death from a mountain trail during one of their trips to the Philippines. While mourning for his wife, he came to understand better the link between grief and headhunting, which he had originally described in naive academic terms. As Rosaldo explains, he became an "insider" to the experience of grieving and rage. He tells of the intense anger he felt at the death of his wife and the rage with which he needed to deal in the grieving process. He came to realize that headhunting is a symbolic process meant both to vent anger at death and to reestablish order in the Ilongot community.

Rosaldo subsequently reinterpreted studies of his own ethnic (Latino/a) community as an insider, thereby overcoming the scholarly descriptions' limitations. Such opportunities are rare, though.

The Critical Approach

A third approach to the study of intercultural communication includes many assumptions of the interpretive approach. For instance, researchers who use the **critical approach** believe in subjective (as opposed to objective) and material reality. They also emphasize the importance of studying the context in which communication occurs—that is, the situation, background, or environment. However, critical researchers usually focus on **macrocontexts,** such as the political and social structures that influence communication. Critical scholars, unlike most social scientists and interpretivists, are interested in the historical context of communication (Putnam & Pacanowsky, 1983). (See Figure 2-3.)

Critical scholars are interested in the power relations in communication. For them, identifying cultural differences in communication is important only in relation to power differentials. In this perspective, culture is, in essence, a battleground—a plan where multiple interpretations come together but a dominant force always prevails. The goal of critical researchers is not only to understand

FIGURE 2-3 This photo of Venezuelans watching television coverage of the World Trade Center attacks underscores the importance of communication in giving meaning to this event. Think about how, using each of the three paradigms, you might approach studying the role of communication in helping people around the world understand this event. (© *Reuters NewMedia Inc./Corbis*)

human behavior but also to change the lives of everyday communicators. Researchers assume that, by examining and reporting how power functions in cultural situations, they can help the average person learn how to resist forces of power and oppression.

The methods preferred by critical scholars are usually **textual analyses,** which sometimes occur within the economic contexts of the culture industries that produce these texts. That is, the scholars generally analyze cultural "products," such as media (TV, movies, journals, and so on), as powerful voices in shaping contemporary culture, rather than observing or participating in face-to-face interactions or conducting surveys.

Applications   In analyzing the events of 9/11, a critical scholar might try to situate the attacks within a larger cultural struggle that has a much longer history than many U.S. Americans might realize. Linguist Noam Chomsky (2001) reflects on the U.S.'s terrorist history:

> The U.S. is, after all, the only country condemned by the World Court for international terrorism—for the "unlawful use of force" for political ends, as the Court put it—ordering the U.S. to terminate these crimes and pay substantial reparations. The U.S. of course dismissed the Court's judgment with contempt. (p. 84)

I think 9/11 is an intercultural issue because what happens in Jerusalem (Palestine) is actually the real definition of terrorism. But people from the West (i.e., the U.S., Canada) don't admit that, and the citizens of those countries don't know what's going on in the outside world. They claim that all Arabs are terrorists, but they don't take a minute to discover the truth. Also, in the news, you don't see what actually is going on in the Middle East, and this is just not fair to the Arab communities around the world.
—Mohammad

As U.S. Americans, we may not want to study our own history on the international scene, because doing so may not bolster positive views of our national identity. But critical scholars would insist that we take history seriously in order to better understand the 9/11 attacks.

Critical scholars might analyze media coverage (both in the United States and abroad) of the attacks. These scholars might also analyze the hesitation of Hollywood to release certain movies after 9/11, such as *Black Hawk Down* (about U.S. troops trapped in war-torn Somalia), and the criticism directed at other films for being released so soon after 9/11, such as *The Sum of All Fears* (about a nuclear bomb exploded by terrorists in Baltimore). The focus on these public discourses, rather than on interpersonal discussions, reflects an important aspect of critical approaches.

Further, critical scholars might analyze how anyone who appeared to be Middle Eastern became vilified and suspect in the aftermath of 9/11, whereas White Americans were not immediately seen as terrorist suspects after the bombing of the Federal Building in Oklahoma City or the mailbox bombs attack across the Midwest, both by White Americans. Understanding the power differences between groups gives us insight into the ways that stereotyping can (and cannot) function for the benefit of some groups and not others.

An example of critical scholarship is Janice Peck's (1993/1994) analysis of a series of *Oprah Winfrey* segments on racism. Based on these segments, Peck identifies three discourses about racism: liberal, therapeutic, and religious. The liberal discourse emphasizes the individual's response to racism and can result in a double bind: Although individual rights must be respected, racism also violates others' rights. The therapeutic discourse sees prejudice and stereotyping as simple operations of human thinking, which can be corrected through education. The religious discourse relies on the notions of "understanding" and equality before God, with racism seen as reflecting a lack of understanding, a failure to recognize others as divine creations.

Peck's main point is that all three ways of talking about racism are centered on individuals and place all responsibility for subjective change on individual actions. She emphasizes that these discourses ignore many of the root causes of

Here are three different student perspectives on the various approaches to studying intercultural communication.

> *I am an engineer, so I think that hypotheses and research are very important in order to describe and predict a subject. On the other hand, it is important to understand the individual more like a person and not like a number.*
> —Liliana

> *I like the interpretive approach. I think that it is important to understand and to actually get involved hands-on to understand something so important and complicated as intercultural communication. Even though outsiders may never fully be considered an insider, they are better off than neither an insider nor an outsider.*
> —Matt

> *Having three different paradigms allows me to view intercultural communication from three different perspectives. I can then incorporate all three into how I interpret other cultures. I personally like the critical view the most because I agree that often cultural groups are in a power struggle against one another, and that's just human nature.*
> —Andrew

racism (e.g., economic and political inequality) and many racist practices (e.g., redlining, the banking practice of automatically denying home mortgage loans to people who live in specific areas).

Another example of a critical study is Tom Nakayama's (1994) analysis of the movie *Showdown in Little Tokyo*, which depicts two Los Angeles police officers investigating a murder. One is European American; the other is of mixed European–Asian American heritage. As Nakayama shows, the narrative, the camera shot sequences, and other aspects of the movie favor the European American character over the Asian American character. For example, the European American police officer is portrayed as more physically attractive, and this character is the one who gets the love interest.

Nakayama emphasizes that this type of relationship between majority and minority ethnic characters in movies is so prevalent in our everyday culture that we don't ever question the superiority of Whites. We identify with this view of the world even though an increasing number of people in the United States do not share it.

A final example of a critical study is Dreama Moon's (1997) investigation of gender and social class communication. In her study, Moon analyzed interviews of White women from working-class backgrounds. She discovered that social class is a "marked feature" in the communication practices in academia that restricts upward mobility. Subtle communication practices that reinforce social class differences are not so invisible to women from working-class backgrounds. Moon shows how culture, social class, and communication work together to reproduce the contemporary social structure. She also identifies some strategies used by these women to resist this process of **social reproduction.**

Strengths and Limitations   The critical approach emphasizes the power relations in intercultural interactions and the importance of social and historical contexts. However, one limitation is that most critical studies do not focus on face-to-face intercultural interaction. Rather, they focus on popular media forms of communication—TV shows, music videos, magazine advertisements, and so on. Such studies, with their lack of attention to face-to-face interactions, may yield less practical results. Thus, for example, although understanding different discourses about racism may give us insights into U.S. race relations, it may not provide individuals with specific guidelines on how to communicate better across racial lines. However, one exception is co-cultural theory, presented in Chapter 6, which is used to understand how people's location in a social hierarchy influences their perceptions of reality regarding, among other things, relational issues or problems (Orbe, 1998).

Also, this approach does not allow for much empirical data. For example, Janice Peck did not measure audience members' reactions to the *Oprah Winfrey* segments; instead, her essay analyzed these TV discourses. Peck's argument rests upon the popularity of the TV program and its influence based upon a large audience.

A DIALECTICAL APPROACH TO UNDERSTANDING CULTURE AND COMMUNICATION

Combining the Three Traditional Paradigms: The Dialectical Approach

The social science, interpretive, and critical approaches operate in interconnected and sometimes contradictory ways. Rather than advocating any one approach, we propose a **dialectical approach** to intercultural communication research and practice (see also Martin, Nakayama, & Flores, 2002). The dialectical approach emphasizes the processual, relational, and contradictory nature of intercultural communication, which encompasses many different kinds of intercultural knowledge.

With regard to the **processual** nature of intercultural communication, it is important to remember that cultures change, as do individuals. For example, the cultural communication of Arabs, U.S. Americans, and others about why the attacks of 9/11 occurred and what to do about them, as described by research studies, provide a static but fleeting picture of the intercultural differences. However, it's important to remember that these patterns are dynamic and ever-changing. The intercultural relationships between Arabs and U.S. Americans will be somewhat different today from what they were when these studies were conducted.

Second, a dialectical perspective emphasizes the relational aspect of intercultural communication study. It highlights the relationship among various aspects of intercultural communication and the importance of viewing these holistically rather than in isolation. The key question becomes, Can we really understand culture without understanding communication, and vice versa? Specifically, can we understand the attacks of 9/11 without looking at the values and beliefs of the various cultural groups that come together on the global scene, the influence of the particular context (U.S. domination and globalization), the history of U.S.–Middle East relations that influence daily intercultural interactions, and so on?

A third characteristic of the dialectical perspective involves holding contradictory ideas simultaneously. This notion may be difficult to comprehend, because it goes against most formal education in the United States, which emphasizes dichotomous thinking. Dichotomies such as "good and evil," "arteries and veins," and "air and water" form the core of our philosophical and scientific beliefs. The fact that dichotomies such as "far and near," "high and low," and "long and short" sound complete, as if the two parts belong together, reveals our tendency to form dichotomies (Stewart & Bennett, 1991). One such dichotomy that emerged after September 11 was that U.S. Americans are good and that anyone who looks Arabic is suspect and potentially evil. However, a dialectical approach requires that we transcend dichotomous thinking in studying and practicing intercultural communication.

Certainly, we can learn something from each of the three traditional approaches, and our understanding of intercultural communication has been enriched by all three. One of our students described how the three perspectives can be useful in everyday communication:

The three paradigms help me understand intercultural communication by giving me insight into how we can work with people. Understanding how to predict communication behavior will make it easier for us to deal with those of other cultures—the social science approach. By changing unfair notions we have [about people from other cultures], we can gain more equality, as in the critical approach. We try to change things. Finally, the interpretive perspective is important so we can see face-to-face how our culture is.

Combining these approaches, as our discussion of the events of 9/11 shows, provides us with extensive insight into the problems and challenges of this and other intercultural ventures. Clearly, if we limit ourselves to a specific research orientation, we may fail to see the complexities of contemporary intercultural interaction in contexts. Although this kind of paradoxical thinking is rather foreign to Western minds, it is quite accepted in many Asian cultures. For example, people doing business in China are advised to recognize this dialectical thinking: "It is not possible to overstate the importance of 'and' versus 'or' thinking. It recurs, in various forms, throughout business in China and the Orient as a whole" (Ambler & Witzel, 2000, p. 197).

In fact, research findings can make a difference in the everyday world. From the social science perspective, we can see how specific communication and cultural differences might create differing worldviews, which can help us to predict intercultural conflicts. An interpretive investigation gives us an opportunity to confirm what we predicted in a hypothetical social science study. This might be the case with the attacks of 9/11. That is, different worldviews of U.S. Americans and Arabs might explain different explanations for why the attacks occurred and what kinds of responses are appropriate. The critical approach to the attacks raises some questions about the reasons for anger with the United States and challenges us to examine our assumptions about the neutrality of intercultural experiences.

Employing these different perspectives is similar to photographing something from different angles. No single angle or snapshot gives us the truth, but taking pictures from various angles gives a more comprehensive view of the subject. The content of the photos, of course, to some extent depends on the interests of the photographer. And the photos may contradict one another, especially if they are taken at different times. But the knowledge we gain from any of these "angles" or approaches is enhanced by the knowledge gained from the others.

However, a dialectical approach requires that we move beyond simply acknowledging the contributions of the three perspectives and accept simultaneously the assumptions of all three. That is, we need to imagine that reality can be at once external *and* internal, that human behavior is predictable *and* creative *and* changeable. These assumptions may seem contradictory, but that's the point. Thinking dialectically forces us to move beyond our familiar categories and opens us up to new possibilities for studying and understanding intercultural communication.

Six Dialectics of Intercultural Communication

We have identified six **dialectics** that characterize intercultural communication and have woven them throughout this book. Perhaps you can think of other dialectics as you learn more about intercultural communication.

Cultural–Individual Dialectic   Intercultural communication is both cultural and individual, or idiosyncratic. That communication is *cultural* means we share communication patterns with members of the groups to which we belong. For example, Sandra, a fifth-generation Italian American, tends to be expressive, like other members of her family. However, some of her communication patterns—such as the way she gestures when she talks—are completely idiosyncratic (that is, particular to her and no one else). Consider another example, that of Angela, who tends to be relationally oriented. Although her role as a woman and the relationships she cultivates in that role are important, being a woman does not completely define her behaviors. In this book, we often describe communication patterns that seem to be related to membership in particular cultural groups. However, it is important to remember that communication for all of us is both cultural and individual. We need to keep this dialectic in mind as we try to understand and develop relationships across cultural differences.

When communicating interculturally, I feel that it is better to think in dialectics because you allow yourself to be more open with others with little bias or barriers. You are also able to better understand yourself as well as others and their cultures. For instance, in the differences–similarities dialectic, when I visited the Bahamas I did not know what to expect. I knew that the majority of people there were Black and that made me feel a bit more comfortable, but I also knew that they were Bahamian and had a different culture than what I was used to in the U.S. To make a long story short, I realize that although we have some similarities as far as appearance, religion, family values, etc., we are still different in some aspects of life as well—differences such as the food we eat, the slang we use, the things we say, and so on and so forth. I also knew that out of respect for their culture, there were certain things that I could not do that I would normally do at home. Luckily, most of the people that I was around realized the same thing and understood that although we came from different places we were still one of the same kind of people.
    —Nicole

Personal–Contextual Dialectic   This dialectic involves the role of context in intercultural relationships and focuses simultaneously on the person and the context. Although we communicate as individuals on a personal level, the context of this communication is important as well. In some contexts, we enact specific social roles that give meaning to our messages. For example, when Tom was teaching at a Belgian university, he often spoke from the social role of professor. But this role did not correspond exactly to the same role in the United States, because Belgian students accord their professors far more respect and distance than do U.S. students. In Belgium, this social role was more important than his communication with the students. In contrast, his communication with students in the United States is more informal.

Differences–Similarities Dialectic   Intercultural communication is characterized by both similarities and differences, in that people are simultaneously similar to and different from each other. In this book, we identify and describe real and important differences between groups of people—differences in values, language, nonverbal behavior, conflict resolution, and so on. For example, Japanese and U.S. Americans communicate differently, just as do men and women. However, there also are many similarities in human experiences and ways of communicating. Emphasizing only differences can lead to stereotyping and prejudice (e.g., that women are emotional or that men are rational); emphasizing only similarities can lead us to ignore the important cultural variations that exist. Therefore, we try to emphasize both similarities and differences and ask you to keep this dialectic in mind.

POINT OF VIEW

This excerpt demonstrates a dialectical tension between dealing honestly with racial difference and misinterpreting or misusing racial information.

> *For a long time, African Americans experienced discrimination not just for being the only race to pass on the genetic disease [sickle cell anemia], but because of the mistaken impression that even those with a single recessive gene—the sickle cell carriers—were somehow physically impaired. In the 1970s, for example, the U.S. Navy and the Air Force Academy restricted training opportunities for blacks with sickle cell trait, policies that were later criticized as discriminatory.*
>
> *Subsequent research revealed that the carriers actually were more healthy in one important respect than people with no sickle cell anemia [gene] at all. In the malaria-infested parts of Africa from which most American blacks' ancestors came, sickle cell carriers were more resistant to malaria than non-carriers. This theory explained why such a devastating disease could perpetuate itself through the generations. . . . Other observations about different racial or ethnic groups' susceptibility to disease have similar explanations. . . . Scientists must regularly confront these racial or ethnic differences, and must deal with them honestly in order to ferret out their origins and implications. . . . While genetic researchers forge ahead in their population-based research, they know from experience that many of their findings may be misinterpreted or possibly even abused. The real burden of care belongs not only to scientists, but to the rest of us.*

Source: From R. M. Henig, "Genetic Misunderstandings: The Linking of Jews with Cancer Is an Accident of Science and How Ethnic Groups Are Studied," *The Washington Post National Weekly Edition*, October 13, 1997, p. 23.

Static–Dynamic Dialectic This dialectic suggests that intercultural communication tends to be at once static and dynamic. Some cultural and communication patterns remain relatively constant, whereas other aspects of cultures (or personal traits of individuals) shift over time—that is, they are dynamic. For example, as we learned in Chapter 1, anti-immigrant sentiment traditionally has been a cultural constant in the United States, although the groups and conditions of discrimination have changed. Thus, the antagonism against Irish and Italian immigrants that existed at the turn of the 20th century has largely disappeared but may linger in the minds of some people. To understand interethnic communication in the United States today, we must recognize both the static and dynamic aspects of these relations.

History/Past–Present/Future Dialectic Another dialectic emphasizes the need to focus simultaneously on the past and the present in understanding intercultural communication. On the one hand, we need to be aware of contemporary forces and realities that shape interactions of people from different cultural groups. On the other hand, we need to realize that history has a significant impact on contemporary events. One of our students described how this dialectic was illustrated in a televised panel discussion on race relations:

> The panelists frequently referred to and talked about the history of different cultural groups in the United States and the present. They also touched on racial conflicts of the past and future possible improvement for certain groups. They were, therefore, communicating in a history/past–present/future dialectical manner. The discussion of past and present were critical to the overall goal of understanding current cultural identity. Without understanding the history of, for example, the slave trade or the Jim Crow laws, can we truly comprehend the African American experience in the United States today? The history of each cultural group plays a major role in the present role of that group.

Privilege–Disadvantage Dialectic   A dialectical perspective recognizes that people may be simultaneously privileged and disadvantaged, or privileged in some contexts and disadvantaged in others. For example, many tourists are in the position of economic privilege because they can afford to travel, but in their travels, they also may be disadvantaged if they do not speak the local language. We can also be simultaneously privileged and disadvantaged due to gender, age, race, socioeconomic status, and other identities. One of our Asian American colleagues relates how he is simultaneously privileged because he is educated, middle class, and male, and disadvantaged because he experiences subtle and overt mistreatment based on his race and accent (Collier, Hegde, Lee, Nakayama, & Yep, 2002, p. 247).

Keeping a Dialectical Perspective

We ask that you keep a dialectical perspective in mind as you read the rest of this book. The dialectics relate in various ways to the topics discussed in the following chapters and are interwoven throughout the text. Keep in mind, though, that the dialectical approach is not a specific theory to apply to all aspects of intercultural communication. Rather, it is a lens through which to view the complexities of the topic. Instead of offering easy answers to dilemmas, we ask you to look at the issues and ideas from various angles, sometimes holding contradictory notions, but always seeing things in processual, relational, and holistic ways.

The dialectical approach that we take in this book combines the three traditional approaches (social science, interpretive, and critical) and suggests four components to consider in understanding intercultural communication: culture, communication, context, and power. Culture and communication are the foreground, and context and power are the backdrop against which we can understand intercultural communication. We will discuss these four components in the next chapter.

SUMMARY

In the chapter, we traced the history of the study of intercultural communication. The field of intercultural communication in the United States began with the Foreign Service Institute, established in 1946. Scholars at the institute drew from different disciplines and emphasized practical ways to facilitate communication among various cultural groups. The perceptions and worldviews of these scholars and other researchers have an impact on the study of intercultural communication. Three contemporary study approaches developed from different philosophical worldviews: the social science approach, the interpretive approach, and the critical approach. Combined, these three approaches form the dialectical perspective. This perspective emphasizes a processual, relational, and holistic view of intercultural communication study and practice and, on occasion, requires that we balance contradictory ideas. These contradictory views form dialectics that shape our study. Intercultural communication is both cultural *and* individual, personal *and* contextual, characterized by differences *and* similarities, static *and* dynamic, oriented to the present *and* the past, and characterized by both privilege *and* disadvantage. And these six dialectics may be just the beginning.

DISCUSSION QUESTIONS

1. How have the origins of the study of intercultural communication in the United States affected its present focus?
2. How did business and political interests influence what early intercultural communication researchers studied and learned?
3. How have the worldviews of researchers influenced how they studied intercultural communication?
4. How have other fields contributed to the study of intercultural communication?
5. What are the advantages of a dialectical approach to intercultural communication?

 Go to the self-quizzes on the Online Learning Center at www.mhhe.com/martinnakayama to further test your knowledge.

ACTIVITIES

1. *Becoming Culturally Conscious.* One way to understand your cultural position within the United States and your own cultural values, norms, and beliefs is to examine your upbringing. Answer the following questions:
   a. What values did your parents or guardians attempt to instill in you?
   b. Why were these values considered important?
   c. What were you expected to do when you grew up?
   d. How were you expected to contribute to family life?
   e. What do you know about your ethnic background?
   f. What was your neighborhood like?

Discuss your answers with classmates. Analyze how your own cultural position is unique and how it is similar to that of others.

2. *Analyzing Cultural Patterns.* Find a text or speech that discusses some intercultural or cultural issues, and analyze the cultural patterns present in the text. Consider, for example, the "I Have a Dream" speech by Martin Luther King, Jr. (Andrews & Zarefsky, 1992), or Chief Seattle's 1854 speech (Low, 1995).

3. *Analyzing a Video.* View a feature film or video (e.g., *Titanic, Soul Food,* or *Dangerous Beauty*) and assume the position of a researcher. Analyze the cultural meanings in the film from each of the three perspectives: social science, interpretive, and critical. What cultural patterns (related to nationality, ethnicity, gender, and class) do you see? What does each perspective reveal? What does each one fail to reveal?

KEY WORDS

Afrocentricity	interpretive approach
collectivist	macrocontexts
communication accommodation theory	paradigm
conceptual equivalence	participant observation
critical approach	perception
cross-cultural training	processual
dialectic	proxemics
dialectical approach	qualitative methods
distance zones	quantitative methods
diversity training	rhetorical approach
emic	Sapir-Whorf hypothesis
ethnography	social reproduction
etic	social science approach
functionalist approach	textual analyses
individualist	translation equivalence
intercultural competence	variable
interdisciplinary focus	worldview

The Online Learning Center at www.mhhe.com/martinnakayama features flashcards and crossword puzzles based on these terms and concepts.

REFERENCES

Allport, G. W. (1979). *The nature of prejudice.* Reading, MA: Addison-Wesley.

Ambler, T., & Witzel, M. (2000). *Doing business in China.* New York: Routledge.

Amundson, A. (2001). A widow's plea for non-violence. In J. Kim et al. (Eds.), *Another world is possible/New world disorder: Conversations in a time of terror* (pp. 37–38). New Orleans: Subway & Elevated Press.

Andrews, J. R., & Zarefsky, D. (1992). *Contemporary American voices: Significant speeches in American history, 1945–present* (pp. 78–81). New York: Longman.

Asante, M. K. (1987). *The Afrocentric idea.* Philadelphia: Temple University Press.

—— (2001). Transcultural realities and different ways of knowing. In V. H. Milhouse, M. K. Asante, & P. O. Nwosu (Eds.), *Transcultural realities: Interdisciplinary perspectives on cross cultural relations* (pp. 71–82). Thousand Oaks, CA: Sage.

Barnlund, D. C., & Yoshioka, M. (1990). Apologies: Japanese and American styles. *International Journal of Intercultural Relations, 14,* 193–205.

Berry, J. W. (1997). Preface. In P. R. Dasen, T. S. Saraswathi, & J. W. Berry (Eds.), *Handbook of cross cultural psychology: Vol. 2. Basic processes and human development* (pp. xi–xvi). Boston: Allyn & Bacon.

Braithwaite, C. (1990). Communicative silence: A cross cultural study of Basso's hypothesis. In D. Carbaugh (Ed.), *Cultural communication and intercultural contact* (pp. 321–328). Hillsdale, NJ: Lawrence Erlbaum.

Brantlinger, P. (1986). Victorians and Africans: The genealogy of the myth of the dark continent. In H. L. Gates Jr. (Ed.), *"Race," writing and difference* (pp. 185–222). Chicago: University of Chicago Press. (Original work published 1985)

Brislin, R. (1999). *Understanding culture's influence on behavior* (2nd ed.). Belmont, CA: Wadsworth.

Burrell, G., & Morgan, G. (1988). *Sociological paradigms and organizational analysis.* Portsmouth, NH: Heinemann.

Carbaugh, D. (1996). *Situating selves: The communication of social identities in American scenes.* Albany: State University of New York Press.

Casmir, F. L. (1994). The role of theory and theory building. In F. L. Casmir (Ed.), *Building communication theories* (pp. 7–41). Hillsdale, NJ: Lawrence Erlbaum.

Chomsky, N. (2001). *9–11.* New York: Seven Stories Press.

Collier, M. J., Hegde, R. S., Lee, W., Nakayama, T. K., & Yep, G. A. (2002). Dialogue on the edges: Ferment in communication and culture. In M. J. Collier (Ed.)., *Transforming communication about culture. International and Intercultural Communication Annual* (Vol. 24, pp. 219–280). Thousand Oaks, CA: Sage.

Delgado, F. (2002). Mass-mediated communication and intercultural conflict. In J. N. Martin, T. K. Nakayama, & L. A. Flores (Eds.), *Readings in intercultural communication: Experiences and contexts* (2nd ed., pp. 351–359). Boston: McGraw-Hill.

Dershowitz, A. (2001, September 28). Preserving civil liberties. *The Chronicle of Higher Education,* p. B9.

Gallois, C., Giles, H., Jones, E., Cargile, A. C., & Ota, H. (1995). Accommodating intercultural encounters: Elaborations and extensions. In R. L. Wiseman (Ed.), *Intercultural communication theory* (pp. 115–147). Newbury Park, CA: Sage.

Garner, T. (1994). Oral rhetorical practice in African American culture. In A. González, M. Houston, & V. Chen (Eds.), *Our voices: Essays in culture, ethnicity and communication* (pp. 81–91). Los Angeles: Roxbury.

Gould, S. J. (1993). American polygeny and craniometry before Darwin: Blacks and Indians as separate, inferior species. In S. Harding (Ed.), *The "racial" economy of science: Toward a democratic future* (pp. 84–115). Bloomington: Indiana University Press. (Original work published 1981)

Gudykunst, W. B. (1998). Individualistic and collectivistic perspectives on communication: An introduction. *International Journal of Intercultural Relations, 22,* 107–134.

—— (2002a). Intercultural communication theories. In W. B. Gudykunst & B. Mody (Eds.), *Handbook of international and intercultural communication* (2nd ed., pp. 183–205). Thousand Oaks, CA: Sage.

—— (2002b). Cross-cultural communication theories. In W. B. Gudykunst & B. Mody (Eds.), *Handbook of international and intercultural communication* (2nd ed., pp. 25–50). Thousand Oaks, CA: Sage.

Gudykunst, W. B., & Nishida, T. (1989). Theoretical perspectives for studying intercultural communication. In M. K. Asante & W. B. Gudykunst (Eds.), *Handbook of international and intercultural communication* (pp. 17–46). Newbury Park, CA: Sage.

Hall, B. J. (1992). Theories of culture and communication. *Communication Theory, 1,* 50–70.

Hall, E. T. (1959). *The silent language.* Garden City, NY: Doubleday.

——— (1966). *The hidden dimension.* Garden City, NY: Doubleday.

Hamlet, J. (2000). Understanding traditional African American preaching. In A. González, M. Houston, & V. Chen (Eds.), *Our voices: Essays in culture, ethnicity and communication* (3rd ed., pp. 92–97). Los Angeles: Roxbury.

Hart, W. B. (1999). Interdisciplinary influences in the study of intercultural relations: A citation analysis of the *International Journal of Intercultural Relations. International Journal of Intercultural Relations, 23,* 575–590.

Heidlebaugh, N. J. (2002, November). *What shall we call an Act of War?: Examination of a Listserv as vernacular rhetoric.* Paper presented at the annual meeting of the National Communication Association, New Orleans.

Hymes, D. (1974). *Foundations in sociolinguistics: An ethnographic approach.* Philadelphia: University of Pennsylvania Press.

Kim, Y. Y. (2001). *Becoming intercultural: An integrative theory of communication and cross-cultural adaptation.* Thousand Oaks, CA: Sage.

Kirkpatrick, J. (2001, September 28). The case for force. *The Chronicle of Higher Education,* p. B16.

Kuhn, T. (1970). *The structure of scientific revolutions* (Rev. ed.). Chicago: University of Chicago Press.

Landis, D., & Bhagat, R. (1996). *Handbook of intercultural training* (2nd ed.). Thousand Oaks, CA: Sage.

Landis, D., & Wasilewski, J. H. (1999). Reflections on 22 years of the *International Journal of Intercultural Relations* and 23 years in other areas of intercultural practice. *International Journal of Intercultural Relations, 23,* 535–574.

Levinson, P. (2001, September 28). Images of unmediated ugliness. *The Chronicle of Higher Education,* p. B15.

Low, D. (1995). Contemporary reinvention of Chief Seattle's 1854 speech. *American Indian Quarterly, 19*(3), 407.

Lutz, C. (2001, September 28). Our legacy of war. *The Chronicle of Higher Education,* p. B14.

Martin, J. N., Nakayama, T. K., & Flores, L. A. (2002). A dialectical approach to intercultural communication. In J. N. Martin, T. K. Nakayama, & L. A. Flores (Eds.), *Readings in intercultural communication: Experiences and contexts* (2nd ed., pp. 3–13). Boston: McGraw-Hill.

Moon, D. (1997). *Deconstructing the 'intra'/'inter' divide: Toward a critical inter/cultural practice.* Unpublished Ph.D. disssertation. Tempe: Arizona State University.

Nakayama, T. K. (1994). Show/down time: "Race," gender, sexuality, and popular culture. *Critical Studies in Mass Communication, 11,* 162–179.

Orbe, M. (1998). *Constructing co-cultural theory: An explication of culture, power and communication.* Thousand Oaks, CA: Sage.

Peck, J. (1993/1994). Talk about racism: Framing a popular discourse of race on *Oprah Winfrey. Cultural Critique, 27,* 89–126.

Philipsen, G. (1990). Speaking "like a man" in Teamsterville. In D. Carbaugh (Ed.), *Cultural communication and intercultural contact* (pp. 11–20). Hillsdale, NJ: Lawrence Erlbaum.

Putnam, L., & Pacanowsky, M. (Eds.). (1983). *Communication and organizations: An interpretive approach.* Newbury Park, CA: Sage.

Rosaldo, R. (1989). *Culture and truth: The remaking of social analysis.* Boston: Beacon Press.

Serpell, R. (1982) Measures of perception, skills and intelligence: The growth of a new perspective on children in a third world country. In W. Hartrup (Ed.), *Review of Child Development Research* (Vol. 6). Chicago: University of Chicago Press.

Singer, M. R. (1987). *Intercultural communication: A perceptual approach.* Englewood Cliffs, NJ: Prentice-Hall.

————. (1998). Culture: A perceptual approach. In M. J. Bennett (Ed.), *Basic concepts of intercultural communication* (pp. 97–110). Yarmouth, ME: Intercultural Press.

Stewart, E. C., & Bennett, M. J. (1991). *American cultural patterns: A cross-cultural perspective* (Rev. ed.). Yarmouth, ME: Intercultural Press.

Swarns, R. (2002, May 5). France returns old remains to homeland. *The Arizona Republic,* p. A28.

Winton, R. (2002, December 21). Hate crimes soar following attacks. *Los Angeles Times,* p. B1.

CULTURE, COMMUNICATION, CONTEXT, AND POWER

In Chapter 2, we touched on the history of intercultural communication studies, examined three theoretical approaches, and outlined an integrated dialectical approach to intercultural communication. In this chapter, we continue our discussion of the dialectical approach and identify four interrelated components or building blocks in understanding intercultural communication: culture, communication, context, and power. As noted previously, culture and communication are the foreground, and context and power form the backdrop against which we can understand intercultural communication. First, we define and describe culture and communication. Then we examine how these two components interact with issues of context and power to enhance our understanding of intercultural communication.

WHAT IS CULTURE?

Culture is often considered the core concept in intercultural communication. One characteristic of culture is that it functions largely at a subconscious level. As John, one of our students, said:

> *We take things for granted . . . when living within our own culture, we are never really reminded of it. When I am walking down the street, people just don't stop to say, "Hey, it's an American." In other words, we don't talk about our own culture too much, because we are living it.*

In this sense, trying to understand our own culture is like trying to explain to a fish that it lives in water. Therefore, we often cannot identify our own cultural backgrounds and assumptions until we encounter assumptions that differ from our own. John goes on to explain that he had the opportunity to "step outside" his culture when he traveled to Canada for a couple of months. In Canada, he was called the "Yankee from the States" and would get into friendly arguments about whose country was better, Canada or the United States (e.g., which country supplied more of the world's food). As John observed, "These kinds of conversations made me realize that I was no longer in my culture and that there is always something to learn outside the walls of our own culture."

Consider another example: During a trip to Paris, Tom learned about a U.S. cultural pattern of shopping. In France, cultural **norms** dictate that shoppers greet the shopkeeper before they begin to select items, whereas in the States, he realized, the norm is to simply start shopping. Indeed, all facets of French life have what is sometimes called *la forme de la politesse* (a structured way of manners). Louis-Bernard Robitaille (1995) explains: "In France, there are an infinite number of rites, terms, and manners that must be assimilated, known and scrupulously respected if one has any intention of surviving in this society" (p. 68). (*En France, il y a un nombre infini des rites, des usages, et des manières qu'il faut assimiler, qu'il faut saisir, et qu'il faut respecter scrupuleusement si l'on a l'intention de vivre en sociéte.*)

Culture has been defined in many ways—from a pattern of perceptions that influence communication to a site of contestation and conflict. Because there are many acceptable definitions of culture, and because it is a complex concept, it is

Our understanding of our own culture is mostly subconscious. But this understanding can be brought to consciousness by having contact with people who differ from us or by exploring our own family background. These students describe an experience when they first became aware of their own culture.

> *I do not remember the exact moment when I was made aware of my culture because my parents have always presented to me as being African American. But what I do remember is explaining to some of my White friends why I couldn't go swimming with them because my hair would frizz up and would take at least two hours to do. While they could wash and go, I had to wash, condition for 20 minutes, then blow dry, press and finally style my hair. My White friends also could not understand why I could only wash my hair once a week while they washed their hair every day.*
> —Diana

> *One of the moments that I was made aware of my own culture was when I was confronted with another. When studying Spanish, I went down to Mexico. I witnessed their* Dia de los Muertos *(Day of the Dead). For this holiday, the people honor the dead and often give offerings of food to the deceased. I found it interesting that although both my culture and theirs shared in the same religion, we still celebrate different religious holidays and honor our dead in different ways.*
> —Andrew

> *Two years ago I was taking a Women's Studies class and a project we were assigned required us to interview a woman who was different from us either by race, age, sexual orientation or ethnicity. I decided to interview my grandma because I didn't know much about my family's history. When I learned that the name we had been calling her by her whole life wasn't her real name, I freaked. Her first name wasn't Edith, but Lorenza! Then I realized that I knew little to nothing about my family's history.*
> —Shara

important to reflect on the centrality of culture in our own interactions. The late British writer Raymond Williams (1983) wrote that culture "is one of the two or three most complicated words in the English language" (p. 89). And this very complexity indicates the many ways in which it influences intercultural communication (Williams, 1981). Culture is more than merely one aspect of the practice of intercultural communication. How we think about culture frames our ideas and perceptions. For example, if we think that culture is defined by nation-states, then communication between a Japanese and an Italian would be intercultural communication because Japan and Italy are different nation-states. However, according to this definition, an encounter between an Asian American from North Carolina and an African American from California would not be intercultural because North Carolina and California are not different nation-states.

In this essay, communication scholar Wen Shu Lee identifies different common uses of the term *culture* and then describes how each definition serves particular interests. She also defends her preferred choice, the sixth definition.

1. Culture = unique human efforts (as different from nature and biology). For example, "*Culture* is the bulwark against the ravages of nature."

2. Culture = refinement, mannerism (as different from things that are crude, vulgar, and unrefined). For example, "Look at the way in which he chows down his food. He has no *culture* at all."

3. Culture = civilization (as different from backward barbaric people). For example, "In countries where darkness reigns and people are wanting in *culture*, it is our mandate to civilize and Christianize those poor souls."

4. Culture = shared language, beliefs, values (as different from language beliefs and values that are not shared; dissenting voices; and voices of the "other"). For example, "We come from the same *culture*, we speak the same language, and we share the same tradition."

5. Culture = dominant or hegemonic culture (as different from marginal cultures). For example, "It is the *culture* of the ruling class that determines what is moral and what is deviant." [This definition is a more charged version of definitions 2, 3, and 4 through the addition of power consciousness.]

6. Culture = the shifting tensions between the shared and the unshared (as different from shared or unshared things). For example, "American *culture* has changed from master/slave, to white only/black only, to anti-war and black power, to affirmative action/multiculturalism and political correctness, to transnational capital and anti-sweatshop campaigns."

Each of these definitions privileges certain interests. Definition 2 privileges high culture and leaves out popular culture. . . . Definition 3 privileges nations that are/were imperialistic, colonizing. . . . Definition 4 privileges a "universal and representative" view of a society, but such a view often represents only a specific powerful group and silences other groups that do not readily share this view. Definition 5 privileges the interaction of the culture authorized by the dominant group/sector/nation—more politically explicit than definitions 2, 3, and 4. Definition 6 is the one I like the most. It is more of a meta view of cultures. It focuses on the "links" between "the shared" and the "little shared." But the sharedness, *the* unsharedness, *and their* links remain not only situated but also unstable, shifting, and contested.

Source: From "Dialogue on the Edges: Ferment in Communication and Culture," by Wen Shu Lee, 2002, *Transforming Communication About Culture*, edited by M. J. Collier et al., pp. 219–280.

We do not advocate a singular definition of culture, because any one definition is too restrictive. A dialectical approach suggests that different definitions offer more flexibility in approaching the topic. We believe that the best approach to understanding the complexities of intercultural communication is to view the concept of culture from many perspectives.

By and large, social science researchers focus not on culture per se but on the *influence* of culture on communication. In other words, such researchers concern themselves with communication differences that result from culture. They pay little attention to how we conceptualize culture or how we see its functions. In contrast, interpretive researchers focus more on how cultural contexts influence communication. Critical researchers, for their part, often view communication—and the power to communicate—as instrumental in reshaping culture. They see culture as the way that people participate in or resist society's structure.

Although research studies help us understand different aspects of intercultural communication, it is important to investigate how we think about culture, not simply as researchers but as practitioners as well. We therefore broaden our scope to consider different views of culture, especially in terms of how they influence intercultural communication.

High Culture and Low Culture

The 19th-century essayist and poet Matthew Arnold, who expressed concern with protecting civilization, defined *culture* as "the best that has been thought and said in the world"—a definition that emphasizes quality. In this context, many Western societies distinguish "high culture" from "low culture."

High culture refers to those cultural activities that are often the domain of the elite or the well-to-do: ballet, symphony, opera, great literature, and fine art. These activities sometimes are framed as *international* because supposedly they can be appreciated by audiences in other places, from other cultures, in different time periods. Their cultural value is seen as transcendent and timeless. To protect these cultural treasures, social groups build museums, symphony halls, and theaters. In fact, universities devote courses, programs, and even entire departments to the study of aspects of high culture.

In opposition to high culture is **low culture,** which refers to the activities of the non-elite: music videos, game shows, professional wrestling, stock car racing, graffiti art, TV talk shows, and so on. Traditionally, low-culture activities have been seen as unworthy of serious study—and so of little interest to museums or universities. The cultural values embedded in these activities were considered neither transcendent nor timeless.

The elitism reflected in the distinction between high and low culture points to the tensions in Western social systems. In recent decades, however, this distinction has begun to break down. Rapid social changes propelled universities to alter their policies and also have affected how we study intercultural communication. For example, the turbulent 1960s brought to the university a powerful new interest in ethnic studies, including African American studies and women's and gay and lesbian issues. These areas of study did not rely on the earlier distinctions between high and low culture. Rather, they contributed to a new conceptual framework by arguing for the legitimacy of other cultural forms that traditionally would have been categorized as low culture but were now framed as **popular culture.**

Although the distinction between high and low cultures has broken down, it has not disappeared. What we study and how we study it have significant implications for how we think about the world. The biases of high culture prevail: In most academic settings, some works are favored and others are shunned. Although this practice is less pervasive than it once was, it continues to reinforce a predominantly European-elitist view of the world.

Shared and Learned Patterns of Belief and Perception

Anthropological Definitions of Culture   Traditional intercultural communication studies have been influenced mostly by definitions of culture proposed by anthropologists and psychologists. Of the two disciplines, anthropology is more concerned with definitions. Even so, the definitions proposed are numerous and varied. In 1952, anthropologists Arthur Kroeber and Clyde Kluckhohn categorized and integrated approximately 150 definitions of culture. Some emphasized culture as a set of patterns of thought and beliefs; others viewed culture in terms of a set of behaviors; still others focused on the nonmaterial aspects of human life or on the material aspects of societies. The proliferation of definitions has not diminished (Baldwin & Lindsley, 1994; Jenks, 1993).

Anthropologist Clifford Geertz's definition of culture, traditionally the most widely accepted one in his field, also has been adopted in communication studies. According to Geertz (1973), culture

> denotes an historically transmitted pattern of meaning embodied in symbols, a system of inherited conceptions expressed in symbolic forms by means of which men communicate, perpetuate and develop their knowledge about and attitudes toward life. (p. 89)

The traditional concept of culture continues to involve learned, shared patterns of belief. According to a more recent definition, reflecting Geertz's influence, culture is

> (1) that set of capacities which distinguishes Homo sapiens as a species and which is fundamental to its mode of adaptation; (2) the learned, cumulative product of all social life; (3) the distinctive patterns of thought, action, and value that characterize the members of a society or social group. (Winthrop, 1991, p. 50)

Psychological Definitions of Culture   Geert Hofstede (1984), a noted social psychologist, defines culture similarly, as the "programming of the mind" and the "interactive aggregate of common characteristics that influence a human group's response to its environment" (p. 21). The social psychological definition of culture is centered in the mind of the individual. Hofstede (1997) explains his notion of culture in terms of a computer program:

> Every person carries within him or herself patterns of thinking, feeling, and potential acting which were learned throughout [his or her] lifetime. Much of [these patterns are] acquired in early childhood, because at that time a person is most susceptible to learning and assimilating. (p. 4)

Hofstede goes on to describe how these patterns are developed through interactions in the social environment and with various groups of individuals—first in the family and neighborhood, then at school and in youth groups, then at college, and so on. Culture becomes a collective experience because it is shared with people who live in and experience the same social environments.

To understand this notion of the collective programming of the mind, Hofstede and other scholars studied organizational behavior at various locations of a multinational corporation; this study is discussed in detail later in the chapter. Both the anthropological and the psychological approaches to understanding culture have been influential in the social science perspective on intercultural communication. Social scientists also have emphasized the role of perception in cultural patterns. They contend that cultural patterns of thought and meaning influence our perceptual processes, which, in turn, influence our behavior:

> Culture is defined as a pattern of learned, group-related perception—including both verbal and nonverbal language attitudes, values, belief system, disbelief systems, and behavior. (Singer, 1987, p. 34)

Definitions Borrowed From Ethnography

Ethnography of communication is a specialized field of study within the communication discipline in which researchers look for symbolic meanings of verbal and nonverbal activities in an attempt to understand patterns and rules of communication. This area of study defines cultural groups rather broadly—for example, as talk show participants or Vietnam War veterans.

Ethnography of communication scholar Donal Carbaugh (1988) suggests that it is best to reserve the concept of culture for patterns of symbolic action and meaning that are deeply felt, commonly intelligible, and widely accessible. Patterns that are deeply felt are sensed collectively by members of the cultural group. Gathering around the coffee machine at work every morning, for example, could be a cultural pattern, but only if the activity holds **symbolic significance,** or evokes feelings that extend beyond itself. Then the activity more completely exemplifies a cultural pattern. Suppose that gathering around the coffee machine each morning symbolizes teamwork, or the desire to interact with colleagues. To qualify as a cultural pattern, the activity must have the same symbolic significance for all members of the group; they must all find the activity meaningful in more or less the same way. Further, all participants must have access to the pattern of action. This does not mean that they must all use the pattern; it only means that the pattern is available to them.

Communication theorist Gerry Philipsen extends Carbaugh's notion of culture by emphasizing that these patterns must endure over time, passed along from person to person. Philipsen (1992) writes:

Culture . . . refers to a socially constructed and historically transmitted pattern of symbols, meaning, premises, and rules. . . . A cultural code of speaking, then, consists of a socially constructed and historically transmitted system of symbols and meanings pertaining to communication—for instance, symbols "Lithuanian" or "communication" and their attendant definitions; beliefs about spoken actions (that a man who uses speech to discipline boys is not a real man); and rules for using speech (that a father should not interrupt his daughter at the dinner table). (pp. 7–8)

These definitions of culture suggested by Philipsen are influenced by communication ethnographer Dell Hymes's (1972) framework for studying naturally occurring speech in depth and in context. The framework comprises eight elements: scene, participant, end, act sequence, key, instrumentality, norm, and genre. In this sequence, the terms form the acronym *SPEAKING*. The *S*cene is the setting of the communication event. The *P*articipants are the people who perform or enact the event. The *E*nd is the goal of the participants in conversation. The *A*ct sequence is the order of phrases during the enactment. The *K*ey is the tone of the conversation. The channel of communication is the *I*nstrumentality. The *N*orms, as you know, are the rules that people follow. And *G*enre is the type or category of talk. By analyzing speech using this descriptive framework, we can gain a comprehensive understanding of the rules and patterns followed in any given speech community. Later in this chapter, we'll provide an example of how the framework can be used to explore cultural communication in context.

Although this notion of culture as shared, learned group patterns has long been the standard in a variety of disciplines, more and more people are beginning to question its utility. One colleague reports that in a class discussion about the definition of culture in which most students were giving the usual definitions, "one student almost indignantly jumped into our discussion and said, 'Do we really have a common culture?'" She then followed with the question "Whose version of a shared and common culture are we talking about?" (Collier, Hegde, Lee, Nakayama, & Yep, 2002, p. 269). Indeed, these are important questions, and so the next section describes an alternative approach to defining culture. (For a challenge to common notions of a "shared" U. S. culture, take the "Test of American Cultural Intelligence.")

Culture as a Contested Zone

The emergence in the 1960s of British cultural studies, which held a critical perspective, brought profound changes to how we think about culture and study communication. Originally motivated largely by the establishment of the Centre for Contemporary Cultural Studies at the University of Birmingham, **cultural studies** was fiercely multidisciplinary and committed to social change.

Proponents believed that divisions between disciplines were arbitrary and ideological and that no single discipline embraced all of the methods and theories needed to generate rich understandings of cultural phenomena. Stuart Hall (not related to Edward Hall), an early and enduring figure in British cultural studies, envisioned the group's task as drawing on intellectual resources to help understand everyday life and its supposed antihumaneness.

This desire to make academic work relevant to everyday life resonated in other fields. Most people, in fact, want to find the connections between what they learn in the classroom and what is occurring in contemporary society. In any case, this movement led to the reconfiguration of the role of the university in society.

Cultural studies soon spread from Britain to Australia, Latin America, and other parts of the world. Due to differing cultural and political situations, the specific construction of cultural studies differs from place to place. In the United States, for instance, cultural studies developed mainly within departments of communication (Grossberg, 1993).

The influence of cultural studies in the field of communication has been profound. In many ways, it has far surpassed that of ethnic studies. The cultural studies movement presents a significant challenge to the distinction between high culture and low culture. In fact, proponents argue that low culture is far more significant because it captures the contemporary and dynamic everyday representations of cultural struggles. As a result of this hierarchy inversion, formerly overlooked cultural phenomena such as soap operas and music videos have become important areas of study.

You may sense that the concept of culture that emerged from this area of inquiry differs markedly from the concept expressed in social science or even interpretive research. However, it is in agreement with concepts found in recent work in anthropology. Many anthropologists have criticized research that categorizes people and characterizes cultural patterns as set, unchanging, and unconnected to issues of gender, class, and history (Keesing, 1994). Recent anthropological research sees cultural processes as dynamic and fluid "organizations of diversity" that extend across national and regional borders within contexts of history and power (Hannerz, 1996).

Many communication scholars are also embracing the critical notions of culture that

> *move beyond hegemonic definition of culture as "shared and transmitted from generation to generation" that assume that we all experience a "common culture" and . . . is passed down from one generation to the next in a linear and seemingly static fashion . . . this is a dangerous myth . . . that works in invisible yet extremely powerful ways to suppress and erase marginalized voices and experiences. (Gust Yep, in Collier et al., 2002, p. 231)*

Viewing culture as a contested site or zone helps us understand the struggles of various groups—Native Americans, Asian Americans, Pacific Islanders, African Americans, Latinos/as, women, gays and lesbians, working-class people,

TEST OF AMERICAN CULTURAL INTELLIGENCE

This test covers basic knowledge about the diverse cultures in the United States today. Answers can be found on pages 105–107.

1. "Chitlings" are a part of which of the following animals?
   a. Horse
   b. Chicken
   c. Pig
   d. Cow
   e. Sheep

2. The Japanese American term "yonsei" means:
   a. A fourth generation Japanese American
   b. A dish of fish and rice
   c. Celebration of the New Year
   d. Love
   e. A profitable business venture

3. Chinese New Year is usually celebrated in which month?
   a. March
   b. December
   c. June
   d. January
   e. February

4. Mexican Independence Day is celebrated on which of the following dates:
   a. April 17th
   b. September 16th
   c. October 10th
   d. May 5th
   e. January 22nd

5. What is the use/purpose of a C.I.B.?
   a. To provide free medical services
   b. To verify Native American ancestry
   c. To document immigrant numbers
   d. To create equal opportunity for women
   e. To insure legal employment in the United States

6. A kiva is:
   a. A Pueblo headdress
   b. A rain god
   c. A cornmeal grinding tool
   d. A sacred, ceremonial structure
   e. An eagle staff

7. What is the name of the African American celebration focusing on African cultural pride and celebrated during the month of December?
   a. Patois
   b. Swahili
   c. Imhotep
   d. Natchez
   e. Kwanzaa

8. The Yiddish term "Shalom" means which of the following:
   a. Hello
   b. Peace
   c. Good-bye
   d. All of the above
   e. None of the above

9. The mythical homeland of the Aztec people is called:
   a. Michoacán
   b. Nuestra Señora de los Angeles de Porciuncula
   c. Aztlán
   d. Teotihuacán
   e. Quetzalcóatl

10. What is the name of the traditional Filipino bamboo stick dance?
   a. Teatro
   b. Pancit Palabok
   c. Umoja
   d. Sipapu
   e. Tinikling

11. The Spanish word "orale" is:
   a. Used to curse at someone in a respectful manner
   b. An expression equivalent to "cool!"
   c. A reference to fast eating
   d. The name of a spicy, chicken dish
   e. An expression to describe a "loud mouth"

12. Which of the following is not the (English) name of a Native American tribe?
   a. Arapaho
   b. Tagalog
   c. Pomo
   d. Cahuilla
   e. Potawatomi

Source: From Intercultural Center, Sonoma State University, www.sonoma.edu/icc/test/test.html.

FIGURE 3-1   You can probably notice many differences among the people in this cultural group despite not having communicated with them. What symbols and non-verbal communication influence your assumptions about them? You are likely to encounter many people who are culturally different from you in everyday life. What influences your decisions about which cultural expressions are more acceptable or less acceptable? (© *Michael Newman/PhotoEdit, Inc.*)

and so on—as they attempt to negotiate their relationships and promote their well-being within U.S. society. By studying the communication that springs from these ongoing struggles, we can better understand several intercultural concerns. Consider, for example, Proposition 227 in California, passed by voters in 1998, which eliminated public funding for bilingual education. The controversy surrounding the passage of this proposition illustrates the concerns of many different cultural groups. Similar debates surrounded the prior passage of Propositions 187 and 209 in California.

Viewing culture as a contested site opens up new ways of thinking about intercultural communication. After all, the individuals in a given culture are not identical, which suggests that any culture is replete with cultural struggles. Thus, when we use terms like *Chinese culture* or *French culture*, we gloss over the heterogeneity, the diversity, that resides in that culture. Yet the ways in which various cultures are heterogeneous are not the same elsewhere as in the United States, which means it would be a mistake to map our structure of differences onto other cultures. (See Figure 3-1.) How sexuality, ethnicity, gender, and class function in other cultures is not necessarily the same as, or even similar to, their function in the United States. By viewing any culture as a contested zone or site of struggle, we can understand the complexities of that culture; we can become more sensitive to how people in that culture live.

Our dialectical approach, though, enables us to accept and see the interrelatedness of these different views. Culture is at once a shared and a learned pattern of beliefs and perceptions that are mutually intelligible and widely accessible. It is also a site of struggle for contested meanings.

WHAT IS COMMUNICATION?

The second component in understanding intercultural communication, **communication,** is as complex as culture. The defining characteristic of communication is meaning, and we could say that communication occurs whenever someone attributes meaning to another person's words or actions. Communication may be understood as a "symbolic process whereby reality is produced, maintained, repaired and transformed" (Carey, 1989, p. 23). This simple definition involves several ideas.

First, communication is *symbolic*. This means that the words we speak and the gestures we make have no inherent meaning, but rather gain their significance from an agreed-upon meaning. Thus, when we use symbols to communicate, we assume that the other person shares our symbol system. Also, these symbolic meanings are conveyed both verbally and nonverbally. Thousands of nonverbal behaviors—gestures, postures, eye movements, facial expressions, and so on—involve shared meaning. Powerful social symbols—for example, flags, national anthems, and Disney logos—also communicate meaning nonverbally. Many of these symbols are material as well; that is, they have physical consequences in the world. For example, when schoolchildren in the United States bring guns to school and kill schoolmates, the symbolism of these acts communicate something while the acts themselves are material.

To make things more complicated, each message has more than one meaning, and perhaps many layers of meaning. For example, the message *I love you* may mean, "I'd like to have a good time with you tonight," or "I feel guilty about what I did last night without you," or "I need you to do me a favor," or "I have a good time when I'm with you," or "I want to spend the rest of my life (or at least the next few hours) with you." When we communicate, we assume that the other person takes the meaning that we intend. However, for individuals from different cultural backgrounds and experiences, this assumption may be faulty.

Second, the *process* by which we negotiate meaning is dynamic. Communication is not a singular event but is ongoing—it relies on other communication events to make sense. When we enter into communication with another person, we simultaneously take in messages through all of our senses. The messages are not discreet and linear; they are simultaneous, with blurry boundaries between beginning and end. When we negotiate meaning, we are creating, maintaining, repairing, or transforming reality. This implies that people are actively involved in the communication process. One person cannot communicate alone.

THE RELATIONSHIP BETWEEN CULTURE AND COMMUNICATION

The relationship between culture and communication is complex. A dialectical perspective assumes that culture and communication are interrelated and reciprocal. That is, culture influences communication, and vice versa. Thus, cultural groups influence the process by which the perception of reality is created and maintained: "All communities in all places at all times manifest their own view of reality in what they do. The entire culture reflects the contemporary model of reality" (Burke, 1985, p. 11). However, we might also say that communication helps create the cultural reality of a community. Let's see how these reciprocal relationships work.

How Culture Influences Communication

Intercultural communication scholars use broad frameworks from anthropology to identify and study cultural differences in communication. For example, researchers Kluckhohn and Strodtbeck (1961) studied contemporary Navajo and descendants of Spanish colonists and European Americans in the Southwest. They extended Geertz's earlier work, which emphasized the centrality of **cultural values** in understanding cultural groups. **Values** are the most deeply felt beliefs shared by a cultural group; they reflect a shared perception of what ought to be, and not what is. Equality, for example, is a value shared by many people in the United States. It refers to the belief that all humans are created equal, even though we must acknowledge that, in reality, there are many disparities, such as in talent, intelligence, or access to material goods.

Kluckhohn and Strodtbeck suggested that members of all cultural groups must answer the following important questions:

- What is human nature?
- What is the relationship between humans and nature?
- What is the relationship between humans?
- What is the preferred personality?
- What is the orientation toward time?

According to Kluckhohn and Strodtbeck, there are three possible responses to each question as they relate to shared values. (See Table 3-1.) Kluckhohn and Strodtbeck believed that, although all responses are possible in all societies, each society has one, or possibly two, preferred responses to each question that reflect the predominant values of that society. Religious beliefs, for example, may reinforce certain cultural values. The questions and their responses become a framework for understanding broad differences in values among various cultural groups. Although the framework was applied originally to ethnic groups, we can extend it to cultural groups based on gender, class, nationality, and so on.

TABLE 3-1	VALUE ORIENTATIONS		
	Range of values		
Human nature	Basically good	Mixture of good and evil	Basically evil
Relationship between humans and nature	Humans dominate	Harmony exists between the two	Nature dominates
Relationships between humans	Individual	Group-oriented	Collateral
Preferred personality	"Doing": stress on action	"Growing": stress on spiritual growth	"Being": stress on who you are
Time orientation	Future-oriented	Present-oriented	Past-oriented

Source: Adapted from *Variations in Value Orientations,* by Kluckhohn and Strodtbeck, 1961.

The Nature of Human Nature   As the table shows, there are three possible responses, or solutions, to basic questions about human nature. One solution is a belief in the fundamental goodness of human nature. Legal practices in a society that holds this orientation would emphasize rehabilitating violators of the law; jails and prisons would be seen as places to train violators to rejoin society as contributing citizens. Religions such as Buddhism and Confucianism tend toward this orientation, focusing on improving the natural goodness of humans.

A second solution reflects a perception of a combination of goodness and evil in human nature. Many groups within the United States hold this value orientation, although there has been a shift in views for many U.S. Americans in the past 50 years. With regard to religious beliefs, there is less emphasis on the fundamental evil of humanity, which many European settlers of the Puritan tradition believed (Kohls, 1996). However, the current emphasis is on incarceration and punishment for violators of the law. For example, consider the increase in "three strikes" legislation and the lack of interest in rehabilitation and reform. Given this orientation, not surprisingly, the United States currently has a higher proportion of citizens incarcerated than any other industrialized country.

According to the third orientation, human nature is essentially evil. Societies that hold this belief would be less interested in rehabilitation of criminals than in punishment. We often have trouble understanding torture or the practice of cutting off hands and other limbs—practices prevalent in many societies in the past—without understanding their orientation to human nature. While he lived in Belgium, Tom was particularly struck by the display of punishments and tortures in the Counts of Flanders Castle in Ghent. Perhaps the key to understanding these cultural practices is an understanding of the Christian view of humans as essentially evil and born in sin.

This student talks about the religious and cultural values that have shaped his attitude toward other people and the world and about the importance of understanding others' values.

> *The family cultural element that has probably shaped my life the most has been my religion and heritage. I was raised in an actively religious family; Mormon values and morals are very strict compared to many religions; some even think they could be considered radical. Mormon values are a higher standard of living. It is taking the golden rule a little further. It is living in service to your fellow man, and turning the other cheek to those who have wronged you. . . . I was also raised in rural areas and small towns throughout my younger years. I have been instilled with those "small town values" and know little of living in major cities of the world. By small town values I simply mean that you would go out of your way to help a neighbor, as opposed to ignoring those around you who need help like most people that live in cities do. . . . I am very close with my immediate family. I hold them very dear to me as the most important people and part of my life. I also have a big extended family as you might guess. . . .*
>
> *Being from America, it is very easy for me to interact with others born and raised for generations in this country, but it is of no help when commuicating with someone from other places. I think that the more I can travel and read about circumstances of others, the better chance I have of understanding why people are as they are. If I know what has shaped their views and their lives, I will know what motivates their actions and words.*
> —Josiah

Relationship Between Humans and Nature In most of U.S. society, humans dominate nature. For instance, scientists seed clouds when we need rain, and engineers reroute rivers and build dams to meet the needs for water, recreation, and power. We control births with drugs and medical devices, and we make snow and ice for the recreational pastimes of skiing and skating. Of course, not everyone in the United States agrees that humans should always dominate nature. Conflicts between environmentalists and land developers often center on disagreements over this value orientation. And, of course, there are variations in how these values play out in different societies. For example, a country like Canada, which generally espouses a "humans over nature" orientation, still seems more concerned with environmental issues than does the United States. As described by a student,

> *Canada is very concerned about protecting their environment, and this is very clear even if you are just traveling through. They are concerned about clean water, clean air and not doing too much logging of their trees, keeping streams free of pollution etc.*

POINT OF VIEW

Korean communication scholars Tae-Seop Lim and Soo-Hyang Choi describe the Korean value of collectivism, as expressed in interpersonal relations and communication.

> *Traditionally, Koreans have valued social relationships more than anything else. Koreans often forgo their own personal interests and the welfare of the groups they belong to for the sake of their interpersonal relationships. Because Koreans emphasize social relationships, the abilities to maintain good interpersonal relationships are also valued. Persons are judged based upon their abilities to maintain successful relationships. Having good relationships with others is considered to reflect one's character as well as competence.*
>
> Che-myon *is what enables a person to face others with dignity. Part of* che-myon, *like the Western concept of face, is personalized and negotiated without interaction. The aspect of* che-myon *that Koreans are really sensitive to, however, is sociological and normative* che-myon. *This is extended to one in relation to the social position one holds.*
>
> Noon-chi *is what makes tacit communication possible. It is a strategy that enables one to figure out the intention, desire, mood, and attitude of the other without exchanging explicit verbal messages. It is similar to the Western notion of "reading between the lines," but is much more complicated than its Western counterpart.* Noon-chi *sometimes reads something out of nothing; that is, it reads the mind of the other even before the other knows his or her own mind.* Noon-chi *is often used to protect each other's* che-myon. *When one needs to perform a certain face-threatening act, if the other figures out one's needs before one expresses them and reacts appropriately, then both parties do not have to endanger their* che-myon. . . .
>
> *[A] relationship needs mutual* jung *to be solid.* Jung *is a type of emotional attachment that grows over time as persons in a relationship make repeated contacts with each other. It functions to make a relationship strongly bonded. As the relationship grows old, love often fades away, but* jung *usually grows deep.*

Source: From "Interpersonal Relationships in Korea," by T.-S. Lim and S.-H. Choi, 1996, *Communication in Personal Relationships Across Cultures*, edited by W. B. Gudykunst, S. Ting-Toomey, and T. Nishida, pp. 122–136.

In societies that believe mainly in the domination of nature over humans, decisions are made differently. Families may be more accepting of the number of children that are born naturally. There is less intervention in the processes of nature, and there are fewer attempts to control what people see as the natural order.

Many Native Americans and Japanese believe in the value of humans living in harmony with nature, rather than one force dominating the other. In this value orientation, nature is respected and plays an integral part in the spiritual and religious life of the community. Some societies—for example, many Arab groups—emphasize aspects of both harmony with and domination of nature. This reminds us that values are played out in very complex ways in any cultural group.

Relationships Between Humans   Some cultural groups value individualism whereas others are more group-oriented. The cultural differences pertaining to these values distinguish two types of societies. Individualism, often cited as a value held by European Americans, places importance on individuals rather than on families, work teams, or other groups (Bellah, Madsen, Sullivan, Swidler, & Tipton, 1985). This characteristic is often cited as the most important European American cultural value. In contrast, people from more collectivistic societies, like those in Central and South America, Asia, and many Arab societies, place a great deal of importance on extended families and group loyalty. In the United States, this is the case in Amish communities and in some Latino/a and Native American communities. A visitor to Mexico described one example of collectivism in that culture:

> *I remember that in public that children always seem to be accompanied by someone older, usually a family member. People went around in family groups—children with older siblings, grandparents, aunts—not nearly so age-segregated as it is here in the U.S.*

The collateral orientation emphasizes the collectivist connection to other individuals (mostly family members) even after death. This orientation is found in cultures in which ancestors are seen as a part of the family and are influential in decisions even though they are not alive. Examples of this include the Asian practice of maintaining a table in the house to honor their ancestors or the Mexican "Day of the Dead" practice of having a picnic near the graves of the family members and leaving food for them. (See Figure 3-2.)

Values may also be related to economic status or rural–urban distinctions. In the United States, for example, working-class people tend to be more collectivistic than middle- or upper-class people. (Working-class people reportedly donate a higher percentage of their time and money to help others.) Historian Roxanne A. Dunbar (1997), who grew up poor in Oklahoma, describes an encounter with middle-class individualism she had while on an extended car trip with her new husband, Jimmy. They passed several stranded motorists, the women sitting in the shade while the men worked on the cars. She was surprised when her husband didn't stop to help:

> *"Why don't we stop?" I asked. No one in my family would ever have passed up a stranded motorist. . . .*
> *"They're hustlers, rob you blind, highway bandits," Jimmy said.*
> *"How do you know?"*
> *"I just know, they use the kids and old people for bait to get you to stop, then rob you, they're transients, fruit pickers, white trash."*

Holidays are significant ways of enacting and transmitting culture and cultural values across the generations. For example, Kwanzaa is an important holiday for many African Americans. What holidays does your family celebrate? What cultural values are being transmitted in those celebrations? (*Lawrence Migdale/Getty Images*)

> *I stared at the sad faces as we passed by and tried to see the con artists and criminals behind the masks. But they merely looked familiar, like my own relatives. (p. 83)*

These cultural values may influence patterns of communication. For example, people who value individualism *tend* also to favor direct forms of communication and to support overt forms of conflict resolution. People in collectivistic societies *may* employ less direct communication and more avoidance-style conflict resolution. Of course, sometimes people belong to cultural groups that hold contradictory values. For example, most U.S. work contexts require highly individualistic communication, which may conflict with the collectivistic family or ethnic backgrounds of some workers. Workers may find it hard to reconcile and live with these competing values. Consider the experience of Lucia, a Native American college student. When one of her uncles passed away during the first week of school, she was expected to participate in family activities. She traveled out of state with her family to his home, helped cook and feed other family members, and attended the wake and the funeral. Then her mother became ill, and she had to care for her. Thus, she missed the first two weeks of school. Some of her professors were sympathetic; others were not. As Lucia describes it,

POINT OF VIEW

Two recent news items in the Belgian newspaper *Le Soir* show apparently contradictory cultural values. In the first, Yves Berger, a writer and U.S. specialist, was asked to explain the sexual affair of President Bill Clinton.

> *In any case, it shows to what extent puritanism is ingrained in the American mentality. This might seem unbelievable as Americans, in daily life, give the opposite appearance.*

> (Elle nous permet en tout cas de mesurer à quel point le puritanisme est une donnée profonde de la mentalité, de la sensibilité américaines. Cela peut évidemment sembler incroyable, tant les Américains donnent quotidiennement le spectacle du contraire.)

Another article in the same newspaper describes the dramatic growth of the U.S. pornography industry.

> *The adult video market is booming and the business figures on the rental and sale of adult videos rose in 1997 to 4.2 billion dollars, according to the annual guide* Adult Video News.

> (Le marché de la vidéo pour adults est en plein boom et le chiffre d'affaires de la location et de la vente des films pornographiques s'est élevé en 1997 à 4,2 millards de dollars, selon le guide annuel *Adult Video News.*)

Sources: From "A bout portant," *Le Soir*, January 7, 1998, p. 2; from "Marché porno en expansion aux Etats-Unis," *Le Soir*, January 7, 1998, p. 11.

she feels almost constantly torn between the demands of her collectivistic family and the demands of the individualistic professors and administration.

Preferred Forms of Activity The most common "activity value" in the United States is the "doing" orientation, which emphasizes productivity. (Remember the expression "Idle hands are the devil's workshop"?) Employment reward systems reflect this value in that workers often must document their progress (e.g., in numbers of sales made or numbers of clients seen). In general, the highest status is conferred on those who "do" (sports figures, physicians, lawyers), rather than on those who "think" (philosophers, professors, priests) (Stewart & Bennett, 1991).

The "growing" orientation emphasizes spiritual aspects of life. This orientation seems to be less prevalent than the other two, perhaps practiced only in Zen Buddhism and as a cultural motif in the United States in the 1960s (Stewart & Bennett, 1991). Some societies, as in Japan, combine both "doing" and "growing" orientations, emphasizing action and spiritual growth. The third solution is to emphasize "being," a kind of self-actualization in which the individual is fused with the experience. Some societies in Central and South America, as well as Greece and Spain, exhibit this orientation.

In an interview that appears in *Le Nouvel Observateur*, François Mas was asked to explain the popularity of the medication Viagra (a remedy for sexual impotence) in the United States. He relates the popularity to the "can do" value of the U.S. American people.

> *Probably the most revealing is the "can do" attitude. This attitude, inherited from the pioneers, is how American society, in general, deals with existing problems. Centered on the concrete and practical applications, and often seen as naive in the view of older cultures, this approach has the advantage of deploying a kind of energy and rejecting opposition to progress.*

> (Le plus révélateur étant le "can do". . . . Cette attitude, héritée de pionniers, est celle de la société américane en général face aux problèmes de l'existence. Centrée sur le réel et les applications pratique, souvent naïve dans son expression aux yeux de cultures plus anciennes, cette approach a l'avantage de déployer une certaine énergie et de refuser l'immobilisme.)

Source: From "Vers un Renouveau Sexuel," *Le Nouvel Observateur*, May 1998, pp. 21–27.

Orientation to Time Most U.S. cultural communities—particularly European American and middle class—seem to emphasize the future. Consider the practices of depositing money in retirement accounts or keeping appointment books that reach years into the future. Other societies—for example, in Spain or Greece—seem to emphasize the importance of the present, a recognition of the value of living fully in and realizing the potential of the present moment. One of our friends described her impression of this value difference after a visit to Mexico:

> *I had a wonderful experience in Mexico. I liked the energy—there was ALWAYS so much going on in the streets, and in the* zocalo, *all hours of the day and night. And when I returned to the U.S., the streets seemed so dead—everyone individually alone in their own little houses here. I felt suddenly so sensory-deprived!! I guess I also liked it partly because it is so different, culturally, from the way I grew up. The emphasis of expressing and focusing on life in the present. I don't want to imply that life is a constant thoughtless fiesta in Mexico, because it's not. But there was a kind of joie de vivre and enjoyment of life NOW that certainly was not present in my family's very constrained, restrained, serious lifestyle! And so Mexico seemed a great contrast!*

Many European and Asian societies strongly emphasize the past, believing that knowledge and awareness of history has something to contribute to an understanding of contemporary life. For example, the Leaning Tower of Pisa was closed for 10 years while Italian workers repaired structural damage on this historic building!

Value Orientations and Cultural Conflict

Of course, not everyone in a society holds the dominant value. Instead, representation follows a normal distribution pattern, with most people clustered near the mean but with a few others spread at various distances around the mean. The range-of-values framework highlighted in Table 3-1 provides a way to map and contrast broad cultural differences between various groups. It can also serve as a way to analyze cultural differences. However, we must avoid reducing people to stereotypes based on these value orientations. After all, not all Amish or all Japanese are group-oriented, and although people in small rural communities may be more collectivistic (more willing to help their neighbors), we cannot say that all city dwellers ignore those around them.

Intercultural conflicts are often due to differences in value orientations. For example, some people feel strongly that it is important to consider how things were done in the past. For them, history and tradition help provide guidance. Values often conflict among participants in international assistance projects in which future-oriented individuals show a lack of respect for traditional ways of doing things. And conflicts may be exacerbated by power differentials, with some values privileged over others. Organizational communication scholars have pointed out that many U.S. workplaces reward extremely individualistic relationships and "doing" behaviors at the expense of more collaborative (and equally productive) work (Buzzanell, 1994).

Geert Hofstede (1984, 1997) proposed a similar framework based on an extensive cross-cultural study of personnel working in IBM subsidiaries in 53 countries. Whereas Kluckhohn and Strodbeck (1961) based their framework on cultural patterns of ethnic communities within the United States, Hofstede examined value differences among national societies. Hofstede identified five areas of common problems. Although the problems were shared by different cultural groups, solutions varied from culture to culture. The problem types are identified as follows:

- Power distance: social inequality, including the relationship with authority
- Individualism versus collectivism: orientation toward the individual or toward groups
- Femininity versus masculinity: the social implications of having been born male or female
- Ways of dealing with uncertainty, controlling aggression, and expressing emotions
- Long-term versus short-term orientation to life

Hofstede then investigated how these various cultural values influenced corporate behavior in various countries. One problem type, individualism versus collectivism, appeared in the Kluckhohn and Strodbeck framework. Let's examine the other problem types more closely.

Power distance refers to the extent to which less powerful members of institutions and organizations within a country expect and accept the unequal dis-

I recently spent two weeks in Mexico City. It was an amazing experience. The contrast between Phoenix and Mexico City totally blew me away, especially the architecture. I mean, just walking down the street you see buildings all around you that are hundreds of years old. We went to the Basilica of the Virgin of Guadalupe, and our guide showed us the exact hill where Juan Diego supposedly saw the Virgin and brought back roses to prove to the priests that he saw her. The priests then built a church exactly right there because that was what the Virgin told Juan to tell the priests to do. Juan Diego is like a national hero in Mexico, and this place where they built these churches is totally sacred. People come from all over Mexico to this exact place, and it is just so hugely important to them.

We also went to Teotihuacán and Templo Mayor. Both are ancient ruins from the Aztecs. These places were really, really amazing. Our guide pointed out for us places where the Spanish built buildings right on top of the ancient structures. It was their way of winning over the natives, of making the Spanish ways take over the ways of the native people. I realized that this change in architecture conveyed a whole history of different cultures and conquest. I was amazed that as I stood there at Templo Mayor, right in the heart of this huge city, I could literally see hundreds of years of history. And the domination also hit me. The Spanish had to build over the temples and other sacred sites of the Aztecs in order to win the hearts of the people. And they needed to make Juan Diego a national hero and make sacred the spot that he is said to have seen the Virgin of Guadalupe. And in order to make all that real to the people, they had to put it all in the architecture.

—Samantha

tribution of power. Denmark, Israel, and New Zealand, for example, value small power distance. Most people there believe that less hierarchy is better and that power should be used only for legitimate purposes. Therefore, the best corporate leaders in those countries are those who minimize power differences. In societies that value large power distance—for example, Mexico, the Philippines, or India—the decision-making process and the relationships between managers and subordinates are more formalized. In addition, people may be uncomfortable in settings in which hierarchy is unclear or ambiguous.

The **masculinity–femininity** value is two-dimensional. It refers to (1) the degree to which gender-specific roles are valued and (2) the degree to which cultural groups value so-called masculine values (achievement, ambition, acquisition of material goods) or so-called feminine values (quality of life, service to others, nurturance, support for the unfortunate). IBM employees in Japan, Austria, and Mexico scored high on the masculine values orientation, expressing a general preference for gender-specific roles, with some roles (e.g., main wage earner) better filled by men and other roles (e.g., homemaker, teacher) by women. In contrast, employees in northern Europe (Denmark, Norway, Sweden, and the Netherlands) tended to rank higher in feminine values orientation, reflecting more gender equality and a stronger belief in the importance of quality of life for all.

Uncertainty avoidance concerns the degree to which people who feel threatened by ambiguous situations respond by avoiding them or trying to establish more structure to compensate for the uncertainty. Societies that have a weak uncertainty avoidance orientation (Great Britain, Sweden, Hong Kong, and the United States) prefer to limit rules, accept dissent, and take risks. In contrast, those with a strong uncertainty avoidance orientation (Greece, Portugal, and Japan) usually prefer more extensive rules and regulations in organizational settings and seek consensus about goals.

Hofstede's original framework contained only four problem types and was criticized for its predominantly western European bias. In response, a group of Chinese researchers developed and administered a similar, but more Asian-oriented, questionnaire to people in 22 countries around the world (Chinese Culture Connection, 1987). Their questionnaire included ideas related to Confucian-based thinking. In comparing their framework to Hofstede's, they concluded that there was, in fact, a great deal of overlap. Indeed, the three dimensions of individualism–collectivism, power distance, and masculinity–femininity seem to be universal. However, uncertainty avoidance seems to be more relevant to Western societies. A fifth dimension that emerged from the Asian study and that seems to apply to both Eastern and Western societies is the **long-term versus short-term orientation,** which reflects a society's search for virtue or truth.

Those with a short-term orientation are concerned with possessing the truth (reflected in the Western religions of Judaism, Christianity, and Islam), focus on quick results in endeavors, and recognize social pressure to conform. Those with a long-term orientation tend to respect the demands of virtue (reflected in Eastern religions such as Confucianism, Hinduism, Buddhism, and Shintoism); to focus more on thrift, perseverance, and tenacity in whatever they attempt; and to be willing to subordinate themselves to a larger purpose.

The main limitation of value frameworks is that they tend to "essentialize" people. In other words, people tend to assume that a particular group characteristic is the essential characteristic of a given member at all times and in all contexts. Writers Tim Ambler and Morgan Witzel (2000), who have spent a great deal of time in China, challenge the validity of these frameworks and promote a dialectical perspective:

> *For many people familiar with both China and the overseas Chinese, . . . this research is not reliable in an oriental context because it falls into the either/or trap. . . . The Chinese are not* either *individualist* or *collective but both at the same time. (p. 70)*

The cultural–individual dialectic reminds us that these value orientations exist on a continuum and are all present, to a greater or lesser extent, in all societies. For example, we could characterize the debate about health care in the United States as a struggle between "masculine" and "feminine" value orientations. Those with a "masculine" orientation believe that each person should take care of him- or herself and be free to achieve and to acquire as many material goods as possible. Others, representing a "feminine" position, believe that everyone should sacrifice a little for the good of the whole and that everyone should be assured access to health care and hospitalization.

The differences–similarities dialectic reminds us that, although people may differ with respect to specific value orientations, they also may hold other value orientations in common. For example, people may have different views on the importance of individual or group loyalty but share a belief in the essential goodness of human nature and find similarity in religious faith and practice. Finally, a static–dynamic dialectic reminds us that, although group-related values tend to be relatively consistent, people are dynamic, and their behavior varies contextually. Thus, they may be more or less individualistic or group-oriented depending on the context.

How Communication Influences Culture

Culture not only influences communication but also is enacted through, and so is influenced by, communication. Scholars of cultural communication describe how various aspects of culture are enacted in speech communities in situ, that is, in contexts. They seek to understand communication patterns that are situated socially and give voice to cultural identity. Specifically, they examine how the cultural forms and frames (terms, rituals, myths, and social dramas) are enacted through structuring norms of conversation and interaction. The patterns are not connected in a deterministic way to any cultural group (Philipsen, 2002).

Researcher Tamar Katriel (1990) examines "griping," a **communication ritual** that takes place among middle-class Israelis. Using the SPEAKING framework (scene, participant, end, act sequence, key, instrumentality, norm, and genre), Katriel analyzes the ritual in the following way: The griping topic must be one related to the domain of public life, and the purpose of the griping is not to solve the problem but to vent pent-up tensions and to affirm the shared reality of being Israeli. The ritual is a deeply felt, widely held, accessible behavioral pattern that affirms the cultural identity of Israelis. Although individuals belonging to other cultural groups may gripe, the activity may not be performed in this systematic cultural way and may not fill the same function.

The instrumentality (or channel) in griping is face-to-face, and the scene (or setting) usually is a Friday night gathering in a private home. Participants may be friends or acquaintances, or even strangers, but not real outsiders. (Katriel describes an embarrassing incident when a couple of gripers discovered that one of the group was merely a visiting Jew, and not a native Israeli.) The key (or tone) of this ritual is one of plaintiveness and frustration. The act sequence comprises an initiation phase, when someone voices a complaint; this is followed by the acknowledgment phase, when others comment on the opener, and then a progression of subthemes. Finally, during the termination phase, everyone intellectually sighs and agrees that it is a problem: "It's no joke, things are getting worse all the time," the participants might say.

FIGURE 3-3   This photo of tourists watching Aztec dancers in Mexico City reflects an earlier context in which Aztec culture was dominant in Mexico. What role does Aztec culture play in Mexican life today? What does this communicate about the continued vitality of Aztec culture in today's Mexico? (*Courtesy Jackie Martinez, Arizona State University*)

It is possible to compare different ways in which cultural norms and forms such as griping enact aspects of the culture and construct cultural identity. For example, although Katriel is not interested in making cross-cultural comparisons, she does allude to the difference between the Israeli griping ritual and a similar communication ritual that many White, middle-class U.S. residents engage in (Katriel & Philipsen, 1990). The communication ritual is a form of close, supportive, and flexible speech aimed at solving personal problems and affirming participants' identities. It is initiated when people sit down together, acknowledge the problem, and negotiate a solution. Katriel identifies similarities in these two rituals: Each fills the function of dramatizing major cultural problems, provides a preferred social context for the venting of problems and frustration, and promotes a sense of community identity (Katriel, 1990).

A related approach from cultural communication studies sees culture as **performative.** If we accept this metaphor, then we are not studying any external (cultural) reality. Rather, we are examining how persons enact and represent their culture's worldviews. (See Figure 3-3.) For example, as Philipsen (1992) reports in his study of Teamsterville, men enact their gender (cultural) roles by remaining silent in many instances, engaging in talk mainly with peers but not with women or children.

These interpretive studies sometimes use cultural values as a way to explain cultural patterns. Kristine Fitch (1994) conducted a cross-cultural study comparing how people in Bogotá, Colombia, and Boulder, Colorado, got others to do what they wanted, a sociolinguistic form known as a *directive*. Fitch found that directives were seen as a problem in both societies, but as different kinds of problems that reflected and reinforced different value orientations. Individuals in Boulder seemed to think that telling someone what to do should be approached carefully so as not to infringe on that person's autonomy—reflecting a value of individualism. In Bogotá, where collectivistic values reign, directives must be negotiated within relationships; there must be enough *confianza* (respect) or authority that one person is required by the social hierarchy to do the other's bidding. As you can see, cultural values can be used to show how culture influences communication or to explain how communication reinforces cultural values.

Culture as Resistance to the Dominant Cultural System

Resistance is the metaphor used in cultural studies to conceptualize the relationship between culture and communication. Borrowing this metaphor, we can try to discover how individuals use their own space to resist the dominant cultural system. For example, we might study the floating bars in New York City—warehouses where people meet (clandestinely and illegally) for a night or two, exchange money, party, and then disappear. The "establishment" does not obtain a liquor license or pay taxes, and so people are circumventing the system. Similarly, workers often find ways to resist extreme individualism and competition in the workplace. For example, flight attendants may collaborate to protect each other from the critical gaze of supervisors (Murphy, 1998). Or students may sign their advisors' names on course registration forms, thereby circumventing the university bureaucracy. We can interpret these behaviors as resistance to the dominant cultural system.

THE RELATIONSHIP BETWEEN COMMUNICATION AND CONTEXT

Context typically is created by the physical or social aspects of the situation in which communication occurs. For example, communication may occur in a classroom, a bar, or a church; in each case, the physical characteristics of the setting influence the communication. People communicate differently depending on the context. Context is neither static nor objective, and it can be multilayered. Context may consist of the social, political, and historical structures in which the communication occurs.

Not surprisingly, the social context is determined on the societal level. Consider, for example, the controversy over the Calvin Klein underwear ads in the early 1990s that used young adolescents as models: many critics viewed the ads as equivalent to pedophilia. The controversy took place in a social context in which pedophilia was seen as perverse or immoral. This meant that any communication that encouraged or fed that behavior or perspective, including advertising, was deemed wrong by the majority of observers. However, pedophilia has not been considered wrong in all societies in all periods of history. To adequately interpret the ads, we would have to know something about the current feelings toward and meanings attached to pedophilia wherever the ads were displayed.

The political context in which communication occurs includes those forces that attempt to change or retain existing social structures and relations. For example, to understand the acts of protesters who throw blood or red paint on people who wear fur coats, we must consider the political context. In this case, the political context would be the ongoing informal debates about animal rights and cruelty to animals farmed for their pelts. In other locales or other eras, the protesters' communicative acts would not make sense or would be interpreted in other ways.

We also need to examine the historical context of communication. For example, the meaning of a college degree depends in part on the particular school's reputation. Why does a degree from Harvard communicate a different meaning than a degree from an obscure state university? Harvard's reputation relies on history—the large endowments given over the years, the important persons who have attended and graduated, and so forth.

THE RELATIONSHIP BETWEEN COMMUNICATION AND POWER

Power is pervasive in communication interactions, although it is not always evident or obvious how power influences communication or what kinds of meaning are constructed. We often think of communication between individuals as being between equals, but this is rarely the case. As communication scholar Mark Orbe (1998) describes it,

> *In every society a social hierarchy exists that privileges some groups over others. Those groups that function at the top of the social hierarchy determine to a great extent the communication system of the entire society. (p. 8)*

Orbe goes on to describe how those people in power, consciously or unconsciously, create and maintain communication systems that reflect, reinforce, and promote their own ways of thinking and communicating. There are two levels of group-related power: (1) the primary dimensions—age, ethnicity, gender, physical abilities, race, and sexual orientation—which are more permanent in nature, and (2) the secondary dimensions—educational background, geographic location, marital status, and socioeconomic status—which are more changeable (Loden & Rosener, 1991). The point is that the dominant communication systems ultimately impede those who do not share the systems. The communication style most valued in college classrooms, for example, emphasizes public speaking and competition (because the first person who raises his or her hand gets to speak). Not all students are comfortable with this style, but those who take to it naturally are more likely to succeed.

Power also comes from social institutions and the roles individuals occupy in those institutions. For example, in the classroom, there is temporary inequal-

It is often difficult to distinguish what is "natural" from what is "cultural." In this selection, author bell hooks tells us how she negotiated her way through one cultural practice related to fashion. Consider what aspects of cultural domination she is resisting, and notice how gender is intertwined with culture.

> GOOD HAIR—*that's the expression. We all know it, begin to hear it when we are small children. When we are sitting between the legs of mothers and sisters getting our hair combed. Good hair is hair that is not kinky, hair that does not feel like balls of steel wool, hair that does not take hours to comb, hair that does not need tons of grease to untangle, hair that is long. Real good hair is straight hair, hair like white folks' hair. Yet no one says so. No one says your hair is so nice, so beautiful because it is like white folks' hair. We pretend that the standards we measure our beauty by are our own invention—that it is questions of time and money that lead us to make distinctions between good hair and bad hair. . . .*
>
> *For each of us, getting our hair pressed is an important ritual. It is not a sign of our longing to be white. It is not a sign of our quest to be beautiful. We are girls. It is a sign of our desire to be women. It is a gesture that says we are approaching womanhood. It is a rite of passage. . . . Secretly I had hoped that the hot comb would transform me, turn the thin good hair into thick nappy hair, the kind of hair I like and long for, the kind you can do anything with, wear in all kinds of styles. I am bitterly disappointed in the new look.*
>
> *A senior in high school, I want to wear a natural, an afro. I want never to get my hair pressed again. It is no longer a rite of passage, a chance to be intimate in the world of women. The intimacy masks betrayal.*

Source: From bell hooks, "Black Is a Woman's Color," *Callaloo 39*, 1989, p. 2.

ity, with instructors having more power. After all, they set the course requirements, give grades, determine who speaks, and so on. In this case, the power rests not with the individual instructor but with the role that he or she is enacting.

Power is dynamic. It is not a simple one-way proposition. For example, students may leave a classroom at any time during a class period, or they may carry on a conversation while the professor is speaking—thus weakening the professor's power over them. They may also refuse to accept a grade and file a grievance with the university administration to have the grade changed. Further, the typical power relationship between instructor and student often is not perpetuated beyond the classroom. However, some issues of power play out in a broader social context. For example, in contemporary society, cosmetic companies have a vested interest in a particular image of female beauty that involves purchasing and using makeup. Advertisements encourage women to feel compelled to participate in this cultural definition. Resistance can be expressed by a refusal to go along with the dominant cultural standards of beauty. Angela, a student from rural Michigan, describes how she resisted the "beauty culture" of her metropolitan university:

> *I came to school, and when I looked around I felt like I was inadequate. I had one of two choices, to conform to what the girls look like here, or to stay the same. I chose to stay true to my "Michigan" self. I felt more confident this way. I still remember looking at all of the blond girls with their fake boobs and black pants, strutting down campus. Four years later, I have a more mature attitude and realized that this culture wasn't for me.*

What happens when someone like Angela decides not to buy into this definition? Regardless of the woman's individual reason for not participating, other people are likely to interpret her behavior in ways that may not match her own reasons. What her unadorned face communicates is understood against a backdrop of society's definitions—that is, the backdrop developed by the cosmetics industry.

Dominant cultural groups attempt to perpetuate their positions of privilege in many ways. However, subordinate groups can resist this domination in many ways too. Cultural groups can use political and legal means to maintain or resist domination, but these are not the only means of invoking power relations. Groups can negotiate their various relations to culture through economic boycotts, strikes, and sit-ins. Individuals can subscribe (or not subscribe) to specific magazines or newspapers, change TV channels, write letters to government officials, or take action in other ways to change the influence of power.

The disempowered can negotiate power in many ways. For instance, employees in a large institution can find ways to reposition themselves or gain power. Students might sign their advisors' signature on their registration schedules if they don't have time to see their advisors.

Power is complex, especially in relation to institutions or the social structure. Some inequities, such as in gender, class, or race, are more rigid than those created by temporary roles such as student or teacher. The power relations between student and teacher, for example, are more complex if the teacher is a female challenged by male students. We really can't understand intercultural communication without considering the power dynamics in the interaction.

A dialectical perspective looks at the dynamic and interrelated ways in which culture, communication, context, and power intersect in intercultural communication interactions. Consider this example: When Tom first arrived in Brussels in January 1998, he asked for a national train schedule from the information office at one of the train stations. Because he does not speak Dutch, he talked to the agent behind the counter in French. The agent gave Tom a copy of the national train schedule in Dutch. When Tom asked if it was available in French, the man politely apologized, saying that it was the end of the season and there were no more available in French. It was clear to Tom that, although both parties followed *la forme de la politesse*, the agent did not want to give him the train schedule in French. Indeed, it was not near the end of the season, because the 1997–1998 train schedule ran from June 1 to May 23.

Many of the Thai managers I spoke with while doing research on American companies in Thailand stressed to me that when working with Thais one needed to be very aware of relationships and the hierarchy in which they exist. A Thai woman I spoke with, who was the secretary to the company's American president, provided this example of the need for attention to the details of relationships:

> *I believe in the United States it is common for a boss to ask the secretary to request some materials from another person or to call people and tell them the boss wants to see them. In the United States, you all look at each other as equals. It is not so important what someone's title is, their age, or time with the company. In Thailand, those things are very important. For example, my boss, who is an American, was always asking me to go call so-and-so and request a meeting or go talk to so-and-so and get some reports from them. By having me do this, the Thais were wondering several things: Why should we deal with her; she is just a secretary, and have I done something wrong that the boss does not want to talk with me? Finally, I got my boss to understand that when he had a request for someone—especially someone who was high-ranking in the company, someone who was much older than me or had been with the company longer than me—I would write a short note to that person, he would sign it, then I would pass the note along. That way, everyone's face was saved, their positions were recognized, and the boss came across as showing that he cared about his personal relationship with everyone. Mind you, I can run over and ask others of my same rank, age, or time with the company for any information or a meeting, but it is important to show respect toward those in high positions.*
> —Chris

From a communication perspective, it might not be at all clear that an intercultural struggle had taken place. None of the traditional signals of conflict were manifested: no raised voices, no harsh words, no curtness. Indeed, the exchange seemed polite and courteous.

From a cultural perspective, however, with various contexts and power differentials in mind, a different view of this intercultural interaction emerges. Belgium is a nation largely divided by two cultures, Flemish and Walloon, although there is a small German-speaking minority in the far eastern part of the country. Belgium is officially trilingual (Dutch, French, German); that is, each language is the official language in its territory. Dutch is the official language in Flanders, and French is the official language in Wallonia, except in the eastern part, where German is the official language. The only part of Belgium that is officially bilingual is the "Brussels-Capital Region."

Just out of college, I went to Japan and lived with a family for a few months. I vividly remember the sense of shock upon realizing the gap between my Japanese homestay family's perception of my status, power, and role compared to my own view of the situation. I had seen the experience as a chance for them to show and teach me various facets of Japanese home life and, reciprocally, as a time for me to study my language books and appreciate them. And I tried to learn as much as I could from Ken, their son, whom I considered a role model. One day, however, after what I suppose was a lengthy period of frustration on her part, my Japanese mother took me aside and said, "You seem to look for learnings behind each of Ken's actions, Douglas-san, but remember that since you are older it is you who must teach and be the responsible one."

—Douglas

There are many historical contexts to consider here. For example, Brussels is historically a Flemish city, located in Flanders (but near the border with Wallonia). Also, the French language dominated in Belgium from the time it gained independence from the Netherlands in 1830 until the early 20th century when Flemish gained parity.

There are social and economic contexts to consider as well. Since the 1960s, Flanders has been more economically powerful than Wallonia. The Brussels-Capital Region, despite being in Flanders, has become increasingly French-speaking; some estimates place the current percentage of francophones at 85–90%. And nearly 30% of Brussels' residents are foreigners, most of whom are francophones. The increasing migration of city dwellers to the suburbs has also caused tensions, because a number of communes located in Flanders now have a francophone majority.

So, although the Brussels-Capital Region is officially bilingual, this is the site of a number of struggles between French and Dutch. Indeed, as many Walloons told Tom, one does not get a sense of the conflict in Wallonia, but it is evident in Brussels. In the context of the various tensions that existed at the time of Tom's arrival in Belgium, the intercultural conflict at the train station is merely a playing out of much larger issues in Belgian society. Tom's entry into that society, as another francophone foreigner, situated his communication interactions in largely prefigured ways.

Although he later secured a French train schedule, he continued to use the Dutch one so he could learn the Dutch names of many Belgian cities as well. In any case, Tom's experience involved various dialectical tensions: (1) being a francophone foreigner versus a traditional Flemish resident, (2) being in an officially bilingual region versus an increasingly francophone one, (3) recognizing the importance of formality and politeness in French versus the nature of this ancient conflict, (4) having abundant opportunities to learn French versus the lack of

ANSWERS TO THE "TEST OF AMERICAN CULTURAL INTELLIGENCE"

1. (c) PIG is the correct answer

   "Chitlings" are the small intestines, usually boiled or fried for eating, and are a traditional African American food. Today there is much controversy concerning the healthiness of this meal. There are also historical connotations related to the time when slaves were given the unwanted "leftovers" of the slave owners (such as the intestines, feet, etc.).

2. (a) A FOURTH GENERATION JAPANESE AMERICAN is the correct answer

   The Japanese have terms depicting each of the various generations of American citizenship.
   First generation = "issei"
   Second generation = "nisei"
   Third generation = "sansei"
   Fifth generation = "gosei"

3. (e) FEBRUARY is the correct answer

   Chinese New Years are usually celebrated in the month of February. The year is begun with the cleaning of the house and the hope for good luck for the coming year. Chinese celebrations are commonly known for the firecrackers (which scare evil spirits away) and lion dances. Luck and good fortune are key elements to New Years activities. By the way, 2004 is the year of the Monkey.

4. (b) SEPTEMBER 16TH is the correct answer

   Contrary to popular belief, Cinco de Mayo is not Mexican Independence. Cinco de Mayo represents the May 5th, 1862 victory, in Puebla, against the French (a war which Mexico eventually lost). September 16th is the day of the "Grito," or shout; the first day of the uprising which led to independence.

5. (b) TO VERIFY NATIVE AMERICAN ANCESTRY is the correct answer

   C.I.B. stands for Certificate of Indian Blood. It is a documentation of Native American ancestry, in order to allow the use of federal programs or services. Most tribes, however, have the ability to determine who is and is not considered a member of the tribe. These individuals may be ineligible for federal services despite tribal recognition.

6. (d) A SACRED, CEREMONIAL STRUCTURE is the correct answer

   A kiva is a ceremonial structure used by the Pueblos. The word originated from the Hopi tribe, of northeastern Arizona.

(continues)

7. (e) KWANZAA is the correct answer

Kwanzaa is an African American creation which promotes cultural pride and addresses social conditions and needs. Despite popular belief, Kwanzaa is not necessarily a celebration intended to replace Christmas, despite its monthly relationship. The celebration stretches from December 26th to January 1st. The seven principles are:
1. Umoja (unity)
2. Kujichagulia (self determination)
3. Ujima (collective work and responsibility)
4. Ujamaa (cooperative economics)
5. Nia (purpose)
6. Kuumba (creativity)
7. Imani (faith)

Other Answers:

Patois is a term describing a linguistic dialect. It is often used for the Jamaican dialect.

Swahili is an African language.

Imhotep was an Egytpian scientist, architect, and physician. Considered by many as the first "multi-genius."

Natchez is the name of a tribe originally from the Mississippi area. Their tribal identity is now extinct.

8. (d) ALL OF THE ABOVE is the correct answer

"Shalom" has many meanings in the Jewish community. Hello, Good-Bye, and Peace are all correct uses.

9. (c) AZTLAN is the correct answer

Aztlán is the mythical homeland of the Aztec people, where, as prophesized by their king, they saw an eagle perched on a cactus, eating a snake. This was where the capital city was to be built, and it was. Today, the site is known as Mexico City. For Chicanos, Aztlán represents all of the Southwest that used to be Mexico before the land loss to the United States.

Other Answers:

Michoacán is a present agricultural and mining state in southern Mexico.

Nuestra Señora de los Angeles de Porciuncula is the original name of present day Los Angeles, CA when it was still a tiny pueblo of Mexico.

opportunities to study Dutch in the United States, and (5) illustrating the economic power of the Flemish in Belgium versus that of the francophones in Brussels. From these dialectical tensions and others, Tom attempted to understand and contextualize his intercultural interaction.

Teotihuacán was a huge (approx. 250,000 people) religious center in Mexico from 300–900 A.D. It was home to the Temples of the Sun and Moon.

Quetzalcóatl was the feathered serpent god of Teotihuacán, representing learning, fine arts, and agriculture.

10. (e) TINIKLING is the correct answer

Tinikling is a dance which displays endurance, coordination, agility, and grace as the dancers step in and out of a pair of bamboo sticks which are opened and closed by two other performers. The speed changes, twists, turns, and step variance make this dance an incredible sight to see.

Other Answers:

Teatro is the Spanish word for theater.

Pancit Palabok is a pasta dish which uses meat, shrimp, and vegetables.

Umoja is one of the principles of Kwanzaa, that of unity.

A Sipapu is the spiritual opening ("emergence" representation) inside a kiva.

11. (b) AN EXPRESSION EQUIVALENT TO "COOL!" is the correct answer

Although "orale" has several uses and meanings, "cool!" is one of them.

12. (b) TAGALOG is the correct answer

Tagalog is one of the many Filipino dialects.

Other Answers:

The *Arapaho* are originally thought to have lived in Minnesota before moving West into present day Wyoming and Colorado.

The *Pomo* ranged from the coastal area to the inland areas of Northern California.

The *Cahuilla* lived in present day Southern California.

The *Potawatomi* lived in Michigan before many moved into other nearby areas and even into the present day Midwest.

Note: All of these tribes are STILL in existence and have diverse modern experiences.

Source: From Intercultural Center, Sonoma State University, www.sonoma.edu/icc/test/test.html.

There are no simple lists of behaviors that are key to successful intercultural interaction. Instead, we encourage you to understand the contexts and dialectical tensions that arise in your intercultural communication experiences. In this way, you will better understand the constraints you face in your interactions. You will also come to a better understanding of the culture you are in and the culture you are from. Although the dialectical perspective makes the investigation of culture and communication far more complex, it also makes it far more exciting and interesting and leads to a much richer understanding.

SUMMARY

In this chapter, we built on the dialectical perspective in outlining several different approaches to understanding the four building blocks of intercultural communication: culture, communication, context, and power. Culture can be viewed as deep-seated patterns of learned, shared beliefs and perception; as deeply felt, commonly intelligible, and widely accessible patterns of symbolic meaning; and/or as contested zones of meaning. Communication is a symbolic process whereby reality is produced, maintained, repaired, and transformed. The relationship between culture and communication is complex. Culture influences communication and is enacted through communication; in turn, communication is a way of contesting and resisting the dominant culture. The context—the physical and social setting in which communication occurs, or the larger political, social, and historical environment—affects that communication. Finally, power is pervasive and plays an enormous, though often hidden, role in intercultural communication interactions. Power relationships, determined largely by social institutions and roles, influence communication.

Now that we have laid the foundation of our approach to intercultural communication, the next step is to examine in depth the role of history in intercultural communication.

DISCUSSION QUESTIONS

1. How have notions of high and low culture influenced people's perspectives on culture?

2. How do the values of a cultural group influence communication with members of other cultural groups?

3. What techniques do people use to assert power in communication interactions?

4. How is culture a contested site?

 Go to the self-quizzes on the Online Learning Center at www.mhhe.com/martinnakayama to further test your knowledge.

ACTIVITIES

1. *Cultural Values.* Look for advertisements in newspapers and popular magazines. Analyze the ads to see if you can identify the social values to which they appeal.

2. *Culture: Deeply Felt or Contested Zone?* Analyze the lyrics of songs you listen to and try to identify patterns in the songs. Then think about your own cultural position and discuss which framework—the one proposed by cultural ethnographies (culture as deeply felt) or the one proposed by cultural studies (culture as a contested zone)—more adequately articulates the connection between culture and communication.

KEY WORDS

communication
communication ritual
context
cultural studies
cultural values
culture
ethnography of
    communication

high culture
long-term versus
    short-term
    orientation
low culture
masculinity–
    femininity value
norms

performative
popular culture
power distance
symbolic significance
uncertainty avoidance
values

 The Online Learning Center at www.mhhe.com/martinnakayama features flashcards and crossword puzzles based on these terms and concepts.

REFERENCES

Ambler, T., & Witzel, M. (2000). *Doing business in China.* New York: Routledge.

Baldwin, J. R., & Lindsley, S. L. (1994). *Conceptualizations of culture.* Tempe: Arizona State University Urban Studies Center.

Bellah, R. N., Madsen, R., Sullivan, W. M., Swidler, A., & Tipton, S. M. (1985). *Habits of the heart: Individualism and commitment in American life.* New York: Harper & Row.

Berger, Y. (1998, January 7). A bout portant. *Le Soir*, p. 2.

Burke, J. (1985). *The day the universe changed.* Boston: Little, Brown.

Buzzanell, P. M. (1994). Gaining a voice: Feminist organizational communication theorizing. *Management Communication Quarterly, 7,* 339–383.

Carbaugh, D. (1988). Comments on "culture" in communication inquiry. *Communication Reports, 1,* 38–41.

Carey, J. W. (1989). *Communication as culture: Essays on media and society.* Boston: Unwin Hyman.

Chinese Culture Connection. (1987). Chinese values and the search for culture-free dimensions of culture. *Journal of Cross-Cultural Psychology, 18,* 143–164.

Collier, M. J., Hegde, R. S., Lee, W., Nakayama, T. K., & Yep, G. A. (2002). Dialogue on the edges: Ferment in communication and culture. In M. J. Collier (Ed.), *Transforming communication about culture. International and Intercultural Communication Annual* (Vol. 24, pp. 219–280). Thousand Oaks, CA: Sage.

Dunbar, R. A. (1997). Bloody footprints: Reflections on growing up poor white. In M. Wray & A. Newitz (Eds.), *White trash: Race and class in America* (pp. 73–86). New York: Routledge.

Fitch, K. L. (1994). A cross-cultural study of directive sequences and some implications for compliance-gaining research. *Communication Monographs, 61,* 185–209.

Geertz, L. (1973). *The interpretation of culture.* New York: Basic Books.

Grossberg, L. (1993). Can cultural studies find true happiness in communication? *Journal of Communication, 43*(4), 89–97.

Hall, S. (1992). Cultural studies and its theoretical legacies. In L. Grossberg, C. Nelson, & P. Treichler (Eds.), *Cultural studies* (pp. 277–294). New York: Routledge.

Hannerz, U. (1996). *Transnational connections.* London: Routledge.

Hofstede, G. (1984). *Culture's consequences.* Beverly Hills, CA: Sage.

———. (1997). *Cultures and organizations: Software of the mind* (Rev. ed.). New York: McGraw-Hill.

hooks, b. (1989). Black is a woman's color. *Callaloo, 39,* 382–388.

Hymes, D. (1972). Models of the interaction of language and social life. In J. Gumperz & D. Hymes (Eds.), *Directions in sociolinguistics: The ethnography of speaking* (pp. 35–71). New York: Holt, Rinehart & Winston.

Jenks, C. (1993). *Culture.* New York: Routledge.

Katriel, T. (1990). "Griping" as a verbal ritual in some Israeli discourse. In D. Carbaugh (Ed.), *Cultural communication and intercultural contact* (pp. 99–112). Hillsdale, NJ: Lawrence Erlbaum.

Katriel, T., & Philipsen, G. (1990). What we need is communication: "Communication" as a cultural category in some American speech. In D. Carbaugh (Ed.), *Cultural communication and intercultural contact* (pp. 77–94). Hillsdale, NJ: Lawrence Erlbaum.

Keesing, R. M. (1994). Theories of culture revisited. In R. Brofsky (Ed.), *Assessing cultural anthropology.* New York: McGraw-Hill.

Kohls, L. R. (1996). *Survival kit for overseas living.* Yarmouth, ME: Intercultural Press.

Kluckhohn, F., & Strodtbeck, F. (1961). *Variations in value orientations.* Chicago: Row, Peterson.

Kroeber, A. L., & Kluckhohn, C. (1952). *Culture: A critical review of concepts and definitions.* New York: Vintage.

Lim, T.-S. & Choi, S.-H. (1996). Interpersonal relationships in Korea. In W. B. Gudykunst, S. Ting-Toomey, & T. Nishida (Eds.), *Communication in personal relationships across cultures* (pp. 122–136). Thousand Oaks, CA: Sage.

Loden, M., & Rosener, J. B. (1991). *Workforce American! Managing employee diversity as a vital resource.* Homewood, IL: Business One Irwin.

Mas, F. (1998, May). Vers un renouveau sexuel. *Le Nouvel Observateur, 1750,* 21–27.

Murphy, A. G. (1998). Hidden transcripts of flight attendant resistance. *Management Communication Quarterly, 11,* 499–512.

Orbe, M. O. (1998). *Constructing co-cultural theory: An explication of culture, power, and communication.* Thousand Oaks, CA: Sage.

Philipsen, G. (1992). *Speaking culturally: Explorations in social communication.* Albany: State University of New York Press.

———. (2002). Cultural communication. In W. B. Gudykunst & B. Mody (Eds.), *Handbook of international and intercultural communication* (2nd ed., pp. 51–67). Thousand Oaks, CA: Sage.

Robitaille, L.-B. (1995, April 15). La terre de la grande complication. *L'actualité,* pp. 67–69.

Singer, M. R. (1987). *Intercultural communication: A perceptual approach.* Englewood Cliffs, NJ: Prentice-Hall.

Stewart, E. C., & Bennett, M. J. (1991). *American cultural patterns: A cross-cultural perspective.* Yarmouth, ME: Intercultural Press.

Williams, R. (1981). The analysis of culture. In T. Bennett, G. Martin, C. Mercer, & J. Woollacott (Eds.), *Culture, ideology and social process: A reader* (pp. 43–52). London: Open University Press.

———. (1983). *Keywords: A vocabulary of culture and society* (Rev. ed). New York: Oxford University Press.

Winthrop, R. H. (1991). *Dictionary of concepts in cultural anthropology.* New York: Greenwood Press.

HISTORY AND INTERCULTURAL COMMUNICATION

Frances Fitzgerald (1972), a journalist who has written about the U.S. involvement in the Vietnam War, analyzes the U.S. cultural orientation to the future rather than the past:

> *Americans ignore history, for to them everything has always seemed new under the sun. The national myth is that of creativity and progress, of a steady climbing upward into power and prosperity, both for the individual and for the country as a whole. Americans see history as a straight line and themselves standing at the cutting edge of it as representatives for all mankind. They believe in the future as if it were a religion; they believe that there is nothing they cannot accomplish, that solutions wait somewhere for all problems.*

This difference in orientation to the past framed the conflict in a very narrow way for the United States. This contrasts greatly with the Vietnamese view of history, especially in the context of their struggles against outside aggression over thousands of years.

You may think it odd to find a chapter about history in a book on intercultural communication. After all, what does the past have to do with intercultural interaction? In this chapter, we discuss how the past is a very important facet of intercultural communication.

The history that we know and our views of that history are very much influenced by our culture. When people of different cultural backgrounds encounter one another, the differences among them can become hidden barriers to communication. However, people often overlook such dynamics in intercultural communication. We typically think of "history" as something contained in history books. We may view history as those events and people, mostly military and political, that played significant roles in shaping the world of today. This chapter examines some of the ways in which history is important in understanding intercultural interaction. Many intercultural interactions involve a dialectical interplay between past and present.

We have found, in the classes we teach, that European American students often want to de-emphasize history. "Why do we have to dwell on the past? Can't we all move on?" they ask. In contrast, some other students argue that without history it is impossible to understand who they are. How do these different viewpoints affect the communication among such students? What is the possibility for meaningful communication interactions among them?

On a larger scale, we can see how history influences intercultural interaction in many different contexts. For example, the ongoing conflict in the West Bank between the Israelis and the Palestinians makes little sense without an understanding of the historical relations among the different groups that reside in the area. Historical antagonisms help explain the present-day animosity felt by many Pakistanis toward Indians. Disputes over the Kashmir region, Indian participation in the struggle for independence of Bangladesh, and conflicts over the Himalayas underscore deep-rooted bases for strife. Likewise, historical antagonisms (including colonization, discrimination, and starvation) help explain the current animosity felt by many Irish toward the British.

How we think about the past very much influences how we think about ourselves and others even here in the United States. Judith went to college in southern Virginia after growing up in Delaware and Pennsylvania. She was shocked to encounter the antipathy that her dormitory suite-mates expressed toward northerners. The suite-mates stated emphatically that they had no desire to visit the North; they felt certain that "Yankees" were unfriendly and unpleasant people.

For Judith, the Civil War was a paragraph in a history book; for her suite-mates, that historical event held a more important meaning. It took a while for friendships to develop between Judith and her suite-mates. In this way, their interactions demonstrated the present–past dialectic. Indeed, this exemplifies the central focus of this chapter: that various histories contextualize intercultural communication. Taking a dialectical perspective enables us to understand how history positions people in different places from which they can communicate and understand other people's messages.

Early in this book, we set forth six dialectical tensions that we believe drive much intercultural interaction. In this chapter, we focus on the history/past–present/future dialectic. As you will see, culture and cultural identities are intimately tied to history, because they have no meaning without history. Yet there is no single version of history; the past has been written in many different ways. For example, your own family has its version of family history that must be placed in dialectical tension with all of the other narratives about the past. Is it important to you to feel positive about who your forebears were and where they came from? We often feel a strong need to identify in positive ways with our past even if we are not interested in history. The stories of the past, whether accurate or not, help us understand why our families live where they do, why they own or lost land there, and so on. We experience this dialectical tension between the past, the present, and the future every day. It helps us understand who we are and why we live and communicate in the ways we do.

In this chapter, we first discuss the various histories that provide the contexts in which we communicate: political, intellectual, social, family, national, and cultural-group histories. We then describe how these histories are intertwined with our various identities, based on gender, sexual orientation, ethnicity, race, and so on. This chapter introduces two identities that have strong historical bases: diasporic and colonial. We pay particular attention to the role of narrating our personal histories. As you read this chapter, think about the importance of history in constructing your own identity and the ways in which the past–present dialectic helps us understand different identities for others in various cultural groups. Finally, we explore how history influences intercultural communication.

FROM HISTORY TO HISTORIES

Many different kinds of history influence our understanding of who we are—as individuals, as family members, as members of cultural groups, and as citizens of a nation. To understand the dialectics in everyday interaction, we need to

FIGURE 4-1   In the United States, the history of racially segregated facilities extends well beyond drinking fountains. Drinking fountains were not segregated by sexual orientation, gender, or some other cultural difference but by race alone. What are some other facilities that were once racially segregated? How does that history help us understand race relations today? Do you know how your family experienced racial privilege and discrimination in the United States? (© *Corbis/Bettmann*)

think about the many histories that help form our different identities. These histories necessarily overlap and influence each other. For example, when Fidel Castro came to power half a century ago, many Cubans fled to the United States. The families that departed have histories about that experience that help them understand their cultural identity. Political histories tell the story of that exodus, but not necessarily the story of every family even though many families' histories were very much influenced by that event. Understanding all of those histories sheds new light on the conflict surrounding the decision in 2000 to return young Elián González to his father in Cuba, rather than permit him to remain in the United States. Identifying the various forms of historical contexts is the first step in understanding how history affects communication. (See Figure 4-1.)

Political, Intellectual, and Social Histories

Some people restrict their notion of history to documented events. Although we cannot read every book written, we do have greater access to written history. When these types of history focus on political events, we call them **political histories.** Written histories that focus on the development of ideas are often called

intellectual histories. Some writers seek to understand the everyday life experiences of various groups in the past; what they document are called **social histories.**

Although these types of history seem more manageable than the broad notion of history as "everything that has happened before now," we must also remember that many historical events never make it into books. For example, the strict laws that forbad teaching slaves in the United States to read kept many of their stories from being documented. **Absent history,** of course, does not mean that the people did not exist, that their experiences do not matter, or that their history has no bearing on us today. To consider such absent histories requires that we think in more complex ways about the past and the ways it influences the present and the future.

Family Histories

Family histories occur at the same time as other histories, but on a more personal level. Often, they are not written down but are passed along orally from one generation to the next. Some people do not know which countries or cities their families emigrated from or what tribes they belonged to or where they lived in the United States. Other people place great emphasis on knowing that their ancestors fought in the Revolutionary War, survived the Holocaust, or traveled the Trail of Tears when the Cherokees were forcibly relocated from the Southeast to present-day Oklahoma. Many of these family histories are deeply intertwined with ethnic-group histories, but the family histories identify each family's participation in these events.

You might talk to members of your own family to discover how they feel about your family's history. Find out, for example, how family history influences their perceptions of who they are. Do they wish they knew more about their family? What things has your family continued to do that your forebears probably also did? Do you eat some of the same foods? Practice the same religion? Celebrate birthdays or weddings in the same way? Often, the continuity between past and present is taken for granted.

National Histories

The history of any nation is important to the people of that nation. We typically learn **national history** in school. In the United States, we learn about the Founding Fathers—George Washington, Benjamin Franklin, John Jay, Alexander Hamilton, and so on—and our national history typically begins with the arrival of Europeans in North America in the 16th century.

U.S. citizens are expected to recognize the great events and the so-called great people (mostly men of European ancestry) who were influential in the development of the nation. In history classes, students learn about the Revolutionary War, Thomas Paine, the War of 1812, the Civil War, Abraham Lincoln, the Great Depression, Franklin D. Roosevelt, and so on. They are told stories, verging on myths, that give life to these events and figures. For example, students

My history is somewhat vague, but I will write what I know.

Father's side: My great-grandfather came to the United States in the late 1800s. He and my great-grandmother came from Yugoslavia. My great-grandfather worked as a coal miner in Hazleton, PA. He died of "black lung." I don't know much about my great-grandmother. My grandfather and grandmother moved to Philadelphia in the 1940s.

Mother's side: My great-grandfather on my mom's side came to the United States in 1908 from Ireland. My great-grandmother is Scottish. As I write this I realize I don't know much about the maternal side of the family. I will definitely find out. I strongly believe it is important to know the history of my family in the United States. It is something to pass on to children and keep the spirit of this country alive!

—Jennifer

The history of my family on my mother's side dates back to before the American Revolution, when my ancestors came over on the Mayflower. Our extensive family history has been documented through Daughters of the American Revolution and passed on through many generations. All of us know we are descendants of Wyndell Trout. My father's side of the family is more recent to the United States and is not as well documented. They are of German-Czechoslovakian heritage.

I believe it is important to understand one's culture and heritage. It makes me feel proud; the fact that all members of my family, including my brother and sister, know who we are gives us a confidence and respect toward others who find pride in their heritage. I often am disappointed by the lack of interest my peers have in their heritage. Many feel they don't need to know, that it doesn't affect them. In my opinion it provides you with a better understanding of yourself.

—Heather

learn about Patrick Henry's "give me liberty or give me death" speech even though the text of the speech was collected by a biographer who "pieced together twelve hundred words from scattered fragments that ear witnesses remembered from twenty years before" (Thonssen, Baird, & Braden, 1970, p. 335). Students also learn about George Washington having chopped down a cherry tree and confessing his guilt ("I cannot tell a lie") although there's no evidence of this story's truth.

National history gives us a shared notion of who we are and solidifies our sense of nationhood. Although we may not fit into the national narrative, we are expected to be familiar with this particular telling of U.S. history so we can understand the many references used in communication. It is one way of constructing cultural discourses. Yet U.S. students seldom learn much about the histories of other nations and cultures unless they study the languages of those

I am the fourth generation of females raised in Philadelphia. My great-grandmother raised me until she died, when I was 13. Her mother was a slave who had 19 children. Charlotte, North Carolina, was the place my great-grandmother said she was born. I care because my grandmother had personal information about why Blacks should be glad slavery is over. She encouraged my family to make use of all of the benefits of freedom. She always said, "Get an education so you can own something, because we couldn't own anything. We couldn't even go to school." So that is why she moved to the city of Philadelphia. She made getting an education a reward instead of a joke.
    —Marlene

I know very little about the history of my family in the United States, although I have bits and pieces of information. For instance, I know that my background is primarily Irish and German on my father's side and Scottish on my mother's side. Both of my parents grew up in the South. I do not know if I am descended from plantation owners. I am not sure about any other parts of my family history because my parents never talked about it. My grandmother is currently gathering information for me about her mother, but my grandfather will not talk about his past. I care about my history because I feel that I should know about where I came from so I can tell my children if they are interested.
    —Ruth

The history of my family in the United States is a short one. I am the first generation of the Cho line. My parents grew up in Asia (Hong Kong and Taiwan) and became naturalized U.S. citizens. I was born in New Jersey, a citizen by birth. The first to be born here: guess it's special, huh?
    —Mimi

countries. As any student of another language knows, it is part of the curriculum to study not only the grammar and vocabulary of the language but also the culture and history of the people who speak that language.

Judith and Tom both studied French. Because we learned a great deal about French history, we understand references to the *ancien régime* (the political system prior to the French Revolution in 1789), *les Pieds-noirs* (colonial French who returned to France during the struggle for Algerian independence in the mid-20th century), *la Bastille* (the notorious prison), and other commonly used terms. The French have their own national history, centering on the development of France as a nation. For example, French people know that they live in the *Veme République* (or Fifth Republic), and they know what that means within the grand narrative of French history.

When Judith lived in Algeria, her French friends spoke of *les Événements* (the events), but her Algerian friends spoke of *la Libération*—both referring to the war between France and Algeria that led to Algerian independence. When Tom lived in France, he also heard the expression *la Libération*, but here it referred to the end of the German occupation in France during World War II. Historical contexts shape language, which means we must search for salient historical features in communicating across cultural differences.

Cultural-Group Histories

Although people may share a single national history, each cultural group within the nation may have its own history. The history may be obscure (hidden), but it is still related to the national history. **Cultural-group histories** help us understand the identities of various groups.

Consider, for example, the expulsion of many Acadians from eastern Canada and their migration to and settlement in Louisiana. These historical events are central to understanding the cultural traits of the Cajuns. The forced removal in 1838 of the Cherokees from Georgia to settlements in what eventually became the state of Oklahoma resulted in a 22% loss of the Cherokee population. This event, known as the Trail of Tears, explains much about the Cherokee Nation. The migration in 1846 of 12,000 Latter Day Saints from Nauvoo, Illinois, to the Great Basin region in the western United States was prompted by anti-Mormon attacks. These events explain much about the character of Utah. The northward migration of African Americans in the early part of the 20th century helps us understand the settlement patterns and working conditions in northern cities such as Cleveland, Detroit, Chicago, and New York. These cultural histories are not typically included in our national history, but they are important in the development of group identity, family histories, and contemporary lives of individual members of these co-cultures.

We prefer to view history as the many stories we tell about the past, rather than one story on a single time continuum. Certainly, the events of families, cultural groups, and nations are related. Even world events are related. Ignorance of the histories of other groups makes intercultural communication more difficult and more susceptible to misunderstandings.

HISTORY, POWER, AND INTERCULTURAL COMMUNICATION

Power is a central dynamic in the writing of history. It influences the content of the history we know and the way it is delivered. Power dictates what is taught and what is silenced, what is available and what is erased. Let's look at what this means.

The Power of Texts

History is extremely important in understanding identity. Think about all of the stories about the past that you have been taught. Yet, as literature professor Fredric Jameson (1981) notes, although history is not a narrative at all, it is ac-

FIGURE 4-2   These young women are playing softball during their incarceration in a U.S. internment camp in Manzanar, California. The internment of U.S. Americans of Japanese ancestry was a significant historical event that points up the importance of race in our society. Although history helps us understand how different cultural groups experienced life in the United States, we do not often focus on the internment experience. When did you learn about the internment of Japanese Americans? Do you think that U.S. Americans still assume that racial characteristics can identify someone as an "American"? (© AP/Wide World Photos)

cessible to us only in textual, narrative form. However, people do not have equal access to the writing and production of these texts.

Political texts reflect the disparities of access to political participation in various countries at various times in history. Some languages have been forbidden, making the writing of texts difficult if not impossible. For example, U.S. government Indian schools forbad Native American children to speak their native languages, which makes it more difficult for people today to understand what this experience was about.

With regard to the language we use to understand history, think about the difference between the terms *internment camp* and *concentration camp*. In 1942, at the height of World War II, after President Franklin Roosevelt signed Executive Order 9066, anyone of Japanese ancestry—whether they were U.S. citizens or not—were rounded up from a restricted zone, including parts of Arizona, Oregon, and Washington and all of California, and placed mostly into ten camps. (See Figure 4-2.) The U.S. federal government used both terms in the 1940s, but

The internment, or mass imprisonment, of Japanese Americans by the U.S. government in the 1940s has led to much discussion about the right term for these camps. What difference does it make if we call them "concentration camps" or "relocation centers"? This entry from the *Encyclopedia of Japanese American History* provides food for thought.

> **Concentration camps.** *Euphemistically called "relocation centers" by the War Relocation Authority (WRA), the concentration camps were hastily constructed facilities for housing Japanese Americans forcibly removed from their homes and businesses on the West Coast during World War II. Located in isolated areas of the United States on either desert or swampland, the camps were usually surrounded by barbed wire and guarded by armed sentries. Although these sentries were presumably in place to protect the inmates from hostile outsiders, their guns usually pointed into the camps instead of away from them. Most inmates were transported to their camp by train from an assembly center between April and September 1942. In all, over 120,000 Japanese Americans served time in these camps.*

Source: From *Encyclopedia of Japanese American History: An A-to-Z Reference from 1868 to the Present*, edited by Brian Niiya, 2001, p. 142.

the historical weight of the German concentration camps of the same era, in which millions of Jews perished, often casts a shadow over our understanding of the U.S. concentration camps. Denotatively, the use of the term *concentration camp* is correct, but connotatively, it invokes quite different responses. You may wish to keep this in mind as you read Chapter 6, which discusses the importance of language and discourse in intercultural communication.

When U.S. Americans are taught history, they also learn a particular way of looking at the world from their history textbooks. This worldview, as James Loewen (1995) tells us, reinforces a very positive White American identity. In his analysis of history textbooks, he notes: "History is furious debate informed by evidence and reason. Textbooks encourage students to believe that history is facts to be learned" (p. 16). Yet these "facts" are often wrong or portray the past in ways that serve the White American identity. For example, he analyzes the way in which Native Americans are depicted in history texts:

> *Even if no Natives remained among us, however, it would still be important for us to understand the alternatives foregone, to remember the wars, and to learn the unvarnished truths about white–Indian relations. Indian history is the antidote to the pious ethnocentrism of American exceptionalism, the notion that European Americans are God's chosen people. Indian history reveals that the United States and its predecessor British colonies have wrought great harm in the world. We must not forget this—not to wallow in our wrongdoing, but to understand and to learn, that we might not wreak harm again. (p. 136)*

But the prevailing value of teaching history lies not in serving the future but in reinforcing a positive cultural identity for White Americans. How does power function in determining which stories are told and how they are told?

The relative availability of political texts and the ways that they reflect powerful inequities are reinscribed in the process of writing history. History writing requires documentation and texts, and, of course, is limited by what is available. In writing history, we often ask ourselves, "What was important?" without asking, "Important to whom? For what purposes?" Once texts are written, they are available for teaching and learning about the past. But the seeming unity of the past, the linear nature of history, is merely the reflection of a **modernist identity,** grounded in the Western tradition.

The Power of Other Histories

We live in an era of rapid change, which causes us to rethink cultural struggles and identities. It may be difficult for you to envision, but at one time a unified story of mankind—the "**grand narrative**"—dominated how people thought of the past, present, and future. This is no longer the case. French philosopher Jean-François Lyotard (1984) writes:

> In contemporary society and culture—postindustrial society, postmodern culture— the grand narrative has lost its credibility, regardless of what mode of unification it uses, regardless of whether it is a speculative narrative or a narrative of emancipation. (p. 37)

In her work on the constructions of White identity in South Africa, communication scholar Melissa Steyn (2001) notes how the grand narrative in South Africa served White interests and led to the establishment of **apartheid.** She writes:

> In drawing on the master narrative, interpreting it and adapting it to the particular circumstances in which they found themselves in the country, whites were able to maintain their advantage as the dominating group that controlled the political, material, and symbolic resources of the country for three centuries. (p. 43)

By telling and retelling one view of the past, White South Africans were able to create a society in which a White minority dominated.

In place of the grand narrative are revised and restored histories that previously were suppressed, hidden, or erased. The cultural movements that are making this shift possible are empowering to the cultural identities involved. Recovering various histories is necessary to rethinking what some cultural identities mean. It also helps us rethink the dominant cultural identity.

For example, on June 30, 1960, at the signing of the treaty granting independence to the former Belgian colony of the Congo (as Zaire), the king of the Belgians, Baudouin, constructed one way of thinking about the past:

> All of our thoughts should be turned toward those who founded the African emancipation and after them, those who made the Congo into what it is today. They

POINT OF VIEW

Since the ending of apartheid in South Africa, there has been a rewriting of the nation's history textbooks in an attempt to forge a new national identity and a different understanding of the past. However, there are strongly contested and very different views about the South African past. Compare, for example, the apartheid view and the post-Apartheid view of the establishment of separate areas for Whites and Blacks during the 1950s and 1960s. Think about how any understanding of history is important in creating cultural identity.

> *Apartheid View: The Group Areas Act is passed, dividing the country by race. Apartheid is an absolute necessity, because all nationalisms are mutually exclusive, and it is in the best interest of both races to live separately from one another. Hence black people must be relocated to "some of the best parts of the country."*

> *Post-Apartheid View: Tens of thousands of black people are violently removed from their homes, entire neighborhoods are bulldozed, and dispossessed residents are forced to move to some of the least fertile and most remote regions of the country, where employment opportunities are scarce, if not nonexistent. Meanwhile, the white minority secures control of the best land and its mineral wealth.*

Source: From Sasha Polakow-Suransky, "Reviving South African History," *The Chronicle of Higher Education,* June 14, 2002, p. A37.

> *merit at the same time our admiration and your recognition since it was they who consecrated all of their efforts and even their lives for a grand ideal, bringing you peace and enriching your homeland materially and morally. They must never be forgotten, not by Belgium, not by the Congo. (quoted in Gérard-Libois & Heinen, 1989, p. 143)*

In response, Patrice Lumumba, who would become prime minister, offered a different view of Belgian colonialism:

> *After eighty years of colonial rule, our wounds are still too fresh and too deep to be chased from our memory. . . . We have known the ironies, the insults, the beatings to which we had to submit morning, noon, and night because we were negroes. Who will forget that they spoke to Blacks with "tu" certainly not because of friendship, but because the honorary "vous" was reserved only for speaking to whites. (p. 147)*

Lumumba's words created a different sense of history. These differences were clear to the people of the time and remain clear today. In this way, the grand narrative of Belgian colonialism has been reconfigured and no longer stands as the only story of the Belgian Congo.

Power in Intercultural Interactions

Power is also the legacy, the remnants of the history that leaves cultural groups in particular positions. We are not equal in our intercultural encounters, nor can we ever be equal. Long histories of imperialism, colonialism, exploitation, wars, genocide, and more leave cultural groups out of balance when they communicate.

Regardless of whether we choose to recognize the foundations for many of our differences, these inequalities influence how we think about others and how we interact with them. They also influence how we think about ourselves—our identities. These are important aspects of intercultural communication. It may seem daunting to confront the history of power struggles. Nevertheless, the more you know, the better you will be positioned to engage in successful intercultural interactions.

HISTORY AND IDENTITY

The development of cultural identity is influenced largely by history. In this next section, we look at some of the ways that cultural identities are constructed through understanding the past. Note how different cultural-group identities are tied to history.

Histories as Stories

Faced with these many levels or types of history, you might wonder how we make sense of them in our everyday lives. Although it might be tempting to ignore them all and merely pretend to be "ourselves," this belies the substantial influence that history has on our own identities.

According to communication scholar Walter Fisher (1984, 1985), storytelling is fundamental to the human experience. Instead of referring to humans as *Homo sapiens,* Fisher prefers to call them *Homo narrans* because it underscores the importance of narratives in our lives. Histories are stories that we use to make sense of who we are and who we think others are.

It is important to recognize that a strong element in our cultural attitudes encourages us to forget history at times. French writer Jean Baudrillard (1988) observes:

> *America was created in the hope of escaping from history, of building a utopia sheltered from history. . . . [It] has in part succeeded in that project, a project it is still pursuing today. The concept of history as the transcending of a social and political rationality, as a dialectical, conflictual vision of societies, is not theirs, just as modernity, conceived precisely as an original break with certain history, will never be ours [France's]. (p. 80)*

The desire to escape history is significant in what it tells us about how our culture negotiates its relation to the past, as well as how we view the relations

We can never escape the past, and in the Polish town that was the site of the in-famous Auschwitz concentration camp, the preservation of this past is seen as hampering economic development. Much of the town is preserved to mark this horrific history. If they cannot escape the past, what options do the townspeople have in this situation?

Andrzej Czarnik was surprised, but hardly shocked, to learn that his home stood on the site of the first gas chamber Nazis used to kill Jews at Auschwitz.

"In this town," he said, "there are human ashes everywhere."

A year ago, Czarnik agreed to an offer to take another house a mile away so the Auschwitz museum could demolish his and erect a memorial.

"What can you do about it?" he said, sitting on a bench outside his new two-story home. "You can't just plant grass everywhere."

It's a familiar refrain among the 43,000 residents of Oswiecim, a poor industrial town in southern Poland, where remnants of the Auschwitz-Birkenau death camp seem to be everywhere. . . .

Frustrated townspeople say that the preserved remains of the camp are symbol enough and that uncertainty over other so-called martyrdom sites hampers sorely needed investment.

The town is hurting from layoffs that began in 1997 when the communist-era Dwory chemicals plant began restructuring. . . .

Jewish appeals to preserve off-camp sites have collided with private-property rights and local fears that Oswiecim could become one big cemetery. . . .

Townspeople say they deserve more understanding, not more off-limits zones.

"We want to live a normal life," said Monika Kos, 21, who has lived all her life in the Pilecki housing block just outside the Auschwitz fence. Built as a camp annex in 1944, the buildings once housed 6,000 female prisoners and a laboratory where some endured sterilization experiments.

Source: From Beata Pasek, "Auschwitz Haunts Town," *The Arizona Republic*, June 9, 2002, p. A24.

of other nations and cultures to their pasts. By ignoring history, we sometimes come to wrongheaded conclusions about others that only perpetuate and rein-force stereotypes. For example, the notion that Jewish people are obsessed with money and are disproportionately represented in the world of finance belies the history of anti-Semitism, whereby Jews were excluded from many professions. The paradox is that we cannot escape history even if we fail to recognize it or try to suppress it.

POINT OF VIEW

The relationships between cultural groups may not always be apparent, depending on how we categorized them in the past. The historical events referred to in this article illuminate the ties between Irish and Mexicans, based in part on their shared religion, Catholicism. Do you know of other connections between cultural groups that may not be apparent to others?

> They were celebrated as war heroes in Mexico, hanged as traitors by the U.S. Army and forgotten back in famine-racked Ireland. This month, Ireland and Mexico honored the quixotic saga of the St. Patrick's Battalion, an ill-starred column of Irish immigrants recruited by the American military to fight in the Mexican-American War. . . .
>
> When the Irishmen defected to the Mexican side and fought American troops under a green silk banner emblazoned with St. Patrick, a shamrock and the traditional harp of Erin, they earned the wrath of the U.S. military and the everlasting admiration of Mexico. For years an obscure historical footnote, the story is being dusted off today as an allegory for the plight of immigrants, a morality tale on the implacability of Manifest Destiny and an example of the bond of Irish-Mexican solidarity in an era of increasingly mutual trade.
>
> The U.S. anti-immigrant press of the time caricatured the Irish with simian features, portraying them as unintelligent and drunk and charging that they were seditiously loyal to the pope. At least 20 people were killed and two churches were burned in anti-Catholic riots in Philadelphia during that era, and a mob in Massachusetts burned a convent.

Source: From Anne-Marie O'Connor, "Mexico, Ireland Recall Immigrant Tale of Divided Loyalties," *The Arizona Republic*, September 18, 1997, p. A17.

> history. It challenges us to have a more inclusive view of history, not merely the chronicling of events of the past, not dominated by the record of men marching forward through time, their paths strewn with the detritus of war and politics and industry and labor. (p. xiii)

Although there is much interest in women's history among contemporary scholars, documenting such **gender histories** is difficult due to the traditional restrictions on women's access to public forums, public documents, and public records. Even so, the return to the past to unearth and recover identities that can be adapted for survival is a key theme of writer Gloria Anzaldúa (1987). She presents *la Llorana* (the crying woman) as a cultural and historical image that gives her the power to resist cultural and gender domination. *La Llorana* is well known in northern Mexico and the U.S. Southwest. This legend tells the story of a woman who killed her children and who now wanders around looking for them and weeping for them. Her story has been retold in various ways, and Anzaldúa rewrites the tale to highlight the power that resides in her relentless crying. This mythical image gives her the power to resist cultural and gender domination:

> *My Chicana identity is grounded in the Indian woman's history of resistance.*
> *The Aztec female rites of mourning were rites of defiance protesting the cultural*
> *changes which disrupted the equality and balance between female and male, and*
> *protesting their demotion to a lesser status, their denigration. Like* la Llorana, *the*
> *Indian woman's only means of protest was wailing. (p. 21)*

Anzaldúa's history may seem distant to us, but it is intimately tied to what her Chicana identity means to her.

Sexual Orientation Histories   In recounting his experiences as a young man whom the police registered as "homosexual," Pierre Seel (1994) recounts how police lists were used by the Nazis to round up homosexuals for internment. The incarceration and extermination of gays, as members of one of the groups deemed "undesirable" by Nazi Germany, is often overlooked by World War II historians. Seel recalls one event in his **sexual orientation history:**

> *One day at a meeting in the SOS Racisme [an antiracism organization] room,*
> *I finished by getting up and recounting my experience of Nazism, my deportation*
> *for homosexuality. I remarked as well the ingratitude of history which erases that*
> *which is not officially convenient for it. (p. 162)*

> (Un jour de réunion, dans la salle de SOS Racisme, je finis par me lever
> et par raconter mon expérience du nazisme, ma déportation pour homo-
> sexualité. Je fis également remarquer l'ingratitude de l'histoire qui gomme
> ce qui ne lui convient pas officiellement.)

This suppression of history reflects attempts to construct specific understandings of the past. If we do not or cannot listen to the voices of others, we miss the significance of historical lessons. For example, a recent legislative attempt to force gays and lesbians to register with the police in the state of Montana ultimately was vetoed by the governor after he learned of the law's similarities to laws in Nazi Germany.

The late Guy Hocquenghem (Hocquenghem & Blasius, 1980), a gay French philosopher, lamented the letting go of the past because doing so left little to sustain and nurture his community:

> *I am struck by the ignorance among gay people about the past—no, more even*
> *than ignorance: the "will to forget" the German gay holocaust. . . . But we aren't*
> *even the only ones who remember, we don't remember! So we find ourselves begin-*
> *ning at zero in each generation. (p. 40)*

How we think about the past and what we know about it help us to build and maintain communities and cultural identities. And our relationships with the past are intimately tied to issues of power. To illustrate, a recent book, *The Pink Swastika: Homosexuality in the Nazi Party*, attempts to blame the Holocaust on German gays and lesbians ("Under Surveillance," 1995). This book, in depicting gays and lesbians as perpetrators, rather than victims, of Nazi atrocities, presents the gay identity in a markedly negative light. However, stories of the horrendous treatment of gays and lesbians during World War II serve to promote a common history and influence intercultural communication among gays and lesbians in France, Germany, the Netherlands, and other nations. Today, there is a monument in Amsterdam that serves to mark that history, to help ensure that we remember that gays and lesbians were victims of the Nazi Holocaust as well.

Racial and Ethnic Histories   The injustices done by any nation are often swept under the carpet. In an attempt to bring attention to and promote renewed understanding of the internment of Japanese Americans during World War II, academician John Tateishi (1984) collected the stories of some of the internees. He notes at the outset that

> *this book makes no attempt to be a definitive academic history of Japanese American internment. Rather it tries to present for the first time in human and personal terms the experience of the only group of American citizens ever to be confined in concentration camps in the United States. (p. vii)*

Although not an academic history, this collection of oral histories provides insight into the experiences of many Japanese Americans. Because this historical event demonstrates the fragility of our constitutional system and its guarantees in the face of prejudice and ignorance, it is not often discussed as significant in U.S. history. For Japanese Americans, however, it represents a defining moment in the development of their community.

Not all histories are so explicitly suppressed. For example, in recounting his personal narrative, writer René Han (1992) tells us:

> *I was born in France. My parents were both Chinese. I am therefore Chinese because they left on my face the indelible imprint of the race. In life, nationality, when it doesn't match with physical traits, is less important than appearance. But I am French. I have never been anything but French and, for nothing in the world, would I be anything else. (p. 11)*

(Je suis né en France. Mes parents étaient, tous les deux, chinois. Je suis donc chinois parce qu'ils ont laissé, sur mon visage, l'empreinte indélébile de la race. Dans la vie d'un homme la nationalité, quand elle ne concorde pas avec les traits, importe moins que l'apparence. Pourtant, je suis français. Je n'ai jamais été que français et, pour rien au monde, je ne voudrais cesser de l'être.)

Nevertheless, disjointedness is a central theme in Han's life:

> *There is my appearance and there is me. Appearance is the way others look at me. For them, I am above all Chinese. For me, it's my own perception that I have of my being. And I never see myself as anything but a Frenchman living in France among other French people. (p. 12)*

(Il y a mon apparence et il y a moi. L'apparence, c'est le regard des autres. Pour eux, je suis, d'abord, un Chinois. Moi, c'est la propre perception que j'ai mon être. Et je ne me suis jamais perçu que comme un Français, un Français vivant en France parmi les autres.)

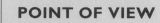
This letter from the President of the United States was sent to all of the surviving Japanese American internees who were in U.S. concentration camps during World War II. In recognizing that there is no way to change mistakes made in the past, what does this letter do? If you were to write this letter, what would you write in the letter? How should we deal with the past, in order to construct better intercultural relations in the future?

THE WHITE HOUSE
WASHINGTON

A monetary sum and words alone cannot restore lost years or erase painful memories; neither can they fully convey our Nation's resolve to rectify injustice and to uphold the rights of individuals. We can never fully right the wrongs of the past. But we can take a clear stand for justice and recognize that serious injustices were done to Japanese Americans during World War II.

In enacting a law calling for restitution and offering a sincere apology, your fellow Americans have, in a very real sense, renewed their traditional commitment to the ideals of freedom, equality, and justice. You and your family have our best wishes for the future.

Sincerely,

GEORGE BUSH
PRESIDENT OF THE UNITED STATES

OCTOBER 1990

The intercultural communication problems that arise in negotiating the complexities of how people view both themselves and others are neither unique to France nor rare. The desire to view the world in discrete units, as if people never migrate, presents problems for intercultural contact.

As you will see in Chapter 5, people often confuse "nationality"—a legal status that denotes citizenship in a particular country—with "race" or "ethnicity." Why do you think this confusion occurs? In what ways do we engage in stereotypes when we assume that, say, French citizens or Mexican citizens must look a certain way? We know that we live in a world of transnational and transcontinental migrations, yet we often react as if we believed otherwise. To illustrate, a U.S. American in the Netherlands was surprised to see people of African and Asian ancestry talking and laughing with Europeans in Dutch. What do you think are the ideological and political underpinnings of such thinking?

Diasporic Histories   The international relationships that many racial and ethnic groups have with others who share their heritage and history are often overlooked in intercultural communication. These international ties may have been created by transnational migrations, slavery, religious crusades, or other historical forces. Because most people do not think about the diverse connections people have to other nations and cultures, we consider these histories to be hidden. In his book *The Black Atlantic*, scholar Paul Gilroy (1993) emphasizes that, to understand the identities, cultures, and experiences of African descendants living in Britain and the United States, we must examine the connections between Africa, Europe, and North America.

A massive migration, often caused by war or famine or persecution, that results in the dispersal of a unified group is called a **diaspora.** The chronicles of these events are **diasporic histories.** A cultural group (or even an individual) that flees its homeland is likely to bring some customs and practices to the new homeland. In fact, diasporic migrations often cause people to cling more strongly to symbols and practices that reflect their group's identity. Over the years, though, people become acculturated to some degree in their new homelands. Consider, for example, the dispersal of eastern European Jews who migrated during or after World War II to the United States, Australia, South America, Israel, and other parts of the world. They brought their Jewish culture and eastern European culture with them, but they also adopted new cultural patterns as they became New Yorkers, Australians, Argentinians, Israelis, and so on. Imagine the communication differences among these people over time. Imagine the differences between these groups and members of the dominant culture of their new homelands.

History helps us understand the cultural connections among people affected by diasporas and other transnational migrations. Indeed, it is important that we recognize these relationships. But we must also be careful to distinguish between the ways in which these connections are helpful or hurtful to intercultural communication. For example, some cultures tend to regard negatively those who left their homeland. Thus, many Japanese tend to look down on Japanese Canadians, Japanese Americans, Japanese Brazilians, Japanese Mexicans, and Japanese

We do not often think about emigration *from* the United States. Nevertheless, many U.S. citizens move to other countries. This excerpt describes how some cultural symbols continue in new contexts. Do these new contexts change the meanings of those symbols?

> More than 2,000 people . . . emigrated to Brazil in the 1860s after the Civil War ended. Rather than endure the devastation of the South they chose to go to Brazil, partly because until 1888, Brazil still allowed slavery, but mainly because Emperor Pedro II, hoping to take advantage of a worldwide cotton shortage, subsidized their journey, guaranteed them freedom of religion and sold them land at 22 cents an acre. . . .
>
> The "confederados" tried to establish plantations along the Amazon. But tropical illnesses ended most of the jungle settlements, and many of the families went home.
>
> Only one colony prospered—the town in São Paulo state they called Vila Americana, later shortened to Americana.
>
> Residents grew not only cotton but watermelons, peaches and pecans. Today, Americana has a population of 2,000,000 and is a thriving textile center, the only city in Brazil with a Confederate flag in its coat of arms.
>
> "For me the Confederate flag means the memory of my ancestors, my history, what I care for most," Jones [a resident of Americana] said. "It has nothing to do with racism. All symbols change their meanings with time; the colors fade and new ones emerge."
>
> Jones is from one of the few Confederado families in Americana who still speak English at home. "I only visited the United States twice, on business. During a trip to Alabama, people were always trying to locate my accent and where I was from. I said I was from the deep, deep Deep South!"

Source: From Candace Piette, "American Thriving in Brazil: Confederates' Descendants Cherish Town's Links to Past," *The Arizona Republic*, December 7, 1997, p. A21.

Peruvians. In contrast, the Irish tend not to look down on Irish Americans or Irish Canadians. Of course, we must remember, too, that many other intervening factors can influence diasporic relationships on an interpersonal level.

Colonial Histories As you probably know, throughout history, societies and nations have ventured beyond their borders. Due to overpopulation, limited resources, notions of grandeur, or other factors, people have left their homelands to colonize other territories. It is important to recognize these **colonial histories** so we can better understand the dynamics of intercultural communication today.

Let's look at the significance of colonialism in determining language. Historically, three of the most important colonizers were Britain, France, and Spain.

As a result of colonialism, English is spoken in Canada, Australia, New Zealand, Belize, Nigeria, South Africa, India, Pakistan, Bangladesh, Zimbabwe, Hong Kong, Singapore, and the United States, among many places in the world. French is spoken in Canada, Senegal, Tahiti, Haiti, Benin, Côte d'Ivoire, Niger, Rwanda, Mali, Chad, and the Central African Republic, among other places. And Spanish is spoken in most of the Western Hemisphere, from Mexico to Chile and Argentina, and including Cuba, Venezuela, Colombia, and Panama.

Many foreign language textbooks proudly display maps that show the many places around the world where that language is commonly spoken. Certainly, it's nice to know that one can speak Spanish or French in so many places. But the maps don't reveal *why* those languages are widely spoken in those regions, and they don't reveal the legacies of colonialism in those regions. For example, the United Kingdom maintains close relations with many of its former colonies, and the queen of England is also the queen of Canada, Australia, New Zealand, and the Bahamas.

Other languages have been spread through colonialism as well, including Portuguese in Brazil, Macao, and Angola; Dutch in Angola, Suriname, and Mozambique; and a related Dutch language, Afrikaans, in South Africa. Russian is spoken in the former Soviet republics of Kazakhstan, Azerbaijan, and Tajikistan. In addition, many nations have reclaimed their own languages in an effort to resist the influences of colonialism. For example, today, Arabic is spoken in Algeria, and Vietnamese is spoken in Vietnam; at one time, French was widely spoken in both countries. And in the recently independent Latvia, the ability to speak Latvian is a requirement for citizenship.

The primary languages that we speak are not freely chosen by us. Rather, we must learn the languages of the societies into which we are born. Judith and Tom, for example, both speak English although their ancestors came to the United States from non-English-speaking countries. We did not choose to learn English among all of the languages of the world. Although we don't resent our native language, we recognize why many individuals might resent a language imposed on them. Think about the historical forces that led you to speak some language(s) and not others. Understanding history is crucial to understanding the linguistic worlds we inhabit, and vestiges of colonialism are often part of these histories.

However, the imposition of language is but one aspect of cultural imperialism. Much colonial history is one of oppression and brutality. To cast off this legacy, many people have looked to **postcolonialism**—an intellectual, political, and cultural movement that calls for the independence of colonialized states and liberation from colonialist *mentalités*, or ways of thinking. The legacy of this cultural invasion often lasts much longer than the political relationship.

Socioeconomic Class Histories   Although we often overlook the importance of socioeconomic class as a factor in history, the fact is that economic and class issues prompted many people to emigrate to the United States. The poverty in Ireland in the 19th century, for example, did much to fuel the flight to the United States; in fact, today, there are more Irish Americans than Irish.

Yet it is not always the socioeconomically disadvantaged who emigrate. After the Russian Revolution in 1917, many affluent Russians moved to Paris. Likewise, many affluent Cubans left the country after Castro seized power in 1959. Today, Canada offers business immigration status to investors who own their own businesses and "who have a net worth, accumulated by their own endeavors, of at least CAD [Canadian dollars] $500,000" ("Immigrant Investor Program Redesign," 1998). Although the program varies somewhat from province to province, the policy ensures that socioeconomic class continues to influence some migrations.

The key point here is that socioeconomic class distinctions are often overlooked in examining the migrations and acculturation of groups around the world. Historically, the kinds of employment that immigrants supplied and the regions they settled were often marked by the kinds of capital—cultural and financial—that they were or were not able to bring with them. These factors also influence the interactions and politics of different groups; for example, Mexican Americans and Cuban Americans, as groups, frequently are at odds with the political mainstream.

INTERCULTURAL COMMUNICATION AND HISTORY

One way to understand specific relationships between communication and history is to examine the attitudes and notions that individuals bring to an interaction; these are the antecedents of contact. A second way is to look at the specific conditions of the interaction and the role that history plays in these contexts. Finally, we can examine how various histories are negotiated in intercultural interaction, applying a dialectical perspective to these different histories.

Antecedents of Contact

We may be able to negotiate some aspects of history in interaction, but it is important to recognize that we bring our personal histories to each intercultural interaction. These personal histories involve our prior experience and our attitudes. Social psychologist Richard Brislin (1981) has identified four elements of personal histories that influence interaction.

First, people bring childhood experiences to interactions. For example, both Judith and Tom grew up hearing negative comments about Catholics. As a result, our first interactions with adherents to this faith were tinged with some suspicion. This personal history did not affect initial interactions with people of other religions.

Second, people may bring historical myths to interactions. These are myths with which many people are familiar. The Jewish conspiracy myth—that Jewish people are secretly in control of U.S. government and business—is one example.

Third, the languages that people speak influence their interactions. Language can be an attraction or a repellent in intercultural interactions. For example,

In this excerpt, intercultural scholar Parker Johnson describes the way in which history affects his everyday experience in the United States. History, although "in the past," continues to affect contemporary cultural experiences.

> *Racism is a lifelong unlearning and relearning process like alcoholism and sexism; it is not a task to be solved and done within a finite moment. It is not solely about "Black–White" relations; there are many other racial, ethnic, and cultural groups. However, our fixation with the "Black–White" paradigm" does reveal our passionate and unreconciled history of slavery which is often subtle and piercing in its manifestations. For example, I drive to Harrisburg [PA] and see the Plantation Inn near the junction of route 15 and the Penn turnpike. Would we ever see a "concentration camp inn" or an "internment camp inn"? We are comfortable with the abominable history of slavery and keep it alive with such symbols. The same is true of the Confederate flag which is so proudly displayed in Gettysburg. It is fundamentally racist to display that flag and ask Black folks to get over slavery with the constant reminder displayed throughout the country. We see slavery with the constant reminder displayed throughout the country. We see no Nazi flags prominently displayed in Germany or the U.S. despite [their] importance to German history. Let's challenge these ideas and reclaim our humanity.*

Source: From Parker Johnson, "Eliminating Racism as a Social Disease," *Hanover Evening Sun*, October 21, 1995, p. 2.

many people from the United States enjoy traveling in Britain because English is spoken there. However, these same people may have little desire, or even be afraid, to visit Russia, simply because it is not an English-speaking country.

Finally, people tend to be affected by recent, vivid events. For example, after the bombing of the World Trade Center in New York, interactions between Arab Americans and other U.S. residents were strained, characterized by suspicion, fear, and distrust. The media's treatment of such catastrophic events often creates barriers and reinforces stereotypes by blurring distinctions between Arabs, Persians, Muslims, and Palestinians. Perhaps recent histories, such as the racially motivated riots in Los Angeles in the mid-1990s, are more influential in our interactions than the hidden or past histories, such as the massacre in 1890 of some 260 Sioux Indians at Wounded Knee in South Dakota or the women's suffrage movement around the turn of the 20th century.

The Contact Hypothesis

The **contact hypothesis** is the notion that better communication between groups of people is facilitated simply by bringing them together and allowing them to interact. Although history does not seem to support this notion, many

How we commemorate the past can create intercultural conflicts, in that many historical events are entangled in contemporary cultural identities. Note how different views of the past can make a difference in how we assign status to the so-called Old Spanish Trail.

> *The Old Spanish Trail, a main corridor of moving Native American slaves, wool products and livestock between Santa Fe, N.M., and Los Angeles in its heyday, 1829 to 1850, is being considered for adoption into the national trail system. The system already includes such historic routes as the Oregon Trail.*
>
> *Alan Downer, the [Navajo] tribe's historic preservation director, said that he was surprised the measure was being considered and that the Navajos had not even been consulted about the project. The trail snakes through about 100 miles of the [tribe's] reservation near the Four Corners area.*
>
> *"I don't think honoring a European culture like this with which the Navajos had such distrust and hostility will be very popular on the reservations," Downer said. "After all, it was used for slave raids and other unsavory activities during a particularly rough time in the tribe's history."*
>
> *Harry Walters, a history professor at the Navajos' Dine College in Tsalie, said he sees "no value" to Navajo culture in recognizing the trail.*
>
> *"All it does is glorify European expansion and land-grabbing," Walters said.*

Source: From Mark Shaffer, "Navajos Protest National Status for Old Spanish Trail," *The Arizona Republic*, June 9, 2002, pp. B1, B8.

public policies and programs in the United States and abroad are based on this hypothesis. Examples include desegregation rulings; the prevalence of master-planned communities like Reston, Virginia; and many international student exchange programs. All of these programs are based on the assumption that simply giving people from different groups opportunities to interact will result in more positive intergroup attitudes and reduced prejudice.

Gordon Allport (1979) and Yehudi Amir (1969), two noted psychologists, have tried to identify the conditions under which the contact hypothesis does and does not hold true. The histories of various groups figure prominently in their studies. Based on these and subsequent studies, psychologists have outlined at least eight conditions that must be met (more or less) to improve attitudes and facilitate intergroup communication (Schwarzwald & Amir, 1996; Stephan & Stephan, 1996). These are particularly relevant in light of increasing diversity in U.S. society in general and the workforce in particular. The eight conditions are as follows:

1. Group members should be of equal status, both within and outside the contact situation. Communication will occur more easily if there is no disparity between individuals in status characteristics (education, socioeconomic status,

and so on). This condition does not include temporary inequality, such as in student–teacher or patient–doctor roles. Consider the implications of this condition for relations among various ethnic groups in the United States. How are we likely to think of individuals from specific ethnic groups if our interactions are characterized by inequality? A good example is the interaction between longtime residents and recent immigrants in the Southwest, where Mexican Americans often provide housecleaning, gardening, and similar services for Whites. It is easy to see how the history of these two groups in the United States contributes to the lack of equality in interaction, leads to stereotyping, and inhibits effective intercultural communication. But the history of relations between Mexican Americans and Whites varies within this region. For example, families of Spanish descent have lived in New Mexico longer than other European-descent families, while Arizona has a higher concentration of recent immigrants from Mexico. Intergroup interactions in New Mexico are characterized less by inequality (Stephan & Stephan, 1989).

2. Strong normative and institutional support for the contact should be provided. This suggests that, when individuals from different groups come together, positive outcomes do not happen by accident. Rather, institutional encouragement is necessary. Examples include university support for contact between U.S. and international students, or for contact among different cultural groups within the university, and local community support for integrating elementary and high schools. Numerous studies have shown the importance of commitment by top management to policies that facilitate intercultural interaction in the workplace (Brinkman, 1997). Finally, institutional support may also mean government and legal support, expressed through court action.

3. Contact between the groups should be voluntary. This may seem to contradict the previous condition, but it doesn't. Although support must exist beyond the individual, individuals need to feel that they have a choice in making contact. If they believe that they are being forced to interact, as with some diversity programs or affirmative action programs, the intercultural interaction is unlikely to have positive outcomes. For example, an air traffic controller was so incensed by a required diversity program exercise on gender differences that he sued the Department of Transportation for $300,000 (Erbe & Hart, 1994). A better program design would be to involve all participants from the beginning. This can be done by showing the benefits of an inclusive diversity policy— one that values all kinds of diversity, and not merely that based on gender, for example. Equally important is the mounting evidence of bottom-line benefits of diverse personnel who work well together (Harris, 1997).

4. The contact should have the potential to extend beyond the immediate situation and occur in a variety of contexts with a variety of individuals from all groups. This suggests that superficial contact between members of different groups is not likely to have much impact on attitudes (stereotypes, prejudice) or result in productive communication. For instance, simply sitting beside someone from another culture in a class or sampling food from different countries is not likely to result in genuine understanding of that person or appreciation for

his or her cultural background (Stephan & Stephan, 1992). Thus, international students who live with host families are much more likely to have positive impressions of the host country and to develop better intercultural communication skills than those who go on "island programs," in which students interact mostly with other foreigners to the host country.

5. Programs should maximize cooperation within groups and minimize competition. For example, bringing a diverse group of students together should not involve pitting the African Americans against the European Americans on separate sports teams. Instead, it might involve creating diversity within teams to emphasize cooperation. Especially important is having a superordinate goal, a goal that everyone can agree on. This helps diverse groups develop a common identity (Gaertner, Dovidio, & Bachman, 1996). For instance, there is a successful summer camp in Maine for Arab and Jewish youths; the camp brings together members of these historically conflicting groups for a summer of cooperation, discussion, and relationship building.

6. Programs should equalize numbers of group members. Positive outcomes and successful communication will be more likely if members are represented in numerical equality. Research studies have shown that being in the numerical minority can cause stress and that the "solo" minority, particularly in beginning a new job, is subject to exaggerated expectations (either very high or very low) and extreme evaluations (either very good or very bad) (Pettigrew & Martin, 1989).

7. Group members should have similar beliefs and values. A large body of research supports the idea that people are attracted to those whom they perceive to be similar to themselves. This means that, in bringing diverse groups of people together, we should look for common ground—similarities based on religion, interests, competencies, and so on. For example, an international group of mothers is working for peace in the Middle East. Although members represent different ethnic groups, they come together with a shared goal—to protect their children from military action between the warring factions in the region.

8. Programs should promote individuation of group members. This means that they should downplay the characteristics that mark the different groups (such as language, physical abilities, or racial characteristics). Instead, group members might focus on the characteristics that express individual personalities.

This list of conditions can help us understand how domestic and international contexts vary (Gudykunst, 1979). It is easy to see how the history within a nation-state may lead to conditions and attitudes that are more difficult to facilitate. For example, historical conditions between African Americans and White Americans may make it impossible to meet these conditions; interracial interactions in the United States cannot be characterized by equality.

Note that this list of conditions is incomplete. Moreover, meeting all of the conditions does not guarantee positive outcomes when diverse groups of people interact. However, the list is a starting place, and it is important to be able to identify which conditions are affected by historical factors that may be difficult to change and which can be more easily facilitated by communication professionals.

Negotiating Histories Dialectically in Interaction

How can a dialectical perspective help us negotiate interactions, given individual attitudes and personal and cultural histories? How can we balance past and present in our everyday intercultural interactions? First, it is important to recognize that we all bring our own histories (some known, some hidden) to interactions. We can try to evaluate the role that history plays for those with whom we interact.

Second, we should understand the role that histories play in our identities, in what we bring to the interaction. Communication scholar Marsha Houston (1997) says there are three things that White people who want to be her friends should never say: "I don't notice you're Black," "You're not like the others," and "I know how you feel." In her opinion, each of these denies or rejects a part of her identity that is deeply rooted in history.

Sometimes it is unwise to ask people where they are "really from." Such questions assume that they cannot be from where they said they were from, due to racial characteristics or other apparent features. Recognizing a person's history and its link to her or his identity in communication is a first step in establishing intercultural relationships. It is also important to be aware of your own historical blinders and assumptions.

Sometimes the past–present dialectic operates along with the disadvantage–privilege dialectic. The Hungarian philosopher György Lukács wrote a book titled *History and Class Consciousness* (1971), in which he argues that we need to think dialectically about history and social class. Our own recognition of how class differences have influenced our families is very much affected by the past and by the conditions members experienced that might explain whom they married, why they lived where they did, what languages they do and do not speak, and what culture they identify with.

Two dialectical tensions emerge here: (1) between privilege and disadvantage, and (2) between the personal and the social. Both of these dialectics affect our view of the past, present, and future. As we attempt to understand ourselves and our situations (as well as those of others), we must recognize that we arrived at universities for a variety of reasons. Embedded in our backgrounds are dialectical tensions between privilege and disadvantage, and the ways in which those factors were established in the past and the present. Then there is the dialectical tension between seeing ourselves as unique persons and as members of particular social classes. These factors affect both the present and the future. In each case, we must also negotiate the dialectical tensions between the past and the present, and between the present and the future. Who we think we are today is very much influenced by how we view the past, how we live, and what culture we believe to be our own.

Geetha Kothari, a native New Yorker, explains her anger at being asked where she is from. How does this question communicate to her that she is not a U.S. American?

> *"Where are you from?"*
>
> *The bartender asks this as I get up from my table. It's quiet at the Bloomfield Bridge Tavern, home of the best pirogies in Pittsburgh. I have just finished eating, just finished telling my boyfriend how much I love this place because it's cheap and simple, not crowded in the early evening, and has good food.*
>
> *"New York."*
>
> *He stares at me, but before he can ask another question, I'm down the stairs in the ladies' room, washing my hot face. When I come up again, I glare at him.*
>
> *"I hate this place," I say to my boyfriend. "That man asked me where I'm from."*
>
> *The man has no reason to ask me that question. We are not having a conversation. I am not his friend. Out of the blue, having said no other words to me, he feels that it is ok for him, a white man, to ask me where I am from. The only context for this question is my skin color and his need to classify me. I am sure he doesn't expect me to say New York. I look different, therefore it's assumed that I must be from somewhere, somewhere that isn't here, America. It would never occur to him to ask my boyfriend, who is white—and Canadian—where he's from.*

Source: From "Where Are You From?" by Geetha Kothari, 1995, *Under Western Eyes: Personal Essays From Asian America*, edited by G. Hongo, pp. 151–173.

SUMMARY

In this chapter, we explored some of the dimensions of history in intercultural communication. Multiple histories are important for empowering different cultural identities. They include political, intellectual, social, family, national, and cultural-group histories. History is constructed through narrative. Our understanding of the events that occur comes to us through our "telling" of the events. Histories that typically are not conveyed in a widespread manner are considered to be hidden. These include histories based on gender, sexual orientation, race, and ethnicity. All kinds of histories contribute to the success or failure of intercultural interaction.

We also looked at the role history plays in intercultural interaction. People bring four elements of personal histories—childhood experiences, historical myths, language competence, and memories of recent political events—to intercultural interactions. Histories of all kinds can affect the interactions between individuals. The contact hypothesis suggests that simply bringing people from diverse groups together will result in positive attitude change. However, at least eight conditions must exist for the contact hypothesis to hold. Group members must be of equal status and have institutional support; contact must be voluntary and extend beyond the superficial; there must be maximum cooperation; participants should be in equal numbers; and contact should promote similarity and individuation of group members.

Finally, a dialectical perspective helps us negotiate interactions, given the effects of different histories. We can recognize that each of us brings our own history to interactions. And we can acknowledge the role that history plays in forming our identities.

DISCUSSION QUESTIONS

1. What are some examples of hidden histories, and why are they hidden?
2. How do the various histories of the United States influence our communication with people from other countries?
3. What kinds of histories are likely to influence your interactions with an international student of the same gender and age?
4. What factors in your experience have led to the development of positive feelings about your own cultural heritage and background? What factors have led to negative feelings, if any?
5. When can contact between members of two cultures improve their attitudes toward each other and facilitate communication between them?
6. How do histories influence the process of identity formation?
7. What is the significance of the shift from history to histories? How does this shift help us understand intercultural communication?
8. Why do some people in the United States prefer not to talk about history? What views of social reality and intercultural communication does this attitude encourage?

 Go to the self-quizzes on the Online Learning Center at www.mhhe.com/martinnakayama to further test your knowledge.

ACTIVITIES

Cultural-Group History. This exercise can be done by individual students or in groups. Choose a cultural group in the United States that is unfamiliar to you. Study the history of this group, and identify and describe significant events in its history. Answer the following questions:

   a. What is the historical relationship between this group and other groups (particularly the dominant cultural groups)?
   b. Are there any historical incidents of discrimination? If so, describe them.
   c. What are common stereotypes about the group? How did these stereotypes originate?

d. Who are important leaders and heroes of the group?

e. What are notable achievements of the group?

f. How has the history of this group influenced the identity of group members today?

REFERENCES

Allport, G. (1979). *The nature of prejudice.* New York: Addison-Wesley.

Amir, Y. (1969). Contact hypothesis in ethnic relations. *Psychological Bulletin, 71,* 319–343.

Anzaldúa, G. (1987). *Borderlands/La frontera: The new mestiza.* San Francisco: Spinsters/Aunt Lute.

Baudrillard, J. (1988). *America* (C. Turner, Trans.). New York: Verso.

Blanchot, M. (1986). *The writing of the disaster* (A. Smock, Trans.). Lincoln: University of Nebraska Press.

Brinkman, H. (1997). Managing diversity: A review of recommendations for success. In C. D. Brown, C. Snedeker, & B. Sykes (Eds.), *Conflict and diversity* (pp. 35–50). Cresskill, NJ: Hampton Press.

Brislin, R. W. (1981). *Cross cultural encounters: Face to face interaction.* New York: Pergamon.

Erbe, B., & Hart, B. (1994, September 16). Employer goes overboard on "gender sensitivity" issue. *The Evansville Courier,* p. A13.

Fanon, F. (1968). *The wretched of the earth* (C. Farrington, Trans.). New York: Grove Press.

Fisher, W. (1984). Narration as a human communication paradigm: The case of public moral argument. *Communication Monographs, 51,* 1–22.

———. (1985). The narrative paradigm: An elaboration. *Communication Monographs, 52,* 347–367.

Fitzgerald, F. (1972). *Fire in the lake: Vietnamese and Americans in Vietnam.* New York: Vintage Books.

Gaertner, S. L., Dovidio, J. F., & Bachman, B. A. (1996). Revisiting the contact hypothesis: The induction of a common ingroup identity. *International Journal of Intercultural Relations, 20,* 271–290.

Gérard-Libois, J., & Heinen, J. (1989). *Belgique-Congo, 1960.* Brussels: Politique et Histoire.

Gilroy, P. (1993). *The Black Atlantic: Modernity and double consciousness.* New York: Verso.

Gudykunst, W. B. (1979). Intercultural contact and attitude change: A review of literature and suggestions for future research. *International and Intercultural Communication Annual, 4,* 1–16.

Han, R. (1992). *Un chinois de Bourgogne, avant-mémoires.* Paris: Librairie Académique Perrin.

Harris, T. E. (1997). Diversity: Importance, ironies, and pathways. In C. D. Brown, C. Snedeker, & B. Sykes (Eds.), *Conflict and diversity* (pp. 17–34). Cresskill, NJ: Hampton Press.

Hocquenghem, G., & Blasius, M. (1980, April). Interview. *Christopher Street, 8*(4), 36–45.

Houston, M. (1997). When Black women talk with White women: Why dialogues are difficult. In A. González, M. Houston, & V. Chen (Eds.), *Our voices: Essays in ethnicity, culture, and communication* (2nd ed., pp. 187–194). Los Angeles: Roxbury.

Immigrant Investor Program Redesign. (1998, December). Guide for applying for permanent residence in Canada: Business applicants. cicnet.ci.gc.ca/press/98/9865-pre.html.

Jameson, F. (1981). *The political unconscious: Narrative as a socially symbolic act.* Ithaca, NY: Cornell University Press.

Johnson, P. (1995, October 21). Eliminating racism as a social disease. *Hanover Evening Sun,* p. 2.

Kothari, G. (1995). Where are you from? In G. Hongo (Ed.), *Under Western eyes: Personal essays from Asian America* (pp. 151–173). New York: Anchor Books/Doubleday.

Loewen, J. W. (1995). *Lies my teacher told me: Everything your American history textbook got wrong.* New York: Touchstone.

Lukács, György. (1971). *History and class consciousness: Studies in marxist dialectics* (R. Livingstone, Trans.). Cambridge, MA: MIT Press.

Lyotard, J.-F. (1984). *The postmodern condition: A report on knowledge* (G. Bennington & B. Massumi, Trans.). Minneapolis: University of Minnesota Press.

Nakano, M. (1990). *Japanese American women: Three generations, 1890–1990.* Berkeley and San Francisco: Mina Press/National Japanese American Historical Society.

Niiya, B. (Ed.). (2001). *Encyclopedia of Japanese American history: An A-to-Z reference from 1868 to the present.* (Updated ed.). New York: Checkmark Books.

O'Connor, A-M. (1997, September 18). Mexico, Ireland recall immigrant tale of divided loyalties. *The Arizona Republic,* p. A17.

Pasek, B. (2002, June 9). Auschwitz haunts town. *The Arizona Republic,* p. A24.

Pettigrew, T. F., & Martin, J. (1989). Organizational inclusion of minority groups: A social psychological analysis. In J. P. VanOudenhoven & T. M. Willemsen (Eds.), *Ethnic minorities: Social psychological perspectives* (pp. 169–200). Amsterdam/Lisse: Swets & Zeitlinger.

Piette, C. (1997, December 7). American thriving in Brazil: Confederates' descendants cherish town's links to past. *The Arizona Republic,* p. A21.

Polakow-Suransky, S. (2002, June 14). Reviving South African history. *The Chronicle of Higher Education,* p. A37.

Schwarzwald, J., & Amir, Y. (1996). Guest editor's introduction: Special issue on prejudice, discrimination and conflict. *International Journal of Intercultural Relations, 20,* 265–270.

Seel, P., with Bitoux, J. (1994). *Moi, Pierre Seel, déporté homosexuel.* Paris: Calmann-Lévy.

Shaffer, M. (2002, June 9). Navajos protest national status for Old Spanish Trail. *The Arizona Republic,* pp. B1, B8.

Stephan, C. W., & Stephan, W. G. (1989). Antecedents of intergroup anxiety in Asian Americans and Hispanic Americans. *International Journal of Intercultural Relations, 13,* 203–216.

———. (1992). Reducing intercultural anxiety through intercultural contact. *International Journal of Intercultural Relations, 16,* 89–106.

Stephan, W. G., & Stephan, C. W. (1996). *Intergroup relations.* Boulder, CO: Westview Press.

Steyn, M. (2001). *"Whiteness just isn't what it used to be": White identity in a changing South Africa.* Albany: State University of New York Press.

Tateishi, J. (1984). *And justice for all: An oral history of the Japanese American detention camps.* New York: Random House.

Thonssen, L., Baird, A. C., & Braden, W. W. (1970). *Speech criticism* (2nd ed.). New York: Ronald Press.

Under surveillance. (1995, December 26). *The Advocate,* p. 14.

PART II

Intercultural Communication Processes

IDENTITY AND INTERCULTURAL COMMUNICATION

Now that we have examined some sociohistorical contexts that shape culture and communication, let us turn to a discussion of identity and its role in intercultural communication. Identity serves as a bridge between culture and communication. It is important because we communicate our identity to others, and we learn who we are through communication. It is through communication—with our family, friends, and others—that we come to understand ourselves and form our identity. Issues of identity are particularly important in intercultural interactions.

Conflicts can arise, however, when there are sharp differences between who we think we are and who others think we are. For example, a female college student living with a family in Mexico on a homestay may be treated protectively and chaperoned when she socializes, which may conflict with her view of herself as an independent person. In this case, the person's identity is not confirmed but is questioned or challenged in the interaction.

In this chapter, we describe a dialectical approach to understanding identity, one that includes perspectives from psychology and communication. We then turn to the development of specific aspects of our social and cultural identity including those related to gender, race or ethnicity, class, religion, and nationality. We describe how these identities are often related to problematic communication—stereotypes, prejudice, and discrimination. We also examine how various identities develop, including an increasingly important identity—that of multicultural individuals. Finally, we discuss the relationship among identity, language, and communication.

A DIALECTICAL APPROACH TO UNDERSTANDING IDENTITY

How do we come to understand who we are? What are the characteristics of **identity?** In this section, we employ both the static–dynamic and the personal–contextual dialectic in answering these questions. There are three main contemporary perspectives on identity. (See Table 5-1.) The social psychological perspective views the self in a static fashion, in relation to the community to which a person belongs—including comparative studies of identity. The communication perspective is more dynamic and recognizes the role of interaction with others as a factor in the development of the self. Finally, the critical perspective views identity even more dynamically—as the result of contexts quite distant from the individual. As you read this chapter, keep in mind that the relationship between identity and intercultural interaction involves both static and dynamic, and both personal and contextual, elements.

A Social Psychological Perspective

The social psychological perspective emphasizes that identity is created in part by the self and in part in relation to group membership. According to this perspective, the self is composed of multiple identities, and these notions of identity are culture bound. How, then, do we come to understand who we are? That de-

TABLE 5-1	THREE PERSPECTIVES ON IDENTITY AND COMMUNICATION	
Social psychological	Communication	Critical
Identity created by self (by relating to groups)	Identity formed through communication with others	Identity shaped through social, historical forces
Emphasizes individualized, familial, and spiritual self (cross-cultural perspective)	Emphasizes avowal and ascribed dimensions	Emphasizes contexts and resisting ascribed identity

pends very much on our cultural background. According to Western psychologists like Erik Erikson, our identities are self-created, formed through identity conflicts and crises, through identity diffusion and confusion (Erikson, 1950, 1968). Occasionally, we may need a moratorium, a time-out, in the process. Our identities are created not in one smooth, orderly process but in spurts, with some events providing insights into who we are and long periods intervening during which we may not think much about ourselves or our identities.

Cross-Cultural Perspectives   In the United States, young people are often encouraged to develop a strong sense of identity, to "know who they are," to be independent and self-reliant, which reflects an emphasis on the cultural value of individualism. However, this is not the case in many other countries, in which there is a more collectivistic orientation. Cross-cultural psychologist Alan Roland (1988) has identified three universal aspects of identity present in all individuals: (1) an individualized identity, (2) a familial identity, and (3) a spiritual identity. Cultural groups usually emphasize one or two of these dimensions and downplay the other(s). Let's see how this works. The **individualized identity** is the sense of an independent "I," with sharp distinctions between the self and others. This identity is emphasized by most groups in the United States, where young people are encouraged to be independent and self-reliant at a fairly early age—by adolescence.

In contrast, the **familial identity,** evident in many collectivistic cultures, stresses the importance of emotional connectedness to and interdependence with others. It also involves a strong identification with the reputation and honor of others in hierarchical groups. For example, in many African and Asian societies, and in some cultural groups in the United States, children are encouraged and expected to form strong, interdependent bonds, first with the family and later with other groups. As one of our students explains,

> to be Mexican American is to unconditionally love one's family and all it stands for. Mexican-Americans are an incredibly close-knit group of people, especially when it comes to family. We are probably the only culture that can actually recite the names of our fourth cousins by heart. In this respect our families are like clans,

Communication scholar Ge Gao contrasts the Western idea of the independent self with the Chinese notion of the interdependent self.

In the Western world, an "individual" signifies an independent entity with free will, emotions and personality. An individual, however, is not conceptualized in this way in the Chinese culture. . . . The incomplete nature of the self is supported by both Taoism and Confucianism even though they differ in many fundamental ways. Taoism defines self as part of nature. Self and nature together complete a harmonious relationship. Self in the Confucian sense is defined by a person's surrounding relations, which often are derived from kinship networks and supported by cultural values such as filial piety, loyalty, dignity, and integrity. . . .

The other-orientation thus is key to an interdependent self. Congruous with the notion of an interdependent self, the Chinese self also needs to be recognized, defined, and completed by others. The self's orientation to others' needs, wishes, and expectations is essential to the development of the Chinese self.

Source: From "Self and Other: A Chinese Perspective on Interpersonal Relationships," by Ge Gao, 1996, *Communication in Personal Relationships Across Cultures*, edited by W. G. Gudykunst, S. Ting-Toomey, and T. Nishida, pp. 83–84.

they go much further than the immediate family and very deep into extended families. We even have a celebration, Dia de los Muertos *(Day of the Dead) that honors our ancestors.*

In these societies, educational, occupational, and even marital choices are made by individuals with extensive family guidance. The goal of the developed identity is not to become independent from others, but rather to gain an understanding of and cultivate one's place in the complex web of interdependence with others. Communication scholar Ge Gao (1996) describes the Chinese sense of self:

The other-orientation thus is key to an interdependent self. Congruous with the notion of an interdependent self, the Chinese self also needs to be recognized, defined, and completed by others. The self's orientation to others' needs, wishes, and expectations is essential to the development of the Chinese self. (p. 84)

In addition, the understanding of the familial self may be more connected to others and situation bound. According to studies comparing North Americans' and East Asians' senses of identity, when asked to describe themselves, the North Americans give more abstract, situation-free descriptions ("I am kind," "I am outgoing," "I am quiet in the morning"), whereas East Asians tend to describe their memberships and relationships to others rather than themselves ("I am a mother," "I am the youngest child in my family," "I am a member of tennis club") (Cross, 2000).

The third dimension is the **spiritual identity,** the inner spiritual reality that is realized and experienced to varying extents by people through a number of outlets. For example, the spiritual self in India is expressed through a structure of gods and goddess and through rituals and mediation. In Japan, the realization of the spiritual self tends more toward aesthetic modes, such as the tea ceremony and flower arranging (Roland, 1988).

Clearly, identity development does not occur in the same way in every society. The notion of identity in India, Japan, and some Latino/a and Asian American groups emphasizes the integration of the familial and the spiritual self, but very little of the more individualized self.

This is not to say that there is not considerable individuality among people in these groups. However, the general identity contrasts dramatically with the predominant mode in most U.S. cultural groups, in which the individualized self is emphasized and there is little attention to the familial self. However, there may be some development of the spiritual self among devout Catholic, Protestant, Jewish, or Muslim individuals.

Groups play an important part in the development of all these dimensions of self. As we are growing up, we identify with many groups, based on gender, race, ethnicity, class, sexual orientation, religion, and nationality (Tajfel, 1981, 1982). And depending on our cultural background, we may develop tight or looser bonds with these groups. By comparing ourselves and others with members of these groups, we come to understand who we are. Because we belong to various groups, we develop multiple identities that come into play at different times, depending on the context. For example, in going to church or temple, we may highlight our religious identity. In going to clubs or bars, we may highlight our sexual orientation identity. Women who join social groups exclusive to women (or men who attend social functions just for men) are highlighting their gender identity.

A Communication Perspective

The communication perspective builds on the notions of identity formation discussed previously but takes a more dynamic turn. That is, it emphasizes that identities are negotiated, co-created, reinforced, and challenged through communication with others; they emerge when messages are exchanged between persons (Hecht, Collier, & Ribeau, 1993). This means that presenting our identities is not a simple process. Does everyone see you as you see yourself? Probably not. To understand how these images may conflict, the concepts of avowal and ascription are useful.

Avowal is the process by which individuals portray themselves, whereas **ascription** is the process by which others attribute identities to them. Sometimes these processes are congruent. For example, we (Judith and Tom) see ourselves as professors and hope that students also see us as professors. We also see ourselves as young, but many students do not concur, ascribing an "old person" identity to us. This ascribed identity challenges our avowed identity. And these conflicting views influence the communication between us and our students.

Different identities are emphasized depending on the individuals we are communicating with and the topics of conversation. For example, in a social conversation with someone we are attracted to, our gender or sexual orientation identity is probably more important to us than other identities (ethnicity, nationality). And our communication is probably most successful when the person we are talking with confirms the identity we think is most important at the moment. In this sense, competent intercultural communication affirms the identity that is most salient in any conversation (Collier & Thomas, 1988). For example, if you are talking with a professor about a research project, the conversation will be most competent if the interaction confirms the salient identities (professor and student) rather than other identities (e.g., those based on gender, religion, or ethnicity).

How do you feel when someone does not recognize the identity you believe is most salient? For example, suppose your parents treat you as a child (their ascription) and not as an independent adult (your avowal). How might this affect communication? One of our students describes how he reacts when people ascribe a different identity than the one he avows:

> *Pretty much my entire life I was seen not as American but as half Mexican. In reality I am 50% Mexican and 50% Dutch. So technically I am half Mexican and half Dutch American. I always say it like that but it was obvious that not everybody saw it like that. I was asked if I was Hawaiian, Persian, and even Italian, but I was able to politely tell them about myself.*

Central to the communication perspective is the idea that our identities are expressed communicatively—in core symbols, labels, and norms. **Core symbols** (or cultural values) tell us about the fundamental beliefs and the central concepts that define a particular identity. Communication scholar Michael Hecht and his colleagues (Hecht, 1998; Hecht, Collier, & Ribeau, 1993) have identified the contrasting core symbols associated with various ethnic identities. For example, core symbols of African American identity may be positivity, sharing, uniqueness, realism, and assertiveness. Individualism is often cited as a core symbol of European American identity. Core symbols are not only expressed but also created and shaped through communication. Labels are a category of core symbols; they are the terms we use to refer to particular aspects of our own and others' identities—for example, *African American, Latino, White,* or *European American.*

Finally, some norms of behavior are associated with particular identities. For example, women may express their gender identity by being more concerned about safety than men. They may take more precautions when they go out at night, such as walking in groups. People might express their religious identity by participating in activities such as going to church or Bible study meetings.

A Critical Perspective

Contextual Identity Formation   The driving force behind a critical approach is the attempt to understand identity formation within the contexts of history, economics, politics, and discourse. To grasp this notion, ask yourself: How and why

FIGURE 5-1 We have many different identities—including gender, ethnicity, age, religion, nationality, and sexuality—that we express in different ways at different times. Celebrations are one way to highlight identity. Here, Sikhs in the northern Indian city of Chandigarh light candles in a temple to celebrate Diwali. Diwali marks the age-old culture of India and celebrates knowledge and the vanquishing of ignorance. (© *Dipak Kumar/Reuters/Getty Images*)

do people identify with particular groups and not others? What choices are available to them?

We are all subject to being pigeonholed into identity categories, or contexts, even before we are born. (See Figure 5-1.) Many parents ponder a name for their unborn child, who is already part of society through his or her relationship to the parents. Some children have a good start at being, say, Jewish or Chicana before they are even born. We cannot ignore the ethnic, socioeconomic, or racial positions from which we start our identity journeys.

To illustrate, French psychoanalyst Jacques Lacan (1977) offers the example of two children on a train that stops at a station. Each child looks out a window and identifies the location: One says that they are in front of the door for the ladies' bathroom; the other says they are in front of the gentlemen's. Both children see and use labels from their seating position to describe where they are; they are on the same train, but they describe their locations differently. Just as we are never "out" of position, we are never "outside" of language and its system that helps define us. And, like the two children, where we are positioned—by language and by society—influences how and what we see and, most importantly, what it means.

The identities that others may ascribe to us are socially and politically determined. They are not constructed by the self alone. We must ask ourselves what drives the construction of particular kinds of identities. For example, the label "heterosexual" is a relatively recent one, created less than a hundred years ago (Katz, 1995). Today, people do not hesitate to identify themselves as "heterosexuals." A critical perspective insists on the constructive nature of this process and attempts to identify the social forces and needs that give rise to these identities.

Resisting Ascribed Identities   When we invoke such discourses about identity, we are pulled into the social forces that feed the discourse. We might resist the position they put us in, and we might try to ascribe other identities to ourselves. Nevertheless, we must begin from that position in carving out a new identity.

French philosopher Louis Althusser (1971) uses the term **interpellation** to refer to this process. He notes that we are pushed into this system of social forces

> by that very precise operation which I have called interpellation or hailing, and which can be imagined along the lines of the most commonplace everyday police (or other) hailing: "Hey you there!" . . . Experience shows that the practical tele-communication of hailings is such that they hardly ever miss their man: verbal call or whistle, the one hailed always recognizes that it is really him who is being hailed. And yet it is a strange phenomenon, and one which cannot be explained solely by "guilt feelings." (p. 163)

This hailing process that Althusser describes operates in intercultural communication interactions. It establishes the foundation from which the interaction occurs. For example, occasionally, someone will ask Tom if he is Japanese, a question that puts him in an awkward position. He does not hold Japanese citizenship, nor has he ever lived in Japan. Yet the question probably doesn't mean to address these issues. Rather, the person is asking what it means to be "Japanese." How can Tom reconfigure his position in relation to this question?

The Dynamic Nature of Identities   The social forces that give rise to particular identities are never stable but are always changing. Therefore, the critical perspective insists on the dynamic nature of identities. For example, the emergence of the European Union has given new meaning to the notion of being "European" as an identity. Similarly, the terrorist attacks of September 11, 2001, have caused many Americans to reconsider what it means to be "American." And the various and sometimes contradictory notions of what it means to be an American highlights the fluidity and dynamic nature of identities. For some, being "American" now means having a renewed patriotism, as described by one of our students:

> To be an American is to be proud. After September 11, a sense of patriotism swept through this country that I have never felt before. Growing up I heard about how patriotic the United States was during WW I and WW II, but I had never experienced it personally. After that day, it was as if racial, religious, and democratic differences had stopped. Even if that tension only stopped temporarily, the point

Writer Philippe Wamba describes how his multicultural identity developed across several continents and languages. His father (from the Republic of the Congo, formerly Zaire) and mother (an African American midwesterner) met and married while attending college in Michigan. His father's career took the family first to Boston (where Phillipe was one of only a few Blacks in his school), then to Dar es Salaam, Tanzania, where he learned flawless Swahili and added a third heritage to his cultural background: "half American, half Zairean, and half Tanzanian." Now an adult, he describes his answer to the question "Where are you from?"

> I used to try to find succinct ways of responding to the question "Where are you from"—simple one-word answers that would satisfy the curious. I envied my friends their ability to state one place confidently and simply say "New York" or "Kenya." . . . For a period, I even referred to myself as a "a citizen of the world," a high-minded moniker, bred of my own boredom and frustration, that used to annoy people. . . . Now I have decided that the succinct answer is always inadequate and that the story of origin is always a complex saga. . . . I have come to reject the idea of a simple, dualized family heritage and the simple bicultural understanding of self I internalized as a child. . . . For a time I lived as a sophisticated cultural chameleon, attempting to blend with my shifting surroundings by assuming the appearance and habits of those around me. . . . In the end I am both African and African American and therefore neither. I envy others their hometowns and unconflicted patriotism, but no longer would I exchange them for my freedom to seek multiple homes and nations and to forge my own.

Source: From "A Middle Passage," by P. Wamba, 1998, *Half and Half: Writers on Growing Up Biracial + Bicultural*, edited by C. C. O'Hearn, pp. 150–169.

> is that it did stop. Our country came together to help, pray, and donate. The feeling of being an American is a sense of feeling and strength and pride.

For others, the events of 9/11 led to more ambivalence about being "American":

> The media showed negative responses that other countries displayed toward Americans. This makes me ponder what I've done, as a White mut American to make people feel this way. I know it is not necessarily my fault but actually American beliefs as a whole. . . . The "cop in the head" feeling occurs in me whenever I see a group of people gathered around speaking a foreign language and staring at me. Maybe it is an insecurity issue within me, aided by rumors I've heard, that initiates this uneasy feeling. I really hope Americans, as a whole, become more accepting of each other so that other countries will see that we can work together with such diversity.

For another example, look at the way that identity labels have changed from "colored" to "Negro" to "Black" to "Afro-American" to "African American."

Although the labels seem to refer to the same group of people, the political and cultural identities of those so labeled are different. Indeed, the contexts in which the terms developed and were used vary considerably.

SOCIAL AND CULTURAL IDENTITIES

People can identify with a multitude of groups. This section describes some of the major types of groups.

Gender Identity

We often begin life with gendered identities. When newborns arrive in our culture, they may be greeted with clothes and blankets in either blue for boys or pink for girls. To establish a **gender identity** for the newborn, visitors may ask if the baby is a boy or a girl. But gender is not the same as biological sex. This distinction is important in understanding how our views on biological sex influence gender identities.

What it means to be a man or a woman in our society is heavily influenced by cultural notions. For example, some activities are considered more masculine or more feminine. Thus, whether people hunt or sew or fight or read poetry can transform the ways that others view them. Similarly, the programs that people watch on television—soap operas, football games, and so on—affect how they socialize with others, contributing to gendered contexts.

As culture changes, so does the notion of what we idealize as masculine or feminine. Cultural historian Gail Bederman (1995) observes:

> Even the popular imagery of a perfect male body changed. In the 1860s, the middle class had seen the ideal male body as lean and wiry. By the 1890s, however, an ideal male body required physical bulk and well-defined muscles. (p. 15)

In this sense, the male body, as well as the female body, can be understood not in its "natural" state but in relation to idealized notions of masculinity and femininity. To know that this man or that woman is particularly good-looking requires an understanding of the gendered notions of attractiveness in a culture.

Our notions of masculinity and femininity change continually, driven by commercial interests and other cultural forces. For example, there is a major push now to market cosmetics to men. However, advertisers acknowledge that this requires sensitivity to men's ideas about makeup:

> Unlike women, most men don't want to talk about makeup, don't want to go out in public to shop for makeup and don't know how to use makeup. The first barrier is getting men to department stores or specialty shops to buy products. (Yamanouchi, 2002, p. D1)

Our expression of gender not only communicates who we think we are but also constructs a sense of who we want to be. Initially, we learn what masculinity and femininity mean in our culture. Then, through various media, we monitor how these notions shift and negotiate to communicate our gendered selves to others.

Consider, for example, the contemporary trend in the United States for women to have very full lips. If one's lips are not naturally full, there is always the option of getting collagen injections or having other body fat surgically inserted into the lips. In contrast, our Japanese students tell us that full lips are not considered at all attractive in Japan. The dynamic character of gender reflects its close connection to culture. Society has many images of masculinity and femininity; we do not all seek to look and act according to a single ideal. At the same time, we *do* seek to communicate our gendered identities as part of who we are.

Gender identity is also demonstrated by communication style. Women's and men's different communication styles sometimes lead to misunderstanding and conflict. For example, sometimes U.S. women make sympathetic noises in response to what a friend says, whereas men say nothing out of respect for the other person's independence. And women may interpret men's silence as not caring. Another area of misinterpretation is the reaction to "troubles talk." Typically, women commiserate by talking about a similar situation they experienced. However, men who follow cultural rules for conversational dominance interpret this as stealing the stage.

Yet another difference arises in storytelling. Men tend to be more linear in telling stories; women tend to give more details and offer tangential information, which men interpret as an inability to get to the point (Tannen, 1990). Men and women also often misinterpret relationship talk. Women may express more interest in the relationship process and may feel better simply discussing it. Men who are problem-solving oriented may see little point in discussing something if nothing is identified as needing fixing (Wood, 1994, pp. 145–148).

Age Identity

As we age, we also play into cultural notions of how individuals our age should act, look, and behave; that is, we develop an **age identity.** As we grow older, we sometimes look at the clothes displayed in store windows or advertised in newspapers and magazines and feel that we are either too old or too young for that "look." These feelings stem from an understanding of what age means and how we identify with people that age.

Some people feel old at 30; others feel young at 40 or 50. There is nothing inherent in age that tells us we are young or old. Rather, our notions of age and youth are all based on cultural conventions. These same cultural conventions also suggest that it is inappropriate to engage in a romantic relationship with someone who is too old or too young.

Our notions of age often change as we grow older ourselves. When we are quite young, someone in college seems old; when we are in college, we do not feel so old. Yet the relative nature of age is only one part of the identity process. Social constructions of age also play a role. Different generations often have different philosophies, values, and ways of speaking. For example, recent data show that today's college freshmen are more liberal politically and more inter-

I think that my being in college with kids just a little older than my son has helped me "learn the language" of the younger generation. So my college classmates have helped me acculturate into the younger generation at a more rapid speed than others my age. When I sit in class with these young people who have graduated from high school and are going to college, it is very easy to focus on these kids as being representative of the younger generation. Then there are the stereotypical "bad" teenagers—the gang members, the druggies, and so on. It isn't fair to generalize the younger generation with these stereotypes, either.

Are the cultural differences of our two age groups just as approachable as in any other intercultural exchange? I believe that they are. By using the skills that I am learning in bridging cultural differences, I am getting better at bridging the generation gap between "old mom" and "18-year-old teenager." Interpersonal skills, flexibility, motivation, attitudes, knowledge, skills, and love are all applicable when communicating interculturally with teenagers.
—Marcia

ested in volunteer work and civic responsibility than were Gen Xers. Scholars who view generations as "cultural groups" say that these characteristics make them similar to the World War I generation—politically curious and assertive, and devoted to a sense of personal responsibility (Sax, Lindholm, Astin, Korn, & Mahoney, 2001).

Sometimes these generational differences can lead to conflict in the workplace. For example, young people who entered the job market during the "dot com" years have little corporate loyalty and think nothing of changing jobs when a better opportunity comes along. This can irritate Baby Boomer workers, who emphasize the importance of demonstrating corporate loyalty, of "paying one's dues" to the establishment while gradually working one's way "up the corporate ladder." Although not all people in any generation are alike, the attempt to find trends across generations reflects our interest in understanding age identity.

Racial and Ethnic Identities

Racial Identity   Race consciousness, or **racial identity,** is largely a modern phenomenon. In the United States today, the issue of race is both controversial and pervasive. It is the topic of many public discussions, from television talk shows to talk radio. Yet many people feel uncomfortable talking about it or think it should not be an issue in daily life. Perhaps we can better understand the contemporary issues if we look at how the notion of race developed historically in the United States.

Current debates about race have their roots in the 15th and 16th centuries, when European explorers encountered people who looked different from themselves. The debates centered on religious questions of whether there was "one family of man." If so, what rights were to be accorded to those who were different? Debates about which groups were "human" and which were "animal" pervaded popular and legal discourse and provided a rationale for slavery. Later, in the 18th and 19th centuries, the scientific community tried to establish a classification system of race, based on genetics and cranial capacity. However, these efforts were largely unsuccessful.

Today, most scientists have abandoned a strict biological basis for classifying racial groups, deferring instead to a social science approach to understanding race. They recognize that racial categories like White and Black are constructed in social and historical contexts.

Several arguments refute the physiological basis for race. First, racial categories vary widely throughout the world. In general, distinctions between White and Black are fairly rigid in the United States, and many people become uneasy when they are unable to categorize individuals. In contrast, Brazil recognizes a wide variety of intermediate racial categories in addition to White and Black. These variations indicate a cultural, rather than a biological, basis for racial classification (Omi & Winant, 1998). Terms like *mulatto* and *Black Irish* demonstrate cultural classifications; terms like *Caucasoid* and *Australoid* are examples of biological classification.

Second, U.S. law uses a variety of definitions to determine racial categories. A 1982 case in Louisiana reopened debates about race as socially created rather than biologically determined. Susie Phipps applied for a passport and discovered that under Louisiana law she was Black because she was $\frac{1}{32}$ African (her great-grandmother had been a slave). She then sued to be reclassified as White. Not only did she consider herself White, inasmuch as she grew up among Whites, but she also was married to a White man. And because her children were only $\frac{1}{64}$ African, they were legally White. Although she lost her lawsuit, the ensuing political and popular discussions persuaded Louisiana lawmakers to change the way the state classified people racially. It is important that the law was changed, but this legal situation does not obscure the fact that social definitions of race continue to exist (Hasian & Nakayama, 1999).

A third example of how racial categories are socially constructed is illustrated by their fluid nature. As more and more southern Europeans immigrated to the United States in the 19th century, the established Anglo and German society tried to classify these newcomers (Irish and Jewish, as well as southern European) as non-White. However, this attempt was not successful because, based on the narrower definition, Whites might have become demographically disempowered. Instead, the racial line was drawn to include all Europeans, and people from outside of Europe (e.g., immigrants from China) were designated as non-White (Omi & Winant, 1998).

Racial categories, then, are based to some extent on physical characteristics, but they are also constructed in fluid social contexts. It probably makes more sense to talk about racial *formation* than racial *categories,* thereby casting race as a complex of social meanings rather than as a fixed and objective concept. How people construct these meanings and think about race influences the ways in which they communicate.

Ethnic Identity   In contrast to racial identity, **ethnic identity** may be seen as a set of ideas about one's own ethnic group membership. It typically includes several dimensions: (1) self-identification, (2) knowledge about the ethnic culture (traditions, customs, values, and behaviors), and (3) feelings about belonging to a particular ethnic group. Ethnic identity often involves a shared sense of origin and history, which may link ethnic groups to distant cultures in Asia, Europe, Latin America, or other locations.

Having an ethnic identity means experiencing a sense of belonging to a particular group and knowing something about the shared experience of group members. For instance, Judith grew up in an ethnic community. She heard her parents and relatives speak German, and her grandparents made several trips back to Germany and talked about their German roots. This experience contributed to her ethnic identity.

For some U.S. residents, ethnicity is a specific and relevant concept. They see themselves as connected to an origin outside the United States—as Mexican American, Japanese American, Welsh American, and so on—or to some region prior to its being absorbed into the United States—Navajo, Hopi, and so on. As one African American student told us, "I have always known my history and the history of my people in this country. I will always be first African American and then American. Who I am is based on my heritage." For others, ethnicity is a vague concept. They see themselves as "American" and reject the notion of **hyphenated Americans.** One of our students explains:

> *I am American. I am not German American or Irish American or Native America. I have never set foot on German or Irish land. I went to Scotland a couple years ago and found a Scottish plaid that was my family crest. I still didn't even feel a real connection to it and bought it as more of a joke, to say, "Look! I'm Scottish!" even though in my heart I know I'm not.*

We'll discuss the issues of ethnicity for White people later.

What, then, does *American* mean? Who defines it? Is there only one meaning, or are there many different meanings? It is important to determine what definition is being used by those who insist that we should all simply be "Americans." If one's identity is "just American," how is this identity formed, and how does it influence communication with others who see themselves as hyphenated Americans (Alba, 1985, 1990; Carbaugh, 1989)?

Racial Versus Ethnic Identity   Scholars dispute whether racial and ethnic identity are similar or different. Some suggest that ethnic identity is constructed by both selves and others but that racial identity is constructed solely by others. They stress as well that race overrides ethnicity in the way people classify others (Cornell & Hartmann, 1998). The American Anthropological Association has suggested that the U.S. government phase out use of the term *race* in the collection of federal data because the concept has no scientific validity or utility.

On the one hand, discussions about ethnicity tend to assume a "melting pot" perspective on U.S. society. On the other hand, discussions about race as shaped

This press release from the American Anthropological Association questions the utility of the term *race* and suggests that the government eliminate it from their data gathering.

> *The government should phase out use of the term "race" in the collection of federal data because the concept has no scientific justification in human biology, according to a statement released today by the American Anthropological Association (AAA).*
>
> *Instead of race, ethnic categories, which better reflect the diversity of the US population, should be used. The AAA statement includes five recommendations for changes in the way the government collects information about its citizens. It addresses the federal Office of Management and Budget (OMB) Directive 15, which designates racial and ethnic categories used in the US census and in innumerable other public and private research projects.*
>
> *The recommendations outlined by the AAA include the immediate need for the OMB to combine the now-separate "race" and "ethnicity" questions into one question for the 2000 Census and to eliminate "race" by the time planning begins for the 2010 Census. Respondents should be allowed to identify more than one category in reporting their ancestry. Additionally, the AAA advocates more research to determine what terms best capture human variability in ways best understood by the American people.*
>
> *. . . Probably the clearest data on human variation come from genetic studies. Genetic data do show differences between groups and these can potentially trace an individual's likely geographic origin. This can be helpful in such applications as health screening. Nevertheless, the data also show that any two individuals within a particular population are as different genetically as any two people selected from any two populations in the world. . . .*

Source: From "AAA Recommends Race Be Scrapped; Suggests New Government Categories," press release/OMB15, September 1997, www.aaanet.org/gvt/obmnews.htm.

by U.S. history allow us to talk about racism. If we never talk about race, but only about ethnicity, can we consider the effects and influences of racism?

Bounded Versus Dominant Identities   One way to sort out the relationship between ethnicity and race is to differentiate between bounded and dominant (or normative) identities (Frankenburg, 1993; Trinh, 1986/1987). Bounded cultures are characterized by groups that are specific but not dominant. For most White people, it is easy to comprehend the sense of belonging in a bounded group (e.g., an ethnic group). Clearly, for example, being Amish means following the *ordnung* (community rules). Growing up in a German American home, Judith's identity included a clear emphasis on seriousness and very little on communicative expressiveness. This identity differed from that of her Italian American friends at college, who seemed much more expressive.

However, what it means to belong to the dominant, or normative, culture is more elusive. *Normative* means "setting the norm for a society." In the United States, Whites clearly are the normative group in that they set the standards for appropriate and effective behavior. Although it can be difficult for White people to define what a normative White identity is, this does not deny its existence or importance. It is often not easy to see what the cultural practices are that link White people together. For example, we seldom think of Thanksgiving or Valentine's Day as White holidays.

Our sense of racial or ethnic identity develops over time, in stages, and through communication with others. These stages seem to reflect our growing understanding of who we are and depend to some extent on the groups we belong to. Many ethnic or racial groups share the experience of oppression. In response, they may generate attitudes and behaviors consistent with a natural internal struggle to develop a strong sense of group identity and self-identity. For many cultural groups, these strong identities ensure their survival.

Religious Identity

Religious identity can be an important dimension of many people's identities, as well as an important site of intercultural conflict. Often, religious identity is conflated with racial or ethnic identity, which makes it difficult to view religious identity simply in terms of belonging to a particular religion. For example, when someone says, "I am Jewish," does it mean that he practices Judaism? That he views Jewish identity as an ethnic identity? Or when someone says, "She has a Jewish last name," is it a statement that recognizes religious identity? With a historical view, we can see Jews as a racial group, an ethnic group, and a religious group.

Drawing distinctions between various identities—racial, ethnic, class, national, and regional—can be problematic. For example, Italians and Irish are often viewed as Catholics, and Episcopalians are frequently seen as belonging to the upper classes. Issues of religion and ethnicity have come to the forefront in the war against Al-Queda and other militant groups. Although those who carried out the attacks against the Pentagon and the World Trade Center were Muslims and Arabs, it is hardly true that all Muslims are Arabs or that all Arabs are Muslims (Feghali, 1997).

Religious differences have been at the root of contemporary conflicts from the Middle East to Northern Ireland, and from India and Pakistan to Bosnia-Herzegovina. In the United States, religious conflicts caused the Mormons to flee the Midwest for Utah in the mid-19th century. And, more recently, religious conflicts have become very real for some Arab Americans as the U.S. government presses the war against terrorism, with many of those people subject to suspicion if not persecution. And militant Muslims in the Middle East and elsewhere see their struggle against the United States as a very serious endeavor and are willing to die for their religious beliefs.

In the United States, we often believe that people should be free to practice whatever religion they wish. Conflicts arise, however, when the religious beliefs of some individuals are imposed on others who may not share those beliefs. For example, some Jews see the predominance of Christmas trees and Christian crosses as an affront to their religious beliefs.

People in some religions communicate and mark their religious differences by their clothing. For example, Hassidic Jews wear traditional, somber clothing, and Muslim women are often veiled according to the Muslim guideline of female modesty. Of course, most religions are not identified by clothing. For example, you may not know if someone is Buddhist, Catholic, Lutheran, or atheist based upon the way he or she dresses. Because religious identities are less salient, everyday interactions may not invoke religious identity.

Class Identity

We don't often think about socioeconomic class as an important part of our identity. Yet scholars have shown that class often plays an important role in shaping our reactions to and interpretations of culture. For example, French sociologist Pierre Bourdieu (1987) studied the various responses to art, sports, and other cultural activities of people in different French social classes. According to Bourdieu, working-class people prefer to watch soccer whereas upper-class individuals like tennis, and middle-class people prefer photographic art whereas upper-class individuals favor less representational art. As these findings reveal, class distinctions are real and can be linked to actual behavioral practices and preferences.

English professor Paul Fussell (1992) shows how similar signs of **class identity** operate in U.S. society. According to Fussell, the magazines we read, the foods we eat, and the words we use often reflect our social class position. At some level, we recognize these class distinctions, but we consider it impolite to ask directly about a person's class background. Therefore, we may use communication strategies to place others in a class hierarchy. Unfortunately, these strategies don't always yield accurate information. For example, people may try to guess your class background by the foods you eat. Some foods are seen as "rich folk's food"—for instance, lamb, white asparagus, brie, artichokes, goose, and caviar. Do you feel as if you are revealing your class background if you admit that these foods are unfamiliar to you? Perhaps not admitting your unfamiliarity is a form of "passing," of representing yourself as belonging to a group you really don't belong to. Another strategy that people may use to guess a person's class background is to ask where that person did her or his undergraduate work.

Most people in the United States recognize class associations even as they may deny that such class divisions exist. What does this apparent contradiction indicate? Most importantly, it reveals the complexities of class issues, particularly in the United States. We often don't really know the criteria for inclusion in a given social class. Is membership determined by financial assets? By educational level? By profession? By family background? These factors may or may not be indicators of class.

Another reason for this apparent contradiction is that people in the majority or normative class (the middle class) tend not to think about class, whereas those in the working class are often reminded that their communication styles and lifestyle choices are not the norm. In this respect, class is like race. For example, terms like *trailer trash* or *white trash* show the negative connotations associated with people who are not middle class (Moon & Rolison, 1998).

A central assumption of the American Dream is that, with hard work and persistence, individuals can improve their class standing, even in the face of overwhelming evidence to the contrary. For example, census data show that the disparity between top and bottom income levels is actually increasing. In 1970, households in the top 20% of the income distribution earned about 44% of all income; by 1998, this figure had increased to 50%. The share of total income received by households in every other income group declined over the same period (U.S. Bureau of the Census, 1999). Scholar Donna Lanston (1995) explains:

> In the myth of the classless society, ambition and intelligence alone are responsible for success. The myth conceals the existence of a class society, which serves many functions. One of the main ways it keeps the working-class and poor locked into a class-based system in a position of servitude is by cruelly creating false hope . . . that they can have different opportunities in life. (p. 101)

Lanston goes on to suggest that another outcome of this myth is that, when poverty persists, the poor are blamed. They are poor because of something they did or didn't do—for example, they were lazy or didn't try hard enough, or they were unlucky. It is a classic case of blaming the victim. And the media often reinforce these notions. As Leonardo DiCaprio's character in the movie *Titanic* shows us, upward mobility is easy enough—merely a matter of being opportunistic, charming, and a little bit lucky.

Working-class individuals who aren't upwardly mobile are often portrayed in TV sitcoms and movies as unintelligent, criminal, or unwilling to do what they have to do to better their lot in life. (Consider, for example, the TV show *Married With Children*.) And members of the real working class, as frequent guests on television talk shows like *Rikki Lake*, *Jerry Springer* and on court shows like *Judge Judy* and *Judge Joe Brown*, are urged to be verbally contentious and even physically aggressive with each other.

The point is that, although class identity is not as readily apparent as, say, gender identity, it still influences our perceptions of and communication with others. Race, class, and sometimes gender identity are interrelated. For example, statistically speaking, being born African American, poor, and female increases one's chances of remaining in poverty. But, of course, race and class are not synonymous. There are many poor Whites, and there are increasing numbers of wealthy African Americans. In this sense, these multiple identities are interrelated but not identical.

National Identity

Among many identities, we also have a **national identity,** which should not be confused with racial or ethnic identity. Nationality, unlike racial or ethnic identity, refers to one's legal status in relation to a nation. Many U.S. citizens can trace their ethnicity to Latin America, Asia, Europe, or Africa, but their nationality, or citizenship, is with the United States.

What is Japanese national identity? I have to say that many things are in the very psyche, the Japanese psyche. They are more than feelings—the way you feel when the spring is around and see cherry blossoms everywhere. You become grateful to the cycle of nature and the promise that spring always comes. Such a feeling that you believe that you share with others, as people talk about it, is a big part of national identity, I think. It is also in big sport events, where you can feel one with others by sharing emotions. It is in the fixation to the food, the meticulous attention and kodawari *(fixation) about food. And it is felt in many folk songs (douyou), which sing a lot about nature, living creatures, etc. In sum, there are so many things about Japanese national identity. But, to me, they are never about the national flag or pledging allegiance to your country.*
—Tamie

Although national identity may seem to be a clear-cut issue, this is not the case when the nation's status is unclear. For example, bloody conflicts erupted over the attempted secession in the mid-1800s of the Confederate States of America from the United States. Similar conflicts erupted in more recent times when Eritrea tried to separate from Ethiopia, and Chechnya from Russia. Less bloody conflicts that involved nationhood led, in the former Czechoslovakia, to the separation of Slovakia and the Czech Republic.

Contemporary nationhood struggles are being played out as Quebec attempts to separate from Canada and as Corsica and Tahiti attempt to separate from France. Sometimes nations disappear from the political map but persist in the social imagination and eventually reemerge, such as Poland, Ukraine, Latvia, Lithuania, and Estonia. Other times national identity may shift in significant ways, as in the United States after the attacks of September 11, 2001, when ideas about national identity seemed to incorporate increased expressions of patriotism. One of our Japanese graduate students explains how her feeling of national identity is much different from what she sees in the United States:

I have seen so many "God bless America," "Proud to be American" messages EVERYWHERE as I have lived here as a Japanese sojourner. . . . Coming from Japan, I don't think I have the same notion of "I am proud about my country." I love my culture, the beauty, the meanings, the spirituality that surround it. But I feel that I have been consciously or subconsciously taught that being proud of your country can be dangerous, misleading, blinding. Look at what happened before 1945—how many people in my country thought about their country and framed the "cause" which led to a disaster (WW II). In fact, I have talked to my Japanese friends about this sentiment and mixed emotion I feel about the concept of "patriotism," and almost all of them agreed with me—we were not taught to be proud of our country in the post–WW II era. Of course, each country has a different his-

165

tory, political situation, so what I am saying here doesn't necessarily translate to other people in other cultures.

It may sound funny, but one thing I would say I am proud of about my country is that I don't have to say I am proud of my country. I am proud that I can see both beautiful and ugly sides of my country's history. I feel free there, for not being pressured by anyone to say that I am proud of my country.

In sum, people have various ways of thinking about nationality, and they sometimes confuse nationality and ethnicity. Thus, we have overheard students asking minority students, "What is your nationality?" when they actually meant, "What is your ethnicity?" This confusion can lead to—and perhaps reflects—a lack of understanding about differences between, say, Asian Americans (ethnic group) and Asians (nationality groups). It can also tend to alienate Asian Americans and others who have been in the United States for several generations but are still perceived as foreigners.

Regional Identity

Closely related to nationality is the notion of **regional identity.** Many regions of the world have separate, but vital and important, cultural identities. The Scottish Highlands is a region of northern Scotland that is distinctly different from the Lowlands, and regional identity remains strong in the Highlands.

Here in the United States, regional identities remain important, but perhaps less so as the nation moves toward homogeneity. Southerners, for example, often view themselves, and are viewed by others, as a distinct cultural group. Similarly, Texas advertises itself as "A Whole Other Country," promoting its regional identity. Although some regional identities can fuel national independence movements, they more often reflect cultural identities that affirm distinctive cuisines, dress, manners, and language. These identities may become important in intercultural communication situations. For example, suppose you meet someone who is Chinese. Whether the person is from Beijing, Hong Kong, or elsewhere in China may raise important communication issues. After all, Mandarin is not understood by Cantonese speakers, although both are dialects of the Chinese language. Indeed, there are many dialects in China, and they certainly are not understood by all other Chinese speakers.

One fairly recent variation in regional identities has to do with the degree of diversity within certain parts of the United States. Data from the 2000 census reveal that the South and the West are the most diverse, along with the coastal Northeast. The Midwest, in contrast, with a few exceptions, remains relatively homogenous (Brewer & Suchan, 2001, pp. 22–23). In addition, the overwhelming majority of multiracial individuals (67%) live in the South and the West (pp. 87–89). What are the implications for identity and intercultural communication? It could mean that people in these areas have more opportunities for understanding and practicing intercultural communication, and so benefit from the diversity. Or they may withdraw into their own groups and protect their racial and ethnic "borders."

Personal Identity

Many issues of identity are closely tied to our notions of self. Each of us has a **personal identity,** but it may not be unified or coherent. A dialectical perspective allow us to see identity in a more complex way. We are who we think we are; at the same time, however, contextual and external forces constrain and influence our self-perceptions. We have many identities, and these can conflict. For example, according to communication scholar Victoria Chen (1992), some Chinese American women feel caught between the traditional values of their parents' culture and their own desire to be Americanized. From the parents' point of view, the daughters are never Chinese enough. From the perspective of many people within the dominant culture, though, it is difficult to relate to these Chinese American women simply as "American women, born and reared in this society" (p. 231). The dialectical tension related to issues of identity for these women reveals the strain between feeling obligated to behave in traditional ways at home and yet holding a Western notion of gender equality. A dialectical perspective sees these contradictions as real and presenting challenges in communication and everyday life.

Our personal identities are important to us, and we try to communicate them to others. We are more or less successful depending on how others respond to us. We use the various ways that identity is constructed to portray ourselves as we want others to see us.

IDENTITY, STEREOTYPES, AND PREJUDICE

The identity characteristics described previously sometimes form the basis for stereotypes, prejudice, and racism. The origins of these have both individual and contextual elements. To make sense out of the overwhelming amount of information we receive, we necessarily categorize and generalize, sometimes relying on **stereotypes**—widely held beliefs about some group. Stereotypes help us know what to expect from others. They may be positive or negative. For example, Asian Americans have often been subjected to the positive "**model minority**" stereotype, which characterizes all Asians and Asian Americans as hardworking and serious. This stereotype became particularly prevalent in the United States during the civil rights movement of the 1960s and 1970s. At that time, Asian Americans were seen as the "good" minority—in contrast to African Americans, who were often confrontative and even militant in their fight for equality.

Even positive stereotypes can be damaging in that they create unrealistic expectations for individuals. Simply because someone is Asian American (or pretty, or smart) does not mean that he or she will excel in school or be outgoing and charming. Stereotypes become particularly detrimental when they are negative and are held rigidly. Research has shown that, once adopted, stereotypes are difficult to discard. In fact, people tend to remember information that

This essay describes how one group, a basketball team with several Native American players, resists an ascribed identity and a stereotype they feel is offensive.

> *Unable to persuade a local school to change a mascot name that offends them, a group of American Indian students at the University of Northern Colorado named their intramural basketball team "The Fighting Whities."*
>
> *The team chose a white man as its mascot to raise awareness of stereotypes that some cultures endure. "The message is, let's do something that will let people see the other side of what it's like to be a mascot" said Solomon Little Owl, a member of the team and director of Native American Student Services at the university.*
>
> *The team, made of American Indians, Hispanics and Anglos, wears jerseys that say "Every thang's going to be all white."*
>
> *The students are upset with Eaton High School for using an American Indian caricature on the team logo. The team is called the Reds.*
>
> *"It's not meat to be vicious, it is meant to be humorous," said Ray White, a Mohawk American Indian on the team. "It puts people in our shoes."*
>
> *Eaton School District superintendent John Nuspl said the school's logo is not derogatory and called the group's criticism insulting. "There's no mockery of Native Americans with this," he said.*

Source: From Associated Press, "Fighting Whities' Mock School's Indian Mascot," March 11, 2002, www.azcentral.com/news/articles/0311fightingwhities-ON.html.

---

supports a stereotype but may not retain information that contradicts it (Hamilton, Sherman, & Ruvolo, 1990).

We pick up stereotypes in many ways, including from the media. In TV shows and movies, older people often are portrayed as needing help, and Asian Americans, African Americans, or Latino/as rarely play leading, assertive roles. Communication scholar Bishetta D. Merritt (2000) analyzes portrayals of African American women on television shows and decries the lack of multidimensional roles. She identifies the kinds of roles that perpetuate stereotypes:

> *Portrayals that receive little or no attention today are the background characters that merely serve as scenery on television programs. These characters include the homeless person on the street, the hotel lobby prostitute, or the drug user making a buy from her dealer. They may not be named in the credits or have recurring roles, but their mere appearance can have an impact on the consciousness of the viewer and, as a result, an impact on the imagery of the African American women. (p. 52)*

We may learn stereotypes from our families and peers. One student described how she learned stereotyping and prejudice from her classmates:

One of my earliest experiences with a person ethnically diverse from me was when I was in kindergarten. A little girl in my class named Adelia was from Pakistan. I noticed that Adelia was a different color from me, but I didn't think it was a bad thing. I got along with her very well. We played the same games, watched the same cartoons, and enjoyed each other's company. Soon I discovered that my other friends didn't like Adelia as much as I did. They didn't want to hold hands with her, and they claimed that she was different from us. When I told them that Adelia was my friend, they didn't want to hold hands with me either. They started to poke fun at me and excluded me from their games. This hurt me so much that I stopped playing with Adelia, and I joined my friends in avoiding her. As a result, Adelia began to resent me and labeled me prejudiced.

Stereotypes can also develop out of negative experiences. If we have unpleasant encounters with people, we may generalize that unpleasantness to include all members of that group, whatever group characteristic we focus on (e.g., race, gender, or sexual orientation). This was demonstrated repeatedly after the attacks of September 11, 2001. Many people of Middle Eastern descent became victims of stereotyping, particularly when traveling. For example, one Arab American software developer from Dallas who was waiting for his flight home from Seattle to leave the gate was told by a flight attendent to take his belongings and get off the plane. Apparently, the pilot had been suspicious of his looks. He was questioned for more than an hour by authorities before being allowed to proceed.

Because stereotypes often operate at an unconscious level and so are persistent, people have to work consciously to reject them. First, they must recognize the stereotype, and then they must obtain information to counteract it. This is not easy because, as noted previously, we tend to "see" behavior that fits our stereotypes and to ignore that which doesn't. For example, if you think that most women are bad drivers, you will tend to notice when a female motorist makes a mistake but to ignore bad male driving. To undo this stereotype, you have to be very vigilant and do something that isn't "natural"—to be very conscious of how you "see" and categorize bad driving, and to note bad driving by both males and females.

Prejudice is a negative attitude toward a cultural group based on little or no experience. It is a prejudgment of sorts. Whereas stereotypes tell us what a group is like, prejudice tells us how we are likely to feel about that group (Newberg, 1994). Scholars disgree somewhat on the origins of prejudice and its relationship to stereotyping. Prejudice may arise from personal needs to feel positive about our own groups and negative about others, or it may arise from perceived or real threats (Hecht, 1998). Researchers Walter Stephan and Cookie Stephan (1996) have shown that tension between cultural groups and negative previous contact, along with status inequalities and perceived threats, can lead to prejudice.

Why do people hold prejudices? Psychologist Richard Brislin (1999) suggests that, just as stereotyping arises from normal cognitive functioning, holding prejudices may serve understandable functions. These functions may not excuse

I fell in love with a first-generation Mexican American. It took many arguments and lots of time before he was accepted into my family. Once everyone saw what an incredible person Gabe is, I think they favored him more than me. . . . He and I had been together for a year and a half and the time had come for me to meet his family. I was extremely nervous because his parents spoke only Spanish and I only spoke English. How was I going to communicate with my boyfriend's family? To my surprise, this was the least of my worries. When we were introduced, I thought his parents were going to faint. I am "white." I am not the same race as this family, and they resented my having a relationship with their son. I must be very naive, but I never thought prejudices would be directed toward me. This was quite an eye-opener for me. . . .

Unfortunately, Gabriel's sisters spoke English. They made quite a point to be rude and neglect me in every conversation they had. I felt terrible. Before I knew it, Gabe's sister, Amelia, pulled me into her room. She began explaining to me how I would never be part of their family. Because I was not of Hispanic descent, I was not worthy to be with her brother. She went on to tell me that her parents hated me. . . . This was really difficult for me to swallow. This family hated me because of something I have absolutely no control over, my race.

I sat there, not sure of what to say or do. I was so hurt and upset, I stood up and yelled. I told her that this is the problem with society. Why, when we have a chance to change what we hate, do we resist? How can we consciously continue doing these things? Basically, the same countless arguments I had with my parents, I had with Gabe's sister. Whatever happened in that room was the most rewarding experience. We continued discussing the problem. By the end of the conversation, we were such good friends. Shortly after that, Gabe's family felt like my family.

The slight taste of prejudice I felt has to be minimal compared to other people's experiences. I am thankful I was fortunate enough to have such an experience early in my life. I honestly have to admit, Amelia changed me for the better.

—Jennifer

prejudice, but they do help us understand why prejudice is so widespread. He identifies four such functions:

1. The utilitarian function. People hold certain prejudices because they can lead to rewards. For example, if your friends or family hold prejudices toward certain groups, it will be easier for you simply to share those attitudes, rather than risk rejection by contradicting their attitudes.

2. The ego-defensive function. People hold certain prejudices because they don't want to believe unpleasant things about themselves. For example, if either of us (Judith or Tom) is not a very good teacher, it will be useful

for us to hold negative stereotypes about students, such as that they are lazy and don't work hard. In this way, we can avoid confronting the real problem—our lack of teaching skills. The same kind of thing happens in the workplace: It is easier for people to stereotype women and minorities as unfit for jobs than to confront their own lack of skill or qualifications for a job.

3. The value-expressive function. People hold certain prejudices because they serve to reinforce aspects of life that are highly valued. Religious attitudes often function in this way. Some people are prejudiced against certain religious groups because they see themselves as holding beliefs in the one true God, and part of their doctrine is the belief that others are wrong. For instance, Judith's Mennonite family held prejudices against Catholics, who were viewed as misguided and wrong. This may also be operating today as some U.S. Americans search for validation of prejudices again Muslims. A more extreme example involves the atrocities committed against groups of people by others who want to retain the supposed values of a pure racial stock (e.g., "ethnic cleansing" by Serbs against Muslims in the former Yugoslavia).

4. The knowledge function. People hold certain prejudices because such attitudes allow them to organize and structure their world in a way that makes sense to them—in the same way that stereotypes help us organize our world. For example, if you believe that members of a certain group are flaky and irresponsible, then you don't have to think very much when meeting someone from that group in a work situation. You already know what they're like and so can react to them more automatically.

Prejudices can serve several of these functions over the life span. Thus, children may develop a certain prejudice to please their parents (utilitarian) and continue to hold the prejudice because it helps define who they are (value-expressive). Brislin (1999) points out that many remedial programs addressing the problem of prejudice fail because of a lack of recognition of the important functions that prejudice fill in our lives. Presenting people with factual information about groups addresses only one function (knowledge) and ignores the more complex reasons that we hold prejudices.

The behaviors that result from stereotyping or prejudice—overt actions to exclude, avoid, or distance—are called **discrimination.** Discrimination may be based on race (racism), gender (sexism), or any of the other identities discussed in this chapter. It may range from subtle nonverbal behavior such as lack of eye contact or exclusion from a conversation, to verbal insults and exclusion from jobs or other economic opportunities, to physical violence and systematic exclusion. Discrimination may be interpersonal, collective, or institutional. In recent years, interpersonal racism has become not only more subtle and indirect but also more persistent. Equally persistent is institutionalized or collective discrimination whereby individuals are systematically denied equal participation in society or equal access to rights in informal and formal ways (Maluso, 1995). Researcher John Lambeth (1998) has investigated the systematic discrimination against African Americans on the nation's highways. In several rigorous controlled studies in numerous states, he has shown that Blacks are much more likely to be stopped by police officers than are non-Blacks (e.g., 4.85 times as likely on the New Jersey Turnpike). This is in spite of evidence from the National Institute of Drug Abuse indicating that African Americans are no more likely than Whites to possess or traffic in drugs.

IDENTITY DEVELOPMENT ISSUES

Minority Identity Development

As mentioned previously, minority group members in the United States tend to develop a sense of racial and ethnic identity much earlier than majority group members. Whites tend to take their culture for granted; although they may develop a strong ethnic identity, they often do not really think about their racial identity (Ferguson, 1990). There probably is a hierarchy of salient identities that change over time and place.

Social psychologists have identified four stages in **minority identity** development. Although these stages center on racial and ethnic identities, they may also apply to other identities such as class, gender, or sexual orientation (Ponterotto & Pedersen, 1993). It is also important to remember that, as with any model, this one represents the experiences of many people, but it is not set in stone. That is, not everyone experiences these phases in exactly the same way. Some people spend more time in one phase than do others; individuals may experience the phases in different ways; and not everyone reaches the final phase.

Stage 1: Unexamined Identity   This stage is characterized by the lack of exploration of ethnicity. At this stage, ideas about identity may come from parents or friends. Minority group members may initially accept the values and attitudes of the majority culture, including negative views of their own group. They may have a strong desire to assimilate into the dominant culture, and they may express positive attitudes toward the dominant group. Or they may simply lack interest in the issue of ethnicity. As one woman in the African American community put it, "Why do I need to learn about who was the first black woman to do this or that? I'm just not too interested" (quoted in Phinney, 1993, p. 68).

Stage 2: Conformity   This stage is characterized by the internalization of the values and norms of the dominant group and a strong desire to assimilate into the dominant culture. Individuals in this phase may have negative, self-deprecating attitudes toward both themselves and their group. A Mexican American writer describes an experience in his youth:

> *I went to the beach quite often—always to the "white" beach at Santa Monica, staying away from the pier, where the Mexicans hung out. But after a long day in the sun I'd come home and notice my skin, which was no longer just brown, but verging on* chocolate. *I clearly remember one time standing in the shower with*

a bar of Irish Spring soap, scrubbing as hard as I could, raking nails across skin, hoping to soften the darkness. (Martinez, 1999, p. 257)

Individuals who criticize members of their own group may be given negative labels such as "Uncle Tom" or "oreo" for African Americans, "banana" for Asian Americans, "apple" for Native Americans, and "Tio Taco" for Chicanos. Such labels condemn attitudes and behaviors that support the dominant White culture. This stage often continues until they encounter a situation that causes them to question prodominant culture attitudes, which initiates the movement to the next stage—an ethnic identity search.

Stage 3: Resistance and Separatism   Many kinds of events can trigger the move to the third stage, including negative ones such as encountering discrimination or name-calling. A period of dissonance, or a growing awareness that not all dominant group values are beneficial to minorities, may also precede this stage. For writer Ruben Martinez (1998), a defining moment was when he was rather cruelly rejected by a White girl whom he had asked to dance at a high school prom:

I looked around me at the dance floor with new eyes: Mexicans danced with Mexicans, blacks with blacks, whites with whites. Who the hell did I think I was? Still, it would take a while for the gringo-hater in me to bust out. It was only a matter of time before I turned away from my whiteness and became the ethnic rebel. It seemed like it happened overnight, but it was the result of years of pent-up rage in me. (p. 256)

Sometimes the move to the next phase happens because individuals who have been denying their racial heritage meet someone from that racial group who exhibits strong cultural connections. This encounter may result in a concern to clarify the personal implications of their heritage. One member of an ethnic group explained the rationale behind attending ethnic fairs: "Going to festivals and cultural events helps me to learn more about my own culture and about myself" (quoted in Phinney, 1993, p. 71). Another person explained: "I think people should know what black people had to go through to get to where we are now" (p. 71).

This stage may be characterized by a blanket endorsement of one's group and all the values and attitudes attributed to the group. At the same time, the person may reject the values and norms associated with the dominant group.

Stage 4: Integration   According to this model, the ideal outcome of the identity development process is the final stage—an achieved identity. Individuals who have reached this stage have a strong sense of their own group identity (based on gender, race, ethnicity, sexual orientation, and so on) and an appreciation of other cultural groups. In this stage, they come to realize that racism and other forms of oppression occur, but they try to redirect any anger from the previous stage in more positive ways. The end result is individuals with a confident and secure identity characterized by a desire to eliminate all forms of injustice, and not merely oppression aimed at their own group.

This essay describes some of the controversy surrounding the increasing diversity in dolls.

> *One girl is black, the second white. But Allister Byrd and Samantha Arvin say the same thing when it comes to playing with dolls. They love them in any color—black, white, brown, you name it.*
>
> *Toy makers are taking note with new doll lines that are more diverse than ever, including the first multiracial Barbie, which was on display last week at the American International Toy Fair in New York. A Mattel spokeswoman says the new Barbie could be viewed as black, Asian and Hispanic—a "mix of cultures in one doll."*
>
> *. . . Some dolls of different races and ethnicities, including black Barbie, have been around for years, but industry experts say an increased demand and awareness of other cultures has spawned a new wave of diverse dolls.*
>
> *. . . At least one line, called the Ghetto Kids, was criticized by some parents and TV commentators because its packaging included hard-hitting doll "biographies" that mentioned parents who were drug addicts or who abandoned and even sold their children.*
>
> *Officials at Chicago-based Teddi's Toys, who created the dolls, have since removed some of the made-up doll background. But they're keeping the Ghetto Kids name as an attention grabber. They also hope information on their Website, including a cartoon series, will spur parents to talk to kids about such topics as smoking, guns, and teen-age pregnancy.*

Majority Identity Development

Rita Hardiman (1994), educator and pioneer in antiracism training, presents a model of **majority identity** development for members of the dominant group that has some similarities to the model for minority group members. She outlines five stages.

Stage 1: Unexamined Identity   The first stage is the same as for minority individuals. In this case, individuals may be aware of some physical and cultural differences, but they do not fear other racial or ethnic groups or feel a sense of superiority.

Stage 2: Acceptance   The second stage represents the internalization, conscious or unconscious, of a racist (or otherwise biased) ideology. This may involve passive or active acceptance. The key point is that individuals are not aware that they have been programmed to accept this worldview.

In the passive acceptance stage, individuals have no conscious identification with being White. However, some assumptions, based on an acceptance of inequities in the larger society, are subtly racist. Consider the following assumptions:

"It's real life, real time," says company founder Tommy Perez, who unveiled a Jewish Ghetto Kid at the New York toy fair. "It doesn't pull many punches."

Some parents say the race issue alone can be touchy, even if diversity among dolls is expanding.

Rob Whitehouse, a father from Akron, Ohio, says he's noticed the looks his fair-haired, fair-skinned 5 year old gets when she totes around her favorite companion, a black Addy doll. . . . "I just say, 'yeah, she loves it'" Whitehouse says. "It's best just to be very matter-of-fact about it."

Marguerite Wright, a clinical psychologist from Oakland, Calif., says that's a good way to handle it. But sometimes, she says, parents insist that their children play with dolls of a certain race, usually their own. "It's just a small step between forcing children to choose dolls according to skin color and forcing them to choose friends according to skin color," say Wright, who addresses the doll issue in her book "I'm Chocolate, You're Vanilla: Raising Healthy Black and Biracial Children in a Race-Conscious World."

Some parents say their children still don't have much choice in dolls because the selection remains overwhelmingly white. Phyllis Redus, who is black, says she often has a hard time finding anything but white dolls in her hometown of Huntsville, Ala. . . .

Source: From "Dolls Getting More Racially Diverse," *Pittsburgh Tribune-Review*, February 20, 2002, www.pittsburghlive.com/x/tribune-review/entertainment/s_18297.html.

- Minority groups are culturally deprived and need help to assimilate.
- Affirmative action is reverse discrimination because people of color are being given opportunities that Whites don't have.
- White culture—music, art, and literature—is "classical"; works of art by people of color are folk art or "crafts."
- People of color are culturally different, whereas Whites have no group identity or culture or shared experience of racial privilege.

Individuals in this stage usually take one of two positions with respect to racial issues and interactions with minorities: (1) They avoid contact with minority group members, or (2) they adopt a patronizing stance toward them. Both positions are possible at the same time.

In contrast, Whites in the active acceptance stage are conscious of their whiteness and may express their feelings of superiority collectively (e.g., join the White Student Union). Some people never move beyond this phase—whether it is characterized by passive or active acceptance. And if they do, it is usually a result of a number of cumulative events. For example, Judith gradually came to realize that her two nieces, who are sisters—one of whom is African American and one of whom is White—had very different experiences growing up. Both girls lived in middle-class neighborhoods, both were honor students in high school, and both went to Ivy League colleges. However, they often had very different experiences. On more than one occasion, the African American girl was followed by security while shopping; she also was stopped several times by police while driving her mother's sports car. Her White sister never had these experiences. Eventually, awareness of this reality prodded Judith to the next stage.

Stage 3: Resistance   The next stage represents a major paradigm shift. It involves a move from blaming minority members for their condition to naming and blaming their own dominant group as a source of racial or ethnic problems. This resistance may take the form of passive resistance, with little behavioral change, or active resistance—an ownership of racism. These individuals may feel embarrassed, try to distance themselves from other Whites, or gravitate toward people of color.

Stage 4: Redefinition   In the fourth stage, people begin to refocus or redirect their energy toward redefining whiteness in nonracist terms. They realize they don't have to accept the definition of White that society has instilled in them. They can move beyond the connection to racism to see positive aspects of being European American and to feel more comfortable being White. Hardiman (1994) states:

> *One of the greatest challenges in all this is to identify what White culture is. Because Whiteness is the norm in the United States society, it is difficult to see. Like fish, whose environment is water, we are surrounded by Whiteness and it is easy to think that what we experience is reality rather than recognizing it as the particular culture of a particular group. And like fish who are not aware of water until they are out of it, White people sometimes become aware of their culture only when they get to know, or interact with, the cultures of people of color. Difficult as this process is, it is necessary to "see the water" before it can be possible to identify ways in which the culture of Whites needs to be redefined beyond racism. (pp. 130–131)*

Stage 5: Integration   As in the final stage of minority identity development, majority group individuals now are able to integrate their whiteness into all other facets of their identity. They not only recognize their identity as White but also appreciate other groups. This integration affects other aspects of social and personal identity, including religion and gender.

Characteristics of Whiteness

What does it mean to be White in the United States? What are the characteristics of a White identity? Is there a unique set of characteristics that define whiteness, just as other racial identities have been described? The film *The Color of Fear*, produced in the early 1990s, addresses these issues by examining the real-life experiences of men from a variety of ethnic and racial backgrounds. Let's look at the dialogue between Victor, who is African American, and David, who is White.

Victor: What I hear from White people is, they talk about being human. They don't talk about themselves as White people. What I want to know is what it means to be White.

David: We don't look at ourselves as part of an ethnic group. I think that's what you're looking for and you're not going to find it.

Victor: Do you know that that means something? The fact that you have no answer to that?

It may be difficult for most White people to describe exactly what cultural patterns are uniquely White, but scholars have tried to do so. For example, scholar Ruth Frankenburg (1993) says that whiteness may be defined not only in terms of race or ethnicity but also as a set of linked dimensions. These dimensions include (1) normative race privilege, (2) a standpoint from which White people look at themselves, others, and society, and (3) a set of cultural practices (often unnoticed and unnamed).

Normative Race Privilege   Historically, Whites have been the normative (dominant) group in the United States and, as such, have benefited from privileges that go along with belonging to the dominant group. However, not all Whites have power, and not all have equal access to power. In fact, at times during U.S. history, some White communities were not privileged and were viewed as separate, or different, if not inferior. Examples include the Irish and Italians in the early 20th century and German Americans during World War II. And as scholars point out, the memory of marginality outlasts the marginality. For example, memories of discrimination may persist in the minds of some Italian Americans although little discrimination exists today. There also are many White people in the United States who are poor and so lack economic power.

There is an emerging perception that being White no longer means automatic privilege, particularly as demographics change in the United States and as some Whites perceive themselves to be in the minority. (See Figure 5-2.) This has led some Whites to feel threatened and "out of place." Charles A. Gallagher (1994), a sociologist, conducted a study in the early 1990s on what it means to be White in the United States today. He surveyed students at Temple University in Philadelphia, asking them how they felt about being White. He also asked the students to estimate the ratio of Whites to Blacks on campus. Many students reported that they thought the ratio was 30% White and 70% Black; that is, they perceived themselves to be in the minority. The actual ratio was 70% White and 30% Black. Students' perceptions affected their sense of identity, which, in turn, can affect intercultural communication.

Gallagher found that many of the students, mostly from working-class families, were very aware of their whiteness. Further, they believed that being White was a liability, that they were being prejudged as racist and blamed for social conditions they personally did not cause. They also claimed that they were denied opportunities that were unfairly given to minority students. One of our White students describes this feeling:

FIGURE 5-2(A)   White culture is difficult to define. White people do not often think of some of their activities as White cultural practices. Sunbathing, for example, is particularly important to some White people. These sunbathers at a resort in Cancun, Mexico, are using their tans to communicate messages to other members of White culture. What kinds of messages might their tans send? (© *Bill Bachmann/The Image Works*)

> *When I was trying to get into college I had to fight for every inch. I didn't have a lot of money to go to school with, so to get a scholarship was of great importance to me. So I went out and bought a book titled* The Big Book of Scholarships. *Ninety percent of the scholarships that this book contained didn't apply to me. They applied to the so-called minorities. . . . I think this country has gone on so long with the notion that white equals wealth or with things like affirmative action, that it has lost sight of the fact that this country is not that way any longer.*

In addition, due to corporate downsizing and the movement of jobs overseas in recent decades, increasing numbers of middle-age White men have not achieved the degree of economic or professional success they had anticipated.

FIGURE 5-2(B)   Not all cultural groups place a high value on suntans. In this photo, a Chinese man holds an umbrella to shield his wife from the sun as she takes a photo of her parents at Tiananmen Square. In this culture, darker skin, particularly on a woman, is seen as more negative than light skin. Gender and racial identities function together to place a low cultural value on suntanning. (© *Reuters/Getty Images*)

They sometimes blame their lack of success on immigrants who will work for less or on the increasing numbers of women and minorities in the workplace. In these cases, whiteness is not invisible; it is a salient feature of the White individuals' identities.

The point is not whether these perceptions are accurate. Rather, the point is that identities are negotiated and challenged through communication. People act on their perceptions, not on some external reality. As the nation becomes increasingly diverse and Whites no longer form a majority in some regions, there will be increasing challenges for all of us as we negotiate our cultural identities. There may be many Whites who feel like the students in Gallagher's study: threatened and outnumbered. How can Whites in the United States incorporate the reality of not belonging to a majority group? Will Whites find inclusive and productive ways to manage this identity change? Or will they react in defensive and exclusionary ways?

One reaction to feeling outnumbered and being a "new member" of an ethnic minority group is to strengthen one's own ethnic identity. For example, White people may tend to have stronger White identities in those U.S. states that have a higher percentage of non-Whites (e.g., Mississippi, South Carolina, Alabama). In these states, the White population traditionally has struggled to protect its racial privilege in various ways. As other states become increasingly

TABLE 5-2 VIEWPOINTS OF MIDDLE-CLASS BLACKS AND WHITES*		

Viewpoint	Percentage of Black respondents agreeing	Percentage of White respondents agreeing
"During the last ten years, tensions between racial and ethnic groups have decreased."	23%	30%
"African Americans have about the same opportunities as whites."	23	58
"African Americans are just about as well off as the average white person—in income."	15	38
"There is only a little or no discrimination against African Americans in our society today."	11	26

*Of the total number of respondents, 323 were Black and 779 were White.
Source: Based on a Washington Post/Kaiser Family Foundation/Harvard University survey, reported in *The Washington Post,* July 11, 2001, p. A1.

less White, we are beginning to see various moves to protect whiteness, as in California with a series of propositions (187, prohibiting undocumented workers from receiving public services; 209, making affirmative action programs illegal in public universities; and 227, banning bilingual education in public schools) and increasing concerns about immigration. Historically, California has enacted measures to ensure that Whites retained dominance in population, as well as in politics, economics, and so on. It is unclear what will happen in California and other states if, as predicted, Whites become a demographic minority group. How do you think that Whites will respond?

A Standpoint From Which to View Society   Opinion polls reveal significant differences in how Whites and Blacks view many issues. For example, according to polls, most African Americans doubted O. J. Simpson's guilt or had no faith in the legal system, whereas most Whites thought Simpson was guilty of murdering two people.

According to a 2001 survey, 34% of Whites, as compared with only 9% of Blacks, think we have overcome the major problems facing racial minorities in the United States (Morin, 2001). How can the perception of race relations be so different for Whites and Blacks? Something about being White and something about being African American influence how we view the world and, ultimately, how we communicate with others. Other results of the survey bear this out. (See Table 5-2.) The researchers concluded that,

> *whether out of hostility, indifference or simple lack of knowledge, large numbers of white Americans incorrectly believe that blacks are as well off as whites in terms*

POINT OF VIEW

These quotes demonstrate the extent to which Whites and Blacks view the world differently and have very different ideas about race relations in the United States. Two Whites offered the following views:

> *I just feel as though the white person is being blamed for everything that goes wrong with the African Americans. Nobody owes any of us anything. Let's get on with our lives and make the best of it. . . . Come on. Everything in the world can't be racial.*
> —Merle Barone, 64, retired department store clerk

> *The percentage of black people that are middle class and the percentage of white people that are middle class I would say are equal.*
> —Gloria Jane Smith, 46, nurse

Three African Americans offered these views:

> *Whites do not want to get it. The reason they don't acknowledge the problems is because then they would have to admit that the system is corrupt and that it's working for their benefit and then they would have to give up something they have and would have to share.*
> —Kolima David Williams, 39, chemist

> *You give an opportunity to a black kid in a corporation and he's supposed to hold his head down, but the manager's sons and daughters don't hold their heads down when they walk around the place. . . . Black kids, they're supposed to be saddened by the fact that they got their jobs because the government said so. What difference does it make if the government said so or if daddy said so?*
> —Ed Smith, director, Leaders for the 21st Century

> *I can't escape the thought that white America, which stopped short of embracing middle-class blacks at the moment we most wanted inclusion, may have already lost its opportunity. The refusal of the larger society to accept us, on our own terms, combined with our unwillingness to return to the ghetto, is likely to result in even more isolation, frustration, and desperation. And, worst of all, more anger.*
> —Sam Fulwood, III, 39, correspondent for the *Los Angeles Times*

Source: From "Across the Racial Divide," by R. Morin, *The Washington Post National Weekly Edition*, October 16–22, 1995, pp. 6–10.

of their jobs, incomes, schooling and health care. . . . These results defy conventional wisdom. They indicate that many whites do not broadly view blacks as particularly disadvantaged or beset by problems that demand immediate attention. Instead, these whites believe exactly the opposite—that African Americans already have achieved economic and social parity. (Morin, 2001, p. A1)

In another study, Frankenburg (1993) interviewed a number of White women, some of whom reported that they viewed being White as less than positive—as artificial, dominant, bland, homogeneous, and sterile. These respondents also saw White culture as less interesting and less rich than non-White culture. In contrast, other women viewed being White as positive, representing what was "civilized," as in classical music and fine art.

A Set of Cultural Practices   Is there a specific, unique "White" way of viewing the world? As noted previously, some views held consistently by Whites are not necessarily shared by other groups. And some cultural practices and core symbols (e.g., individualism) are expressed primarily by Whites and significantly less by members of minority groups. These cultural practices are most clearly visible to those who are not White, to those groups who are excluded (Helms, 1994). For example, in the fairy tale of Snow White, the celebration of her beauty—emphasizing her beautiful, pure white skin—is often seen as problematic by people who are not White.

Multiracial and Multicultural People

Multicultural people are those who grow up "on the borders" of two or more cultures. They often struggle to reconcile two very different sets of values, norms, and lifestyles. Some are multicultural as a result of being born to parents from different cultures or adopted into families that are racially different from their own family of origin. Others are multicultural because their parents lived overseas and they grew up in cultures different from their own, or because they spent extended time in another culture as an adult or married someone from another cultural background. Let's start with those who are born into biracial or multiracial families.

According to the most recent census, the United States has almost 7 million multiracial people—that is, people whose ancestry includes two or more races (Brewer & Suchan, 2001). (See Figure 5-3.) The 2000 census was the first one in which people were given the option of selecting several categories to indicate their racial identities. This rapidly growing segment of our population must be understood in its historical context. The United States has a long history of forbidding miscegenation (the mixing of two races). The law sought not to prevent *any* interracial marriage but to protect "whiteness"; interracial marriage between people of color was rarely prohibited or regulated (Root, 2001). Thus, in 1957, the state of Virginia ruled the marriage of Mildred Jeter (African American and Native American heritage) and Peter Loving (White) illegal. The couple fought to have their marriage legalized for almost 10 years. Finally, in 1967, the Supreme Court ruled in their favor, in *Loving v. Virginia*, overturning 200 years of antimiscegenation legislation.

The development of racial identity for the children of parents like the Lovings is a fluid process of complex transactions between the child and the broader social environment (Nance & Foeman, 2002). Whereas majority and minority identities seem to develop in a fairly linear fashion, biracial children may cycle through three stages: (1) awareness of differentness and resulting dissonance, (2) struggle for acceptance, and (3) self-acceptance and -assertion. And as they mature, they may experience the same three phases with greater intensity and awareness.

FIGURE 5-3   There are increasing numbers of multiracial individuals and families in the United States. For the first time, the 2000 census included the option of individuals marking multiple backgrounds, although many multiracial people still chose to mark one race only. Some multiracial people identify more strongly with one of their racial identities than the others, while other multiracial people try to balance their identification with multiple racial identities. (© *Tom Stewart Photography/Corbis*)

In the first stage, multiracial children realize that they are different from other children—they may feel that they don't fit in anywhere. Tiffany, whose mother is White and father is Black, describes her experience:

Growing up I had kids make fun of me because they said I did not know what color I was. That really hurt me as a kid because even at a young age, I started questioning my own race.

At the next stage, struggle for acceptance, multiracial adolescents may feel that they have to choose one race or the other—and indeed this was Tiffany's experience:

During my teenage years I still was a little confused about my race because I would only choose one side. When people asked me what color I was I would tell them I was black because I was embarrassed about being mixed. I was afraid of not being accepted by the black community if I said I was mixed. . . . I would go around telling people that I am black and would get mad if someone said I was white. I never thought about being mixed with both black and white.

After being torn between the two (or more) races, multiracial individuals may reach the third stage, of self-acceptance and self-assertion. Tiffany describes how this happened for her:

This essay describes some of the complexities and controversies surrounding the "new" multiracial category used for the first time in the 2000 census, illustrating how race is a dynamic notion that changes depending on individuals and context.

The 2000 Census marked a fundamental change in how we measure race in the United States. Rather than insist that every person in the country iden- tify with only one racial group, as have all previous U.S. censuses, it invited multiracial identification. . . . Yet the first census count of the multiracial pop- ulation will be far from definitive.

My reasons for believing this are both personal and professional. Consider the following reactions to my 3 year old daughter. When she and my wife were at a hospital in New Mexico, a white nurse asked if she spoke Spanish. While they waited in line at a grocery store in Ann Arbor, an African American bagger leaned over to my daughter and said, "I know you've got soul." As they made their way through O'Hare International Airport in Chicago, a white airline worker commented to my wife that our daughter "has a great tan."

The nurse in New Mexico saw a white woman with a bronze-skinned child and concluded that, like many people in the Southwest, our daughter was part Latino. In the predominantly black-and-white context of Michigan, the grocery store bagger interpreted these same cues as indicative of black heritage. By contrast, the white airline worker, who for historical reasons has probably had little personal experience with multiracial children, used the more salient frame of sun tanning to reconcile the incongruity between my wife and daughter's physical characteristics.

Now consider the results from a national survey of adolescents. When more than 10,000 middle and high school students were asked to report their race on separate school and home surveys, about 12 percent failed to provide consistent responses. Seven percent reported being multiracial on only one of the surveys and nearly 3 percent of the youth switched between single-race groups. Multiracial reports were almost twice as likely on the school survey,

I can recall a time when I had to spend Christmas with my mother's side of the family. This was the first time I met her side of the family and I felt myself being scared. Honestly, I have never been around a lot of white people, and when I was there I realized that I am mixed and this is who I am and I cannot hide it any- more. . . . From then on I claimed both sides.

And she goes on to demonstrate her self-acceptance and -assertion:

Being mixed is wonderful, and most importantly, being mixed taught me many things especially growing up. It taught me how to be strong, not to worry about what other people think and to just be myself. It also taught me not to like only one color and that all colors are beautiful. My race made me who I am today.

which was self-administered, as on the home survey, which was administered by an interviewer.

These examples illustrate that rather than being a fixed characteristic, one's race is constantly being negotiated. Race depends not just on ancestry—my wife identifies as white and I as black—but also on the verbal, physical and cultural cues we project to others, their interpretation of these cues and the setting in which this exchange occurs. . . . Although most people who answered the 2000 Census probably did not give the race question much thought, its new wording certainly caused some people to contemplate which response they should give for the racially mixed members of their household. . . .

So as the Census Bureau begins releasing its official count of multi-racial Americans, we should all be a little skeptical about the numbers. If the 2000 race question had specifically asked for all of the racial groups known to be in a person's background, the count of multiracials would be much larger. Alternatively, if it had asked for the race or races that others most often consider this person to be, then the count of multiracials would almost certainly be much smaller.

This is not to say that the limited space available on the census could have been used to capture all of the complexities of race. Rather, my point is that because race can and, from people like my daughters, does vary across observers and contexts, we must employ more sophisticated ways of measuring race if we hope to understand the multiracial population. More complex approaches will likely show that the size and characteristics of the multiracial population vary significantly from Census 2000 estimates. We should all keep this is mind before using the census count of multiracials to support statements about the social, political and legal consequences of race in contemporary American society.

Source: From "The Multiracial Count," by D. R. Harris, *The Washington Post*, March 24, 2001, p. A21

I am strong and I know my race. I no longer have to deny what my race is or who I am.

In addition to growing up in biracial or multiracial homes, individuals develop multicultural identities for other reasons. For example, **global nomads** grow up in many different cultural contexts because their parents moved around a lot (e.g., missionaries, international business employees, or military families). Children of foreign-born immigrants may also develop multicultural identities. Foreign-born immigrants in the United States represent one of the fastest-growing segments—almost a third of the current foreign-born population arrived in the United States since 1990. These include refugees from war zones like Kosovo and the Balkans, and migrants who come to the United States to escape dire economic conditions. They often struggle to negotiate their identities, torn between family expectations and their new American culture. Khoa, a first-generation Vietnamese American, describes how important his family's values are:

> *What does it mean to be "Asian" then? Being Asian is being proud of my heritage, my family, and the values that they have passed down to you. I am proud of my parents' discipline upon me. . . . I learned very early in life the differences between right and wrong. . . . I am proud that my parents taught me to respect my elders. I value the time I spend with my grandparents. I love the time I spend with my uncles and aunts, and my cousins. Having a deep love and honest respect for my family, both immediate and extended, is what being "Asian" means to me.*

Then he recounts the struggle to reconcile being both Vietnamese and American:

> *There are a few things, though, that my parents believe in that I do not agree with. I think it is important that you know where you came from and to have pride in your nationality. However, I do not think that just because I am Vietnamese I am obligated to marry a Vietnamese girl. A Vietnamese girl is not any better or worse than any other girl of another nationality.*

Like Khoa, multicultural adolescents often feel pulled in different directions as they develop their own identities.

A final category of multicultural people includes those who have intense intercultural experiences as adults—for example, people who maintain long-term romantic relationships with members of another ethnic or racial group or who spend extensive time living in other cultures. All multicultural people may feel as if they live in cultural margins, struggling with two sets of cultural realities: not completely part of the dominant culture but not an outsider, either.

Social psychologist Peter Adler (1974) describes the multicultural person as someone who comes to grips with a multiplicity of realities. This individual's identity is not defined by a sense of belonging; rather, it is a new psychocultural form of consciousness. Milton Bennett (1993) describes how individuals can develop an "ethnorelative" perspective based on their attitudes toward cultural difference. The first, and most ethnocentric, stage involves the denial or ignoring of difference. The next stage occurs when people recognize difference but attach negative meaning to it. A third stage occurs when people minimize the effects of difference—for example, with statements like "We're really all the same under the skin" and "After all, we're all God's children." Bennett recognizes that minority and majority individuals may experience these phases differently. In addition, minority individuals usually skip the first phase. They don't have the option to deny difference; they are often reminded by others that they are different.

The remainder of the stages represent a major shift in thinking—a paradigm shift—because positive meanings are associated with difference. In the fourth phase (acceptance), people accept the notion of cultural difference; in the fifth phase (adaptation), they may change their own behavior to adapt to others. The final phase (integration) is similar to Peter Adler's (1974) notion of a "multi-cultural person."

According to Adler, multicultural individuals may become **culture bro-kers**—people who facilitate cross-cultural interaction and reduce conflict. And, indeed, there are many challenges and opportunities today for multicultural people, who can reach a level of insight and cultural functioning not experienced by others. One of our students, who is Dutch (ethnicity) and Mexican (national-ity), describes this:

> *Being the make-up I am to me means I come from two extremely proud cultures. The Dutch in me gives me a sense of tradition and loyalty. The Mexican side gives me a rich sense of family as well as closeness with not only my immediate family, with my aunts, uncles, and cousins as well. My unique mix makes me very proud of my identity. To me it means that I am proof that two parts of the world can unite in a world that still believes otherwise.*

However, Adler (1974) also identifies potential stresses and tensions associ-ated with multicultural individuals:

They may confuse the profound with the insignificant, not sure what is really important.

They may feel multiphrenic, fragmented.

They may suffer a loss of their own authenticity and feel reduced to a vari-ety of roles.

They may retreat into existential absurdity. (p. 35)

Communication scholar Janet Bennett (1993) provides insight into how being multicultural can be at once rewarding *and* challenging. She describes two types of multicultural individuals: (1) *encapsulated marginals*, who become trapped by their own marginality, and (2) *constructive marginals*, who thrive in their marginality.

Encapsulated marginals have difficulty making decisions, are troubled by ambiguity, and feel pressure from both groups. They try to assimilate but never feel comfortable, never feel "at home." In contrast, constructive marginal people thrive in their marginal existence and, *at the same time*, recognize the tremendous challenges. They see themselves (rather than others) as choice makers. They rec-ognize the significance of being "in between," and they are able to make com-mitments within the relativistic framework. Even so, this identity is constantly being negotiated and explored; it is never easy, given society's penchant for su-perficial categories. Writer Ruben Martinez (1998) describes the experience of a constructive marginal:

> *And so I can celebrate what I feel to be my cultural success. I've taken the far-flung pieces of myself and fashioned an identity beyond that ridiculous, fraying old border between the United States and Mexico. But my "success" is still marked by anxiety, a white noise that disturbs whatever raceless utopia I might imagine. I feel an uneasy tension between all the colors, hating and loving them all, perceiv-ing and speaking from one and many perspectives simultaneously. The key word*

here is "tension": nothing, as yet, has been resolved. My body is both real and un-
real, its color both confining and liberating. (p. 260)

IDENTITY AND LANGUAGE

The labels that refer to particular identities are an important part of intercultural communication. These labels do not, of course, exist outside of their relational meanings. It is the relationships—not only interpersonal but social—that help us understand the importance of the labels.

Communication scholar Dolores Tanno (2000) describes her own multiple identities reflected in the various labels applied to her. For instance, the label "Spanish" was applied by her family and designates an ancestral origin in Spain. The label "Mexican American" reflects two important cultures that contribute to her identity. "Latina" reflects cultural and historical connectedness with others of Spanish descent (e.g., Puerto Ricans and South Americans), and "Chicana" promotes political and cultural assertiveness in representing her identity. She stresses that she is all of these, that each one reveals a different facet of her identity: symbolic, historical, cultural, and political.

In emphasizing the fluidity and relational nature of labels, communication scholar Stuart Hall (1985) notes that,

> *at different times in my thirty years in England, I have been "hailed" or interpel-*
> *lated as "coloured," "West-Indian," "Negro," "black," "immigrant." Sometimes*
> *in the street; sometimes at street corners; sometimes abusively; sometimes in a*
> *friendly manner; sometimes ambiguously. (p. 108)*

Hall underscores the dynamic and dialectic nature of identity and the self as he continues:

> *In fact I "am" not one or another of these ways of representing me, though I have*
> *been all of them at different times and still am some of them to some degree. But,*
> *there is no essential, unitary "I"—only the fragmentary, contradictory subject*
> *I become. (pp. 108–109)*

These and other labels construct relational meanings in communication situations. The interpersonal relationships between Hall and the other speakers are important, but equally important are such labels' social meanings.

IDENTITY AND COMMUNICATION

Identity has a profound influence on intercultural communication processes. We can employ some of the dialectics identified in earlier chapters to illuminate this relationship. First, we can use the individual–cultural dynamic to examine the issues that arise when we encounter people whose identities we don't know. In intercultural communication interactions, mistaken identities are often exacerbated and can create communication problems.

Sometimes we assume knowledge about another person's identity based on his or her membership in a particular cultural group. When we do so, we are ignoring the individual aspect. Taking a dialectical perspective can help us recognize and balance both the individual and the cultural aspects of another's identity. This perspective can guide the ways that we communicate with that person (and conceivably with others). "The question here is one of identity: Who am I perceived to be when I communicate with others? . . . My identity is very much tied to the ways in which others speak to me and the ways in which society represents my interests" (Nakayama, 2000, p. 14).

Think about the assumptions you might make about others based on their physical appearance. What do you "know" about people if you know only that they are from, say, the South, or Australia, or Pakistan? Perhaps it is easier to think about the times that people have made erroneous assumptions about you based on limited information—assumptions that you became aware of in the process of communication. Focusing solely on someone's nationality, place of origin, education, religion, and the like can lead to mistaken conclusions about the person's identity.

Now let's turn to the static–dynamic dialectic. The problem of erroneous assumptions has increased during the information age, due to the torrent of information about the world and the dynamic nature of the world in which we live. We are bombarded daily with information from around the globe about places and people. This glut of information and intercultural contacts has heightened the importance of developing a more complex view of identity.

Given the many identities that we all negotiate for ourselves in our everyday interactions, it becomes clear how our identities and those of others make intercultural communication problematic. We need to think of these identities as both static and dynamic. We live in an era of information overload, and the wide array of communication media only serve to increase the identities we must negotiate. Consider the relationships that develop via e-mail, for example. Some people even create new identities as a result of online interactions. We change who we are depending on the people we communicate with and the manner of our communication. Yet we also expect some static characteristics from the people with whom we communicate. We expect others to express certain fixed qualities; these help account for why we tend to like or dislike them and how we can establish particular communication patterns with them. The tensions that we feel as we change identities from e-mail to telephone to mail to fax and other communication media demonstrate the dynamic and static characters of identities.

Finally, we can focus on the personal–contextual dialectic of identity and communication. Although some dimensions of our identities are personal and remain fairly consistent, we cannot overlook the contextual constraints on our identity.

SUMMARY

In this chapter, we explored some of the facets of identity and the ways in which identities can be problematic in intercultural communication. We used several dialectics to frame our discussion. Identities are both static (as described by social psychologists) and dynamic (as described by communication and critical scholars). They are created by the self and by others in relation to group membership. They may be created for us by existing contexts and structures. When these created identities are incongruent with our sense of our own identity, we need to challenge and renegotiate them.

Identities are multiple and reflect gender, ethnicity, sexual orientation, race, religion, class, nationality, and other aspects of our lives. Identities also develop in relation to minority and majority group membership. The development of such identities may follow several stages for individuals of either group.

Identity is expressed through language and labels. Keeping in mind the many dynamics in people's lives can help minimize faulty assumptions about their identities. It is important to remind ourselves that identities are complex and subject to negotiation.

DISCUSSION QUESTIONS

1. How do our perceptions of our own cultural identity influence our communication with others?

2. What are some ways in which we express our identities?

3. How does being White affects one's experience in the United States?

4. What are the roles of avowal and ascription in the process of identity formation?

5. What are some of the ways in which members of minority cultures and members of majority cultures develop their cultural identities?

 Go to the self-quizzes on the Online Learning Center at www.mhhe.com/martinnakayama to further test your knowledge.

ACTIVITIES

1. *Stereotypes in Your Life.* List some of the stereotypes you have heard about U.S. Americans. Then answer the following questions:

   a. How do you think these stereotypes developed?
   b. How do they influence communication between U.S. Americans and people from other countries?

2. *Stereotypes in Prime-Time TV.* Watch four hours of television during the next week, preferably during evening hours when there are more commercials. Record the number of representatives of different identity groups (ethnic, racial, gender, age, class, and so on) that appear in the commercials; also record the role that each person plays. Answer the following questions:

   a. How many different groups were represented?
   b. What groups were most represented? Why do you think this is so?
   c. What groups were least represented? Why do you think this is so?

d. What differences (if any) were there in the roles that members of the various groups played? Did one group play more sophisticated or more glamorous roles than others?

e. In how many cases were people depicted in stereotypical roles—for example, African Americans as athletes, or women as homemakers?

f. What stereotypes were reinforced in the commercials?

g. What do your findings suggest about the power of the media and their effect on identity formation and intercultural communication? (Think about avowal, ascription, and interpellation.)

KEY WORDS

age identity	gender identity	national identity
ascription	global nomads	personal identity
avowal	hyphenated Americans	prejudice
class identity	identity	racial identity
core symbols	individualized identity	regional identity
culture brokers	interpellation	religious identity
discrimination	majority identity	spiritual identity
ethnic identity	minority identity	stereotypes
familial identity	model minority	

The Online Learning Center at www.mhhe.com/martinnakayama features flashcards and crossword puzzles based on these terms and concepts.

REFERENCES

Adler, P. (1974). Beyond cultural identity: Reflections on cultural and multicultural man. *Topics in Culture Learning,* (Vol. 2, pp. 23–40). Honolulu: East-West Center.

Alba, R. D. (1985). The twilight of ethnicity among Americans of European ancestry: The case of Italians. *Ethnic and Racial Studies, 8,* 134–158.

———. (1990). *Ethnic identity: The transformation of white America.* New Haven, CT: Yale University Press.

Althusser, L. (1971). Ideology and ideological state apparatuses (notes towards an investigation). In B. Brewster (Trans.), *Lenin and philosophy and other essays* (pp. 134–165). London: NLB.

Bederman, G. (1995). *Manliness and civilization: A cultural history of gender and race in the United States, 1880–1917.* Chicago: University of Chicago Press.

Bennett, J. M. (1993). Cultural marginality: Identity issues in intercultural training. In R. M. Paige (Ed.), *Education for the intercultural experience* (pp. 109–136). Yarmouth, ME: Intercultural Press.

Bennett, M. J. (1993). Towards ethnorelativism: A developmental model of intercultural sensitivity. In R. M. Paige (Ed.), *Education for the intercultural experience* (pp. 21–72). Yarmouth, ME: Intercultural Press.

Bourdieu, P. (1987). *Distinction: A social critique of the judgment of taste* (R. Nice, Trans.). Cambridge, MA: Harvard University Press.

Brewer, C. A., & Suchan, T. A. (2001). *Mapping Census 2000: The geography of U.S. diversity* (U.S. Census Bureau, Census Special Reports, Series CENSR/01-1). Washington, DC: U.S. Government Printing Office.

Brislin, R. (1999). *Understanding culture's influence on behavior* (2nd ed.). Belmont, CA: Wadsworth.

Carbaugh, D. (1989). *Talking American: Cultural discourse on* Donahue. Norwood, NJ: Ablex.

Chen, V. (1992). The construction of Chinese American women's identity. In L. F. Rakow (Ed.), *Women making meaning* (pp. 225–243). New York: Routledge.

Collier, M. J., & Thomas, M. (1988). Cultural identity: An interpretive perspective. In Y. Y. Kim & W. B. Gudykunst (Eds.), *Theories in intercultural communication* (pp. 99–122). Newbury Park, CA: Sage.

Cornell, S., & Hartmann, D. (1998). *Ethnicity and race: Making identities in a changing world.* Thousand Oaks, CA: Pine Forge Press.

Cross, S. E. (2000). What does it mean to "know thyself" in the United States and Japan?: The cultural construction of the self. In T. J. Owens (Ed.), *Self and identity through the life course in cross-cultural perspective* (pp. 159–180). Stamford, CT: JAI Press.

Erikson, E. (1950). *Childhood and society.* New York: Norton.

———. (1968). *Identity: Youth and crisis.* New York: Norton.

Feghali, E. (1997). Arab cultural communication patterns. *International Journal of Intercultural Relations, 21,* 345–378.

Ferguson, R. (1990). Introduction: Invisible center. In R. Ferguson, M. Gever, T. M. Trinh, & C. West (Eds.), *Out there: Marginalization and contemporary cultures* (pp. 9–14). New York and Cambridge: New Museum of Contemporary Art/MIT Press.

Frankenburg, R. (1993). *White women, race matters: The social construction of whiteness.* Minneapolis: University of Minnesota Press.

Fussell, P. (1992). *Class: A guide through the American status system.* New York: Touchstone Books. (Original work published 1979)

Gallager, C. A. (1994). White construction in the university. *Socialist Review, 1/2,* 167–187.

Gao, G. (1996). Self and other: A Chinese perspective on interpersonal relationships. In W. G. Gudykunst, S. Ting-Toomey, & T. Nishida (Eds.), *Communication in personal relationships across cultures* (pp. 81–101). Thousand Oaks, CA: Sage.

Hall, S. (1985). Signification, representation, ideology: Althusser and the poststructuralist debates. *Critical Studies in Mass Communication, 2,* 91–114.

Hamilton, D. L., Sherman, S. J., & Ruvolo, C. M. (1990). Stereotype-based expectancies: Effects on information processing and social behavior. *Journal of Social Issues, 46,* 35–60.

Hardiman, R. (1994). White racial identity development in the United States. In E. P. Salett & D. R. Koslow (Eds.), *Race, ethnicity and self: Identity in multicultural perspective* (pp. 117–142). Washington, DC: National MultiCultural Institute.

Hasian, M., Jr., & Nakayama, T. K. (1999). Racial fictions and cultural identity. In J. Sloop & J. McDaniels (Eds.), *Treading judgment.* Boulder, CO: Westview Press.

Hecht, M. L. (1998). Introduction. In M. L. Hecht (Ed.), *Communicating prejudice* (pp. 3–23). Thousand Oaks, CA: Sage.

Hecht, M. L., Collier, M. J., & Ribeau, S. A. (1993). *African American communication: Ethnic identity and cultural interpretation.* Newbury Park, CA: Sage.

Helms, J. (1994). *A race is a nice thing to have: A guide to being a white person.* Topeka, KS: Content Communication.

Katz, J. (1995). *The invention of heterosexuality.* New York: Dutton.

Lacan, J. (1977). The agency of the letter in the unconscious or reason since Freud. In A. Sheridan (Trans.), *Écrits: A selection* (pp. 146–178). New York: Norton. (Original work published 1957)

Lambeth, J. (1998, August 24). DWB is not a crime: The numbers show that police unfairly and unconstitutionally pull over more cars driven by Blacks. *The Washington Post National Weekly Edition,* p. 23.

Lanston, D. (1995). Tired of playing monopoly? In M. L. Andersen & P. H. Collins (Eds.), *Race, class, and gender: An anthology* (2nd ed., pp. 100–110). Belmont, CA: Wadsworth.

Maluso, D. (1995). Shaking hands with a clenched fist: Interpersonal racism. In B. Lott & D. Maluso (Eds.), *The social psychology of interpersonal discrimination* (pp. 50–79). New York: Guilford.

Martinez, R. (1998). Technicolor. In C. C. O'Hearn (Ed.) *Half and half: Writers on growing up biracial + bicultural* (pp. 245–264). New York: Pantheon Books.

Merritt, B. D. (2000). Illusive reflections: African American women on primetime television. In A. Gonzalez, M. Houston, & V. Chen (Eds.), *Our voices: Essays in culture, ethnicity and communication* (3rd ed., pp. 47–53). Los Angeles: Roxbury.

Moon, D. G., & Rolison, G. L. (1998). Communication of classism. In M. L. Hecht (Ed.), *Communicating prejudice* (pp. 122–135). Thousand Oaks, CA: Sage.

Morin, R. (1995, October 16–22). Across the racial divide. *The Washington Post National Weekly Edition*, pp. 6–10.

———. (2001, July 11). Misperceptions cloud Whites' view of Blacks. *The Washington Post*, p. A01.

Nakayama, T. K. (2000). Dis/orienting identities: Asian Americans, history, and intercultural communication. In A. González, M. Houston, & V. Chen (Eds.), *Our voices: Essays in ethnicity, culture, and communication* (3rd ed., pp. 13–20). Los Angeles: Roxbury.

Nance, T. A., & Foeman, A. K. (2002). On being biracial in the United States. In J. N. Martin, T. K. Nakayama, & L. A. Flores (Eds.), *Readings in intercultural communication: Experiences and contexts* (pp. 53–62). Boston: McGraw-Hill.

Newberg, S. L. (1994). Expectancy-confirmation processes in stereotype-tinged social encounters: The moderation of social goals. In M. P. Zanna & J. M. Olson (Eds.), *Ontario symposium on personality and social psychology: Vol 7. The psychology of prejudice* (pp. 103–130). Hillsdale, NJ: Lawrence Erlbaum.

Omi, M., & Winant, H. (1998). Racial formation. In P. S. Rothenberg (Ed.), *Race, class and gender in the United States* (pp. 26–35). New York: St. Martin's Press.

Phinney, J. S. (1993). A three-stage model of ethnic identity development in adolescence. In M. E. Bernal & G. Knight (Eds.), *Ethnic identity* (pp. 61–79). Albany: State University of New York Press.

Ponterotto, J. G., & Pedersen, P. B. (1993). *Preventing prejudice* (Chaps. 4 & 5). Newbury Park, CA: Sage.

Roland, A. (1988). *In search of self in India and Japan: Towards a cross-cultural psychology.* Princeton, NJ: Princeton University Press.

Root, M. P. P. (2001). *Love's revolution: Interracial marriage.* Philadelphia: Temple University Press.

Sax, L. J., Lindholm, J. A., Astin, A. W., Korn, W. S., & Mahoney, K. M. (2001). *The American freshman: National norms for fall 2001.* Los Angeles: UCLA Graduate School of Education and Information Studies.

Stephan, W., & Stephan, C. (1996). Predicting prejudice: The role of threat. *International Journal of Intercultural Relations, 20,* 409–426.

Tajfel, H. (1978). Social categorization, social identity and social comparison. In H. Tajfel (Ed.), *Differentiation between social groups* (pp. 61–76). London: Academic Press.

———. (1981). *Human categories and social groups.* Cambridge: Cambridge University Press.

———. (1982). *Social identity and intergroup relations.* Cambridge: Cambridge University Press.

Tannen, D. (1990). *You just don't understand: Women and men in conversation.* New York: Morrow.

Tanno, D. (2000). Names, narratives, and the evolution of ethnic identity. In A. González, M. Houston, & V. Chen (Eds.), *Our voices: Essays in ethnicity, culture, and communication* (3rd ed., pp. 25–28). Los Angeles: Roxbury.

Trinh, T. M. (1986/1987). Difference: A special third world women issue. *Discourse*, 8.

Wamba, P. (1998). A middle passage. In C. C. O'Hearn (Ed.), *Half and half: Writers on growing up biracial + bicultural* (pp. 150–169). New York: Pantheon Books.

U.S. Bureau of the Census. 'Share of aggregate income received by each fifth and top 5 percent of households (all races) 1967–1998.' Accessed November 18, 1999. www.census.gov/hhes/income/histinc/h02.html.

Wood, J. T. (1994). *Gendered lives: Communication, gender, and culture*. Belmont, CA: Wadsworth.

Yamanouchi, K. (2002, May 19). Cosmetic companies market products aimed at men, *Arizona Republic*, p. D1.

LANGUAGE AND INTERCULTURAL COMMUNICATION

As this book shows, intercultural communication involves far more than merely language, but language clearly cannot be overlooked as a central element in the process. This chapter focuses on the verbal aspects of intercultural communication; the next chapter focuses on the nonverbal elements.

The social science approach generally focuses on language and its relation to intercultural communication; the interpretive approach focuses on contextual uses of linguistic codes; and the critical approach emphasizes the relations between discourse and power. This chapter uses a dialectical perspective to explore how language works dynamically in intercultural contexts. With the personal–contextual dialectic, we can consider not only how language use operates on an individual level but also how it is influenced by context. We also use the static–dynamic dialectic to distinguish between language and discourse, to identify the components of language, and to explore the relationship between language, meaning, and perception. Although it may seem that the components of language are static, the *use* of language is a dynamic process.

In this chapter, we also explore cultural variations of language. Then we discuss the relationship between language and power, and between language and identity, and examine issues of multilingualism, translation, and interpretation. Finally, we look at language policies and politics.

THE STUDY OF LANGUAGE: THINKING DIALECTICALLY

Language Versus Discourse

French theorists who laid the early foundations for the structural study of language distinguished what they called *la langue* and *la parole. La langue* refers to the entire system of **language**—its theoretical conceptualization. For example, when we consider what is English, should we include the various forms of English spoken around the world—for example, in South Africa, Ireland, Zimbabwe, Australia, New Zealand, Singapore, Hong Kong, Nigeria, and Kenya? Do we include the different kinds of English that have been spoken in the past, such as Old English and Middle English? How about the various forms of **pidgin** or **creole?** As you can see, thinking about English is very complex indeed.

In contrast, *la parole* refers to language in use, or **discourse.** We think about discourse by focusing on how language is actually used by particular communities of people, in particular contexts, for particular purposes. Because there are so many different ways of expressing a given idea, the selection of one approach over another is critical to the study of communication. To illustrate, think about the discourse that you typically use to communicate with your parents. How does it differ from the discourse you use with your friends? How does your discourse change when you speak at a wedding or a funeral? Note that the changing communities and contexts influence the discourse that you use. What other communities and contexts can you identify that might invoke particular discursive patterns?

Sometimes specific words and phrases are embedded with a specific history that listeners may find problematic. Consider expressions like "I'm not your slave," "Boy, this job is like slave labor," and "My professor is a nazi." The experience of slavery or the Holocaust—or other horrific historical events—is not always taken so metaphorically.

The Components of Language

Linguistics is just one of many ways to think about language. Linguists generally divide up the study of language into four parts: semantics, syntactics, pragmatics, and phonetics. Each part highlights a different aspect of the way language works.

Semantics   **Semantics** is the study of meaning—that is, how words communicate the meanings we intend in our communication. The emphasis in semantics is on the generation of meaning, focusing on a single word. For example, think about a chair. Do we define *chair* by its shape? Does a throne count as a chair? Do we define it by its function? If we sit on a table, does that make it a chair?

Syntactics   **Syntactics** is the study of the structure, or grammar, of a language— the rules for combining words into meaningful sentences. One way to think of syntactics is to consider how the order of the words in a sentence creates a particular meaning. For example, the word order in "The red car smashed into the blue car" makes a big difference in the meaning of the sentence. "The blue car smashed into the red car" means something else entirely.

In French, there is a difference between *Qu'est-ce que c'est?* and *Qu'est-ce que c'est que ça?* and *C'est quoi, ça?* Although all three questions mean "What is that?" they each emphasize something different. (Most accurately translated, they mean "What's that?" "What's *that?*" and "That is *what?*") This illustrates that in French meaning often depends more on syntax than on the emphasis of single words in a sentence; this is often the case for English as well.

Pragmatics   **Pragmatics** is the study of how meaning is constructed in relation to receivers, how language is actually used in particular contexts in language communities. For example, if someone says, "That's a cool outfit," you might interpret it variously depending upon the intonation, your relationship with the speaker, the locale, and so on. The person might be mocking the outfit, or flirting with you, or simply giving a compliment. The meaning does not come from the words or the word order alone.

Phonetics   **Phonetics** is the study of the sound system of language—how words are pronounced, which units of sounds (phonemes) are meaningful for a specific language, and which sounds are universal. Because different languages use different sounds, it is often difficult for non-native speakers to learn how to pronounce some sounds.

There have been a few different times when an accent has affected my perception of a person. Usually, when the person with the accent is a male, I find it to be attractive. This may seem funny, but I think a lot of people feel this way. At first, I want to ask a whole bunch of questions: where the person is from, what it's like there, and so on. Then I realize I may be sticking my nose where it doesn't belong. So then I try to back down and not be so forward.
  —Lyssa

French, for example, has no equivalent for the voiced "th" sound (as in *mother*) or the unvoiced "th" sound (as in *think*) in English. French speakers often substitute similar sounds to pronounce English words containing "th." In contrast, English speakers often have a difficult time pronouncing the French "r" (as in *la fourrure*), which is produced further back in the mouth than in English.

The Japanese language has a sound that is between the English "r" and "l." This makes it difficult for Japanese speakers to pronounce some English words, especially those in which the "r" and "l" sounds are both used—for example, the word *gorilla*. It also is difficult for English speakers to pronounce Japanese words that contain the "r/l" sound—for example, *ramen* and *karaoke*.

The **International Phonetic Alphabet (IPA)** helps linguists transcribe the pronunciation of words in different languages. The IPA was developed in 1889 by linguists who realized that it was impossible to transcribe unfamiliar languages without a common notation system. It is based primarily on the Latin alphabet but has been modified over the years to accommodate sounds that weren't easily represented by the Latin alphabet. Most languages have from 15 to 50 meaningful sound units, but the total number of all sound units for all languages is in the hundreds (West, 1975). (See Figure 6-1.)

Language and Meaning

Universal Dimensions of Meaning Intercultural communication scholars are interested in many issues concerning the universality of language. They may look for aspects of structure or meaning that are the same in all languages. They may explore the rules of speaking and using language. The study of comparative linguistics helps us see the diversity of communication systems.

Intercultural communication scholars are also concerned with the role of **translation** and **interpretation**—that is, how people understand each other when they speak different languages. Because we cannot learn every language in the world, spoken now or in the past, we often rely on translators and interpreters to help us span linguistic gaps. What are the parameters of this mode of communication? How do we understand how this communication process works?

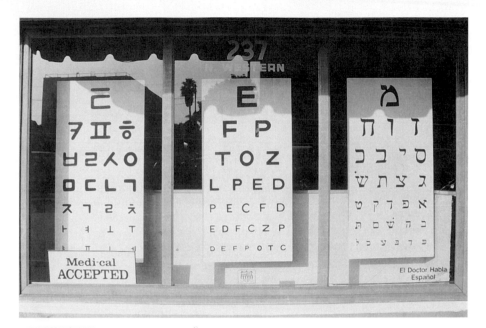

FIGURE 6-1 Language is an important aspect of intercultural communication. The particular symbols used in any language are arbitrary and have no meaning in and of themselves, as these multilanguage optometrist charts illustrate. Language symbols communicate meaning only when used in particular contexts. (© *Bill Aron/Getty Images*)

Finally, scholars are concerned with the power of language and the ways in which discourse may be used to oppress or hurt individuals or groups of people. Language is based on a system of differences. *Cat* and *hat*, for example, sound different, and it is precisely this difference that communicates the meaning. Many differences are arbitrary or cultural. For example, when you learned the mnemonic device "ROY G BIV" to remember the colors of the rainbow (*R*ed, *Or*ange, *Y*ellow, *G*reen, *B*lue, *I*ndigo, *V*iolet), were you aware that different languages classify colors in different ways? The system of difference in any language influences how we perceive and classify the entire world, including peoples and cultures. In short, language becomes a way of regulating societies through how we view the world.

Charles Osgood (1975), a noted psychologist, spent many years investigating the cross-cultural universals of meanings. He found that there are similar dimensions of meaning in many language groups; people everywhere can reflect on a word and characterize meaning for that word according to its value, potency, and activity. On the basis of these three dimensions, Osgood developed the **semantic differential**—a way of measuring attitudes or affective meaning.

For example, we can measure the **evaluative dimension** of meaning for the word *abortion*. (In other words, we can determine whether the word has a good or bad meaning for us.) We can also identify the **potency dimension** of the word—whether it evokes a strong or weak reaction. Finally, we can determine the activity associations. The **activity dimension** of *abortion*, for example, might be "fast" or "slow." For women who have experienced abortion, it may seem a long, drawn-out experience.

These dimensions are probably related to core perceptions and survival reactions; confronting unknown stimuli triggers these dimensions of meaning. The most powerful is the evaluative dimension; it is important to find out if something is good or bad. But we also need to know if it is strong or weak, fast or slow.

Cross-Cultural Comparisons of Meaning   It is useful to understand these dimensions in making cross-cultural comparisons. For example, people in the United States tend to have a negative evaluation of Monday, the first day of the workweek, and a positive evaluation of Friday. In contrast, many Arabic speakers who are Muslims have a negative evaluation of Saturday, their first day of the week after the holy day, Friday. By using this etic (universal) conceptual framework, we can measure people's affective responses to words such as *leisure* or *work*. Comparing the responses can help us understand cultural variations. It can also help us understand cultural expressions such as "Monday morning blues" or "T.G.I.F.," which may not communicate the same meanings in other cultures.

As you think dialectically about intercultural communication messages, consider these various approaches to meaning. In part, this means that you need to free yourself of the need to find the "true" meaning of a word, phrase, expression, or message. Instead, think about the factors that contribute to producing meaning. Note the dialectical tensions between what is said, how it is said, when and whom, and so on. Then consider how you synthesized and interpreted the meaning as you did.

Language and Perception

How much of our perception is shaped by the particular language we speak? Do English speakers see the world differently from, say, Arabic speakers? Is there anything about the particular language we speak that constrains or shapes our perception of the world? These questions are at the heart of the "political correctness" debate. We can address these questions from two points of view: the nominalist and the relativist.

The Nominalist Position   According to the **nominalist position,** perception is not shaped by the particular language we speak. Language is simply an arbitrary "outer form of thought." Thus, we all have the same range of thoughts, which we express in different ways with different languages. This means that any thought can be expressed in any language, although some may take more or fewer words. The existence of different languages does not mean that people have different thought processes or inhabit different perceptual worlds. After all, a tree may be an *arbre* in French and an *arbol* in Spanish, but we all perceive the tree in the same way.

The Relativist Position   According to the **relativist position,** the particular language we speak, especially the structure of that language, determines our thought patterns, our perceptions of reality, and, ultimately, important cultural components. This position is best represented by the Sapir-Whorf hypothesis. As you may recall from Chapter 2, this hypothesis was proposed by Edward Sapir (1921), a linguist, and his student, Benjamin Whorf (1956), based on linguistic research they conducted in the 1930s and 1940s on Native American languages. They proposed that language is not merely an "instrument for voicing ideas but is itself the shaper of ideas, the guide for the individual's mental activity" (Hoijer, 1994, p. 194). According to the Sapir-Whorf hypothesis, language defines our experience. For example, there are no possessives (*his/her/our/your*) in the Navajo language; we might conclude, therefore, that the Navajo think in a particular way about the concept of possession. Another example is the variation in verb forms in English, Spanish, and French. In English and Spanish, the present continuous verb form is frequently used; thus, a student might say, "I am studying" or *"Estoy estudiando."* A French speaker, in contrast, would use the simple present form, *"J'étudie."* The Sapir-Whorf hypothesis suggests that, based on this variation in verb form, French, English, and Spanish speakers may think differently about movement or action.

Another frequently cited example involves variation in color vocabulary. The Navajo use one word for blue and green, two words for two different colors of black, and one word for red; these four words form the vocabulary for primary colors in Navajo culture. The Sapir-Whorf hypothesis suggests that English and Navajo speakers perceive colors differently. Other examples of variations in syntax and semantics reflect differences in perception.

The Sapir-Whorf hypothesis has had tremendous influence on scholarly thinking about language and its impact on everyday communication. It questions the basic assumption that we all inhabit the same perceptual world, the same social reality.

The **qualified relativist position** takes a more moderate view of the relationship between language and perception. Proponents recognize the power of language but see language as a tool rather than a mirror of perception. This view allows for more freedom than the Sapir-Whorf hypothesis. As you read the research findings that follow, you may see the wisdom of the qualified relativist position.

Recent Research Findings

Communication scholar Thomas M. Steinfatt (1989) summarizes three areas of research that investigate the Sapir-Whorf hypothesis: (1) children's **language acquisition,** (2) cross-cultural differences in language, and (3) cognitive development of children who are deaf. As you will see, most of the research in these areas does not support a strict interpretation of the Sapir-Whorf hypothesis.

Language Acquisition in Children   If language structures thought, then language must precede, and only subsequently influence, thought. This raises the question of whether it is possible to think without language. B. F. Skinner, Jean Piaget, Lev Vygotsky, and other psychologists have long wrestled with this question. As their works indicate, they seem to conclude that language and thought are so closely related that it is difficult to speak of one as initiating influence over the other. Their works thus do not provide evidence for a strong relativist position.

Cross-Cultural Differences in Language   Do groups with different language labels perceive the world in different ways? One study compared perception of color variations in U.S. English speakers and the Dani of western New Guinea, who classify colors into roughly two groups, light and dark (Heider & Oliver, 1972). The researchers showed a paint chip to an individual, removed the paint chip, showed the person the same chip along with others, and then asked her or him to identify the original paint chip. There was little difference in the responses of the U.S. English speakers and the Dani, who were able to identify the original paint chip even though their language may not contain a word for that color.

Consider a more familiar example. Many men in the United States might identify someone's shirt as "red," whereas women viewing the same shirt might call it "cranberry" or "cherry" or "scarlet." Both the men and the women recognize the color distinctions, but men tend to use fewer words than women to distinguish colors.

Another example of cross-cultural research involves variations in verb forms. The Chinese language has no counterfactual verb form (illustrated by "If I had known, I *would have gone*, but I did not"). Researchers constructed stories using the counterfactual form and found that the Chinese respondents understood the concept of counterfactual and could answer questions appropriately even though this structure is not present in Chinese (Au, 1983, 1984, 1985; Bloom, 1981, 1984). There is no evidence that Chinese speakers are unable to think in terms of counterfactuals; rather, they simply do not normally express thoughts using such constructions. Although these research examples do not support the nominalist position, they do not provide strong evidence for the relativist position either.

Cognition of Children Who Are Deaf   Researchers have also tried to determine if children who are deaf or who have limited language use have diminished ability in perception or logical thinking. The children with disabilities had the same semantic or categorizing competence, and the same level of cognitive skill, as those children who could hear. The children were deficient in purely linguistic skills and short-term memory storage. The researchers concluded that children who are deaf do not seem to have a different worldview (Rhodda & Grove, 1987).

CULTURAL VARIATIONS IN LANGUAGE

Language is powerful and can have tremendous implications for people's lives. For example, uttering the words *I do* can influence lives dramatically. Being called names can be hurtful and painful, despite the old adage "Sticks and stones can break my bones, but words will never hurt me."

A recent Russian dictionary translates Russian idioms into English. Idiomatic expressions reveal a lot about what people think is important. According to Michael Specter, Russian seems to have abundant idioms about God, food, and the soul.

> *"Without this type of idiomatic expression people simply could not communicate," said Yevgeny N. Shiryaev, deputy director of the Russian Academy of Sciences Institute of Russian Language and an expert on the development of common speech. "Words would not add up properly. And of course the type of idioms we often rely on—earthy, physical phrases—tell a lot about our culture."*
>
> *A Russian could pretty much convey the entire range of human emotion with reference only to kasha, the grain dish. Nobody round here would argue with this notion, for example: "Kashu maslom ne isportish," which means, literally, you cannot spoil kasha with too much butter. What it really means, of course, is you can't have too much of a good thing—and in Russia a good thing is usually, well, food, soaked in butter.*
>
> *God's name is invoked in every imaginable way. If somebody is a complete loser he is "ni bogu svechka ni chyortu kocherga"—neither a candle to God nor a rod to the devil, i.e., useless. But not even God can compare with the soul. No word has more significance in the Russian language than* dusha, *or soul. . . . Russian souls are also always being engraved upon, trampled upon, put aside, unburdened, and burdened.*
>
> *The Russian people are so practical. After all, "Snyavshi golovu, po volosam ne plachut"—or, once your head has been cut off, there's no use crying about your hair. Now doesn't that make "there's no use crying over spilled milk" seem a little pathetic?*

Source: From Michael Specter, "The Rich Idioms of Russian: Verbal Soul Food of a Culture," *The New York Times,* August 20, 1995, p. E3.

The particular language we use predisposes us to think in particular ways and not in others. For example, the fact that English speakers do not distinguish between a formal and an informal *you* (as in German, with *du* and *Sie,* or in Spanish, with *tu* and *usted*) may mean that English speakers think about formality and informality differently than do German or Spanish speakers. In Japanese, formality is not simply noted by *you;* it is part of the entire language system. Nouns take the **honorific** "o" before them, and verbs take more formal and polite forms. Thus, "*Doitsu-go ga dekimasen* [I—or you, he, she, we, they—don't speak German]" is more polite and formal than "*Doitsu-go ga dekinai.*"

In other languages, the deliberate use of nonformal ways of speaking in more formal contexts can be insulting to another person. For example, French speakers may use the "tu" form when speaking to their dog or cat, but it can be insulting to use the "tu" form in a more formal setting when speaking to relative strangers. Yet it may be permissible to use the "tu" form in more social settings with relative strangers, such as at parties or in bars. Here, pragmatics becomes important. That is, we need to think about what else might be communicated by others and whether they shift to more informal ways of speaking.

Variations in Communication Style

Communication style combines both language and nonverbal communication. It is the **tonal coloring,** the **metamessage,** that contextualizes how listeners are expected to receive and interpret verbal messages. A primary way in which cultural groups differ in communication style is in a preference for high- versus low-context communication. A **high-context communication** style is one in which "most of the information is either in the physical context or internalized in the person, while very little is in the coded, explicit, transmitted part of the message" (Hall, 1976, p. 79). This style of communication emphasizes understanding messages without direct verbal communication. People in long-term relationships often communicate in this style. For example, one person may send a meaningful glance across the room at a party, and his or her partner will know from the nonverbal clue that it is time to go home.

In contrast, in **low-context communication,** the majority of meaning and information is in the verbal code. This style of communication, which emphasizes explicit verbal messages, is highly valued in many settings in the United States. Interpersonal communication textbooks often stress that we should not rely on nonverbal, contextual information. It is better, they say, to be explicit and to the point, and not to leave things ambiguous. However, many cultural groups around the world value high-context communication. They encourage children and adolescents to pay close attention to contextual cues (body language, environmental cues), and not simply the words spoken in a conversation (Gudykunst & Matsumoto, 1996).

William Gudykunst and Stella Ting-Toomey (2003) identify two major dimensions of communication styles: direct versus indirect and elaborate versus understated.

Direct Versus Indirect Styles   This dimension refers to the extent to which speakers reveal their intentions through explicit verbal communication and emphasizes low-context communication. A direct communication style is one in which verbal messages reveal the speaker's true intentions, needs, wants, and desires. An indirect style is one in which the verbal message is often designed to camouflage the speaker's true intentions, needs, wants, and desires. Most of the time, individuals and groups are more or less direct depending on the context.

Many English speakers in the United States favor the direct speech style as the most appropriate in most contexts. This is revealed in statements like "Don't beat around the bush," "Get to the point," and "What exactly are you trying to say?" Although "white lies" may be permitted in some contexts, the direct style emphasizes honesty, openness, forthrightness, and individualism.

However, some cultural groups prefer a more indirect style, with the emphasis on high-context communication. Preserving the harmony of relationships

POINT OF VIEW

The following poem was written by communication scholar Cristina González during her fieldwork investigating the sharing of Native American spirituality. It is based on an actual conversation between a Native American male and an Irish American male. The poem shows the difference between direct and indirect, and between low- and high-context, communication styles. The poet tells us how direct, explicit communication can be perceived by people who value more indirect, contextual communication.

THAT WHITE THING

Sometimes I wish I could just
Quit.
Quit talking to white people.
Just zaps your energy
When they do that
White thing
What do you mean?

See?!
It's that
White thing
Always have to explain.
Can't just talk.
Will you show me how?
Man, you just don't get it!
I'm sure glad I'm not white
Never just listening
      —Cristina González, 1997

has a higher priority than being totally honest. Thus, a speaker might look for a "soft" way to communicate that there is a problem in the relationship, perhaps by providing contextual cues (Ueda, 1974). Some languages have many words and gestures that convey the idea of "maybe." For example, three Indonesians studying in the United States were invited by their advisor to participate in a cross-cultural training workshop. They did not want to participate, nor did they have the time. But neither did they want to offend their professor, whom they held in high regard. Therefore, rather than tell him they couldn't attend, they simply didn't return his calls and didn't show up to the workshop.

An international student from Tunisia told Judith and Tom that he had been in the United States for several months before he realized that if someone was asked for directions and didn't know the location of the place, that person should tell the truth instead of making up a response. He explained that he had been taught that it was better to engage in conversation, to give *some* response, than to disappoint the person by revealing that he didn't know.

Different communication styles are responsible for many problems that arise between men and women and between persons from different ethnic groups. These problems may be caused by different priorities for truth, honesty, harmony, and conflict avoidance in relationships.

Elaborate Versus Understated Styles   This dimension of communication styles refers to the degree to which talk is used. The elaborate style involves the use of rich, expressive language in everyday talk. For example, the Arabic language has many metaphorical expressions used in everyday speech. In this style, a simple assertive statement means little; the listener will believe the opposite.

In contrast, the understated style values succinct, simple assertions, and silence. Amish people often use this style of communication. A common refrain is, "If you don't have anything nice to say, don't say anything at all." Free self-expression is not encouraged. Silence is especially appropriate in ambiguous situations; if one is unsure of what is going on, it is better to remain silent.

The exact style falls between the elaborate and the understated, as expressed in the maxim "Verbal contributions should be no more or less information than is required" (Grice, 1975). The exact style emphasizes cooperative communication and sincerity as a basis for interaction.

In international negotiations, visible differences in style can contribute to misperceptions and misunderstandings. For example, in December 1998, after meeting resistance to arms inspections in Iraq, British and U.S. military forces bombed Baghdad. Russian president Boris Yeltsin (1998, December 17), opposed to this military action, gave a speech that used a direct style:

> *Russia demands that actions involving the use of military force be stopped immediately, that restraint and prudence be shown and that a further escalation of the conflict be prevented because an escalation of the conflict would be fraught with the most dramatic consequences not only for finding a settlement of the Iraq problem but also for stability in the region as a whole.*
>
> *A solution to the Iraq problem can be achieved only through political and diplomatic means on the basis of complying with UN Security Council resolutions and international law. (news.bbc.co.uk/hi/english/events/crisis_in_the_gulf/ texts_and_transcripts/newsid_237000/237086.stm)*

President Bill Clinton (1998, December 19) also spoke in a more direct style in his justification for the bombings:

> *So long as Saddam remains in power, he will remain a threat to his people, his region and the world.*
>
> *With our allies, we must pursue a strategy to contain him and to constrain his weapons of mass destruction programme while working toward the day Iraq has a government willing to live at peace with its people and with its neighbours. (news.bbc.co.uk/hi/english/events/crisis_in_the_gulf/texts_and_transcripts/ newsid_239000/239145.stm)*

For his part, Iraqi president Saddam Hussein (1998, December 21) spoke in a much more indirect and elaborate style in response to the bombings:

In the name of God, the merciful, the compassionate. Our great people, gallant men of our valiant armed forces and glorious women in the Iraq of glory, Jihad and virtue, you are now in the fifth day after the night of 16–17 December, when a new aggression was started by the enemies of God and the nation. With it, resistance and combat started once again in the course of the immortal Mother of Battles.

God has wanted it to be a source of honour, pride, glory and blessing for you in this life and in the hereafter. The Almighty, if He wills, will make it a source of shame and disgrace and the guilt of a major crime in this life and in the hereafter for its perpetrators, the enemies of God and humanity. May God have mercy on the souls of our righteous martyrs and may they be the happy dwellers of Paradise. (news.bbc.co.uk/hi/english/events/crisis_in_the_gulf/texts_and_transcripts/ newsid_239000/239287.stm)

These different uses of language communicate different things to their culturally disparate audiences. As they also demonstrate, it is not easy to interpret language use from other people's perspectives.

Taking a dialectical perspective, though, should help us avoid stereotyping specific groups (such as Arabic or English speakers) in terms of communication style. We should not expect any group to use a particular communication style all the time. Instead, we might recognize that style operates dynamically and is related to context, historical forces, and so on. Furthermore, we might consider how tolerant we are when we encounter others who communicate in very different ways and how willing or able we are to alter our own style to communicate better.

Variations in Contextual Rules

Understanding some of the cultural variations in communication style is useful. A dialectical perspective reminds us that the particular style we use may vary from context to context. Think of the many contexts in which you communicate during the day—classroom, family, work, and so on—and about how you alter your communication to suit these contexts. You may be more direct with your family and less direct in classroom settings. Similarly, you may be more instrumental in task situations and more affective when socializing with your friends.

Many research studies have examined the rules for the use of socially situated language in specific contexts. They attempt to identify contexts and then "discover" the rules that apply in these contexts for a given speech community. Researchers Jack Daniel and Geneva Smitherman (1990) studied the communication dynamics in Black churches. They first identified the priorities among congregation members: unity between the spiritual and the material, the centrality of religion, the harmony of nature and the universe, and the participatory, interrelatedness of life. They then described a basic communication format, the call-response, in both the traditional religious context and secular life contexts. In church, the speaker and audience interact, with sermons alternating with music. In secular life, call-response takes the form of banter between the rapper (rhetor) and others in the social group.

At a recent exhibit on Ellis Island devoted to the so-called concentration camps in which thousands of Japanese Americans were confined during World War II, some Jewish organizations objected to the exhibit's use of the term *concentration camps*. This led to a much broader discussion about the use of related terms in everyday discourse in the United States, to which this journalist alludes.

> *"We cannot tell people, 'Don't use our words,'" said Elie Wiesel, the Nobel Peace Prize–winning author, who survived Auschwitz to chronicle the Nazi Holocaust. "All we can say is: 'Think about it. Suffering has a past.' Those of us who respect language should remember what a concentration camp really was in Germany."*
>
> *"Nazi," as in Jerry Seinfeld's "Soup Nazi," is glibly tossed at a nasty person, as though the Nazis simply had bad manners. Ted Turner likens Rupert Murdoch to "the late Führer." Johnnie L. Cochran, Jr., compares the detective Mark Fuhrman to Hitler. Kenneth W. Starr's tactics are attacked by a White House loyalist as something that "smacks of the Gestapo."*

Source: From Clyde Haberman, "Defending Jews' Lexicon of Anguish," *The New York Times*, March 13, 1998, p. B1.

Daniel and Smitherman (1990) go on to discuss problems that can occur in Black–White communication:

> *When the Black person is speaking, the white person, because call-response is not in his cultural heritage, obviously does not engage in the response process, remaining relatively passive, perhaps voicing an occasional, subdued, "mmmmmmmhm." Judging from the white individual's seeming lack of involvement in the communication, the Black communicator gets the feeling that the white isn't listening to him . . . and the white person gets the feeling that the Black person isn't listening because he keeps interrupting. (p. 39)*

People communicate differently in different speech communities. Thus, the context in which the communication occurs is a significant part of the meaning. Although we might communicate in one way in one speech community, we might change our communication style in another. Understanding the dynamics of various speech communities helps us see the range of communication styles.

DISCOURSE: LANGUAGE AND POWER

Recall that discourse refers to language in use. This means that all discourse is social. The language that is used—the words and the meanings that are communicated—depends not only on the context but also on the social relations that are part of that interaction. For example, bosses and workers may use the same words, but the meanings that are communicated are not always the same. A boss and a worker may both refer to the company personnel as a "family." To the boss, this may mean "one big happy family," whereas to a disgruntled employee, it may mean a "dysfunctional family." To some extent, the disparity is due to the inequality between boss and worker, to the power differential.

Co-Cultural Communication

The co-cultural communication theory, proposed by communication scholar Mark Orbe (1998), describes how language works between dominant and nondominant groups—or **co-cultural groups.** Groups that have the most power (Whites, men, heterosexuals) consciously or unconsciously formulate a communication system that supports their perception of the world. This means that co-cultural group members (ethnic minorities, women, gays) must function in communication systems that often do not represent their experiences. Nondominant groups thus find themselves in dialectical struggles: Do they try to adapt to the dominant communication style, or do they maintain their own styles? Women in large, male-dominated corporations often struggle with these issues. Do they adapt a male corporate style of speaking, or do they assert their own style?

In studying how communication operates with many different dominant and co-cultural groups, Orbe has identified three general orientations: nonassertive, assertive, and aggressive. Within each of these orientations, co-cultural individuals may emphasize assimilation, accommodation, or separation in relation to the dominant group. These two sets of orientations result in nine types of strategies (Table 6-1). The strategy chosen depends on many things, including preferred outcome, perceived costs and rewards, and context. These nine types of strategies vary from nonassertive assimilation, in which co-cultural individuals emphasize commonalities and avert controversy, to nonassertive separation, in which they avoid or maintain interpersonal barriers. Assertive assimilation strategies include manipulating stereotypes; assertive accommodation strategies include educating others, using liaisons, and communicating self. Aggressive assimilation involves strategies like ridiculing self and mirroring; aggressive accommodating involves confronting others; and aggressive separation involves attacking or sabotaging others.

Semiotics

The study of **semiotics,** or semiology, offers a useful approach to examining how different discursive units communicate meaning. The process of producing meaning is called **semiosis.** A particularly useful framework for understanding semiosis comes from literary critic Roland Barthes (1980). In his system, meaning is constructed through the interpretation of **signs**—combinations of signifiers and signifieds. **Signifiers** are the culturally constructed, arbitrary words or symbols we use to refer to something else, the **signified.** For example, the word *man* is a signifier that refers to some signified, an adult male human being.

TABLE 6-1   CO-CULTURAL COMMUNICATION ORIENTATIONS

	Separation	Accommodation	Assimilation
Nonassertive	Avoiding Maintaining interpersonal barriers	Increasing visibility Dispelling stereotypes	Emphasizing commonalities Developing positive face Censoring self Averting controversy
Assertive	Communicating self Intragroup networking Exemplifying strengths Embracing stereotypes	Communicating self Intragroup networking Using liaisons Educating others	Extensive preparation Overcompensating Manipulating stereotypes Bargaining
Aggressive	Attacking Sabotaging others	Confronting Gaining advantage	Dissociating Mirroring Strategic distancing Ridiculing self

Source: From *Constructing Co-Cultural Theory: An Explication of Culture, Power, and Communication,* by Mark Orbe, 1998, p. 110.

Obviously, *man* is a general signifier that does not refer to any particular individual. The relationship between this signifier and the sign (the meaning) depends on how the signifier is used (e.g., as in the sentence "There is a man sitting in the first chair on the left") or on our general sense of what *man* means. Here, the difference between the signifier and the sign rests on the difference between the word *man* and the meaning of that word. At its most basic level, *man* means an adult human male, but the semiotic process does not end there, because *man* carries many other layers of meaning. Barthes calls these layers **myths.** The expression "Man is the measure of all things," for example, has many levels of meaning, including the centering of male experience as the norm. *Man* may or may not refer to any particular adult male, but it provides a concept we can use to construct particular meanings based on the way the sign *man* functions. What does *man* mean when someone says, "Act like a real man!"

What comes to mind when you think of the term *man?* How do you know when to use this signifier (and when not to use it) to communicate to others? Think of all of the adult males you know: How do they "fit" under this signifier? In what ways does the signifier reign over their behaviors, both verbal and nonverbal, to communicate particular ideas about them?

Intercultural communication is not concerned solely with the cultural differences in verbal systems, although that is certainly a central interest. Semiotics can be useful in unraveling the ways that the cultural codes regulate verbal and nonverbal communication systems, as we will see in the next chapter. That is, semiotics allows us one way to "crack the codes" of other cultural frameworks. The goal is to establish entire systems of semiosis and the means by which those systems create meaning. We are not so much interested in the discrete, individual signifiers, as in the ways that signifiers are combined and configured.

The use of these semiotic systems relies on many codes taken from a variety of sources: economics, history, politics, religion, and so on. For example, when Nazi swastikas were spray-painted on Jewish graves in Lyon, France, in 1992, the message they communicated relied on semiotic systems from the past. The history of the Nazi persecution of Jews during World War II is well known: The power behind the signifier, the swastika, comes from that historical knowledge and the codes of anti-Semitism that it invokes to communicate its message. Relations from the past influence the construction and maintenance of intercultural relations in the present.

Because we seek the larger semiotic systems, we need to be aware of the cultural contexts that regulate the semiotic frameworks. When we are in different cultural contexts, the semiotic systems transform the communication situations. Consider the following observation by writer Edmundo Desnoes (1985), who discusses the work of photographer Susan Meiselas on her trip to Nicaragua. Desnoes notes that Meiselas "discovered one of the keys to understanding Latin America: a different context creates a different discourse. What she saw and what she shot in Nicaragua could not be plucked away and packaged in New York" (p. 39). That is, the photographs that Meiselas took could not communicate what she saw and experienced and wanted to express. The U.S. context necessarily would be regulated by a different semiotic system that would construct different signs and assign different meanings for the images.

It is wise to be sensitive to the many levels of cultural context that are regulated by different semiotic systems. In other words, it's a good idea to avoid framing the cultural context simply in terms of a "nation." Nation-states have other cultural contexts within their borders—for example, commercial and financial districts, residential areas, and bars, which are all regulated by their own semiotic systems. Consider the clothes that people might wear to a bar; wearing the same clothes in a business setting would not communicate the same message.

Discourse and Social Structure

Just as organizations have particular structures and specific positions within them, societies are structured so that individuals occupy social positions. Differences in **social positions** are central to understanding intercultural communication. For one thing, not all positions within the structure are equivalent; everyone is not the same. When men whistle at an attractive woman walking by, it has a different force and meaning than if women were to whistle at a man walking by.

Power is a central element, by extension, of this focus on social position. For instance, when a judge in court says what he or she thinks *freedom of speech* means, it carries much greater force than when a neighbor or a classmate gives an opinion about what the phrase means. When we communicate, we tend to note (however unconsciously) the group membership and positions of communication participants. To illustrate, consider the previous example. We understand how communication functions, based on the group membership of the judge (as a member of the judicial system) and of the neighbors and classmates; we need know nothing about their individual identities.

Groups also hold different positions of power in the social structure. Because intercultural contact occurs between members of different groups, the positions of the groups affect communication. Group differences lend meaning to intercultural communication because, as noted previously, the concept of differences is key to language and the semiotic process.

The "Power" Effects of Labels

We often use labels to refer to other people and to ourselves. Labels, as signifiers, acknowledge particular aspects of our social identity. For example, we might label ourselves or others as "male" or "female," indicating sexual identity. Or we might say we are "Canadian" or a "New Englander," indicating a national or regional identity. The context in which a label is used may determine how strongly we feel about the label. On St. Patrick's Day, for example, someone may feel more strongly about being an Irish American than about being a woman or a student or a Texan.

Sometimes people feel trapped or misrepresented by labels. They might complain, "Why do we have to have labels? Why can't I just be me?" These complaints belie the reality of the function of discourse. It would be nearly impossible to communicate without labels. People rarely have trouble when labeled with terms they agree with—for example, "man," "student," "Minnesotan," or "Australian." Trouble arises, however, from the use of labels that they don't like or that they feel inaccurately describe them. Think about how you feel when someone describes you using terms you do not like.

Labels communicate many levels of meaning and establish particular kinds of relationships between speaker and listener. Sometimes people use labels to communicate closeness and affection for others. Labels like "friend," "lover," and "partner" communicate equality. Sometimes people intentionally invoke labels to establish a hostile relationship. Labels like "White trash" and "redneck" intentionally communicate inequality. Sometimes people use labels that are unintentionally offensive to others. When this happens, it demonstrates the speaker's ignorance, lack of cultural sensitivity, and connection to the other group. The use of terms such as "Oriental" and "homosexual" communicates negative characteristics about the speaker and establishes distance between the speaker and listener.

Discourse is tied closely to social structure, so the messages communicated through the use of labels depend greatly on the social position of the speaker. If the speaker and listener are close friends, then the use of particular labels may not lead to distancing in the relationship or be offensive. But if the speaker and listener are strangers, then these same labels might invoke anger or close the lines of communication.

Furthermore, if the speaker is in a position of power, then he or she has potentially an even greater impact. For example, when politicians use discourse that invokes racist, anti-Semitic, or other ideologies of intolerance, many people become concerned because of the influence they may have. These concerns were raised in the 2002 presidential elections in France over candidate Jean-Marie Le Pen, whose comments over the years have raised concerns about anti-immigrant, anti-Semitic discourse. Similar concerns have arisen over the political discourse of Austria's Joerg Haider and Louisiana's David Duke. Of course, political office is not the only powerful position from which to speak. Fundamentalist Christian leaders have caused concern with their anti-gay discourse.

Judith and Tom collaborated on a study about reactions to labeling. We asked White students which of the following they preferred to be called: White, Caucasian, White American, Euro-American, European American, Anglo, or WASP. They did not favor such specific labels as "WASP" or "European American," but seemed to prefer a more general label like "White." We concluded that they probably had never thought about what labels they preferred to be called: As we noted in Chapter 5, the more powerful aspects of identity seem to go unnoticed; for many people, whiteness just "is," and the preferred label is a general one that does not specify origin or history. Individuals from powerful groups generally do the labeling of others; they themselves do not get labeled (Martin, Krizek, Nakayama, & Bradford, 1996). For example, when men are asked to describe their identities, they often forget to specify gender as part of their identity. Women, in contrast, often include gender as a key element in their identity. This may mean that men are the defining norm and that women exist in relation to this norm. We can see this in the labels we use for men and women and for people of color. We rarely refer to a "male physician" or a "White physician," but we do refer to a "female doctor" or a "Black doctor."

This "invisibility" of being White may be changing. Apparently, Whites are becoming increasingly more conscious of their White identity, which may change the practice of labeling. Perhaps as the White norm is challenged by changing demographics, by increased interaction in a more diverse United States, and by racial politics, more Whites may think about the meaning of labels for their own group.

MOVING BETWEEN LANGUAGES

Multilingualism

People who speak two languages are often called **bilingual;** people who speak more than two languages are considered **multilingual.** Rarely do bilinguals speak both languages with the same level of fluency. More commonly, they prefer to use one language over another, depending on the context and the topic.

This article describes a recently appointed British commission to investigate the reluctance of the English to study other languages, in contrast to other European countries where it is not unusual for people to speak two or three languages.

> *Sir Peter Parker, the former chairman of British Rail and the chairman of the Languages for Export campaign, who speaks French and Japanese, said, "It is desperately important to speak the language of the customer. English may now be the lingua franca of the world, but this is an ambiguous blessing. For people in Europe, to speak three languages is not uncommon."*
>
> *Alan Mois, the president of the National Association of Language Advisers, who is coordinating the commission, said the English suffered from physical isolation from the rest of Europe and from a sense of superiority, a hangover from the British Empire. With even German companies now suggesting to their executives that English is a better language to speak in the boardroom than their own, English people also had more of a problem deciding which foreign language they should learn.*
>
> *A background paper for the commission says, "The UK's reputation for arrogance in the eyes of other countries and for occasional intolerance of national and cultural difference are no doubt partly linked with our traditional failure when abroad to show willingness to use other languages than English."*
>
> *"While this might be an oversimple stereotype," it continues, "it remains a fact that we as a nation all too readily accept our supposed incapacity in languages, and have hitherto given the matter low political priority."*

Source: From Jonathan Petre and Catherine Elsworth, "McDonald to Tackle Language Failure," *The Sunday Telegraph*, March 22, 1998, p. 5.

Sometimes entire nations are bilingual or multilingual. Belgium, for example, has three national languages (Dutch, German, and French), and Switzerland has four (French, German, Italian, and Romansh).

On either the individual or the national level, multilinguals must engage in language negotiation. That is, they need to work out, whether explicitly or implicitly, which language to use in a given situation. These decisions are sometimes clearly embedded in power relations. For example, French was the court language during the reign of Catherine the Great in 18th-century Russia. French was considered the language of culture, the language of the elite, whereas Russian was considered a vulgar language, the language of the uneducated and the unwashed. Special-interest groups in many U.S. states, especially Arizona and California, have attempted to pass laws declaring English the official language. These attempts reflect a power bid to determine which language will be privileged.

Sometimes a language is chosen as a courtesy to others. For example, Tom joined a small group going to see the fireworks display at the Eiffel Tower on

POINT OF VIEW

For francophones in Belgium, intercultural communication practices rely on borrowing words and phrases from numerous languages, including Flemish, English, and local dialects. In a Belgian newsmagazine, this writer reflects on the utility of English words in walking the tightrope between the two major Belgian languages, Flemish (Dutch) and French.

Our country is already somewhat surrealist. But its language is in the process of becoming more and more cryptic. . . . The influence of Vondel's language [Flemish] is another Belgian particularity, although the principle source of contamination remains English. As all over the world, it is explained by the importance of the United States and the acculturation that they exercise on the rest of the world. But, for us, anglicisms also appear as a solution to our [language] community problems. Some people or some institutions that want to conserve a national (or federal) image, for example, have the tendency to run back to English, as it is perceived a "neutral language," to get out of answering the question of linguistic precedence or . . . to avoid the costs accrued from translation or printing.

(Notre pays avait déjà quelque chose de surréaliste. Mais son langage est en train de devenir de plus en plus crypté. . . . Cette influence de la langue de Vondel est une autre particularité belge, bien que la principale source de contamination reste l'anglais. Comme partout dans le monde, elle s'explique par l'importance des Etats-Unis et l'acculturation qu'ils exercent sur le reste du monde. Mais, chez nous, l'anglicismes apparaissent aussi comme une solution à nos problèmes communautaires. Certaines personnes ou institutions qui veulent conserver une image nationale (ou fédérale) par exemple, tendance à recourir à l'anglais, perçu comme une "langue neutre," pour se dispenser de répondre à la question de la préséance linguistique ou . . . pour éviter des frais accrus de traduction ou d'imprimés.)

Source: From Dorothée Klein, "Le Français Sens Dessus Dessous," *Le Vif/L'Express,* March 20, 1998, pp. 20–21.

Bastille Day one year. (Bastille Day is a French national holiday, celebrated on July 14, to commemorate the storming of the Bastille prison in 1789 and the beginning of the French Revolution.) One woman in the group asked, *"Alors, on parle français ou anglais?* [Are we speaking French or English?]" Because one man felt quite weak at English, French was chosen as the language of the evening.

The reasons that people become bilingual reflect trends identified in Chapter 1—changes that drive the need for intercultural communication. Bilingualism results from these imperatives, as people move from one country to another, as businesses expand into international markets, and so on. More personal imperatives also drive people to become bilingual. Alice Kaplan (1993), a French professor at Duke University, notes: "Speaking a foreign language is, for me and my students, a chance for growth, for freedom, a liberation from the ugliness of our received ideas and mentalities" (p. 211). Many people use foreign languages to escape from a legacy of oppression in their own languages.

Perhaps it is easier to think of language as a "prisonhouse," to borrow Fredric Jameson's (1972) metaphor. All of the semantic, syntactic, pragmatic, and phonetic systems are enmeshed in a social system from which there is no escape, except through the learning of another language. Consider the case of Sam Sue (1992), a Chinese American born and raised in Mississippi, who explains his own need to negotiate these social systems—often riddled by stigmatizing stereotypes—by changing the way he speaks:

> *Northerners see a Southern accent as a signal that you're a racist, you're stupid, or you're a hick. Regardless of what your real situation is. So I reacted to that by adapting the way I speak. If you talked to my brother, you would definitely know he was from the South. But as for myself, I remember customers telling my dad, "Your son sounds like a Yankee." (p. 4)*

Among the variations in U.S. English, the southern accent unwittingly communicates many negative stereotypes. Escaping into another accent is, for some, the only way to escape the stereotypes.

Learning another language is never easy, but the rewards of knowing another language are immense. Language acquisition studies have shown that it is nearly impossible for individuals to learn the language of a group of people they dislike. For instance, Tom was talking to a student about meeting the program's foreign language requirement. The student said, "I can't take Spanish. I'm from California." When Tom said that he did not understand what she meant, she blurted that she hated Mexicans and wouldn't take Spanish under any circumstances. As her well-entrenched racism suggested, she would indeed never learn Spanish.

An interesting linguistic phenomenon known as **interlanguage** has implications for the teaching and learning of other languages. Interlanguage refers to a kind of communication that emerges when speakers of one language are speaking in another language. The native language's semantics, syntactics, pragmatics, and phonetics often overlap into the second language and create a third way of communicating. For example, many English-speaking female students of German might say, *"Ich bin ein Amerikanerin,"* which is incorrect German but is structured on the English way of saying, "I am an American." The correct form is *"Ich bin Amerikanerin."* The insertion of *"ein"* reveals the English language overlap.

In his work on moving between languages, Tom has noted that this creation of other ways of communicating can offer ways of resisting dominant cultures. He notes that "the powerful potential of translation for discovering new voices can violate and disrupt the systemic rules of both languages" (Nakayama, 1997, p. 240). He gives the example of *"shiros,"* which is used by some Japanese Americans to refer to Whites. *Shiro* is the color white, and adding an *s* at the end is the English grammatical way to pluralize words. Tom explains:

People react negatively to being stereotyped by their speech, in this case a southern accent.

"Just because we talk slow doesn't mean we think slow," others point out. On the East Coast they seem to think there's something funny about riding around in a pickup truck. Well in the Deep South, we don't think it's all that natural to hurtle through the dark in a crowded subway.

It's the women of the South who feel the greatest need to look at all this with a sense of humor, but it doesn't help when these belles have to keep explaining that the size of one's hairdo has never been directly disproportionate to the size of one's IQ.
—Marilyn Schwartz

I loved Georgia. I took up for Georgia. I had a Georgia public school education. I had a Georgia accent, and it burned me when someone from the North would run down the South, and Georgia in particular. I hated it when New Yorkers would ask, upon hearing me speak, "Where are you from? Texas?"

"No," I'd say. "Georgia."

And then they would say, with a laugh, "Well, shut yo' mouth, you-all."

That wasn't funny. In the first place, nobody had said "Shut yo' mouth" in the South in a hundred years, and Yankees were always screwing up "you-all."

"You-all" was never used in singular sense. If I were addressing one person, I would never ask "Would 'you-all' like something to drink?" I would just use "you." And if I were addressing two or more persons, I wouldn't say, "Would you-all like something to drink?" I would use the contraction, "y'all."
—Lewis Grizzard

Sources: From Marilyn Schwartz, *New Times in the Old South, or Why Scarlett's in Therapy and Tara's Going Condo,* 1993, p. 12; and Lewis Grizzard, *If I Ever Get Back to Georgia, I'm Gonna Nail My Feet to the Ground,* 1990, p. 312.

Using the color for people highlights the overlay of the ideology of the English language onto Japanese and an odd mixing that probably would not make sense to people who speak only English or Japanese, or those who do not live in the spaces between them. (p. 242n)

Different people react differently to the dialectical tensions of a multilingual world. Some work hard to learn other languages and other ways of communicating, even if they make numerous errors along the way. Others retreat into their familiar languages and ways of living. The dialectical tensions that arise over different languages and different systems of meaning are played out around the world. But these dialectical tensions never disappear; they are always posing new challenges for intercultural communicators.

Translation and Interpretation

Because no one can learn all of the languages in the world, we must rely on translation and interpretation—two distinct but important means of communicating across language differences. The European Union (EU), for example, has a strict policy of recognizing all of the languages of its constituent members. Hence, many translators and interpreters are hired by the EU to help bridge the linguistic gaps.

Translation generally refers to the process of producing a written text that refers to something said or written in another language. The original language text of a translation is called the **source text;** the text into which it is translated is the **target text.**

Interpretation refers to the process of verbally expressing what is said or written in another language. Interpretation can either be simultaneous, with the interpreter speaking at the same time as the original speaker, or consecutive, with the interpreter speaking only during the breaks provided by the original speaker.

As we know from language theories, languages are entire systems of meaning and consciousness that are not easily rendered into another language in a word-for-word equivalence. The ways in which different languages convey views of the world are not equivalent, as we noted previously. Consider the difficulty involved simply in translating names of colors. The English word *brown* might be translated as any of these French words, depending on how the word is used: *roux, brun, bistre, bis, marron, jaune,* and *gris* (Vinay & Darbelnet, 1977, p. 261).

Issues of Equivalency and Accuracy   Some languages have tremendous flexibility in expression; others have a limited range of words. The reverse may be true, however, for some topics. This slippage between languages is both aggravating and thrilling for translators and interpreters. Translation studies traditionally have tended to emphasize issues of **equivalency** and accuracy. That is, the focus, largely from linguistics, has been on comparing the translated meaning with the original meaning. However, for those interested in the intercultural communication process, the emphasis is not so much on equivalence as on the bridges that people construct to cross from one language to another.

Many U.S. police departments are now hiring officers who are bilingual, as they must work with a multilingual public. In Arizona, like many other states, Spanish is a particularly important language. Let's look at a specific case in which a police detective for the Scottsdale (Arizona) Police Department explained an unusual phrase:

> *Detective Ron Bayne has heard his share of Spanish phrases while on the job. But he recently stumped a roomful of Spanish-speaking police officers with an unusual expression.*
>
> *A suspect said,* "Me llevaron a tocar el piano *[They took me to play the piano].*"
>
> *"I knew it couldn't mean that," said Bayne, a translator for the Scottsdale Police Department. "But I had no idea what it really meant." (Meléndez, 2002, p. B1)*

A SACRED LANGUAGE (ON CONTEMPLATING THE ENGLISH-ONLY MOVEMENT IN ARIZONA)

I speak to you
because I like you.
You, the man.
But, do not ask me to
replace my language.
My language is sacred.
Do not tear down the
bridges to my Spanish
island.
No one will see its
beauty.
Do not banish my
language.
Because you, the man, will
begin generations of
ignorance.
Do not attempt to destroy
my language.
Yours is not superior.
I say, learn my beautiful
language as
I have learned yours.
My language, the language of
a many people, cannot banish.
For we are a strong many.

  —Laura Laguna (Guadalupe, Arizona)

This slang term, popular with undocumented aliens, highlights the differences between "street" Spanish and classroom Spanish. It also points to the importance of context in understanding meaning. In this context, we know that the police did not take a suspect to play a piano. Instead, this suspect was saying that the police had fingerprinted him. The varieties of expression in Spanish reflect social class and other differences that are not always communicated through translation or interpretation.

Yet the context for interpreters and translators must also be recognized. The need for Spanish speakers in the U.S. Southwest represents only the tip of the "linguistic iceberg." The recent attacks on the World Trade Center have created another need for translators and interpreters:

> The CIA is looking for a few good speakers of Pashto. And Farsi, Dari and Arabic, too.

> *Backed with new funds from the White House in the wake of the Sept. 11 terrorist attacks, the spy agency has embarked on an urgent mission to reinforce its depleted ranks of specialists in the languages and cultures of other central Asia nations.*
>
> *It is a part of the world the United States virtually ignored for the last decade. (Strobel, 2001)*

The changing context for intelligence work has changed the context for translators and interpreters as well, to say nothing of the languages that are highly valued. These issues, while beyond the scope of equivalency and accuracy, are an important part of the dynamic of intercultural communication.

The Role of the Translator or Interpreter   We often assume that translators and interpreters are "invisible," that they simply render into the target language whatever they hear or read. The roles that they play as intermediaries, however, often regulate how they render the original. Tom believes that it is not always appropriate to translate everything that one speaker is saying to another, in exactly the same way, because the potential for misunderstanding due to cultural differences might be too great. Translation is more than merely switching languages; it also involves negotiating cultures. Writer Elisabeth Marx (1999) explains:

> *It is not sufficient to be able to translate—you have to comprehend the subtleties and connotations of the language. Walter Hasselkus, the German chief executive of Rover, gave a good example of this when he remarked: "When the British say that they have a 'slight' problem, I know that it has to be taken seriously." There are numerous examples of misunderstandings between American English and British English, even though they are, at root, the same language. (p. 95)*

It might be helpful to think of translators and interpreters as cultural brokers who must be highly sensitive to the contexts of intercultural communication.

We often assume that anyone who knows two languages can be a translator or an interpreter. Research has shown, however, that high levels of fluency in two languages do not necessarily make someone a good translator or interpreter. The task obviously requires the knowledge of two languages. But that's not enough. Think about all of the people you know who are native English speakers. What might account for why some of them are better writers than others? Knowing English, for example, is a prerequisite for writing in English, but this knowledge does not necessarily make a person a good writer. Because of the complex relationships between people, particularly in intercultural situations, translation and interpretation involve far more than linguistic equivalence, which traditionally has been the focus.

In his 1993 book *Contemporary Translation Theories*, linguist Edwin Gentzler speculates that the 1990s "might be characterized as experiencing a boom in translation theory" (p. 181). In part, this "boom" was fueled by a recognition that the traditional focus in translation studies is too limiting to explain the wide variety of ways that meanings might be communicated. Gentzler concludes: "With

Translation can create amusing and interesting intercultural barriers. Consider the following translation experiences.

1. A Canadian importer of Turkish shirts destined for Quebec used a dictionary to help him translate into French the label "Made in Turkey." His final translation: "Fabriqué en Dinde." True, "dinde" means "turkey." But it refers to the bird, not the country, which in French is Turquie.

2. An Otis Engineering Corp. display at a Moscow exhibition produced as many snickers among the Russians as it did praise. Company executives were not happy to learn that a translator had rendered in Russian a sign identifying "completion equipment" as "equipment for orgasms."

3. Japan's Olfa Corp. sold knives in the United States with the warning "Caution: Blade extremely sharp. Keep out of children."

4. In one country, the popular Frank Perdue Co. slogan, "It takes a tough man to make a tender chicken," read in local language something akin to "It takes a sexually excited man to make a chicken affectionate."

5. One company in Taiwan, trying to sell diet goods to expatriates living there, urged consumers to buy its product to add "roughage" to their systems. The instructions claimed that a person should consume enough roughage until "your tool floats." Someone dropped the "s" from "stool."

6. How about the Hong Kong dentist who advertised "Teeth extracted by the latest Methodists."

7. Or the hotel in notoriously polluted Mexico City that proclaimed: "The manager has personally passed all the water served here."

8. General Motors Corp.'s promotion in Belgium for its car that had a "body by Fisher" turned out to be, in the Flemish translation, "corpse by Fisher."

Source: From Laurel Delaney, "8 Global Marketing Gaffes," 2002. www.marketingprofs.com/Perspect/delany2.asp

such insight, perhaps we will be less likely to dismiss that which does not fit into or measure up to our standards, and instead open ourselves to alternative ways of perceiving—in other words, to invite real intra- and intercultural communication" (p. 199).

The field of translation studies is rapidly becoming more central to academic inquiry, as it moves from the fringes to an area of inquiry with far-reaching consequences for many disciplines. These developments will have a tremendous impact on how academics approach intercultural communication. Perhaps intercultural communication scholars will begin to play a larger role in the developments of translation studies.

LANGUAGE AND IDENTITY

In the previous chapter, we discussed cultural identity and its complexities. One part of our cultural identity is tied to the language(s) that we speak. As U.S. Americans, we are expected to speak English. If we travel to Nebraska, we assume that the people there speak English. When we travel around the world, we expect Russians to speak Russian, Koreans to speak Korean, and Indonesians to speak Indonesian. But things get more involved, as we noted in Chapter 4, when we consider why Brazilians speak Portugese, Congolese speak French, and Australians speak English. The relationship between language and culture becomes more complicated when we look at the complexity of cultural identities at home and abroad.

When Tom was at the Arizona Book Festival recently, a White male held up a book written in Chinese and asked Tom what it was about. "I don't read Chinese," Tom replied. "Well you should," he retorted and walked away. Two assumptions seem to be at work here: (1) Anyone who looks Asian must be Chinese, and (2) Asian Americans should be able to speak their ancestral languages. This tension has raised important identity questions for Asian Americans. Writer Henry Moritsugu (1992), who was born and raised in Canada and who later immigrated to the United States, explains:

> There is no way we could teach our children Japanese at home. We speak English. It wasn't a conscious effort that we did this. . . . It was more important to be accepted. . . . I wish I could speak the language better. I love Japanese food. I love going to Japanese restaurants. Sometimes I see Japanese groups enjoying themselves at karaoke bars . . . I feel definitely Western, more so than Asian. . . . But we look Asian, so you have to be aware of who you are. (p. 99)

The ability to speak another language can be important in how people view their group membership.

Many Chicana/os also have to negotiate a relationship to Spanish, whether or not they speak the language. Communication scholar Jacqueline Martinez (2000) explains:

> It has taken a long time for me to come to see and feel my own body as an ethnic body. Absent the capacity to express myself in Spanish, I am left to reach for less tangible traces of an ethnic self that have been buried under layers of assimilation into Anglo culture and practice. . . . Yet still there is a profoundly important way in which, until this body of mine can speak in Spanish, gesture in a "Spanishly" way, and be immersed in Spanish-speaking communities, there will remain ambiguities about its ethnic identification. (p. 44)

Although some people who migrate to the United States retain the languages of their homelands, many other U.S. American families no longer speak the language of their forebears. Historically, bilingualism was openly discouraged in the United States. Writer Gloria Anzaldúa (1987) recalls how she was discouraged from speaking Spanish:

This writer explains the resentment of many people around the globe toward U.S. Americans—not only because of the dominance of English but also because of the intimate connections between culture and language. What kinds of resentments are created by the spread of English and U.S. American culture around the world?

> One night, I went to a theater (which was not so much a movie theater as a video theater) to see "Kundun," a Hollywood movie, not yet released in Japan, about the Dalai Lama. A lot of young Americans were hanging around drinking cola. They all burst into laughter at lines in English that I could not make out.
>
> English is flooding not just the Internet; it is infiltrating deeper and deeper into India, Nepal and even the remoter countries of Africa. And when those countries transmit their culture to the world, they use English. As the boundaries between nations weaken, and the globe becomes more and more borderless, the various cultures and languages do not engage in a reciprocal give-and-take based on equal rights. Even in the flow of culture and language, there is a relationship of the strong and the weak that is determined by their underlying political and economic strength.
>
> Even though I realize that nothing can be done about this, I am not comfortable when I see Americans go to other countries and live just the way they do in America and assume that everybody speaks English. It's not just Muslim fundamentalist terrorists; people around the world are beginning to harbor a latent enmity toward Americans, and at times like these I can understand these feelings. This is not a happy situation either for Americans or people of other countries.

Source: From R. Yampolsky, "The Written Word," *Japan Times*, January 29, 1999, p. 16.

> I remember being caught speaking Spanish at recess—that was good for three licks on the knuckles with a sharp ruler. I remember being sent to the corner of the classroom for "talking back" to the Anglo teacher when all I was trying to do was tell her how to pronounce my name. If you want to be American, speak "American." If you don't like it, go back to Mexico where you belong. (p. 53)

Even today we often hear arguments in favor of making English the official language of the nation. The interconnections between cultural identity and language are indeed strong.

What about the challenges facing cultural groups whose languages are nearing extinction. Whereas millions of people speak Chinese, Japanese, and Spanish, some languages are spoken by only a handful of people. One Osage Indian laments:

> "Even though I am painfully aware of what needs to be said and how to say it, my words usually fall upon noncomprehending ears, for only a handful of Osage

Indians can speak or understand our tribal language. And, after each such occasion, I often silently lament that this may be the last time the Osage language is publicly spoken and that within a mere 10 years it might not ever be heard again." (quoted in Pratt & Buchanan, 2000, p. 155)

Many Native American tribes are currently working to save their tribal languages, but they face enormous challenges. Yet it is their culture and identity that are at risk.

The languages we speak and the languages others think we should speak can create barriers in intercultural communication. Why might some U.S. Americans assume that someone whose ancestors came from China continues to speak Chinese while someone whose ancestors came from Germany or Denmark is assumed to no longer speak German or Dutch? Here, again, we can see how identity, language, and history create tensions between who we think we are and who others think we are.

Code Switching

Code switching is a technical term in communication that refers to the phenomenon of changing languages, dialects, or even accents. People code switch for several reasons: (1) to accommodate the other speakers, (2) to avoid accommodating others, or (3) to express another aspect of their cultural identity.

Linguistics professor Jean-Louis Sauvage (2002) studied the complexity of code switching in Belgium, which involves not only dialects but languages as well. He explains the practical side of code switching:

For example, my house was built by a contractor who sometimes resorted to Flemish subcontractors. One of these subcontractors was the electrician. I spoke Dutch to him but had to use French words when I referred to technical notions that I did not completely understand even in French. This was not a problem for the electrician, who knew these terms in Dutch as well as in French but would have been unable to explain them to me in French. (p. 159)

Given the complex language policies and politics in Belgium, code switching takes on particularly important political meaning. Who code switches and who does not is a frequent source of contestation.

In her work on code switching, communication scholar Karla Scott (2000) discusses how the use of different ways of communicating creates different cultural contexts and different relationships between the conversants. Based on a series of interviews with Black women, she notes "the women's shared recognition that in markedly different cultural worlds their language use is connected to identity" (p. 246). She focuses on the use of the words *girl* and *look* as they relate to communicative practices in different contexts. She identifies three areas in which code switching occurs with *girl:* "(1) in discourse about differences between Black and White women's language use, (2) in discourse about being with other Black women, and (3) in uses of '*girl*' as a marker in discourse among participants during the interview" (p. 241). The use of *look* in code switching occurs in three contexts as well: "(1) in discussions and descriptions of talking like a Black woman versus White women's talk, (2) in the women's reports of interactions with Whites, both male and female, and (3) in the women's reports of interactions with Black men" (p. 243). *Girl* creates a sense of solidarity and shared identity among Black women, whereas *look* is particularly important in White-dominated contexts, as it asserts a different identity. Thus, code switching between these two words reflects different ways of communicating and different identities and relationships among those communicating.

LANGUAGE POLITICS AND POLICIES

Some nations have multiple official languages. For instance, Canada has declared English and French to be the official languages. Here in the United States, there is no official national language, although English is the de facto national language. Yet the state of Hawai'i has two official languages, English and Hawaiian. Laws or customs that determine which language is spoken where and when are referred to as **language policies.** These policies often emerge from the politics of language use. As mentioned previously, the court of Catherine the Great of Russia used not Russian but French, which was closely tied to the politics of social and economic class. The history of colonialism also influences language policies. Thus, Portuguese is the official national language of Mozambique, and English and French are the official national languages of Cameroon. (See Figure 6-2.)

Language policies are embedded in the politics of class, culture, ethnicity, and economics. They do not develop as a result of any supposed quality of the language itself. Belgium provides an excellent example. When Tom was in Belgium, he was shocked to hear a professor tell his francophone students that they should not be ashamed to be French speakers, because France and French speakers have made tremendous contributions to the world. Why would the students be ashamed of their language? Currently, the French-speaking part of Belgium is not doing as well economically as the Flemish part. The notion of being ashamed of speaking French would have been unthinkable in the court of Catherine the Great. But this has nothing to do with the language itself. The shifting character of language and intercultural communication is highlighted in the case of French. Attitudes toward language—and those who speak that language—are influenced by economic and social contexts and by the power of various linguistic groups.

After gaining its independence from the Netherlands in 1830, Belgium chose French as its national language. Some historians see this choice as a reaction against the rule of the Dutch. However, following protests by the Flemings, Dutch was added as a national language in 1898 and Belgium became bilingual. In 1962, a linguistic border was drawn across the country to mark the new language policies, demarcating which language would be the official language of each region. As a consequence, Belgium's oldest university, the Catholic

FIGURE 6-2   Tensions between English and French speakers—shown by this photo taken near Montreal's Olympic Stadium—have led to the creation of language policies in Quebec. Some U.S. states have attempted to implement language policies as well, as "English-only" laws. Do these language policies reduce or exacerbate intercultural communication problems? Why do some languages face more difficulty in their survival than others? (*Courtesy T. K. Nakayama*)

University of Leuven—located in Flanders, bilingual at the time—found itself at the center of a linguistic conflict. In 1968, the *Walen Buiten* (Walloons Out) movement demanded that the French-speaking part of the university leave Flanders. As a consequence, the government split the university and built a new city and a new campus for the French-speaking part across the linguistic border in a city now called Louvain-la-Neuve (New Leuven). In 1980, Belgians divided their country into three communities (Dutch, French, and German) and three regions (Brussels, Flanders, and Wallonia). As a result of these language politics, Dutch is the official language in Flanders and French is the language of Wallonia (except in the eastern cantons, where German is spoken).

Although many Belgians may speak Dutch and French, the decision to speak one language or the other in particular contexts communicates more than linguistic ability. For some Belgians, it is rude not to speak the official language of the region they are in at the moment; for others, it is more important to be accommodating, to try to speak the language of the other person. Other Belgians insist on speaking "their" language. Each of these communication decisions in a multilingual context reflects a range of political and social commitments.

Although some people predict the end of the Belgian state as a result of these linguistic differences, others don't see these differences as divisive. Along the linguistic border, feelings about the language politics range from embracing bilingualism to embracing monolingualism (Engels, 1998). In any case, the Belgian example is only one; not all multilingual nations are discussing dissolution, and not all multilingual nations create language territories. Yet we can view the language politics and policies of Belgium in dialectical tension with the history of the language groups, economic relations, and political power. The majority of Belgians are Flemings (Dutch speaking), and Flanders is currently doing better economically; in the past, however, the French-speaking region, Wallonia, has been stronger economically and has been more populous. These shifting trends exacerbate the problems of intercultural communication and drive the need for language policies.

LANGUAGE AND GLOBALIZATION

In a world in which people, products, and ideas can move easily around the globe, rapid changes are being made in the languages spoken and learned. Globalization has sparked increased interest in some languages while leaving others to disappear.

The dream of a common international language has long marked Western ways of thinking. Ancient Greeks viewed the world as filled with Greek speakers or those who were *barbaroi* (barbarians). The Romans attempted to establish Latin and Greek, which led to the subsequent establishment of Latin as the learned language of Europe. Latin was eventually replaced by French, which was spoken, as we have noted, throughout the elite European communities and became the **lingua franca** of Europe. More recently, Esperanto was created as an international language, and although there are Esperanto speakers, it has not attained wide international acceptance. Today, Ancient Greek and Latin, as well as French, still retain some of their elite status, but "English is the de facto language of international communication today" (Tsuda, 1999, p. 153).

Many native English speakers are happy with the contemporary status of the language. They feel much more able to travel around the world, without the burden of having to learn other ways of communicating, given that many people around the world speak English. Having a common language also facilitates intercultural communication, but it can also create animosity among those who must learn the other's language. Dominique Noguez (1998) explains:

> *In these language affairs, as in many other moral or political affairs—tolerance, for example—is the major criteria for reciprocity. Between comparable languages and equal countries, this must be: I speak and learn your language and you speak and learn mine. Otherwise, it's sadomasochism and company—the sadist being simply the one with the gall to say to another: "I am not speaking your language, therefore speak mine!" This is what Anglo-Saxons have been happily doing since at least 1918. (p. 234)*

> (En ces affaires de langue, comme en bien d'autres affaires morales ou politiques—la tolerance, par exemple—le critère majeur, c'est la réciprocité. Entre langues comparables et pays égaux, ce devrait être: je parle et enseigne votre langue et vous parlez et enseignez la mienne.

Harumi Befu, emeritus professor at Stanford University, discusses the consequences of English domination for monolingual Americans.

> . . . *Instead of language enslavement and intellectual imperialism, however, one more often is told of the benefit of learning a second language, such as English. For example, non-native English speakers can relativize their own language and appreciate each language on its own terms. It was Goethe who said that one who does not know a foreign language does not know his/her own language. . . .*
>
> *Thanks to the global dominance of their country, American intellectuals have acquired the "habitus" (Bourdieu) of superiority, whereby they exercise the license of expressing their thoughts in English wherever they go instead of showing respect to locals through expending efforts to learn their language. This privileged position, however, spells poverty of the mind.*
>
> *For their minds are imprisoned in a single language; they are unable to liberate their minds through relativizing English. In short, other things being equal, monolingual Americans (not all Americans are monolingual) are the most provincial and least cosmopolitan among those who traffic in the global interlinguistic community—a price they pay for the strength of the country backing them.*

Source: From H. Befu, "English Language Intellectual Imperialism and Its Consequences," *Newsletter: Intercultural Communication,* 37 (Intercultural Communication Institute, Kanda University of International Studies, Japan), June 2000, p. 1.

Autrement, c'est sadomasochisme et compagnie—le sadique étant tout simplement celui qui l'aplomb de declarer à l'autre: "Je ne parle pas votre langue, parlez donc la mienne!" C'est ce que font, avec assez de bonheur, les Anglo-Saxons depuis au moins 1918.)

Learning a foreign language is never easy, of course, but the dominance of English as the lingua franca raises important issues for intercultural communication.

What is the relationship between our four touchstones and this contemporary linguistic situation? That is, how do culture, communication, power, and context play out in the domination of English? First, the intimate connections between language and culture mean that the diffusion of English is tied to the spread of U.S. American culture around the world. Is this a new form of colonialism? If we consider issues of power, what role does the United States play in the domination of English on the world scene? How does this marginalize or disempower those who are not fluent in English in intercultural communication? What kinds of resentment might be fostered by forcing people to recognize their disempowerment?

In what intercultural contexts is it appropriate to assume that others speak English? For English speakers, this is a particularly unique context. Latvians, for

English is the world's 900-pound gorilla. The most widely used language world-wide, it is becoming the lingua franca of industry, commerce, and finance.

It happened independently, in the pragmatic world of commerce and competition.

And it isn't stuffy, old-British English people want to learn. It's American English. But let's not gloat.

Sure, it's wonderful to grow up speaking a language whose devilish "i" before "e" except after "c" intricacies could scare a matador. And it's a privilege to be born into the lap of world economic eminence.

So feel good.

Feel lucky.

But don't feel too smug.

After all, those people struggling with the power of the silent "e" will soon be able to call themselves fluent in a foreign language. Most of the Americans who can say that are recent immigrants.

Source: From: "Plan to Go Global? Best Speak English—Mother Tongue for Industry, Commerce and Finance," June 5, 2002, *The Arizona Republic*, p. B8.

example, cannot attend international meetings and assume that others will speak Latvian; and Albanians will have difficulty transacting international trade if they assume that others know their language.

SUMMARY

In this chapter, we explored many dimensions of language and discourse in intercultural communication. Discourse, or language in use, always has a social context. Linguists study four basic components of language as they investigate how language works: Semantics is the study of meaning, syntax the study of structure, pragmatics the study of context, and phonetics the study of the sound system of the language.

Some dimensions of meaning are universal, at least to many language groups. People in different cultures can characterize the meaning of a phrase according to three criteria: the phrase's value, its potency, and its level of activity. The particular language we speak influences our perception, but it does not totally determine our perception.

Languages exhibit many cultural variations, both in communication style and in the rules of context. Cultural groups may emphasize the importance of verbal (low-context) or nonverbal (high-context) communication. Two important types of communication styles are the direct/indirect and the elaborate/

succinct. The context in which the communication occurs is a significant part of the meaning.

Understanding the role of power in language use is important. Dominant groups, consciously or unconsciously, develop communication systems that require nondominant groups (or co-cultural groups) to use communication that doesn't fit their experiences. The effects of power are also revealed in the use of labels, with the more powerful people in a society labeling the less powerful. Individuals who occupy powerful positions in a society often don't think about the ways in which their positions are revealed in their communication.

Another language issue is that of multilingualism. Individuals learn languages for different reasons, and the process is often a rewarding one. The complexity of moving between languages is facilitated by interpretation and translation, in which issues of equivalency and accuracy are crucial. Being a good translator or interpreter requires more than merely fluency in two languages.

Some nations have multiple official languages, and others have no official national language. Language use is often tied to the politics of class, culture, ethnicity, and economics. The issue of what language should be spoken when, to whom, and why becomes quite complex.

Through globalization, English has become the new international language. But there are both positive and negative implications of English as the lingua franca.

DISCUSSION QUESTIONS

1. Why is it important for intercultural communication scholars to study both language and discourse?

2. What is the relationship between our language and the way we perceive reality?

3. What are some cross-cultural variations in language use and communication style?

4. What aspects of context influence the choice of communication style?

5. What does a translator or an interpreter need to know to be effective?

6. Why is it important to know the social positions of individuals and groups involved in intercultural communication?

7. Why do some people say that we should not use labels to refer to people but should treat everybody as individuals? Do you agree?

8. Why do people have such strong reactions to language policies, as in the "English-only" movement?

9. In what ways is the increasing and widespread use of English around the world both a positive and a negative change for U.S. Americans?

 Go to the self-quizzes on the Online Learning Center at www.mhhe.com/martinnakayama to further test your knowledge.

ACTIVITIES

1. *Regional Language Variations.* Meet in small groups with other class members and discuss variations in language use in different regions of the United States (accent, vocabulary, and so on). Identify perceptions that are associated with these variations.

2. *"Foreigner" Labels.* Meet in small groups with other class members and generate a list of labels used to refer to people from other countries who come to the United States—for example, "immigrants" and "aliens." For each label, identify a general connotation (positive, negative, mixed). Discuss how connotations of these words may influence our perceptions of people from other countries. Would it make a difference if we referred to them as "guests" or "visitors"?

3. *Values and Language.* Although computer-driven translations have improved dramatically over earlier attempts, translation is still intensely cultural. Communication always involves many layers of meaning, and when you move between languages, there are many more opportunities for misunderstanding. Try to express some important values that you have (e.g., freedom of the press) on this Web site, and see how they are retranslated in five different languages: http://www.tashian.com/multibabel/

KEY WORDS

activity dimension
bilingual
co-cultural groups
code switching
communication style
Creole
discourse
equivalency
evaluative dimension
high-context communication
honorific
interlanguage
International Phonetic Alphabet (IPA)
interpretation
la langue

language acquisition
language politics
la parole
lingua franca
low-context communication
metamessage
multilingual
myths
nominalist position
phonetics
pidgin
potency dimension
pragmatics
qualified relativist position

relativist position
semantic differential
semantics
semiosis
semiotics
signified
signifiers
signs
social positions
source text
syntactics
target text
tonal coloring
translation

OLC The Online Learning Center at www.mhhe.com/martinnakayama features flashcards and crossword puzzles based on these terms and concepts.

REFERENCES

Anzaldúa, G. (1987). *Borderlands/la frontera: The new mestiza.* San Francisco: Spinsters/ Aunt Lute.

Au, T. K. (1983). Chinese and English counterfactuals: The Sapir-Whorf hypothesis revisited. *Cognition, 15*, 155–187.

———. (1984). Counterfactuals: In reply to Alfred Bloom. *Cognition, 17*, 239–302.

———. (1985). Language and cognition. In L L. Lloyd & R. L. Schiefelbusch (Eds.), *Language perspectives II*. Baltimore: University Park Press.

Barthes, R. (1980). *Elements of semiology* (A. Lavers & C. Smith, Trans.). New York: Hill & Wang. (Original work published 1968)

Befu, H. (2000, June). English language intellectual imperialism and its consequences. *Newsletter: Intercultural Communication, 37* (Intercultural Communication Institute, Kanda University of International Studies, Japan), p. 1.

Bloom, A. (1981). *The linguistic shaping of thought: A study in the impact of language on thinking in China and the West*. Hillsdale, NJ: Lawrence Erlbaum.

———. (1984). Caution—the words you use may affect what you say: A response to Terry Kitfong Au's "Chinese and English counterfactuals: The Sapir-Whorf hypothesis revisited." *Cognition, 17*, 275–287.

Daniel, J. L., & Smitherman, G. (1990). How I got over: Communication dynamics in the Black community. In D. Carbaugh (Ed.), *Cultural communication and intercultural contact* (pp. 27–40). Hillsdale, NJ: Lawrence Erlbaum.

Delaney, L. (2002). 8 global marketing gaffes. www.marketingprofs.com/Perspect/delany2.asp

Desnoes, E. (1985). The death system. In M. Blonsky (Ed.), *On signs* (pp. 39–42). Baltimore: Johns Hopkins University Press.

Engels, P. (1998, April 24–30). La frontière à saute-mouton. *Le Vif/L'Express, 242*, pp. 40–45.

Grice, H. (1975). Logic and conversation. In P. Cole & J. Morgan (Eds.), *Syntax and semantics: Vol. 3. Speech acts*. New York: Academic Press.

Grizzard, L. (1990). *If I ever get back to Georgia, I'm gonna nail my feet to the ground*. New York: Ballantine Books.

Gudykunst, W. B., & Matsumoto, Y. (1996). Cross-cultural variability of communication in personal relationships. In W. B. Gudykunst, S. Ting-Toomey, & T. Nishida (Eds.), *Communication in personal relationships across cultures* (pp. 19–56). Thousand Oaks, CA: Sage.

Gudykunst, W. B., & Ting-Toomey, S. (2003). *Communicating with strangers: An approach to intercultural communication* (4th ed.). New York: McGraw-Hill.

Haberman, C. (1998, March 13). Defending Jews' lexicon of anguish. *The New York Times*, p. B1.

Hall, E. T. (1976). *Beyond culture*. Garden City, NY: Doubleday.

Heider, E. R., & Oliver, D. C. (1972). The structure of the color space in naming and memory for two languages. *Cognitive Psychology, 8*, 337–354.

Hoijer, H. (1994). The Sapir-Whorf hypothesis. In L. Samovar & R. E. Porter (Eds.), *Intercultural communication: A reader* (pp. 194–200). Belmont, CA: Wadsworth.

Jameson, F. (1972). *The prisonhouse of language*. Princeton, NJ: Princeton University Press.

Klein, D. (1998, March 20). Le français sens dessus dessous. *Le Vif/L'Express*, pp. 20–21.

Martin, J. N., Krizek, R. L., Nakayama, T. K., & Bradford, L. (1996). Exploring whiteness: A study of self-labels for White Americans. *Communication Quarterly, 44*, 125–144.

Martinez, J. (2000). *Phenomenology of Chicana experience and identity: Communication and transformation in praxis*. Lanham, MD: Rowan & Littlefield.

Marx, E. (1999). *Breaking through culture shock*. London: Nicholas Brealey.

Meléndez, M. (2002, April 7). Police try to connect, reach out in Spanish. *The Arizona Republic*, p. B1.

Moritsugu, H. (1992). To be more Japanese. In J. F. J. Lee (Ed.), *Asian Americans* (pp. 99–103). New York: New Press.

Nakayama, T. K. (1997). Les voix de l'autre. *Western Journal of Communication, 61*(2): 235–242.

Noguez, D. (1998). *La colonisation douce: Feu la langue française, carnets, 1968–1998.* Paris: Arléa.

Orbe, M. P. (1998). *Constructing co-cultural theory: An explication of culture, power, and communication.* Thousand Oaks, CA: Sage.

Osgood, C. E., May, W. H., & Miron, M. S. (1975). *Cross-cultural universals of meaning.* Urbana: University of Illinois Press.

Petre, J., & Elsworth, C. (1998, March 22). McDonald to tackle language failure. *The Sunday Telegraph*, p. 5.

Plan to go global? Best speak English—mother tongue for industry, commerce and finance. (2002, June 5). *The Arizona Republic*, p. B8.

Pratt, S. B., & Buchanan, M. C. (2000). Wa-zha-zhe-i-e: Notions on a dying ancestral language. In A. Gonzàley, M. Houston, & U. Chen (Eds.), *Essays in culture, ethnicity, and communication* (3rd ed., pp. 155–163). Los Angeles: Roxbury.

Rhodda, M., & Grove, C. (1987). *Language, cognition, and deafness.* Hillsdale, NJ: Lawrence Erlbaum.

Sapir, E. (Ed.). (1921). *Language: An introduction to the study of speech.* New York: Harcourt, Brace & World.

Sauvage, J.-L. (2002). Code-switching: An everyday reality in Belgium. In J. N. Martin, T. K. Nakayama, & L. A. Flores (Eds.), *Readings in intercultural communication: Experiences and contexts* (2nd ed., pp. 156–161). New York: McGraw-Hill.

Scott, K. D. (2000). Crossing cultural borders: "Girl" and "look" as markers of identity in Black women's language use. *Discourse & Society, 11*(2): 237–248.

Specter, M. (1995, August 20). The rich idioms of Russian: Verbal soul food of a culture. *New York Times*, p. E3.

Steinfatt, T. M. (1989). Linguistic relativity: Toward a broader view. In S. Ting-Toomey & F. Korzenny (Eds.), *Language, communication and culture* (pp. 35–78). Newbury Park, CA: Sage.

Stroebel, W. P. (2001, November 16). Language, cultural void: CIA urgently seeks Afghan, central Asian linguists. *Detroit Free Press.* www.freep.com/news/nw/terror2001/spies16_20011116.htm

Sue, S. (1992). Growing up in Mississippi. In J. F. J. Lee (Ed.), *Asian Americans* (pp. 3–9). New York: New Press.

Swartz, M. (1993). *New times in the Old South, or why Scarlett's in therapy and Tara's going condo.* New York: Crown.

Tsuda, Y. (1999). The hegemony of English and strategies for linguistic pluralism: Proposing the ecology of language paradigm. In M. Tehranian (Ed.), *Worlds apart: Human security and global governance* (pp. 153–167). New York: Tauris.

Ueda, K. (1974). Sixteen ways to avoid saying "no" in Japan. In J. C. Condon & M. Saito (Eds.), *Intercultural encounters with Japan* (pp. 185–192). Tokyo: Simul Press.

Vinay, J. P., & Darbelnet, J. (1977). *Stylistique comparée du français et de l'anglais: Méthode de traduction.* Paris: Marcel Didier.

West, F. (1975). *The way of language: An introduction.* New York: Harcourt Brace Jovanovich.

Whorf, B. L. (1956). *Language, thought and reality.* Cambridge, MA: MIT Press.

Yampolsky, R. (1999, January 29). The written word. *Japan Times*, p. 16.

NONVERBAL CODES AND CULTURAL SPACE

Nonverbal elements of cultural communication are highly dynamic and play an important role in understanding intercultural communication. Reading nonverbal communication within various cultural spaces can be a key to survival, depending upon the situation. Consider the following scenario:

> *"It's your first day with your FTO (Field Training Officer). He drives the squad. You're too nervous to drive. You don't know where you're going anyway. And all this stuff is coming at you. The police radio's on; you can't make sense out of it; your FTO's talking to you constantly; you're hearing all these sounds from the street, languages you've never heard. You're seeing things you've never seen before. You're confused as hell.*
>
> *"Suddenly, your FTO stops the squad and says, 'Okay, let's get out, kid.' He jumps out and flings somebody against the wall and takes a gun off of him.*
>
> *"You're looking at him in total disbelief. How'd he know that? This guy must be the Great Carnac. Ten years later you've got a kid driving with you and you see something and you fling somebody against a wall. And the kid's looking at you like how did he know? And you know it's not magic." (quoted in Fletcher, 1992, pp. 137–139)*

Communication scholar Connie Fletcher goes on to note: "Urban police officers are one group for whom taking 'everyday life' for granted by screening out the discomfiting or confusing elements can have tragic consequences for both cops and citizens" (p. 135).

You may never become a police officer, but you certainly will find yourself in many intercultural communication situations and cultural spaces. Your own nonverbal communication may create additional problems and, if the behaviors are inappropriate for the particular cultural space, may exacerbate existing tensions. In other cases, your use of nonverbals might reduce tension and confusion.

The first part of this chapter focuses on the importance of understanding nonverbal aspects of intercultural communication. We can examine nonverbal communication in terms of the personal–contextual and the static–dynamic dialectics. Although nonverbal communication can be highly dynamic, personal space, gestures, and facial expressions are fairly static patterns of specific nonverbal communication codes. These patterns are the focus of the second part of this chapter. Finally, we investigate the concept of cultural space and the ways in which cultural identity is shaped and negotiated by the cultural spaces (home, neighborhood, and so on) that people occupy.

As urban police officers know, there is no guidebook to "reading the streets." The nonverbals of the street change constantly. For the same reason, we believe it is useless to list nonverbals to memorize. Instead, it will be more beneficial for you to learn the framework of nonverbal communication and cultural spaces so you can tap into the nonverbal systems of whatever cultural groups become relevant to your life. Understanding communication is a matter of understanding how to think dialectically about *systems* of meaning, and not discrete elements. Nonverbal intercultural communication is no exception.

DEFINING NONVERBAL COMMUNICATION: THINKING DIALECTICALLY

In this chapter, we discuss two forms of communication beyond speech. The first includes facial expression, personal space, eye contact, use of time, and conversational silence. (What is not said is often as important as what is spoken.) The second includes the cultural spaces that we occupy and negotiate. **Cultural spaces** are the social and cultural contexts in which our identity forms—where we grow up and where we live (not necessarily the physical homes and neighborhoods, but the cultural meanings created in these places).

In thinking dialectically, we need to consider the relationship between the nonverbal behavior and the cultural spaces in which the behavior occurs, and between the nonverbal behavior and the verbal message. Although there are patterns to nonverbal behaviors, they are not always culturally appropriate in all cultural spaces. Remember, too, that some nonverbal behaviors are cultural, whereas others are idiosyncratic, that is, peculiar to individuals.

Comparing Verbal and Nonverbal Communication

Recognizing Nonverbal Behavior   Both verbal and nonverbal communication are symbolic, communicate meaning, and are patterned—that is, are governed by contextually determined rules. Societies have different nonverbal languages, just as they have different spoken languages. However, some differences between nonverbal and verbal communication codes have important implications for intercultural interaction.

Let's look at some examples of these differences. The following incident occurred to Judith when she was new to Algeria, where she lived for a while. One day she stood at her balcony and waved to one of the young Algerian teachers, who was walking across the school yard. Several minutes later, the young teacher knocked on the door, looking expectantly at Judith, as if summoned. Because Judith knew that it was uncommon in Algeria for men to visit women they didn't know well, she was confused. Why had he come to her door? Was it because she was foreign? After a few awkward moments, he left. A few weeks later, Judith figured it out: In Algeria (as in many other places), the U.S. "wave" is the nonverbal signal for "come here." The young teacher had assumed that Judith had summoned him to her apartment. As this example illustrates, rules for nonverbal communication vary among cultures and contexts.

Let's consider another example. Two U.S. students attending school in France were hitchhiking to the university in Grenoble for the first day of classes. A French motorist picked them up and immediately started speaking English to them. They wondered how he knew they spoke English. Later, when they took a train to Germany, the conductor walked into their compartment and berated them in English for putting their feet on the opposite seat. Again, they wondered how he had known that they spoke English. As these examples suggest, nonverbal communication entails more than gestures—even our appearance can

I have a couple of good friends who are deaf, and it is evident that body language, eye contact, and visual communication are far more important in our conversations than between two hearing people. I found that both of my friends, who lived very close to me, would much rather stop by my house than call me on the relay. I can see the cultural implications of space and distance. We keep in touch mostly by using e-mail. It's funny because the e-mails that I get from those guys have more commonly used slang words than most of my hearing friends use. The question is: Do my friends understand the slang, make it a part of their language, and create a sign for it, or do they know the words through somewhat of a verbal exchange with the hearing?
—Andrea

communicate loudly. The students' appearance alone probably was a sufficient clue to their national identity. One of our students explains:

When I studied abroad in Europe, London more specifically, our clothing as a nonverbal expression was a dead giveaway that we were from America. We dressed much more casual, wore more colors, and had words written on our T-shirts and sweatshirts. This alone said enough; we didn't even have to speak to reveal that we were Americans.

As these examples also show, nonverbal behavior operates at a subconscious level. We rarely think about how we stand, what gestures we use, and so on. Occasionally, someone points out such behaviors, which brings them to the conscious level. Consider one more example, from our student Suzanne:

I was in Macedonia and I was traveling in a car, so I immediately put on my seat belt. My host family was very offended by this because buckling my seat belt meant I didn't trust the driver. After that I rode without a seat belt.

When misunderstandings arise, we are more likely to question our verbal communication than our nonverbal communication. We can search for different ways to explain verbally what we mean. We can also look up words in a dictionary or ask someone to explain unfamiliar words. In contrast, it is more difficult to identify nonverbal miscommunications or misperceptions.

Learning Nonverbal Behavior   Whereas we learn rules and meanings for language behavior in grammar and language arts lessons, we learn nonverbal meanings and behaviors by more implicit socialization. No one explains, "When you talk with someone you like, lean forward, smile, and touch the person frequently, because that will communicate that you really care about him or her." In many contexts in the United States, such behaviors communicate immediacy and positive meanings (Burgoon & LePoire, 1999). But how is it interpreted if someone does not display these behaviors?

237

Sometimes, though, we learn strategies for nonverbal communication. Have you ever been told to shake hands firmly when you meet someone? You may have learned that a limp handshake indicates a weak person. Likewise, many young women learn to cross their legs at the ankles and to keep their legs together when they sit. These strategies combine socialization and the teaching of nonverbal codes.

Coordinating Nonverbal and Verbal Behaviors   Nonverbal behaviors can reinforce, substitute for, or contradict verbal behaviors. For example, when we shake our heads and say "no," we are reinforcing verbal behavior. When we point instead of saying "over there," we are substituting nonverbal behavior for verbal communication. If we tell a friend, "I can't wait to see you," and then don't show up at the friend's house, our nonverbal behavior is contradicting the verbal message. Because nonverbal communication operates at a less conscious level, we tend to think that people have less control over their nonverbal behavior. Therefore, we often think of nonverbal behaviors as conveying the "real" messages.

What Nonverbal Behavior Communicates

Although language is an effective and efficient means of communicating explicit information, nonverbal communication conveys **relational messages**—how we really feel about other people. Nonverbal behavior also communicates **status** and power. For example, a supervisor may be able to touch subordinates, but it is usually unacceptable for subordinates to touch a supervisor. Broad, expansive gestures are associated with high status; conversely, holding the body in a tight, closed position communicates low status.

In addition, nonverbal behavior communicates **deception.** Early researchers believed that some nonverbal behaviors (e.g., avoiding eye contact or touching or rubbing the face) indicated lying. However, as more recent research has shown, deception is communicated by fairly idiosyncratic behaviors and seems to be revealed more by inconsistency in nonverbal communication than by specific nonverbal behaviors (Freeley & Young, 1998; Henningsen, Cruz, & Morr, 2000).

Most nonverbal communication about affect, status, and deception happens at an unconscious level. For this reason, it plays an important role in intercultural interactions. Both pervasive and unconscious, it communicates how we feel about each other and about our cultural groups.

THE UNIVERSALITY OF NONVERBAL BEHAVIOR

Most traditional research in intercultural communication focuses on identifying cross-cultural differences in nonverbal behavior. How do culture, ethnicity, and gender influence nonverbal communication patterns? How universal is most nonverbal communication? Research traditionally has sought to answer these questions.

FIGURE 7-1   Nonverbal behavior can vary among cultures, in different settings, and with gender. In this photo, two men are conversing in Israel. Note the nonverbal behavior of these men—their postures, eye contact, physical contact, and facial expressions. These behaviors convey an informal social relationship among friends. How might these same nonverbal behaviors be interpreted in different settings? With strangers? (© *Frank Siteman/Stock, Boston*)

As we have observed in previous chapters, it is neither beneficial nor accurate to try to reduce individuals to one element of their identity (gender, ethnicity, nationality, and so on). Attempts to place people in discrete categories tend to reduce their complexities and to lead to major misunderstandings. However, we often classify people according to various categories to help us find universalities. For example, although we may know that not all Germans are alike, we may seek information about Germans in general to help us communicate better with individual Germans. In this section, we explore the extent to which nonverbal communication codes are universally shared. We also look for possible cultural variations in these codes that may serve as tentative guidelines to help us communicate better with others. (See Figure 7-1.)

Recent Research Findings

Research investigating the universality of nonverbal communication has focused on three areas: (1) the relationship of human behavior to that of primates (particularly chimpanzees), (2) nonverbal communication of sensory-deprived children who are blind or deaf, and (3) on facial expressions.

Chimpanzees and humans share many nonverbal behaviors. For example, both exhibit the eyebrow flash—a slight raising of the eyebrow that communicates recognition—one of the most primitive and universal animal behaviors. Primates and humans also share some facial expressions. Researcher Stephan Suomi (1988) concluded, after many animal studies, that "there are compelling parallels between specific facial expressions universally displayed by rhesus monkey infants and those expressed by human infants and young children and universally interpreted as indicative of basic emotional states" (p. 136). However, communication among monkeys, with fewer facial blends, or combinations of expressions, appears to be less complex than that among humans. Suomi points out that monkeys, with their basic communicative capabilities, "are clearly not the equivalent of furry little humans with tails" (p. 139).

Researcher Irenäus Eibl-Eibesfeldt (1988) conducted studies that compared the facial expressions of children who were blind with those of sighted children and found many similarities. Even though the children who were blind couldn't see the facial expressions of others to mimic them, they still made the same expressions. This suggests some innate, genetic basis for these behaviors.

Indeed, many cross-cultural studies support the notion of some universality in nonverbal communication, particularly in **facial expressions.** Several facial gestures seem to be universal, including the eyebrow flash just described, the nose wrinkle (indicating slight social distancing), and the "disgust face" (a strong sign of social repulsion). It is also possible that grooming behavior is universal (as it is in animals), although it seems to be somewhat suppressed in Western societies (Schiefenhovel, 1997). Recent findings indicate that at least six basic emotions—including happiness, sadness, disgust, fear, anger, and surprise—are communicated by similar facial expressions in most societies. Expressions for these emotions are recognized by most cultural groups as having the same meaning (Ekman & Friesen, 1987; Ekman & Keltner, 1997; Matsumoto, Franklin, Choi, Rogers, & Tatani, 2002).

Although research may indicate universalities in nonverbal communication, some variations exist. The evoking stimuli (i.e., what causes the nonverbal behavior) may vary from one culture to another. Smiling, for example, is universal, but what prompts a person to smile may be culture specific. Similarly, there are variations in the rules for nonverbal behavior and the contexts in which nonverbal communication takes place. For example, people kiss in most cultures, but there is variation in who kisses whom and in what contexts. When French friends greet each other, they often kiss on both cheeks but never on the mouth. Friends in the United States usually kiss on greeting only after long absence, with the kiss usually accompanied by a hug. The rules for kissing also vary along gender lines.

Finally, it is important to look for larger cultural patterns in the nonverbal behavior, rather than trying simply to identify all of the cultural differences. Researcher David Matsumoto (1990) suggests that, although cultural differences in nonverbal patterns are interesting, noting these differences is not sufficient. Studying and cataloging every variation in every aspect of nonverbal behavior would be an overwhelming task. Instead, he recommends studying nonverbal communication patterns that vary with other cultural patterns, such as values.

For example, Matsumoto links cultural patterns in facial expressions with cultural values of power distance and individualism versus collectivism. Hypothetically, cultural groups that emphasize status differences will tend to express emotions that preserve these status differences. Matsumoto also suggests that within individualistic cultures the degree of difference in emotional display between ingroups and outgroups is greater than the degree of difference between the same groups in collectivistic societies. If these theoretical relationships hold true, we can generalize about the nonverbal behavior of many different cultural groups.

Nonverbal Codes

Proxemics   As you may recall from Chapter 2, proxemics is the study of how people use personal space, or the "bubble" around us that marks the territory between ourselves and others. O. M. Watson (1970), a proxemics specialist, investigated nonverbal communication between Arab and U.S. students after hearing many complaints from each group about the other. The Arab students viewed the U.S. students as distant and rude, while the U.S. students saw the Arab students as pushy, arrogant, and rude. As Watson showed, the two groups were operating with different rules concerning personal space. Watson's research supports Edward Hall's (1976) observations about the cultural variations in how much distance individuals place between themselves and others. Hall distinguished contact cultures from noncontact cultures. He described **contact cultures** as those societies in which people stand closer together while talking, engage in more direct eye contact, use face-to-face body orientations more often while talking, touch more frequently, and speak in louder voices. He suggested that societies in South America and southern Europe are contact cultures, whereas those in northern Europe, the United States, and the Far East are **noncontact cultures**—in which people tend to stand farther apart when conversing, maintain less eye contact, and touch less often.

Of course, many other factors besides regional culture determine how far we stand from someone. Gender, age, ethnicity, context, and topic all influence the use of personal space. In fact, some studies have shown that regional culture is perhaps the least important factor. For example, in Algeria, gender might be the overriding factor, as unmarried young women and men rarely stand close together, touch each other, or maintain direct eye contact.

Eye Contact   **Eye contact** often is included in proxemics because it regulates interpersonal distance. Direct eye contact shortens the distance between two people, whereas less eye contact increases the distance. Eye contact communicates meanings about respect and status and often regulates turn-taking.

Patterns of eye contact vary from culture to culture. In many societies, avoiding eye contact communicates respect and deference, although this may vary from context to context. For many U.S. Americans, maintaining eye contact communicates that one is paying attention and showing respect.

The first time I came to the United States I stayed for over two years without returning home. My first trip home was really hard because I had forgotten a lot of my native language and I spent most of my time translating everything in my head first before I could express it in proper French. I also had a lot of problems readapting to French society and the way of doing things. One of my worst episodes was going to a post office and being very angry at the people around me because I perceived them as not knowing how to properly behave in a public space: They didn't form a waiting line but seemed to be packed in front of the teller, and they were also very close to each other without respecting the personal space that I had been accustomed to while living in the United States.

—Denis

When they speak with others, most U.S. Americans look away from their listeners most of the time, looking at their listeners perhaps every 10–15 seconds. When a speaker is finished taking a turn, he or she looks directly at the listener to signal completion. However, some cultural groups within the United States use even less eye contact while they speak. For example, some Native Americans tend to avert eye gaze during conversation.

Facial Expressions   As noted earlier in this chapter, there have been many investigations of the universality of facial expressions. Psychologists Paul Ekman and Wallace Friesen (1987) conducted extensive and systematic research in non-verbal communication. They showed pictures of U.S. Americans' facial expressions reflecting six emotions thought to be universal to people in various cultural groups. They found that people in these various cultures consistently identified the same emotions reflected in the facial expressions in the photographs.

However, Ekman and Friesen's studies have been criticized for a few reasons. First, the studies don't tap into universality; that is, people may be able to recognize and identify the six emotions because of exposure to media. Also, the researchers presented a limited number of responses (multiple-choice answers) when they asked respondents to identify emotions expressed.

Later studies improved on this research. Researchers took many photographs, not always posed, of facial expressions of members from many different cultural groups; then they asked the subjects to identify the emotion expressed by the facial expression. They showed these photographs to many different individuals in many different countries, including some without exposure to media. Their conclusion supports the notion of universality of facial expressions. Specifically, basic human emotions are expressed in a fairly finite number of facial expressions, and these expressions can be recognized and identified universally (Boucher & Carlson, 1980; Ekman & Friesen, 1987; Ekman & Keltner, 1997).

Chronemics   **Chronemics** concerns concepts of time and the rules that govern its use. There are many cultural variations regarding how people understand and use time. Edward Hall (1976) distinguished between monochronic and polychronic time orientation. People who have a **monochronic** concept of time regard it as a commodity: Time can be gained, lost, spent, wasted, or saved. In this orientation, time is linear, with one event happening at a time. In general, monochronic cultures value being punctual, completing tasks, and keeping to schedules. Most university staff and faculty in the United States maintain a monochronic orientation to time. Classes, meetings, and office appointments start when scheduled; faculty members see one student at a time, hold one meeting at a time, and keep appointments except in the case of emergency. Family problems are considered poor reasons for not fulfilling academic obligations—for both faculty and students.

In contrast, in a **polychronic** orientation, time is more holistic, and perhaps more circular: Several events can happen at once. Many international business negotiations and technical assistance projects falter and even fail because of differences in time orientation. For example, U.S. businesspeople often complain that meetings in the Middle East do not start "on time," that people socialize during meetings, and that meetings may be canceled because of personal obligations. Often, tasks are accomplished *because* of personal relationships, not in spite of them. International students and business personnel observe that U.S. Americans seem too tied to their schedules; they suggest that U.S. Americans do not care enough about relationships and often sacrifice time with friends and family in order to complete tasks and keep appointments.

Silence   Cultural groups may vary in the degree of emphasis placed on silence, which can be as meaningful as language. One of our students recalls his childhood:

> *I always learned while growing up that silence was the worse punishment ever. For example, if the house chore stated clearly that I needed to take the garbage out, and I had not done so, then my mother would not say a word to me. And I would know right away that I had forgotten to do something.*

In most U.S. American contexts, silence is not highly valued. Particularly in developing relationships, silence communicates awkwardness and can make people feel uncomfortable. According to scholar William B. Gudykunst's (1983) uncertainty reduction theory, the main reason for communicating verbally in initial interactions is to reduce uncertainty. In U.S. American contexts, people employ active uncertainty reduction strategies, such as asking questions. However, in many other cultural contexts, people reduce uncertainty using more passive strategies—for example, remaining silent, observing, or perhaps asking a third party about someone's behavior.

In a classic study on the rules for silence among the western Apache in Arizona, researcher Keith Basso (1970) identified five contexts in which silence is appropriate: (1) meeting strangers, (2) courting someone, (3) seeing friends after

Almost anyone who has been to Thailand will tell you that the feet are regarded [in value] as the lowest part of the body and the head, the highest. Therefore, people should take steps to ensure that their feet do not end up pointing directly at someone, and they should not pat others on the head. With this in mind, I'm sure you can understand my shock when the following incident was related to me by a Thai man who worked for an American multinational in Bangkok. He was in the sales department and was responsible for showing a new expatriot around. The expat was an expert in a new technology the company wished to introduce into the Thai market, so the Thai man figured he would take the guy around to some of the customers who might be interested in the new product. During the first meeting with a customer, the Thai man sat horrified as the expat reclined back in his chair and put his feet on the customer's desk—with the soles of his feet pointing directly at the customer. This is the ultimate insult. "I could not believe it!" the Thai man said. "I mean, this guy is from the company headquarters. He should know better! If some average American made this mistake, I would understand—just as an average Thai might make a mistake in the United States. But this guy was from a big multinational whose business depends on successfully dealing with another culture. I couldn't believe it."

—Chris

a long absence, (4) getting cussed out, and (5) being with people who are grieving. Verbal reticence with strangers is directly related to the conviction that the establishment of social relationships is a serious matter that calls for caution, careful judgment, and plenty of time.

In courting, western Apaches can go without speaking for a long time. Similarly, encounters between individuals who have been apart for a while may call for silence. For example, parents and children may remain silent for a time after the children have returned from boarding school, waiting to see if the returnees have changed in some way.

The western Apaches also believe that silence is an appropriate response to an individual who becomes enraged and starts insulting and criticizing others. The silence represents acknowledgment that the angry person is not really him- or herself—that the person has temporarily taken leave of his or her senses, is not responsible for his or her behavior, and therefore may be dangerous. In this instance, silence seems the safest course of action. Being with people who are sad or bereaved also calls for silence, for several reasons. First, talking is unnecessary because everyone knows how it feels to be sad. Second, intense grief, like intense rage, results in personality changes and personal instability.

Basso hypothesized that the underlying commonality in these social situations is that participants perceive their relationships vis-à-vis one another to be ambiguous and/or unpredictable and that silence is an appropriate response to uncertainty and unpredictability. He also suggested that this same contextual rule may apply to other cultural groups.

Communication scholar Charles Braithwaite (1990) tried to find out if Basso's rule applied to other communities. He compiled ethnographic accounts from 13 speech communities in which silence seems to play a similar role; these groups included Warm Springs (Oregon) Indians, Japanese Hawaiians, and 17th-century Quakers. Braithwaite extended Basso's rule when he determined that in many communities silence is not simply associated with uncertainty. Silence also is associated with social situations in which a known and unequal distribution of power exists among participants.

Cultural Variation or Stereotype?

As noted previously, one of the problems with identifying cultural variations in nonverbal codes is that it is tempting to overgeneralize these variations and stereotype people. For example, psychologist Helmut Morsbach (1988) cautions us about comparing Japanese and Western attitudes toward silence. Based on his research and extensive experience in Japan, he identifies some of the subtleties of cultural patterns of silence. For instance, the television is on continuously in many Japanese homes, and tape-recorded comments about beauty are transmitted at Zen gardens. So, although many scholars suggest that silence might be a cultural ideal, things may be different in practice. In very specific situations (such as in mother–daughter relationships or in the hiding of true feelings), there may be more emphasis on silence in Japan than in comparable U.S. situations. Also, when communicating with strangers, the Japanese view silence as more negative than it is in the United States (Hasegawa & Gudykunst, 1998).

In any case, we would be wise to heed Morsbach's warning about generalizations. Cultural variations are tentative guidelines that we can use in intercultural interaction. They should serve as examples, to help us understand that there is a great deal of variation in nonverbal behavior. Even if we can't anticipate how other people's behavior may differ from our own, we can be flexible when we do encounter differences in how close someone stands or how she or he uses eye contact or conceptualizes time.

Prejudice is often based on nonverbal aspects of behavior. That is, the negative prejudgment is triggered by physical appearances or behavior. The following excerpt from a news article underscores the importance of physical appearances in prejudice:

> In December, an Asian American male was hit with a glass bottle at his business in San Francisco by an inebriated European American male. The assailant's threats included "I'm not gonna leave, you f——ing gook or Jap or whatever you are. I'm gonna smash your windows and smash you. Go back to wherever you came from." (Cacas, 1995, p. 8)

As in many instances of hate crimes, the victim's appearance was more significant than his specific cultural heritage. From these kinds of experiences with prejudice, victims develop imaginary "maps" that tell them where they belong and

A close friend I used to have in high school was very intelligent. He took honors classes and did great in school. He was Hispanic and dressed more or less like a "cholo," with baggy pants and long shirts. When he went to speak with his counselor upon entering university, the counselor came to the conclusion that my friend was going to take easy classes rather than honors classes. His mother, who had accompanied him to the advising meeting, couldn't believe what the counselor was saying! My friend's appearance obviously caused the counselor to come to a conclusion about who and what type of person my friend was.

—Adriana

where they are likely to be rejected. They may even start to avoid places and situations in which they do not feel welcome (Marsiglia & Hecht, 1998). Can you identify places you've been where you or others were not welcome?

Semiotics and Nonverbal Communication

In Chapter 6, we introduced semiotics—the study of the signs and symbols of communication and their meanings. Semiotics is a useful tool for examining the various ways that meaning is created in advertisements, clothing, tattoos, and other cultural artifacts. Semioticians have been attentive to the context in which the signifiers (words and symbols) are placed in order to understand which meanings are being communicated. For example, wearing certain kinds of clothes in specific cultural contexts may communicate unwanted messages.

Yet cultural contexts are not fixed and rigid. Rather, they are dynamic and fleeting, as Marcel Proust (1981) noted in writing about Paris in *Remembrance of Things Past:*

> *The reality that I had known no longer existed. It sufficed that Mme Swann did not appear, in the same attire and at the same moment, for the whole avenue to be altered. The places we have known do not belong only to the world of space on which we map them for our own convenience. None of them was ever more than a thin slice, held between the contiguous impressions that composed our life at that time; the memory of a particular image is but regret for a particular moment; and houses, roads, avenues are as fugitive, alas, as the years. (p. 462)*

As this excerpt shows, there is no "real" Paris. The city has different meanings at different times for different people, and for different reasons. For example, executives of multinational corporations moving into Paris see the city quite differently from immigrants arriving in Paris for personal reasons. Therefore, to think about cultural contexts as dynamic means that we must often think about how they change and in whose interests they change.

DEFINING CULTURAL SPACE

At the beginning of this book, we provided some background information about where we grew up. Our individual histories are important in understanding our identities. As writer John Preston (1991) explains, "Where we come from is important to who we are" (p. xi). There is nothing in the rolling hills of Delaware and Pennsylvania or the red clay of Georgia that biologically determined who Judith and Tom are. However, our identities are constructed, in part, in relation to the cultural milieu of the Mid-Atlantic region or the South. Each region has its own histories and ways of life that help us understand who we are. Our decision to tell you where we come from was meant to communicate something about who we think we are. So, although we can identify precisely the borders that mark out these spaces and make them real, or material, the spaces also are cultural in the ways that we imagine them to be.

The discourses that construct the meanings of cultural spaces are dynamic and ever changing. For example, the Delaware that Judith left behind and the Georgia that Tom left behind are not characterized by the same discourses that construct those places now. In addition, the relationship between those cultural spaces and our identities is negotiated in complex ways. For example, both of us participated in other, overlapping cultural spaces that influenced how we think about who we are. Thus, just because someone is from, say, Rhode Island or Samoa or India does not mean that his or her identity and communication practices are reducible to the history of those cultural spaces.

What is the communicative (discursive) relationship between cultural spaces and intercultural communication? Recall that we define cultural space as the particular configuration of the communication (discourse) that constructs meanings of various places. This may seem like an unwieldy definition, but it underscores the complexity of cultural spaces. A cultural space is not simply a particular location that has culturally constructed meanings. It can also be a metaphorical place from which we communicate. We can speak from a number of social locations, marked on the "map of society," that give added meaning to our communication. Thus, we may speak as parents, children, colleagues, siblings, customers, Nebraskans, and a myriad of other "places." All of these are cultural spaces.

Cultural Identity and Cultural Space

Home   Cultural spaces influence how we think about ourselves and others. One of the earliest cultural spaces we experience is our home. As noted previously, nonverbal communication often involves issues of status. The home is no exception. As English professor Paul Fussell (1983) notes, "Approaching any house, one is bombarded with class signals" (p. 82). Fussell highlights the semiotic system of social class in the American home—from the way the lawn is maintained, to the kind of furniture within the home, to the way the television is situated.

These signs of social class are not always so obvious from all class positions, but we often recognize the signs.

Even if our home does not reflect the social class to which we aspire, it may be a place of identification. We often model our own lives on the patterns from our childhood homes. Although this is not always the case, the home can be a place of safety and security. African American writer bell hooks (1990) remembers:

> *When I was a young girl the journey across town to my grandmother's house was one of the most intriguing experiences. . . . I remember this journey not just because of the stories I would hear. It was a movement away from the segregated blackness of our community into a poor white neighborhood [where] we would have to pass that terrifying whiteness—those white faces on porches staring down on us with hate. . . . Oh! that feeling of safety, of arrival, of homecoming when we finally reached the edges of her yard. (p. 41)*

Home, of course, is not the same as the physical location it occupies or the building (the house) at that location. Home is variously defined in terms of specific addresses, cities, states, regions, and even nations. Although we might have historical ties to a particular place, not everyone has the same relationship between those places and their own identities. Indeed, the relationship between place and cultural identity varies. Writer Steven Saylor (1991) explains:

> *Texas is a long way, on the map and otherwise, from San Francisco. "Steven," said my mother once, "you live in another country out there." She was right, and what I feel when I fly from California to Texas must be what an expatriate from any country feels returning to his childhood home. . . . Texas is home, but Texas is also a country whose citizenship I voluntarily renounced. (p. 119)*

The discourses surrounding Texas and giving meaning to Texas no longer "fit" Saylor's sense of who he is or wants to be. We all negotiate various relationships to the cultural meanings attached to the particular places or spaces we inhabit. Consider writer Harlan Greene's (1991) relationship to his hometown in South Carolina:

> *Now that I no longer live there, I often think longingly of my hometown of Charleston. My heart beats faster and color rushes to my cheek whenever I hear someone mentioning her; I lean over and listen, for even hearing the name casts a spell. Mirages rise up, and I am as overcome and drenched in images as a runner just come from running. I see the steeples, the streets, the lush setting. (p. 55)*

Despite his attachment to Charleston, Greene does not believe that Charleston feels the same way toward him. He explains: "But I still think of Charleston; I return to her often and always will. I think of her warmly. I claim her now; even though I know she will never claim me" (p. 67).

The complex relationships we have between various places and our identities resist simplistic reduction. These three writers—hooks, Saylor, and Greene—have negotiated different sentiments toward "home." In doing so, each demonstrates the complex dialectical tensions that exist between identity and location.

FIGURE 7-2   Many cities abound with multiple cultural spaces. In this photo, several different cultural contexts are adjacent and emphasize the increasing significance of multiculturalism. How would people in this urban place experience cultural spaces differently from people who live in less diverse cultural spaces? How might it influence their intercultural communication patterns? (© *Robert Brenner/PhotoEdit, Inc.*)

Neighborhood   One significant type of cultural space that emerged in U.S. cities in the latter 19th and early 20th centuries was the ethnic or racial neighborhood. (See Figure 7-2.) By law and custom, and under different political pressures, some cities developed segregated neighborhoods. Malcolm X (Malcolm X & Haley, 1964), in his autobiography, tells of the strict laws that governed where his family could live after their house burned down:

> *My father prevailed on some friends to clothe and house us temporarily; then he moved us into another house on the outskirts of East Lansing. In those days Negroes weren't allowed after dark in East Lansing proper. There's where Michigan State University is located; I related all of this to an audience of students when I spoke there in January, 1963. . . . I told them how East Lansing harassed us so much that we had to move again, this time two miles out of town, into the country. (pp. 3–4)*

The legacy of "White-only" areas pervades the history of the United States and the development of its cultural geography. Neighborhoods exemplify how power influences intercultural contact. Thus, some cultural groups defined who got to live where and dictated the rules by which other groups lived. These rules were enforced through legal means and by harassment. For bell hooks and Malcolm X, the lines of segregation were clear and unmistakable.

In San Francisco, different racial politics constructed and isolated China-town. The boundaries that demarcated the acceptable place for Chinese and Chinese Americans to live were strictly enforced through violence:

The sense of being physically sealed within the boundaries of Chinatown was im-pressed on the few immigrants coming into the settlement by frequent stonings which occurred as they came up Washington or Clay Street from the piers. It was perpetuated by attacks of white toughs in the adjacent North Beach area and downtown around Union Square, who amused themselves by beating Chinese who came into these areas. "In those days, the boundaries were from Kearny to Powell, and from California to Broadway. If you ever passed them and went out there, the white kids would throw stones at you," Wei Bat Liu told us. (Nee & Nee, 1974, p. 60)

In contrast to Malcolm X's exclusion from East Lansing, the Chinese of San Francisco were forced to live in a marked-off territory. Yet we must be careful not to confuse the experience of Chinese in San Francisco with the experiences of all Chinese in the United States. For example, a different system developed in Savannah, Georgia, around 1900:

Robert Chung Chan advised his kinsmen and the other newly arrived Chinese to live apart from each other. He understood the distrust of Chinatowns that Cau-casians felt in San Francisco and New York. . . . Robert Chung Chan, probably more than anyone else, prevented a Chinatown from developing in Savannah. (Pruden, 1990, p. 25)

Nor should we assume that vast migrations of Chinese necessarily led to the development of Chinatowns in other cities around the world. The settlement of Chinese immigrants in the 13th Arrondissement of Paris, for example, reflects a completely different intersection between cultures: "There is no American-style Chinatown [*Il n'y a pas de Chinatown à la américaine*]" in Paris (Costa-Lascoux & Yu-Sion, 1995, p. 197).

Within the context of different power relations and historical forces, settle-ment patterns of other cultural groups created various ethnic enclaves across the U.S. landscape. For example, many small towns in the Midwest were settled by particular European groups. Thus, in Iowa, Germans settled in Amana, Dutch in Pella, and Czechs and Slovaks in Cedar Rapids. Cities, too, have their neighbor-hoods, based on settlement patterns. South Philadelphia is largely Italian Amer-ican, South Boston is largely Irish American, and Overtown in Miami is largely African American. Although it is no longer legal to mandate that people live in particular districts or neighborhoods based on their racial or ethnic back-grounds, the continued existence of such neighborhoods underscores their his-torical development and ongoing functions. Economics, family ties, social needs, and education are some factors in the perpetuation of these cultural spaces.

The relationships among identity, power, and cultural space are quite com-plex. Power relations influence who (or what) gets to claim who (or what), and under what conditions. Some subcultures are accepted and promoted within a

This writer describes the ongoing debate over the "meaning" of the Confederate flag—whether it represents hallowed traditions or symbolizes racism.

> *The flag has always been around but grew into a prominent symbol among students during the 1960s, as the civil rights movement and its demand for racial equality swept the South. Then the confederate flag became an expression of defiance across Dixie and, at Ole Miss, it really took off after enrollment of the school's first black student, James Meredith, in 1962. . . .*
>
> *Carmen Hoskins, a black graduate student, calls the flag "the symbol I hate. To them, it represents tradition, but it was one of hatred and slavery. They all swear it doesn't represent that anymore. But I don't care how many 'heritage—not hate' T-shirts I see; things have not changed that much. Get real.". . .*
>
> *But at the alumni association meeting, no one was predicting an easy solution. As he was sworn in, newly elected association president Frank Triplett, who graduated in 1955, also appealed for students and graduates to move on.*
>
> *"Change is inevitable," said Triplett, who noted in his invocation that "there is no progress without pain." But, he noted later, "This is painful for a lot of people."*

Source: From Donald P. Baker, "Waving the Past in the Future's Face," *The Washington Post National Weekly Edition*, October 13, 1997, p. 30.

particular cultural space, others are tolerated, and still others may be unacceptable. Identifying with various cultural spaces is a negotiated process that is difficult (and sometimes impossible) to predict and control. The key to understanding the relationships among culture, power, people, and cultural spaces is to think dialectically.

Regionalism   Ongoing regional and religious conflict, as well as nationalism and ethnic revival, point to the continuing struggles over who gets to define whom. Such conflicts are not new, though. In fact, some cultural spaces (such as Jerusalem) have been sites of struggle for many centuries.

Although regions are not always clearly marked on maps of the world, many people identify quite strongly with particular regions. **Regionalism** can be expressed in many ways, from symbolic expressions of identification to armed conflict. Within the United States, people may identify themselves or others as southerners, New Englanders, and so on. In Canada, people from Montreal might identify more strongly with the province of Quebec than with their country. Similarly, some Corsicans might feel a need to negotiate their identity with France. Sometimes people fly regional flags, wear particular kinds of clothes, celebrate regional holidays, and participate in other cultural activities to communicate their regional identification. However, regional expressions are not always simply celebratory, as the conflicts in Kosovo, Chechnya, Eritrea, Tibet, and Northern Ireland indicate.

National borders may seem straightforward, but they often conceal conflicting regional identities. To understand how intercultural communication may be affected by national borders, we must consider how history, power, identity, culture, and context come into play. Only by understanding these issues can we approach the complex process of human communication.

Changing Cultural Space

Chapter 8 discusses in greater detail the intercultural experiences of those who traverse cultural spaces and attempt to negotiate change. In this chapter, however, we want to focus on some of the driving needs of those who change cultural spaces.

Travel   We often change cultural spaces when we travel. Traveling is frequently viewed as an unimportant leisure activity, but it is more than that. In terms of intercultural communication, traveling changes cultural spaces in ways that often transform the traveler. Changing cultural spaces means changing who you are and how you interact with others. Perhaps the old saying "When in Rome, do as the Romans do" holds true today as we cross cultural spaces more frequently than ever.

On a recent trip to Belgium, Tom flew nonstop on British Airways from Phoenix to London and then on to Brussels. Because the entire flight was conducted in English, Tom did not have a sense of any transition from English to French. Unlike flying the now defunct Sabena (Belgian National Airlines) from the United States to Belgium, flying British Airways provided no cultural transition space between Arizona and Belgium. Thus, when he got off the plane in Brussels, Tom experienced a more abrupt cultural and language transition, from an English environment to a Flemish/French environment.

Do you alter your communication style when you encounter travelers who are not in their traditional cultural space? Do you assume that they should interact in the ways prescribed by your cultural space? These are some of the issues that travel raises.

Migration   People also change cultural spaces when they relocate. Moving, of course, involves a different kind of change in cultural spaces than traveling. In traveling, the change is fleeting, temporary, and usually desirable; it is something that travelers seek out. However, people who migrate do not always seek out this change. For example, in recent years, many people have been forced from their strife-torn homelands in Rwanda and in Bosnia and have settled elsewhere. Many immigrants leave their homelands simply so they can survive. But they often find it difficult to adjust to the change, especially if the language and customs of the new cultural space are unfamiliar.

This student explains her difficulty in knowing when she is in Japan as she moves through the airport and onto the airplane. How are these cultural spaces different from national borders?

Whenever I am at LAX [Los Angeles International Airport] on the way back to Japan, my sense of space gets really confused. For example, I fly into LAX from Phoenix, and as I line up at the Korean Air check-in counter, I see so many Asian-looking people (mostly Japanese and Koreans). Then, as I proceed, getting past the stores (e.g., duty-free shop) and walk further to the departure gate, I see a lot less Americans and, eventually and pratically, NOBODY but Asian-looking people (except for a very limited number of non-Asian-looking passengers on the same flight). So, when I wait at the gate, hearing Japanese around me, I get confused—"Where am I? Am I still in the U.S.? Or, am I already back in Japan?" This confusion gets further heightened when I go aboard and see Japanese food served for meals and watch a Japanese film or TV program on the screen. So, to me, arriving at the Narita International Airport is not the moment of arriving in Japan. It already starts while I am in the U.S. This is just one of the many examples of postmodern cultural spaces that I have experienced in my life.
—Sakura

Even within the United States, people may have trouble adapting to new surroundings when they move. Tom remembers that when northerners moved to the South they often were unfamiliar with the custom of banks closing early on Wednesday or with the traditional New Year's Day foods of black-eyed peas and collards. Ridiculing the customs of their new cultural space simply led to further intercultural communication problems.

Postmodern Cultural Spaces

Space has become increasingly important in the negotiation of cultural and social identities, and so to culture more generally. As Leah Vande Berg (1999) explains, scholars in many areas "have noted that identity and knowledge are profoundly spatial (as well as temporal), and that this condition structures meaningful embodiment and experience" (p. 249). **Postmodern cultural spaces** are places that are defined by cultural practices—languages spoken, identities enacted, rituals performed—and they often change as new people move in and out of these spaces. Imagine being in a small restaurant when a large group of people arrives, all of whom are speaking another language. How has this space changed? Whose space is it? As different people move in and out of this space, how does the cultural character change?

Inspired by her experiences in various airports around the world, Elisabeth Marx uses airport architecture as a type of cultural lens to understand each culture. How do these physical spaces reflect the cultures that built them? What can we learn about cultural space by thinking about airports? If you know of people who have traveled to other airports, what have they told you about them? How does your city's airport reflect your area's culture?

GERMANY

I always find it interesting to look at airports, airport architecture, the way the services are handled and the general atmosphere to get a first impression of a country, its society and culture. Landing at Frankfurt Airport, particularly the new Terminal 2, is impressive: it is glitzy and big, with glass walls, expensive materials, generous planning and a logical layout— everything you would expect in Germany. However, it takes ages to get through passport control: every single passport is scrutinized and put through an electronic detection system, resulting in large queues of people waiting to get to the luggage area and out of the airport. Is this a colossal system that does not seem to be terribly efficient at times, or is efficiency simply defined in a different way?

FRANCE

Landing at Charles de Gaulle Airport is like being in a 1960s science fiction movie. Its interesting, space-age design illustrates France's affinity for technical advances and modernist architecture and the importance of engineering within its culture. But is design more important than efficiency? To the newcomer, the airport is slightly confusing as you have the impression of running round in circles. However, there is no doubt that there is always an interesting and surprising angle to consider.

In his study of listening among the Blackfeet, Donal Carbaugh (1999) reports that listening is intimately connected to place as a cultural space. It is both a physical location and a cultural phenomenon. Through his cultural informant, Two Bears, Carbaugh notes that

in his oral utterance to us about "listening," in this landscape, he is commenting about a non-oral act of listening to this landscape. This nonverbal act is itself a deeply cultural form of action in which the Blackfeet persona and the physical place become intimately linked, in a particularly Blackfeet way. (p. 257)

But these places are dynamic, and "listening" is not limited to fixed locations: "Some kinds of places are apparently more appropriate for this kind of Blackfeet

UK

"Arriving at Heathrow is like arriving in a third world country," commented a self-critical British friend. The main Heathrow building with its three terminals always seems to be in a state of chaos with permanent attempts at improvement, leaving the traveler in a similar state of confusion. Although Heathrow has improved dramatically over the years and has extensive shopping facilities, its rather slapdash approach towards airport architecture may reflect the UK's "layperson" approach. The British are pragmatic and have a low-key attitude to adversity: they don't get too upset and may not seek perfectionism at all costs; they are also prepared to change and to be flexible. This may be one of their strong points when it comes to business.

USA

Landing at San Francisco Airport is at first a pleasant experience—a great location for an airport and a smooth transition through immigration; there are efforts to show off the Californian flora and a distinctly personal touch in a greeting from the city's mayor. However, this personal greeting is a continuous tape and when you have to hear it for the third time in three minutes, you are getting slightly tired of this noise pollution—is this a symptom of the automatized, "have a nice day" service orientation in the USA?

CHINA

Beijing Airport, 1992, on holiday—landing in a daze after a harrowing flight. Glad to be alive and being processed through the airport—there is a clear separation in the treatment of foreigners and PRC [People's Republic of China] Chinese. Fortunately, I am met by an American friend who is a fluent Chinese speaker and has lived in China for years—an example of a translator with the right links whom every western businessperson needs in China.

Source: From Elisabeth Marx, *Breaking Through Culture Shock*, 1999, pp. 79, 82, 84–85, 88, 91.

'listening' than are others, although—according to Two Bears—'just about anywhere' might do" (p. 257). Physical place, in this sense, can become a cultural space in that it is infused with cultural meanings. Think about how the same physical place might have a different meaning to someone from a different cultural group.

The fluid and fleeting nature of cultural space stands in sharp contrast to the 18th- and 19th-century notions of space, which promoted land ownership, surveys, borders, colonies, and territories. No passport is needed to travel in the postmodern cultural space, because there are no border guards. The dynamic nature of postmodern cultural spaces underscores its response to changing cultural needs. The space exists only as long as it is needed in its present form.

Postmodern cultural spaces are both tenuous and dynamic. They are created within existing places, without following any particular guide: There is no marking off of territory, no sense of permanence or official recognition. The postmodern cultural space exists only while it is used.

The ideology of fixed spaces and categories is currently being challenged by postmodernist notions of space and location. Phoenix, for example, which became a city relatively recently, has no Chinatown, or Japantown, or Koreatown, no Irish district, or Polish neighborhood, or Italian area. Instead, people of Polish descent, for example, might live anywhere in the metropolitan area but congregate for special occasions or for specific reasons. On Sundays, the Polish Catholic mass draws many people from throughout Phoenix. When people want to buy Polish breads and pastries, they can go to the Polish bakery and also speak Polish there. Ethnic identity is only one of several identities that these people negotiate. When they desire recognition and interaction based on their Polish heritage, they can meet that wish. When they seek other forms of identification, they can go to places where they can be Phoenix Suns fans, or community volunteers, and so on. Ethnic identity is neither the sole factor nor necessarily the most important one at all times in their lives.

The markers of ethnic life in Phoenix are the urban sites where people congregate when they desire ethnic cultural contact. At other times, they may frequent other locations in expressing other aspects of their identities. In this sense, the postmodern urban space is dynamic and allows people to participate in the communication of identity in new ways (Drzewiecka & Nakayama, 1998).

Cultural spaces can also be metaphorical, with historically defined places serving as sources of contemporary identity negotiation in new spaces. In her study of academia, Olga Idriss Davis (1999) turns to the historical role of the kitchen in African American women's lives and uses the kitchen legacy as a way to rethink the university. She notes that "the relationship between the kitchen and the Academy [university] informs African American women's experience and historically interconnects their struggles for identity" (p. 370). In this sense, the kitchen is a metaphorical cultural space that is invoked in an entirely new place, the university. Again, this postmodern cultural space is not material but metaphoric, and it allows people to negotiate their identities in new places.

SUMMARY

In this chapter, we examined both nonverbal communication principles and cultural spaces. Nonverbal communication operates at a subconscious level. It is learned implicitly and can reinforce, substitute for, or contradict verbal behaviors.

Nonverbal behaviors can communicate relational meaning, status, and deception. Nonverbal codes are influenced by culture, although many cultures share some nonverbal behaviors. Nonverbal codes include proxemics, eye contact, facial expressions, chronemics, and silence. Sometimes cultural differences in nonverbal behaviors can lead to stereotyping of other cultures. Semiotics is one approach to studying nonverbal communication, including cultural practices related to clothing styles and advertising. Cultural space influences cultural identity. Cultural spaces such as homes, neighborhoods, regions, and nations relate to issues of power and intercultural communication. Two ways of changing cultural spaces are travel and migration. Postmodern cultural spaces are tenuous and dynamic, accommodating people with different cultural identities.

DISCUSSION QUESTIONS

1. How does nonverbal communication differ from verbal communication?
2. What are some of the messages that we communicate through our nonverbal behaviors?
3. Which nonverbal behaviors, if any, are universal?
4. How do our cultural spaces affect our identities?
5. What role does power play in determining our cultural spaces?
6. What is the importance of cultural spaces to intercultural communication?
7. How do postmodern cultural spaces differ from modernist notions of cultural space?

 Go to the self-quizzes on the Online Learning Center at www.mhhe.com/martinnakayama to further test your knowledge.

ACTIVITIES

1. *Cultural Spaces.* Think about the different cultural spaces in which you participate (clubs, churches, concerts, and so on). Select one of these spaces and describe when and how you enter and leave it. As a group, discuss the answers to the following questions:
   a. Which cultural spaces do many students share? Which are not shared by many students?
   b. Which cultural spaces, if any, are denied to some people?
   c. What factors determine whether a person has access to a specific cultural space?
2. *Nonverbal Rules.* Choose a cultural space that you are interested in studying. Visit this space on four occasions to observe how people there interact. Focus on one aspect of nonverbal communication (e.g., eye contact or proximity). List some rules that seem to govern this aspect of nonverbal communication. For example, if you are focusing on proximity, you might describe, among other things, how far apart people tend to stand when conversing. Based on your observations, list some prescriptions about proper (expected) nonverbal behavior in this cultural space. Share your conclusions with the class. To what extent do other students share your

conclusions? Can we generalize about nonverbal rules in cultural spaces? What factors influence whether an individual follows unspoken rules of behavior?

chronemics	facial expressions	regionalism
contact cultures	monochronic	relational messages
cultural space	noncontact cultures	status
deception	polychronic	
eye contact	postmodern cultural spaces	

 The Online Learning Center at www.mhhe.com/martinnakayama features flashcards and crossword puzzles based on these terms and concepts.

REFERENCES

Baker, D. P. (1997, October 13). Waving the past in the future's face. *The Washington Post National Weekly Edition*, p. 30.

Basso, K. (1970). "To give up on words": Silence in western Apache culture. *Southwestern Journal of Anthropology, 26*, 213–320.

Boucher, J. D., & Carlson, G. E. (1980). Recognition of facial expression in three cultures. *Journal of Cross Cultural Psychology, 11*, 263–280.

Braithwaite, C. A. (1990). Communicative silence: A cross-cultural study of Basso's hypothesis. In D. Carbaugh (Ed.), *Cultural communication and intercultural contact* (pp. 321–327). Hillsdale, NJ: Lawrence Erlbaum.

Burgoon, J. K., Buller, D. B., & Woodall, W. G. (1996). *Nonverbal communication: The unspoken dialogue* (2nd ed.). New York: Harper & Row.

Burgoon, J. K., & LePoire, B. A. (1999). Nonverbal cues and interpersonal judgments: Participant and observer perceptions of intimacy, dominance, composure and formality. *Communication Monographs, 66*, 105–124.

Cacas, S. (1995, August 4). Violence against APAs on the rise. *Asian Week*, pp. 1, 8.

Carbaugh, D. (1999). "Just listen": "Listening" and landscape among the Blackfeet. *Western Journal of Communication, 63*(3), 250–270.

Costa-Lascoux, J., & Yu-Sion, L. (1995). *Paris-XIIIe, lumières d'Asie.* Paris: Éditions Autrement.

Davis, O. I. (1999). In the kitchen: Transforming the academy through safe spaces of resistance. *Western Journal of Communication, 63*(3), 364–381.

Drzewiecka, J. A., & Nakayama, T. K. (1998). City sites: Postmodern urban space and the communication of identity. *Southern Communication Journal, 64*, 20–31.

Eibl-Eibesfeldt, I. (1988). Social interactions in an ethological, cross-cultural perspective. In F. Poyatos (Ed.), *Cross cultural perspectives in nonverbal communication* (pp. 107–130). Lewiston, NY: Hogrefe.

Ekman, P., & Friesen, W. V. (1987). Universals and cultural differences in the judgments of facial expressions of emotion. *Journal of Personality and Social Psychology, 53*, 712–717.

Ekman, P., & Keltner, D. (1997). Universal facial expressions of emotion: An old controversy and new findings. In U. Segerstråle & P. Molnár (Eds.), *Nonverbal communication: Where nature meets culture* (pp. 27–46). Mahwah, NJ: Lawrence Erlbaum.

Fletcher, C. (1992). The semiotics of survival: Street cops read the street. *Howard Journal of Communications, 4*(1, 2), 133–142.

Freeley, T. H., & Young, M. J. (1998). Humans as lie detectors: Some more second thoughts. *Communication Quarterly, 46*, 109–126.

Fussell, P. (1983). *Class.* New York: Ballantine Books.

Greene, H. (1991). Charleston, South Carolina. In J. Preston (Ed.), *Hometowns: Gay men write about where they belong* (pp. 55–67). New York: Dutton.

Gudykunst, W. B. (1983). Uncertainty reduction and predictability of behavior in low and high context cultures. *Communication Quarterly, 31*, 49–55.

Hall, E. T. (1976). *Beyond culture.* Garden City, NY: Doubleday.

Hasegawa, T., & Gudykunst, W. B. (1998). Silence in Japan and the United States. *Journal of Cross-Cultural Psychology, 29*, 668–684.

Henningsen, D. D., Cruz, M. G., & Morr, M. C. (2000). Pattern violations and perceptions of deception. *Communication Reports, 13*, 1–9.

hooks, b. (1990). *Yearning: Race, gender, and cultural politics.* Boston: South End Press.

Malcolm X, & Haley, A. (1964). *The autobiography of Malcolm X.* New York: Grove Press.

Marsiglia, F. F., & Hecht, M. L. (1998). Personal and interpersonal interventions. In M. L. Hecht (Ed.), *Communicating prejudice* (pp. 287–301). Thousand Oaks, CA: Sage.

Marx, E. (1999). *Breaking through culture shock.* London: Nicholas Brealey.

Matsumoto, D. (1990). Cultural influences on facial expressions of emotion. *Southern Communication Journal, 56*, 128–137.

Matsumoto, D., Franklin, B., Choi, J.-W., Rogers, D., & Tatani, H. (2002). Cultural influences in the expression and perception of emotion. In W. B. Gudykunst & B. Mody (Eds.), *Handbook of international and intercultural communication* (2nd ed., pp. 107–127). Thousand Oaks, CA: Sage.

Morsbach, H. (1988). The importance of silence and stillness in Japanese nonverbal communication: A cross cultural approach. In F. Poyatos (Ed.), *Cross cultural perspectives in nonverbal communication* (pp. 201–215). Lewiston, NY: Hogrefe.

Nee, V. G., & Nee, B. D. B. (1974). *Longtime Californ': A documentary study of an American Chinatown.* Boston: Houghton Mifflin.

Preston, J. (1991). Introduction. In J. Preston (Ed.), *Hometowns: Gay men write about where they belong* (pp. xi–xiv). New York: Dutton.

Proust, M. (1981). *Swann in love: Remembrance of things past* (C. K. S. Moncrieff & T. Kilmartin, Trans.). New York: Vintage.

Pruden, G. B., Jr. (1990). History of the Chinese in Savannah, Georgia. In J. Goldstein (Ed.), *Georgia's East Asian connection: Into the twenty-first century: Vol. 27. West Georgia College studies in the social sciences* (pp. 17–34). Carrollton: West Georgia College.

Saylor, S. (1991). Amethyst, Texas. In J. Preston (Ed.), *Hometowns: Gay men write about where they belong* (pp. 119–135). New York: Dutton.

Schiefenhovel, W. (1997). Universals in interpersonal interactions. In U. Segerstråle & P. Molnár (Eds.), *Nonverbal communication: Where nature meets culture* (pp. 61–79). Mahwah, NJ: Lawrence Erlbaum.

Suomi, S. J. (1988). Nonverbal communication in nonhuman primates: Implications for the emergence of culture. In U. Segerstråle & P. Molnár (Eds.), *Nonverbal communication: Where nature meets culture* (pp. 131–150). Mahwah, NJ: Lawrence Erlbaum.

Vande Berg, L. R. (1999). An introduction to the special issue on "spaces." *Western Journal of Communication, 63*(3), 249.

Watson, O. M. (1970). *Proxemic behavior: A cross cultural study.* The Hague: Mouton.

PART III

Intercultural Communication Applications

UNDERSTANDING INTERCULTURAL TRANSITIONS

In Chapter 7, we discussed how we define and move through various cultural spaces. In this chapter, we look more specifically at how we move between cultural contexts. People travel across cultural boundaries for many different reasons: for work, study, or adventure, or in response to political or other events. A recent *National Geographic* story highlights a high school in Falls Church, Virginia, whose student body indicates the tremendous migration that is going on around the world. The high school opened in 1959 with 1,616 students, mostly European Americans. In the year 2000, the 1,400-member student population came from 70 different countries, and more than half learned English as a second language!

> *"It's as if you took the whole human race and threw it up in the air—and everyone ended up here," says Mel Riddle, principal of the school. "Everybody's a minority here—and that's the best mix of all." (quoted in Swerdlow, 2001, pp. 44–45)*

Among the languages spoken by the students are Italian, Korean, Persian, Russian, Turkish, French, and Hindi. One of the students, Thuy-Lan Phan, came to the United States with his family in 1993 after her father had spent six years as a political prisoner in Vietnam. Although some students, like Phan, came from regions plagued by war, civil unrest, or extreme poverty, most students' families emigrated simply to find a better life—like most world migrants. Some students are here because their parents were recruited for jobs in the Washington, DC, area. And some students are third- and fourth-generation Italian and Irish and other European Americans. A few are exchange students, spending a year in the United States for the cultural experience. As one student, Kevin Wiafe, whose family left Ghana in 1980, put it, he is inspired by "curiosity and adventure."

This high school reflects the changing face of the United States and reflects what is happening in many countries around the world, and this pattern of migration has tremendous implications for intercultural communication. Migration is changing the makeup of populations everywhere—and migration doesn't have to be defined in terms of crossing national borders. For example, China has the largest rural-to-urban migration, and Asia in general has substantial intraregional migrations (e.g., Thais migrating to Taiwan for jobs). Singapore has a million foreign workers among its 2.1 million workers, and Thailand and Malaysia also have substantial numbers of foreign workers. And the same thing is happening in Europe: Britain and France each have 7% foreign-born populations, and immigrants now constitute nearly 10% of Germany's population. And 17% of residents in Canada are foreign-born.

The oil-exporting Middle East countries have huge numbers of foreign workers (e.g., 70% of the labor force in Saudi Arabia in 2000), but they also have 45% of the world's refugees (Martin & Widgren, 2002). In contrast, some regions are losing more people than they are gaining—many African and Caribbean nations have more emigration than immigration. Reductions in a region's population also have implications for intercultural communication. For example, the "brain drain" from Africa has resulted in many young Africans seeking edu-

In this article, the author describes the high cost of losing educated professionals for many African countries.

> *Africa is losing as much as US $4 billion a year through top professionals seeking better jobs abroad, according to research by a senior economist at Addis Ababa University. Dr. Dejene Aredo argues that 20,000 professionals each year leave the continent for new jobs in the west. "It is a problem, because there is a huge deficit of manpower in developing countries." . . . He said that for every 100 professionals sent abroad for further training between 1982 and 1997, 35 failed to return home.*
>
> *"In Ethiopia alone we have one full professor in economics—in the United States they have more than 100. We don't have enough highly skilled manpower," he said.*
>
> *Dejene argues that countries should put policies in place that restrict the flow of educated migrants. He also says western governments should pay compensation for drawing the best talent away from developing countries. He believes that higher wages, better access to information and the dominance of western culture and values act as a magnet to professionals.*
>
> *"Today if you visit colleges and universities in this country you will not find any lecturers who have been there for more than seven or eight years," he said. He pointed out that the majority of senior lecturers had been lured abroad by lucrative university posts and by political freedoms.*
>
> *"The main reason people go is politics," he added. "Across Africa I still think the main reason people go is political, the lack of development, democratisation and human rights. . . . And some may leave simply for better opportunities."*

Source: From UN Integrated Regional Information Networks. "Braindrain Reportedly Costing $4 Billion a Year," April 30, 2002. allafrica.com/stories/200204300167.html

cation abroad and then settling there, depriving their home countries of needed educational and technological expertise.

What can we learn about cultural transitions from these particular intercultural experiences? Why do people travel across cultural boundaries? Why are some transitions easy for some people and more difficult for others? Why do some people choose to adapt and others resist adaptation? What can we learn about culture and communication from these experiences?

We begin this chapter by discussing characteristics of three groups of travelers (migrants). We define culture shock and examine how migrants resist or adapt to new cultural contexts. Using a dialectical framework, we also identify four ways in which migrants and hosts can relate. Then we turn our attention to the individual experience of dealing with cultural transitions. We identify four models of individual adaptation: (1) the anxiety and uncertainty management model, (2) the U-curve model, (3) the transition model, and (4) the communication system model. Finally, we explore the relationship between identity, context, and adaptation, and examine the contexts of intercultural transitions.

TYPES OF MIGRANT GROUPS

A dialectical perspective requires that we examine intercultural transitions on both a personal and a contextual level (Berry, 1992). On the personal level, we can look at individual experiences of adapting to new cultural contexts. But we also can examine the larger social, historical, economic, and political contexts in which these personal transitions occur. To understand cultural transitions, we must simultaneously consider both the individual migrant groups and the contexts in which they travel.

Migration may be long-term or short-term and voluntary or involuntary. A **migrant** is an individual who leaves the primary cultural contexts in which he or she was raised and moves to a new cultural context for an extended period. For instance, exchange students, sojourns are relatively short-term and voluntary, and these transitions occur within a structured sociopolitical context. In contrast, Thuy-Lan Phan's family's sojourn is a long-term one, an experience of being forced to relocate due to an unstable sociopolitical context. Cultural transitions may vary in length and in degree of voluntariness. We can identify four types of migrant groups based on these criteria. (See Figure 8-1.)

Voluntary Migrants

There are two groups of voluntary travelers: sojourners and immigrants. **Sojourners** are those travelers who move into new cultural contexts for a limited time and a specific purpose. They are often people who have freedom and the means to travel. This includes international students who go abroad to study and technical assistance workers, corporate personnel, and missionaries who go abroad to work for a specific period. Some domestic sojourners move from one region to another within their own country for a limited time to attend school or work (e.g., Native Americans who leave their reservations).

Another type of voluntary traveler is the immigrant, first discussed in Chapter 1. Families that voluntarily leave one country to settle in another exemplify this type of migrant. Although many U.S. Americans believe that most immigrants come to the United States in search of freedom, the truth is that most come for economic reasons. There is often a fluid and interdependent relationship between the countries that send and those that receive immigrants. Countries like the United States welcome working immigrants, even issuing special visas and developing programs (such as the *bracero* program of the 1940s between the United States and Mexico) during times of economic prosperity (Oboler, 1995). Currently, there are only five major countries that officially welcome international migrants as permanent residents: the United States, Canada, Australia,

FIGURE 8-1   People have always traveled from their homelands, but with the increasing technological ease of travel, people are moving much more than ever before. Sojourners, business travelers, tourists, immigrants, and refugees have very different reasons for traveling. These people are waiting for international arrivals at the Atlanta airport. How might their reasons for traveling shape their intercultural experiences? (© *Jeff Greenberg/PhotoEdit, Inc.*)

Israel, and New Zealand. Altogether, these countries accept 1.2 million immigrants a year, a small percentage of the estimated annual global immigration—and these countries can quickly restrict immigration during economic downturns. However, most migrants who move to another country are not accepted as official immigrants. And due to shifts in economic and political policy, family members of migrants may be trapped in the home country, unable to join the rest of the family in the new home country.

International migration is a global fact of life in the 21st century. According to the Population Reference Bureau, at least 160 million people were living outside their country of birth or citizenship in 2000, an increase of about 25% since 1990. Most of this international migration occurs not from developing countries to industrialized countries but from one developing country to another (Martin & Widgren, 2002).

The voluntariness of immigration is more variable than absolute. Some migrants feel that they have a choice in moving whereas others may not. The decision to migrate usually is made while other factors intervene. The three main reasons that people migrate are asylum seeking, family reunification, and economics (Featherstone, 2002).

One of the influences on adaptation is ethnicity and country of origin. Meri Nana-Ama Danquah, whose family came to the United States from Ghana when she was six, describes how difficult it was for her to make this transition, partly because they came from Africa.

> *Being black made the transition from Africa to America extremely difficult because it introduced another complex series of boundaries. In a racially divided country, it isn't enough for an immigrant to know how to float in the mainstream. You have to know how to retreat to your margin, where to place your hyphen. You have to know that you are no longer just yourself, you are now an Asian American, a Latin American, an Irish American, or in my case a black American. . . .*
>
> *The white Americans—children and adults—I met attacked me with verbal "kindness," not verbal cruelty. Their branding came in the form of adjectives, not nouns—special, exceptional, different, exotic. These words, which flowed so freely from the lips of teachers, parents, and fellow students, were intended to excuse me from my race, to cage me like some zoo animal being domesticated; these words, I realized years later, were intended to absolve those white people from their own racism. I was among the black people to whom many white people were referring when they said, "Some of my best friends." . . . I was complimented for not talking like "them," not acting like "them," not looking like "them"—"them" being black Americans, the only other physical reflections I had of myself besides my family. But, of course, that wasn't acceptance; it was tolerance.*
>
> *The one place where I found acceptance was in the company of other immigrants. Together, we concentrated on our similarities, not our differences, because our differences were our similarities. Still, I secretly envied the other foreign kids because I believed that their immigrant experience was somehow more authentic than mine. Unlike me, they were not caught in the racial battlefield of black and white, their ethnicity was visible. Mine invariably faded to black. They spoke languages that were identifiable. Everybody's heard of Spanish, Korean, Chinese, even Arabic. The few people who had heard of Ga and Twi colonially labeled them dialects, not languages.*

Source: From "Life as an Alien," by Meri Nana-Ama Danquah, 1988, *Half+Half*, edited by C. C. O'Hearn, pp. 105–106.

Involuntary Migrants

There are two types of migrants who move involuntarily: **long-term refugees** and **short-term refugees.** According to one estimate, 14 million people have left their home countries since 1979 because of superpower struggles (e.g., in Afghanistan, Angola, and Cambodia) and, more recently, because of internal ethnic strife (e.g., in the former Yugoslavia and in Rwanda). Long-term refugees are

POINT OF VIEW

This article describes the experience of one group of short-term refugees—the thousands of Native American youths who were taken from their homes and sent to "boarding schools" from the 1880s through the 1960s. Richard H. Pratt, a zealous army officer, spearheaded this movement, believing that removing these children from their culture would force their assimilation into mainstream society.

Whether toddlers or teens, they were taken from home and shipped thousands of miles to dreary barracks. Their hair was cut, they were given new names, and each was assigned a number.

The United States government began their brutal attempt at social engineering in 1879. Breaking rebellious Indians by indoctrinating their children in Anglo ways was considered a cost-effective alternative to war. But the personal cost to native Americans was incalculable. . . .

They were literally kidnapped, loaded on wagons or trains, and all of them thought at any moment they were going to die. When the children arrived at the schools, it was the first time they'd been away from home. . . .

Contagious diseases often swept through the schools, and exposure to the elements took the lives of many runaways. . . . For decades, there was little criticism of this abusive program from a nation steeped in dime novels about "the savage Indian." Instead, magazines such as Harper's Weekly *praised the schools. . . .*

Vocational training was central to the boarding-school mission. Indian teens worked at various tasks—girls setting tables and cooking meals, boys repairing shoes or pushing wheelbarrows.

Pratt's misguided vision was never fully realized, as most children eventually returned to their families and old ways of life. By the 1960s, tribes wrestled control of the schools away from the federal government. Today, only four boarding schools remain, and attendance is voluntary.

Robin Tsosie, a Navajo who went to Arizona's Leupo Indian School from kindergarten through second grade, describes his experience there as "scary." "They were very strict. We had to always have our hair braided and wear dresses. . . . It was heartbreaking," he says. "It brings back bad memories. It's sad that we were forced to change our identities when all we wanted to do was be ourselves. We now have to teach our kids where we came from."

"It was a sad era when they tried to put American/European values on their culture," says Dorothy Allenson of Cape Coral, Fla. "I hope it was just ignorance and not something else."

Countless native Americans are still grappling with their boarding-school ordeals. But they no longer suffer quietly.

Source: From T. Vanderpool, "Lesson No. 1: Shed Your Indian Identity," *Christian Science Monitor*, April 2, 2002, p. 14.

those like Phan's family, forced to relocate permanently because of war, famine, and oppression. Long-term refugees include those who left Rwanda during the war in 1993, and the war in the former Yugoslavia in the mid-1990s.

One of our students, Naida, describes how her family fled Bosnia to become refugees and then immigrants in the United States:

> *During the year 1992, civil war erupted in my home country, Bosnia. Overnight my life shifted from a peaceful existence to fear, persecution, and anxiety. My family and I were forcefully taken to a concentration camp, where we witnessed the blind rage of mankind expressed through physical and mental abuses, humiliation, destruction, rapes, and killings. Six months later, we were among the 5,000 people released. We returned home to fight for simple survival. At the age of 16, I found myself spending my days planning ways for my family to escape. My family and I were again forced from our home and experienced three years of uncertainty, fear and anger. The life we knew and had taken for granted was abruptly changed by others' political agendas. Having our basic human rights violated was the experience that literally changed my life.*

Her family was eventually rescued by the International Red Cross in 1995 and transported to Phoenix, Arizona. She describes the difficulty of being a refugee and yearning for her past life:

> *I witnessed this part of my life in confusion; I wanted tears but they were hiding. I let a loud scream, but my face was numb. I understood just how fortunate we were to have had the opportunity to leave my war-torn country and live in peace again. I don't think I realized the magnitude and the burden of our experiences until a year later, after my family and I were well situated in Phoenix. I kept thinking about thousands of Bosnian people left behind still living in danger and kept praying for them. Then nostalgia settled in—despite the horrors I witnessed in Bosnia, I wanted to return to my hometown. I disliked everything about my new home.*

There are also cases of domestic refugees who are forced, for short or indefinite periods, to move within a country. Examples include the Japanese Americans sent to internment camps during World War II; the Cherokees forcibly removed in 1838 from their own nation, New Echota, to Oklahoma (the devastating Trail of Tears); and the Mormons, who fled the East and eventually settled in Utah and elsewhere in the West. Populations also relocate temporarily because of natural disasters, such as hurricanes or floods. This mass migration of refugees presents complex issues for intercultural communication, pointing to the importance of context. The complex communication issues involve culture shock, identity, and adaptation.

CULTURE SHOCK

Individuals face many challenges of transition in new cultural contexts. **Culture shock** is a relatively short-term feeling of disorientation, of discomfort due to the unfamiliarity of surroundings and the lack of familiar cues in the environ-

The majority of individuals and families that emigrate from other countries have the ability to positively confront the obstacles of a new environment. Dr. Carmen Guanipa, a psychologist, suggests specific ways to combat stress produced by culture shock.

- Develop a hobby.
- Be patient; the act of immigrating is a process of adaptation to new situations. It is going to take time.
- Learn to include a regular form of physical activity in your routine. This will help combat the sadness and loneliness in a constructive manner. Exercise, swim, take an aerobics class, etc.
- Practice relaxation and meditation. These are proven to be very positive for people who are passing through periods of stress.
- Maintain contact with your ethnic group. This will give you a feeling of belonging and will reduce your feelings of loneliness and alienation.
- Maintain contact with the new culture. Learn the language. Volunteer in community activities that allow you to practice the language you are learning. This will help you feel less stress about language and useful at the same time.
- Allow yourself to feel sad about the things that you have left behind: your family, your friends, etc.
- Recognize the sorrow of leaving your old country. Accept the new country. Focus your power on getting through the transition.
- Pay attention to relationships with your family and at work. They will serve as support for you in difficult times.
- Find ways to live with the things that don't satisfy you 100%.
- If you feel stressed, look for help. There is always someone or some service available to help you.

Source: From Carmen Guanipa, Department of Counseling and School Psychology, San Diego State University, 1998. edweb.sdsu.edu/people/Cguanipa/cultshok.htm

ment. Kalvero Oberg, the anthropologist who coined the term *culture shock*, suggests that it is like a disease, complete with symptoms (excessive hand washing, irritability, and so on). If it is treated properly (that is, if the migrant learns the language, makes friends, and so on), the migrant can "recover," or adapt to the new cultural situation and feel at home (Oberg, 1960). One international student described her experience:

> *The first year was the toughest . . . the everyday experience of some of the simplest things (such as making friends, going out on a date, talking with your American professors, and so on) created a significant level of anxiety and stress. I remember*

during the final week of my second semester, I had a severe chest pain. I also started crying as I was writing up final papers. I had no idea why this was happening to me . . . everything seemed different. And it was a very, very difficult time for me.

Although most individuals experience culture shock during the period of transition to a new culture, they are less likely to experience it if they maintain separateness because culture shock presumes cultural contact. For instance, military personnel who live abroad on U.S. bases and have very little contact with members of the host society often experience little culture shock. In fact, the very structure of military bases and military housing is designed to insulate military personnel from the host society.

Almost all migrants who cross cultural boundaries, whether voluntarily or not, experience culture shock. They then face a long-term process of more or less adapting to the new culture. However, for many individuals, the long-term adaptation is not easy. Some people actively resist assimilation in the short term. For example, many students from Muslim countries, especially females, often continue to wear traditional clothing while living in the United States, thus actively resisting participating in U.S. popular culture. Others resist assimilation in the long term, as is the case with some religious groups, like the Amish and the Hutterites. Some would like to assimilate but are not welcome in the new culture, as is the case with many immigrants to the United States from Latin America. And some people adapt to some aspects of the new culture but not to others.

In sum, the relationship between host society and migrants is complicated. Continuing with the theme of the personal–contextual dialectic, let's look at how hosts and migrants can relate.

MIGRANT–HOST RELATIONSHIPS

There are four ways in which migrants may relate to their new cultures: They can assimilate, remain separate, integrate, or become marginalized.

Assimilation

In an **assimilation** mode, the individual does not want to maintain an isolated cultural identity but wants to maintain relationships with other groups in the new culture. And the migrant is more or less welcomed by the new cultural hosts. When this course is freely chosen by everyone, it creates the archetypal "melting pot." The central focus in assimilation is not on retaining one's cultural heritage. Many immigrant groups, particularly those from Europe, follow this mode of adapting in North America. For them, assimilating may not require adjusting to new customs. The same religions dominate, eating practices (the use of forks, knives, and spoons) are the same, and many other cultural practices (clearly originated in Europe) are already familiar. However, when the dominant group forces assimilation, especially on immigrants whose customs are different from those of the host society, it creates a "pressure cooker." This mode of relating often entails giving up or losing many aspects of the original culture, including language. One of our students, Rick, describes the process:

> *I am Mexican American and I grew up in a household where we took part in cultural events, but we never discussed why we did them. I am always asked if I know how to speak Spanish. I guess people ascribe this to my appearance. My parents speak Spanish fluently, as well as English, but they never taught my siblings or myself because they did not want us to have any problems when we entered school, as they did.*

And some people question why immigrants need to give up so much to assimilate. As one of our students said, "Why must we lose our history to fit into the American way of life? I suppose that, because race is such a sensitive issue in our country, by not discussing culture and race we feel it makes the issue less volatile." A recent study of African Americans and Hispanic Americans showed the effects of society's pressure on groups to assimilate. According to the study, the more experiences people had with ethnic or racial discrimination (on the job, in public settings, in housing, and in dealings with police), the less importance they assigned to maintaining their own cultural heritage. This suggests that heavy doses of discrimination can discourage retention of immigrants' original cultural practices (Ruggiero, Taylor, & Lambert, 1996).

Separation

There are two forms of **separation.** The first is when migrants choose to retain their original culture and avoid interaction with other groups. This is the mode followed by groups like the Amish, who came to the United States from Europe in the 18th century. They maintain their own way of life and identity and avoid prolonged contact with other groups. Many strict religious groups actively resist the influence of the dominant society. The Amish, for example, do not participate in U.S. popular culture; they don't have televisions or radios, go to movies, or read mainstream newspapers or books. An important point here is that these groups choose separation, and the dominant society respects their choice.

However, if such separation is initiated and enforced by the dominant society, the condition constitutes a second type of separation, **segregation.** Many cities and states in the United States historically had quite restrictive codes that dictated where members of various racial and ethnic groups could and could not live. For example, Oregon passed legislation in 1849 excluding Blacks from the state; it was not repealed until 1926 (Henderson, 1999, p. 74). You may recall the excerpt in Chapter 7 from Malcolm X's autobiography in which he notes that his family could not live in East Lansing, Michigan, because it was for Whites only. An example of de facto segregation is the practice of redlining, in which banks refuse loans to members of particular ethnic groups. This practice perpetuates ethnic segregation.

Scholar Suzanne Oboler (1995) explains that many migrants from Latin America experience discrimination as they strive to make it in the United States. Maria, an immigrant from the Dominican Republic, reports:

"The American teachers are always trying to sidetrack my daughter. They give her bad advice. They tell her she'll never make it. I remember staying up so many nights talking with her. I always said to her: Look, life is like this. Some people don't want others to go up in life, because the more uneducated people there are, the more people there are to be exploited." (p. 149)

Some people, realizing that they have been excluded from the immigrant advancement version of the melting pot by legal or informal discriminatory practices, in turn promote a separate mode of relating to the host culture. They may demand group rights and recognition but not assimilation.

Integration

Integration occurs when migrants have an interest both in maintaining their original culture and language and in having daily interactions with other groups. This differs from assimilation in that it involves a greater interest in maintaining one's own cultural identity. Immigrants can resist assimilation in many ways— for example, by insisting on speaking their own language in their home. One immigrant from Ghana, Meri, describes her home:

"English was spoken only in the presence of people who could not communicate in any of our languages (Ga or Twi). It wasn't as if my parents forbad me to speak English, but if I addressed either of them in English, the response I got was always in Ga. . . . My mother still insists upon conversing with me in Ga. When it appeared as though I was losing fluency, she became adamant and uncompromising about this; in her mind, to forget one's mother tongue was to place the final sever in the umbilical cord. I do believe that she was right, but over the years I have praised and cursed her for this." (quoted in O'Hearn, 1998, p. 102)

Meri also describes how her family participated in other aspects of American life, such as enjoying American music: "We listened to reggae, calypso, high life, jazz and sometimes R&B. We listened to country music—Kenny Rogers and Willie Nelson" (p. 103).

Other immigrants, like Asian Indians in the United States, maintain a strong sense of their ethnic identity by celebrating Indian holidays like Navarātrī, the Hindu festival that celebrates cosmic good over evil. Communication scholar Radha Hegde (2000) describes how these kinds of celebrations

provide a connection and sense of affirmation to immigrants, playing an important part in the process of redefining selfhood and establishing a sense of community in the new environment. . . . To immigrants like myself, these are opportunities to enjoy being Indian and to savor the colors, clothes, tastes, and sounds of a home left behind. (p. 129)

Migrant communities can actively resist assimilation in many ways. They may refuse to consume popular culture products (TV, radio, movies) or the fashions of the host society, often for many generations. In any case, integration depends on the openness and willingness of those in the dominant society to accept the cultures of others.

Marginalization

Marginalization occurs when individuals or groups express little interest in maintaining cultural ties with either the dominant culture or the migrant culture. This situation of being out of touch with both cultures may be the result of actions by the dominant society—for example, when the U.S. government forced Native Americans to live apart from other members of their nations. However, the term *marginalization* has come to describe, more generally, individuals who live on the margin of a culture, not able to participate fully in its political and social life as a result of cultural differences. For example, women from overseas who marry U.S. military men may find themselves living in relatively isolated parts of the country upon their husbands' return to the States. These women, sometimes called "war brides," become marginalized by the dominant society. They cannot find a local community of people with whom to share their native culture and language, nor can they participate in U.S. culture as a result of linguistic, cultural, and sometimes prejudicial barriers. These women may also be rejected by their husband's families, leading to further marginalization.

Combined Modes of Relating

Immigrants and their families often combine these four different modes of relating to the host society—for example, integrating in some areas of life and assimilating in others. They may desire economic assimilation (via employment), linguistic integration (bilingualism), and social separation (marrying someone from the same group and socializing only with members of their own group). One of our students, Nancy, describes how she grew up assimilating in terms of the language but still retaining some of her Vietnamese cultural background:

> As I grew up, I thought of myself as Vietnamese, but American at the same time. Being born in the United States made my perspective of being American the dominant of the two nationalities. Going to school from kindergarten until today, going from one job to the next, watching TV, and going on the Internet have all influenced the way I perceive my way of life. I have to admit that I am "whitewash." However, it is only because of the places I have been in and what and who I have been surrounded by in my entire life. Everyone is like that. . . . Even though I am a true American (like not having my Vietnamese accent anymore), I still try to do things related to my own cultural background. After all, I am proud to be Vietnamese and I am not ashamed of it.

In some families, individual members choose different paths of relating to the larger culture. This can cause tensions when children want to assimilate and parents prefer a more integrative mode. This was true of the high school students in Falls Church, Virginia, referred to at the beginning of the chapter. When

This excerpt from *National Geographic* describes the students at a high school in Falls Church, Virginia, where the student body comes from 70 different countries and many different language groups. The author comments on the similarities and differences of this diverse student body.

People of different colors and textures go in, and a mixture that appears homogeneous comes out. Everyone has a backpack. Most boys wear jeans and T-shirts; many girls wear short skirts or tight pants, showing a bit of bare midriff. Boys and girls wear earrings and talk about the same music.

But running beneath the sameness in fashion and attitude is a current of ethnic soul—a diversity that many of the students cling to even as they conform. They may sense that they are losing their family stories in the blender. . . .

The student's ethnic awareness coupled with the sense of losing their ethnic identity creates a subtle tension, even in the relatively benign atmosphere of the high school. "Hey Italian," evokes a response of "Hey, mulatto!" Pakistani girls are teased about wearing pajamas to school.

"I'm forgetting Arabic," says one student. "I can feel it fading away, being sucked away from me." "It's part of becoming American," says a friend. . . .

"We feel better with our own people," explains one student when I ask about apparently segregated groups in the cafeteria, which has a distinct geography that all the students can readily map out. Groups that sit together include Pakistani, Spanish-speakers, Moroccan, freshmen, cheerleaders, slackers, and nerds. Blacks who have recently arrived from Africa do not sit with the black Americans. Some tables are frequented by students who live in the same apartment building.

Despite such boundaries, most tables appear just plain mixed. At what looks like a typical table I pass out a piece of paper and ask everyone to write down his or her ethnic background. The results: "half Greek, half Middle eastern," "Greek," "Saudi Arabian," "Bolivian," "African American," "Hispanic," "white (American)," "Russian," "African," "Pakistani," "confused," "mixed—black with . . ."

These are normal American teenagers, I think, wondering how I'll get them to discuss immigration issues. Then I realize that they've already taught me the most important lesson. Young people whose backgrounds span the spectrum of human cultures are becoming "normal American teenagers" and in the process they will change America. We may not know yet what the change will mean, but the kids themselves know they are at the heart of something significant. As one boy, speaking simply and confidently, told me: "We make America more interesting."

Source: From J. Swerdlow, "Changing America," *National Geographic*, *200*(3), September 2001, pp. 59–60.

asked what they thought about the cultural rules that their parents tried to enforce, the Sikh students said they rebelled when their parents wouldn't let them cut their hair. Some of the Muslim girls argued with their parents about what kinds of dresses they could wear. And some of the Asian students rejected their parents' decree that they marry another Asian.

As these experiences indicate, one of the more difficult aspects of adaptation involves religion. How do immigrants pass on their religious beliefs to their children in a host country with very different religious traditions? Or should they? Aporva Dave, an honors student at Brown University, was curious about this question and conducted (along with another student) a study as an honors thesis. He interviewed members of South Asian Indian families that, like his own, had immigrated to the United States. He was curious about how strictly the parents followed the Hindu religion, how strongly they wanted their children to practice Hinduism in the future, and how the children felt about following the religious practices of their parents. In general, as expected, the children had a tendency to move away from the traditional practices of Hinduism, placing more emphasis on Hindu values than on Hindu practices (e.g., prayer). Although many of the parents themselves prayed daily, most were more concerned that their children adopt the morals and values of Hinduism. The parents seemed to understand that assimilation requires a move away from strict Hindu practices. Most viewed Hinduism as a progressing, "living" religion that would change but not be lost. And many spoke of Hinduism as becoming more attractive as a religion of the future generation.

However, the study also revealed that children raised in the same house could have very different attitudes toward adaptation and religion. For example, two sisters who participated in the study were raised with "moderately" religious parents who worship weekly, read religious articles, and spend much time thinking about God. One sister followed the traditions of the parents: she prays every day, spends time reading religious scriptures, and is committed to marrying a Hindi. The other sister does not practice Hinduism and places emphasis on love in making a marriage decision. These kinds of differences can sometimes make communication difficult during the adaptation process.

As individuals encounter new cultural contexts, they have to adapt to some extent. This adaptation process occurs in context, varies with each individual, and is circumscribed by relations of dominance and power in so-called host cultures. Let's look more closely at this process.

CULTURAL ADAPTATION

Cultural adaptation is the long-term process of adjusting to and finally feeling comfortable in a new environment (Kim, 2001). Immigrants who enter a culture more or less voluntarily and who at some point decide to—or feel the need to—adapt to the new cultural context experience cultural adaptation in a positive way.

Marco's parents sent him to the United States in 1993 because they thought it would be easier to combine sports and academic studies in a U.S. high school than a German high school. Marco's career goal is to become a professional tennis player. He describes his initial culture shock and his ultimate adaptation to life here.

> *The first semester at American high school, I experienced culture shock, even though I had visited the States several times before with my parents. . . . Even though I studied English since the fifth grade in Germany and understood most of what people said, it was hard to get used to the American slang. I was really close to going back home to Germany, because I was frustrated and had to get used to the new living conditions. . . .*
>
> *Sometimes it confuses me, and I don't know in which of these two worlds I belong, because I wonder where in 10 years I am going to be living and working. First, I was intimidated by the unfamiliarity of the school, but I recovered from culture shock soon, because I adapted to the new cultural situation and living arrangements with my new family and the language. I have lived here in the United States for about a fourth of my life, and sometimes I feel like I am American even though I am still a German citizen. At the same time, my friends in Germany refer to me as the "American," but here I am perceived as being German. Living here in the U.S. has taught me a great deal about being German—maybe more than I could have found out living in Germany, because here I see everything through different eyes. . . .*
>
> *I still consider myself German . . . but if people ask me where I am from I sometimes answer that I am from California, and they would never find out that I was not. I don't even consider the fears I once had about coming to the U.S. and experiencing another culture anymore, because over the years it has become such a ritual to me that it is no longer a big issue. It feels like I am able to switch back and forth between two different cultures without having anxiety.*
>
> —Marco

This section describes specific models of cultural adaptation, the contexts that enable or hamper adaptation, and the outcomes of adaptation.

Models of Cultural Adaptation

The Anxiety and Uncertainty Management Model   Communication theorist William Gudykunst (1995, 1998) stresses that the primary characteristic of relationships in intercultural adaptation is ambiguity. The goal of effective intercultural communication can be reached by reducing anxiety and seeking information, a process known as **uncertainty reduction.** There are several kinds of uncertainty. **Predictive uncertainty** is the inability to predict what someone will say or do. We all know how important it is to be relatively sure how people will respond to us. **Explanatory uncertainty** is the inability to explain why people behave as they do. In any interaction, it is important not only to predict how someone will behave but also to explain why the person behaves in a particular way. How do we do this? Usually, we have prior knowledge about someone, or we gather more information about the person. One of our students, Linda, describes her interactions with a Swedish exchange student:

> *I remember feeling very uncomfortable and unsure about how to communicate with her. I think one of the problems I had initially in getting to know my friend was that I was unsure of what to expect. . . . I felt unsure about what kind of personality she had. Will she be hostile toward me if I say something that offends her? . . . I can remember asking simple questions about her hobbies, her family, and why she wanted to be a foreign exchange student. Basically, I was seeking to reduce my own uncertainty so that I could better predict her behavior. . . . The experience was a very positive one.*

Migrants also may need to reduce the anxiety that is present in intercultural contexts. Some level of anxiety is optimal during an interaction. Too little anxiety may convey that we don't care about the person, and too much causes us to focus only on the anxiety and not on the interaction. One student recalls her anxiety about communicating during a visit to Italy: "Once I decided to let go of my anxiety and uncertainty, I was much better at assessing behavior and attitudes [of Italians] and thereby increasing my understanding of aspects of the Italian culture."

This model assumes that to communicate effectively we will gather information to help us reduce uncertainty and anxiety. How do we do this? The theory is complicated; however, some general suggestions for increasing effectiveness are useful. The theory predicts that the most effective communicators (those who are best able to manage anxiety and predict and explain others' behaviors) (1) have a solid self-concept and self-esteem, (2) have flexible attitudes (a tolerance for ambiguity, empathy) and behaviors, and (3) are complex and flexible in their categorization of others (e.g., able to identify similarities and differences and avoid stereotypes). The situation in which communication occurs is important in this model. The most conducive environments are informal, with support from and equal representation of different groups. Finally, this model requires that people be open to new information and recognize alternative ways to interpret information.

Of course, these principles may operate differently according to the cultural context; the theory predicts cultural variability. For example, people with more individualistic orientations may stress independence in self-concepts and communities; self-esteem may become more important in interactions. Individualists also may seek similarities more in categorizing. (See also Witte, 1993.)

The U-Curve Model   Many theories describe how people adapt to new cultural environments. The pattern of adaptation varies depending on the circumstances and the migrant, but some commonalities exist. The most common theory is the **U-curve theory** of adaptation. This theory is based on research conducted by a

Norwegian sociologist, Sverre Lysgaard (1995), who interviewed Norwegian students studying in the United States. This model has been applied to many different migrant groups.

The main idea is that migrants go through fairly predictable phases in adapting to a new cultural situation. They first experience excitement and anticipation, followed by a period of shock and disorientation (the bottom of the U-curve); then they gradually adapt to the new cultural context. Although this framework is simplistic and does not represent every migrant's experience, most migrants experience these general phases at one time or another.

The first phase is the anticipation or excitement phase. When a migrant first enters a new cultural context, he or she may be excited to be in the new situation and only a little apprehensive. This was the case for Helga María, who moved from Iceland to the United States so that her mother could attend graduate school in Florida. She describes the excitement of moving to the States:

> *I packed all my belongings in a box and said good-bye to my friends and family thinking that I was going on a long vacation to America. My friends envied me and I was excited too; I mean, how much better could it get, going to Florida, the sunshine state, the state of Disneyland, white sand and blue water beaches. I thought about walking downtown Hollywood and perhaps visiting some of the movie celebrities. The travel date finally arrived. My grandma cried as we walked toward our gate at the airport, but I still felt as if we were just going on a long, fun vacation. . . . I remember how huge the supermarket was, the first time we went buying groceries. Every aisle had more and more food and I wanted to taste all the different types of candy and cakes. Even the bread was different, so soft and it felt like a pillow.*

Although moving was mostly fun for Helga María, someone adapting to a new job in a new region of the country may experience more apprehension than excitement during the first part of the transition. The same would be true for, say, an international student from East Africa who experiences prejudice in the first months at a U.S. college, or for refugees who are forced to migrate into new cultural contexts.

The second phase, culture shock, happens to almost everyone in intercultural transitions. And for Helga María, it happened pretty quickly:

> *The first few weeks, I really liked the hot weather, to never have to worry about being cold when outside, and to be able to go to the beach often. But then after a few weeks, when my school started, it became rather tiring. I could hardly be outside for more than five minutes without looking like I just came out of the shower. The bus, or what the students called the "cheese wagon," was the same way, with nice warm leather seats and no air conditioning. I walked around from class to class feeling almost invisible. Thankfully, I could understand some of what people were saying, but not communicate back to them.*

For Helga María's mother, Erla, it was even harder:

> *The first semester in Pensacola was one of the hardest in our lives. My husband stayed at home and I went to the university. I am glad that I didn't really know*

POINT OF VIEW

In this essay, Grant Pearse, a New Zealander of mixed ethnicity, writes about his experience as a student in the United States. Note his description of conflicting feelings: simultaneously missing his home, enjoying his life in his host country, and feeling uncomfortable with the emphasis on individuality.

AN INDIVIDUAL, BUT NOT TOTALLY

Whatever the reason people come to the United States, whether it is for escape from economic, political or social unrest, or for adventure or just to experience another country, we're all faced with one thing and that is that our home culture is different from the one we experience here. . . .

I think of when my mother died in New Zealand and I went back. While standing in line at the supermarket, my mother's best friend came up to me and we embraced for about 10 minutes, just standing there in line at the supermarket, hugging and weeping. Then this friend invited me to her home for a special New Zealand meal, so that I wouldn't forget that this was my home.

In the Maori traditions, the body lies in the house, just as my mother did, with a Tongan tapa cloth draped over our sturdy coffee table, and the casket on top. Then people come and visit, bring food and gifts of money. I miss the singing, the vehemence, the subtle harmonies so unrehearsed and yet so moving as to bring change into a soul. I miss the participation at the grave site, each of the family shoveling the earth onto the coffin in the final gesture of love.

Yet I love my new home here in the United States with its beauty and excitement, but am torn by its adoration of individuality and lack of community. I believe that I am an individual but not totally, as I can never separate myself from my relationship to a family, a community, the earth and God. What I do enhances these groups, and what I fail to do, fails these groups. I can't give up the Polynesian attitude that if everyone else can't rise with me, it is not worth rising at all.

Source: From C. C. Ottesen, *L.A. Stories: The Voices of Cultural Diversity,* 1993, p. 39.

what I was getting into. I missed my colleagues, my work, and my family at home. I felt so ignorant, unintelligent, and old when I first started. I walked from one building to another, between classes. I kept my mouth shut, and when I tried to speak, the southern instructors often didn't understand what I was trying to say. This was awful. I often thought whether throwing myself and my family into this situation had been the right decision. There I was studying with young kids, working so hard that it was affecting my health, paying a large amount of money for it and the money wasn't even mine. It was the Icelandic government's money. Maybe my friends were right after all; I was being crazy and selfish. But here we were, and not about to give up.

Not everyone experiences culture shock when they move to a new place. For example, migrants who remain isolated from the new cultural context may experience minimal culture shock. As noted previously, U.S. military personnel, as well as diplomatic personnel, often live in compounds overseas where they associate mainly with other U.S. Americans and have little contact with the indigenous cultures. Similarly, spouses of international students in the United States sometimes have little contact with U.S. Americans. In contrast, corporate spouses may experience more culture shock because they often have more contact with the host culture: placing children in schools, setting up a household, shopping, and so on.

During the culture shock phase, migrants like Helga María and her family may experience disorientation and a crisis of identity. Because identities are shaped and maintained by cultural contexts, experiences in new cultural contexts often raise questions about identities. For example, Judy, an exchange teacher in Morocco, thought of herself as a nice person. Being nice was part of her identity. But when she experienced a lot of discipline problems with her students, she began to question the authenticity of her identity. When change occurs to the cultural context of an identity, the conditions of that identity also change.

The third phase in Lysgaard's model is adaptation, in which migrants learn the rules and customs of the new cultural context. As Erla says, "After the first semester, we started adapting pretty well. My daughters made new friends and so did my husband and I. I got used to studying, and started looking at it as any other job. My daughters learned how to speak English very well." Like Helga María, Erla, and the rest of their family, many migrants learn a new language, and they figure out how much of themselves to change in response to the new context. Remember Naida, the immigrant from Bosnia? After several years here in the States, she, too, has adapted. But she also acknowledges that life here still has its challenges:

> *I live in freedom and peace, and these are the things that life has to offer, and I must not take them for granted. I must take advantage of them. Life itself is a great gift, and many of us forget to acknowledge that and to appreciate what we have. I need to be thankful that I have stable and peaceful life, a roof over my head, and food to eat. Unlike in some other parts of the world, here I have the opportunity to educate myself, and to make things better, and I must take advantage of it and appreciate it. I should know. I also know that I am going to experience many setbacks, disappointments, and emotional crises in my life, but I want to look forward, beyond that and learn.*

However, this phase may be experienced very differently if the sociopolitical context is not conducive to individual adaptation. This was the experience of Maria and her sister, who migrated from Greece to Germany:

> *Unfortunately, I am also the victim of discrimination at the moment. I am applying for a job here in Germany, and although I have finished the German university with an excellent grade and I have the permission to work here, I always get*

This excerpt of an article that appeared in *The Washington Post* describes the sometimes ambivalent attitudes toward non-White immigrants in Australia. These attitudes are similar to those in the United States.

> *Australian Danh Ngoc Phung fled her native Vietnam by boat 20 years ago and eventually found her way to this busy suburb south of Sydney, where she opened a pharmacy and raised six children. Now 65, she is a classic immigrant success story: She owns two pharmacies, two of her children are pharmacists, one is an architect, and three own small businesses. "It's been good for us here," she said.*
>
> *Far too good for some Australians, who wish she would just go home. Phung and other Asian immigrants are keenly aware that they are in the crosshairs of this country's divisive debate about race relations, immigration and the identity of a mainly European nation at the far end of Asia.*
>
> *"I'm scared sometimes," Phung said, noting an increase in verbal and physical abuse of Asians in the last year. "But there's nothing I can do about it except remind my children not to go out at night—it's dangerous."*
>
> *Since World War II, Australia has grown from a land of 7 million people of almost purely British and Irish descent into a multihued melting pot of 18 million people, almost a quarter of them born overseas. The transition generally has been smooth, unmarked by the sporadic violence toward immigrants in parts of Europe and the United States. . . .*
>
> *The government's "White Australia" immigration policy, which officially ended in 1973, required immigrants to be of European descent. . . . Australia's changing makeup has been welcomed by many who see a new richness in the nation's culture, food and lifestyle. But some people feel uneasy watching comfortable old traditions such as cold ale and hot meat pies being replaced by Singha beer from Thailand and Vietnamese pho soup.*

Source: From Kevin Sullivan, "'White Australia' in Identity Crisis: Many Fear Asian Immigrants Are Taking Away Jobs, Culture," *Washington Post*, December 6, 1997, p. A1.

rejected because of my nationality! All the other students from my university have already found a job, only because they are German!! The same experience I had in the UK. And I was only looking for a temporary job!! Of course discrimination exists in my own country as well, but strangely not to the people of the so-called "industrially developed countries"! But what really shocked me is a recent experience from my sister. She had an interview in a German IT company, and she was told that she was not allowed to take the job because of her "different" accent and her "dark hair"!!! So how can we still speak from "really developed" countries and great technological progress in the year 2002 when the abilities and knowledge of an individual are determined from his hair or skin colour??? I think that a cultural adaptation will only take place if we all first learn to respect one another!!

Although the U-curve seems to represent the experiences of many short-term sojourners, it may be too simplistic for other types of migrants (Berry, 1992). A more accurate model represents long-term adaptation as a series of U-curves. Migrants alternate between feeling relatively adjusted and experiencing culture shock; over the long term, the sense of culture shock diminishes.

The Transition Model   Recently, culture shock and adaptation have been viewed as a normal part of human experience, as a subcategory of transition shock. Janet Bennett (1998), a communication scholar, suggests that culture shock and adaptation are just like any other "adult transition." Adult transitions include going away to college for the first time, getting married, and moving from one part of the country to another. These experiences share common characteristics and provoke the same kinds of responses.

All transition experiences involve change, including some loss and some gain, for individuals. For example, when people marry, they may lose some independence, but they gain companionship and intimacy. When international students come to the United States to study, they leave their friends and customs behind but find new friends and new ways of doing things.

Cultural adaptation depends in part on the individual. Each person has a preferred way of dealing with new situations. Psychologists have found that most individuals prefer either a "flight" or a "fight" approach to unfamiliar situations. Each of these approaches may be more or less productive depending on the context. Migrants who prefer a **flight approach** when faced with new situations tend to hang back, get the lay of the land, and see how things work before taking the plunge and joining in. Migrants who take this approach may hesitate to speak a language until they feel they can get it right, which is not necessarily a bad thing. Taking time out from the stresses of intercultural interaction (by speaking and reading in one's native language, socializing with friends of similar background, and so on) may be appropriate. Small periods of "flight" allow migrants some needed rest from the challenges of cultural adaptation. However, getting stuck in the "flight" mode can be unproductive. For example, some U.S. students abroad spend all of their time with other American students and have little opportunity for intercultural learning.

A second method, the **fight approach,** involves jumping in and participating. Migrants who take this approach use the trial-and-error method. They try to speak the new language, don't mind if they make mistakes, jump on a bus even when they aren't sure it's the right one, and often make cultural gaffes. For example, Bill, a U.S. exchange teacher in France, took this approach. His French was terrible, but he would speak with anyone who would talk to him. When he and his wife first arrived in their town late at night, he went to the Hôtel de Ville (City Hall) and asked for a room! His wife, Jan, was more hesitant. She would speak French only when she knew she could get the grammar right, and she would study bus schedules for hours rather than risk getting on the wrong bus or asking a stranger. Getting stuck in the "fight" mode can also be unproductive. Migrants who take this approach to the extreme tend to act on their surroundings with little flexibility and are likely to criticize the way things are done in the new culture.

Neither of these preferences for dealing with new situations is inherently right or wrong. Individual preference is a result of family, social, and cultural influences. For example, some parents encourage their children to be assertive, and others encourage their children to wait and watch in new situations. Society may encourage individuals toward one preference or the other. A third alternative is the "flex" approach, in which migrants use a combination of productive "fight" or "flight" behaviors. The idea is to "go with the flow" while keeping in mind the contextual elements. Hostile contexts (such as racism or prejudice) may encourage extreme responses, but a supportive environment (tolerance) may encourage more productive responses.

The Communication System Model   The three approaches discussed so far concentrate on the psychological feelings of migrants, on how comfortable they feel. What role does communication play in the adaptation process? For an answer, we turn to a model of adaptation developed by communication scholar Young Yun Kim (1977, 2001). Kim suggests that adaptation is a process of stress, adjustment, and growth. As individuals experience the stress of not fitting in with the environment, the natural response is to seek to adjust. This process of adjustment represents a psychic breakdown of previously held attitudes and behaviors—ones that worked in original cultural contexts. This model fits very well with our dialectical approach in its emphasis on the interconnectedness of individual and context in the adaptation process.

Adaptation occurs through communication. That is, the migrant communicates with individuals in the new environment and gradually develops new ways of thinking and behaving. In the process, the migrant achieves a new level of functioning and acquires an intercultural identity. Of course, not everyone grows in the migrant experience. Some individuals have difficulty adapting to new ways. According to the cognitive dissonance theorists of the 1950s, individuals typically have three options when confronting ideas or behaviors that do not fit with previously held attitudes: They can (1) reject the new ideas, (2) try to fit them into their existing frameworks, or (3) change their frameworks (Festinger, 1957).

Communication may have a double edge in adaptation: Migrants who communicate frequently in their new culture adapt better but also experience more culture shock. Beulah Rohrlich and Judith Martin (1991) conducted a series of studies of U.S. American students living abroad in various places in Europe. They discovered that those students who communicated the most with host culture members experienced the most culture shock. These were students who spent lots of time with their host families and friends in many different communication situations (having meals together, working on projects together, socializing, and so on). However, these same students also adapted better and felt more satisfied with their overseas experience than the students who communicated less. Along the same lines, communication scholar Stephanie Zimmerman

(1995), in a recent study, found that international students who interacted most often with U.S. American students were better adapted than those who interacted less.

Dan Kealey (1996), who worked for many years with the Canadian International Development Agency, conducted studies of overseas technical assistance workers in many different countries. Kealey and his colleagues tried to understand what characterized effective workers and less effective workers. They interviewed the Canadian workers, their spouses, and their host country coworkers. They discovered that the most important characteristics in adaptation were the interpersonal communication competencies of the workers.

In one study, Kealey (1989) found that those who communicated more in the host country experienced a greater degree of culture shock and had more initial difficulty in adapting to the new country. These people also were rated by their host country coworkers as more successful. As with the student sojourners, for these workers, communication and adaptation seem to be a case of "no pain, no gain." Intercultural interaction may be difficult and stressful but ultimately can be highly rewarding.

Specifically, how does communication help migrants adapt? There seem to be three stages in this process of adaptation: (1) taking things for granted, (2) making sense of new patterns, and (3) coming to understand new information. Scholar Ling Chen (2000) interviewed Chinese international students and described how they experienced these three phases.

In the first phase, migrants realize that their assumptions are wrong and need to be altered. Chen describes the experiences of one of the students she interviewed, Mr. An. He was arriving in the middle of the night at his new U.S. university, but he wasn't worried. In China, student housing is always arranged for by university officials. However, in conversations on the plane with a friendly seatmate named Alice, he began to realize that his expectations of having a place to stay were probably a mistake. He was grateful when Alice offered her home. Mr. An explained: "Alice said she could put me up for the night, that I could live in her house until I found a place. . . . I was surprised but also very grateful" (Chen, p. 221).

In the second stage, migrants slowly begin to make sense of new patterns, through communication experiences. The first step in making sense for Mr. An took place the next day, when he went to the International Students Office. A clerk handed him a map and told him to find his own housing. Although he had heard that people in the United States were individualistic and independent, this cultural pattern was now a living experience for him. The dorms were full, but Mr. An learned how to seek alternatives. He explained how he began to make sense of the experience: "I started to better understand the meaning of independence. I felt I really understood America and was overjoyed [to find] there was a Chinese Student Association on campus. This meant that maybe I could get help from them" (p. 224).

As migrants begin to make sense of their experiences and interactions in new cultural contexts, they come to understand them in a more holistic way. This en-

When I first arrived in Belgium, I watched a lot of TV. I always liked to watch TV before I left the United States, so it was a good way for me to learn French. And it was certainly a lot easier and less painful than trying to talk with Belgians. I always hated that pained look they got on their faces when I would screw up the language in my halting speech.
    —Jesse

ables them to fit the new information into a pattern of cultural understanding. Again, this happens through communication with members of the host country and others who implicitly or explicitly explain the new cultural patterns. Mr. An stayed in touch with Alice for a while, but this changed over time. He explained:

> *One day I realized I had not called Alice in a long time, then it occurred to me that she rarely called me; I was the one who usually made the calls. . . . I just didn't get around to calling her again, but now I don't feel guilty about it. She didn't seem to mind one way or the other. I've learned that many Americans are ready to help others, but never see them again afterwards. (p. 226)*

At that point, Mr. An understood the U.S. cultural emphasis on helpful intervention, and he was able to make sense of his friendship with Alice—as a momentary helping relationship. As Chen notes, "Coming to a tentative understanding is the last stage in a cycle of sense-making. . . . In the long run, however, this new perspective will never be completely fulfilled by one's accumulation of knowledge" (p. 227). As Chen points out, there are always more sense-making cycles.

Mass media also play a role in helping sojourners and immigrants adapt. Radio, television, movies, and so on are powerful transmitters of cultural values, readily accessible as sources of socialization for newcomers. The mass media may play an especially important role in the beginning stages of adaptation. When sojourners or immigrants first arrive, they may have limited language ability and limited social networks. Listening to the radio or watching TV may be the primary source of contact at this stage, one that avoids negative consequences of not knowing the language (Nwanko & Onwumechili, 1991).

Individual Influences on Adaptation

Many individual characteristics—including age, gender, preparation level, and expectations—can influence how well migrants adapt (Ward, 1996). But there is contradictory evidence concerning the effects of age and adaptation. On the one hand, younger people may have an easier time adapting because they are less fixed in their ideas, beliefs, and identities. Because they adapt more completely, though, they may have more trouble when they return home. On the other hand, older people may have more trouble adapting because they are less flexible. However, for that very reason, they may not change as much and so have less trouble when they move back home (Kim, 2001).

Level of preparation for the experience may influence how migrants adapt, and this may be related to expectations. Many U.S. sojourners experience more culture shock in England than in other European countries, because they expect little difference between life there and life here in the United States (Weissman & Furnham, 1987). In contrast, sojourners traveling to cultures that are very different expect to experience culture shock. The research seems to show that overly positive and overly negative expectations lead to more difficulty in adaptation; apparently, positive but realistic or slightly negative expectations prior to the sojourn are best (Martin, Bradford, & Rohrlich, 1995).

Context and Adaptation

Cultural adaptation depends on the context. Some contexts are easier to adapt to than others, and some environments are more accepting. Young Yun Kim (2001) writes about the receptivity of the host environment and the degree to which the environment welcomes newcomers. She maintains that in a country like Japan, which emphasizes homogeneity, people may be less welcoming toward outsiders than in less homogeneous settings, as in many contexts in the United States. Communication scholar Satoshi Ishii (2001) explains the ambivalent feelings of contemporary Japanese toward foreigners and traces their historical roots: "Since ancient times the Japanese have consistently held not positive–negative dichotomous feelings but the conventional welcome–nonwelcome and inclusion–exclusion ambivalence in encountering and treating . . . strangers" (p. 152). Similarly, many Muslim societies tend to be fairly closed to outsiders. In these societies, the distinction between ingroup (family and close friends) and outgroup (everyone else) is very strong.

The relative status and power of sojourners and host groups also influence adaptation. For instance, African students often find it more difficult to adapt to U.S. colleges because of racism. In fact, one study found that two sources of stress for many international students in the United States were perceived discrimination and hatred (Sandhu & Asrabadi, 1994). According to a University of Minnesota study, international students came to see themselves as their group was perceived. Those students who thought their group was perceived positively (e.g., Scandinavians) adapted more easily, whereas those who felt discrimination against their group (e.g., many Africans) experienced more difficulty (Morris, 1960). Similarly, it can be difficult for women to adapt in many contexts because of their relatively lower status.

Class issues often enter into the picture. Sometimes immigrant workers are seen as necessary but are not really welcomed into the larger society because of their class (which is often fused with racial differences). For example, many of the Latin American immigrants interviewed by scholar Suzanne Oboler (1995) expressed the opinion that the prejudice and discrimination directed at them was the result of the social and class distance between Hispanics and "Americans."

> *When I moved to Arizona from San Francisco to go to school, it was a big shock. I was used to seeing many different kinds of people—Asian Americans, African Americans. At my new university in Phoenix, almost everyone is White. And I was treated differently in Phoenix than I was at home. I often got passed by at the supermarket while the clerk waited on someone who was White. Some of the children who lived in my apartment complex followed me one day, yelling, "Chink, Chink, Chinaman."*
>   —Lois

And sometimes the discrimination and class issues result in conflict between recent migrants and emigrants from the same country who have been in the host country for a long time. For example, Mexicans have come in increasing numbers to work in the carpet plants in the Southeast and in the meatpacking plants in the Midwest. This has led to tension between those Latinos/as who have worked hard to achieve harmony with Whites and to attain middle-class status, and the newcomers, who are usually poor and have lower English proficiency. The older Latinos/as feel caught between the two—ridiculed by Whites for not speaking English correctly and now by recently arrived Mexicans for mangling Spanish. This resentment between old and new immigrants has always been present in America—from the arrival of the first Europeans.

However, there is an upside to the arrival of these new immigrants. Journalist Arian Campo-Flores (2001), writing about the relationships between these two groups in one Midwest town, observes:

> *Cultural collisions can be as enriching as they are threatening. . . . Older Chicanos have learned to adjust, too. In fact many say that the fresh infusion of Hispanic culture brought by immigrants has revitalized their identity as Latinos. Their girls are celebrating* quinceaneras, *the equivalent of "sweet 16" parties. They're singing to their departed relatives at the cemetery. They've resuscitated their language . . . both communities have recognized that their complexions will become only more richly hued. And Chicanos, who in a way are the arbiters between what the towns used to be and what they've become, are uniquely qualified to lead. (p. 51)*

The United States is not the only country grappling with an influx of new workers. When Germany needed low-cost laborers, the country brought in many Turkish guestworkers, but these immigrants were not necessarily welcomed into German society. Citizenship and other signs of entry into German society were not easily obtainable, and many immigrants (or those perceived to be immigrants) were victims of violent attacks. In fact, one travel guidebook even warned non-White tourists in Germany that

> *in certain regions, tourists of color or members of certain religious groups may feel threatened by local residents. Neo-Nazi skinheads in the large cities of former East*

Germany, as well as in Western Germany, have been known to attack foreigners, especially non-whites. (Larsson, 1998, p. 25)

Economic changes that resulted from the reuniting of East and West Germany have reduced the need for guestworkers.

Which groups of migrants do you think have a positive image in the United States? Which groups do you think have a negative image? Which groups of international students do you think U.S. students would want to meet and socialize with? Which groups would students not want to meet? The stereotypes of various cultural groups should make it easy for you to sense which groups would face resistance from U.S. Americans in trying to adapt to U.S. culture.

Outcomes of Adaptation

Much of the early research on cultural adaptation concentrated on a single dimension. More recent research emphasizes a multidimensional view of adaptation and applies best to voluntary transitions. There are at least three aspects, or dimensions, of adaptation: (1) psychological health, (2) functional fitness, and (3) intercultural identity (Kim, 2001). Again, we must note that these specific aspects are dialectically related to the contexts to which individuals adapt.

Part of adapting involves feeling comfortable in new cultural contexts. **Psychological health** is the most common definition of adaptation, one that concentrates on the emotional state of the individual migrant (Berry, Kim, Minde, & Mok, 1987). Obviously, the newcomer's psychological well-being will depend somewhat on members of the host society. As mentioned previously, if migrants are made to feel welcome, they will feel more comfortable faster. But if the host society sends messages that migrants don't really belong, psychological adjustment becomes much more difficult.

Achieving psychological health generally occurs more quickly than the second outcome, **functional fitness,** which involves being able to function in daily life in many different contexts (Ward, 1996). Some psychologists see adaptation mainly as the process of learning new ways of living and behaving (Ward, Bochner, & Furnham, 2001). That is, they view the acquisition of skills as more important than psychological well-being. They have tried to identify areas of skills that are most important for newly arrived members of a society to acquire. Specifically, newcomers to a society should learn the local rules for politeness (e.g., honesty), the rules of verbal communication style (e.g., direct, elaborate), and typical use of nonverbal communication (e.g., proxemic behavior, gestures, eye gaze, facial expressions). An international student from Japan describes how frustrating it can be to not feel "functionally fit" in a new culture:

I will never forget when I first went to the Subway sandwich shop. I knew what BLT stands for and I ordered one. After that I just wanted to sit back, relax, and wait for my BLT to show up right in front of me. A second later, the man over the counter asked me, "What kind of bread would you like?" "What kind of cheese would you like?" Of course, we have bread and cheese in Japan. But I was not familiar with the names of all the different kinds of cheese (e.g., provolone, Swiss,

American, etc). I responded, "Ah, well, how about . . . the yellow one over there, the half circle one." "Oh, you mean, Provolone?" At that time, I was a mature 26-year-old woman from Japan. But at this sandwich shop, I was feeling like a 3-year-old, not knowing these "basic" things.

Obviously, this outcome of becoming functionally fit takes much longer and also depends on the cooperation of the host society. Newcomers will become functionally fit more quickly if host members are willing to communicate and interact with them. Even so, it takes most migrants a long time to function at an optimal level in the new society.

Another potential outcome of adaptation is the development of an **intercultural identity,** a complex concept. Social psychologist Peter Adler (1975) writes that the multicultural individual is significantly different from the person who is more culturally restricted. One student describes her change in identity after living abroad for a year:

The year I studied abroad in France was crucial to developing my identity. Not only was I interacting among French people, but I also dealt with intercultural relations among other international students and American exchange students. I developed a new identity of myself and braved a complete transformation of self. All my intercultural experiences have helped me to become a more competent and understanding person.

The multicultural person is neither a part of nor apart from the host culture; rather, this person acts situationally. But the multicultural life is fraught with pitfalls and difficulty. Multicultural people run the risk of not knowing what to believe or how to develop ethics or values. They face life with little grounding and lack the basic personal, social, and cultural guidelines that cultural identities provide.

IDENTITY AND ADAPTATION

How individual migrants develop multicultural identities depends on three issues. One is the extent to which migrants want to maintain their own identity, language, and way of life compared to how much they want to become part of the larger new society. Recall that the immigrant–host culture relationship can be played out in several ways. Immigrants to the United States often are encouraged to "become American," which may entail relinquishing their former cultural identity. (See Figure 8-2.) For example, Mario and his family emigrated from Mexico to Germany when Mario's father took a new job. Mario and his siblings have taken different paths with respect to their relationship to Mexican culture. Mario, the oldest child, has tried to keep some Mexican traditions. His brother, who was very young when the family migrated to Germany, did not learn to speak Spanish at home but is now trying to learn it in college.

The second issue that affects how migrants develop multicultural identities is the extent to which they have day-to-day interactions with others in the new

FIGURE 8-2   These immigrant children are learning about Thanksgiving in ways that serve White dominant culture. How could this adaptation process be offensive? In what ways is it offensive to contemporary native peoples to see their culture and religion mocked by these paper outfits? (© *Tony Freeman/PhotoEdit, Inc.*)

society. Some migrants find it painful to deal with the everyday prejudices that they experience and so retreat to their own cultural groups.

The third issue that affects how migrants relate to their new society involves the ownership of political power. In some societies, the dominant group virtually dictates how nondominant groups may act; in other societies, nondominant groups are largely free to select their own course. For instance, Tom learned that when his mother first went to grammar school she had to pick an "American name" because her own name "was too hard to pronounce." As a first-grader, she chose the name "Kathy" because she thought it sounded pretty. This kind of forced assimilation reflects the power of dominant groups over nondominant groups. In this case, *American* means "English" or "British," even though we are a nation of emigrants from all parts of the world. Looking at how migrants deal with these identity issues in host culture contexts can help us understand different patterns of contact (Berry, 1992).

Adapting on Reentry

When migrants return home to their original cultural contexts, the same process of adaptation occurs and may again involve culture, or reentry, shock. Sometimes this adaptation is even more difficult because it is so unexpected. Coming home,

Living in the Borderlands means you fight hard to
resist the gold elixir beckoning from the bottle,
the pull of the gun barrel,
the rope cruising the hollow of your throat;
In the Borderlands
you are the battleground
where enemies are kin to each other;
you are at home, a stranger,
the border disputes have been settled
the volley of shots have shattered the truce
you are wounded, lost in action
dead, fighting back;
To live in the Borderlands means
the mill with the razor white teeth wants to shred off
your olive-red skin, crush out the kernel, your heart
pound you pinch you roll you out
smelling like white bread but dead;
To survive the Borderlands
you must live sin fronteras
be a crossroads.

Gabacha—a Chicano term for a white woman
Rajetas—literally, "split," that is, having betrayed your word
Burra—donkey
Buey—oxen
Sin fronteras—without borders

Source: From G. Anzaldua, *Borderlands/La Frontera: The New Mestiza*, 1999, pp. 216–217.

several languages (Spanish, English, and Nuhuatl), and in prose (the academic) and poetry (the artistic and spiritual):

> *I will no longer be made to feel ashamed of existing. I will have my voice: Indian, Spanish, white. I will have my serpent's tongue—my woman's voice, my sexual voice, my poet's voice. I will overcome the tradition of silence. (p. 81)*

Technological developments have made global travel much easier, and we can change cultural contexts as never before. Yet the movement between cultures is never as simple as getting on a plane (Clifford, 1992). David Mura (1991), a Japanese American from the Midwest, went to live in Japan and wrote about his experiences there:

> *Japan helped me balance a conversation which had been taking place before I was born, a conversation in my grandparents' heads, in my parents' heads, which, by*

my generation, had become very one-sided, so that the Japanese side was virtually silenced. My stay helped me realize that a balance, which probably never existed in the first place, could no longer be maintained. In the end, I did not speak the language well enough; I did not have enough attraction to the culture. In the end, the society felt to my American psyche too cramped, too well defined, too rule-oriented, too polite, too circumscribed. I could have lived there a few more years if I had had the money and the time, but eventually I would have left. I would not have become one of those Americans who finds in Japan a surrounding society which nourishes and confirms their own sense of identity. Either I was American or I was one of the homeless, one of the searchers for what John Berger calls a world culture. But I was not Japanese. (p. 370)

The entanglements of history, identity, language, nonverbal communication, and cultural spaces are all salient concerns for understanding these global movements.

THINKING DIALECTICALLY ABOUT INTERCULTURAL TRANSITIONS

Understanding the process of adaptation in intercultural transitions depends on several dialectical tensions. Unfortunately, there are no easy answers. Think about how the privilege–disadvantage dialectic structures some kinds of intercultural transitions. For example, businesspeople who live abroad while working for transnational corporations often are economically privileged: They receive additional pay, housing relocation money, and so on. They also meet many people through work and can afford to travel in their new host location. In contrast, refugees often lack financial resources in their new host location, which may have been chosen out of sheer necessity. They may have few opportunities to meet other people, travel in their new homeland, or purchase basic necessities. In this way, they may not view their new environment in the same way as a more privileged migrant. These dialectical differences shape the intercultural migrant's identity and the changes that this identity undergoes.

We might also invoke the personal–contextual dialectic. Often, in adapting to new cultural contexts, people may find themselves challenged to be culturally competent by behaving in ways that may be contradictory to their personal identities. For example, a Muslim woman may feel that she can't wear her chador in certain U.S. contexts and thus can't express her religious identity. The dialectic calls for a balance between the individual and contextual demands.

SUMMARY

In this chapter, we highlighted the main issues in moving from one culture to another. We stressed the importance of a dialectical perspective in examining the migration needs at both an individual level and a sociopolitical level. Migrant groups vary in the length of the migration and the degree of voluntariness. Given these two criteria, there are four types of migrants: sojourners (short-term voluntary), immigrants (long-term voluntary), and refugees (long-term or short-term involuntary). With regard to short-term culture shock and longer-term cultural adaptation, some migrant groups resist rather than adapt to the host culture. There are four modes of relationships between migrants and host cultures: assimilation, separation, integration, and marginalization.

Four models can be used to explain adaptation issues: the anxiety and uncertainty management model, the U-curve model, the transition model, and the communication system model. Communication plays a crucial role in migration. Individual characteristics such as age, gender, preparation level, and expectations influence how well people adapt to new cultures. They can affect the personal outcomes of adaptation, which include good psychological health, functional fitness, and an intercultural identity. Cultural adaptation and identity are interrelated in many ways. Migrants who return to their original homes also face readjustment, or cultural reentry. Those who make frequent or multiple border crossings often develop multicultural identities.

DISCUSSION QUESTIONS

1. Why does culture shock occur to people who make cultural transitions?
2. Why are adaptations to cultures difficult for some people and easier for others?
3. What is the role of communication in the cultural adaptation process?
4. How do relations of power and dominance affect adaptation?
5. What factors affect migration patterns?
6. What dialectical tensions can you identify in the process of adapting to intercultural transitions?

 Go to the self-quizzes on the Online Learning Center at www.mhhe.com/martinnakayama to further test your knowledge.

ACTIVITIES

Culture Shock. Meet with other students in your class in small groups and explore your own experiences of cultural adaptation. Find out how many students experienced culture shock during the first year of college. What did it feel like? How many experienced culture shock when traveling abroad? How about reentry shock? If there are differences in students' experience, explore why these differences exist. Are they due to differences in individual experience? In contexts?

KEY WORDS

assimilation	fight approach	intercultural identity
cultural adaptation	flight approach	long-term refugee
culture shock	functional fitness	marginalization
explanatory uncertainty	integration	migrant

multicultural identity
predictive uncertainty
psychological health
segregation

separation
short-term refugee
sojourners
transnationalism

U-curve theory
uncertainty reduction
W-curve theory

OLC   The Online Learning Center at www.mhhe.com/martinnakayama features
flashcards and crossword puzzles based on these terms and concepts.

REFERENCES

Adler, P. (1975). The transition experience: An alternative view of culture shock. *Journal of Humanistic Psychology, 15*, 13–23.

Anzaldúa, G. (1999). *Borderlands/La frontera: The new mestiza* (2nd ed.). San Francisco: Aunt Lute Press.

Al-Shaykh, H. (1995). *Beirut blues.* New York: Anchor Books.

Bennett, J. M. (1998). Transition shock: Putting culture shock in perspective. In M. J. Bennett (Ed.), *Basic concepts in intercultural communication: Selected readings* (pp. 215–224). First published in 1977, in N. C. Jain (Ed.), *International and Intercultural Communication Annual, 4*, 45–52.

Berry, J. W. (1992). Psychology of acculturation: Understanding individuals moving between two cultures. In R. W. Brislin (Ed.), *Applied cross cultural psychology* (pp. 232–253). Newbury Park, CA: Sage.

Berry, J. W., Kim, U., Minde, T., & Mok, D. (1987). Comparative studies of acculturative stress. *International Migration Review, 21*, 491–511.

Black, J. S., & Gregersen, H. B. (1999). *So you're coming home.* San Diego: Global Business.

Campo-Flores, A. (2001, September 18). Brown against brown. *Newsweek,* 49–51.

Chen, L. (2000). How we know what we know about Americans: How Chinese sojourners account for their experiences. In A. González, M. Houston, & V. Chen (Eds.), *Our voices: Essays in culture, ethnicity and communication* (3rd ed., pp. 220–227). Los Angeles: Roxbury.

Clifford, J. (1992). Traveling cultures. In L. Grossberg, C. Nelson, & P. Treichler (Eds.), *Cultural studies* (pp. 96–116). New York: Routledge.

Danquah, M. N.-A. (1998). Life as an alien. In C. C. O'Hearn (Ed.), *Half+half.* New York: Pantheon Books.

Dave, A. (2000). Hinduism in America. Honors thesis, Brown University. www.brown.edu/Departments/AmCiv/Studentprojects/apurva/Results.htm

Featherstone, J. (2002, April 1). International migration: Work flows. *Financial Times Expatriate.*

Festinger, L. (1957). *A theory of cognitive dissonance.* Stanford, CA: Stanford University Press.

Gudykunst, W. B. (1995). Anxiety uncertainty management (AUM) theory: Current status. In R. L. Wiseman (Ed.), *Intercultural communication theory* (pp. 8–58). Newbury Park, CA: Sage.

————. (1998). Applying anxiety/uncertainty management (AUM) theory to intercultural adjustment training. *International Journal of Intercultural Relations, 22*, 187–227.

Hegde, R. S. (1998). Swinging the trapeze: The negotiation of identity among Asian Indian immigrant women in the United States. In D. V. Tanno & A. González (Eds.), *Communication of identity across cultures* (pp. 34–55). Thousand Oaks, CA: Sage.

————. (2000). Hybrid revivals: Defining Asian Indian ethnicity through celebration. In A. González, M. Houston, & V. Chen (Eds.), *Our voices: Essays in culture, ethnicity and communication* (3rd. ed., pp. 133–138). Los Angeles: Roxbury.

Henderson, M. (1999). *Forgiveness: Breaking the chain of hate*. Wilsonville, OR: Book-Partners.

Ishii, S. (2001). The Japanese welcome-nonwelcome ambivalence syndrome toward Marebito (Ijin) Gaijin strangers: Its implications for intercultural communication research. *Japan Review, 13*, 145–170.

Kealey, D. J. (1989). A study of cross-cultural effectiveness: Theoretical issues, practical applications. *International Journal of Intercultural Relations, 13*, 387–427.

———. (1996). The challenge of international personnel selection. In D. Landis & R. S. Bhagat (Eds.), *Handbook of intercultural training* (2nd ed., pp. 81–105). Thousand Oaks, CA: Sage.

Kim, Y. Y. (1977). Communication patterns of foreign immigrants in the process of acculturation. *Human Communication Research, 41*, 66–76.

———. (2001). *Becoming intercultural: An integrated theory of communication and cross-cultural adaptation*. Thousand Oaks, CA: Sage.

Kim, Y. Y., & Gudykunst, W. B. (Eds.). (1988). *Cross cultural adaptation: Current approaches*. International and Intercultural Communication Annual 11. Newbury Park, CA: Sage.

Larsson, M. O. (Ed.). (1998). *Let's go: Germany*. New York: St. Martin's Press.

Lysgaard, S. (1955). Adjustment in a foreign society: Norwegian Fulbright grantees visiting the United States. *International Social Science Bulletin, 7*, 45–51. Thousand Oaks, CA: Sage.

Martin, J. N. (1984). The intercultural reentry: Conceptualizations and suggestions for future research. *International Journal of Intercultural Relations, 8*, 115–134.

———. (1986). Communication in the intercultural reentry: Student sojourners' perceptions of change in reentry relationships. *International Journal of Intercultural Relations, 10*, 1–22.

Martin, J. N., Bradford, L., & Rohrlich, B. (1995). Comparing predeparture expectations and post-sojourn reports: A longitudinal study of U.S. students abroad. *International Journal of Intercultural Relations, 19*, 87–110.

Martin, J. N., & Harrell, T. (1996). Reentry training for intercultural sojourners. In D. Landis & R. S. Bhagat (Eds.), *Handbook of intercultural training* (2nd ed., pp. 307–326). Thousand Oaks, CA: Sage.

Martin, P., & Widgren, J. (2002). International migration: Facing the challenge. *Population Bulletin, 57*, 1–43.

Morris, R. (1960). *The two way mirror: National status in foreign students' adjustment*. Minneapolis: University of Minnesota Press.

Mura, D. (1991). *Turning Japanese: Memoirs of a sansei*. New York: Anchor Books.

Nwanko, R. N., & Onwumechili, C. (1991). Communication and social values in cross-cultural adjustment. *Howard Journal of Communications, 3*, 99–111.

Oberg, K. (1960). Cultural shock: Adjustment to new cultural environments. *Practical Anthropology, 7*, 177–182.

Oboler, S. (1995). *Ethnic labels, Latino lives: Identity and the politics of (re)presentation in the United States*. Minneapolis: University of Minnesota Press.

Ottesen, C. C. (1993). *L.A. stories: The voices of cultural diversity* (p. 39). Yarmouth, ME: Intercultural Press.

Rohrlich, B., & Martin, J. N. (1991). Host country and reentry adjustment of student sojourners. *International Journal of Intercultural Relations, 15*, 163–182.

Ruggiero, K. M., Taylor, D. M., & Lambert, W. E. (1996). A model of heritage culture maintenance. *International Journal of Intercultural Relations, 20*, 47–67.

Sandhu, D. S., & Asrabadi, B. R. (1994). Development of an acculturative stress scale for international students: Preliminary findings. *Psychological Reports, 75*, 435–448.

Storti, C. (2001). *The art of coming home* (2nd ed.). Yarmouth, ME: Nicholas Brealey/Intercultural Press.

Swerdlow, J. L. (2001, September). Changing America. *National Geographic, 200* (3), 42–61.

Sullivan, K. (1997, December 6). "White" Australia in identity crisis: Many fear Asian immigrants are taking away jobs, culture. *Washington Post*, p. A1.

Vanderpool, T. (2002, April 2). Lesson no. 1: Shed your Indian identity. *Christian Science Monitor*, p. 14.

Ward, C. (1996). Acculturation. In D. Landis & R. S. Bhagat (Eds.), *Handbook of intercultural training* (2nd ed., pp. 125–147). Thousand Oaks, CA: Sage.

Ward, C., Bochner, S., & Furnham, A. (2001). *The psychology of culture shock* (2nd ed.). East Sussex: Routledge. (Simultaneously published in USA by Taylor & Francis, Philadelphia, PA.)

Weissman, D., & Furnham, A. (1987). The expectations and experiences of a sojourning temporary resident abroad: A preliminary study. *Human Relations, 40*, 313–326.

Witte, K. (1993). A theory of cognitive and negative affect: Extending Gudykunst and Hammer's theory of uncertainty and anxiety reduction. *International Journal of Intercultural Relations, 17*, 197–216.

Zimmerman, S. (1995). Perceptions of intercultural communication competence and international student adaptation to an American campus. *Communication Education, 44*, 321–335.

FOLK CULTURE, POPULAR CULTURE, AND INTERCULTURAL COMMUNICATION

Although we often think of museums as repositories of culture, we know that many facets of our culture are not displayed in museums. For example, museums of fine arts are filled with paintings, sculptures, and other artwork, but these pieces reveal little about the lifestyles or values of the cultural groups that created them. Even contemporary art installations provide little evidence of how people live today.

This chapter explores two kinds of culture that are often overlooked by intercultural communication scholars but that play an important role in the construction, maintenance, and experience of culture, particularly in intercultural interactions. These two kinds of culture are folk culture and popular culture.

LEARNING ABOUT CULTURES
WITHOUT PERSONAL EXPERIENCE

As discussed in Chapter 8, people can experience and learn about other cultures by traveling to and relocating and living in other regions. But there will always be many places around the world that we have not visited and where we have not lived. How do we know about places we have never been? Much of what we know probably comes from popular culture—the media experience of films, television, music, videos, books, and magazines that most of us know and share. How does this experience affect intercultural communication?

Neither Tom nor Judith has ever been to Brazil, Nigeria, India, Russia, or China. Yet both of us hold tremendous amounts of information about these places from the news, movies, TV shows, advertisements, and more. The kind and quality of information we all have about other places is influenced by popular culture. But the views that the media portray supplement the information we get from other sources. For example, audiences that see the movie *Black Hawk Down* are likely to be familiar with the military mission in Mogadishu, the attempt to end the civil war in Somalia, and the famine relief efforts. In this sense, popular culture is pervasive.

Unlike popular culture, folk culture is often overlooked as a player in the development of cultural identity, perhaps because it is less obvious and less driven by financial interests. Yet many folk traditions are deeply embedded in the history of a culture, and their perpetuation can be extremely important to members of that cultural group. Popular culture, in contrast, is less inward looking and appeals to people far beyond those who produced it. In many ways, it is helpful to view popular culture as both contrary and complementary to folk culture.

The complexity of these two kinds of culture is often overlooked. People express concern about the social effects of popular culture—for example, the influence of television violence on children, the role of certain kinds of music in causing violent behavior by some youths, and the relationship between heterosexual pornography and violence against women. Yet most people look down on the study of folk and popular culture, as if these forms of culture convey nothing of lasting significance. Then, too, people tend to be interested in folk traditions

I was on my way to Rome from Newark last summer. Since I took the Polish Airlines, I had to make a stopover there in Warsaw. During my first morning in Warsaw, I got up, took a shower, and turned on the TV, just out of curiosity to see what was showing. I guess I expected to hear Polish, some local news and dramas, etc.

The first thing that jumped at me from the TV screen was Ricky Martin! Then followed Destiny's Child! I was shocked! U.S. popular culture really is everywhere! And I thought I already knew that! But I didn't expect it, all the way in Poland.

—Mina

only if they are members of the specific cultural group that holds those traditions. So, on the one hand, we are concerned about the power of popular culture; on the other, we don't look on popular culture as a serious area of academic research. This inherent contradiction can make it difficult to investigate and discuss folk and popular culture.

As U.S. Americans, we are in a unique position in relationship to popular culture. Products of U.S. popular culture are well known and circulate widely on the international market. The popularity of U.S. movies such as *Spider-Man* and *Star Wars: Episode II*, of U.S. music stars such as Jennifer Lopez and Madonna, and of U.S. television shows from *I Love Lucy* to *Will and Grace* and *Friends* creates an uneven flow of texts between the United States and other nations. Scholars Elihu Katz and Tamar Liebes (1987) have noted the "apparent ease with which American television programs cross cultural and linguistic frontiers. Indeed, the phenomenon is so taken for granted that hardly any systematic research has been done to explain the reasons why these programs are so successful" (p. 419).

In contrast, U.S. Americans are rarely exposed to popular culture from outside the United States. Exceptions to this largely one-way movement of popular culture include pop music stars who sing in English, such as Ricky Martin (Puerto Rican), Shakira (Colombian), and Céline Dion (French Canadian). Consider how difficult it is to find foreign films or television programs throughout most of the United States. Even when foreign corporations market their products in the United States, they almost always use U.S. advertising agencies— collectively known as "Madison Avenue." The apparent imbalance of cultural texts globally not only renders U.S. Americans more dependent on U.S.-produced popular culture but also can lead to cultural imperialism, a topic we discuss later in this chapter.

The study of popular culture has become increasingly important in the communication field, whereas the study of folk culture is developing far more slowly. Although intercultural communication scholars traditionally have overlooked folk culture and popular culture, we believe that both are significant influences in intercultural interaction.

What Is Folk Culture?

Folk culture is not the national culture of a nation-state, nor is it high culture or low culture. **Folk culture** is something else entirely: It is the traditional expressive culture shared within cultural groups, and it often includes particular customs, creative arts, rituals, and cultural products that are usually not produced for financial gain. Although folklorists often look to the past to study traditional culture, they are also interested in how traditions are played out in contemporary society to form cultural-group identities. As folklore specialist Simon Bronner (1986) reminds us, folklore studies have "made culture more concrete and more complex, by pointing to the many expressions of America's cultures, and, in so doing, . . . reminded the nation of social worlds beneath its surface" (p. 129).

Participating in folk rituals and maintaining folk traditions usually have no relationship to profit and are not controlled by any particular industry such as advertising or media. Nor are such rituals and traditions necessarily a nationwide phenomenon. For example, the celebration of Oktoberfest in Germany is laden with rituals that differ from one region to another. These differences mark cultural groups. Although the annual celebrations may be open to outsiders, they express and confirm discrete cultural identities and group memberships.

The social functions that folk culture serves are quite different from those served by popular culture. Folk culture is not meant to be packaged and exported around the globe, whereas the goal of most popular culture industries is to sell their products elsewhere. Therefore, folk culture and folk rituals are not in evidence everywhere and cannot always be practiced by everyone. Some rituals, such as the celebration of New Year's Day, differ widely from one cultural group to another. And they are subject to change. In the South, many southerners have special foods they eat for good luck, wealth, and health in the new year. Japanese also have special foods that they prepare for the new year, which are quite different from the foods that southerners prepare. They also have a number of important rituals that celebrate the new year as a new beginning. What special rituals and foods are important to your family at New Year's? If members of one cultural group move to a new location, they may continue to try to celebrate New Year's Day according to tradition to maintain their cultural group identity. Over time, though, they may adjust their rituals to suit their new location.

Increasingly, however, many popular culture industries use folk culture to situate their products as different. Cultural differences are often highlighted in travel advertisements, for example. After all, why spend a lot of money to travel to a faraway place if you do not see that locale as much different from a nearby destination? In this sense, folk culture may be exaggerated to serve the needs of travel advertisements, product endorsements, and international business concerns (O'Barr, 1994). Hence, the distinction between folk culture and popular culture remains important, but the distinction can become blurred. Given the powerful economic forces behind popular culture and its importance in intercultural interaction, we devote the rest of this chapter to popular culture.

What Is Popular Culture?

In Chapter 3, we examined various approaches to the study of culture, including a distinction between "high culture" and "low culture," which has been reconceptualized as **popular culture.** Barry Brummett (1994), a contemporary rhetorician, offers the following definition: "Popular culture refers to those systems or artifacts that most people share and that most people know about" (p. 21). According to this definition, television, music videos, and popular magazines are systems of popular culture. In contrast, the symphony and the ballet do not qualify as popular culture because most people cannot identify much about them.

So, popular culture often is seen as populist—including forms of contemporary culture that are made popular by and for the people. John Fiske (1989), professor of communication arts, explains:

> *To be made into popular culture, a commodity must also bear the interests of the people. Popular culture is not consumption, it is culture—the active process of generating and circulating meanings and pleasures within a social system: culture, however industrialized, can never be adequately described in terms of the buying and selling of commodities. (p. 23)*

In his study of popular Mexican American music in Los Angeles, ethnic studies professor George Lipsitz (1990) highlights the innovative, alternative ways that marginalized social groups are able to express themselves. In this study, he demonstrates how popular culture can arise by mixing and borrowing from other cultures: "The ability of musicians to learn from other cultures played a key role in their success as rock-and-roll artists" (p. 140). The popular speaks to—and resonates from—the people, but it does so through multiple cultural voices. Lipsitz continues:

> *The marginality of Chicano rock-and-roll musicians has provided them with a constant source of inspiration and a constant spur toward innovation that gained them the attention of mainstream audiences. But this marginal sensibility amounts to more than novelty or personal eccentricity; it holds legitimacy and power as the product of a real historical community's struggle with oppression. . . . As Chicano musicians demonstrate in their comments about their work, their music reflects a quite conscious cultural politic that seeks inclusion in the American mainstream by transforming it. (p. 159)*

Intercultural contact and intercultural communication play a central role in the creation and maintenance of popular culture. Yet, as Lipsitz points out, the popular is political and pleasurable, which further complicates how we think about popular culture.

There are four significant characteristics of popular culture: (1) It is produced by culture industries, (2) it differs from folk culture, (3) it is everywhere,

FIGURE 9-1   Fans are one type of consumer of popular culture. In this photo, fans of Ricky Martin are expressing their affection for him in various ways, during an appearance he made on the *Today Show*. How might people express their resistance to or avoidance of Ricky Martin's music? (© *AP/Wide World Photos*)

and (4) it fills a social function. As Fiske (1989) points out, popular culture is nearly always produced within a capitalist system that sees the products of popular culture as commodities that can be economically profitable. They are produced by what are called **culture industries.** The Disney Corporation is a noteworthy example of a culture industry because it produces amusement parks, movies, cartoons, and a plethora of associated merchandise. As mentioned previously, folk culture, by contrast, arises apart from any drive for financial profit. It emerges from needs that are not satisfied by the dominant culture.

Popular culture is ubiquitous. We are bombarded with it, every day and everywhere. On average, U.S. Americans watch more than 40 hours of television per week. Movie theaters beckon us with the latest multimillion-dollar extravaganzas, nearly all U.S.-made. Radio stations and music TV programs blast us with the hottest music groups performing their latest hits. (See Figure 9-1.) And we are inundated with a staggering number of advertisements and commercials daily.

It is difficult to avoid popular culture. Not only is it ubiquitous, but it also serves an important social function. How many times have you been asked by friends and family for your reaction to a recent movie or TV program? Academicians Horace Newcomb and Paul Hirsch (1987) suggest that television serves as a cultural forum for discussing and working out our ideas on a variety of topics, including those that emerge from the programs themselves. Television, then, has a powerful social function—to serve as a forum for dealing with social issues.

A recent example of the power of television overseas was evident in the 2002 World Cup soccer games. The World Cup is an enormous sporting event around the world, although it is not so popular in the United States. In Moscow, the Russian team's games had been televised until the Russians lost a match to Japan. This loss, which was shown on giant outdoor screens, led to a huge riot. The BBC (2002) reported:

> *Authorities in Moscow are to stop televising World Cup games on giant outdoor screens after thousands of football fans went on the rampage in the city, leaving two dead and many others injured.*
>
> *The violence happened in the centre of Moscow on Sunday after Russia went down 1–0 to Japan, severely denting the country's chances of progressing to the second round of the tournament. (news.bbc.co.uk/hi/english/world/europe/ newsid_2034000/2034878.stm)*

National identity, cultural pride, and other factors were blamed for this riot. How important are sports teams in the United States? How do U.S. Americans respond when their teams win or lose? How is this related to cultural identity?

The ways that people negotiate their relationships to popular culture are complex, and it is this complexity that makes understanding the role of popular culture in intercultural communication so difficult. Clearly, we are not passive recipients of this deluge of popular culture. We are, in fact, quite active in our consumption of or resistance to popular culture, a notion that we turn to next.

CONSUMING AND RESISTING POPULAR CULTURE

Consuming Popular Culture

Faced with this onslaught of **cultural texts,** people negotiate their ways through popular culture in quite different ways. Popular culture texts do not have to win over the majority of people to be "popular." People often seek out or avoid specific forms of popular culture. For example, romance novels are the best-selling form of literature, but many readers have no interest in such books. Likewise, whereas many people enjoy watching soap operas or professional wrestling, many others find no pleasure in those forms of popular culture.

Stuart Hall's (1980) encoding/decoding model might be helpful here. Hall is careful to place "meaning" at several stages in the communication process, so that it is never fixed but is always being constructed within various contexts. Thus, in his model, he places **encoding**—or the construction of textual meaning by popular culture institutions—within specific social contexts. **Decoding**—the interpretation of the text's meaning by receivers—is performed by various audiences in different social contexts, whose members have different interests at stake. In this way, the meaning(s) of various popular culture texts can be seen as negotiated throughout the communication process. The "real meaning" of any

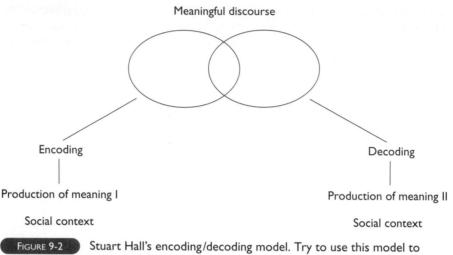

Meaningful discourse

Encoding

Production of meaning I

Social context

Decoding

Production of meaning II

Social context

FIGURE 9-2 Stuart Hall's encoding/decoding model. Try to use this model to discuss how different people might arrive at different interpretations of your favorite TV show.

popular culture text cannot simply be located in either the senders or the receivers. Although this model may seem to suggest tremendous unpredictability in popular culture, people do not create just any meaning out of these texts. We are always enmeshed in our social identities, which help guide our interpretations as decoders. Encoders, in turn, rely on these larger identity formations to help them fashion their texts to sell to particular markets. (See Figure 9-2.)

There is some unpredictability in how people navigate popular culture. After all, not all men enjoy watching football, and not all women like to read romance novels. However, some profiles emerge. Advertising offices of popular magazines even make their **reader profiles** available to potential advertisers. These reader profiles portray what the magazine believes its readership "looks" like. Although reader profiles do not follow a set format, they generally detail the average age, gender, individual and household incomes, and so on of their readership. The reader profile for *Vogue*, for example, will not look like the reader profile for *Esquire*.

Each magazine targets a particular readership and then sells this readership to advertisers. The diversity of the U.S. American population generates very different readerships among a range of magazines, in several ways. Let's explore some of the ways that this diversity is played out in the magazine market.

How Magazines Respond to the Needs of Cultural Identities   A wide range of magazines respond to the different social and political needs of groups with different cultural identities. You may already be familiar with magazines geared toward a male or a female readership. But many other kinds of magazines serve important functions for other cultural groups. For example, *Ebony* is one of many magazines that cultivate an African American readership. Similar magazines exist for other cultural identities. *Hispanic Magazine*, published in Florida, targets a

Latino/a audience; *The Advocate* claims to be the national newsmagazine for gays and lesbians. These magazines offer information and viewpoints that are generally unavailable in other magazines. They function as a discussion forum for concerns that mainstream magazines often overlook. They also tend to affirm, by their very existence, these other cultural identities, which sometimes are invisible or are silenced in the mainstream culture.

In addition, many non–English language newspapers circulate among readers of specific ethnic groups, serving the same functions as the magazines just mentioned. However, because their production costs are low, they are better able to survive and reach their limited readerships. For instance, newspapers printed in Cantonese, Spanish, Vietnamese, Japanese, French, Korean, Arabic, Polish, Russian, Navajo, and other languages reach non-English-speaking readers in the United States.

How Readers Negotiate Consumption   Readers actively negotiate their way through cultural texts such as magazines—consuming those that fulfill important cultural needs and resisting those that do not. Hence, it is possible to be a reader of magazines that reflect various cultural configurations; that is, someone might read several women's magazines and Spanish language newspapers and magazines, as well as *Newsweek* and *Southern Living.*

Cultural Texts Versus Cultural Identities   We must be careful not to conflate the magazines with the cultural identities they are targeting. After all, many publications offer different points of view on any given topic. Thus, there is no single, unified "Asian American position" on immigration reform or any "Latino position" on affirmative action. Rather, there can be a preponderance of opinions on some issues. These often are played out through popular culture forums.

It is important to remember that cultural populations other than readers of mainstream texts can participate in different cultural forums—with different discussions and information. For example, an article in *The Rafu Shimpo*, the Los Angeles Japanese daily news, highlighted yet another hate crime against an Asian American. In this case, a European American man repeatedly stabbed a Chinese American man at a grocery store in Novato, a city in the San Francisco Bay Area. The reality of living in a society that expresses racism, homophobia, xenophobia, and anti-Semitism through hate crimes is often lost on those who rely on mainstream media. These issues make a tremendous difference in how we perceive social reality on a day-to-day basis.

People come together through cultural magazines and newspapers to affirm and negotiate their relationships with their cultural identities. In this way, the texts resemble cultural spaces, which we discussed in Chapter 7. However, magazines are but one example of how popular culture can function. Not all popular culture texts are easily correlated to particular cultural groups. Think about the various TV programs, movies, mass-market paperbacks, and tabloids that flood our everyday lives. The reasons that people enjoy some over others cannot easily be determined. People negotiate their relationships to popular culture in complex ways.

Resisting Popular Culture

Sometimes people actively seek out particular popular culture texts to consume; other times they resist cultural texts. But resistance to popular culture is a complex process. Avoiding certain forms of popular culture is one kind of resistance, but resistance can occur in a variety of ways. Let's look at the recent controversy that erupted over a series of Abercrombie & Fitch T-shirts that appeared in the company's Spring 2002 catalog.

> *Among the collection were T-shirts with depictions of slant-eyed, conical-hat wearing men with slogans like, "Wong Brothers Laundry: Two Wongs Can Make it White," "Get Your Buddha on the Dance Floor," and "Wok-N-Bowl: Chinese Food and Bowling." (Salinas, 2002)*

Following a storm of protest from Asian American groups, the T-shirts were pulled from stores and are no longer sold (you can see these T-shirts at www.boycottaf.com).

Let's consider why these T-shirts created negative feelings, as well as how Asian American groups resisted the circulation of these products. There was a mixed reaction to the T-shirts among Asian Americans: Some were not offended by the shirts, but others were incensed. It is important to note that all members of any cultural group have diverse reactions to various popular images. For example, not all women are offended by the Hooters restaurant/bar chain, which features scantily clad waitresses.

If we return to our four touchstones to understand this controversy, we can see how communication, culture, power, and context play out in this example. Asian Americans are a relatively small market segment in general. With whom is Abercrombie & Fitch likely communicating? Who might have been the target audience for these T-shirts? What kinds of cultural attitudes might be perpetuated among non–Asian Americans through these products? Think about who is communicating with whom. What kind of power differential is at work here when non–Asian Americans can create and market these kinds of products to non–Asian Americans.

The context is important as well. As noted previously, we need to consider historical contexts as one arena for understanding intercultural contact. In this case, the images on these T-shirts gain their meaning from the history of Asian immigrants in the United States. Brown University professor Robert Lee (1999) reminds us: "Since popular culture is a significant arena in which the struggle over defining American nationality occurs, it also plays a critical role in defining race" (p. 6). Lee continues his analysis by focusing on popular images of Asians and Asian Americans. Many of these stereotypical images are reflected in the Abercrombie & Fitch T-shirts.

Lee (1999) also tells us that "subordinated groups offer resistance to the hegemony of elite culture; they create subaltern popular cultures and contest for a voice in the dominant public sphere" (p. 6). In this sense, many Asian Americans felt that these historical and stereotypical images continued to mark Asian Americans as somehow not American. For example, Terry Fung, a Chinese

This writer, in a University of California newsmagazine, addresses the controversy over the marketing and selling of T-shirts that some feel are racist. To see these T-shirts, go to www.boycottaf.com, as they are no longer on sale.

> *The focus of Abercrombie & Fitch's marketing angle has been to celebrate whiteness. While somewhat different from the White Pride ideologies of racial supremacists (but not too far off), they have promoted, as the meaning of their brand, the lifestyle of the rich and affluent offspring of WASPs. As one commenter on Plastic.com noted, "I'm Scot-Irish-German. . . . and I don't feel Caucasian enough to shop there."*
>
> *But what does it say when a company that is so staunch in its whiteness acknowledges its non-white customers with shirts that make fun of their ethnicity? And so to add levity, ethnic jokes are used? Also, notice that the Asian characters are in roles of servitude. They make pizza, run the bowling alleys, wash the laundry and deliver the hoagies that are enjoyed by people at leisure. They work, and their work is menial. On the other hand, none of the Abercrombie models are working. Even Abercrombie's other T-shirts, with topics like road trips, music fests, beach life, and sex, all emphasize leisure. It's as if they're resurrecting the old racial hierarchy where whites are of the privileged class to be served and minorities are designated their servants. Abercrombie is welcoming Asians into their gated community, but only if they're houseboys or girls, not their peers. . . .*
>
> *But Abercrombie's business is whiteness, and some of us are buying it. Some are willing to do anything to remove any trait of difference from their appearance. . . . And what easier way to express one's self-hate than with a T-shirt, priced at $24.95, and sold in a store where everything else is whitewashed?*

Source: From Kevin Lee, "Pimped by Abercrombie & Fitch," *Hard Boiled, 5.5.* May 2002. www.hardboiled.org/5.5/55-08-af.html

American online marketer, reflected on seeing the T-shirts: "I was so shocked that I just stood there staring at the shirts for a good two to three minutes. . . . Now the anger is setting in. I have a few pieces of clothing from Abercrombie. Now I don't want to wear anything from there anymore" (quoted in Kang & Kato, 2002).

Here we see a clear example of a group's resistance to popular culture and popular images, because they construct Asian and Asian American identity in undesirable ways. Indeed, people often resist particular forms of popular culture by refusing to engage in them. For example, some people feel the need to avoid television and even decide not to own televisions. Some people refuse to go to movies that contain violence or sexuality because they do not find pleasure in such films. These kinds of conscious decisions are often based on concerns about the ways that cultural products should be understood as political.

Resistance to popular culture can also be related to social roles. Likewise, some people have expressed concern about the supposedly homophobic or racist ideologies embedded in Disney films such as *Aladdin* (Boone, 1995). *Aladdin* plays into Western fears of homosexuality and the tradition of projecting those concerns on Arab culture. Resistance stems mainly from concerns about the representation of various social groups. Popular culture plays a powerful role in how we think about and understand other groups. More recently, the Disney film *Pocahontas* has been criticized for its rewriting of the European encounters with Native Americans. According to communication scholars Derek Buescher and Kent Ono (1996), this film "helps audiences unlearn the infamous history of mass slaughter by replacing it with a cute, cuddly one" (p. 128).

REPRESENTING CULTURAL GROUPS

As noted at the beginning of this chapter, people often are introduced to other cultures through the lens of popular culture. These introductions can be quite intimate, in ways that tourists may not experience. For example, movies may portray romance, familial conflict, or a death in the family; the audience experiences the private lives of people they do not know, in ways that they never could simply as tourists.

Yet we must also think about how these cultural groups are portrayed through that lens of popular culture. Not everyone sees the portrayal in the same way. For example, you may not think that the TV shows *Friends* and *Everybody Loves Raymond* represent quintessential U.S. American values and lifestyles. But some viewers may see it as their entree into how U.S. Americans (or perhaps European Americans) live.

In his critical study of the martial arts movie *Showdown in Little Tokyo*, Tom Nakayama (1994) argues that popular culture representations help us understand identities in relationship to other identities. In this movie, the cultural identities of the Japanese (as the "bad guys") had to be understood in their narrative relationship to the "good guys" (two Los Angeles police officers). Images portraying other identities—based on race, gender, or sexual orientation—fueled the movie's narrative. In this way, the relationships among the various identities were negotiated and constructed by Hollywood.

In a recent study on television coverage of affirmative action and African Americans, communication researchers Alexis Tan, Yuki Fujioka, and Gerdean Tan (2000) found that more negative coverage increased negative stereotypes about African Americans. However, they also found that "positive TV portrayals did not lead to positive stereotypes, nor did they influence opinions" (p. 370). They conclude that "negative portrayals are remembered more than positive portrayals, are more arousing and therefore are more influential in the development of stereotypes" (p. 370). Given this dynamic, it is clear how TV news coverage can continue to marginalize and reinforce negative stereotypes, even if the reports also present positive information about minority groups. Would the

A Belgian student describes his first impressions on arriving in the United States.

When I first landed at JFK Airport, I felt like I was going crazy. When I was younger, I only knew about America through television, radio, books, and movies. Even if people don't like America, it is still like a dream-land because it is a place where everything is big, where movies are made, especially police movies. American movies are very well made, with special effects, and so the first time I saw the real America, it was like in the movies. The police in the airport were like cowboys, wearing sunglasses, big mustaches, with badges everywhere and they were big and unafraid, like cowboys. You must respect the customs lines, and all the rules are very strict.

When we left the airport to go to Manhattan, we saw really poor neighborhoods near the airport. I wondered, is America really so poor with small houses? The houses look like they are made of wood and flimsy, unlike the brick ones in Belgium. Once you cross into Manhattan, however, you understand that in America you either have money or you don't. There are majestic cities and poverty; you can get lots of money or nothing. It is another way of living. In Belgium, you do not have to struggle so much for money. Once you have a job in Belgium, there are lots of job protections. In Belgium, if you want to live, you don't have to work.

—Christophe

same results occur if the researchers were to study the Abercrombie & Fitch T-shirts, instead of television?

Migrants' Perceptions of Mainstream Culture

Ethnographers and other scholars have crossed international and cultural boundaries to examine the influence of popular culture. In an early study, Elihu Katz and Tamar Liebes (1987) set up focus groups to see how different cultural groups perceived the popular 1980s TV drama *Dallas:*

There were ten groups each of Israeli Arabs, new immigrants to Israel from Russia, first and second generation immigrants from Morocco, and kibbutz members. Taking these groups as a microcosm of the worldwide audience of Dallas, we are comparing their readings of the program with ten groups of matched Americans in Los Angeles. (p. 421)

Katz and Liebes found that the U.S. Americans in Los Angeles were much less likely to perceive *Dallas* as portraying life in the United States. In contrast, the Israelis, Arabs, and immigrants were much more inclined to believe that this television show was indeed all about life in the United States. Katz and Liebes note: "What seems clear from the analysis, even at this stage, is that the non-Americans consider the story more real than the Americans. The non-

Americans have little doubt that the story is about 'America'; the Americans are less sure" (p. 421). The results of this study are not surprising, but we should not overlook what they tell us about the intercultural communication process. We can see that these popular culture images are often more influential in constructing particular ways of understanding other cultural groups than our own.

Another study (Lee & Cho, 1990) that focused on immigrants to the United States yielded similar results. The researchers asked female Korean immigrants why they preferred watching Korean TV shows (which they had to rent at the video store) instead of U.S. programs. The respondents stated that, because of the cultural differences, the Korean shows were more appealing. Yet, as one respondent noted,

> *"I like to watch American programs. Actors and actresses are glamorous and the pictures are sleek. But the ideas are still American. How many Korean women are that independent? And how many men commit incest? I think American programs are about American people. They are not the same as watching the Korean programs. But I watch them for fun. And I learn the American way of living by watching them." (p. 43)*

Here, both consumption of and resistance to U.S. television are evident. This woman uses U.S. television to learn about the U.S. American "way of living," but she prefers to watch Korean shows because they relate to her cultural identity. As she says, "I like the Korean programs because I get the sense of what's going on in my country" (p. 43).

The use of popular culture to learn about other cultures should not be surprising. After all, many teachers encourage their students to use popular culture in this manner, not only to improve their language skills but also to learn many of the nuances of another culture. When Tom was first studying French, his French professor told the students that *Le dernier métro* (*The Last Metro*), a film by director François Truffaut, was playing downtown. The point, of course, was to hear French spoken by natives. But Tom remembers being amazed at the subtle references to anti-Semitism, the treatment of lesbianism, and the film's style, which contrasted sharply with that of Hollywood films.

Popular Culture and Stereotyping

In what ways does reliance on popular culture create and reinforce stereotypes of different cultures? As we noted at the outset of this chapter, neither author has had the opportunity to travel all over the world. Our knowledge about other places, even places we have been, is largely influenced by popular culture. For people who do not travel and who interact in relatively homogeneous social circles, the impact of popular culture may be even greater.

Film studies scholar Richard Dyer (1993) tells us that

> *the effectiveness of stereotypes resides in the way they invoke a consensus. . . . The stereotype is taken to express a general agreement about a social group, as if that agreement arose before, and independently of, the stereotype. Yet for the most part it is* from *stereotypes that we get our ideas about social groups. (p. 14)*

Dyer makes an important observation that stereotypes are connected to social values and social judgments about other groups of people. These stereotypes are powerful because they function to tell us how "we" value and judge these other groups.

Because some of these stereotypes are negative, they have negative consequences for members of that social group. In his study of the controversy at the University of North Dakota over their mascot, the Fighting Sioux, communication scholar Raúl Tovares (2002) points to the climate at sporting events, which highlights the ways in which stereotypes, cultural values, and popular culture images can come together. (See Figure 9-3.) He explains:

> *Hockey and football games have become sites where offensive images of Native Americans are common. Students from NDSU show up at athletic events with cartoonish images of bison forcing themselves sexually on Native Americans. At "sporting" events, it is not uncommon to hear phrases such as "kill the Sioux," "Sioux suck," "f——k the Sioux," and "rape Sioux women." Such phrases, many Native American students claim, are a direct result of the Fighting Sioux logo. (p. 91)*

Think about the ways that this mascot might circulate on jackets, T-shirts, cartoons, and other popular culture forms. How does popular culture represent an important site for negotiating this cultural identity? Why do non–Native Americans have a dominant voice and more power in these representations?

Many familiar stereotypes of ethnic groups are represented in the media. Scholar Lisa Flores (2000) describes the portrayal of a diverse group of high school students in the television show *Matt Waters*. Flores focuses her analysis on Angela, a Puerto Rican student. According to Flores, there is a strong theme of assimilation at work in this show. She notes that

> *to follow the seeming logic of this assimilationist politics requires an initial belief in the goal of a single, unified American culture expressed in a harmonious community such as that found within the* Matt Waters *community. The assimilationist perspective also mandates an assumption that ethnic minorities cannot maintain cultural difference except in rejection of all of dominant or mainstream society. (pp. 37–38)*

She turns to Chicana feminism to show how we can resist these popular culture representations.

African American women also traditionally have been portrayed stereotypically on TV, especially in the 1950s and 1960s, when the roles they held were secondary (e.g., as domestics). Scholar Bishetta Merritt (2000) also reminds us of the African American female characters who often appear as background scenery: the person buying drugs, the homeless person on the sidewalk, the hotel lobby prostitute. Merritt points out that these women still project images, even if they aren't the focus:

> *If the majority of black women the television audience is exposed to are homeless, drug-addicted, or maids, and if viewers have no contact with African American women other than through television, what choice do they have but to believe that*

FIGURE 9-3   Concern about sports mascots centers on issues of how they are interpreted and how they create barriers to intercultural communication. This woman's concern that Indian mascots reflect racism is not always understood by sports fans. Although many people know that these mascots are offensive to some, what might drive people to resist changing sports mascots? How does this conflict demonstrate the diversity that resides within U.S. culture? (© Steve Skjold/PhotoEdit, Inc.)

Although I feel that race is an emotionally charged issue, I do feel that media have a lot to do with it. Whenever a crime is committed, if it is someone who is colored or from a different ethnic group than White America, the media always state what color the person is or what the person's ethnicity is. Unfortunately, this paints a bad picture of the rest of the group. This then leads to stereotyping. If the media would not focus so much on the color or ethnicity of the person committing the crime, and if people would not be so ignorant to the fact that this one person does not represent the whole group, then, in my opinion, prejudice would eventually decline.

I think stereotyping and prejudice also come about because of ingroups and reference groups. Ingroups are the people who want to use the term we. *Reference groups are the groups that we want to be part of, to belong to. If the media state that some Black man robbed a bank, then a White person may state that we (the ingroup of Whites) should not put up with criminals from the Black community (the outgroup). That person may say about his own racial or ethnic group, "I don't know anyone who has ever committed a crime." Although this may be the case, it does not necessarily mean that no Whites have ever committed a crime. This leads back to the media. They seem to paint a negative picture of a whole race. Also, if a White person, for instance, committed a crime, this same man would try to use the scapegoat theory and/or make an excuse for the crime.*

—Brad

all women of this ethnic background reflect this television image? . . . It is, therefore, important, as the twenty-first century approaches and the population of this country includes more and more people of color, that the television industry broaden the images of African American women to include their nuances and diversity. (p. 53)

What about those ethnic groups that simply don't appear except as infrequent stereotypes—for example, Native Americans and Asian Americans? How do these stereotypes influence intercultural interaction? Do people behave any differently if they don't hold stereotypes about people with whom they are interacting? Two communication researchers, Valerie Manusov and Radha Hegde (1993), investigated these questions in a study in which they identified two groups of college students: those who had some preconceived ideas about India (which were fairly positive) and those who didn't. Manusov and Hegde asked all of the students to interact, one at a time, with an international student from India who was part of the study.

When the students with preconceptions talked with the Indian student, they interacted differently than those who had no expectations. Specifically, students from the former group relied less on small talk, covered more topics, and asked fewer questions within each topic. Overall, their conversations were more like

This essay points out the problem of stereotypes perpetuated by the media.

WHAT'S AMERICAN?

Say the words "quintessentially American kid" to most anyone, and the image that comes to mind is one of a white American—blond-haired, blue-eyed, etc.

Why is it that an African-American kid is never referred to as a quintessentially American kid? Why not a Hispanic child, an Asian child or an Indian child? Are they not just as American? Part of the reason for the slight is that stereotyping is ages old, as compelling as it is devastating.

In the wake of the recent school shootings that have rocked America, the hypocrisy of stereotyping people reached another insulting crescendo. . . .

Kip Kinkel, the 15-year-old boy who allegedly killed his parents and two classmates in Oregon last month, was described in Newsweek *magazine as having "an innocent look that is part Huck Finn and part Alfred E. Newman—boyish and quintessentially American."*

You knew he was white. . . .

The New York Times *and* Newsweek *also described Kinkel with words such as "skinny," "slight," "diminutive," "freckle-faced," with an "innocent look." Luke Woodham, convicted recently in Mississippi of killing two students, was the "chubby, poor kid at Pearl High School who always seemed to get picked on." Mitchel Johnson and Andrew Golden, who allegedly killed four girls and a teacher in Jonesboro, Arkansas, were "little boys." Andrew Wurst, who allegedly killed a teacher in Edinboro, Pennsylvania, was a "shy and quirky eighth grader with an offbeat sense of humor." . . .*

When's the last time a black child who allegedly committed a comparable crime was described in such wholesome detail, instead of as cold or adultlike?

The danger in such description is that black children are demonized in people's minds, making it easier to dismiss their humanity and easier to mete out more harsh and unfair judgments and punishment than whites receive.

Source: From "What's American? When Is the Last Time You Heard a Young Black Suspect Described as 'Innocent-Looking' or 'Shy'?" *The Post Standard*, July 3, 1998, p. A6.

those between people who know each other. The students with the preconceptions also were more positive about the conversation.

What can we learn from this study? Having some information and positive expectations may lead to more in-depth conversations and positive outcomes than having no information. But what happens when negative stereotypes are present? It is possible that expectations are fulfilled in this case too.

For example, in several studies at Princeton University, Whites interviewed both White and Black "job applicants" who were actually part of the study and were trained to behave consistently, no matter how interviewers acted toward

Popular culture—and movies, in particular—is an important place to begin to understand our society and our own identities. This excerpt discusses how movies can both help and hurt individuals' understanding of their own identities and those of others.

> *Over the years, Hollywood's given me great and terrible things—a culture as tangible as the mix of race and ethnicity I grew up around—and somewhere between my "reel" and "real" lives lie my deepest beliefs and my greatest fears, my nightmares and my dreams. As a kid and now an adult with a perpetual identity crisis, Hollywood has been a constant mirror for me, and what I've screened has resulted in validation and self-loathing, vindication and betrayal (I of it, and it of me). I was raised in a swirl of cultures that at times melded seamlessly and at others clashed violently—a contradiction that exists at the very heart of Hollywood, the tension between its most noble and most debased instincts.*
>
> > *For starters, I think I'd hate white people if it wasn't for Hollywood. This is not to say that I haven't hated some white people, and sure, the entire race, on occasion. But how can you hate someone you're on such intimate terms with—on screen and off?*

Source: From "Technicolor," by Rubén Martínez, 1998, *Half and Half: Writers on Growing Up Biracial and Bicultural*, edited by C. C. O'Hearn, p. 248.

them. The interviews were videotaped. The interviewers clearly behaved differently toward Blacks: Their speech deteriorated, they made more grammatical errors, they spent less time, and they showed fewer "immediacy" behaviors—that is, they were less friendly and less outgoing. In a second study, interviewers were trained to be either "immediate" or "nonimmediate" as they interviewed White job applicants. A panel of judges watched the videotapes and agreed that those applicants interviewed by the "nonimmediate" interviewer performed less well and were more nervous. This suggests that the African American applicants in the first study never had a chance: They were only reacting to the nonimmediate behavior of the interviewers. Mark Snyder (1998) summarizes: "Considered together, the two investigations suggest that in interracial encounters, racial stereotypes may constrain behavior in ways to cause both blacks and whites to behave in accordance with those stereotypes" (p. 455).

U.S. POPULAR CULTURE AND POWER

One of the dynamics of intercultural communication that we have highlighted throughout this text is power. In considering popular culture, we need to think about not only how people interpret and consume popular culture but also how these popular culture texts represent particular groups in specific ways. If people

FIGURE 9-4 James Dean remains a popular cultural icon in the United States and abroad. This 1996 photo shows that one of his films, *East of Eden,* continues to play in Tokyo. How does Dean's popularity in Japan contrast with the absence of a similar popular Japanese male star in the United States? What might explain this disparity? Think about the issues of cultural imperialism raised in this chapter. (*Courtesy T. K. Nakayama*)

largely view other cultural groups through the lens of popular culture, then we need to think about the power relations that are embedded in these popular culture dynamics.

Global Circulation of Images and Commodities

As noted previously, much of the internationally circulated popular culture is U.S. popular culture. U.S.-made films, for example, are widely distributed by an industry that is backed by considerable financial resources. Some media scholars have noted that the U.S. film industry earns far more money outside the United States than from domestic box office receipts (Guback, 1969; Guback & Varis, 1982). This situation ensures that Hollywood will continue to seek overseas markets and that it will have the financial resources to do so. A recent film, *Spider-Man*, exemplifies this economic position of Hollywood. Although the producers and distributors certainly made a considerable amount of money from the domestic screenings, they earned significant amounts of money from non-U.S. showings as well. (See Figure 9-4.)

Many other U.S. media are widely available outside of the United States, including television and newspapers. (Cable News Network [CNN] was even available in Iraq during the Gulf War.) For example, MTV is broadcast internationally. And *The International Herald Tribune*, published jointly by *The New*

I think American pop culture has a major effect on other nations, especially during this past century. One example is blue jeans . . . these are completely and totally American and have been adopted all over the world. I have also noticed in my travels that American music and pop stars seem to gain notoriety and are sometimes even more popular than they are at home. Also there seem to be many American TV shows that are shown overseas, and they may not always be the example of what is going on in American TV programming. When traveling abroad, running into evidence of American pop culture is sometimes a weird experience. Sometimes it is a proper representation of what is going on in America, and other times it is a gross distortion in perception. It has helped me define and redefine my culture better and what I value as an American and what I value as a human being.

—Kati

York Times and *The Washington Post*, is widely available in some parts of the world. The implications of the dominance by U.S. media and popular culture have yet to be determined, although you might imagine the consequences.

Not all popular culture comes from the United States. For example, James Bond is a British phenomenon, but the famous character has been exported to the United States. In their study of the popularity of the Bond series, scholars Tony Bennett and Janet Woollacott (1987) note that in the Bond film *A License to Kill* "the threat to the dominance of white American male culture is removed not by a representative of that culture, and certainly not by a somewhat foppish English spy, but by the self-destruction of the forces ranged against it" (pp. 293–294). Here, a British character becomes a hero for U.S. and international audiences through the U.S. film industry. It is not always easy to know what is and what is not U.S. popular culture.

The television show *The Weakest Link* also originated in Britain and eventually spread to over 70 countries, including the United States. Yet the cultural values of the show are not universal, and cultural discontent can occur. For example, "the Thai version of the TV quiz show has reduced contestants to tears, provoked national outrage and drawn an official plea to the producers to show mercy. Even the prime minister says he's a bit upset" (Noikorn, 2002, p. A31). The cultural value embedded in the humiliation of the contestants "goes against the grain in Thailand, where politeness is a supreme virtue and disagreement is often expressed by smiling" (p. A31). The global circulation of popular culture that reflects Western cultural values may have an uneven impact. After all, we are not often recipients of popular culture from Thailand.

Much popular culture that is expressed in non-English languages has a difficult time on the global scene. Although Céline Dion, who sings in English, has been able to reach a worldwide audience, a fellow French Canadian, Garou, who sings in French, has not reached the same level of notoriety. Still, Garou

323

(Pierre Garand) is extremely popular in the francophone world. His album *Seul* was the top-selling album in France in 2001, and he sold "1.5 million copies in Europe (France, Belgium, Switzerland) (*1.5 million d'exemplaires en Europe [France, Belgique, Suisse]*)" (Arseneault, 2001, p. 76). He is so popular in France, that he "cannot have a private life, nor walk alone. There's no question that if he goes to restaurants or bars, he will be harassed, if not to say attacked" (*En Europe, Garou ne peut pas avoir une vie privée, ni se promener seul. Pas question pour lui de sortir dans les restos ou dans les bars sans se faire harceler, pour ne pas dire agresser*) (p. 76). Have you ever heard of Garou? To reach a worldwide audience, must he sing in English? Garou wants "to attack the American market with an album in English next year" (*s'attaquer au marché américain avec un album en anglais dès l'année prochaine*) (p. 80). What does this tell us about popular culture? What does it tell us about the unequal power relations that are evident in popular culture? How does it influence how we think about the world? (See Figure 9-5.)

Cultural Imperialism

It is difficult to measure the impact of the U.S. and Western media and popular culture on the rest of the world. But we do know that we cannot ignore this dynamic. The U.S. government in the 1920s believed that having U.S. movies on foreign screens would boost the sales of U.S. products because the productions would be furnished with U.S. goods. The government thus worked closely with the Hays Office (officially, the Motion Picture Producers and Distributors of America) to break into foreign markets, most notably in the United Kingdom (Nakayama & Vachon, 1991).

Discussions about **media imperialism, electronic colonialism,** and **cultural imperialism,** which began in the 1920s, continue today. The interrelationships between economics, nationalism, and culture make it difficult to determine with much certainty how significant cultural imperialism might be. The issue of cultural imperialism is complex because the definition is complex. In his survey of the cultural imperialism debates, scholar John Tomlinson (1991) identifies five ways of thinking about cultural imperialism: (1) as cultural domination, (2) as media imperialism, (3) as nationalist discourse, (4) as a critique of global capitalism, and (5) as a critique of modernity (pp. 19–23). Tomlinson's analysis underscores the interrelatedness of issues of ethnicity, culture, and nationalism in the context of economics, technology, and capitalism—resources that are distributed unevenly throughout the world. To understand the concerns about cultural imperialism, therefore, it is necessary to consider the complexity of the impact of U.S. popular culture. There is no easy way to measure the impact of popular culture, but we should be sensitive to its influences on intercultural communication. Let's look at some examples.

In the Gulf War of 1991, U.S. troops and allies fought the Iraqis for control of Kuwait. Demanding that Iraq relinquish Kuwait and determined to reestablish Kuwait's independence, the United States attacked Baghdad. Media coverage highlighted the air strikes in these attacks, and many U.S. homes, malls, and

FIGURE 9-5   French Canadian singer Garou
holds up his World's Best-Selling Canadian Male
Artist award during the 2002 World Music Awards
ceremony in Monaco. How important is the English
language in the circulation of popular culture products (e.g., movies, songs, and television shows)?
Would you be willing to sing in a language other
than your native language? (© *Reuters/Getty Images*)

businesses were festooned with yellow ribbons in support of U.S. and allied
troops. At that time, French writer Jean Baudrillard published a series of articles
(called *"La guerre du golfe n'aura pas eu lieu,"* or "The Gulf War Did Not Take
Place") in a Paris-based newspaper, *Libération*. In these articles, he argued that
the Gulf War was a media simulation, that we had no access to truth. Our reliance on media images, rather than on reality, made us very reliant on popular
culture. Yet, as he argues, we need not play into that game:

I arrived in Moscow, Russia, spent three days with my host family, and was then sent to what is called a Pioneer Camp. This camp was basically a scout camp designed to indoctrinate the youth in preparation for Communist Party membership. At that point I had no knowledge of the Russian language or culture and there wasn't a single person at the camp (of 300 students) who spoke English. Needless to say, I mastered the art of nonverbal communication very quickly.

In terms of the initial interaction, those around me and I lacked both linguistic and cultural competence. The frustration accumulated for a few days, until we had a little dance one evening. As it turned out, the Billy Joel song "We Didn't Start the Fire" was the favorite song of the older students and, although they didn't understand the lyrics, they could sing along. We played that song over and over again until we were all friends. We found similarity. That one similarity factor brought us to a level of closeness that was unbelievably intense.
—Katrina

The true belligerents are those who thrive on the ideology of the truth of this war, despite the fact that the war itself exerts its ravages on another level, through faking, through hyper-reality, the simulacrum, through all those strategies of psychological deterrence that make play with facts and images, with the precession of the virtual over the real, of virtual time over real time, and the inexorable confusion between the two. If we have no practical knowledge of this war—and such knowledge is out of the question—then let us at least have the skeptical intelligence to reject the probability of all information, of all images whatever their source. (quoted in Norris, 1992, pp. 193–194)

Baudrillard's rejection of the war coverage is one tactic for dealing with the media hype and barrage of images. Theorist Christopher Norris warns against such a position, because it encourages us to forget that many people, mostly Iraqis, were killed in the war; it was not simply a movie.

Sometimes the Western images are imported and welcomed by the ruling interests in other countries. For example, the government of the Ivory Coast in West Africa has used foreign (mostly French) media to promote its image of a "new" Ivoirien cultural identity. The government purchased a satellite dish that permits 1,400 hours of French programming annually, which represents 77% of all programming. But it has been criticized by many for borrowing heavily from the Western media—for inviting cultural imperialism:

While television, as mirror, sometimes reflects multiple Ivoirien cultures, the latter are expected to acquiesce to a singular national culture in the image of the Party, which is also synonymous with a Western cultural image. . . . The cultural priority is openness for the sake of modernization in the quest of the Ivoirien national identity. (Land, 1992, p. 25)

In all of these examples, popular culture plays an enormous role in explaining relations around the globe. It is through popular culture that we try to understand the dynamics of other cultures and nations. Although these representations are problematic, we also rely on popular culture to understand many kinds of issues: the conflict in Kashmir between India and Pakistan, the sex abuse scandals in the Catholic Church, the conflict in the West Bank between Israelis and Palestinians, and the breakup of the former Soviet Union. For many of us, the world exists through popular culture.

SUMMARY

In this chapter, we touched on folk culture but focused on popular culture. For many people, popular culture is one of the primary modes of intercultural experience. The images produced by culture industries such as film and television enable us to "travel" to many places. As a forum for the development of our ideas about other places, we rely heavily on popular culture. For example, many people who have never been to Somalia or the Middle East or studied much about Islam have very strong ideas about these topics. Military issues overseas are prominent in many U.S. news reports and form the backdrop in U.S. films such as *Black Hawk Down* and *Three Kings*. The United States imports very little popular culture from these parts of the world.

It is significant that much of our popular culture is dominated by U.S.-based culture industries, considering how we use popular culture as a form of intercultural communication. Not all popular culture emerges from the United States, but the preponderance is from either the United States or western Europe. And it contributes to a power dynamic—cultural imperialism—that affects intercultural communication everywhere.

There are four important characteristics of popular culture: Popular culture is produced by culture industries; it is distinct from folk culture; we find it everywhere; and it serves social functions. Individuals and groups can determine the extent to which they are influenced by popular culture. That is, we may consume or resist the messages of popular culture. Our cultural identities are significant in how we negotiate our interaction with popular culture.

Popular culture is an important force in the way we understand other cultural groups. We tend to rely more heavily on media images when we consider cultural groups with which we have little or no personal experience. However, we need to be aware of stereotypes as we try to understand intercultural interaction.

Despite the importance of popular culture, many people find important aspects of their cultural identities enacted through folk culture. The holidays we celebrate— the foods we prepare and eat, the clothes we wear, the decorations we make—reflect the significance of folk culture. As we noted in this chapter, folk culture is not produced by large corporations for profit; hence, many folk rituals remain local. However, the distinction between popular culture and folk culture is blurred when folk culture serves the needs of popular culture. For example, folk culture is often used in popular culture products to create a sense of uniqueness.

A great deal of popular culture is produced in the United States and circulates globally. The imbalance between the exchange of U.S. popular culture and other popular culture texts has raised concerns about cultural imperialism.

DISCUSSION QUESTIONS

1. Why do people select some popular culture forms over others?

2. How do the choices you make about what forms of popular culture to consume influence the formation of your cultural identity?

3. What factors influence culture industries to portray cultural groups as they do?

4. How does the portrayal of different cultural groups by the media influence intercultural interactions with those groups?

5. What stereotypes are perpetuated by U.S. popular culture and exported to other countries?

6. How do our social roles affect our consumption of popular culture?

7. What strategies can people apply to resist popular culture?

OLC Go to the self-quizzes on the Online Learning Center at www.mhhe.com/martinnakayama to further test your knowledge.

ACTIVITIES

1. *Popular Culture.* Meet with other students in small groups and answer the following questions:

   a. Which popular culture texts (magazines, TV shows, and so on) do you watch or buy? Why?

   b. Which popular culture texts do you choose *not* to buy or watch? Which do you *not* like? Why?

   c. Think about and discuss why people like some products compared to others. (For example, do they support our worldview and assumptions?)

2. *Ethnic Representation in Popular Culture.* For a week, keep a log of the TV shows you watch. Record the following information for each show and discuss in small groups:

   a. How many different ethnic groups were portrayed in this show?
   b. What roles did these ethnic groups have in the show?
   c. What ethnic groups were represented in the major roles?
   d. What ethnic groups were represented in the minor roles?
   e. What ethnic groups were represented in the good-guy roles?
   f. What ethnic groups were represented in the bad-guy roles?
   g. What types of roles did women have in the show?
   h. What intercultural interaction occurred in the show?

i. What was the outcome of the interaction?

j. How do the roles and interactions support or refute common stereotypes of the ethnic groups involved?

KEY WORDS

cultural imperialism
cultural texts
culture industries

decoding
electronic colonialism
encoding

folk culture
media imperialism
reader profiles

 The Online Learning Center at www.mhhe.com/martinnakayama features
flashcards and crossword puzzles based on these terms and concepts.

REFERENCES

Arseneault, M. (2001, December 15). Il chante avec les loups. *L'actualité*, pp. 76–82.

Bennett, T., & Woollacott, J. (1987). *Bond and beyond: The political career of a popular culture hero.* New York: Methuen.

BBC (British Broadcasting Corporation) News. (2002, June 10). Moscow riot prompts World Cup rethink. news.bbc.co.uk/hi/english/world/europe/newsid_2034000/2034878.stm

Boone, J. A. (1995). Rubbing Aladdin's lamp. In M. Dorenkamp & R. Henke (Eds.), *Negotiating lesbian and gay subjects* (pp. 149–177). New York: Routledge.

Bronner, S. J. (1986). *American folklore studies: An intellectual history.* Lawrence: University Press of Kansas.

Brummett, B. (1994). *Rhetoric in popular culture.* New York: St. Martin's Press.

Buescher, D. T., & Ono, K. A. (1996). Civilized colonialism: *Pocahontas* as neocolonial rhetoric. *Women's Studies in Communication, 19,* 127–153.

Dyer, R. (1993). *The matter of images: Essays on representations.* New York: Routledge.

Fiske, J. (1989). *Understanding popular culture.* New York: Routledge.

Flores, L. (2000). Challenging the myth of assimilation: A Chicana feminist perspective. In Mary Jane Collier (Ed.), *Constituting cultural difference through discourse* (pp. 26–46). International and Intercultural Communication Annual 12. Thousand Oaks, CA: Sage.

Guback, T. (1969). *The international film industry: Western Europe and America since 1945.* Bloomington: Indiana University Press.

Guback, T., & Varis, T. (1982). *Transnational communication and cultural industries.* Paris: Unesco.

Hall, S. (1980). Encoding/decoding. In S. Hall, D. Hobson, A. Lowe, & P. Willis (Eds.), *Culture, media, language.* London: Hutchinson.

Kang, C., & Kato, D. (2002, April 18). New line of clothing backfires. *San Jose Mercury News.* www.bayarea.com/mld/bayarea/3088530.htm

Katz, E., & Liebes, T. (1987). Decoding *Dallas:* Notes from a cross-cultural study. In H. Newcomb (Ed.), *Television: The critical view* (4th ed., pp. 419–432). New York: Oxford University Press.

Land, M. (1992). Ivoirien television, willing vector of cultural imperialism. *The Howard Journal of Communications, 4,* 10–27.

Lee, K. (2002, May). Pimped by Abercrombie & Fitch. *Hard Boiled, 5.5.* www.hardboiled.org/5.5/55-08-af.html

Lee, M., & Cho, C. H. (1990, January). Women watching together: An ethnographic study of Korean soap opera fans in the U.S. *Cultural Studies, 4*(1), 30–44.

Lee, R. G. (1999). *Orientals: Asian Americans in popular culture.* Philadelphia: Temple University Press.

Lipsitz, G. (1990). *Time passages: Collective memory and American popular culture.* Minneapolis: University of Minnesota Press.

Manusov, V., & Hegde, R. (1993). Communicative outcomes of stereotype-based expectancies: An observational study of cross-cultural dyads. *Communication Quarterly, 41,* 338–354.

Martínez, R. (1998). Technicolor. In C. C. O'Hearn (Ed.), *Half and half: Writers on growing up biracial and bicultural* (pp. 245–264). New York: Pantheon Books.

Merritt, B. D. (2000). Illusive reflections: African American women on primetime television. In A. González, M. Houston, & V. Chen (Eds.), *Our voices* (3rd ed., pp. 47–53). Los Angeles: Roxbury.

Nakayama, T. K. (1994). Show/down time: "Race," gender, sexuality and popular culture. *Critical Studies in Mass Communication, 11*(2), 162–179.

Nakayama, T. K., & Vachon, L. A. (1991). Imperialist victory in peacetime: State functions and the British cinema industry. *Current Research in Film, 5,* 161–174.

Newcomb, H., & Hirsch, P. M. (1987). Television as a cultural forum. In H. Newcomb (Ed.), *Television: The critical view* (4th ed., pp. 455–470). New York: Oxford University Press.

Noikorn, U. (2002, May 5). Shame is name of game: Thai "Weakest Link" provokes outrage. *The Arizona Republic,* p. A31.

Norris, C. (1992). *Uncritical theory: Postmodernism, intellectuals, and the gulf war.* Amherst: University of Massachusetts Press.

O'Barr, W. (1994). *Culture and the ad: Exploring otherness in the world of advertising.* Boulder, CO: Westview Press.

Salinas, R. A. C. (2002, April 19). How Asian Americans beat retail racism through unity and the Internet. www.politicalcircus.com/archive/article_701.shtml

Snyder, M. (1998). Self-fulfilling stereotypes. In P. Rothenburg (Ed.), *Race, class and gender in the United States* (4th ed., pp. 452–457). New York: St. Martin's Press.

Tan, A., Fujioka, F., & Tan, G. (2000). Television use, stereotypes of African Americans and opinions on affirmative action: An affective model of policy reasoning. *Communication Monographs, 67*(4), 362–371.

Tomlinson, J. (1991). *Cultural imperialism.* Baltimore: Johns Hopkins University Press.

Tovares, R. (2002). Mascot matters: Race, history, and the University of North Dakota's "Fighting Sioux" logo. *Journal of Communication Inquiry, 26*(2), 76–94.

What's American? When is the last time you heard a young black suspect described as "innocent-looking" or "shy"? (1998, July 3). *The Post Standard,* p. A6.

CULTURE, COMMUNICATION, AND INTERCULTURAL RELATIONSHIPS

How do we develop relationships with people who differ from us in terms of age, ethnicity, religion, class, or sexual orientation? Think about friends who differ from you in any of these ways. How did you get to know them? Are these relationships any different from those that are characterized by similarity? Why do we develop relationships with some people and not with others?

There may be almost as many reasons for relationships as there are relationships themselves. Some relationships develop because of circumstances (e.g., working on a course project with another student). Some develop because of proximity or repeated contact (e.g., with neighbors in dorms or apartments). Others develop because of a strong physical attraction or a strong similarity (e.g., same interests, attitudes, or personality traits). Sometimes relationships develop between dissimilar people, simply because they are different. There seems to be some truth to *both* adages: "Birds of a feather flock together" and "Opposites attract."

What is the role of communication in intercultural relationships? And how do contexts (social, historical, political) influence our relationships? In this chapter, we explore the benefits and challenges of intercultural relationships, examine how relationships develop over time, and identify some cultural differences in relational development and maintenance. Throughout the chapter, we emphasize a dialectical perspective on intercultural relationships—both friendship and romantic. Contextual issues exist along with individual relational issues, so for each of these topics we'll examine contextual issues.

BENEFITS AND CHALLENGES OF INTERCULTURAL RELATIONSHIPS

Benefits

Most people have a variety of **intercultural relationships** that may feature differences in age, physical ability, gender, ethnicity, class, religion, race, or nationality. The potential rewards and opportunities in these relationships are tremendous. The key to these relationships often involves maintaining a balance between differences and similarities. One example is the relationship between Judith and a Chicana colleague. When they first met, they thought they had little in common, coming as they did from very different ethnic and cultural backgrounds. But once they found commonality in their academic work, they discovered that they actually had a great deal in common. For instance, both come from large religious families, both have parents who contributed a great deal to their communities, and both are close to their older sisters and their nieces. Through the relationship, they also have learned a lot about each other's different worlds.

The benefits of such relationships include (1) acquiring knowledge about the world, (2) breaking stereotypes, and (3) acquiring new skills. You can probably think of a lot more. In intercultural relationships, we often learn specific information about unfamiliar cultural patterns and languages. Nancy, an undergrad-

Young people often encounter disapproval for interethnic relationships, some-times from both sides. Thomas Matthew Pilgrim and Robert Brown, from Athens, Georgia, are good friends. They describe how they got together and how they each each get some static from their respective friends and family.

Thomas: *Ask anybody in Athens about me and Robert, they'll say that we are always together. I'm 15. He's 17. We think just alike, act just alike and dress just alike. If he wasn't black and if I wasn't white, people could think that we were brothers. A brother in every sense of the word.*

I'm part Mexican. I'm probably the only white person in Athens with their hair braided. I just did it because it's long; it's hard to keep up with. Most of the people I know are black or Mexican. As far as I know they don't have a problem with me. But there's always got to be an odd person that has to say something. One woman said, "Look, white boy, why you got your hair braided?" I just stopped caring what people think about me. [My] family are just really big ——. All they like are people with the same skin as them. But race doesn't matter to me and my sister. And Robert and the other people I hang with don't care that I'm white. They were who I stuck with when I first moved here two and a half years ago. They took to me and really helped me. He's my best friend.

Robert: *I was going to fight him at first. I'm not going to lie. The homeboys I used to hang around with were like, "Hey man, look at that white boy." But my friend Jason knew Matt, so it was cool. I asked him his name. I told him mine. We started chilling from there. All my friends are black except for Matthew. It'd be about 30 of us and Matt. . . . He fits right in with me. He acts like everybody else that I hang around with. I don't care that he's white. If you want to find me, you look for Matt. Every day, all day, we hang out. We play basketball, beat each other up, listen to rap. We have fun. . . .*

Source: From "'Hometown Homeboys,' What They Were Thinking About Race," *New York Times Magazine*, special issue (How Race Is Lived in America), July 16, 2000, p. 26.

uate student, describes how she learned about culture and religion through her relationship with her boyfriend:

My family and I are Buddhists; however, we are not very religious. We still cele-brate the holidays and traditions, but we do not attend the temple often. Anyway, my boyfriend, being Catholic, asked me to go to his church for an Easter celebra-tion one year. I decided to go because I am an open person and not restricted to be-lieving in just one religion. Anyhow, I went to his church, and I must say it was a good learning experience and a fun one, too. I was glad that I went to see what "Catholics" do to celebrate Easter.

A romance or a close intercultural friendship may be the vehicle through which we learn something about history. Jennifer, a student in one of our classes,

FIGURE 10-1   College students often benefit from the experience of forming intercultural relationships. Through these relationships, we can learn about other cultural groups, as well as gain additional insight into our own cultural backgrounds. How often do you come into contact with people who are different from you? How often do you seek out intercultural friendships? (© *Chuck Savage/Corbis*)

told us how she learned more about the Holocaust from her Jewish friends and about the Middle Passage from her African American friends. These are examples of **relational learning**—learning that comes from a particular relationship but generalizes to other contexts. Relational learning is often much more compelling than knowledge gained from books, classes, and so on. And once we develop one close intercultural relationship, it becomes much easier to form others. (See Figure 10-1.)

Intercultural relationships also can help break stereotypes. Andy, a student at Arizona State University, told us about how he used to view Mexicans as lazy. This opinion was formed from media images, discussions with friends, and political speeches about immigration in the Southwest. However, when he met and made friends with emigrants from rural Mexico, his opinion changed. He saw that in everyday life his friends were anything but indolent. They had family responsibilities and sometimes worked two jobs to make ends meet. Later, we'll discuss how breaking stereotypes actually works in relationships.

We often learn how to do new things in intercultural relationships. Through her friendships with students in the United States and abroad, Judith has learned to make paella (a Spanish dish) and *nopalitos con puerca* (a cactus-and-pork stew), to play bridge in French, and to downhill ski. Through intercultural relationships, newcomers to a society can acquire important skills. Andy's immigrant friends often ask him for help with new tasks and activities, such as buying car insurance or shopping for food. When Tom first moved to France, his new French friends helped him navigate the university cafeteria. All of these potential benefits can lead to a sense of interconnectedness with others and can establish a lifelong pattern of communication across differences. We also hope that it helps us become better intercultural communicators.

Challenges

Intercultural relationships are unique in several ways, and as such present particular challenges. By definition, they are characterized by cultural differences in communication style, values, and perceptions. The dissimilarities probably are most prominent in the early stages of relational development, when people tend to exchange less personal information. However, if some commonality is established and the relationship develops beyond the initial stages, these cultural differences may have less of an impact because all relationships become more idiosyncratic as they move to more intimate stages. There seems to be an interplay of both differences and similarities in intercultural relationships. The differences are a given, and the challenge can be to discover and build on the similarities—common interests, activities, beliefs, or goals.

Negative stereotyping often comes into play in intercultural relationships. As we discussed in Chapter 5, stereotypes are a way of categorizing and processing information but are detrimental when they are negative and are held rigidly. Sometimes people must work to get information that can counteract the stereotype. Navita Cummings James (2000), a communication scholar, describes the beliefs and stereotypes about White people passed along to her from her family:

- Whites can be violent and treacherous.
- Whites have an inferiority complex that compels them to "put down" Blacks and other minorities.
- White men are arrogant, and White women are lazy.
- "Good" Whites are the exception.

More importantly, James goes on to describe how she did not let these stereotypes become "an intellectual prison of my self identity or beliefs about Whites" (p. 45). Through intercultural relationships and effort, her beliefs evolved and the stereotypes diminished. She learned that race is not a predictor of intelligence but that income and opportunities are. She learned that all people, regardless of color, deserve to be treated with dignity and respect. And she made definite choices about how to relate to others and to cultivate a variety of friends, and not merely African Americans.

Another challenge in intercultural relationships involves the anxiety that people often experience initially. Some anxiety is present in the early stages of any relationship, but the anxiety is greater in intercultural relationships. Anxiety

I have a group of African American friends that have really allowed me to understand the relationship between the individual and culture. We live in a world that constantly defines and redefines a cultural group through stereotypes. But since I consider this group of people as my friends, and we share a lot of the same interests, I have to look past those cultural stereotypes. . . . They are a part of African American culture, but overlooking their individual identity would be like reading the beginning and ending of a book without reading the rest of it.

While I perceive my friends as African Americans and certainly notice their cultural identities, I am also aware of their individual identities. By using this dialectical approach, I am more apt to see how individuals and their respective cultures interact. This way, I think we are on the same page, and we understand one another better. The idea is not to focus more on one side, but to balance your perspective and see things as a whole, both the individual and cultural identities together.

—Oliver

arises from concern about possible negative consequences. We may be afraid that we'll look stupid or that we'll offend someone because we're unfamiliar with that person's language or culture. Differences in age do not usually evoke such anxiety, but differences in physical ability, class, or race are likely to—at least initially. For example, a student describes his experience of being on a soccer team with players from Kenya, Jamaica, Egypt, and Mexico:

In our first meeting, we were to get acquainted with everyone and introduce ourselves. At the end of the meeting, we all stood around talking—reducing anxiety. Eventually, our conversations were directed toward self-disclosure and relating our experiences. I believe this helped me prepare for more experiences along this line.

The level of anxiety may be higher if one or both parties have negative expectations based on a previous interaction or on stereotypes (Stephan & Stephan, 1992). In contrast, intercultural interactions in which one or both parties have few negative expectations and no negative prior contact probably have less anxiety. For example, one student tells of traveling to New Zealand as an 18-year-old on a sports team:

I remember quite vividly experiencing uncertainty and anxiety and being forced to deal with it. Eighteen years old in a foreign land, and forced to deal with factors I did not know existed. . . . As I look back, I see that I was merely experiencing what I would later come to know as uncertainty and anxiety management.

The student goes on to describe how, with few negative preconceptions and no real language barrier, he quickly found similarity with people he met and had "truly an unforgettable experience."

Writer Letty Cottin Pogrebin (1987) emphasizes that intercultural relationships take more "care and feeding" than do those relationships between people who are very similar. Intercultural relationships are often more work than ingroup relationships. A lot of the work has to do with explaining—explaining to themselves, to each other, and to their respective communities.

First, in some way, conscious or unconscious, we ask ourselves: What is the meaning of being friends with someone who is not like me? Am I making this friend out of necessity, for my job, or because everyone I'm around is different from me in some way? Am I making this friend because I want to gain entry into this group for personal benefit? Because I feel guilty?

Second, we explain to each other. This is the process of ongoing mutual clarification, one of the healthiest characteristics of intercultural relationships. It is the process of learning to see from the other's perspective. For example, Judith discovered that, even when she thought she was being very indirect with her Japanese students, they still thought she was being rather direct! In this way, Judith came to understand that others can interpret events and conversation in very different ways.

Third, people who cross boundaries often have to explain this to their respective communities. Thus, your friends may question your close relationship with someone who is much older or is of a different ethnicity. This may be especially true for those who date someone from a different culture. For example, one of our students recounted how his friend terminated an intercultural relationship because of his parents' attitudes:

> *My Jewish friend was dating a Christian girl he met during his freshman year in college. He proposed marriage when they both graduated last year. But throughout their relationship, the parents of my friend let it be known that they were not happy with the fact that they were dating. My friend and his girlfriend are no longer seeing one another. My friend has told me he believes the parents' disapproval of the relationship was one of the reasons for their eventual split.*

Historically, the biggest obstacles to boundary-crossing friendships have come not from minority communities but from majority communities (McCullough, 1998). Those in the majority (e.g., Whites) have the most to gain by maintaining social inequality and are less likely to initiate boundary-crossing friendships. In contrast, minority groups have more to gain. Developing intercultural relationships can help them survive—economically, professionally, and personally.

Finally, in intercultural relationships, individuals recognize and respect the differences. In these relationships, we often have to remind ourselves that we can never know exactly what it's like to walk in another person's shoes. Furthermore, those in the majority group tend to know less about those in minority groups than vice versa. As Pogrebin (1992) stated, "Mutual respect, acceptance, tolerance for the faux pas and the occasional closed door, open discussion and patient mutual education, all this gives crossing friendships—when they work at all—a special kind of depth" (p. 318). Perhaps this is especially true of interracial relationships in the United States. Pat, an African American woman, describes the importance of honesty and openness in her relationship with her friend Rose, who is White:

> *"Rose is one of the few White women that I have an honest, direct relationship with. . . . She is very aware that I am a Black woman and she is a White woman. . . . I care about her very deeply. . . . And I am committed to our friendship and I respect her a whole lot. . . . I like her values. I like how she thinks about people, about nature, her integrity and her principles. . . . It is her willingness to make race her issue." (quoted in McCullough, 1998, p. 193)*

CULTURAL DIFFERENCES IN NOTIONS OF FRIENDSHIP

What are the characteristics of a friend? How do notions of friendship vary across cultures? To some people, a friend is someone to see or talk with occasionally, someone to do things with—go to a movie, discuss interests, maybe share some problems. This person might be one of many friends. If the friend moves away, the two people might eventually lose contact, and both might make new friends. Other people, however, view friendship much more seriously. For them, a friendship takes a long time to develop, includes many obligations (perhaps lending money or doing favors), and is a lifelong proposition.

Friendships are seen in very different ways around the world. For example, in most Western cultures, these relationships are seen as mostly voluntary and spontaneous, in contrast to family or work relationships. Although our friendships may be more constrained than we think (we do form relationships with people who are often very similar to ourselves), nonetheless, we enter into them voluntarily (Bell & Coleman, 1999).

Cultural differences in notions about friendships are related to ideas discussed earlier—ideas about identity and values. In societies that stress values like individualism and independence, as is the case in most Western cultures, it makes sense to view friendship and romance as voluntary relationships. However, people who view the self always in relation to others—that is, collectivists—hold a notion of friendship that is also less individual-oriented and less spontaneous (Carrier, 1999). For example, in China, where the value of collectivism is very strong, friendships are long-term and involve obligations:

> *The meaning of friendship itself differs from the American version. Chinese make few casual, short-term acquaintanceships as Americans learn to do so readily in school, at work, or while out amusing themselves. Once made, however, Chinese friendships are expected to last and to give each party very strong claims on the other's resources, time and loyalty. (Gates, 1987, p. 6)*

Friendship in China cannot be understood without attention to an important related concept, **quanxi**—"relationships of social connection built on shared identities such as native place, kinship or attending the same school" (Smart,

POINT OF VIEW

In collectivist cultures, like Taiwan, relationships are very important and often involve a positive sense of interdependence and involvement with others.

The Taiwanese view of relationships is grounded in the concept of family. In Taiwanese culture, family is considered the most important environment shaping appropriate communication. Maintaining good relationships provides the foundation of social harmony. Taiwanese are guided by several principles in maintaining relationships with others: gan qing, ren qing, bao, lian, *and* mian.

GAN QING

Tainwanese relationship partners expect to provide mutual aid and care to one another. Gan qing *refers to this sense of interdependency.*

REN QING AND BAO

Ren qing *is somewhat equivalent to Western notions of "favor," but functions more as a mechanism regulating personal relationships. If one asks* ren qing *from someone, he or she has to return it eventually or be considered "heartless." This reciprocating behavior is* bao. Ren qing *and* bao *are often used interchangeably. A person understands* ren qing *if he or she knows how to reciprocate* (bao).

LIAN AND MIAN

. . . one would not risk harming his/her relationship by not paying back the ren qing. *Such behavior may affect their* lian *and* mian. *Taiwanese conceptualize "face" in two ways:* lian *(face) and* mian *(image).* Lian *represents a person's personal integrity and moral character, and* mian *is a person's public image. These concepts reflect Taiwanese collectivist notions of face. One's behavior not only affects one's own* lian *and* mian, *but also their family and friends'* lian *and* mian.

Source: From T. C.-C. Chen, J. A. Drzewiecka, and P. M. Sias, "Dialectical Tensions in Taiwanese International Student Friendship," *Communication Quarterly, 49,* 2001, p. 57.

1999, p. 120). It is through *quanxi* that things get done (e.g., jobs acquired or bureaucratic snafus resolved), often "through the back door." Although "connections" are important in the United States, they are not viewed in so positive a light. Here, one should not have to resort to connections to get something done. In China, in contrast, being able to get something done through connections, or *quanxi*, is seen as very positive, and so these relationships are purposefully cultivated. *Quanxi* is not the same thing as friendship, but friendship provides an acceptable base on which *quanxi* can be built (Smart, 1999).

This emphasis in China on cultivating close relationships, filled with obligations (and always open to *quanxi*), can be a bit overwhelming to people from Western cultures, but it can also be rewarding. A prominent journalist, Fox Butterfield (1982), who spent many years in China, describes these rewards:

> *Friendship in China offered assurances and an intimacy that we have abandoned in America; it gave the Chinese psychic as well as material rewards that we have lost. We ourselves did feel close to the Wangs [their Chinese friends], but as Westerners, the constant gift giving and obligations left us uneasy. (p. 47)*

There are other cultures in which friendships are explicitly cultivated for economic gain. Scholars have pointed out that economics and friendship may be especially closely linked under political regimes (e.g., the former Soviet Union) that offer limited economic choices. In such contexts, it seems logical that friends will help each other out economically and that economics will play a significant role in friendship (Abrahams, 1999).

In some cultures, family and friend relationships are inextricably intertwined. Anthropologist Mario Aguilar (1999) describes life in a small, pastoral community in Kenya where people work on their land and interact primarily with their extended family. In many communities and cultures like these, primary social relationships start with the extended family. Of course, friendships and relationships with those who are not kin develop, but the Western distinction between kinship and friendship is not so clear.

Researcher Elizabeth Gareis (1995) conducted an in-depth study of intercultural relationships among U.S. American and international students and concluded that the term *friend* may have different meanings for different cultural groups. In the United States, the term *friend* "is broad and applies to many different kinds of relationships" (p. 21). Shyam, a student from India, describes U.S. Americans:

> *"They try to have a lot of friends; they don't meet the same people again and again all the time. . . . In India close friends are together most of the time, day after day after day [they] hang out together. My impression is, Americans probably don't do that; they try to meet different people." (quoted in Gareis, p. 96)*

It's probably more accurate to say that what most people in the world consider simply a "friend" is what a U.S. American would consider a "close friend." A German student explains that in Germany people are hardly able to call somebody a friend, even if they have known that person for more than a year. Only if they have a "special emotional relationship" can they call the person a friend (p. 128). For most U.S. Americans, the "special emotional relationship" is reserved for a so-called good or close friend.

Communication scholar Dean Barnlund's (1989) study of Japanese and U.S. students revealed many similarities in how the two groups defined and developed friendships. In general, the principles of similarity and proximity played an important role. Both groups tended to be attracted to individuals similar in age and nationality and to those around them. And both groups used the same words to describe characteristics of a friend: *trust, respect, understanding,* and *sincerity.*

However, the study also revealed differences in certain characteristics of friends. Whereas both U.S. and Japanese students described similar characteristics of "friend," they ordered these characteristics differently. The Japanese students listed togetherness, trust, and warmth as the top characteristics; the U.S. students named understanding, respect, and sincerity. Barnlund links these different priorities to cultural values: The Japanese list emphasizes relational harmony and collectivism, whereas the U.S. list reflects the importance of honesty and individuality. For many U.S. Americans, relationships are based on and strengthened by honesty and understanding, even if it hurts sometimes.

Barnlund's study focused on European American students. Researcher M. J. Collier (1991) conducted a similar study that investigated Latino/a, African American, and European American students' notions of friendships. She found that these three groups had many ideas in common regarding the characteristics of close friendship. Their definitions of *friendship* focused on two characteristics: trust and acceptance.

More recently, Collier conducted a study with these three groups and Asian Americans in which she investigated conversational rules in close friendships (Collier, 1996). Again, she found many similarities in how these groups thought about close friendship. However, she also found some differences. For instance, Latino/a, Asian American, and African American students said that it took, on average, about a year to develop a close friendship; European Americans felt that it took only a few months. She also found differences in what each group thought was important in close friendships: "Latinos emphasized relational support, Asian Americans emphasized a caring, positive exchange of ideas, African Americans emphasized respect and acceptance and Anglo [European] Americans emphasized recognizing the needs of individuals" (p. 315). Clearly, such distinctions affect how people of different cultural groups develop friendships.

CULTURAL DIFFERENCES IN RELATIONAL DEVELOPMENT

Relationships seem to develop in phases. You probably have acquaintances— people you don't know very well, with whom you are in the early stages of a friendship and are just getting to know. And you probably have friends—people you know very well, with whom you have passed through several friendship phases. These phases are continuous, fluid, and overlapping; they include initial attraction, and the exploratory and stability phases. We are especially interested in how communication in these various phases may differ across cultures.

For relationships to develop, individuals first must be attracted to each other. Next, in the **exploratory phase,** people try to discover more about each other by discussing nonintimate topics. They make small talk and try to find common ground, in a sense "auditioning" for future interaction. Most relationships don't go beyond this stage. In the **stability phase,** as individuals get to know each other better, they rely on more idiosyncratic information to guide their actions

POINT OF VIEW

In some societies, the development of relationships is intricately related to issues of status and formality. Communication scholar Wintilo Garcia explains how these issues are expressed in Mexican Spanish.

> *The Mexican use of the Spanish words* tu *and* usted *signals the immediacy and status of the relational partners.* Tu *is the informal application of the pronoun* you. *It is common that individuals refer to their friends, family members, or children by this form of the word. The word* usted *is the formal form of the pronoun* you. *Cultural norms and rules require individuals to use this form when addressing new acquaintances, older people, professional (white-collar) people, and people who possess some sort of power. . . . In Mexico, as relationships become more intimate, the form of address changes. This often occurs over time where people who were once referred to by* usted *will later be referred to by* tu. *. . . Usually this transformation is initiated by the person who holds a perceived higher class. This is reasonable because high class individuals are perceived to possess more power in the relationship. In Mexico, the usual request phrase from the high class player is* tuteame *(interpreted as you "tu" me), which implies a desire for relational equality. In order for this request to be fulfilled, relational players must negotiate the pattern of communication. . . . For example, if a student normally addresses professors by the title* Doctor G *and* Doctor T, *it implies a status and class difference. In general, to change this form of address, the professor must initiate the request.*

Source: From "Respeto: A Mexican Base for Interpersonal Relationships," by Wintilo Garcia, in *Communication in Personal Relationships Across Cultures*, edited by W. B. Gudykunst, S. Ting-Toomey, and T. Nishida, 1996, pp. 137–155.

and expectations. The interaction in this phase of development is more intense; there is more active participation and greater mutual awareness. Conversations have more depth and cover more topics, and the communication becomes more personal. Cultural differences affect relational development at each of these stages.

Initial Attraction

Why do we enter into relationships with some people and not others? There are four primary principles of relational attraction: proximity, physical attraction, similarity, and complementarity. These vary somewhat from culture to culture.

Proximity   One of the most powerful principles of relational attraction in the United States is the **proximity principle:** People form relationships with those who are in close proximity—people with whom they work, play, worship, or share other activities. The Hollywood portrayal of relationships between people who randomly encounter each other is romantic but is not often substantiated in real life. Films like *Titanic* show relationships developing across class and cultural backgrounds. This makes for good fantasy; however, most individuals tend to meet and develop relationships with people whom they encounter in their daily lives. This means that we tend to be attracted to individuals from similar social, economic, and cultural backgrounds.

However, proximity is not as important to relational development in many other cultural contexts. As communication scholars Akbar Javidi and Manoochehr Javidi (1991) point out, in many Eastern countries, a person's background (family, ethnicity, religion, and so on) is more important than who he or she is as an individual. Communication scholar Kristine Fitch (1990/1991) describes similar patterns in Colombia, where personal compatibility is not key to romantic relationships. Rather, the major factor that determines whether the relationship will work is whether friends and families like each other.

To acknowledge the personal–contextual dialectic, let's also explore the context in which relationships happen. Many societies are structured so that individuals do not often come in contact with people who differ from them. When they do, it is usually in highly imbalanced power situations—for example, when someone hires a maid or a gardener. In the United States, people tend to live in neighborhoods and work in places that are segregated by race and class. Writers Allan and Florence Bérubé (1997) describe the segregation of class in growing up in a trailer park:

> *"Did you ever experience other people looking down on us because we lived in a trailer park?" I ask my mom.*
> *"Never," she tells me.*
> *"But who were your friends?"*
> *"They all lived in the trailer park."*
> *"What about the neighbors who lived in houses up the street?"*
> *"Oh, they didn't like us at all," she says. "They thought people who lived in trailers were all low-life and trash. They didn't really associate with us."*
> *(pp. 17–18)*

The principle of proximity has implications for intercultural relationships. How many people do you meet in the course of a day who are different from you in terms of age, gender, ethnicity, socioeconomic status, and sexual orientation? According to this principle, the more diverse your daily contacts, the more opportunities you have to develop intercultural relationships.

Physical Attraction   Another reason we're attracted to certain people is that we like the way they look. In fact, physical attraction may be the most important aspect in the very beginning of relationships, at least in the United States. Like the principle of proximity, the principle of physical attraction has implications for intercultural relationships. The standards for physical attractiveness, though, are culturally based. Notions of attractiveness are defined for us and are reinforced by what we see on TV and film and in other media. When we look at the cultural constructions of sexuality and race, we can see how truly complex the problems of culturally influenced standards of beauty are. Popular culture often depicts ethnic and racial characteristics in untruthful ways. For example, African American men frequently are depicted as highly sexually driven. Writer Kobena Mercer's (1994) critique of Robert Mapplethorpe's photographs of nude Black men exposes this stereotype. Mercer argues that these photographs play into racist stereotypes about Black male sexuality as a fetish.

Similarly, Asian and Asian American women are portrayed in popular culture texts and discourses as erotic, exotic, and submissive, and thus as highly attractive to Caucasian men (Root, 2001). One young man, Shane, describes his attraction to Asian women:

> *"I think they're so exotic. Really, what concerns me about the girl is the eyes, and the Asian women have beautiful eyes, the form and the shape of them. It's a plus for me. I had another Asian girlfriend before. And I like their skin color; tannish, not just white, white, white. A girl with color. It's just different; its more sexual. It's not just like Plain Jane." ("Talking About Race," 2000, p. 59)*

This kind of attraction has spawned an entire business of mail-order Asian brides. Communication scholar Rona Halualani (1995) analyzed how these businesses perpetuate and market stereotypes of Asian women as idealized wives—submissive, sexual, and eager to please men. In contrast, Asian men are often stereotyped in ways that downplay their masculinity (Eng, 2001). In response to these social discourses, some Asian American groups have hosted Asian male beauty pageants and produced calendars featuring attractive Asian men.

Of course, we all want to believe that we choose our relational partners outside of the influences of these social discourses. That is, we all want to believe that we fell in love with this man or this woman because he or she is "special." Yet, if we want to understand the problems and dynamics of intercultural communication, we must be attentive to these larger social discourses about racial and sexual identities. Our relationships are strongly influenced by social and cultural ideas about interracial, intercultural, heterosexual, gay, lesbian, and intergenerational romance. In whatever ways people view their own relationships, other people can be quite influential in the development of those relationships through their support, silence, denial, or hostility.

Similarity   The principles of similarity and complementarity are especially relevant to intercultural communication. These two principles also operate dialectically. According to the **similarity principle,** we tend to be attracted to people whom we perceive to be similar to ourselves. And there is evidence that this principle works for many cultural groups (Osbeck & Moghaddam, 1997; Tan & Singh, 1995). Social psychologist Donn Byrne and his associates conducted a series of studies on this principle of attraction. They discovered that many individuals didn't really know if the people they were attracted to were similar to themselves. Most of the studies concentrated on similarity of attitudes—belief in God, political opinions, and so on (Byrne, 1971; Byrne & Blaylock, 1963).

Finding people who agree with our beliefs confirms our own beliefs and provides us with **cognitive consistency.** (If we like ourselves, we probably will like others who share our views.) In addition, we may explicitly seek partners who hold the same beliefs and values due to deep spiritual, moral, or religious convictions. Also, if we're friends with people who are like us, we can better predict their behavior than if they are different from us. We may be attracted to people whom we perceive to be similar in personality, although the research is less conclusive on this point. Or we may simply perceive greater similarity in people we like. In this sense, similarity is based not on whether people actually are similar but on the perception of a similar trait. This process of discovery is crucial in developing relationships (Duck & Barnes, 1992). In fact, when people think they're similar, they have higher expectations about future interactions (La-Gaipa, 1987).

Complementarity   In intercultural relationships, we may be attracted to persons who are somewhat different from ourselves. The differences that form the basis of attraction may involve personality traits and may contribute to complementarity, or balance, in the relationship. This describes the **complementarity principle.** For example, an introverted individual may seek a more outgoing partner, or a spendthrift may be attracted to an individual who is more careful with money. Some individuals are attracted to people simply because they have a different cultural background. Intercultural relationships present intriguing opportunities to experience new ways of living in and looking at the world.

Most of us seek a balance between novelty and predictability in our relationships. The degree to which we seek more or less novelty depends on both individual differences and social influences. When Judith was in college, she wanted to socialize with international students, whose different backgrounds and experiences seemed intriguing. Growing up, Judith had had little opportunity to interact with people who were different from her. In contrast, Tom sought out other Asian Americans when he was in college. This difference may be due more to the paucity of Asian Americans in the Deep South during the 1970s than to any substantial traits of his.

Most people are attracted to some differences but not others. In fact, society seems to accept some relationships of complementarity better than others. For example, dating across nationalities tends to be more acceptable than dating across class lines. But this similarity–difference dialectic may operate differently in Eastern countries, where people tend to shape their interpersonal relations in accordance with various levels of hierarchy, which is determined by gender, age, and background. Some fairly explicit guidelines govern these vertical relationships. For example, in most Eastern cultures, respect and loyalty toward older people is absolute, and differences in sex, status, and rank are maximized (Dodd, 1983; Javidi & Javidi, 1991). In family and work relationships, then, the complementarity principle applies in that the differences are a given. In other relationships, such as friendships, the similarity principle may be stronger. The complementarity–similarity dialectic is at the heart of understanding intercultural relationships. It seems likely that the similarity and complementarity principles operate in intercultural relationships. Although we may be attracted initially by

Traditionally, when studying other cultures, people focus on the differences, appreciating and respecting them. However, the dialectic that includes differences and similarities takes this process one step further. It not only expresses the importance of respecting differences but also points up the basic human needs and wants that we all possess. In our multicultural society, it is important to recognize the similarities among ourselves.

> *It is apparent that most cultures share some common bonds. Human emotions are the same throughout the world. Knowing that someone laughs, cries, and is scared the same as you creates an empathy that is important to understanding other cultures. This point of view allows us to form bonds and brings us closer to the people of the other culture.*
>
> *Emotions are universal, and being able to see someone as you see yourself can lead to a deep respect and appreciation for the other person. Using this dialectic myself, I have already begun to blur the lines that divide me from people of other cultures. Where I once might have been scared or nervous to approach someone different, I am now curious to see how the person is the same. It is a very rewarding feeling to break down these barriers and become enlightened by someone of a different culture. I've learned that the physical differences that at first seem so apparent begin to fade away as people of different cultures communicate with one another. No matter where we come from, what our language or skin color, we all bleed red, and that makes us the same.*
> —Danielle

differences, some common ground or similarity must be established for the relationship to develop, flourish, and be mutually satisfying over time (Hatfield & Rapson, 1992).

Exploratory Interaction

Cultural differences often come into play in the very beginning stages of relational development, in initial interactions. Different cultural rules govern how to regard strangers. In some cultural communities, all strangers are viewed as sources of potential relationships; in others, relationships can develop only after long and careful scrutiny. For example, in traditional German Mennonite society, strangers, especially those outside the religious group, are regarded with suspicion and not as potential friends. In contrast, many U.S. Americans are known to disclose personal information in very public contexts. One international student observes:

> *One thing that was very different from what I was used to in Iceland was that people, even people that I didn't know at all, were telling me their whole life stories, or so it felt like. Even some women at the checkout line at the supermarket were talking about how many times they had been married or divorced or about*

the money they had, which in my culture, we are not used to just telling anyone about.

The renowned communication scholar Dean Barnlund (1989), along with his colleagues, found many differences in relational development in their students in Japanese and U.S. colleges. Students in both countries were asked about their interactions with strangers and friends and about their views on friendship and more intimate relationships. The U.S. American students were more open and receptive to strangers; they talked to strangers in many different contexts— perhaps at a bus stop, in line at the grocery store, or in classes. In contrast, the Japanese students talked to significantly fewer strangers than did U.S. Americans over the same period.

Barnlund suggests that these differences may be due to different cultural patterns, such as a preference for high- or low-context communication. As discussed in Chapter 6, many cultures in the United States emphasize low-context communication, in which information is contained more in the words than the background of the situation (the context) (Gudykunst & Matsumoto, 1996). Other cultures, such as Japanese, prefer more high-context communication, in which background (contextual) information about someone is important in determining whether (or how) to pursue a relationship with the person:

> *Members of high context cultures, such as most non-Western cultures, are interested in gathering background (demographic) information, such as what high school or university a person attended, his or her hometown, the company for which he or she works, the father's occupation, and religious background. . . . People are able to reduce uncertainty and obtain a high level of accuracy in predicting others' future behaviors by making a rich array of dependable inference from these types of information. (Javidi & Javidi, 1991, p. 135)*

In a high-context culture, relationships will not develop as easily without background or contextual information. For example, Yuichi, a Japanese student, had just begun his graduate work at a university in the midwestern United States. The department held its annual get-acquainted potluck, at which students and faculty chatted informally. Yuichi was panic stricken in this situation because he couldn't tell who was a member of the faculty and who was a student. Because he had no prior information about the individuals present (and couldn't determine their status from the way they dressed), he was uncertain about how to act and communicate. He was worried that he would address someone too informally or formally. The difficulty he experienced was not shared by others at the potluck, to whom status and position were less important in communication. Similar cultural differences affect communication at other stages of relational development.

The Stability Phase

Friendships   As relationships develop in **intimacy** in the stability phase, the friends share more personal and private information. Researchers Tamar Katriel and Gerry Philipsen (1990) describe a U.S. American "communication ritual" between good friends, in which the individuals "sit down and talk" or "talk it out." This kind of communication differs from "mere talk," and we recognize it as such. The ritual involves specific phases: One person presents a problem, the other person affirms the problem, and a discussion ensues. Although there is some attempt at resolution, the primary function of this ritual is to affirm participants' identities and engender intimacy. According to Katriel and Philipsen, this ritual also reinforces the unspoken but understood cultural rules that define many intimate relationships in the United States.

Over a half century ago, Kurt Lewin (1948), a renowned psychologist, conducted a classic cross-cultural study in self-disclosure whose findings still hold true today. Lewin proposed that the personal/private self can be modeled as three concentric circles representing three areas of information we share with others. The first circle is an outer boundary that includes superficial information about ourselves and our lives—our general interests, our daily life, and so on. The middle circle includes more personal information—perhaps our life history, our family background, and so on. Then there is the inner core, which includes very personal and private information, some of which we share with no one. These spheres of information may correspond with the phases in relational development. Thus, in the exploratory stage, people exchange some personal information, and in the stability phase, they may disclose more intimate information.

According to Lewin, there is the most variation in the extent to which the outer area is more or less permeable. For example, for many European Americans, the outer boundary is highly permeable; they may disclose a wide range of relatively superficial information with many people, even those they don't know well, in many contexts. The middle, or second, area is less permeable; this information is shared with fewer people and in fewer contexts. And information in the inner area is shared with very few. In contrast, for many other cultural and ethnic groups, the outer boundary is much more closed. International students in the United States often remark that U.S. students seem superficial. That is, U.S. students welcome interaction with strangers and share information of a superficial nature—for example, before class or at a party. When some international students experience this, they assume that they are moving into the exploratory "friend" phase (the middle circle), only to discover that the U.S. student considers the international student to be merely an acquaintance. A student from Singapore explains:

> I learned in the first couple months that people are warm yet cold. For example, I would find people saying "Hi" to me when I'm walking on campus or asking me how I am doing. It used to make me feel slighted that even as I made my greeting back to them, they were already a mile away. Then when real interaction occurs—for example, in class—somehow I sense that people tend to be very superficial and false. Yet they disclose a lot of information—for example, talking about personal relationships, which I wasn't comfortable with. I used to think that because of such self-disclosure you would share a special relationship with the other person, but it's not so because the same person who was telling you about her personal relationship

yesterday has no idea who you are today. Now I have learned to not be offended or feel slighted by such incidences.

There also are cultural differences in how much nonverbal expression is encouraged. Again, according to Barnlund's and other studies, U.S. Americans expressed much more intimacy nonverbally than did the Japanese respondents (Nishida, 1996).

Romantic Relationships   Some intimate relationships develop into **romantic relationships.** Several studies have compared the development of these types of intimate relationships across cultures. For example, communication researcher Gao Ge (1991) compared romantic heterosexual relationships among Chinese and U.S. American young people. Based on interviews with students about their romantic relationships, she identified common themes of openness, involvement, shared nonverbal meanings, and relationship assessment. However, there were some variations between the two groups. The U.S. American students emphasized the importance of physical attraction, passion, and love, which Gao interprets as a reflection of a more individualistic orientation. In contrast, the Chinese students stressed the importance of their partners' connectedness to their families and other relational connections, reflecting a more collectivistic orientation.

In a more recent study, Gao (2001) compared intimacy, passion, and commitment in Chinese and U.S. American heterosexual romantic relationships. Based on her previous research and on cultural values, she predicted that intimacy and passion would be higher for U.S. couples, given that passion and intimacy are more individually-centered relationship goals. She also predicted that commitment—a more collectivistic relational value—would be higher for Chinese couples. She found that passion *was* significantly higher in U.S. American couples than in Chinese couples but that the amount of intimacy and commitment did not vary cross-culturally. This may mean that intimacy is a universal dimension of romantic relationships, but the finding about commitment is more puzzling. Gao speculates that this finding may be due to the fact that all the couples in her study were in advanced stages of serious relationship, at which time commitment is more universally expected. Her hypothesis about commitment may have applied to couples in earlier stages in their relationships.

This was confirmed in a similar study comparing North American, Japanese, and Russian beliefs about romantic love. In this study, North Americans emphasized romantic love, passionate love, and love based on friendship more than did the Japanese or Russians. Other, more collectivistic cultural groups emphasized the acceptance of the potential mate by family members and commitment over romantic or passionate love (Sprecher et al., 1994).

Research on the development of romantic relationships in the United States has focused on the importance of the individual's autonomy. Togetherness is important as long as it doesn't interfere too much with a person's freedom. Being open, talking things out, and retaining a strong sense of self are seen as specific strategies for maintaining a healthy intimate relationship. This emphasis on autonomy—trying to balance the needs of two "separate" individuals—in relationships can be difficult. Also, extreme individualism makes it challenging for either partner to justify sacrificing or giving more than she or he is receiving. All of this leads to fundamental conflicts in trying to reconcile personal freedom with relational obligations (Dion & Dion, 1988). In fact, one study found that people who held extremely individualistic orientations experienced less sense of love, care, trust, and physical attraction toward their partners in romantic relationships (Dion & Dion, 1991). These problems are less common in collectivistic societies.

Gay and Lesbian Relationships

Most of the discussion so far was derived from research on heterosexual friendships and romantic relationships. Much less information is available about gay and lesbian relationships. What we do know is that these relationships are a fact of society: Homosexuality has existed in every society and in every era (Chesebro, 1981, 1997).

What we know about gay and lesbian relationships is often in contrast to the "model" of heterosexual relationships. Gay and lesbian relationships may be intracultural or intercultural. Although there are many similarities between gay/lesbian and straight relationships, they may differ in several areas, including the roles of same-sex friendships and cross-sex friendships and the relative importance of friendships.

Same-sex friendship relationships may have different roles for gay and straight males in the United States. Typically, U.S. males are socialized toward less self-expression and emotional intimacy. Most heterosexual men turn to women for emotional support; often, a wife or female romantic partner, rather than a same-sex friend, is the major source of emotional support.

This was not always the case in the United States, and it is not the case today in many countries, where male friendship often closely parallels romantic love. In India, for example, "men are as free as women to form intimate friendships with revelations of deep feelings, failures, and worries and to show their affection physically by holding hands" (Gareis, 1995, p. 36). Same-sex friendships and romantic relationships both may involve expectations of undying loyalty, deep devotion, and intense emotional gratification (Hammond & Jablow, 1987). This seems to be true as well for gay men, who tend to seek emotional support from same-sex friendships (Sherrod & Nardi, 1988). However this differentiation doesn't seem to hold for straight women and lesbians, who more often seek intimacy through same-sex friendships. That is, they seek intimate friendships with women more than with men.

The role of sexuality also may be different in heterosexual relationships than in gay and lesbian relationships. In heterosexual relationships, friendship and sexual involvement sometimes seem mutually exclusive. As the character Harry said to Sally in the film *When Harry Met Sally*. . . . "Men can never be friends with women. The sex thing always gets in the way." Cross-sex friendships always seem ambiguous because of the "sex thing."

I had a friend who was lesbian and with whom I used to work at a car dealership. In class, we talked about the theory that we are attracted by dissimilarities, but only after we interact with the dissimilar person. I can relate to this theory. When I first met Yvette, I was nervous and wasn't sure whether I wanted to become friends with her. Before I even met her, I made fun of her behind her back, along with my other coworkers. It was only after I got to know her that I realized a person's sexuality is insignificant in developing a relationship. I was threatened by what I didn't understand or know.

After I got to know Yvette, I came to appreciate our differences. She has become a real friend and confidante. I found her sexuality to be not only interesting but refreshingly different. I met her girlfriend and went out to dinner with them. Because I have allowed myself to let down my barriers with her, it has become easier to let down my barriers with other people whose culture is different from mine. However, sometimes I still make the mistake of patronizing on the basis of dissimilarities without fully getting to know the person. This is something I have a feeling we all need to work on!

—Shannon

This ambiguity does not seem to hold in gay and lesbian relationships. Friendships can start with sexual attraction and involvement but endure after sexual involvement is terminated. There is frequently a clear distinction between "lover" and "friend" for both gays and lesbians similar to the "incest taboo" among a family of friends (Nardi, 1992, p. 114). Close friendships may play a more important role for gays than for straights. Gays and lesbians often suffer discrimination and hostility from the straight world (Nakayama, 1998), and they often have strained relationships with their families. For these reasons, the social support from friends in the gay community can play a crucial role. Sometimes friends act as family, as one young man explains:

"Friends become part of my extended family. A lot of us are estranged from our families because we're gay and our parents don't understand or don't want to understand. That's a separation there. I can't talk to them about my relationships. I don't go to them; I've finally learned my lesson: family is out. Now I've got a close circle of good friends that I can sit and talk to about anything. I learned to do without the family." (quoted in Nardi, 1992, p. 110)

Many of the issues in heterosexual romantic relationships apply to gay/lesbian couples as well. However, some relational issues, especially those pertaining to permanence and relational dissolution, are unique to gay partners.

In the United States, there is little legal recognition of permanent gay and lesbian relationships. At the time of this writing, only Vermont recognizes same-sex civil unions. In fact, many states have passed laws stating that only marriages between a man and a women will be recognized (Wehmeyer, 2002). The federal government also has passed the Defense of Marriage Act, which allows states to not recognize same-sex marriages registered in other states. These political and legal actions have implications for the development and maintenance, as well as the termination, of gay and lesbian relationships in the United States.

Some countries, however, formally recognize same-sex relationships and thereby create different social conditions for gay and lesbian relationships. Same-sex relationships, like heterosexual relationships, are profoundly influenced by the cultural contexts in which they occur. In Denmark, for example, gay and lesbian couples are allowed to marry (Bech, 1992), and Vietnam does not stipulate that marriage must be between members of the opposite sex ("Mariage Vietnamien Lesbien," 1998). In one canton (state) in Switzerland, gay couples have the same rights and obligations as heterosexual couples (Swissinfo, 2002). In other countries, gay relationships might be recognized as partnerships but not have all rights and privileges accorded nongay married couples. For example, in France, the Civil Solidarity Pact allows same-sex couples to register their unions and gain inheritance, housing, and social welfare rights (ABC Online, 1999). Germany and Australia grant similar rights, and in addition, foreign partners there are eligible for a permanent residence permit (Cole, 2001; Hart, 1992). However, in many places in the world, the social contexts are problematic for gay partners in permanent relationships.

Regardless of one's position on the desirability of gay and lesbian marriage, it is important to understand the implications for same-sex relationships, which include issues of dissolution. The dissolution of heterosexual relationships often is delayed due to family and societal pressures, religious beliefs, child custody battles, and so on. However, some gay relationships probably terminate much earlier because they are not subject to these pressures. This also may mean that, even though they are shorter lived, gay and lesbian relationships are happier and more mutually productive (Bell & Weinberg, 1978).

RELATIONSHIPS ACROSS DIFFERENCES

Intercultural Relationship Dialectics

As you may have noticed from the studies discussed so far in this chapter, much of the research on intercultural friendships and romantic relationships has focused on comparing U.S. Americans (particularly White Americans) with other cultural groups. Unfortunately, comparisons of these groups' families, marriages, friendships, and work relationships with our own often leads to stereotyping. A dialectical way of thinking about relationships can help us avoid stereotyping.

Researcher Leslie A. Baxter (1993) suggests that a dialectical model explains the dynamics of relationships. She and her colleagues have identified several basic dialectical tensions in relationships: novelty–predictability, autonomy–connection, and openness–closedness (Baxter & Montgomery, 1996). That is, we can simultaneously feel the need to be both connected and autonomous in relationships with our parents, friends, and romantic partners. We may also feel the need simultaneously for novelty and predictability and the need to be open and yet private in our relationships. According to a recent study, Taiwanese students in close relationships experience these same dialectical tensions (Chen, Drzewiecka, & Sias, 2001).

We can extend the notion of dialectical tensions to encompass the entire relational sphere (Chen, 2002; Martin, Nakayama, & Flores, 2002).

Differences–Similarities Dialectic   As noted earlier, this is perhaps the most relevant dialectic to a discussion of relationships. Real, important differences exist between various cultural groups, and these differences come into play in intercultural relationships. However, there are also many similarities in human experiences and ways of communicating. Although we have pointed out some of these differences pertaining to relational development, we have also tried to highlight some of the similarities regarding the development and maintenance of relationships. To be successful in intercultural relationships, it is important for individuals to consider these two notions *at the same time*. Tamie, a student from Japan, explains how this dialectic works in her relationship with her roommate/friend Hong-Ju, a Korean graduate student:

> *We are both women and about the same age—30. Both of us are pursuing a Ph.D. degree and aspire to become successful professional scholars and educators. When we cook in our apartment, there are several common foods (e.g., rice, dried seaweed) while our eating styles may be different; (e.g., Hong-Ju's cooking tends to include more spicy food than mine). We also share some common cultural values (e.g., importance of respect for elders). Yet, Hong-Ju is married (a long-distance marriage), and I am single. Finally, we both consider ourselves as "not so typical" Korean or Japanese women. Hong-Ju's long-distance marriage and my staying single even in my 30s are usually considered as nontraditional in our respective countries. Eventually, this "nontraditionalness" creates in both of us a shared and proud sense of identity and bond.*

Cultural–Individual Dialectic   Communication in intercultural relationships is both cultural and individual, that is, idiosyncratic. We have described various cultural differences that exist in value orientations, in both nonverbal and verbal communication. Although we have provided some generalizations about how various cultural groups differ, it is important to remember that communication is both cultural and individual. Tamie describes how she deals with this cultural–individual dialectic in her classroom teaching:

> *I have become very aware of cultural differences between U.S. classrooms and Japanese classrooms. In terms of my teaching style, I have noticed myself delivering the course content in a more linear, straightforward, fast-paced manner than I would in Japan. Therefore, there is definitely a certain cultural expectation that I am aware of as I teach in the U.S. However, I am also aware that there are also unique individual styles and preferences among U.S. students—some students are*

outspoken and comfortable in speaking up, others take more time before speaking up, as they reflect and think more holistically. So, this cultural–individual dialectic is always at work in my intercultural teaching experience here in the U.S.

Privilege–Disadvantage Dialectic   We have stressed the importance of (and the difficulty of understanding) power and power differentials in intercultural relationships. People may be simultaneously privileged and disadvantaged, or privileged in some contexts and disadvantaged in others. For example, Laura, a bilingual university student, feels at a greater advantage in settings in which conversations take place in Spanish and English than she does in all-English settings. Her friends who speak only English probably feel the opposite. People in more powerful positions in particular need to be sensitive to power differentials, which may be less obvious to them.

Personal–Contextual Dialectic   This dialectic involves the role of context in intercultural relationships. Communication is both personal and contextual, or social. To illustrate, one of our students, Amy, describes how individuals

feel more comfortable talking more casually with people close to them and act more socially proper when in formal situations. It's kind of the same thing when I'm with my friends. My attitude, word pronunciation, and vocabulary changes when I'm around my friends compared to when I'm with a professor or with my boss.

This example shows how conscious we can be of the different communication styles we use for different contexts.

Static–Dynamic Dialectic   This dialectic suggests that people and relationships are constantly in flux, responding to various personal and contextual dynamics. Intercultural relationships are no different in this regard. When Judith first met her friend Patricia (a third-generation, Mexican American, older student), Patricia was single and had just transferred to Arizona State University from a community college. At that time, both were living alone (Judith was in a commuter marriage), but both were close to their families. Patricia is now married, has a daughter, and has almost completed her graduate education. In this context, Judith and Patricia cannot respond to each other as the people they were five years ago, but must respond to each other as they are now. Changes occur very slowly sometimes, but we need to remind ourselves that relationships are both static and dynamic.

History/Past–Present/Future Dialectic   Rather than trying to understand relationships by examining the relational partners alone, it is helpful to consider the contexts in which relationships occur. Often, this means the historical context. As noted in Chapter 4, cultural groups have different relationships with each other; some of these relationships are more positive, and others more negative. For example, the historical and continuing hostility between the United States and Cuba means that each cultural group has fewer opportunities to meet people from the other nation and thus fewer opportunities to develop relationships. One student, John, gives his views on the past–present dialectic:

> *I don't feel as if people should feel guilty about what their family, ethnic group, or country did in the past, but they should definitely empathize with those their ancestors have hurt, understand what they did, understand the implications of what they did, and understand how the past (whether we have ties to it or not) greatly affects the present.*

Communicating in Intercultural Relationships

Now that we have considered various ways of thinking dialectically about intercultural relationships, let's turn our attention to how we communicate across cultural differences. As we've noted, intercultural relationships may be very similar to intracultural relationships. However, there may be some unique characteristics that can guide our thinking about communicating in these relationships.

Based on interviews with U.S. and Japanese students who were friends, researcher Sandra Sudweeks and colleagues (1990) identified competence, similarity, involvement, and turning points as characterizing important aspects of intercultural relationships. For example, the students talked about the importance of linguistic and cultural competence. At first, language was a common issue. Even when people speak the same language, they sometimes have language difficulties that can prevent relationships from flourishing. The same holds true for cultural information. Dissimilarity may account for the initial attraction, but these students mentioned the importance of finding some *similarity* in their relationships that transcended the cultural differences. For example, they looked for a shared interest in sports or other activities. Or they were attracted by similar physical appearance, lifestyle, or attitude. Sometimes shared religious beliefs can help establish common bonds (Graham, Moeai, & Shizuru, 1985).

Relationships take time to develop; students interviewed by Sudweeks and colleagues mentioned how important it was that the other person make time for the relationship. This is one aspect of involvement. Intimacy of interaction is another element, as are shared friendship networks. According to the study, sharing the same friends is more important for Japanese students than for U.S. American students because the Japanese students had left their friendships behind.

Finally, the students mentioned significant occurrences that were related to perceived changes in the relationship—turning points that moved the relationship forward or backward. For example, asking a friend to do a favor or to share an activity might be a turning point. The students remarked that if the other person refused the relationship often didn't develop beyond that point. However, a turning point of understanding—**self-disclosure**—may move the relationship to a new level.

Another communication scholar, Brenda J. Allen (2000), gives us an example of a turning point. She describes her relationship across sexual orientation lines with a colleague in her department:

We found that we had similar ideas about issues, activities and improvement on our own critical thinking skills in the classroom. . . . [We] were both baby boomers from the Midwest, only months apart in age. We also came from lower-class families, and religion played a strong role in our childhood. (p. 179)

Allen describes the turning point in their relationship when her friend revealed that she was gay: "As a heterosexual I had never before given much thought to sexual orientation or gays 'coming out of the closet.' Thanks to Anna, I have become far more sensitive and enlightened" (p. 180).

The process of dealing with differences, finding similarities, and moving beyond stereotypes and prejudice is summed up by a U.S. American student talking about her relationship with a Singaporean friend:

"We just had different expectations, different attitudes in the beginning, but at the end we were so close that we didn't have to talk about it. . . . After we erased all prejudices, that we thought the other person has to be different, after we erased that by talking, we just understood each other." (quoted in Gareis, 1995, p. 136)

Intercultural Dating and Marriage

Why do people date others from different cultural backgrounds? Probably for the same reasons we form any intercultural relationship. We are attracted to them, the relationship offers benefits—increased knowledge about the world and the breaking of stereotypes. This has been the experience of Peiting, a Tawainese American dating Paul, a Danish exchange student: "Dating Paul offers me this whole new perspective of life as a Caucasian and a Dane." Also, she encounters ideas that differ from those of most of her U.S. American friends: "We'll talk for hours about American films, about Danish government, even about variations in our countries attitudes toward drinking" (quoted in Russo, 2001).

Several decades ago, researcher Phillip E. Lampe (1982) investigated interethnic dating among students attending a college in Texas. He discovered that the reasons students gave for dating within and outside their own ethnic group were very similar: They were attracted to the other person, physically and/or sexually. In contrast, the reasons students gave for not dating someone within or outside their own ethnic group were very different. The main reason for not dating *within* the ethnic group was lack of attraction. However, the reasons for not dating *outside* the ethnic group were not having an opportunity to do so and not having thought about it. Lampe interpreted this distinction in responses as reflecting the social and political structure of U.S. American society. That is, most individuals, by the time they reach adolescence, have been taught that it is better to date within one's ethnic and racial group and probably have had very little opportunity to date interethnically.

Have things changed since Lampe's study? Many people assume that they have, that U.S. Americans today are much more open to intercultural relationships. We decided to conduct a study similar to Lampe's to find out. What we found was somewhat surprising and confirms how individual dating experiences

One day during the first few months of our relationship, my American girl-friend and I went to a beach that was famous for sunsets. We walked up to the top of a sand dune and stood there to enjoy the sunset. I did not find it as romantic as she did because I saw such sunsets every day. "It is not different from the other sunsets I have seen in my life," I thought. Slowly she got closer to me while we were talking about anything we could talk about. Then her hand held my hand. I froze and looked around to see if people were watching us. It seemed people did not really care, or maybe they pretended not to notice our presence. After a while, she started hugging me. I pretended it was OK, though my eyes tried to find out if people were looking at us. When it came to the point that she wanted to kiss me, I held her arms and slowly pushed her away from me.

She was at least discouraged, if not disappointed, hurt, and confused. We did not talk to each other. It seemed as if we did not know each other. When we had dinner at a nearby restaurant, I saw tears in her eyes. "Just tell me the truth if you do not love me," she said. I did not really understand what she meant, because the fact that I did not kiss her at the top of the dunes did not mean I didn't love her. I felt uncomfortable with the people who seemed to watch us. Maybe one of them knew us, our friends, our colleagues, relatives, and so on. It would be embarrassing if those people knew what we were doing at the beach. Public displays of affection are not accepted by my community.

—Api

and societal contexts are still closely related (Martin, Bradford, Chitgopekar, & Drzewiecka, 2003). Like Lampe's respondents, about 60% of our respondents said they had dated interculturally, with Mexican Americans doing so more frequently than African American or Whites. Many of the remaining 40% gave the same reasons as respondents in Lampe's study for not dating interculturally: They had no desire or no opportunity. So, even though Lampe's study was conducted in the early 1980s, the same conditions seem to hold, at least in some parts of the United States, particularly for African Americans and Whites. The reality remains that most Americans live, go to school, and worship in segregated groups (Stephan, 1999). And this was certainly true in our study, as 80% of the White students said they grew up in all-White neighborhoods.

We also found that the social context and past experiences were a strong influence on whether young people dated interculturally. Not surprisingly, those who did date interculturally were more likely to have grown up in ethnically diverse neighborhoods and to have more ethnically diverse acquaintances and friends. In addition, they came from families in which other family members had dated interculturally. This suggests that family attitudes play a big role. Indeed, other studies confirm that families often instill negative attitudes regarding interracial friendships or romantic relationships (Harris & Kalbfleisch, 2000; Kouri & Lasswell, 1993; Mills, Daly, Longmore, & Kilbride, 1994). And these

Diana, a native of Singapore, is ethnically Chinese, and Rogan is a White American; both are students at Georgetown University. The couple met early during the fall semester and have been dating since. This newspaper article describes how people react to them as an intercultural couple.

> *While both Rogan and Diana's parents accept their current relationship, Diana's family is somewhat more apprehensive toward the situation. "They don't mind if I date Rogan now, in college, but they see it as temporary," she said. "Their ideal, for something long term, would be a Chinese boy."*
>
> *The couple feels they haven't experienced negative reactions from the Georgetown community. They have, however, encountered some awkward moments because of other students' stereotypes. During the early months of their relationship, the two often headed out for the night with Rogan's close friend, Larry. Larry is also of Chinese descent. "When I met Rogan's friends, they often thought I was dating Larry," Diana recalled. While the problem faded with time, Diana did feel annoyed at the assumptions others automatically made based on appearances.*
>
> *Despite the problems encountered the couple see many advantages to dating outside their cultural groups. . . . [Rogan] feels especially struck with the new viewpoint Diana's culture brings to the relationship. "We have to think differently, but it keeps it interesting," he stated. It's also really cool to be with someone who doesn't always want to go down to the Tombs for a burger. Instead Diana will cook some great meal I've never even heard of."*
>
> *While intercultural relationships may present difficulties, Rogan and Diana still have the typical ebb and flow of a traditional couple. "We do have our arguments," Diana said. Rogan's still upset that I didn't know who was playing in the Super Bowl. But I guess that would probably happen with any boy."*

Source: From R. Russo, "Intercultural Relationships Flourish Despite Differences," *The Hoya* (Georgetown University student newspaper), February 9, 2001.

attitudes are learned at a very young age. As Derryck, a young Black child said, when asked about his relationship with his white friend, "Black and white kids can be friends with each other, if you're in the same class. But they can't get married, because they don't match. They can't have a kid together" ("Talking About Race", 2000, p. 47). Interracial friendships may be more accepted in elementary school, but they are less accepted in teenage years (Graham & Cohen, 1997).

Finally, whether individuals date interculturally may also depend on the region of the country in which they grow up. A study conducted in California, for example, showed a slightly higher incidence of intercultural dating there than we found in our study (Tucker & Mitchell-Kernan, 1995). As the 2000 census shows, there is more diversity in the West and Southwest. Given what we know

FIGURE 10-2 Weddings are one way that people mark their cultural and relational identities. This is a photo of an Indian wedding in South Africa. Many Indians migrated to South Africa in the 19th century, and today there are more than a million Indian South Africans. How might this relationship face different issues than relationships among majority group members? (© *David Turnley/Corbis*)

about the influence of context on interpersonal relationships, we would expect more diverse schools and neighborhoods, and thus more opportunity for intercultural contact in these areas.

Permanent Relationships

In spite of substantial resistance to intercultural (especially interracial) romantic relationships, increasing numbers of people are marrying across racial and ethnic lines, so much so that scholar Maria P. P. Root (2001) says we are in the midst of a "quiet revolution." Who is most likely to intermarry in the United States? According to Root, women (except for Black women) intermarry more than men. Also, older rather than younger people tend to intermarry, except where similar-size groups live in proximity to one another. For example, in Hawaii, California, and Arizona, younger persons are more likely to intermarry. In addition, later generations of immigrants have higher rates of intermarriage than earlier ones. (See Figure 10-2.)

Why are the rates of intermarriage so low for certain groups? The answer has to do with various contextual issues related to gender and social status. For example, there are fewer objections to Asian American–White than to Black–

White marriages. Gender stereotypes come into play in that Asian women are, even now, viewed as traditionally feminine, subservient, and obedient, as well as petite—making them attractive as partners for White men. This has led to increasing numbers of Asian American women intermarrying. The same is true for Latinas and Native American women, but not Black women. As Root observes, blackness for them still has caste connotations, which means they are partnered in intermarriages less than any other group. White women, in contrast, intermarry more frequently.

The larger social discourses on interracial relationships should not be ignored. Columnist Hoyt Sze (1992) notes:

> *Naturally, people outmarry [marry outside their racial group] for love. But we must ask ourselves how much of this love is racist, unequal love. Unfortunately, interracial love is still inextricably linked to colonialism. How else does one explain the disproportional rates at which Asian American women and African American men marry out? Is it just a coincidence that the mainstream media objectify the same groups as "exotic-erotic" playthings? I know that Asian American men and African American women aren't fundamentally lacking in attractiveness or desirability. (p. 10)*

If we try to understand romantic love only on the interpersonal level, how might we explain the high rates of outmarriage by some groups and not others?

In any case, the current trend to intermarry may change things. As the rates of intermarriage continue to increase, these families will produce more children who challenge the current race and gender stereotypes, and the structural barriers to intermarriage will be eroded. As Root (2001) observes, "Intermarriage has ripple effects that touch many people's lives. It is a symbolic vehicle through which we can talk about race and gender and reexamine our ideas about race" (p. 12). And the fact is that younger people do have more tolerant attitudes about intermarriage. Although intermarriage will not solve all intercultural problems, the increasing numbers of multicultural people will have a positive impact.

What are the major concerns of couples who marry interculturally? One study compared experiences of inter- and intracultural couples. Their concerns, like those of dating couples, often involved dealing with pressures from their families and from society in general. An additional issue involved raising children. Sometimes these concerns are intertwined. Although many couples are concerned with raising children and dealing with family pressures, those in intercultural marriages deal with these issues to a greater extent. They are more likely to disagree about how to raise the children and are more likely to encounter opposition and resistance from their families about the marriage (Graham, Moeai, & Shizuru, 1985).

Writer Dugan Romano (1997) interviewed couples in which one spouse came from another country to identify challenges of these international marriages. Some are common problems faced by most couples, including friends, politics, finances, sex, in-laws, illness and suffering, and children. But some issues are exacerbated in these intercultural marriages; these involve values, eating and

POINT OF VIEW

Most people describe their reasons for intermarriage in terms of romantic love. Mariel, a 24-year-old Chicana raised in a suburb of Los Angeles, reflected on what influenced her decision to marry her Black husband and how fortunate she was that her family approved.

> I was really active in La Raza and feel committed to my people, so I always thought I would marry a Chicano guy. I love my older brothers and even thought I might marry one of their friends. When I went away to college. . . . I was just exposed to so many people. My political ideals didn't change. But I met my husband in my second year. He was very supportive of my commitments. We just started doing things together, studying, talking, going to parties. He fit in well with my friends and I liked his friends. It was like we would go to parties and there were all sorts of people there and I'd find I always had more in common with him than just about anyone in a room. We had really good talks. And music. We both loved music and movies. So one thing led to another. I tried to talk myself out my feelings for him, thinking I should just keep it as good friends, but then I thought, "Shouldn't the man I marry be my best friend?" My family liked him. I mean, like, if my brothers didn't like him, this would have been real hard. They have a lot of influence on me even though I make up my own mind. We talked a lot about what it meant to marry someone different than your own cultural background. But I realized I didn't have to give up my commitment to my people. We believed in the same issues. Now it might have been different if he was white. I'm not sure how that would have gone over.

Source: From M. P. P. Root, *Love's Revolution: Interracial Marriage*, 2001, pp. 7–8.

drinking habits, gender roles, attitudes regarding time, religion, place of residence, stress, and ethnocentrism.

Of course, every husband and wife develop their own idiosyncratic way of relating to each other, but intercultural marriage poses consistent challenges. Romano also points out that most couples have their own systems for working out the power balance in their relationships, for deciding who gives and who takes. She identifies four styles of interaction: submission, compromise, obliteration, and consensus. Couples may adopt different styles depending on the context.

The **submission style** is the most common. In this style, one partner submits to the culture of the other partner, abandoning or denying his or her own. The submission may occur in public, whereas in private life the relationship may be more balanced. Romano points out that this model rarely works in the long run. People cannot erase their core cultural background, no matter how hard they try.

In the **compromise style,** each partner gives up some of his or her culturally bound habits and beliefs to accommodate the other person. Although this may seem fair, it really means that both people sacrifice things that are important to them. For example, the Christian who gives up having a Christmas tree and celebrating Christmas for the sake of a Jewish spouse may eventually come to resent the sacrifice.

In the **obliteration style,** both partners deal with differences by attempting to erase their individual cultures. They may form a new culture, with new beliefs and habits, especially if they live in a country that is home to neither of them. This may seem to be the only way for people whose backgrounds are completely irreconcilable to survive. However, because it's difficult for people to completely cut themselves off from their own cultural backgrounds, obliteration is not a viable long-term solution.

The style that is the most desirable, not surprisingly, is the **consensus style,** which is based on agreement and negotiation. It is related to compromise in that both partners give and take, but it is not a tradeoff; rather, it is a win-win proposition. Consensus may incorporate elements of the other models. On occasion, one spouse might temporarily "submit" to the other's culture or temporarily give up something to accommodate the other. For example, while visiting her husband's Muslim family, a Swiss wife might substantially change her demeanor, dressing more modestly and acting less assertive. Consensus requires flexibility and negotiation. Romano stresses that couples who are considering permanent international relationships should prepare for the commitment by living together, spending extended time with the other's family, learning the partner's language, studying the religion, and learning the cuisine. The couple should also consider legal issues like their own and their children's citizenship, finances and taxation, ownership of property, women's rights, and divorce.

CONTEXTS OF INTERCULTURAL RELATIONSHIPS

It is important to consider intercultural relationships in the contexts in which they emerge. What kinds of persecution might individuals in intercultural relationships encounter? What social institutions might discourage such relationships? Think, for example, how much more difficult it would be to have an interracial relationship if such marriages were illegal, if you attended racially segregated educational institutions, if your church leaders preached against them, or if your own family discouraged them. Some of these contexts no longer apply, of course. For example, public schools no longer can segregate based on race. But what kinds of social restrictions continue to discourage the development of intercultural relationships? And who benefits today, on a social level, from such relationships? These questions are well worth considering.

As noted in Chapter 4, history is an important context for understanding intercultural interactions and relationships. Many U.S. men in military service during various wars have returned to the United States with wives whom they

This poem was written by a student, honoring her grandmother, who died several years ago. The poem shows how the Spanish language was an important part of her relationship with her grandmother.

I can hear your words
Assembled into tales of childhood.

Memories of your mother spoken to me
In a language of love and innocence.

The food that you made
With your hands, I remember
Tasting Sonora.

Fig trees in the summer became
Eagerly fruitless and cinnamon
Was your perfume.

My soul swayed to the
Sounds of your Spanish song.

I remember that you sang
To me. Maybe, the same song
You shared with your children.

I must confess, your pain and
Your tears I do not know.

But I remember you. I
Remember you in Spanish.
—Laura Laguna

met and married while stationed abroad. And many of the servicemen who experienced such intercultural relationships argued successfully against miscegenation laws, or laws that prohibited interracial marriages.

An example of the role that history and politics can play in intercultural communication can be seen in the experiences of William Kelly (2001), a communication scholar who lived in Japan for many years. He recounts his experiences when he first went to Japan to teach English 25 years ago. There were few U.S. Americans in Japan, and they were treated with great deference. In retrospect, he realizes that he was quite arrogant in his view of the Japanese:

> I expected Japanese to assimilate to my culture. I also felt superior to them. Due to their culture, I believed that Japanese would never reach the goals of individual, freedom, rational thought in daily life and speaking English like a U.S. American. Therefore they would always remain aspiring U.S. Americans, not capable of achieving equality. (p. 7)

His relationship with the Japanese can best be understood in the context of the history of U.S.-Japanese relations. As we learned in Chapter 1, Asians in the United States were treated very badly in the late 18th and early 19th centuries. (Remember the Oriental Exclusion Act of 1882 as well as the Johnson-Read Act of 1924, which severely restricted Japanese immigration to United States.) Then came World War II and the internment of Japanese Americans, followed by the U.S. occupation of Japan. As a result, in the 1960s, 1970s, and 1980s, although the Japanese deferred to U.S. economic and political superiority, there was restrained resentment, and sometimes outright racism, toward U.S. Americans living in Japan. For example, in the 1980s, U.S. Americans in Japan could not enter certain establishments, obtain loans, or have the same jobs as Japanese.

This example reveals the importance of the material and the symbolic realm in understanding culture. Kelly explains:

> It was the material conditions of white U.S. power and privilege that led me to assume a stance of superiority in relation to the Japanese people I encountered. The communication grooves that I unthinkingly entered when I began living in Japan were the outcome of a colonial relationship between the United States and Japan. . . . Japanese racial discrimination against whites has often been a defensive measure to keep members of a powerful nation within well-defined spheres. The goal has been to maintain a private area of Japanese people where the overbearing Western presence was absent and where Japanese could be "themselves." (p. 9)

Over the years, Kelly developed a different way of relating to Japanese. This came about primarily as a result of his encounters with U.S. Americans in Japan who were truly respectful of the Japanese. They learned Japanese, had many Japanese friends, and tried to adapt to the Japanese way of life—thereby achieving a more equal power balance. Eventually, he says, he was able to reach a level of understanding that accepted both similarities and differences between Japan and the United States.

Kelly points out that his efforts to communicate with Japanese people in a truly respectful manner were assisted by the diminishing of the unequal power relations between the United States and Japan:

> By the 1990s, there were many Japanese who had experienced the West that were no longer so positive about Westerners, and especially Americans. They expected white people to learn the Japanese language and communicate in a more Japanese way. . . . Many Japanese had gone overseas to work or study and there was less of an inferiority complex among Japanese towards white Americans. European Americans had been very gradually losing their place of privilege. (p. 11)

All this points to the effect of power on hierarchical relations of communication. Though power does not determine communication patterns in any simple causal sense, it does have an impact on the direction communication takes within intercultural relations. Although U.S.-Japanese communication is still affected in numerous ways by the legacy of the U.S. occupation of Japan, increased economic power has given the Japanese people a new sense of pride.

There are other examples of how colonial histories framed relationships. The British, for example, constructed myriad intercultural relationships, recognized or not, within the lands they colonized. Writer Anton Gill (1995), in his book *Ruling Passions*, discusses various ways in which the colonialists tried to engage in or to avoid intercultural relations, as well as the legacy of interracial children left in their wake. He was concerned with British social policies in the colonies, particularly as they related to offspring, who were often unwanted and abandoned.

The dialectical tension rests, on the one hand, in the social, political, and economic contexts that make some kinds of intercultural relationships possible and, on the other hand, in the desires and motives of the partners involved. There are no easy explanations for whom we meet, when we meet them, and under what conditions we might have a relationship. Different cultural groups have different demographics, histories, and social concerns. Scholar Harry Kitano and his colleagues (1984) discuss some of these issues for Asian Americans. Scholars Robert Anderson and Rogelis Saenz (1994) apply the demographics of Mexican American communities to argue for the importance of larger structural factors—such as proximity—in understanding interracial marriage.

SUMMARY

In this chapter, we examined some aspects of forming relationships with people who are both similar to and different from ourselves. Through intercultural relationships, we can acquire specific and general knowledge beyond our local communities, break stereotypes, and acquire new skills. Developing relationships with people who are different from ourselves offers special challenges, such as coping with differences, tending to stereotype, dealing with anxiety, and having to explain ourselves to others.

There are three phases of relational development: initial attraction, exploration, and stabilization. There also are cultural variations in how relationships develop during these different phases. In initial attraction, two principles— proximity and physical attraction—seem to be more important in European American society than in other societies. Two other principles—similarity and complementarity—seem to operate for most people in most cultures. These two principles of relationships are especially important for intercultural relationships, because differences are inherent in such relationships; individuals are simultaneously drawn to the similarities and differences of other people.

Gay relationships are similar in many ways to heterosexual relationships, but they differ in other aspects. In gay relationships, friendship and sexual involvement are not mutually exclusive, as often seems to be the case for heterosexuals. Gay men seem to seek more emotional support from same-sex friends than heterosexual men do. Friendships may play a special role in gay relationships, because gays often experience strained relationships with their families.

We can view relationships through the competing tensions of differences–similarities, cultural–individual, privilege–disadvantage, personal–contextual, history/past–present/future, and static–dynamic dialectics. These dialectics help us avoid stereotyping. They also help us understand the specific ways of communicating in intercultural relationships.

Intercultural dating and marriage, particularly in the United States, are still not very common and are often disapproved of by families and by society. Due to societal structures, there may be little opportunity or desire to date across differences. We must take into account the broader social, political, and historical environments in which relationships develop. The contexts in which we move and live may or may not provide us with opportunities and support for developing intercultural relationships.

DISCUSSION QUESTIONS

1. What are some of the benefits of intercultural relationships?
2. What factors contribute to our forming relationships with some people and not with others?
3. How is the development of intercultural relationships different from that of intracultural relationships?
4. What challenges do intercultural couples face when they decide to make their relationships permanent?
5. What are the advantages of taking a dialectical perspective on intercultural relationships?

 Go to the self-quizzes on the Online Learning Center at www.mhhe.com/martinnakayama to further test your knowledge.

ACTIVITIES

1. *Intercultural Relationships.* List all of your friends to whom you feel close. Identify any friends on the list who are from other cultures. Answer the following questions, and discuss your answers with other class members.
   a. Do people generally have more friends from their own culture or from other cultures? Why?
   b. In what ways are intercultural friendships different from or similar to friendships with people from the same culture?
   c. What are some reasons people might have for not forming intercultural friendships?
2. *Friendship Dialectics.* Choose one friend who is different from you. Describe a situation or situations in which you experienced the dialectics discussed in this chapter. (Hint: Think of the ways in which the two of you are both similar and different (age, gender, background, interests, personality, and so on). Think of the ways your relationship has both changed and stayed the same (attitudes, experiences, interests, and so on).

KEY WORDS

cognitive consistency
complementarity principle
compromise style
consensus style
exploratory phase
intercultural relationships

intimacy
obliteration style
orientation phase
proximity principle
relational learning
romantic relationships

self-disclosure
similarity principle
stability phase
submission style

 The Online Learning Center at www.mhhe.com/martinnakayama features flashcards and crossword puzzles based on these terms and concepts.

REFERENCES

ABC News Online. (1999, October 14). France grants equal legal rights to gay couples. Australian Broadcasting Corporation.

Abrahams, R. (1999). Friends and networks as survival strategies in North-East Europe. In S. Bell & S. Coleman (Eds.), *The anthropology of friendship* (pp. 155–168). New York: Berg.

Aguilar, M. I. (1999). Localized kin and globalized friends: Religious modernity and the 'educated self' in East Africa. In S. Bell & S. Coleman (Eds.), *The anthropology of friendship* (pp. 169–184). New York: Berg.

Allen, B. J. (2000). Sapphire and Sappho: Allies in authenticity. In A. Gonzalez, M. Houston, & V. Chen (Eds.), *Our voices: Essays in culture, ethnicity and communication*, 3rd ed., (pp. 179–183). Los Angeles: Roxbury.

Anderson, R. N., & Saenz, R. (1994). Structural determinants of Mexican American intermarriage, 1975–1980. *Social Science Quarterly*, 75(2), 414–430.

Barnlund, D. S. (1989). *Communication styles of Japanese and Americans: Images and reality.* Belmont, CA: Wadsworth.

Baxter, L. A. (1993). The social side of personal relationships: A dialectical perspective. In S. Duck (Ed.), *Social context and relationships* (pp. 139–165). Newbury Park, CA: Sage.

Baxter, L. A., & Montgomery, B. (1996). *Relating: Dialogues and dialectics.* New York: Guilford Press.

Bech, H. (1992). Report from a rotten state: "Marriage" and "homosexuality" in "Denmark." In K. Plummer (Ed.), *Modern homosexualities: Fragments of lesbian and gay experience* (pp. 134–150). New York: Routledge.

Bell, A. P., & Weinberg, M. S. (1978). *Homosexualities: A study of diversity between men and women.* New York: Simon & Schuster.

Bell, S., & Coleman, S. (1999). The anthropology of friendship: Enduring themes and future possibilities. In S. Bell & S. Coleman (Eds.), *The anthropology of friendship* (pp. 1–20). New York: Berg.

Bérubé, A., & Bérubé, F. (1997). Sunset Trailer Park. In M. Wray & A. Newitz (Eds.), *White trash: Race and class in America* (pp. 15–40). New York: Routledge.

Butterfield, F. (1982). *Alive in the bitter sea.* Toronto: Bantam Books.

Byrne, D. (1971). *The attraction paradigm.* New York: Academic Press.

Byrne, D., & Blaylock, B. (1963). Similarity and assumed similarity of attitudes between husbands and wives. *Journal of Abnormal and Social Psychology*, 67, 636–640.

Carrier, J. G. (1999). People who can be friends: Selves and social relationships. In S. Bell & S. Coleman, *The anthropology of friendship* (pp. 21–28). New York: Berg.

Chen, L. (2002). Communication in intercultural relationships. In W. B. Gudykunst & B. Mody (Eds.), *Handbook of international and intercultural communication* (pp. 241–258). Thousand Oaks, CA: Sage.

Chen, T. C.-C., Drzewiecka, J. A., & Sias, P. M. (2001). Dialectical tensions in Taiwan-ese international student friendships. *Communication Quarterly, 49*, 57–66.

Chesebro, J. W. (Ed.). (1981). *Gayspeak: Gay male and lesbian communication.* New York: Pilgrim Press.

———. (1997). Ethical communication and sexual orientation. In J. M. Makau & R. C. Arnett (Eds.), *Communication ethics in an age of diversity* (pp. 126–154). Bloomington: University of Illinois Press.

Cole, D. (2001, July 31). Germany opens door to gay marriage. *Agence Presse.* www .gfn.com/archives/story.phtml?sid=9975.

Collier, M. J. (1991). Conflict competence within African, Mexican and Anglo American friendships. In S. Ting-Toomey & F. Korzenny (Eds.), *Cross-cultural interpersonal communication* (pp. 132–154). Newbury Park, CA: Sage.

———. (1996). Communication competence problematics in ethnic friendships. *Communication Monographs, 63*, 314–346.

Dion, K. K., & Dion, K. L. (1991). Psychological individualism and romantic love. *Journal of Social Behavior and Personality, 6*, 17–33.

Dion, K. L., & Dion, K. K. (1988). Romantic love: Individual and cultural perspectives. In R. Sternberg & M. Barnes (Eds.), *The psychology of love* (pp. 264–289). New Haven, CT: Yale University Press.

Dodd, H. C. (1983). *Dynamics of intercultural communication.* Dubuque, IA: Brown.

Duck, S., & Barnes, M. K. (1992). Disagreeing about agreement: Reconciling differences about similarity. *Communication Monographs, 59*, 199–208.

Eng, D. L. (2001). *Racial castration: Managing masculinity in Asian America.* Durham, NC: Duke University Press.

Fitch, K. (1990/1991). A ritual for attempting leave-taking in Colombia. *Research on Language and Social Interaction, 24*, 204–224.

Gao, G. (1991). Stability of romantic relationships in China and the United States. In S. Ting-Toomey & F. Korzenny (Eds.), *Cross-cultural interpersonal communication* (pp. 99–115). Newbury Park, CA: Sage.

———. (2001). Intimacy, passion, and commitment in Chinese and U.S. American romantic relationships. *International Journal of Intercultural Relations, 25*, 329–342.

Garcia, W. (1996). Respeto: A Mexican base for interpersonal relationships. In W. B. Gudykunst, S. Ting-Toomey, & T. Nishida (Eds.), *Communication in personal relationships across cultures* (pp. 137–155). Thousand Oaks, CA: Sage.

Gareis, E. (1995). *Intercultural friendship: A qualitative study.* Lanham, MD: University Press of America.

Gates, H. (1987). *Chinese working-class lives.* Ithaca, NY: Cornell University Press.

Gill, A. (1995). *Ruling passions: Sex, race and empire.* London: BBC Books.

Graham, J. A., & Cohen, R. (1997). Race and sex factors in children's sociometric ratings and friendship choices. *Social Development, 6*, 355–372.

Graham, M. A., Moeai, J., & Shizuru, L. S. (1985). Intercultural marriages: An intra-religious perspective. *International Journal of Intercultural Relations, 9*, 427–434.

Gudykunst, W. B., & Matsumoto, Y. (1996). Cross-cultural variability of communication in personal relationships. In W. B. Gudykunst, S. Ting-Toomey, & T. Nishida (Eds.), *Communication in personal relationships across cultures* (pp. 19–56). Thousand Oaks, CA: Sage.

Halualani, R. T. (1995). The intersecting hegemonic discourses of an Asian mail-order bride catalog: Pilipina "oriental butterfly" dolls for sale. *Women's Studies in Communication, 18*(1), 45–64.

Hammond, D., & Jablow, A. (1987). Gilgamesh and the Sundance Kid: The myth of male friendship. In H. Brod (Ed.), *The making of masculinities: The new men's studies* (pp. 241–258). Boston: Allen & Unwin.

Harris, T. M., & Kalbfleisch, P. J. (2000). Interracial dating: The implications of race for initiating a romantic relationship. *The Howard Journal of Communications, 11*, 49–64.

Hart, J. (1992). A cocktail of alarm: Same-sex couples and migration to Australia, 1985–1990. In K. Plummer (Ed.), *Modern homosexualities: Fragments of lesbian and gay experience* (pp. 121–133). New York: Routledge.

Hatfield, E., & Rapson, R. L. (1992). Similarity and attraction in close relationships. *Communication Monographs, 59,* 209–212.

James, N. C. (2000). When Miss America was always white. In A. González, M. Houston, & V. Chen (Eds.), *Our voices: Essays in culture, ethnicity and communication* (3rd ed., pp. 42–46). Los Angeles: Roxbury.

Javidi, A., & Javidi, M. (1991). Cross-cultural analysis of interpersonal bonding: A look at East and West. *Howard Journal of Communications, 3,* 129–138.

Katriel, T., & Philipsen, G. (1990). What we need is communication: Communication as a cultural category in some American speech. In D. Carbaugh (Ed.), *Cultural communication and intercultural contact* (pp. 77–94). Hillsdale, NJ: Lawrence Erlbaum.

Kitano, H. H. L., Yeung, W.-T., Chai, L., & Hatanaka, H. (1984). Asian-American interracial marriage. *Journal of Marriage and the Family, 56,* 179–190.

Kelly, W. (2001 November). *Applying a critical approach to intercultural relations: The case of U.S-Japanese communication.* Paper presented at the annual meeting of the National Communication Association, Atlanta.

Kouri, K. M., & Lasswell, M. (1993). *Black-white marriages.* New York: Haworth Press.

LaGaipa, J. J. (1987). Friendship expectations. In R. Burnett, P. McGee, & D. Clarke (Eds.), *Accounting for relationships* (pp. 134–157). London: Methuen.

Lampe, P. (1982). Interethnic dating: Reasons for and against. *International Journal of Intercultural Relations, 6,* 115–126.

Lewin, K. (1948). Some social psychological differences between the United States and Germany. In G. Lewin (Ed.), *Resolving social conflicts.* New York: Harper.

Mariage vietnamien lesbien. (1998, May). *Illico, 32*–33.

Martin, J. N., Bradford, L., Chitgopekar, A. S., & Drzewiecka, J. A. (2003, June). Interethnic dating relationships among U.S. college students: Have they changed in the past 15 years? *Howard Journal of Communications, 14.*

Martin, J. N., Nakayama, T. K., & Flores, L. A. (2002). A dialectical approach to intercultural communication. In J. N. Martin, T. K. Nakayama, & L. A. Flores (Eds.), *Readings in intercultural communication,* 2nd ed. (pp. 3–13). Boston: McGraw-Hill.

McCullough, M. W. (1998). *Black and White women as friends: Building cross-race friendships.* Cresskill, NJ: Hampton Press.

Mercer, K. (1994). *Welcome to the jungle.* New York: Routledge.

Mills, J. K., Daly, J., Longmore, A., & Kilbride, G. (1995). A note on family acceptance involving interracial friendships and romantic relationships. *The Journal of Psychology, 129*(3), 349–351.

Nakayama, T. K. (1998). Communication of heterosexism. In M. L. Hecht (Ed.), *Communication of prejudice* (pp. 112–121). Thousand Oaks, CA: Sage.

Nardi, P. M. (1992). That's what friends are for: Friends as family in the gay and lesbian community. In K. Plummer (Ed.), *Modern homosexualities: Fragments of lesbian and gay experience* (pp. 108–120). New York: Routledge.

Nishida, T. (1996). Communication in personal relationships in Japan. In W. B. Gudykunst, S. Ting-Toomey, & T. Nishida (Eds.), *Communication in personal relationships across cultures* (pp. 102–121). Thousand Oaks, CA: Sage.

Osbeck, L. M., & Moghaddam, F. M. (1997). Similarity and attraction among majority and minority groups in a multicultural context. *International Journal of Intercultural Relations, 21,* 113–123.

Pogrebin, L. C. (1987). *Among friends.* New York: McGraw-Hill.

———. (1992). The same and different: Crossing boundaries of color, culture, sexual preference, disability, and age. In W. B. Gudykunst, & Y. Y. Kim (Eds.), *Readings on communicating with strangers* (pp. 318–336). New York: McGraw-Hill.

Romano, D. (1997). *Intercultural marriage: Promises and pitfalls* (2nd ed.). Yarmouth, ME: Intercultural Press.

Root, M. P. P. (2001). *Love's revolution: Interracial marriage.* Philadelphia: Temple University Press.

Russo, R. (2001, February 9). Intercultural relationships flourish despite differences. *The (Georgetown) Hoya.*

Sherrod, D., & Nardi, P. M. (1988). *The nature and function of friendship in the lives of gay men and lesbians.* Paper presented at the annual meeting of the American Sociological Association, Atlanta.

Smart, A. (1999). Expression of interest: Friendship and *quanxi* in Chinese societies. In S. Bell & S. Coleman (Eds.), *The anthropology of friendship* (pp. 119–136). New York: Berg.

Sprecher, S., Aron, A., Hatfield, E., Cortese, A., Potapova, E., & Levitskaya, A. (1994). Love: American style, Russian style, and Japanese style. *Personal Relationships, 1,* 349–369.

Stephan, W. G. (1999). *Reducing prejudice and stereotyping in schools.* New York: Teachers College Press.

Stephan, W., & Stephan, C. (1992). Reducing intercultural anxiety through intercultural contact. *International Journal of Intercultural Relations, 16,* 89–106.

Sudweeks, S., Gudykunst, W. B., Ting-Toomey, S., & Nishida, T. (1990). Developmental themes in Japanese–North American relationships. *International Journal of Intercultural Relations, 14,* 207–233.

Swissinfo. (2002, April 18). Gay couples to enjoy equal rights in Zurich. www2.swissinfo .org/sen/swissinfo.html.

Sze, H. (1992, July 24). Racist love. *Asian Week,* pp. 10, 24.

Talking about race. (2000, July 16). *New York Times Magazine,* special issue (How Race Is Lived in America).

Tan, D., & Singh, R. (1995). Attitudes and attraction. *Personality and Social Psychology Bulletin, 21,* 975–986.

Tucker, M. B., & Mitchell-Kernan, C. (1995). Social structure and psychological correlates of interethnic dating. *Journal of Social and Personal Relationships, 12,* 341–361.

Wehmeyer, P. (2002, March 7). California bars gay marriage. ABC News.com. http:// abc.net.au/news/1999/10/item199991014042553_1.htm.

CULTURE, COMMUNICATION, AND CONFLICT

The need to understand intercultural conflict seems more important now than ever. One thing we can be sure of is that conflict is inevitable. Conflicts are happening all around the world, as they always have, and at many different levels: interpersonal, social, national, and international. For example, at the interpersonal level, friends or romantic partners may disagree about their relationship among themselves or with friends and family. At the social level, cultural differences of opinion regarding the importance of preserving the environment compared with the importance of developing industry may fuel conflict between environmentalists and business interests.

An example of cultural conflict at the international level is the ongoing disagreement between the United States and a number of countries concerning capital punishment. France, in particular, has been very critical of the U.S. policy on the death penalty. French officials refused to extradite the man accused of murdering a New York doctor who performed abortions—doing so only when the U.S. prosecutor agreed to not seek the death penalty. Similarly, France criticized the decision by the Justice Department to seek the death penalty in the trial of Zacarias Moussaoui, a French citizen of Moroccan origin suspected of being the 20th hijacker in the 9/11 terrorist attacks. This disagreement has severely strained Franco-U.S. relations (Blocker, 2002).

Conflict also may arise from mediated communication. U.S. television, film, and other media have dominated the world market for many years. People in many other countries feel that this cultural dominance stunts their economic growth and imposes U.S. cultural values. This domination has led to resentment and conflict (Delgado, 2002).

There are three significant approaches to understanding conflict. One is the interpersonal approach, which focuses on how cultural differences cause conflict and influence the management of the conflict. The other two approaches—the interpretive and the critical—focus more on intergroup relationships and on cultural, historical, and structural elements as the primary sources of conflict. These three approaches emphasize different aspects of the individual–contextual dialectic.

Understanding intercultural conflict is especially important because of the relationship between culture and conflict. That is, cultural differences can cause conflict, and once conflict occurs, cultural backgrounds and experiences influence how individuals deal with it. Culture shapes what people consider valuable and worth fighting over; it influences official positions taken and interpretations of others' actions (Ross, 1993a). We should say up front that little is known about how to deal effectively with intercultural conflict. Most research to date in the United States applies almost exclusively to majority culture members. Our challenge is to review this body of research, take what can be applied in intercultural contexts, and perhaps suggest some new ways to think about conflict.

In this chapter, then, we identify characteristics of intercultural conflict, extending our dialectical perspective, and outline two broad orientations to conflict. We examine intercultural conflict in interpersonal contexts, incorporating more interpretive and critical theories into our understanding of conflict. We also examine how cultural background can influence conflict management. Finally, we discuss guidelines for viewing and engaging in conflict across cultural borders.

CHARACTERISTICS OF INTERCULTURAL CONFLICT

One way to think about **intercultural conflict** is from a dialectical perspective, applying many of the same dialectics discussed in Chapter 10. Let's see how this works in an actual dispute that arose in a junior high school in France. The principal of the school refused to let three Muslim girls wear their *chadors*—the scarves traditionally worn by Muslim women to cover their hair in public. In response, the family called in representatives of two Islamic fundamentalist organizations to talk to the principal (Ross, 1993b). The principal defended his action on the grounds of separation of church and state. A high-ranking government official said that, if the school could not persuade the family to change its mind, the girls' education came first, and they should not be expelled. This recommendation did not satisfy anyone, and the dispute quickly became part of a broader national discourse on immigration, integration, and religious and human rights. The issue was never satisfactorily resolved on the national level; it only faded from view after media coverage decreased and the nation turned its attention elsewhere.

The key point is that disputes often are more complicated than they first appear. We can invoke the various dialectics to illuminate the complexity of this conflict. For example, the dispute can be seen as rooted in personal actions taken by the principal and three students. But at the same time, the context in which the dispute occurred is important—a school setting in a town characterized by tension between emigrants from North Africa and native-born French. Similarly, the individual–cultural dialectic can be invoked. That is, the conflict occurred among several individuals—the principal and the three students, as well as family members, clerics, and government officials. But the conflict was also cultural, with the backgrounds of the disputants (French and North African) reflecting different values and religious beliefs and practices. Also, the history–present dialectic helps us understand the conflict. The details of the dispute itself were important, but the history of negative feelings toward immigrants fed the dispute and helped push it onto the national stage. For many years, tensions have been high between North African immigrants (France's largest minority) and native-born French. The French often see the North Africans as showing little interest in integrating, while the North Africans bemoan consistent discrimination in jobs, housing, social services, and social interaction. In this historical context, right-wing politicians used the dispute to point out the supposed evils of immigration and the problems created by foreigners.

Another important historical point was the belief of educators in France that the important role of secular education in promoting democratic values had been increasingly eroded. These teachers, already feeling their authority threatened, linked the scarf incident to other examples of Muslim students refusing to attend

Australia had a program (continued into the 1970s) to remove Aboriginal children from their homes and place them with White foster parents or in institutions. As with the Indian Boarding Schools in the United States, the practice assumed that, by denying these individuals access to Aboriginal culture, Australia would become a wholly Western country. This essay describes the recent "Journey of Healing" undertaken by many Australians to acknowledge this atrocity and move toward forgiveness and reconciliation.

In 1992 the Australian High Court made a momentous decision recognizing traditional indigenous land title in common law. This overthrew the 2000-year-old constitutional myth that Australia was an empty land when the whites arrived. Progress was being made toward creating attitudes of respect between the races. But one issue kept raising its head—the continuing effect of the policies of removing Aboriginal children from their parents. . . .

The commission of inquiry visited every state and territory capital and most regions of Australia. . . . A total of 777 people and organizations provided evidence or submission; 535 were indigenous people most of whom had been abducted as children. [One commission member describes the testimony]: "This inquiry was like no other I have undertaken. For these people to reveal what had happened to them took immense courage and every emotional stimulus they could muster. They weren't speaking with their mind; they were speaking from the heart. And my heart had to open if I was understand it. At each session, the tape would be turned on and we would wait. I would look into the face of the person who was to speak to us. I would see the muscles straining to hold back the tears. And then hesitantly, words would come. We heard the story, told with the person's whole being, reliving experiences which had been buried deep, sometimes for decades."

The 680-page report was finished in April 1997 and contained 54 recommendations that ranged over compensation and apologies, education, standards for indigenous children in state care, the juvenile justice system,

gym classes or objecting to biology, music, and even art classes on religious grounds.

Intercultural conflict may be characterized by ambiguity, which causes us to resort quickly to our default style—the style that we learned growing up—in handling it. If your preferred way of handling conflict is to deal with it immediately and you are in a conflict situation with someone who prefers to avoid it, the conflict may become exacerbated as you both retreat to your preferred style. As the confronting person becomes increasingly confrontational, the avoider simply retreats further.

Issues surrounding language may be important to intercultural conflict. One student, Stephanie, described a situation that occurred when she was studying in Spain. She went to an indoor swimming pool with her host family sisters. Be-

counseling services and research. It called for a national apology. . . . The report shook the conscience of Australia. . . . On their own initiative, many community groups, Aboriginal and non-Aborignial, came together and launched a plan to hold a Sorry Day on 26 May 1998. . . . The idea spread rapidly . . . eventually more than 1200 . . . books were distributed in which some 40,000 people wrote personal messages. . . . A look through these books conveys a sense of a grieving nation reaching out to its Aboriginal people. . . . On National Sorry Day, the books were handed to elders of the "stolen generations" in hundreds of ceremonies in cities, towns and rural centers. . . .

In Adelaide, South Australia, a national monument to the stolen generations was unveiled. . . . In Melbourne, Victoria, the lord mayor handed the keys of the city to representatives of the stolen generations, and the city churches rang their bells. . . . In Sydney, New South Wales, thousands rallied at the Opera House. State legislatures passed resolutions.

Lois "Lowitja" O'donoghue, the first and only Aboriginal to address the United Nations General Assembly, said the day was "a milestone on the road to reconciliation." . . . At the age of two she was taken from her family and did not meet her mother for thirty years. In response to one apology, she said, "We forgive you for the part you played in the removal of children from our mothers, families, culture, our land and our language. But never ask us to forget the pain and anguish we have endured over years. . . ."

On May 26, 1999, the Journey [of Healing] was launched all over the country. . . . Australia faces difficult issues, as it grapples with a fair distribution of land between its Aboriginal and non-Aboriginal inhabitants. In my country, these issues have provoked bitter conflict. The Journey of Healing gives hope that Australians will move beyond the conflict and develop creative solutions that might be of use elsewhere.

Source: From Michael Henderson, *Forgiveness: Breaking the Chain of Hate*, 1999, pp. 26–39.

ing from Arizona, she was unaccustomed to swimming in such cold water, so she went outside to sun bathe. Her "sisters" asked her why she didn't swim with them. Stephanie explains:

At that point I realized they thought I should really be with them. . . . I didn't know how to express myself well enough to explain to them. . . . I tried, but I don't think it worked very well. So I just apologized. . . . I did basically ignore the conflict. I would have dealt with it, but I felt I did not have the language skills to explain myself effectively, so I did not even try. . . . That is why I had such a problem, because I could not even express what I would have liked to.

When individuals don't know the language well, it is very difficult to handle conflict effectively. At the same time, silence is not always a bad thing. Sometimes it provides a "cooling off" period, allowing things to settle down. Depending on the cultural context, silence can be very appropriate.

Intercultural conflict also may be characterized by a combination of orientations to conflict and conflict management styles. Communication scholar Sheryl Lindsley (1999) interviewed managers in *maquiladoras*—sorting or assembly plants along the Mexican-U.S. border—and found many examples of conflict. For example, Mexican managers thought that U.S. managers were often rude and impolite in their dealings with each other and the workers. The biggest difference between U.S. Americans and Mexicans was in the way that U.S. Americans expressed disagreement at management meetings. One Mexican manager explained:

> *"When we are in a meeting together, the U.S. American will tell another manager, 'I don't like what you did.' . . . Mexicans interpret this as a personal insult. They have a difficult time understanding that U.S. Americans can insult each other in this way and then go off and play golf together. . . . Mexicans would be polite, perhaps tell the person in private, or make a suggestion, rather than confronting." (quoted in Lindsley, 1999, p. 158)*

As Lindsley points out, the conflict between the Mexican and U.S. American managers in their business meetings needs to be understood as a dialectical and "layered" process in which individual, dyadic, societal, and historical forces are recognized.

TWO ORIENTATIONS TO CONFLICT

Is conflict good or bad? Should conflict be welcomed because it provides opportunities to strengthen relationships? Or should it be avoided because it can only lead to problems for individuals and groups? What is the best way to handle conflict when it arises? Should people talk about it directly, deal with it indirectly, or avoid it?

It's not always easy to figure out the best way to deal with conflict. And what does culture have to do with it? To answer some of these questions, we first describe two very different ways of thinking about conflict. Then we outline some of the ways in which culture and conflict are related. (See Figure 11-1.)

Conflict as Opportunity

The "opportunity" orientation to conflict is the one most commonly represented in U.S. interpersonal communication texts. **Conflict** is usually defined as involving a perceived or real *incompatibility* of goals, values, expectations, processes, or outcomes between two or more *interdependent* individuals or groups (Cupach & Canary, 1997; Wilmot & Hocker, 2001). According to theologian and mediator David Augsburger (1992), this approach to conflict is based on four assumptions:

FIGURE 11-1   There are many different kinds of conflicts; this particular conflict reflects elements of both interpersonal and social conflict. Usually, conflicts arise because of incompatibilities of values, interests, or goals. How would the two orientations (conflict as opportunity versus conflict as destructive) view this type of conflict? (© Robert Brenner/PhotoEdit, Inc.)

1. Conflict is a normal, useful process.
2. All issues are subject to change through negotiation.
3. Direct **confrontation** and conciliation are valued.
4. Conflict is a necessary renegotiation of an implied contract—a redistribution of opportunity, release of tensions, and renewal of relationships.

Let's examine these assumptions more fully.

Conflict may be a difficult process, but it ultimately offers an opportunity for strengthening relationships. Although this orientation to conflict recognizes that many people don't enjoy conflict, it emphasizes the potentially positive aspects. The main idea is that working through conflict constructively results in stronger, healthier, and more satisfying relationships (Canary, Cupach, & Messman, 1995). From this perspective, there are additional benefits for groups working through conflict: They can gain new information about other people or groups, diffuse more serious conflict, and increase cohesiveness (Filley, 1975).

Consider the second and third assumptions. Individuals should be encouraged to think of creative, and even far-reaching, solutions to conflict. Furthermore, the most desirable response to conflict is to recognize it and work through it in an open, productive way. In fact, many people consider conflict-free relationships to be unhealthy. In relationships without conflict, they suggest, partners are ignoring issues that need to be dealt with (Canary, Cupach, & Messman, 1995). Finally, because conflict represents a renegotiation of a contract, it is worthy of celebration.

This Western-based approach to conflict suggests a neutral-to-positive orientation, but it is not shared by all cultural groups. Let's look at another orientation.

Conflict as Destructive

Many cultural groups view conflict as ultimately unproductive for relationships, a perspective that may be rooted in spiritual or cultural values. Although we must be cautious about generalizing, this viewpoint is generally shared by many Asian cultures (reflecting the influence of Confucianism and Taoism) and in the United States by some religious groups, such as Quakers and the Amish. According to Augsburger (1992), four assumptions underly this perspective:

1. Conflict is a destructive disturbance of the peace.
2. The social system should not be adjusted to meet the needs of members; rather, members should adapt to established values.
3. Confrontations are destructive and ineffective.
4. Disputants should be disciplined.

Again, let's examine these assumptions. Consider the first one: Most Amish, for example, think of conflict not as an opportunity to promote personal growth but as almost certain to destroy the fabric of interpersonal and community harmony. When conflict does arise, the strong spiritual value of **pacifism** dictates a nonresistant response, such as avoidance or silence. Consider the second assumption, that members of society should adapt to existing values. Among the Amish, the nonresistant stance of *Gelassenheit*, or "yieldedness," forbids the use of force in human relations. Thus, the Amish avoid legal and personal confrontation whenever possible (Kraybill, 1989). This avoidance of conflict extends to a refusal to participate in military activities. For instance, during World War II, the federal government granted alternatives to military service for young Amish men. As a result, most Amish conscientious objectors received agricultural deferments, allowing them to work on their farms or on other agricultural projects. Amish children are instructed to turn the other cheek in any conflict situation, even if it means getting beaten up by the neighborhood bully. This emphasis extends to personal and business relationships; that is, the Amish would prefer to lose face or money than to escalate conflict. Similarly, cultural groups influenced by Buddhist, Taoist, Confucian, and Shinto traditions share a common tendency toward avoidance of confrontation and verbal aggression and absence of direct expression of feelings (Toupin, 1980).

Cultural groups that see conflict as destructive often avoid low-level conflict. However, another appropriate response is to seek intervention from a third party, or **intermediary.** On an informal level, a friend or colleague may be asked to intervene. For example, a Taiwanese student at a U.S. university was offended by the People's Republic of China flag that her U.S. American roommate unwittingly displayed in their dorm room. The Taiwanese student went to the international student advisor and asked him to talk to her roommate about the flag. Intermediaries are also used by those who think that interpersonal conflict provides opportunities, mainly in formal settings. For example, people hire lawyers to mediate disputes or negotiate commercial transactions, or they engage counselors or therapists to resolve or manage relational conflicts. Whereas confronting conflict is ultimately desirable, intervention is a less desirable option.

Finally, consider the fourth assumption, that disputants should be disciplined. Discipline is a means of censuring conflict. After all, communities celebrate their success in regaining harmony; they do not celebrate members' contribution to community change and growth through conflict. An example of how a community censures rather than facilitates conflict involves a Maori who was addressing other Maori from New Zealand. His speech turned nasty; he was using swear words and making scathing comments:

> *A woman went up to him, laying her hand on his arm and speaking softly. He shook her off and continued. The crowd now moved back from him as far as possible, and as if by general agreement, the listeners dropped their gaze to their toes until all he could see was the tops of their heads. The speaker slowed, faltered, was reduced to silence, and then sat down. (Augsburger, 1992, p. 80)*

This emphasis on nonviolence and pacifism may contrast with mainstream U.S. values, but as noted previously, many cultural groups practice a nonviolent approach to human and group relations. What are the basic principles of nonviolence applied to interpersonal relations? As Hocker and Wilmot (1991) point out, our language makes it difficult even to talk about this approach. Words and phrases like *passive resistance* and *pacifism* sound lofty and self-righteous. Actually, nonviolence is not the absence of conflict, and it is not a simple refusal to fight. Rather, it is a difficult (and sometimes risky) orientation to interpersonal relationships. The "peacemaking" approach (1) strongly values other people and encourages their growth, (2) attempts to de-escalate conflicts or keep them from escalating once they start, and (3) favors creative negotiations to resolve conflicts when they arise. We'll discuss this approach in detail later.

Researcher Stella Ting-Toomey (1997) describes how these two orientations—conflict as opportunity and conflict as destructive—are based on different underlying cultural values involving identity and face-saving. In the more individualistic approach, espoused by most interpersonal communication textbooks, the concern is how individuals can save their own dignity. The more communal approach espoused by both Amish and Japanese cultures and by other collectivistic groups is more concerned with maintaining interpersonal harmony and saving the dignity of others. For example, in classic Chinese thought, social harmony is the goal of human society—in personal virtue, marriage, family, village, and nation. Writer John C. Wu (1967) explains:

> *If one is entangled in conflict, the only salvation lies in being so clear-headed and inwardly strong that he is always ready to come to terms by meeting the opponent*

halfway. To carry the conflict to the bitter end has evil effects even when one is in the right, because the enmity is then perpetuated. (p. 227)

Cultural Differences in Conflict Views

Anthropologists have long been interested in how various cultures differ in the amount of conflict tolerated and the strategies for dealing with conflict. Why are some cultures more prone to conflicts whereas others have a low incidence of conflict? Anthropologist Marc Howard Ross (1993a, b) spent many years investigating this question, studying views and norms regarding conflicts in small preindustrial cultures and in modern industrialized nations. According to Ross, in some cultures, conflict tends to be minimized and dealt with constructively; in other cultures, conflicts abound.

The reasons for this variation seem to lie in both structural and individual and interpersonal characteristics. Take two examples, Northern Ireland and Norway. Northern Ireland has been the scene of conflict for many years between two divided religious groups, Catholic and Protestant, with incompatible interests. These groups live in segregated communities, and members hold powerful stereotypes. In addition to a powerful class and socioeconomic hierarchy, there is a history of discrimination against Catholics in housing and jobs. Reasons for this conflict may also originate from a more personal level, such as male gender identity conflict, the absence of affection and warmth, a lack of social trust, and emotional distance between fathers and children—none of the predispositions useful in dealing with political differences in a democratic society.

In contrast, Norway traditionally has a low incidence of internal conflict, though Norwegians have fought with outsiders in the past. Certainly, social homogeneity is a structural plus (although there are some strong regional differences). There are also extensive "moralnets"—people who provide support to individuals in times of need, such as extended family, friends, and neighbors. Involvement in voluntary associations (characterized by attachments that are more instrumental than emotional) and overlapping social networks make it difficult for communities to divide into permanent factions. A strong collective sense of responsibility is expressed in a variety of ways, including an emphasis on equality and status leveling, attentiveness to community norms, and conformity and participation, with or without personal commitment.

On a more personal level, Norwegians are socialized to avoid conflict. There are high levels of maternal nurturance and supervision, as well as high levels of paternal involvement, and little is demanded of young children. Norwegians learn early in life that overt aggression or even indirect confrontation of others is unacceptable. Emotional self-control over negative feelings is important. And there are few aggressive models in the popular culture—newspapers do not sensationalize crime, television features little violence and no boxing, and films are controlled. For example, *E.T.* was considered too violent for children under age 12 (Ross, 1993b).

Low-conflict societies share several characteristics (Ross, 1993b). These include interpersonal practices that build security and trust; a strong linkage between individual and community interests, and high identification with the community so that individuals and groups in conflict trust that its interests are their own; a preference for joint problem solving, which leaves ultimate control over decisions in the hands of the disputants; available third parties, sometimes in the form of the entire community, to facilitate conflict management; an emphasis on the restoration of social harmony that is often at least as strong as the concern with the substantive issues in a dispute; the possibility of exit as a viable option; and strategies of conflict avoidance.

THE INTERPERSONAL APPROACH TO CONFLICT

Perhaps if everyone agreed on the best way to view conflict, there would be less of it. But the reality is that different orientations to conflict may result in more conflict. In this section, which takes an interpersonal approach, we identify five different types of conflict and some strategies for responding to conflict.

Types of Conflict

There are many different types of conflict, and we may manage these types in different ways. Communication scholar Mark Cole (1996) conducted interviews with Japanese students about their views on conflict and found most of the same general categories as those identified in the United States. These categories include the following:

- Affective conflict
- Conflict of interest
- Value conflict
- Cognitive conflict
- Goal conflict

Affective conflict occurs when individuals become aware that their feelings and emotions are incompatible. For example, suppose someone finds that his or her romantic love for a close friend is not reciprocated. The disagreement over their different levels of affection causes conflict.

A conflict of interest describes a situation in which people have incompatible preferences for a course of action or plan to pursue. For example, one student described an ongoing conflict with an ex-girlfriend: "The conflicts always seem to be a jealousy issue or a controlling issue, where even though we are not going out anymore, both of us still try to control the other's life to some degree. You could probably see that this is a conflict of interest." Another example of a conflict of interest is when parents disagree on the appropriate curfew time for their children.

Value conflict, a more serious type, occurs when people differ in ideologies on specific issues. For example, suppose Mario and Melinda have been dating for several months and are starting to argue frequently about their religious views,

Conflicts arise for many reasons. Religion is a common cause of conflict in inter-cultural relationships. Note how this student dealt with religious differences in her marriage.

> *I just recently got married. I am Caucasian and my husband is Hispanic. He comes from a large, traditional family. My family background does not include many specific traditions. His family is very religious, and I grew up virtually without religion. When I became pregnant, his family told me that the baby would be baptized Catholic and raised Catholic. They also told me that they did not view our marriage as being legitimate (because we were not "married in God's eyes," that is, the Catholic Church). This was hard for me to deal with at first. I felt that I was being pressured to become someone I wasn't. But I agreed to go to church and learn Catholicism.*
> —Stacy

particularly as related to abortion. Melinda is pro-choice and has volunteered to do counseling in an abortion clinic. Mario, a devout Catholic, is opposed to abortion under any circumstances and is very unhappy about Melinda's volunteer work. This situation illustrates value conflict.

Cognitive conflict describes a situation in which two or more people become aware that their thought processes or perceptions are incongruent. For example, suppose Marissa and Derek argue frequently about whether Marissa's friend Jamal is paying too much attention to her; Derek suspects that Jamal wants to have a sexual encounter with Marissa. Their different perceptions of the situation constitute cognitive conflict.

Goal conflict occurs when people disagree about a preferred outcome or end state. For example, suppose Bob and Ray, who have been in a relationship for 10 years, have just bought a house. Bob wants to furnish the house slowly, making sure that money goes into the savings account for retirement, whereas Ray wants to furnish the house immediately, using money from their savings. Bob and Ray's individual goals are in conflict with each other.

Strategies and Tactics for Dealing With Conflict

The ways in which people respond to conflict may be influenced by their cultural backgrounds. Most people deal with conflict the way they learned to while growing up and watching those around them deal with contentious situations. Conflict strategies usually reflect how people manage themselves in relational settings. For example, they may prefer to preserve their own self-esteem rather than help the other person save face (Ting-Toomey, 1994; Ting-Toomey & Oetzel, 2002).

Although individuals have a general predisposition to deal with conflict in particular ways, they may choose different tactics in different situations. People

When I was back home in Singapore, my parents never really taught me about how to deal with conflict. I was never encouraged to voice my opinions, and, I guess because I'm a girl, sometimes my opinions are not highly valued. I think society also taught me to maintain harmony and peace, and that meant avoiding conflict. I practiced silence and had to learn quietly to accept the way things are at school and especially at work.

When I first came to the United States, I tried to be more vocal and to say what was on my mind. But even then I would restrain myself to a point where I couldn't help it any longer and then I would try to come across as tactfully as possible. I used to think about when I was back in Singapore, when I dealt with conflict in such a way: If I could not remove the situation, then I would remove myself from the situation. But now, after learning to be more independent, more vocal, and more sure of myself, I know that I can remain in the situation and perhaps try to resolve some if not all of it.

—Jacqueline

are not necessarily locked into a particular strategy. There are at least five specific styles of managing conflicts (Rahim, 1986; Rahim & Magner, 1995; Thomas & Kilmann, 1974):

- Dominating
- Integrating
- Compromising
- Obliging
- Avoiding

The **dominating style** reflects high concern for the self and low concern for the other person. It has been identified with having a win-lose orientation and with forcing behavior to win one's position. The behaviors associated with this style include loud and forceful verbalization, which may be counterproductive to conflict resolution. However, this view may indicate a Eurocentric bias, because members of some cultural groups (including African Americans) see these behaviors as appropriate in many contexts (Speicher, 1994).

The **integrating style** reflects high concern for both the self and the other person and involves an open and direct exchange of information in an attempt to reach a solution acceptable to both parties. This style is seen as effective in most conflicts because it attempts to be fair and equitable. It assumes collaboration, empathy, objectivity, creativity, and recognition of feelings. However, it requires a lot of time and energy (Folger, Poole, & Stutman, 1993).

The **compromising style** reflects a moderate degree of concern for both the self and the other person. This style involves sharing and exchanging information

383

in such a way that both individuals give up something to find a mutually acceptable solution. Sometimes this style is less effective than the integrating approach because people feel forced to give up something they value and so have less commitment to the solution.

The **obliging style** describes a situation in which one person in the conflict plays down the differences and incompatibilities and emphasizes commonalities that satisfy the concerns of the other person. Obliging may be most appropriate when one individual is more concerned with the relationship itself than with specific issues. This is often true of hierarchical relationships in which one person has more status or power than the other. However, a pattern of obliging can result in psuedosolutions, especially if one person or the other resents the constant accommodation, so the strategy can eventually backfire.

Finally, the **avoiding style** reflects, supposedly, a low concern for both the self and the other person. In the dominant U.S. cultural contexts, a person who uses this style is often viewed negatively, as attempting to withdraw, sidestep, deny, or bypass the conflict. However, in some cultural contexts, this is an appropriate strategy that, if used by both parties, may result in more harmonious relationships. For example, avoidance can allow individuals to think of some other response, especially if they have trouble "thinking on their feet." Avoidance may also be appropriate if the issue is trivial, if the relationship itself is unimportant to one person, or if others can better manage the conflict (Wilmot & Hocker, 2001).

There are many reasons that we tend to favor a particular conflict style in our interactions. A primary influence is family background; some families prefer a certain conflict style, and children come to accept this style as normal. For instance, the family may have settled conflict in a dominating way, with the person having the strongest argument (or muscle) getting his or her way.

Sometimes people try to reject the conflict styles they saw their parents using. Consider the following examples. One student, Bill, remembers hearing his parents argue long and loud, and his father often used a dominating style of conflict management. He vowed that he would never deal with conflict this way in his own family, and he has tried very hard to keep his vow. Another student, Stephanie, describes how she has changed her style of dealing with conflict as she has grown older:

> *I think as a child I was taught to ignore conflict and especially to not cause conflict. When I was growing up, I saw my mom act this way toward my father and probably learned that women were supposed to act this way toward men. As a teenager, I figured out that this just wasn't how I wanted to be. Now I like conflict, not too much of it, but I definitely cannot ignore conflict. I have to deal with it or else I will worry about it. So I deal with it and get it over with.*

It is important to recognize that people deal with conflict in a variety of ways, for a variety of reasons. A word of caution is in order about conflict management styles. Conflict specialists William Wilmot and Joyce Hocker (2001) warn that we should not think of preferred styles as static and set in stone. Rather, they suggest that purely individual styles really do not exist, because we are each influenced by others in interaction. Therefore, our conflict management styles are not static across settings and relationships. For example, people may use dominating styles at work and avoid conflict at home; or they may use avoiding styles at work and compromise at home. And they may use different styles with different partners. For instance, with coworkers, individuals may tend to collaborate and work through conflict issues; with the boss, they may tend to employ more avoiding strategies. In addition, our styles often change over the course of a conflict and over the life span. For example, individuals who tend to avoid conflict may learn the benefits of engaging and working through conflicts.

Gender, Ethnicity, and Conflict

The relationship between gender and conflict management styles is not clear. Some studies show some gender differences, and others do not. For example, in some studies investigating gender differences among U.S. young people, women report that they are more collaborative in their styles than do men, who report themselves as being more competitive. However, in studies of older adults investigating conflict management styles in the workplace, these gender differences disappear (Wilmot & Hocker, 2001, p. 166).

The relationship between ethnicity, gender, and conflict management is even more complex. Do males and females of different ethnic backgrounds prefer different ways of dealing with conflict? Researcher Mary Jane Collier (1991) investigated this issue in a study in which she asked African American, White American, and Mexican American students to describe conflicts they had had with close friends and the ways they dealt with the conflicts. She also asked them what they should (and should not) have said and whether they thought that males and females handle conflict differently.

Collier found that male and female ethnic friends differed in their ideas about the best ways to deal with conflict. African American males and females offered generally similar descriptions of a problem-solving approach (integration style) as appropriate behavior in conflict management. (One friend said, "I told him to stay in school and that I would help him study." Another explained, "We decided together how to solve the problem" [p. 147].) The males tended to emphasize that appropriate arguments should be given, information should be offered, and opinions should be credible, whereas the females generally emphasized appropriate assertiveness without criticism. (One man complained, "She pushed her own way and opinion and totally disregarded mine" [p. 147].) Some of these findings seem to contradict earlier studies comparing African American and White communication styles. These contradictions might be due to differences among the groups studied (e.g., comparing working-class African Americans and middle-class Whites). Furthermore, because these studies are based on very small samples, we should interpret their findings tentatively.

White males and females generally seemed to focus on the importance of accepting responsibility for their behavior. Males in particular mentioned the importance of being direct. (They used expressions like "getting things in the open" and "say right up front" [p. 145].) Females talked about the importance of

We often do not know which cultural attitudes are important to others until we do something that violates those expectations. As this example shows, jokes are not always simply jokes, but indicators of more deeply held cultural attitudes.

> *My intercultural conflict was between my family, being Roman Catholic, and that of my ex-boyfriend of two years, who was Jewish. My family is one of those Catholic families that only really considers practicing at Christmas and Easter. I never thought that religion was a big deal until I started dating someone who was not even Christian. I had remembered overhearing my parents talk about interreligious relationships. They used to joke around with me (or so I thought) about bringing home Jewish boys from college. So at first when I started to date Shaun, I didn't tell my parents he was Jewish until about three months into the relationship. My mother, being the outspoken one in the family, had a fit, saying that if I married a Jewish man that I would be excommunicated from the Catholic Church and basically go to hell! My dad, who isn't much of a talker, didn't say much, except that he never asked about Shaun, when in previous relationships he usually gave me the third degree.*
> —Dana

concern for the other person and the relationship, and for situational flexibility. (One woman explained, "She showed respect for my position and I showed respect for hers" [p. 146].)

Mexican American males and females tended to differ in that males described the importance of talking to reach a mutual understanding. (One man wanted to "make a better effort to explain." Another said that he and his partner "stuck to the problem until we solved it together" [p. 147].) Females described several kinds of appropriate reinforcement of the relationship. In general, males and females in all groups described females as more compassionate and concerned with feelings, and males as more concerned with winning the conflict and being "right."

It is important to remember that, whereas ethnicity and gender may be related to ways of dealing with conflict, it is inappropriate (and inaccurate) to assume that any one person will behave in a particular way because of his or her ethnicity or gender.

Value Differences and Conflict Styles

Another way to understand cultural variations in intercultural conflict resolution is to look at how cultural values influence conflict management. Cultural values in individualistic societies differ from those in collectivistic societies. Individualistic societies place greater importance on the individual than on groups like the family or the work group. Individualism is often cited as the most important of European American values, as reflected in the autonomy and independence encouraged in children. For example, children in the United States are often encouraged to leave home after age 18, and older parents generally prefer to live on their own rather than with their children. In contrast, collectivistic societies often place greater importance on extended families and loyalty to groups.

Yoko, a Japanese student, recounted a conflict she had with U.S. American student, Linda, with whom she was working on a class project. Linda seemed to take a very competitive, individualistic approach to the project, saying things like "I did this on the project" or referring to it as "my project." Yoko became increasingly irritated and less motivated to work on the project. She finally said to Linda, "Is this your project or our project?" Linda seemed surprised and didn't apologize, but only defended herself. The two women continued to work on the project, but with a strained relationship.

Although these values have been related to national differences, they also may be true for other groups. For example, European Americans may value individualism more than do Latinos/as, and women may value collectivism more than do men.

These contrasting values may influence communication patterns. Several studies have established that people from individualistic societies tend to be more concerned with saving their own self-esteem during conflict, to be more direct in their communication, and to use more controlling, confrontational, and solution-oriented conflict management styles. In contrast, people from collectivistic societies tend to be more concerned with preserving group harmony and with saving the other person's dignity during conflict. They may use a less direct conversational style and may use avoiding and obliging conflict styles instead (Ting-Toomey et al., 2000). However, there is some evidence that not all collectivistic societies prefer indirect ways of dealing with conflict. How someone chooses to deal with conflict in any situation depends on the type of conflict and the relationship she or he has with the other person (Cai & Fink, 2000; Smith, Dugan, Peterson, & Leung, 1998).

A recent study found that Japanese college students tended to use the avoiding style more often with acquaintances than with best friends in some types of conflicts (conflicts of values and opinions). In contrast, they used the integrating style more with best friends than with acquaintances. In interest conflicts, they used a dominating style more with acquaintances than with best friends (Cole, 1996). This suggests that with outgroup members, as with acquaintances, for whom harmony is not as important, the Japanese use dominating or avoiding styles (depending on the conflict type). However, with ingroup members like best friends, the way to maintain harmony is to work through the conflict with an integrating style.

INTERPRETIVE AND CRITICAL APPROACHES TO SOCIAL CONFLICT

Both the interpretive and the critical approaches tend to emphasize the social and cultural aspects of conflict. In these perspectives, conflict is far more complex than the ways that interpersonal conflict is enacted. It is deeply rooted in cultural differences in the social, economic, and historical contexts.

Social conflict arises from unequal or unjust social relationships between groups. Consider, for example, the social conflict in northern Wisconsin between many Whites and Native Americans over fishing rights. Communication theorist Brad Hall (1994) concludes, in part, that "actual intercultural interactions which display the conflict (and generally receive the bulk of attention) are but the tip of the iceberg in understanding the complexities of such conflicts" (p. 82). Let's look more closely at the social, economic, and historical contexts of this contemporary conflict. This area of Wisconsin is heavily dependent on tourism and fishing. However, supposed overfishing by the Anishinabe (Chippewa) is being blamed for economic downturns in the area, leading to uneasy social relationships. A treaty was signed in 1837 giving the Anishinabe year-round fishing rights in exchange for the northern third of Wisconsin. Awareness of these factors is necessary to understanding the complexities of the current conflict.

These complexities are embedded in cultural differences. In addition, the conflict may be motivated by a desire to bring about social change. In **social movements,** individuals work together to bring about social change. They often use confrontation as a strategy to highlight the injustices of the present system. So, for example, when African American students in Greensboro, North Carolina, sat down at White-only lunch counters in the 1960s, they were pointing out the injustices of segregation. Although the students were nonviolent, their actions drew a violent reaction that, for many people, legitimized the claims of injustice.

Historical and political contexts also are sources of conflict. Many **international conflicts** have arisen over border disputes. For example, Argentina and the United Kingdom both claimed the Islas Malvinas (or Falkland Islands) in the south Atlantic, which led to a short war in 1982. Disputes between France and Germany over the Alsace-Lorraine region lasted much longer—from about 1871 to 1945. Similar disputes have arisen between Japan and Russia over islands north of Japan. The historical reasons for such conflicts help us understand the claims of both sides. Contextualizing intercultural conflict can help us understand why the conflict occurs and identify ways to resolve those conflicts.

Social Contexts

How we manage conflict may depend on the particular context or situation. For example, we may choose to use an avoiding style if we are arguing with a close friend about serious relational issues in a movie theater. In contrast, we may feel freer to use a more confrontational style at a social movement rally.

Nikki, a student working part-time at a restaurant, recalls an incident involving a large group of German tourists. The tourists thought she had added a 15% tip to the bill because they were tourists; they hadn't realized that it was the company policy when serving large groups. Nikki explains that she was much more conciliatory when dealing with this group in the restaurant than she would have been in a more social context. She thought the tourists were rude, but she practiced good listening skills and took more of a problem-solving approach than she would have otherwise.

Jacqueline, from Singapore, is annoyed by U.S. Americans who comment on how well she speaks English, because English is her first language even though she is ethnically Chinese. She used to say nothing in response; now sometimes she retorts, "So is yours," reflecting her struggle against the stereotype that Asians cannot speak English. In this context, the social movement against racism gives meaning to the conflict that arises for Jacqueline.

Many conflicts arise and must be understood against the backdrop of large-scale social movements designed to change contemporary society. For example, the women's suffrage movement of the early 20th century was not an individual effort but a mass effort to win women the right to vote in the United States. Many similar contemporary social movements give meaning to conflicts. These include movements against racism, sexism, and homophobia and movements in support of animal rights, the environment, free speech, and civil rights. College campuses are likely locations for much activism. Journalist Tony Vellela (1988) comments: "It may have subsided, and it certainly changed, reflecting changing times and circumstances, but progressive student political activism never really stopped after the much-heralded anti–Vietnam War era" (p. 5).

There is, of course, no comprehensive list of existing social movements. They arise and dissipate, depending on the opposition they provoke, the attention they attract, and the strategies they use. As part of social change, social movements need confrontation to highlight the perceived injustice.

Confrontation, then, can be seen as an opportunity for social change. In arguing for a change, Dr. Martin Luther King, Jr. (1984) emphasized the importance of nonviolent confrontation:

> *Nonviolent resistance is not a method for cowards; it does resist. . . . [It] does not seek to defeat or humiliate the opponent, but to win his friendship and understanding. The nonviolent resister must often express his protest through noncooperation or boycotts, but he realizes that these are not ends themselves; they are merely means to awaken a sense of moral shame in the opponent. (pp. 108–109)*

This type of confrontation exposes the injustices of society and opens the way for social change. Although nonviolence is not the only form of confrontation employed by social movements, its use has a long history—from Mahatma Gandhi's struggle for India's independence from Britain, to the civil rights struggle in the United States, to the struggle against apartheid in South Africa. In each case, images of violent responses to nonviolent protesters tended to legitimize the social movements and delegitimize the existing social system. For example, in the 1950s, and 1960s, the televised images of police dogs attacking schoolchildren and riot squads turning fire hoses on peaceful protesters in Birmingham, Alabama, swung public sentiment in favor of the civil rights movement.

Some social movements have also used violent forms of confrontation. Groups such as Action Directe in France, the Irish Republican Army, Earth First, and independence movements in Corsica, Algeria, Kosovo, and Chechnya have all been accused of using violence. As a result, they tend to be labeled as terrorists rather than mere protesters. Even the suggestion of violence can be threatening to the public. For example, in 1964, Malcolm X (1984) spoke in favor of civil rights: "The question tonight, as I understand it, is 'The Negro Revolt and Where Do We Go From Here?' or 'What Next?' In my little humble way of understanding it, it points toward either the ballot or the bullet" (p. 126). Malcolm X's rhetoric terrified many U.S. Americans, who then refused to give legitimacy to his movement. To understand communication practices such as these, it is important to study their social contexts. Social movements highlight many issues relevant to intercultural interaction.

Economic Contexts

Many conflicts are fueled by economic problems, which may be expressed in cultural differences: Many people find it easier to explain economic troubles by pointing to cultural differences or by assigning blame. For example, in the United States, we have heard many arguments about limiting immigration, with attention focusing largely on non-European immigrants. Concerns about illegal immigrants from Mexico far overshadow concerns about illegal immigrants from, say, Ireland. And discussions about the contributions to society made by different immigrant groups tend to favor European immigrants. Writer Andrew Hacker (1997) compares the median household income of U.S. Americans of various backgrounds, pointing out the lack of attention given to less successful U.S. Americans of some European heritages:

> We rarely hear media pundits pondering aloud why the Irish lag so far behind the Greeks in median income, and why all four Scandinavian nationalities fall in the bottom half of the European roster. But it has been deemed best not to accentuate distinctions, and rather to reserve remarks of that sort for members of another race. (p. 158)

Indeed, U.S. Americans of French ancestry and Dutch ancestry earn less (and therefore contribute less?) than U.S. Americans who trace their ancestry to the Philippines, India, Lebanon, China, Thailand, Greece, Italy, Poland, and many other countries. And yet we do not hear calls for halting immigration from France or the Netherlands. In what ways is the economic argument really hiding a racist argument?

We might also ask who benefits from this finger-pointing. Paul Kivel (1996) suggests that blaming immigrants, people of color, and Jews for economic problems diverts attention from the decision makers who are responsible for the problem.

As the economic contexts change, we see more cultural conflict taking place. The former East Germany, for example, now has many more racially motivated attacks as the region attempts to rebuild its economy. Prejudice and stereotyping that lead to conflict are often due to perceived economic threats and competition. In this sense, economics fuels scapegoating and intercultural conflict and is an important context for understanding intercultural conflict.

Historical and Political Contexts

Most of us recall the childhood saying "Sticks and stones may break my bones, but words will never hurt me." In fact, we know that derogatory words can be a

FIGURE 11-2   Intercultural conflicts occur not only on the interpersonal level but also between groups. In this photo, Tzotzil Indians and aid workers are returning to their abandoned houses in the villages of Chenalho, in the Mexican state of Chiapas. They fled their homes nearly four years earlier when dozens of Indians were killed by paramilitary gunmen. How might the history of this region help us understand this intercultural conflict? (© *Reuters/Getty Images*)

powerful source of conflict. The force that many derogatory words carry comes from their historical usage and the history of oppression to which they refer. As we noted in Chapter 4, much of our identity comes from history. It is only through understanding the past that we can understand what it means to be members of particular cultural groups. For example, understanding the history of Ireland helps give meaning to Irish American identity.

Sometimes identities are constructed in opposition to or in conflict with other identities. When people identify themselves as members of particular cultural groups, they are marking their difference from others. These differences, when infused with historical antagonism, can lead to conflicts. Consider, for example, the modern-day conflicts in Bosnia-Herzegovina. These did not emerge from interpersonal conflicts among the current inhabitants but rather, in large part, reflect centuries-old antagonisms between cultural groups. The contemporary participants are caught in a historical web that has pitted cultural identities against one another.

These dynamics are at work all around the world. Historical antagonisms become part of cultural identities and practices that place people in positions of conflict. Whether in the Middle East, Northern Ireland, Rwanda, Uganda, Nigeria, Sri Lanka, East Timor, Kosovo, or Chechnya, these historical antagonisms lead to various forms of conflict. (See Figure 11-2.)

When people witness conflict, they often assume that it is caused by personal issues between individuals. By reducing conflict to the level of interpersonal interaction, we lose sight of the larger social and political forces that contextualize these conflicts. People are in conflict for reasons that extend far beyond personal communication styles.

MANAGING INTERCULTURAL CONFLICT

Productive Versus Destructive Conflict

One way to think about conflict across cultures is in terms of what is more or less successful conflict management or resolution. Given all of the variations in how people deal with conflict, what happens when there is conflict in intercultural relationships?

Scholar David Augsburger (1992) suggests that productive intercultural conflict is different from destructive conflict in four ways. First, in productive conflict, individuals or groups narrow the conflict in terms of definition, focus, and issues. In destructive conflict, they escalate the issues or negative attitudes. For example, if a partner says, "You never do the dishes" or "You always put me down in front of my friends," the conflict is likely to escalate. Instead, the partner could focus on a specific instance of being put down.

Second, in productive conflict, individuals or groups limit conflict to the original issue. In destructive conflict, they escalate the conflict from the original issues, with any aspect of the relationship open for reexamination. For example, guests on talk shows about extramarital affairs might initially refer to a specific affair and then expand the conflict to include numerous prior arguments.

Third, in productive conflict, individuals or groups direct the conflict toward cooperative problem solving. For example, a partner may ask, "How can we work this out?" In contrast, in destructive conflict, strategies involve the use of power, threats, coercion, and deception. For example, an individual might threaten his or her partner: "Either you do what I want, or else." Finally, in productive conflict, individuals or groups trust leadership that stresses mutually satisfactory outcomes. In destructive conflict, they polarize behind single-minded and militant leadership.

Competition Versus Cooperation

As you can see, the general theme in destructive conflict is competitive escalation, often into long-term negativity. The conflicting parties have set up a self-perpetuating, mutually confirming expectation. "Each is treating the other badly because it feels that the other deserves to be treated badly because the other treats it badly and so on" (Deutsch, 1987, p. 41).

How can individuals and groups promote cooperative processes in conflict situations? The general atmosphere of a relationship will promote specific processes and acts (Deutsch, 1973). For instance, a *competitive* atmosphere will promote coercion, deception, suspicion, and rigidity, and lead to poor communication. In contrast, a *cooperative* atmosphere will promote perceived similarity, trust, and flexibility, and lead to open communication. The key is to establish a positive, cooperative atmosphere in the beginning stages of the relationship or group interaction. It is much more difficult to turn a competitive relationship into a cooperative one once the conflict has started to escalate.

Essential to setting a cooperative atmosphere is exploration. Whereas competition often relies on argumentation, cooperation relies on exploration. Exploration may be done in various ways in different cultures, but it has several basic steps. The parties must first put the issue of conflict on hold and then explore other options or delegate the problem to a third party. Blaming is suspended, so it's possible to generate new ideas or positions. "If all conflicting parties are committed to the process, there is a sense of joint ownership of the recommended solution. . . . [M]oving toward enemies as if they were friends exerts a paradoxical force on them and can bring transcendence" (Hocker & Wilmot, 1991, p. 191).

However, exploration does not have to be logically consistent or rational. As Augsburger (1992) points out, "Exploration can be provocative, speculative, and emotional" (p. 61). It should encourage individuals to think of innovative and interesting solutions to the conflict at hand. For example, Bill and David were having an ongoing disagreement about a project they were working on, and their relationship was becoming more and more strained. One day, Bill spontaneously suggested that they go out to eat together and really talk about the problem. David was surprised because they did not normally socialize—their relationship revolved around work. They talked about the problem, spent some time getting to know each other, and found they had some things in common. Although the problem didn't magically go away, it became easier to manage. Bill's spontaneous invitation to talk helped facilitate the resolution of the conflict.

Dealing With Conflict

There are no easy answers in dealing with intercultural conflict. Sometimes, we can apply the principles of dialectics; other times, we may need to step back and show self-restraint. Occasionally, though, it may be more appropriate to assert ourselves and not be afraid of strong emotion. Here, we offer seven suggestions for dealing with conflict:

1. Stay centered and do not polarize.
2. Maintain contact.
3. Recognize the existence of different styles.
4. Identify your preferred style.
5. Be creative and expand your style repertoire.
6. Recognize the importance of conflict context.
7. Be willing to forgive.

Xenophobia—the fear of foreigners or strangers—is sometimes tied to social class differences. Note the assumptions made about immigrants in this conflict. Is it possible to have a more satisfying resolution to this conflict? How might that be achieved?

My conflict is between my in-laws and myself. This conflict has existed for years and has caused many problems and heartaches in our lives.

It is now hard to pinpoint when the problems began. My husband and I went to visit my now father-in-law when we were first dating, and he gave me the third degree. I was on my very best behavior, but when we said our goodbyes, he insisted that I go back to California (I was just visiting here and still lived in California), and surely I would be able to find a new job there. I did not take this very seriously at the time, but through later conflicts became aware that my husband's family is prejudiced against Germans (as well as Mexicans, African Americans, and immigrants of all sorts).

Since then, many difficult situations have occurred, including a rather violent outbreak with my husband's grandmother and aunt, in which I was referred to as "the German whore," who was "just with him to get her green card" and was "after his money." None of these clichés apply in my case. I have never been a whore, I had a green card prior to meeting my husband, and I was unaware at this point of my in-laws' wealth.

This conflict, I believe, is about prejudice against foreigners, and specifically, immigrants. There seems to be a perception within my husband's family that I am only taking, not giving anything. There is also an assumption that I come from a poor family because my family is not college-educated, which a generation ago only a very small percentage of the German population was. There is a misunderstanding of the educational system in Germany, the apprenticeship system, through which people are trained and able to make very good and profitable careers. My father, for example, had a more respectable social standing and earned far more than my husband's father, who was college-educated. Another issue was that I had not yet received a college degree.

Unfortunately, the way I have dealt with this conflict after many years of being emotionally abused is to ignore his family. They never even call our house anymore now, and will only visit if expressly invited by my husband, which to me has meant some stress reduction. But I also feel very sorry that these misunderstandings exist; they exist because of cultural differences. I do not believe that his family is aware of their prejudicial behavior. The entire problem is said to exist because I am disrespectful and from a supposedly lower class.

—Heidi

Let's look at these guidelines in more detail.

Stay Centered and Do Not Polarize   It's important to move beyond traditional stereotypes and either-or thinking. David Augsburger (1992) elaborates on this approach to dealing with conflict:

> *Immediately challenge the intrusion of either-or thinking, traditional stereotypes, and reductionistic explanations of the other's motives as simple while seeing your own as complex. Sustain the conflicting images of reality, one from the antagonist and one of your own, in parallel co-existence within your mind. Be open to a third, centered perspective that may bring a new synthesis into view. (p. 66)*

The parties involved must practice self-restraint. It's okay to get angry, but it's important to move past the anger and to refrain from acting out feelings. For example, Jenni and her coworker both practiced self-restraint and stayed centered in a recent disagreement about religion. Jenni explains:

> *My friend is a devout Catholic and I am a devout Mormon. She asked me about where we get some of our doctrine and how it relates to the Bible. We never really solved our differences, but compromised and "agreed to disagree." This was necessary to keep our friendship and respect as coworkers. I felt bad that she couldn't see the points I was coming from. I do think it turned out for the best, though, because we don't feel tension around each other.*

Maintain Contact   This does not mean that the parties have to stay in the conflict situation—sometimes it's necessary to step away for a while. However, the parties should not cut off the relationship. Rather, they should attempt a dialogue rather than isolate themselves from each other or engage in fighting. **Dialogue** differs from normal conversation in that it is

> *slow, careful, full of feeling, respectful and attentive. This movement toward an apparently opposing viewpoint must be learned; few develop this approach to others without a deep sense of the importance of each human being, and a belief in collaboratively searching for new solutions that honor each person. (Wilmot & Hocker, 2001, p. 257)*

Dialogue is possible only between two persons or two groups whose power relationship is more or less in balance. Dialogue offers an important opportunity to come to a richer understanding of intercultural conflicts and experiences.

Our student John experienced an intercultural conflict in an accounting class in which his maintaining contact paid off. He was placed in a group with three Japanese students who were all friends. He recalls:

> *Right from the beginning things were quite awkward; their mathematics abilities far exceeded mine. After only two days, they had met twice without me and completed part of the assignment. I had been left out of the decision-making process.*

Rather than avoiding the problem, however, he decided to invite them all over to his house to talk about the project. Everyone was able to loosen up and

In dealing with intercultural conflicts, this author suggests, people should start with a different assumption about the reasons behind the conflict. Is it possible to approach and resolve intercultural conflicts without such an attitude, without giving the benefit of the doubt?

I'm challenged by Gandhian principles to understand—indeed, to know—that the proper response to institutional injustice is action. But it must be wrapped in love. Therein is the power. And the difficulty. Loving one's enemy is to bury deep one's egoistic tendencies. It requires "a supraconsciousness," the Trappist monk and Gandhian scholar Thomas Merton said, advocating: ". . . the strength of heart which is capable of liberating the oppressed and the oppressor together. . . . In any event, without that capacity for pity, neither of them will be able to recognize the truth of their situation: a common relationship in a common complex of sin."

This coming together—this reconciliation, which often seems so impossible to achieve in racial matters but which must never be given up as an impossibility—can often start, indeed, one by one—giving the other person the benefit of the doubt, assuming somebody just misspoke or misunderstood.

Source: From Patricia Raybon, *My First White Friend: Confessions on Race, Love, and Forgiveness*, New York: Penguin, 1996, p. 158.

discuss what had gone wrong, and the conflict was handled productively: "Although I was unhappy with the way things went during the earlier parts of the project, the end result was three new acquaintances and an A in accounting."

Recognize the Existence of Different Styles Conflict is often exacerbated because of the unwillingness of partners to recognize management style differences. Communication scholar Barbara L. Speicher (1994) analyzes a conflict that occurred between two student leaders on the same committee: the chair, Peter, an African American male, and Kathy, a European American female who was president of the organization. The two had a history of interpersonal antagonism. They disagreed on how meetings should be run and on how data should be collected in a particular project they were working on. They interviewed the other participants afterwards and learned that most thought the conflict was related mainly to the interpersonal history of the two and to the issue at hand, but not to either race or gender.

Speicher then describes how her analysis of videotapes of the conflict showed that both Kathy and Peter adhered to cultural norms for communication between Blacks and Whites in the United States:

Peter was assertive, took the floor when he had an important point to make and became loud and emphatic as the conflict accelerated. . . . The Eurocentric discom-

*fort with and disapproval of his adamancy led to either silence (avoidance) or at-
tempts to calm him down and diminish rather than resolve the conflict. (p. 204)*

Speicher notes that part of the problem was due to differences in perceptions
of rationalism—"the sacred cow of Western thought"—and emotionalism. In
Western thought, these two behaviors often are seen as mutually exclusive. But
this is not so in Afrocentric thinking. Peter believed that he was being rational,
giving solid evidence for each of his claims, and also being emotional. To his Eurocentric colleagues, his high affect seemed to communicate that he was taking
something personally, that his vehemence precluded rationality or resolution.
Speicher suggests that perhaps we need to rethink the way we define conflict
competence. From an Afrocentric point of view, one can be emotional and rational and still be deemed competent.

Speicher also points out the danger of attributing individual behavior to
group differences: "While such work can help us understand one another, it can
also encourage viewing an interlocutor as a representative of a group (stereotyping) rather than as an individual" (p. 206). However, she goes on to say that in
this particular case

*failure to recognize cultural differences led to a negative evaluation of an individ-
ual. The problems that emerged in this exchange were attributed almost exclusively to Peter's behavior. The evaluation was compounded by the certainty on the
part of the European Americans, as expressed in the interviews, that their interpretation was the correct one, a notion reinforced by the Eurocentric literature on
conflict. (p. 206)*

This particular combination of differing but complementary styles often
results in damaged relationships and frozen agendas—the rational/avoiding–
emotional/confronting "dance." Other combinations may be problematic but
less overtly damaging. For example, two people with assertive emotional styles
may understand each other and know how to work through the conflict. Likewise, things can work if both people avoid open conflict, particularly in long-
term committed relationships (Pike & Sillars, 1985). Jointly avoiding conflict
does not necessarily mean that it goes away, but it may give people time to think
about how to deal with the conflict and talk about it.

Identify Your Preferred Style   Although people may change their way of dealing with conflict based on the situation and the type of conflict, most tend to
use the same style in most situations. For example, Tom and Judith both prefer
an avoiding style. If we are pushed into conflict or feel strongly that we need to
resolve a particular issue, we can speak up for ourselves. However, we both prefer more indirect means of dealing with current and potential conflicts. We often choose to work things out on a more personal, indirect level.

It is also important to recognize which conflict styles "push your conflict
button." Some styles are more or less compatible; it's important to know which
styles are congruent with your own. If you prefer a more confronting style and

you have a disagreement with someone like Tom or Judith, it may drive you crazy.

Be Creative and Expand Your Style Repertoire   If a particular way of dealing with conflict is not working, be willing to try a different style. Of course, this is easier said than done. As conflict specialists William Wilmot and Joyce Hocker (2001) explain, people often seem to get "frozen" into a conflict style. For example, some people consistently deny any problems in a relationship, whereas others consistently escalate small conflicts into large ones.

There are many reasons for getting stuck in a conflict management style, according to Wilmot and Hocker. The style may have developed during a time when the person felt good about him- or herself—when the particular conflict management style worked well. Consider, for example, the high school athlete who develops an aggressive style on and off the playing field—a style that people seem to respect. A limited repertoire may be related to gender differences. Some women get stuck in an avoiding style, whereas some men get stuck in a confronting style. A limited repertoire also may come from cultural background— a culture that encourages confronting conflict or a culture (like Judith's and Tom's) that rewards avoiding conflict. A combination of these reasons is the likely cause of getting stuck in the use of one conflict management style. For example, even though Tom and Judith prefer an avoiding style, we have occasionally found it effective to be more assertive and direct in intercultural conflicts in which the dominant communication style was more confrontational.

In most aspects of intercultural communication, adaptability and flexibility serve us well—and conflict communication is no exception. This means that there is no so-called objective way to deal with conflict. Many times, as in other aspects of relationships, it's best simply to listen and not say anything. One strategy that mediators use is to allow one person to talk for an extended time while the other person listens.

Recognize the Importance of Conflict Context   As noted earlier in this chapter, it is important to understand the larger social, economic, political, and historical contexts that give meaning to many types of conflict. Conflict arises for many reasons, and it is misleading to think that all conflict can be understood within the interpersonal context alone. For example, when one student, George, went home for a family reunion, everyone seemed to be talking about their romantic relationships, spouses, children, and so on. When George, who is gay, talked about his own partner, George's uncle asked why gay people had to flaunt their lifestyle. George reactly angrily. The conflict was not simply between George and his uncle; it rests in the social context that accepts straight people talking frequently and openly about their relationships but that does not validate the same discussion of romantic relationships from gay people. The same talk is interpreted differently because of the social context.

People often act in ways that cause conflict. However, it is important to let the context explain the behavior as much as possible. Otherwise, the behavior may not make sense. Once you understand the contexts that frame the conflict, whether cultural, social, historical, or political, you will be in a better position to understand and conceive of the possibilities for resolution. For example, Savina, who is White, was shopping with her friend Lashieki. The employee at the cash register referred to someone as "that black girl," and Lashieki, who is African American, demanded, "Why did they have to refer to her as that black girl?" Lashieki's response can only be understood by knowing something about the context of majority–minority relations in the United States. That is, Whites are rarely referred to by color, whereas people of color are often defined solely on the basis of race.

Be Willing to Forgive   A final suggestion for facilitating conflict, particularly in long-term relationships, is to consider forgiveness. This means letting go of— not forgetting—feelings of revenge (Lulofs, 1994). This may be particularly useful in intercultural conflict (Augsburger, 1992).

Teaching forgiveness between estranged individuals is as old as recorded history; it is present in every culture and is part of the human condition (Arendt, 1954). Forgiveness can be a healthy reaction. Psychologists point out that blaming others and feeling resentment lead to a victim mentality. And a lack of forgiveness may actually lead to stress, burnout, and physical problems (Lulofs, 1994).

There are several models of forgiveness. Most include an acknowledgment of feelings of hurt and anger and a need for healing. In a forgiveness loop, forgiveness is seen as socially constructed and based in communication. If someone is in a stressed relationship, he or she can create actions and behaviors that make forgiveness seem real; then he or she can communicate this to the other person, enabling the relationship to move forward. An example of forgiveness on a national level involves the National Sorry Day and the Journey of Healing, which serve to acknowledge and apologize for the wretched treatment of Aboriginals by non-Aboriginal Australians. Another example is the Truth and Reconciliation committee in South Africa, formed to investigate and facilitate the healing of racial wounds as a result of apartheid. The committee hears stories of the atrocities that were committed, but the ultimate goal is forgiveness, not revenge (Henderson, 1999).

Forgiveness may take a long time. It is important to distinguish between what is forgiveness and what is not, because false forgiveness can be self-righteous and obtrusive; it almost nurtures past transgression. As writer Roxane Lulofs (1994) explains, forgiveness is not

> *simply forgetting that something happened. It does not deny anger. It does not put us in a position of superiority. It is not a declaration of the end of all conflict, of ever risking again with the other person (or anybody else). It is not one way. . . . We do not forgive in order to be martyrs to the relationship. We forgive because it is better for us and better for the other person. We forgive because we want to act freely again, not react out of past pain. . . . [It] is the final stage of conflict and is the one thing that is most likely to prevent repetitive, destructive cycles of conflict. (pp. 283–284, 289)*

POINT OF VIEW

Conflict specialist David Augsburger identifies six key Western assumptions—conflict myths—and notes their inadequacies in intercultural settings.

1. **People and problems can be separated cleanly; interests and positions can be distinguished sharply. . . .** In most cultures of the world, equal attention must be given to both person and problem, to relationship and goals and to private interests as well as public positions if a creative resolution is to be reached.

2. **Open self-disclosure is a positive value in negotiations. An open process of public data shared in candid style is assumed necessary for trust. . . .** "Open covenants, openly arrived at," Woodrow Wilson insisted, as did Harry Truman, were the basis for setting up the United Nations. However, when constituents can hear what is being sacrificed in reaching an agreement, then compromise becomes improbable and often impossible precisely because of that openness. The real negotiation is done in corridors or behind closed doors, and is announced publicly when agreements have been reached. Virtually nothing of any substance is agreed on in the official public UN debates.

3. **Immediacy, directness, decisiveness, and haste are preferred strategies in timing.** The Western valuation that time is money can press the negotiator to come to terms prematurely. Many different cultures find that the best way to reach an agreement is to give the matter sufficient time to allow adjustments to be made, accommodations to emerge, and acceptance to evolve and emerge. Believing that "time is people," they are in less haste to reach closure.

4. **Language employed should be reasonable, rational, and responsible.** In some cultures, deprecative language, extreme accusations and vitriolic

Mediation

Sometimes two individuals or groups cannot work through conflict on their own. They may request an intermediary, or one may be assigned to intervene. In some societies, these third parties may be rather informal. In Western societies, though, they tend to be built into the legal and judicial system. For example, lawyers or counselors may act as mediators to settle community or family disputes.

Contemporary Western **mediation** models often ignore cultural variations in conflict processes. Fortunately, more scholars and mediators are looking at other cultural models that may work better in intercultural conflicts. Augsburger (1992) suggests that the culturally sensitive mediator engages in conflict transformation (not conflict resolution or conflict management). The conflict transformer assists disputants to think in new ways about the conflict—for example, to transform attitudes by redirecting negative perceptions. This requires a com-

expressions are used as a negotiating power tactic. Admiral Joy, the senior UN delegate to the armistice talks at the end of the Korean War, has told of a note that was exchanged between North Korean delegates. In Korean characters large enough to be read by the noncommunist representatives, the note proclaimed, "These imperialist errand boys are lower than dogs in a morgue." Joy states that this was "the ultimate Korean insult." In a similar show of disregard for diplomatic courtesy, Huang Hua, the senior Chinese representative at Panmunjom (and subsequently Chinese ambassador to the United Nations) repeatedly referred to American ambassador Arthur H. Dean as a "capitalist crook, rapist, thief, robber of widows, stealer of pennies from the eyes of the dead, [and] mongrel of uncertain origin."

5. **No is no and yes is yes (an affirmation is absolute, a negation final).** In some cultures, one does not say no to an offer; requests are not phrased to elicit negations; when an offer is affirmed, the real meanings are weighed and assessed carefully. Many negotiators have left a meeting with a perceived agreement only to find that the real position was more subtle, more concealed, and the reverse of their public expectations. A Mexican proverb advises, "There are a hundred ways of saying no, without saying it."

6. **When an agreement is reached, implementation will take care of itself as a logical consequence.** The agreements negotiated may mean different things to parties in a reconciliation. Built-in processes, ongoing negotiations, open channels for resolving problems as they arise in ongoing interpretation, and circumstances that would warrant renegotiation are all useful elements for ensuring ongoing success.

Source: From D. Augsburger, *Conflict Mediation Across Cultures*, 1992, pp. 206–208.

mitment by both parties to treat each other with goodwill and mutual respect. Of course, this is often much easier said than done. Behavior can be transformed by limiting all action to collaborative behavior; this can break the negative cycle but requires a commitment to seek a noncoercive process of negotiation even when there has been intense provocation. For example, in the recent Northern Ireland agreement, mediation resulted in commitment by most people to change the vision of Northern Ireland, in spite of horrendous provocation on the part of some extremists.

Traditional societies often use mediation models based on nondirect means. The models vary but share many characteristics. Whereas North American mediation tends to be more formal and structured, involving direct confrontation and communication, most traditional cultural models are more communally based, with involvement by trusted leaders. Indirect communication is preferred in order to permit individuals to save face. In addition, the process is more dynamic, directed toward resolving tension in the community—the responsibility of the disputants to their larger community is central (Augsburger, 1992, p. 204).

Augsburger provides the example of mediation in the Gitksan Nation, in northwest British Columbia, where mediation of disputes begins with placement of the problem "in the middle of the table." Everyone involved—including those in authority and the witnesses—must make suggestions in a peaceful manner until they come to a decision all can live with. Even conflicts ending in murder are resolved in this consensus-oriented fashion. For instance, "land would be transferred as compensation to help deal with the pain of the loss. The murderer might be required to give up his or her name and go nameless for a period to show respect for the life taken" (p. 213). Eventually, however, the land or anything else that was given up would be returned, "when the pain has passed and time has taken care of the grief" (p. 213). Augsburger points out that this traditional communal approach to mediation is based on collectivistic beliefs that make individualistic solutions to conflicts unacceptable.

Contemporary mediatiors have learned some lessons from the traditional non-Western models, and mediation is used increasingly in the United States and other countries to resolve conflicts. Mediation is advantageous because it relies on the disputing parties' active involvement in and commitment to the resolution. Also, it represents the work of all involved, so it's likely to be more creative and integrative. Finally, mediation is often cheaper than adversarial legal resolution (Hocker & Wilmot, 2001, p. 276).

SUMMARY

In this chapter, we took various approaches to understanding conflict. Intercultural conflict may be characterized by various dialectics, ambiguity, language issues, and combinations of conflict management styles. There are two very different cultural orientations to conflict—conflict as opportunity and conflict as destructive—as well as various cultural differences in viewing conflict. The interpersonal approach to understanding conflict focuses on cultural differences, types of conflict (affective conflict, conflict of interest, value conflict, cognitive conflict, and goal conflict), and conflict styles (dominating, integrating, compromising, obliging, and avoiding). The choice of conflict style depends on cultural background and on gender and ethnicity. For example, people from individualistic cultures may tend to use dominating styles, whereas people from collectivistic cultures may prefer more integrating, obliging, and avoiding styles. However, the type of conflict and the relationship the disputants have will mediate these tendencies.

The interpretive and critical approaches focus on intergroup relationships and emphasize the contexts of conflict. Conflicts arise against the backdrop of existing social movements—for example, in reaction to racism, sexism, and homophobia. Some social movements use nonviolent means of dealing with these conflicts; others confront conflict with violence.

Conflict may be productive or destructive. Productive conflict is more likely to be managed or resolved. One theme of destructive conflict is a competitive atmosphere. A cooperative atmosphere is more conducive to conflict management or resolution. Suggestions for dealing with intercultural conflicts include staying centered, maintaining contact, recognizing the existence of different conflict management styles, identifying a preferred style, being creative and expanding one's conflict style repertoire, recognizing the importance of conflict context, and being willing to forgive.

Transforming methods of mediation are commonly used in many cultures. A conflict transformer helps the disputing parties change their attitudes and behaviors.

DISCUSSION QUESTIONS

1. How does the "conflict as opportunity" orientation differ from the "conflict as destructive" orientation?
2. Why is it important to understand the context in which intercultural conflict occurs?
3. How are conflict strategies used in social movements?
4. How does an attitude of forgiveness facilitate conflict resolution?
5. What are some general suggestions for dealing with intercultural conflict?

Go to the self-quizzes on the Online Learning Center at www.mhhe.com/martinnakayama to further test your knowledge.

ACTIVITIES

Cultures in Conflict. For this assignment, work in groups of four. As a group, select two countries or cultural groups that are currently in conflict or that have historically been in conflict. In your group, form two pairs. One pair will research the conflict from the perspective of one of the two cultural groups or countries; the other pair will research the conflict from the perspective of the other group or country. Use library and community resources (including interviews with members of the culture if possible). Outline the major issues and arguments. Explore the role of cultural values, and political, economic, and historical contexts that may contribute to the conflict. Be prepared to present an oral or written report of your research.

KEY WORDS

avoiding style	dominating style	mediation
compromising style	integrating style	obliging style
conflict	intercultural conflict	pacifism
confrontation	intermediary	social conflict
dialogue	international conflict	social movements

 The Online Learning Center at www.mhhe.com/martinnakayama features flashcards and crossword puzzles based on these terms and concepts.

REFERENCES

Arendt, H. (1954). *The human condition.* Chicago: University of Chicago Press.

Augsburger, D. (1992). *Conflict mediation across cultures.* Louisville, KY: Westminster/John Knox Press.

Blocker, J. (2002, April 1). France/U.S.: Criticism tempered on decision to seek death penalty for Moussaoui. Radio Free Europe/Radio Liberty. www.rferl.org/nca/features/2002/04/01042002055307.asp.

Cai, D. A., & Fink, E. L. (2002). Conflict style differences between individualists and collectivists. *Communication Monographs, 69,* 67–87.

Canary, D. J., Cupach, W. R., & Messman, S. J. (1995). *Relationship conflict.* Thousand Oaks, CA: Sage.

Cupach, W. R., & Canary, D. J. (1997). *Competence in interpersonal conflict.* New York: McGraw-Hill.

Cole, M. (1996). *Interpersonal conflict communication in Japanese cultural contexts.* Unpublished dissertation, Arizona State University, Tempe.

Collier, M. J. (1991). Conflict competence within African, Mexican, and Anglo American friendships. In S. Ting-Toomey & F. Korzenny (Eds.), *Cross-cultural interpersonal communication* (pp. 132–154). Newbury Park, CA: Sage.

Delgado, F. (2002). Mass-mediated communication and intercultural conflict. In J. N. Martin, T. K. Nakayama, & L. A. Flores (Eds.), *Readings in intercultural communication: Experiences and contexts* (2nd ed., pp. 351–359). New York: McGraw-Hill.

Deutsch, M. (1973). *The resolution of conflict: Constructive and destructive processes.* New Haven, CT: Yale University Press.

———. (1987). A theoretical perspective on conflict and conflict resolution. In D. Sandole & I. Sandole-Staroste (Eds.), *Conflict management and problem solving.* New York: New York University Press.

Filley, A. C. (1975). *Interpersonal conflict resolution.* Glenview, IL: Scott, Foresman.

Folger, J. P., Poole, M. S., & Stutman, R. K. (1993). *Working through conflict: Strategies for relationships, groups, and organizations* (2nd ed.). New York: HarperCollins.

Hacker, A. (1997). *Money: Who has how much and why.* New York: Scribner.

Hall, B. "J." (1994). Understanding intercultural conflict through kernel images and rhetorical visions. *The International Journal of Conflict Management, 5*(1), 62–86.

Henderson, M. (1999). *Forgiveness: Breaking the chain of hate.* Wilsonville, OR: BookPartners.

Hocker, J. L., & Wilmot, W. W. (1991). *Interpersonal conflict* (3rd ed.). Dubuque, IA: Brown.

King, M. L., Jr. (1984). Pilgrimage in nonviolence. In J. C. Albert & S. E. Albert (Eds.), *The sixties papers: Documents of a rebellious decade* (pp. 108–112). New York: Praeger. (Original work published 1965)

Kivel, P. (1996). *Uprooting racism: How white people can work for racial justice.* Gabriola Islands, BC: New Society.

Kraybill, D. (1989). *The riddle of Amish culture.* Baltimore: Johns Hopkins University Press.

Lindsley, S. L. (1999). A layered model of problematic intercultural communication in U.S.-owned *maquiladoras* in Mexico. *Communication Monographs, 66,* 145–167.

Lulofs, R. S. (1994). *Conflict: From theory to action.* Scottsdale, AZ: Gorsuch Scarisbrick.

Malcolm X. (1984). The ballot or the bullet. In J. C. Albert & S. E. Albert (Eds.), *The sixties papers: Documents of a rebellious decade* (pp. 126–132). New York: Praeger. (Original work published in 1965)

Pike, G. R., & Sillars, A. L. (1985). Reciprocity of marital communication. *Journal of Social and Personal Relationships, 2,* 303–324.

Rahim, M. A. (1986). *Managing conflict in organizations.* New York: Praeger.

Rahim, M. A., & Magner, N. R. (1995). Confirmatory factor analysis of the styles of handling interpersonal conflict: First-order factor model and its invariance across groups. *Journal of Applied Psychology, 80,* 122–132.

Ross, M. H. (1993a). *The culture of conflict: Interpretations and interests in comparative perspective.* New Haven, CT: Yale University Press.

———. (1993b). *The management of conflict: Interpretations and interests in comparative perspective.* New Haven, CT: Yale University Press.

Smith, P. B, Dugan, S., Peterson, M. F., & Leung, K. (1998). Individualism/collectivism and the handling of disagreement: A 23-country study. *International Journal of Intercultural Relations, 22,* 351–367.

Speicher, B. L. (1994). Interethnic conflict: Attribution and cultural ignorance. *Howard Journal of Communications, 5,* 195–213.

Thomas, K., & Kilmann, R. H. (1974). *Thomas-Kilmann conflict MODE instrument.* Tuxedo, NY: Xicom.

Ting-Toomey, S. (1997). Intercultural conflict competence. In W. R. Cupach & D. J. Canary (Eds.), *Competence in interpersonal conflict* (pp. 120–147). New York: McGraw-Hill.

Ting-Toomey, S., & Oetzel, J. G. (2002). Cross-cultural face concerns and conflict styles: Current status and future directions. In W. B. Budykunst & B. Mody (Eds.), *Handbook of international and intercultural communication* (2nd ed., pp. 141–163). Thousand Oaks, Ca: Sage.

Ting-Toomey, S., Yee-Jung, K. K., Shapiro, R., Garcia, W, Wright, T. J., & Oetzel, J. G. (2000). Ethnic/cultural identity salience and conflict styles in four U.S. ethnic groups. *International Journal of Intercultural Relations, 24,* 47–81.

Toupin, A. (1980). Counseling Asians: Psychotherapy in the context of racism and Asian-American history. *American Journal of Orthopsychiatry, 50,* 76–86.

Vellela, T. (1988). *New voices: Student political activism in the '80s and '90s.* Boston: South End Press.

Wilmot, W. W., & Hocker, J. L. (2001). *Interpersonal conflict* (6th ed.). New York: McGraw-Hill.

Wu, J. C. H. (1967). Chinese legal and political philosophy. In C. Moore (Ed.), *The Chinese mind.* Honolulu: East-West Center, University of Hawaii.

THE OUTLOOK FOR INTERCULTURAL COMMUNICATION

Now that we are nearing the end of our journey through this textbook, you might ask, How do you really know whether you are a good intercultural communicator? We have covered a lot of topics and discussed some ideas that will help you be a better communicator. You can't learn how to be a good communicator merely by reading books, though. Just as in learning to be a good public speaker or a good relational partner, it takes experience. In this chapter, we want to leave you with some specific ideas and suggestions for improving your skills in communicating across cultures.

We can approach intercultural competence in several ways. We begin this chapter with the social science approach, identifying specific components of competence: motivation, knowledge, attitudes, behaviors, and skills. We then turn to interpretive and critical approaches, emphasizing the contextual issues in competence. Finally, we continue our dialectical perspective, combining individual and contextual elements to offer specific suggestions for improving intercultural relations by building alliances and coalitions across cultures.

THE COMPONENTS OF COMPETENCE

What are the things we have to know, the attitudes and behaviors, to make us competent communicators? Do we have to be motivated to be good at intercultural communication? Communication scholars Brian Spitzberg and William Cupach (1989) studied interpersonal communication competence in U.S. contexts from a social science perspective, and other scholars have tried to apply their findings in intercultural contexts (Chen & Starosta, 1996). These studies resulted in a list of basic components, or building blocks, of intercultural communication competence (e.g., having respect for others) (Wiseman, 2002). We present these components here because we think they serve as a useful starting point. However, we offer three cautionary notes. First, this is only a starting point. Second, the basic components are interrelated; it is difficult to separate motivation, knowledge, attitudes, behaviors, and skills. Third, it is important to contextualize these components—to ask ourselves, Who came up with these components? Are they applicable to everyone? For example, if a group of Native American scholars came up with guidelines for what it takes to be interculturally competent, would these guidelines apply to every cultural context?

Individual Components

Motivation   Perhaps the most important dimension of communication competence is **motivation.** If we aren't motivated to communicate with others, it probably doesn't matter what other skills we possess. We can't assume that people always want to communicate. This is a difficult idea to wrestle with, especially for those of us who have dedicated our lives to studying and understanding intercultural communication! And yet, motivation is an important aspect of developing intercultural competence.

Why might people not be motivated to engage in intercultural communication? One reason is that members of large, powerful groups often think they don't need to know much about other cultures; there is simply no incentive. In contrast, people from less powerful groups have a strong incentive to learn about and interact with more powerful groups. For example, female managers in corporations are motivated to learn about and adjust to the dominant male norms, Latinos/as are motivated to learn European American norms, and visitors overseas are motivated to learn about and adjust to the norms of foreign cultures. The survival of these less powerful groups often depends on members' motivation to succeed at intercultural interaction.

Sometimes people can *become* motivated to learn about other cultures and to communicate interculturally. For example, the events of 9/11 motivated many U.S. Americans to become more aware of how U.S. worldviews and behavior, on both a personal and a political level, are intertwined with those in other cultures and countries. As an essay in the *Christian Science Monitor* reported, educators scrambled to incorporate more material about Islam and the Middle East in their curricula, in order to help students make some sense out of the historical and political reasons for the terrorist attacks.

> *For educators, the rush for knowledge has been gratifying. But to some, it dramatically underscores the fact that an inward-looking America routinely fails to ground its citizens in the complexities of world history. Most schools serve up little or no material related to the Middle East or a basic understanding of Islam. "Maybe there are courses about the Middle East in some of the more affluent school districts," says Bill Schechter, a history teacher at Lincoln-Sudbury Regional High School in Sudbury, Mass. "But in most schools there's just a bit about the crusades in world history, and then 30 minutes at some point during the school year to talk about the current crisis." (Coeyman, 2001, n.p.)*

A second reason that people aren't motivated is because intercultural communication can be uncomfortable. As discussed previously, anxiety, uncertainty, and fear are common aspects of intercultural interactions. And yet, moving out of our "communication comfort zone" often leads to insights into other individuals, groups, and cultures. One of our students, Kati, explains:

> *If you keep your eyes open and your mind aware, you can learn something new about intercultural communication every day. . . . I think that you learn the most by traveling and/or making a conscious effort to interact with those in another culture or nation or race. Especially being thrust outside of your "comfort zone" (most Americans never get out of their comfort zone) will force you to see the diverse beauty and differences in other cultures.*

Psychologist Beverly Tatum (1997) suggests that people don't address delicate intercultural issues out of fear—fear of being isolated from friends and family members who may be prejudiced and not motivated themselves. She points out that this fear and the resulting silences have huge costs to us, as individuals and society. Individually, when we are not motivated to reach out across cultural

The following anecdote illustrates how complicated intercultural communication can be. It concerns a well-intentioned individual trying to be sensitive to one group (Native Americans) but inadvertently ignoring the feelings and sensibilities of another (Japanese).

> *I participated in a week-long cross-cultural seminar last summer in which the participants were from a mix of domestic and international cultural groups. On the first day, as an icebreaker, we took turns introducing the person to the left. There were several international students, including an older Japanese woman, who had a little trouble with English. She introduced her partner in halting English but made only one mistake; she said that her partner (a White American woman) was "Native American." She meant to say that her partner was born in America, but her English wasn't quite fluent.*
>
> *Immediately, one of the other members of the group raised her hand and said, "I have an ouch," and proceeded to tell the group how important it was that we be honest and tell others when things were bothering us. She said, further, that it bothered her that this woman had been called a Native American when she was not. She emphasized how important it was that people be labeled accurately. She meant well. But the Japanese woman was mortified. She was embarrassed about her English to begin with, and she was really embarrassed at being singled out as being incorrect in her language. She did not say anything at the time. None of the rest of us in the group knew how distressed she was. As soon as the session was over, she went to the workshop leaders and asked to be transferred out of the group.*
>
> —Mary

divides, we suffer from distorted perception (we don't really know how individuals from other cultures may view us or a particular situation) and a lack of personal growth. On the societal level, when we are not motivated to embrace other cultures and other ways of thinking and behavior, our organizations suffer from a loss of productivity and human potential (not everyone gets the opportunity to contribute ideas).

Third, motivation is lacking in contexts in which historical events or political circumstances have resulted in communication breakdowns. For example, it is understandable, given the history of animosity in the Middle East, that Israeli and Arab students would not be motivated to communicate with each other. It is also understandable why a Serbian student would not want to room with a Croatian student, or why a Greek Cypriot would not want to forge a friendship with a Turkish Cypriot, given that these two ethnic communities have been engaged in one of the most protracted international disputes of all time.

To use an example closer to home, many Blacks and Whites in the United States are not motivated to forge friendships with each other. This may be partly due to social pressure. With regard to cross-race friendships, Mary McCullough (1998) describes the hostile treatment meted out to African Americans and Whites when introducing their cross-race partners and friends:

> *For example, Eileen's father made racist jokes to her, in the absence of her Black friends. . . . Most of the negative feedback comes from Whites, but not all . . . some comes from Black kin and non-kin networks and is directed, again, primarily at Black members. For example, Eleanor's brother-in-law asked, "How can you even think of having a White girl for a friend?" Lana, in her effort to sustain friendship within both Black and White women's groups at college, encountered challenges from her Black sorority sisters about not being Black enough, selling out. (p. 191)*

The point here is that it doesn't matter how good a communicator you are if you are not motivated to use those communication skills. For some people, the first step in developing intercultural communication competence may be to examine their motivation to reach out to others who are culturally different.

Knowledge   The **knowledge** component comprises various cognitive aspects of communication competence; it involves what we know about ourselves and others, and about various aspects of communication. Perhaps most important is **self-knowledge**—knowing how you may be perceived as a communicator and what your strengths and weaknesses are. How can you know what these are? Sometimes you can learn by listening to what others say and by observing how they perceive you. One student describes her attempts to become a better intercultural communicator:

> *Honestly, I feel it begins within yourself. I feel that if each person in our class opens his or her eyes just a little more than what they were before coming into class it will make a difference. This class has really opened my eyes to other people's opinions and feelings.*

Acquiring self-knowledge is a long and sometimes complicated process. It involves being open to information coming in many different ways. A White student describes her growing awareness of what it means to be White in the United States after listening to Chicano and African American guest speakers:

> *They each spoke about their experiences that they have had [with others prejudging them]. . . . We discover our White identity by listening to others. We hear these hardships that they have had to endure and we realize that we never have had to experience that. You learn a lot about yourself that way. . . . By listening to our guests speak today, I realized that sometimes other ethnicities might not view my culture very highly.*

We often don't know how we're perceived because we don't search for this information or because there is not sufficient trust in a relationship for people to reveal such things. Of course, knowledge about how other people think and be-

POINT OF VIEW

In his book *The Rage of a Privileged Class*, Ellis Cose describes the many practical ways in which race affects the everyday lives of people. This excerpt illustrates how difficult it is to know what it's like to be somebody else, because our very knowledge is shaped by our experiences.

> *In the workplace, the continuing relevance of race takes on a special force, partly because so much of life, at least for middle-class Americans, is defined by work, and partly because even people who accept that they will not be treated fairly in the world often hold out hope that their work will be treated fairly — that even a society that keeps neighborhoods racially separate and often makes after-hours social relations awkward will properly reward hard labor and competence. What most African Americans discover, however, is that the racial demons that have plagued them all their lives do not recognize business hours — that the stress of coping extends to a nonwork world that is chronically unwilling (or simply unable) to acknowledge the status their professions ought to confer.*
>
> *The coping effort, in some cases, is relatively minor. It means accepting the fact, for instance, that it is folly to compete for a taxi on a street corner with whites. It means realizing that prudence dictates dressing up whenever you are likely to encounter strangers (including clerks, cops, and doormen) who can make your life miserable by mistaking you for a tramp, a slut, or a crook. And it means tolerating the unctuous boor whose only topic of party conversation is blacks he happens to know. But the price of this continual coping is not insignificant. In addition to creating an unhealthy level of stress, it puts many in such a war state of mind that insults are seen where none were intended, often complicating communications even with sensitive, well-meaning whites who unwittingly stumble into the racial minefield.*

Source: From Ellis Cose, *The Rage of a Privileged Class*, 1993, pp. 55–56.

have will help you be a more effective communicator. However, learning about others in only abstract terms can lead to stereotyping. It is often better to learn through relational experience, as this student did:

> *I know that four or five years ago being gay did not have the same effect on me that it does now. My friend Jack told me a couple of years ago that he was gay, and we have had many discussions on the topic. I have a new understanding of what it means to be gay. A few years ago I didn't take a stance on whether it was right or wrong to be gay, and if anyone made a joke I would laugh. Now that I gained experience from Jack, I respect his way of life and would always support him. This point is valid because the more one experiences things with other people from different backgrounds, the more one will be able to respect and understand other people.*

Of course, we can't know everything about all cultures or develop relationships with people from all cultural groups, so it's important to develop some general knowledge about cultural differences. For example, in this book, we have described cultural variations in both verbal and nonverbal communication. To avoid stereotyping, perhaps it is better simply to be aware of the range in thought and behavior across cultures, and not to assume that, because someone belongs to a particular group, he or she will behave in a particular way. One way to achieve this is to expand our mental "category width," or the range of things we can include in one category. For example, can "snake" be included in the category of "foods" as well as the category of "scary thing to be avoided"? Psychologist Richard Detweiler (1980) measured category width among Peace Corps volunteers and discovered that those with more flexible categories tended to be more successful in their work as volunteers.

Linguistic knowledge is another important aspect of intercultural competence. Awareness of the difficulty of learning a second language helps us appreciate the extent of the challenges that sojourners and immigrants face in their new cultural contexts. Also, knowing a second or third language expands our communication repertoire and increases our empathy for culturally different individuals. For example, as Judith struggles through her conversational Spanish class, she is reminded again of how difficult it is to accomplish ordinary things in a second language. And when she sits in class and worries that the instructor might call on her, she is reminded of the anxiety of many international students and immigrants trying to navigate a new country and language.

Attitudes   Many **attitudes** contribute to intercultural communication competence, including tolerance for ambiguity, empathy, and nonjudgmentalness.

Tolerance for ambiguity refers to the ease in dealing with situations in which much is unknown. Whether we are abroad or at home, interacting with people who look different from us and who behave in ways that are strange to us requires a tolerance for ambiguity. When Judith was studying Spanish in Mexico recently, she was struck by the range of attitudes of her fellow students from the United States. Some seemed very tolerant of the classroom procedures in Mexico, but others seemed to want the classes to be run as they would be in the States.

Tolerance for ambiguity is one of the most difficult things to attain. As mentioned previously, people have a natural preference for predictability; uncertainty can be disquieting. Nick, an exchange student in Mexico, discusses how tolerance and language ability are particularly important—and problematic—in stressful situations:

I had lost my wallet in the marketplace and asked my wife to wire money to me. I couldn't figure out which Western Union location (there are many) I was supposed to go to to pick up my money. I finally went to the central post office, only to be told that my money had been delivered somewhere else—and I couldn't understand where. I was frustrated, tired and worried—and my language skills were deteriorating rapidly! Fortunately, I pulled myself together, tried to be patient,

In his book *Last Watch of the Night*, Paul Monette points out that it is important to recognize the many forms of intolerance most of us experience as we grow up. This excerpt is from a speech he gave at the Library of Congress during National Book Week. The writer he refers to, Urvashi Vaid, is a lesbian who has written about issues of tolerance. Think about how the intolerance around you may affect you and how difficult it is sometimes to be tolerant of the many diversities you encounter.

> *Most of our families do the very best they can to bring us up whole and make us worthy citizens. But it's a very rare person who manages to arrive at adulthood without being saddled by some form of racism or sexism or homophobia. It is our task as grownups to face those prejudices in ourselves and rethink them. The absolute minimum we can get out of such a self-examination is tolerance, one for another. We gay and lesbian people believe we should be allowed to celebrate ourselves and give back to the larger culture, make our unique contributions—but if all we get is tolerance, we'll take it and build on it.*
>
> *We don't know what history is going to say even about this week, or where the gay and lesbian revolution is going to go. But we are a revolution that has come to be based very, very strongly on diversity. We have to fight like everyone else to be open in that diversity; but I love Urvashi Vaid's idea that it's not a matter of there being one of each on every board and every faculty and every organization. It's a matter of being each in one. You'll pardon my French, but it's not so hard to be politically correct. All you have to do is not be an ——.*

Source: From Paul Monette, *Last Watch of the Night*, 1994, pp. 122–123.

and joked with the postal workers. It took six hours to get my money, but by the end of the day, I had my money and had made some new friends at the post office!

Empathy refers to the ability to know what it's like to "walk in another person's shoes." Empathic skills are culture-bound. We cannot really view the world through another person's eyes without knowing something about his or her experiences and life. To illustrate, suppose a U.S. American and a Japanese have been introduced and are conversing. The Japanese responds to the U.S. American's first remark with a giggle. The U.S. American feels pleasurable empathic sensations and makes an impulsive comment, indicating a congenial, accepting reaction. However, the Japanese observer now feels intensely uncomfortable. What the U.S American doesn't realize is that the giggle may not mean that the Japanese is feeling pleasure. Japanese often giggle to indicate embarrassment and unease. In this case, the U.S. American's "empathy" is missing the mark. In this sense, empathy is the capacity to imagine oneself in another role, within the context of one's cultural identity.

Intercultural communication scholars have attempted to come up with a more culturally sensitive view of empathy. For example, Ben Broome (1991, 1993) stresses that, in order to achieve empathy across cultural boundaries, people must forge strong relationships and strive for the creation of shared meaning in their interpersonal encounters. However, because this is difficult to achieve when people come from very different cultural backgrounds, Broome suggests that this shared meaning must be seen as both provisional and dynamic, that understanding is not an all-or-nothing proposition. In addition, cross-cultural empathy must integrate both thinking and feeling—we must try to understand not only what others *say* (content) but also how they *feel* (empathy). Finally, he reminds us that to achieve cross-cultural empathy we must seek to understand the context of both others' lived experiences and the specific encounters.

Magoroh Maruyama (1970), an anthropologist-philosopher, agrees that achieving cross-cultural empathy and trying to see the world exactly as the other person sees is very difficult. She describes the process as **transpection,** a postmodern phenomenon that often involves trying to learn foreign beliefs, assumptions, perspectives, and feelings in a foreign context. Transpection, then, can be achieved only with practice and requires structured experience and self-reflection.

Communication scholar Milton Bennett (1998) suggests a "Platinum Rule" ("Do unto others as *they themselves* would have done unto them") instead of the Golden Rule ("Do unto others as *you* would have done unto you") (p. 213). This, of course, requires movement beyond a culture-bound sympathy or empathy for others.

Achieving **nonjudgmentalism** is much easier said than done. We might like to think that we do not judge others according to our own cultural frames of reference, but it is very difficult. One of our colleagues recalls being at a university meeting at which a group of Icelandic administrators and a group of U.S. American faculty were discussing implementing a study-abroad exchange program. The Icelandic faculty were particularly taciturn, and our colleague wanted to lighten up the meeting a little. Eventually, however, she realized that the taciturnity probably reflected different norms of behavior. She had unknowingly judged the tenor of the meeting based on her own style of communication.

The **D.I.E. exercise** is helpful in developing a nonjudgmental attitude (Wendt, 1984). It involves making a distinction between description (D), interpretation (I), and evaluation (E) in the processing of information. Descriptive statements convey factual information that can be verified through the senses (e.g., "There are 25 chairs in the room" and "I am 5 feet tall"). Interpretive statements attach meaning to the description (e.g., "You must be tired"). Evaluative statements clarify how we feel about something (e.g., "When you're always tired, we can't have any fun together"). Only descriptive statements are nonjudgmental.

This exercise can help us recognize whether we are processing information on a descriptive, interpretive, or evaluative level. Confusing the different levels can lead to misunderstanding and ineffective communication. For example, if I think a student is standing too close to me, I may interpret the behavior as "This student is pushy," or I may evaluate it as "This student is pushy, and I don't like pushy students." However, if I force myself to describe the student's behavior, I may say to myself, "This student is standing 8 inches away from me, whereas most students stand farther away." This observation enables me to search for other (perhaps cultural) reasons for the behavior. The student may be worried about a grade and may be anxious to get some questions answered. Perhaps the student is used to standing closer to people than I am. Or perhaps the student really is pushy.

It is impossible to always stay at the descriptive level. But it is important to know when we are describing and when we are interpreting. Most communication is at the interpretive level. For example, have you ever been set up for a blind date and asked for a description of the person? The descriptions you might get (e.g., tall, dark, handsome, nice, kind, generous) are not really descriptions; rather, they are interpretations that reflect individual and cultural viewpoints (Wendt, 1984).

Behaviors and Skills   Behaviors and skills are another component of intercultural competence. What are the most competent behaviors? Are there any universal behaviors that work well in all cultural contexts? At one level, there probably are. Communication scholar Brent D. Ruben devised a list of universal behaviors that actually includes some attitudes. These behaviors are a display of respect, interaction management, ambiguity tolerance, empathy, relational rather than task behavior, and interaction posture (Ruben, 1976, 1977; Ruben & Kealey, 1979).

Some general behaviors seem applicable to many cultural groups and contexts (Koester & Olebe, 1988; Olebe & Koester, 1989). However, these skills become problematic when we try to apply them in specific ways. For example, being respectful works well in all intercultural interactions, and many scholars identify this particular skill as important (Collier, 1988; Martin & Hammer, 1989). However, how one expresses respect behaviorally may vary from culture to culture and from context to context. For example, European Americans show respect by making direct eye contact, whereas some Native Americans show respect by avoiding eye contact.

In one research project, we asked European American and Chicano students to identify nonverbal behaviors that they thought would be seen as competent. They identified some of the same behaviors (smiling, direct eye contact, nice appearance, and so on), but they assigned different levels of importance to various behaviors depending on the context (Martin, Hammer, & Bradford, 1994). There seem to be two levels of behavioral competence. The macro level includes many culture-general behaviors, such as be respectful, show interest, act friendly, and be polite. Then there is the micro level, at which these general behaviors are implemented in culture-specific ways.

It is important to be aware of these different levels of behaviors and be able to adapt to them. Let's see how this works. In one study, Mitch Hammer and his colleagues evaluated the effectiveness of a cross-cultural training program for Japanese and U.S. American managers in a joint venture (a steel company) in Ohio. One goal was to determine if the managers' intercultural communication skills had improved significantly. The research team used a general behavioral framework of communication competence that included the following dimensions: immediacy, involvement, other orientation, interaction management, and social relaxation (Hammer, Martin, Otani, & Koyama, 1990). The two groups (Japanese managers and U.S. American managers) rated these dimensions differently. The U.S. Americans said that the most important dimension was involvement (how expressive one is in conversation), whereas the Japanese managers said that the other orientation (being tuned in to the other person) was most important. The researchers also judged how well each group of managers adapted to the other group's communication style. They videotaped the interaction and asked Japanese raters to judge the U.S. American managers on how well they adapted to the Japanese style, and vice versa. For example, good interaction management for the Japanese meant initiating and terminating interaction, and making sure everyone had a chance to talk; for U.S. Americans, it meant asking opinions of the Japanese, being patient with silence, and avoiding strong disagreement and assertive statements. As this example shows, intercultural communication competence means being able to exhibit or adapt to different kinds of behaviors, depending on the other person's or group's cultural background.

William Howell (1982), a renowned intercultural scholar, investigated how top CEOs made decisions. He found, to his surprise, that they did not follow the analytic process prescribed in business school courses—analysis of cost, benefits, and so on. Rather, they made decisions in a very holistic way. That is, they reflected on the problem and talked about it with their friends and counterparts in other companies, then they would ignore the problem for a while, coming back to it when their minds were fresh to frame the answer. Howell emphasized that intercultural communication is similar, that only so much can be gained by conscious analysis, and that the highest level of communication competence requires a combination of holistic and analytic thinking. He identified four levels of intercultural communication competence: (1) unconscious incompetence, (2) conscious incompetence, (3) conscious competence, and (4) unconscious competence.

Unconscious incompetence is the "be ourself" approach, in which we are not conscious of differences and do not need to act in any particular way. Sometimes this works. However, being ourselves works best in interactions with individuals who are very similar to us. In intercultural contexts, being ourselves often means that we're not very effective and don't realize our ineptness.

At the level of **conscious incompetence,** people realize that things may not be going very well in the interaction, but they are not sure why. Most of us have experienced intercultural interactions in which we felt that something wasn't quite right but couldn't quite figure out what it was. This describes the feeling of conscious incompetence.

As instructors of intercultural communication, we teach at a conscious, intentional level. Our instruction focuses on analytic thinking and learning. This describes the level of **conscious competence.** Reaching this level is a necessary part of the process of becoming a competent communicator. Howell would say that reaching this level is necessary but not sufficient.

POINT OF VIEW

In this essay, S. L. Rosen discusses the powerful stereotyping (or essentializing) of Asian people—referred to as Orientalism. By way of illustration, he analyzes a description of Japanese taken from a travelers' guidebook.

Orientalism is a total misseeing of the other through a veil of interpretations of reality which are relatively impenetrable and resistant to change. . . . Orientalism as cultural myth has been articulated through metaphors which characterize the East in ways which emphasize its strangeness and otherness . . . the Oriental person is a single image, a sweeping generalization; an essentialized image which carries with it the taint of inferiority.

To give one powerful example of this essentializing process of image formation which is entailed by Orientalism, we quote from a book entitled When Cultures Collide *by Richard D. Lewis (1982), a kind of manual for people traveling and doing business around the world to help them understand the various cultures they come in contact with. By no means the worst of its kind, Lewis' book expresses very well the way we use metaphors to trivialize another culture in a totalistic way, so as to make it easier to capture it in the network of our own understandings.*

- Japanese children are encouraged to be completely dependent and keep a sense of interdependence throughout their lives.

- Everything must be placed in context in Japan.

- Japanese are constrained by their thought processes in a language very different from any other.

- They do not like meeting newcomers.

- They represent their group and cannot therefore pronounce on any matters without consultation and cannot initiate an exchange of views.

- Westerners are individuals, but the Japanese represent a company which represents Japan.

- As we all know, Japanese do not like to lose face.

- The Japanese go to incredible lengths to be polite. . . .

This kind of Orientalism [essentializing] carries with it the implication that Asian people are much more conformist than we are, and less respecting of the dignity of individual rights, i.e., inferior. Social and cognitive psychology tells us that stereotyping is a kind of mental schema making designed to help us grasp reality—to make things more understandable and less threatening; these mental schema such as stereotypes provide us with the illusion of understanding by dividing up and categorizing the flux of experience into easily manageable cognitive maps. Orientalism has been the prevalent mode by which this cognitive need to schematize has manifested itself in apprehending Asian people.

Source: From S. L. Rosen, "Japan as Other: Orientalism and Cultural Conflict," *Intercultural Communication, 4,* 2000. www.immi.se/intercultural

Unconscious competence is the level at which communication goes smoothly but is not a conscious process. You've probably heard of marathon runners "hitting the wall," or reaching the limits of their endurance. Usually, inexplicably, they continue running past this point. Communication at the unconscious competent level is like this. This level of competence is not something we can acquire by consciously trying to. It occurs when the analytic and holistic parts are functioning together. When we concentrate too hard or get too analytic, things don't always go easier.

Have you ever prepared for an interview by trying to anticipate every question and forming every answer, and then not done very well? This silent rehearsing—worrying and thinking too hard—is called the "internal monologue." According to Howell, people should avoid this extraneous and obstructive activity, which *prevents* them from being successful communicators (Howell, 1979). You've also probably had the experience of trying unsuccessfully to recall something, letting go of it, and then remembering it as soon as you're thinking about something else. This is what unconscious competence is—being well prepared cognitively and attitudinally, but knowing when to "let go" and rely on your holistic cognitive processing.

Contextual Components

As we have stressed throughout this book, an important aspect of being a competent communicator is understanding the context in which communication occurs. Intercultural communication happens in many contexts. An interpretive perspective reminds us that a good communicator is sensitive to these contexts. (See Figure 12-1.)

We have emphasized that *many* contexts can influence intercultural communication. For instance, by focusing only on the historical context, you may overlook the relational context; by emphasizing the cultural context, you may be ignoring the gender or racial contexts of the intercultural interaction; and so on. It may seem difficult to keep all of these shifting contexts in mind. However, by analyzing your own intercultural successes and failures, you will come to a better understanding of intercultural communication.

Another aspect of context is the communicator's position within a speech community. Reflect on your own social position in relation to various speech communities and contexts. For example, if you are the only woman in a largely male environment, or the only person of color in an otherwise White community, you may face particular expectations or have people project motivations onto your messages. Recognizing your own relation to the speech community and the context will help you better understand intercultural communication.

A critical perspective reminds us that individuals' competence may be constrained by the political, economic, and historical contexts. Intercultural communication scholar Mary Jane Collier (1998) reflects:

> *I have come to see that competence, a central issue in my early work, is a construct that is based on implicit privilege. . . . Relevant questions from postcolonial critics*

FIGURE 12-1   These people are preparing food for the elderly as part of a "Meals on Wheels" program. Work settings such as this often provide opportunities for multicultural interaction and the chance to form intercultural alliances. How do these interactions help one become a better intercultural communicator? (© *Bob Daemmrich/ Getty Images*)

include, "Competence and acceptance from whom? Who decides the criteria? Who doesn't? Competent or acceptable on the basis of what social and historical context?" (p. 142)

For example, characteristics of effective communication for women in the United States have changed dramatically in the last 50 years. In the 1960s, an "effective" female communicator was expected to be rather passive (both verbally and nonverbally), indirect, and nurturing. Assertive women met with disapproval and sanctions. Today, the "effective" female is expected to behave rather differently from this. As the 21st century unfolds, there is a broader range of acceptable behaviors that define competence for females. They may be unassertive in some contexts, but they are also free, and even expected, to be more assertive in many contexts. Similarly, effective Black communicators in the 1960s were expected to be nonassertive in verbal and nonverbal style. Blacks like Muhammad Ali who went against these expectations were severely sanctioned. In short, we need to understand that notions of communication competence depend on specific social, political, and historical contexts. And we need to question who is setting these standards.

These are important questions raised by the critical perspective that force us to rethink intercultural communication competence. Indeed, you now have the skills to push your own thinking about intercultural communication—both strengths and weaknesses—as it helps and hinders your ability to communicate.

APPLYING KNOWLEDGE ABOUT INTERCULTURAL COMMUNICATION

Now that we have taken you down the path of intercultural communication, we would like to conclude with specific suggestions for becoming better intercultural communicators. Our dialectical approach recognizes the important role of individual skills *and* contextual constraints in improving intercultural relations. The dialectical perspective also emphasizes the relational aspects of intercultural communication. Perhaps the first step in applying our knowledge to intercultural communication is to recognize the connectedness of humans and the importance of dialogue.

Entering Into Dialogue

In order to recognize and embrace our connectedness even to people who are different from us, we have to engage in true dialogue. True dialogue is different from conversation, which can be one-sided, strident, and ego focused. "True dialogue is characterized by authenticity, inclusion, confirmation, presentness, spirit of mutual equality, and supportive climate" (Stewart, 1997, p. 120). What does this mean for intercultural communicators? Authenticity means that we approach others knowing ourselves, recognizing our social location, and admitting that we might be uneasy or make mistakes in intercultural interactions (or that we might be racist). True dialogue reflects feelings of mutual equality and supportiveness. This means that we promote reciprocity and solicit equal contributions from all. It's not a one-sided conversation.

But how can we *really* hear the voices of those who come from cultures very different from our own—and especially those who have not been heard from? As you think about all the messages you hear every day, the most obvious voices and images are often the most privileged. To resist the tendency to focus only on the loudest, most obvious voices, we should strive for "harmonic discourse." This is discourse in which all voices "retain their individual integrity, yet combine to form a whole discourse that is orderly and congruous" (Stewart, 1997, p. 119).

Any conciliation between cultures must reclaim the notion of a voice for *all* interactants. In intercultural contexts, there are two options for those who feel left out—exit or expression. When people feel excluded, they often simply shut down, physically or mentally abandoning the conversation. When this happens, their potential contributions—to some decision, activity, or change—are lost. Obviously, the preferred alternative is to give voice to them. People's silence is broken when they feel that they can contribute, that their views are valued. And those who have historically been silenced sometimes need an invitation. Or those who have a more reserved conversation style may need prompting, as was the case with this traveler from Finland:

> *I was on a business trip in England with some colleagues. We visited universities, where we were shown different departments and their activities. The presenters*

There are many small interventions we might make in everyday life to change what we take for granted. Note how this student has learned to use intercultural relationships as a part of her antiracism struggle.

> *I am beginning to see the long-term benefits of intercultural relationships: acquiring knowledge about the world, breaking stereotypes, and acquiring new skills. I did not have any stereotypes of Brazilians before I met Anna, but I tell all my family and friends about her, so if any of them had any prior stereotypes, they may think differently now. I have also found that when you are friends with a person of a different culture, it tends to promote some sort of peace and unity in some small way. If I am with someone of a different culture, people are less likely to make racial remarks of any kind in front of them. For example, a coworker of mine often tells jokes about gay or Black people in front of workers that are White and seemingly heterosexual. When I bring a friend into work or go out with work friends that are of a different culture (Spanish, Ukrainian, or Brazilian), he will not tell these jokes. Although my friends are not even of the culture that he makes fun of, I think he is not sure of how his jokes will go over with people he sees as being "ethnic." Regardless, the jokes stop, and that is a step toward preventing racial discrimination.*
>
> —Michele

spoke volubly, and we, in accordance with Finnish speaking rules, waited for our turn in order to make comments and ask questions. However, we never got a turn; neither had we time to react to the situations.

In sum, one way to become a more competent communicator is to work on "dialogue" skills by trying to engage in true dialogue. It's important to work on speaking and listening skills. A second step is to become interpersonal allies with people from other cultures.

Becoming Interpersonal Allies

The dialectical approach involves becoming allies with others, in working for better intergroup relations. But we need a new way to think about multiculturalism and cultural diversity—one that recognizes the complexities of communicating across cultures and that addresses power issues. Otherwise, we can get stuck within a competitive framework: If we win something, the other person or group loses, and we can *only* win if others lose. This kind of thinking can make us feel frustrated and guilty.

The goal is to find a way in which we can achieve equitable unity despite holding many different and contradictory truths, a unity based on conscious

In outlining specific ways in which White people can fight racism, Paul Kivel lists questions they can ask to better understand specific contexts in which they live and work.

Workplace

1. What is the gender, race and class composition in your workplace? Which groups hold which positions?

2. Who, by race, gender and class, has the power to make decisions about hiring, firing, wages and working conditions in your workplace? Who gets promoted and who doesn't?

3. Is hiring non-discriminatory? Are job openings posted and distributed? Do they attract a wide variety of applicants? Are certain groups excluded? Does the diversity of your workplace reflect the diversity of the wider community?

4. Are there "invisible" workers, people who cook, clean or do maintenance, for example, who are not generally noticed or paid well?

5. What is the racial composition of the people who actually own your workplace? Who makes money from the profits of your work?

Religion

1. What is your religious upbringing?

2. What did you learn about people of color in Sunday school or sermons? About Jewish people?

3. Was your religious community all white? Was the leadership of your religious organization all white?

coalition, a unity of affinity and political kinship, in which we all win. Paul Kivel (1996) suggests a "both/and" dialectic:

> *In this framework we assume that the needs and perspectives of different parties are not necessarily conflicting. Using this approach allows us to embrace both sides' perspectives and draw up a solution that includes elements of each. . . . There may be as many "truths" as there are people or groups involved in the process. There is usually common ground on which we can build our decisions. Finding that common ground needs to be a process in which everyone is included. . . . In a democratic multicultural process, everyone is included. [This] takes time, inclusion and more complex decision-making processes than most of us are used to participating in. (pp. 204–205)*

How can we do this? We first identify what **intercultural alliances** might look like. Communication scholar Mary Jane Collier (1998) interviewed many

4. What attitudes were expressed about people of color through discussion of missionary work, charity or social problems?

5. What do you know about the history of resistance to racism in your religious denomination?

Home and Family

1. Were people of color and racism talked about in your childhood home? Think about particular incidents when it was. Was there tension around it? What was the general tone? Who initiated discussions and who resisted them?

2. Was there silence in your home on issues of racism or anti-Semitism? What did you learn from the silence?

3. As a child, what stories, TV shows or books influenced you the most in your attitudes about people of color? What do you carry with you from that exposure?

4. Talk with your partner, housemates and friends about [racial] issues. Notice the whiteness of your surroundings out loud to family and friends. This needn't be done aggressively or with great anger. You don't need to attack other people. Ask questions, notice things out loud, express your concerns and give other people room to think about and respond to what you say.

5. If you did a room-by-room assessment of your home today, would you find a diversity of images and items? If the answer is no, what do you and other family members lose because of that lack? How does it contribute to racial prejudice and discrimination?

Source: From Paul Kivel, *Uprooting Racism: How White People Can Work for Racial Justice*, 1996, pp. 182–183, 199, 222.

people in intercultural friendships and identified three issues that characterize intercultural alliances. The first has to do with power and privilege: Intercultural friends recognize and try to understand how ethnic, gender, and class differences lead to power and try to manage these power issues.

Communication scholar Karen L. Dace (1994) describes how difficult it is to understand power issues in interracial relationships. Her findings are based on observation of a semester-long interracial discussion group at her university. She describes how difficult it was for the students to discuss the topic openly and honestly. Although the White students quizzed the Black students about their attitudes and experiences, they didn't really want honest answers from them:

Much of the discussion involved talking about interactions African-American students had with European-American students and faculty members. On several occasions, the African-American students talked about being excluded from activities.

> *For example, . . . [they talked about] being told not to pledge during a European-American sorority rush, being the only African-American member of a small class at the university and the only person in the class not invited to a party thrown by another classmate. Still others talked about what they perceived to be racist comments made during lectures by some faculty members. (p. 23)*

Dace observes that in most cases the White students suggested that these experiences were not "reality" and asked the African American students to "prove" that they had actually experienced racism. People who have not often experienced feelings of powerlessness or been discriminated against have a hard time recognizing their impact.

Being on two different sides of the power issue can challenge individuals in intercultural relationships. For example, Eleanor, an African American woman, and her friend Mairead, who is White, describe how they negotiate this issue in their own relationship. Often the only African American participating in discussions of race, Eleanor says she gets tired of "educating white girls" about racism. Mairead recognizes the problem of unwittingly saying or doing racist things and "hurting my friend." This is not merely a matter of benign faux pas, but is an ongoing source of oppression for Black women, something with far deeper implications than simply saying the right thing in a social situation involving equals (McCullough, 1998, p. 83). Eleanor sometimes needs to withdraw from her White friends to restore herself. For her part, Mairead recognizes that she needs to educate herself about issues of racism. And the two women realize that negotiating time-out from a friendship or time to work on personal issues alone is one aspect of intercultural friendship in a racially segregated society.

Collier's (1998) second component of intercultural alliances has to do with the impact of history: Intercultural friends recognize that people from historically powerful groups view history differently than do those who belong to less powerful groups. As we learned in Chapter 4, history often plays an important part in intercultural interactions. One of our colleagues describes how she and her friend Michael had very different views on history:

> *I was always amazed at how often my friend Michael talked about his relatives' experience during the Holocaust—even though his family wasn't directly involved. He was constantly told as he was growing up that prejudice against Jews could easily lead to another holocaust—and that he always had to be vigilant against anti-Semitism. For me, not being Jewish, I used to get impatient with him, but after learning more about the history and getting to know Michael better, I realize that this is an important part of who he is, and I've actually learned a lot from him about the experiences of a group of people that I knew little about. And I appreciate that side of him better.*

History also plays a part in Black–White relationships. We're often struck by how, in discussions about race in our classes, White students go to great lengths to affirm that they aren't racist, often telling stories about friends and family members—who, unlike them, are racist. They seem to want to be absolved of past or present responsibilities where race was concerned. And Whites expect persons of color to communicate in ways that are friendly, comfortable, and absolving. In this case, true dialogue for Whites involves a genuine commitment to listening, to not being defensive, and to recognizing the historical contexts that impact us all. True intercultural friends accept rather than question others' experiences, particularly when historical inequities and power issues are involved. They recognize the importance of historical power differentials and affirm others' cultural experiences even when this calls into question their own worldviews.

Collier's (1998) third component of intercultural alliances has to do with orientations of affirmation: Intercultural friends value and appreciate differences and are committed to the relationship even when they encounter difficulties and misunderstandings. For example, our student Shara comes from a cultural background that emphasizes commitment to family and family obligations. Her friend Kati has very little contact with her parents and siblings. They aren't estranged; they just aren't close. Kati would like to spend time with Shara on holidays, but Shara always spends holidays with her family, who live in another state. This issue has caused tension between the two over the years. But they each realize that these different values are important aspects of their identities. And in complex and dialectical ways, they learn from each other. Shara sometimes envies Kati for her relative freedom and lack of family obligations. But she also feels sorry for Kati that she doesn't have the kind of family support to back her up when she needs help. Similarly, Kati envies Shara's relationships with her large, extended family and all the activities and help they provide. But she also sometimes feels sorry for Shara that she never seems to have any time for herself.

What are some specific communication strategies people can use in becoming allies? Paul Kivel (1996) lists suggestions that people of color have given to White people who want to be allies. Note that some of the suggestions are contradictory, underscoring a dialectical perspective. Being an ally requires that we learn to speak up *and* listen.

> *Find out about us.*
> *Don't take over.*
> *Speak up.*
> *Provide information.*
> *Take risks.*
> *Don't take it personally.*
> *Understanding.*
> *Don't make assumptions.*
> *Don't assume you know what's best for me.*
> *Talk to other white people.*
> *Interrupt jokes and comments.*
> *Don't ask me to speak for my people. (p. 102)*

Similarly, Beverly Tatum (1997) gives some guidelines for people who want to engage in cross-cultural dialogue. She suggests that they look for role models—those who are effective intercultural communicators. One of Judith's role models is Amalia, a director of a learning center, a multicultural setting in a relatively

Yom Kippur is a Jewish holiday focused on themes of repentance and a return to the faith. The following Yom Kippur prayer shows the importance of being willing to transform and forgive, to adopt a new view toward others.

ON TURNING

Now is the time for turning. The leaves are beginning to turn from green to red to orange. The birds are beginning to turn and are heading once more toward the south. The animals are beginning to turn to storing their food for the winter.

For leaves, birds and animals turning comes instinctively, but for us, turning does not come so easily.

It takes an act of will for us to make a turn. It means breaking old habits. It means admitting that we have been wrong, and this is never easy. It means losing face. It means saying I am sorry. It means recognizing that we have the ability to change. These things are terribly hard to do.

But unless we turn, we will be trapped forever in yesterday's ways. Lord help us to turn—from callousness to sensitivity, from hostility to love, from pettiness to purpose, from envy to contentment, from carelessness to discipline, from fear to faith.

Turn us around, oh, Lord, and bring us back toward You. Revive our lives at the beginning. And turn us toward each other, Lord, for in isolation, there is no life.

Source: From: H. Henderson, *Forgiveness: Breaking the Chain of Hate*, 1999, p. 177.

poor town in Arizona. Although Amalia is highly educated and extremely competent, she is humble and works tirelessly to promote dialogue among various ethnic groups in Arizona. She accepts people whatever their social station or economic location. And she follows Tatum's second guideline, which is that people should work in whatever sphere they can. Amalia certainly influences the people who are around her. For your part, you might not be able to influence public policy or promote grandiose schemes to facilitate intercultural dialogue, but you can influence the people around you to adopt the principles of effective intercultural communication.

Building Coalitions

As we have emphasized throughout this book, there are many identities and contexts that give meaning to who you really are. That is, your identities of gender, sexual orientation, race, region, religion, age, social class, and so on gain specific meaning and force in different contexts. Coalitions can arise from these multiple identities. There are many good examples, such as the Seeds of Peace project, which brings together Jewish and Palestinian young people to work toward peace and harmony. Other local coalitions work to promote dialogue between Blacks and Whites, and between gays and straights.

Consider the following example: A group of plantation owners in Hawaii felt that they could resist a workers' alliance by continually hiring workers from different ethnic groups. These ethnic groups, they reasoned, would be too busy with interethnic conflicts to organize any kind of intercultural coalition to challenge the labor system. Ethnic studies historian Ronald Takaki (1983) explains:

> *In order to control a wage-earning working class, planters imported laborers from different countries and created a multiethnic work force. They ethnically diversified and divided the working class, pitting different groups of workers against each other. Eventually, however, laborers of different nationalities began to develop a new consciousness and an understanding of the need for a new politics which transcended ethnicity. (p. 162)*

Some contexts that arise in the future may cause you to rethink many of your identities. The rhetoric that people use to mobilize coalitions may speak to you in various ways. As you strive to build better intercultural relations, you may need to transcend some of your identities, as the workers in Hawaii did, or you may reinforce other identities. These shifting identities allow you to build coalitions among seemingly different peoples, to foster positive intercultural relationships for a better world.

Coalitions, which are built of multiple identities, are never easy to build. In the process, you may find that some of your own identities feel neglected or injured. Part of the process is the commitment to work through these emotional blows, rather than simply withdrawing to the safety of older identities. Work your way to a richer, more meaningful life by navigating between safety and stability, and change.

Forgiveness and Transformation

Sometimes the cultural divide simply seems too huge. Sometimes there are grievances perpetrated by one cultural group upon another or by one individual on another that are so brutal as to make the suggestions listed above sound hollow and idealistic. What can we say to the widow of Daniel Pearl, the *Wall Street Journal* writer who was brutally murdered in Pakistan? He and his wife were known for promoting intercultural understanding in their personal and professional lives. Or to Pauline Mitchell, the mother of Fred Martinez, a Native American who was brutally murdered because he was *nadleeh* (a Native American term meaning "two spirited—with spirit of both male and female"). His mother described the horror of his death: "He'd been chased, beaten with a rock. He had been left to bleed, with a fractured skull, alone in the dark in a little canyon. . . ."

POINT OF VIEW

In this essay, the writer addresses the complexities of the notion of forgiveness. He begins the essay talking about the delayed justice in the case of the 1958 bombing of the Black church in Birmingham, Alabama, that killed four little girls. Roy Wilkins, a long-time civil rights advocate, has always been a firm believer in the merits of forgiveness.

But events like the bombing in Birmingham help Mr. Wilkins recognize the limitations of forgiveness. In some cases, people can free their hearts of hatred without forgiving. Birmingham, he said, might be one of those cases. "I really don't think it is necessary to forgive every act," he said. "Where forgiveness applies to the Birmingham situation is what has happened in that city, and this is that blacks, by and large, have entered in the life of the city and they don't hold Bull Connor against white people who live in the city." A more personal forgiveness is made difficult in Birmingham because the killers have not sought it; Mr. Cherry denied his guilt even after the verdict. "There has to be some show of respect or remorse," said Mr. Jones, the prosecutor. "For there to be true forgiveness, it has to come from both sides."

Yet that did not happen, at least at first, in the case of Amy Biehl, a Fulbright scholar from Southern California who was stoned and stabbed to death in South Africa in 1993. Her killing stunned that country, but more shocking for many people was the forgiving response of her parents, Peter J. and Linda Biehl.

The Biehls quit their jobs to work full time on racial reconciliation. They testified in favor of political amnesty for the killers. They even offered two of them jobs. "To us it is liberating to forgive," Mr. Biehl, who died on March 31, once said.

At the time, Biehl's crusade seemed preposterous, almost beyond human. But that view changed in the past decade as forgiveness evolved into a

We would like to return to the notion of forgiveness that we introduced in Chapter 11. Although limited and problematic, forgiveness is an option for promoting intercultural understanding and reconciliation. As we noted, forgiveness is more than a simple rite of religious correctness; it requires a deep intellectual and emotional commitment during moments of great pain. It also requires a letting go, a moving on, a true transformation of spirit. Dean Murphy (2002), writing in the *New York Times*, reports how scholars, leaders, and other individuals live out the concept of forgiveness. One example is Archbishop Desmond Tutu, the Nobel Laureate and chairman of South Africa's Truth and Reconciliation Commission, and an advocate of forgiveness. He puts it in the context of the African concept of *ubuntu*—that a person is only a person through other people. Again, the importance of human connection and relationships emerges. Tutu

more mainstream tool of holistic healing, conflict resolution and self-help. . . . The Rev. Michael Lapsley, who was an anti-apartheid activist, talked about Sept. 11 forgiveness on a recent visit to New York. He is familiar with the notion of the facelessness of some evildoers—when he was a chaplin for the African National Congress he lost an eye and both hands after he opened an anonymous letter bomb in 1990.

Forgiveness, Father Lapsley says, is a matter of choice, and since the American government ultimately responded militarily to the terror attacks, many Americans never examined any alternative. Yet because so many world-wide shared in America's horror and grief over Sept. 11, he explained, "Your pain has been acknowledged. That gives you freedom to take a position away from war and hatred and revenge."

But what about hunting down the perpetrators? What about justice?

In June, the Rev. Myrna Bethke, a member of the September Eleventh Families for Peaceful Tomorrows, will travel to Kabul with an interfaith delegation. Ms. Bethke, a Methodist minister in Freehold, N. J., had a brother who was killed at the World Trade Center.

She says she has forgiven his killers, but makes a distinction between retaliation, which she is against, and consequences, which she is for. She is going to Kabul in part to help remind herself that the people there have names and faces—making it harder to want to retaliate against them.

Forgiving her brother's killing, she says, released her from a tremendous burden. "You are free to live again," Ms. Bethke said.

Source: From Dean Murphy, "Beyond Justice: The Eternal Struggle to Forgive," *New York Times*, May 26, 2002, Section 4, p. 1.

says that forgiveness can be seen as an act of self-interest, because forgivers are released from the bonds that hold them captive to the forgiven. (See Figure 12-2.)

And many have stressed this aspect—that people can't be consumed by the wrongs that others have done to them, because then their oppressors have won. According to civil rights advocate Roger Wilkins, "If you are consumed by rage, even at a terrible wrong, you have been reduced" (quoted in Murphy, 2002, p. 1). Religious and medical professionals also advocate the healing benefits of forgiveness.

Forgiveness has been likened to a train. People get on the train but must make various stops before forgiveness becomes a way off. The trick is not to miss your stop. And perhaps we might remember these cautionary words from Philip Yancy, an award-winning Christian author who writes about grace and

FIGURE 12-2   After the end of apartheid in
South Africa, the Truth and Reconciliation Commission (TRC) set up hearings to examine human rights
abuses under apartheid and open up the past to reexamination. Crowds in this photo are cheering as
former President P. W. Botha is found guilty of con-
tempt for ignoring a summons to testify about the
State Security Council. Many White South Africans
were shocked by the revelations made by the TRC.
How might forgiveness function to overcome this
horrible past, including torture, murders, and other
human rights violations revealed by these hearings?
(© *Reuters/Getty Images*)

forgiveness in the face of atrocities and brutality: "The only thing harder than
forgiveness is the alternative" (quoted in Henderson, 1999, p. 176).

WHAT THE FUTURE HOLDS

We live in exciting times. The world is changing rapidly, but not necessarily in
a positive direction for intercultural relations. We see a move toward larger political entities, such as the European Union (EU). This relatively new political

giant has even adopted a single currency, the euro. The population and economic power of the EU surpasses that of the United States, and the EU has standardized many regulations among its member states. Yet the unification of much of Europe has not led to a strong European identity. Instead, there has been a retreat to earlier, regional identities. France offers one example of such a retreat, as the national identity is challenged by the resurgence of regional identities conquered in the past (Touraine, Dubet, Hegedus, & Wieviorka, 1981).

The appearance of regional dictionaries, the upsurge in folk celebrations, and the continual resurgence of small subnational identities has the potential to diversify Europe. Will these movements lead to a stronger Europe, or will they degrade into a series of conflicts, similar to what has happened in the former Yugoslavia?

And, of course, there is the ongoing struggle between fundamentalist Islamic groups and many national governments. The struggle has been variously characterized as a clash of civilizations, a struggle between religions, and an uprising of the Middle East against the cultural imperialism of the West. In any case, it is hard to know how to view this struggle from an intercultural communication perspective.

There are no easy answers to what the future holds. But it is important to think dialectically about these issues, to see the dialectical tensions at work throughout the world. For example, a fractured, fragmented Europe is in dialectical tension with a unified Europe. We can see the history/past–present/future dialectic at work here: The fragmented Europe returns to its historical roots, but the unified Europe represents a forward-looking attempt to deal with the global economy. As a unifying force, a global economy also creates fragmentation.

The task of this book has been to help you begin to think dialectically, to begin to see the many contradictions and tensions at work in the world. Understanding these contradictions and tensions is key to understanding the events themselves. We acknowledge that there are no easy answers to the challenge of intercultural communication, but we hope that we have given you the groundwork to begin your own intercultural journeys.

Continue to push yourself to see the complexities of life, and you will have taken an important step toward successful intercultural communication. Have the confidence to engage in intercultural communication, but be aware that there is always more to learn.

SUMMARY

In this chapter, we focused on the outlook for intercultural communication. The individual components of intercultural communication competence include motivation, knowledge, attitudes, behaviors, and skills. The levels of competence are unconscious incompetence, conscious incompetence, conscious competence, and unconscious competence. Competence has interpretive and critical contextual components, and contexts are both dynamic and multiple. One approach to improving intercultural relations recognizes both individual and contextual elements of competence: entering into dialogue, building alliances and coalitions, and, finally, recognizing the importance of forgiveness and transformation.

DISCUSSION QUESTIONS

1. In what ways is the notion of intercultural competence helpful? In what ways is it limiting?

2. How can you be an interpersonal ally? How do you know if you are being an ally?

3. How might you better assess your unconscious competence and unconscious incompetence?

4. How might the European Union affect the United States?

5. How does your own social position (gender, class, age, and so on) influence your intercultural communication competence? Does this competence change from one context to another?

 Go to the self-quizzes on the Online Learning Center at www.mhhe.com/martinnakayama to further test your knowledge.

ACTIVITIES

1. *Global Trends and Intercultural Communication.* Identify and list global trends that are likely to influence intercultural communication in the future. Reflect on the contexts and dialectics that might help you better understand these trends.

2. *Roadblocks to Communication.* Identify and list some of the biggest roadblocks to successful intercultural communication in the future. In what ways will the increasingly global economy be a positive or negative factor in intercultural communication?

3. *Strategies for Becoming Allies.* In a dialogue with someone who is culturally different from you, generate a list of ways that each of you might become an ally of the other. Note the specific communication strategies that will help you become each other's allies.

KEY WORDS

attitudes	knowledge	transpection
conscious competence	linguistic knowledge	unconscious
conscious incompetence	motivation	competence
D.I.E. exercise	nonjudgmentalism	unconscious
empathy	self-knowledge	incompetence
intercultural alliances	tolerance for ambiguity	

 The Online Learning Center at www.mhhe.com/martinnakayama features flashcards and crossword puzzles based on these terms and concepts.

REFERENCES

Arnett, R. C. (1997). Communication and community in an age of diversity. In J. M. Makau & R. C. Arnett (Eds.), *Communication ethics in an age of diversity* (pp. 27–47). Chicago: University of Illinois Press.

Bennett, M. J. (1998). Overcoming the Golden Rule: Sympathy and empathy. In M. J. Bennett (Ed.), *Basic concepts in intercultural communication: Selected readings* (pp. 191–214). Yarmouth, ME: Intercultural Press.

Broome, B. J. (1991). Building shared meaning: Implications of a relational approach to empathy for teaching intercultural communication. *Communication Education, 40,* 235–249.

———. (1993). Managing differences in conflict resolution: The role of relational empathy. In D. J. D. Sandole & H. van der Merwe (Eds.), *Conflict resolution theory and practice: Integration and application* (pp. 97–111). Manchester, England: Manchester University Press.

Chen, G. M., & Starosta, W. J. (1996). Intercultural communication competence: A synthesis. In B. R. Burleson (Ed.), *Communication yearbook, 19* (pp. 353–383). Thousand Oaks, CA: Sage.

Coeyman, M. (2001, October 16). The rush to rewrite history. *Christian Science Monitor.* http://www.csmonitor.com/2001/1016/p13s1-lekt.html.

Collier, M. J. (1988). A comparison of conversations among and between domestic culture groups: How intra- and intercultural competencies vary. *Communication Quarterly, 36,* 122–144.

———. (1998). Researching cultural identity: Reconciling interpretive and postcolonial perspectives. In D. V. Tanno & A. González (Eds.), *Communication and identity across cultures* (pp. 122–147). Thousand Oaks, CA: Sage.

———. (2002). Intercultural friendships as interpersonal alliances. In J. N. Martin, T. K. Nakayama, & L. A. Flores (Eds.), *Readings in intercultural communication: Experiences and contexts* (pp. 301–310). Boston: McGraw-Hill.

Cose, E. (1993). *The rage of a privileged class.* New York: HarperCollins.

Dace, K. L. (1994). Dissonance in European and African American communication. *The Western Journal of Black Studies, 18,* 18–26.

Deetz, S., Cohen, D., & Edley, P. P. (1997). Toward a dialogic ethic in the context of international business organization. In F. L. Casmir (Ed.), *Ethics in intercultural communication* (pp. 183–223). Mahwah, NJ: Lawrence Erlbaum.

Detweiler, R. A. (1980). Intercultural interaction and the categorization process: A conceptual analysis and behavioral outcome. *International Journal of Intercultural Relations, 4,* 275–295.

Hammer, M. R., Martin, J. N., Otani, M., & Koyama, M. (1990, March). *Analyzing intercultural competence: Evaluating communication skills of Japanese and American managers.* Paper presented at the First Annual Intercultural and International Communication Conference, California State University, Fullerton.

Henderson, H. (1999). *Forgiveness: Breaking the chain of hate.* Wilsonville, OR: BookPartners.

Howell, W. (1979). Theoretical directions in intercultural communication. In M. Asante, E. Newmark, & C. Blake (Eds.), *Handbook of intercultural communication.* Beverly Hills, CA: Sage.

Howell, W. S. (1982). *The empathic communicator.* Belmont, CA: Wadsworth.

Imahori, T., & Lanigan, M. L. (1989). Relational model of intercultural communication competence. *International Journal of Intercultural Relations, 13,* 269–286.

Kivel, P. (1996). *Uprooting racism: How White people can work for racial justice.* Gabriola Island, BC: New Society Publishers.

Koester, J., & Olebe, M. (1988). The behavioral assessment scale for intercultural communication effectiveness. *International Journal of Intercultural Relations, 12,* 233–246.

Martin, J. N., & Hammer, M. R. (1989). Behavioral categories of intercultural communication competence: Everyday communicators' perceptions. *International Journal of Intercultural Relations, 13,* 303–332.

Martin, J. N., Hammer, M. R., & Bradford, L. (1994). The influence of cultural and situational contexts on Hispanic and non-Hispanic communication competence behaviors. *Communication Quarterly, 42,* 160–179.

Maruyama, M. (1970). *Toward a cultural futurology.* Paper presented at the annual meeting of the American Anthropological Association, published by the Training Center for Community Programs, University of Minnesota, Minneapolis.

McCullough, M. W. (1998). *Black and White women as friends: Building cross-race friendships.* Cresskill, NJ: Hampton Press.

Monette, P. (1994). *Last watch of the night.* New York: Harcourt Brace.

Murphy, D. E. (2002, May 26). Beyond justice: The eternal struggle to forgive. *New York Times.*

Olebe, M., & Koester, J. (1989). Exploring the cross-cultural equivalence of the behavioral assessment scale for intercultural communication. *International Journal of Intercultural Relations, 13,* 333–347.

Rosen, S. L. (2000). Japan as other: Orientalism and cultural conflict. *Intercultural Communication, 4.* www.immi.se/intercultural.

Ruben, B. D. (1976). Assessing communication competency for intercultural adaptation. *Group and Organization Studies, 1,* 334–354.

———. (1977). Guidelines for cross cultural communication effectiveness. *Group and Organization Studies, 2,* 470–479.

Ruben, B. D., & Kealey, D. J. (1979). Behavioral assessment of communication competence and the prediction of cross-cultural adaptation. *International Journal of Intercultural Relations, 3,* 15–47.

Spitzberg, B. H., & Cupach, W. R. (1989). *Handbook of interpersonal communication competence research.* New York: Springer-Verlag.

Stewart, L. P. (1997). Facilitating connections: Issues of gender, culture, and diversity. In J. M. Makau & R. C. Arnett (Eds.), *Communication ethics in an age of diversity* (pp. 111–125). Chicago: University of Illinois Press.

Takaki, R. (1983). The making of a multiethnic working class in Hawaii. *Critical perspectives of Third World America, 1,* 151–163.

Tatum, B. (1997). *Why are all the Black kids sitting together in the cafeteria?* (pp. 193–206). New York: Basic Books.

Touraine, A., Dubet, F., Hegedus, Z., & Wieviorka, M. (1981). *Le pays contre l'État: Luttes occitanes.* Paris: Éditions du Seuil.

Wendt, J. (1984). D.I.E.: A way to improve communication. *Communication Education, 33,* 397–401.

Wiseman, R. L. (2002). Intercultural communication competence. In W. B. Gudykunst & B. Mody (Eds.), *Handbook of international and intercultural communication* (2nd ed., pp. 207–224). Thousand Oaks, CA: Sage.

Wood, J. T. (1997). Diversity in dialogue: Commonalities and differences between friends. In J. M. Makau & R. C. Arnett (Eds.), *Communication ethics in an age of diversity* (pp. 5–26). Chicago: University of Illinois Press.

Glossary

absent history Any part of history that was not recorded or that is missing. Not everything that happened in the past is accessible to us today, because only some voices were documented and only some perspectives were recorded.

activity dimension In semantics, the extent of alertness, liveliness, or energy that a word evokes. (See **evaluative dimension** and **potency dimension.**)

Afrocentricity An orientation toward African or African American cultural standards, including beliefs and values, as the criteria for interpreting behaviors and attitudes.

age identity The identification with the cultural conventions of how we should act, look, and behave according to our age.

Anglocentrism Using Anglo or White cultural standards as the criteria for interpretations and judgments of behaviors and attitudes.

apartheid A policy that segregated White and Black people in South Africa.

ascription The process by which others attribute identities to an individual.

assimilation A type of cultural adaptation in which an individual gives up his or her own cultural heritage and adopts the mainstream cultural identity. (See **cultural adaptation.**)

attitudes An individual's dispositions or mental sets. As a component of intercultural communication competence, attitudes include tolerance for ambiguity, empathy, and nonjudgmental-ness. (See also **tolerance for ambiguity, empathy,** and **nonjudgmental.**)

avoiding style A conflict management strategy characterized in U.S. cultural contexts by a low concern for the self and others. In some other cultural contexts, however, this strategy may be seen as tactical in maintaining harmonious relationships.

avowal The process by which an individual portrays him- or herself.

bilingual The ability to speak two languages fluently or at least competently.

chronemics The concept of time and the rules that govern its use.

class identity A sense of belonging to a group that shares similar economic, occupational, or social status.

co-cultural group Nondominant cultural groups that exist in a national culture, such as African American or Chinese American.

code switching A technical term in communication that refers to the phenomenon of changing languages, dialects, or even accents.

cognitive consistency Having a logical connection between existing knowledge and a new stimulus.

collectivistic The tendency to focus on the goals, needs, and views of the ingroup rather than individuals' own goals, needs, and views. (Compare with **individualistic.**)

colonial histories The histories that legitimate international invasions and annexations.

colonialism (a) The system by which groups with diverse languages, cultures, religions, and identities were

G-1

united to form one state, usually by European power; (b) the system by which a country maintains power over other countries or groups of people to exploit them economically, politically, and culturally.

communication   A symbolic process whereby reality is produced, maintained, repaired, and transformed.

communication accommodation theory   The view that individuals adjust their verbal communication to facilitate understanding.

communication ritual   A set form of systematic interactions that take place on a regular basis.

communication style   The metamessage that contextualizes how listeners are expected to accept and interpret verbal messages.

complementarity principle   A principle of relational attraction that suggests that sometimes we are attracted to people who are different from us.

compromise style   A style of interaction for an intercultural couple in which both partners give up some part of their own cultural habits and beliefs to minimize cross-cultural differences. (Compare with **consensus style, obliteration style,** and **submission style.**)

compromising style   A conflict management strategy that involves sharing and exchanging information to the extent that both individuals give up something to find a mutually acceptable decision.

conceptual equivalence   The similarity of linguistic terms and meanings across cultures. (See also **translation equivalence.**)

conflict   The interference between two or more interdependent individuals or groups of people who perceive incompatible goals, values, or expectations in attaining those ends.

confrontation   Direct resistance, often to the dominant forces.

conscious competence   One of four levels of intercultural communication competence, the practice of intentional, analytic thinking and learning.

conscious incompetence   One of four levels of intercultural communication competence, the awareness that one is not having success but the inability to figure out why.

consensus style   A style of interaction for an intercultural couple in which partners deal with cross-cultural differences by negotiating their relationship. (Compare with **compromise style, obliteration style,** and **submission style.**)

contact cultures   Cultural groups in which people tend to stand close together and touch frequently when they interact—for example, cultural groups in South America, the Middle East, and southern Europe. (See **noncontact cultures.**)

contact hypothesis   The notion that better communication between groups is facilitated simply by putting people together in the same place and allowing them to interact.

core symbols   The fundamental beliefs that are shared by the members of a cultural group. *Labels*, a category of core symbols, are names or markers used to classify individual, social, or cultural groups.

creole   The form of language that emerges when speakers of several languages are in long-lasting contact with each other; creole has characteristics of both languages.

critical approach   A metatheoretical approach that includes many assumptions of the interpretive approach but that focuses more on macrocontexts, such as the political and social structures that influence communication. (Compare with **interpretive approach** and **functionalist approach.**)

cross-cultural training   Training people to become familiar with other cultural norms and to improve their interactions with people of different domestic and international cultures.

cultural adaptation　A process by which individuals learn the rules and customs of new cultural contexts.

cultural-group histories　The history of each cultural group within a nation that includes, for example, the history of where the group originated, why the people migrated, and how they came to develop and maintain their cultural traits.

cultural imperialism　Domination through the spread of cultural products.

cultural space　The particular configuration of the communication that constructs meanings of various places.

cultural studies　Studies that focus on dynamic, everyday representations of cultural struggles. Cultural studies is multidisciplinary in nature and is committed to social change.

cultural texts　Cultural artifacts (magazines, TV programs, movies, and so on) that convey cultural norms, values, and beliefs.

cultural values　The worldview of a cultural group and its set of deeply held beliefs.

culture　Learned patterns of behavior and attitudes shared by a group of people.

culture brokers　Individuals who act as bridges between cultures, facilitating cross-cultural interaction and conflict.

culture industries　Industries that produce and sell popular culture as commodities.

culture shock　A relatively short-term feeling of disorientation and discomfort due to the lack of familiar cues in the environment.

deception　The act of making someone believe what is not true.

demographics　The characteristics of a population, especially as classified by age, sex, and income.

dialectic　(a) A method of logic based on the principle that an idea generates its opposite, leading to a reconciliation of the opposites; (b) the complex and paradoxical relationship between two opposite qualities or entities, each of which may also be referred to as a *dialectic.*

dialectical approach　An approach to intercultural communication that integrates three approaches—functionalist (or social science), interpretive, and critical—in understanding culture and communication. It recognizes and accepts that the three approaches are interconnected and sometimes contradictory.

dialogue　Conversation that is "slow, careful, full of feeling, respectful and attentive" (Wilmot & Hocker, 2001, p. 257).

diaspora　A massive migration often caused by war, famine, or persecution that results in the dispersal of a unified group.

diasporic histories　The histories of the ways in which international cultural groups were created through transnational migrations, slavery, religious crusades, or other historical forces.

D.I.E. exercise　A device that helps us determine if we are communicating at a descriptive, interpretive, or evaluative level. Only descriptive statements are nonjudgmental.

discourse　The ways in which language is actually used by particular communities of people, in particular contexts, for particular purposes.

discrimination　Behaviors resulting from stereotypes or prejudice that cause some people to be denied equal participation or rights based on cultural group membership, such as race.

distance zones　The area, defined by physical space, within which people interact, according to Edward Hall's theory of proxemics. The four distance zones for individuals are intimate, personal, social, and public. (See also **proxemics.**)

diversity   The quality of being different.

diversity training   The training meant to facilitate intercultural communication among various gender, ethnic, and racial groups in the United States.

dominating style   A conflict management strategy whereby an individual achieves his or her goal at the expense of others' needs.

electronic colonialism   Domination or exploitation utilizing technological forms.

emic   A term stemming from *phonemic.* The emic way of inquiry focuses on understanding communication patterns from inside a particular cultural community or context. (Compare with **etic.**)

empathy   The capacity to "walk in another person's shoes."

enclaves   (a) The territories that are surrounded by another country's territory; (b) cultural minority groups that live within a larger cultural group's territory.

equivalency   An issue in translation, the condition of being equal in meaning, value, quantity, and so on.

ethics   Principles of conduct that help govern behaviors of individuals and groups.

ethnic histories   The histories of ethnic groups.

ethnic identity   (a) A set of ideas about one's own ethnic group membership; (b) a sense of belonging to a particular group and knowing something about the shared experience of the group.

ethnocentrism   (a) An orientation toward one's own ethnic group; (b) a tendency to elevate one's own culture above others.

ethnography   A discipline that examines the patterned interactions and significant symbols of specific cultural groups to identify the cultural norms that guide their behaviors, usually based on field studies.

ethnography of communication   A specialized area of study within communication. Taking an interpretive perspective, scholars analyze verbal and nonverbal activities that have symbolic significance for the members of cultural groups to understand the rules and patterns followed by the groups. (See **interpretive approach.**)

etic   A term stemming from *phonetic.* The etic inquiry searches for universal generalizations across cultures from a distance. (Compare with **emic.**)

evaluative dimension   In semantics, the value-oriented associations of a word—whether the word has a good or bad meaning for us. (See **activity dimension** and **potency dimension.**)

explanatory uncertainty   In the process of cultural adaptation, uncertainty that stems from the inability to explain why people behave as they do. (See **cultural adaptation.**)

exploratory phase   The second phase of relational development, in which people try to discover commonalities in the other by seeking information about them. (See also **orientation phase** and **stability phase.**)

eye contact   A nonverbal code, eye gaze, that communicates meanings about respect and status and often regulates turn-taking during interactions.

facial expressions   Facial gestures that convey emotions and attitudes.

family histories   The body of knowledge shared by family members and the customs, rituals, and stories passed from one generation to another within a family.

field studies   Formal investigations conducted by researchers in the target culture. The purpose of field studies is to gain insiders' insights.

fight approach   A trial-and-error approach to coping with a new situation. (Compare with **flight approach.**)

flight approach   A strategy to cope with a new situation, being hesitant or withdrawn from the new environment. (Compare with **fight approach.**)

folk culture   Traditional and nonmainstream cultural activities that are not financially driven.

functional fitness   The ability to function in daily life in many different contexts.

functionalist approach   A study of intercultural communication, also called the *social science approach*, based on the assumptions that (1) there is a describable, external reality, (2) human behaviors are predictable, and (3) culture is a variable that can be measured. This approach aims to identify and explain cultural variations in communication and to predict future communication. (Compare with **critical approach** and **interpretive approach.**)

gender histories   The histories of how cultural conventions of men and women are created, maintained, and/or altered.

gender identity   The identification with the cultural notions of masculinity and femininity and what it means to be a man or a woman.

global nomads   People who grow up in many different cultural contexts because their parents relocated.

global village   A term coined by Marshall McLuhan in the 1960s that refers to a world in which communication technology unites people in remote parts of the world.

grand narrative   A unified history and view of humankind.

heterogeneity   Consisting of different or dissimilar elements.

hidden histories   The histories that are hidden from or forgotten by the mainstream representations of past events.

high-context communication   A style of communication in which much of the information is contained in the contexts and nonverbal cues rather than expressed explicitly in words. (Compare with **low-context communication.**)

high culture   The cultural activities that are considered elite, including opera, ballet, and symphony. (Compare with **low culture,** or **popular culture.**)

honorific   A term or expression that shows respect.

hyphenated Americans   U.S. Americans who identify not only with being U.S. citizens but also as members of ethnic groups.

identity   The concept of who we are. Characteristics of identity may be understood differently depending on the perspectives that people take—for example, social psychological, communication, or critical perspectives.

identity management   The way individuals make sense of their multiple images concerning the sense of self in different social contexts.

identity tourism   A concept that refers to people taking on the identities of other races, gender, classes, or sexual orientation for recreational purposes.

immigrants   People who come to a new country, region, or environment to settle more or less permanently. (Compare with **sojourners.**)

incompatibility   A state of incongruity in goals, values, or expectations between two or more individuals.

individualistic   The tendency to emphasize individual identities, beliefs, needs, goals, and views rather than those of the group. (Compare with **collectivistic.**)

integrating style   A conflict management strategy characterized by the open and direct exchange of information in an attempt to reach a solution acceptable to both parties.

integration   A type of cultural adaptation in which individuals maintain both their original culture and their daily interactions with other groups. (See also **cultural adaptation.**)

intellectual histories   Written histories that focus on the development of ideas.

intercultural alliances   Bonds between individuals or groups across cultures characterized by a shared recognition of power and the impact of history and by an orientation of affirmation.

intercultural communication   The interaction between people of different cultural backgrounds.

intercultural competence   The ability to behave effectively and appropriately in interacting across cultures.

intercultural conflict   Conflict between two or more cultural groups.

intercultural identity   Identity based on two or more cultural frames of reference.

intercultural relationships   Relationships that are formed between individuals from different cultures.

interdisciplinary   Integrating knowledge from different disciplines in conducting research and constructing theory.

interlanguage   A kind of communication that emerges when speakers of one language are speaking in another language. The native language's semantics, syntactics, pragmatics, phonetics, and language styles often overlap and create a third way of communicating.

intermediary   In a formal setting, a professional third party, such as a lawyer, real estate agent, or counselor, who intervenes when two parties are in conflict. Informal intermediaries may be friends or colleagues who intervene.

international conflicts   Conflicts between two or more nations.

International Phonetic Alphabet   An alphabet developed to help linguists transcribe the pronunciation of words in different languages.

interpellation   The communication process by which one is pulled into the social forces that place people into a specific identity.

interpretation   The process of verbally expressing what is said or written in another language.

interpretive approach   An approach to intercultural communication that aims to understand and describe human behavior within specific cultural groups based on the assumptions that (1) human experience is subjective, (2) human behavior is creative rather than determined or easily predicted, and (3) culture is created and maintained through communication. (Compare with **critical approach** and **functionalist approach.**)

intimacy   The extent of emotional closeness.

knowledge   As an individual component of intercultural communication competence, the quality of knowing about oneself (that is, one's strengths and weaknesses), others, and various aspects of communication.

la langue   The entire system of a language. (Compare with *la parole.*)

language acquisition   The process of learning language.

language policies   Laws or customs that determine which language will be spoken, when and where.

la parole   In linguistics or semiotics, a term that means discourse or language in use. (Compare with *la langue.*)

lingua franca   A commonly shared language that is used as a medium of communication between people of different languages.

linguistic knowledge   Knowledge of other languages besides one's native language or of the difficulty of learning a second or third language.

long-term refugees   People who are forced to relocate permanently because of war, famine, and oppression.

long-term versus short-term orientation   A cultural variability dimension that reflects a cultural-group orientation toward virtue or truth. The long-term orientation emphasizes virtue whereas the short-term orientation emphasizes truth.

low-context communication A style of communication in which much of the information is conveyed in words rather than in nonverbal cues and contexts. (Compare with **high-context communication.**)

low culture The non-elite activities seen as the opposite of high culture—for example, movies, rock music, and talk shows. In the past, low culture was considered unworthy of serious study. With the rise of cultural studies, however, the activities that are associated with low culture have become important representations of everyday human lives. (Compare with **high culture.** See also **popular culture.**)

macrocontexts The political, social, and historical situations, backgrounds, and environments that influence communication.

majority identity A sense of belonging to a dominant group.

maquiladoras Assembly plants or factories (mainly of U.S. companies) established on the U.S.-Mexican border and using mainly Mexican labor.

marginalization A type of cultural adaptation in which an individual expresses little interest in maintaining cultural ties with either the dominant culture or the migrant culture. (See **cultural adaptation.**)

masculinity/femininity value A cultural variability dimension that concerns the degree of being feminine—valuing fluid gender roles, quality of life, service, relationships, and interdependence—and the degree of being masculine—emphasizing distinctive gender roles, ambition, materialism, and independence.

media imperialism Domination or control through media.

mediation The act of resolving conflict by having someone intervene between two parties.

melting pot A metaphor that assumes that immigrants and cultural minorities will be assimilated into the U.S. majority culture, losing their original cultures.

metamessage The meaning of a message that tells others how they should respond to the content of our communication based on our relationship to them; also known as *tonal coloring.*

metaphors Figures of speech that contain implied comparisons, in which a word or a phrase ordinarily and primarily used for one thing is applied to another.

migrant An individual who leaves the primary cultural context in which he or she was raised and moves to a new cultural context for an extended time. (See also **immigrant** and **sojourner.**)

minority identity A sense of belonging to a nondominant group.

mobility The state of moving from place to place.

model minority A positive stereotype that characterizes all Asians and Asian Americans as hardworking and serious and so a "good" minority.

modernist identity The identity that is grounded in the Western tradition of scientific and political beliefs and assumptions—for example, the belief in external reality, democratic representation, liberation, and independent subjects.

motivation As an individual component of intercultural communication competence, the desire to make a commitment in relationships, to learn about the self and others, and to remain flexible.

multicultural identity A sense of in-betweenness that develops as a result of frequent or multiple cultural border crossings.

multilingual The ability to speak more than two languages fluently or at least competently.

multinational corporations Companies that have operations in two or more nations.

multiphrenia The splitting of the individual psychologically into multiple selves.

myths (a) Theories or stories that are widely understood and believed; (b) in semiotics, the layers of meaning beneath a signifier. (See **semiotics, signified,** and **signifier.**)

national history A body of knowledge based on past events that influenced a country's development.

national identity National citizenship.

nativistic Extremely patriotic to the point of being anti-immigrant.

nominalist position The view that perception is not shaped by the particular language one speaks. (Compare with **relativist position** and **qualified relativist position.**)

noncontact cultures Cultural groups in which people tend to maintain more space and touch less often than people do in contact cultures. For instance, Great Britain and Japan tend to have noncontact cultures. (See **contact cultures.**)

nonjudgmental Free from evaluating according to one's own cultural frame of reference.

norms The rules that people follow or the standards to which they adhere as members of a culture.

obliging style A conflict management strategy characterized by playing down differences and incompatibilities while emphasizing commonalities.

obliteration style A style of interaction for an intercultural couple in which both partners attempt to erase their individual cultures in dealing with cultural differences. (Compare with **compromise style, consensus style,** and **submission style.**)

orientation phase The first phase of relational development in which people use categorical or noninterpersonal information, including social role, age, and similarity to others. (See also **exploratory phase** and **stability phase.**)

pacifism Opposition to the use of force under any circumstances.

paradigm A framework that serves as the worldview of researchers. Different paradigms assume different interpretations of reality, human behavior, culture, and communication.

perception The process by which individuals select, organize, and interpret external and internal stimuli to create their view of the world.

performative Acting or presenting oneself in a specific way so as to accomplish some goal.

phonetics The study of the sound system of a language.

pidgin A mixed language incorporating the vocabulary of one or more languages, having a very simplified form of the grammatical system of one of these, and not used as the main language of any of its speakers.

political histories Written histories that focus on political events.

popular culture A new name for *low culture*, referring to those systems or artifacts that most people share and that most people know about, including television, music, videos, and popular magazines.

postcolonialism An intellectual, political, and cultural movement that calls for the independence of colonialized states and also liberation from colonialist ways of thinking.

postmodern cultural spaces Places that are defined by cultural practices—languages spoken, identities enacted, rituals performed—and that often change as new people move in and out of these spaces.

potency dimension In semantics, the degree to which a word evokes a strong or weak reaction. (See **activity dimension** and **evaluative dimension.**)

power distance A cultural variability dimension that concerns the extent to which people accept an unequal distribution of power.

pragmatics The study of how meaning is constructed in relation to receivers and how language is actually used in particular contexts in language communities.

predictive uncertainty A sense of uncertainty that stems from the inability to predict what someone will say or do.

prejudice An attitude (usually negative) toward a cultural group based on little or no evidence.

processual Refers to how interaction happens rather than to the outcome.

proxemics The study of how people use personal space.

proximity principle A principle of relational attraction suggesting that individuals tend to develop relationships with people with whom they are in close contact.

psychological health The state of being emotionally comfortable in a cultural context.

qualified relativist position A moderate view of the relationship between language and perception. This position sees language as a tool rather than a prison. (Compare with **nominalist position** and **relativist position.**)

qualitative methods Research methods that attempt to capture people's own meanings for their everyday behavior in specific contexts. These methods use participant observation and field studies.

quantitative methods Research methods that employ numerical indicators to capture and ascertain the relationships among variables. These methods use survey and observation.

quanxi A Chinese term for relational network.

racial histories The histories of non-mainstream racial groups.

racial identity Identifying with a particular racial group. Although in the past racial groups were classified on the basis of biological characteristics, most scientists now recognize that race is constructed in fluid social and historical contexts.

reader profiles Portrayals of readership demographics prepared by magazines.

regional identity Identification with a specific geographic region of a nation.

regionalism Loyalty to a particular region that holds significant cultural meaning for that person.

relational learning Learning that comes from a particular relationship but generalizes to other contexts.

relational messages Messages (verbal and nonverbal) that communicate how we feel about others.

relativist position The view that the particular language individuals speak, especially the structure of the language, shapes their perception of reality and cultural patterns. (Compare with **nominalist position** and **qualified relativist position.**)

religious identity A sense of belonging to a religious group.

rhetorical approach A research method, dating back to ancient Greece, in which scholars try to interpret the meanings or persuasion used in texts or oral discourses in the contexts in which they occur.

romantic relationships Intimate relationships that comprise love, involvement, sharing, openness, connectedness, and so on.

Sapir-Whorf hypothesis The assumption that language shapes our ideas and guides our view of social reality. This hypothesis was proposed by Edward Sapir, a linguist, and his student, Benjamin Whorf, and represents the relativist view of language and perception. (See **relativist position.**)

segregation The policy or practice of compelling groups to live apart from each other.

self-disclosure Revealing information about oneself.

self-knowledge Related to intercultural communication competence, the quality of knowing how one is perceived as a communicator, as well as one's strengths and weaknesses.

self-reflexivity A process of learning to understand oneself and one's position in society.

semantic differential A way of measuring the attitude or affective meaning of a word, based on three dimensions—value, potency, and activity. (See **activity dimension, evaluative dimension,** and **potency dimension.**)

semantics The study of words and meanings.

semiosis The process of producing meaning.

semiotics The analysis of the nature of and relationships between signs in language.

separation A type of cultural adaptation in which an individual retains his or her original culture while interacting minimally with other groups. Separation may be voluntary, or it may be initiated and enforced by the dominant society, in which case it becomes segregation.

sexual orientation histories The historical experiences of gays and lesbians.

short-term refugees People who were forced for a short time to move from their region or country.

short-term versus long-term orientation See **long-term versus short-term orientation.**

signified In semiotics, anything that is expressed in arbitrary words, or signifiers. (See **semiotics** and **signifiers.**)

signifiers In semiotics, the culturally constructed, arbitrary words or symbols that people use to refer to something else. (See **semiotics.**)

signs In semiotics, the meanings that emerge from the combination of signifiers and signifieds. (See **semiotics, signified,** and **signifiers.**)

similarity principle A principle of relational attraction suggesting that individuals tend to be attracted to people whom they perceive to be similar to themselves.

social conflict Conflict that arises from unequal or unjust social relationships between groups.

social histories Written histories that focus on everyday life experiences of various groups in the past.

social movements Organized activities in which individuals work together to bring about social change.

social positions The places from which people speak that are socially constructed and thus embedded with assumptions about gender, race, class, age, social roles, sexuality, and so on.

social reproduction The process of perpetuating cultural patterns.

social science approach See **functionalist approach.**

sojourners People who move into new cultural contexts for a limited period of time and for a specific purpose, such as for study or business.

source text The original language text of a translation. (See also **target text.**)

stability phase The last phase of relational development, in which interactions are more intense and active, and conversations have more depth and breadth. (See also **orientation phase** and **exploratory phase.**)

status The relative position an individual holds in social or organizational settings.

stereotypes Widely held beliefs about a group of people.

submission style A style of interaction for an intercultural couple in which one partner yields to the other partner's cultural patterns, abandoning or denying his or her own culture. (Compare with **compromise style, consensus style,** and **obliteration style.**)

symbolic significance   The importance or meaning that most members of a cultural group attach to a communication activity.

syntactics   The study of the structure, or grammar, of a language.

target text   The new language text into which the original language text is translated. (See also **source text.**)

textual analysis   Examination of cultural texts such as media—TV, movies, journalistic essays, and so on.

tolerance for ambiguity   The ease with which an individual copes with situations in which a great deal is unknown.

tonal coloring   See **metamessage.**

translation   The process of producing a written text that refers to something said or written in another language.

translation equivalence   The linguistic sameness that is gained after translating and back-translating research materials several times using different translators. (See also **conceptual equivalence.**)

transnationalism   The activity of migrating across the borders of one or more nation-states.

transpection   Cross-cultural empathy.

U-curve theory   A theory of cultural adaptation positing that migrants go through fairly predictable phases—

excitement/anticipation, shock/disorientation, adaptation—in adapting to a new cultural situation.

uncertainty avoidance   A cultural variability dimension that concerns the extent to which uncertainty, ambiguity, and deviant ideas and behaviors are avoided.

uncertainty reduction   The process of lessening uncertainty in adapting to a new culture by seeking information.

unconscious competence   One of four levels of intercultural communication competence, the level at which an individual is attitudinally and cognitively prepared but lets go of conscious thought and relies on holistic cognitive processing.

unconscious incompetence   One of four levels of intercultural communication competence, the "be yourself" level at which there is no consciousness of differences or need to act in any particular way.

variable   A concept that varies by existing in different types or different amounts and that can be operationalized and measured.

W-curve theory   A theory of cultural adaptation that suggests that sojourners experience another U-curve upon returning home. (See **U-curve theory** and **sojourners.**)

worldview   Underlying assumptions about the nature of reality and human behavior.

Credits

TEXT

Chapter 1 Page 13, from http://www.prb.org/AmeristatTemplate.cfm?Section=Estimates, "Changing American Pie," *Popular Reference Bureau*, www.amerstat.org. Used by permission; Page 15, from Bernardo M. Ferdman, "Supreme Court Shows Pitfalls in Doing Right Thing," *Sunday Times Union*, September 17, 1989. Used by permission of the publisher; Page 18, from Craig Ray, "The Potential of Immigrants," *Nations Business*, August, 1998; Page 20, from Eric Schmitt, "Analysis of Census Finds Segregation along with Diversity," *The New York Times*, April 3, 2001. Used by permission of the publisher; Page 26, from Jennifer Sharples, "A Cross-Cultural Conundrum," *Bangkok Post Sunday Magazine*, May 28–June 3, 1995. Used by permission of the author; Page 30, from Ben Feinberg, "What Students Don't Learn Abroad," *The Chronicle Review*, May 3, 2002. Used by permission of the author;   **Chapter 2** Page 45, from Rachel L. Swarns, "France Returns Old Remains to Homeland," *The Arizona Republic*, May 5, 2002. Used with permission; Page 47, from Paul Levinson, "Images of Unmediated Ugliness," *The Chronicle Review*, September 28, 2001. Used by permission of the author; Page 50, from Richard Winton, "Hate Crimes Soar Following Attacks," *Los Angeles Times*, December 21, 2001. Copyright © 2001, *Los Angeles Times*. Reprinted with permission; Page 54, from Alan M. Dershowitz, "Preserving Civil Liberties," *The Chronicle Review*, September 28, 2001. Used by permission of the author; Page 54, from Jeane Kirkpatrick, "The Case for Force," *The Chronicle Review*, September 28, 2001. Used by permission of the author; Page 54, from Catherine Lutz, "Our Legacy of War," *The Chronicle Review*, September 28, 2001. Used by permission of the author; Page 66, from Robin Marantz Henig, "Genetic Misunderstandings: The Linking of Jews With Cancer Is an Accident of Science and How Ethnic Groups Are Studied," *Washington Post National Weekly Edition*, October 13, 1997. Copyright © 1997 Robin Marantz Henig. Reprinted by permission of the author;   **Chapter 3** Page 101, from bell hooks, "Black Is a Woman's Color," *Callaloo*, 12:2 (Spring 1989). Copyright © 1989 The Johns Hopkins University Press. Reprinted by permission of the publisher; Page 105, from Natchee Blu Barnd, "Test of American Cultural Intelligence," *Intercultural Center*. Used by permission of the author;   **Chapter 4** Page 120, from *Encyclopedia of Japanese-American History* edited by Brian Niiya. Copyright © 2001, 1993 by The Japanese American National Museum. Reprinted by permission of Facts On File, Inc.; Page 122, by Sasha Polakow-Suransky, "Reviving South African History," originally published in *The Chronicle of Higher Education*, June 14, 2002. Used by permission of the author; Page 124, from Beata Pasek, "Auschwitz Haunts Town," *The Arizona Republic*, June 9, 2002. Used with permission; Page 127, from Anne-Marie O'Connor, "Mexico, Ireland Recall Immigrant Tale of Divided Loyalties." Copyright © 1997 *Los Angeles Times*. Reprinted with permission; Page 132, from Candace Piette, "American Thriving in Brazil: Confederates' Descendants Cherish Town's Links to Past," *The Arizona Republic*, December 7, 1997. Used with permission; Page 135, Parker Johnson, "Eliminating Racism as a Social Disease," *Hanover Evening Sun*, October 21, 1995. Used with permission; Page 136, from Mark Shaffer, "Navajos Protest National Status for Old Spanish Trail," *The Arizona Republic*, June 9, 2002. Used with permission; Page 140, from Geeta Kothari, "Where Are You

From?" Copyright © 1994 Geeta Kothari. Used by permission of the author; **Chapter 5** Page 161, from "AAA Recommends 'Race' Be Scrapped; Suggests New Government Categories." Press Release/OMB15. Originally published Sept. 8, 1997 by *The American Anthropological Association;* Page 168, from "'Fighting Whities' mock School's Indian Mascot," *The Arizona Republic,* March 11, 2002. Reprinted with permission of The Associated Press; Page 174, from Martha Irvine, "Dolls Getting More Racially Diverse," *Pittsburgh Tribune-Review,* February 20, 2002. Reprinted with permission of The Associated Press; Page 176, from the film "The Color of Fear," 1993. Used with permission from Stir-Fry Seminars and Consulting, 470 3rd Street, Oakland, CA 94607, 1-800-370-7847; Page 180, from Richard Morin, "Misperceptions Cloud Whites' View of Blacks," *The Washington Post,* July, 11, 2001. Copyright © 2001 *The Washington Post.* Reprinted with permission; Page 181, from Richard Morin, "Across the Racial Divide," *The Washington Post National Weekly Edition,* October 16–22, 1995. Copyright © 1995 *The Washington Post;* Page 184, from David Harris, "The Multiracial Count, " *The Washington Post,* March 24, 2001. Used by permission of the author; **Chapter 6** Page 203, from Michael Specter, "The Rich Idioms of Russian: Verbal Soul Food of a Culture," *The New York Times,* August 20, 1995. Copyright © 1995 *The New York Times.* Used with permission of the publisher; Page 205, used with permission of Cristina Gonzalez; Page 214, from Jonathan Petre and Catherine Elsworth, "McDonald to Tackle Language Failure," *The Sunday Telegraph,* March 22, 1998. Copyright © 1998 Telegraph Group Limited, London. Reprinted by permission of the publisher; Page 218, from Mel Melendez, "Police Try to Connect, Reach out in Spanish," *The Arizona Republic,* April 7, 2002. Used with permission; Page 219, used with permission of Laura Laguna; Page 221, from Laurel J. Delaney, Founder, *Chicago-Based Globe-Trade.com* (http://globetrade.com) which helps entrepreneurs and small businesses go global. She can be reached at idelaney@globetrade.com; Page 223, from Robert Yampolsky, "The Written Word," *Japan Times,* January 29, 1999. Used with permission; Page 228, from Harumi Befu, "English Language Intellectual Imperialism and Its Consequences," *Newsletter: Intercultural Communication,* June 2000. Used by permission of the author; **Chapter 7** Page 251, from Donald P. Baker, "Waving the Past in the Future's Face," *Washington Post National Weekly Edition,* October 13, 1997. Copyright © 1997 *The Washington Post.* Reprinted with permission; Page 254, from Elisabeth Marx © *Breaking through Culture Shock: What You Need to Succeed in International Business.* Reprinted with permission of Nicholas Brealey Publishing, London. Copyright © 1999; **Chapter 8** Page 265, "Brain Drain Reportedly Costing $4 Billion a Year," http://allafrica.com/stories/printable/200204300167.html, April 30, 2002. Copyright © 2002 *Intergrated Regional Information Networks.* UN Disclaimer: The above article was written by the UN humanitarian information unit IRIN, but may not necessarily reflect the views of the United Nations. For further information or a free subscription contact IRIN@ocha.unon.org or http://www.irinnews.org. Used by permission; Pages 268, 274 "Life as An Alien." Copyright © 1998 by Meri Nana-Ama Danquah, from *Half and Half* by Claudine Chiawei O'Hearn. Copyright © 1998 by Claudine Chiawei O'Hearn. Used by permission of *Pantheon Books,* a division of Random House, Inc.; Page 269, from Tim Vanderpool, "Lesson No. 1: Shed Your Indian Identity," *The Christian Science Monitor Publishing Society,* April 2, 2002. Used by permission of the author; Page 271, from Carmen Guanipa, "How to Fight Culture Shock," *Amigos* Website, http://edweb.sdsu.edu/people/cguanipa/cultshok.htm. Used by permission of the author; Page 276, from Joel Swerdlow, "Changing America," *National Geographic,* September, 2001. Used by permission of the publisher; Page 283, from Kevin Sullivan, "'White Australia' in Identity Crisis: Many Fear Asian Immigrants Are Taking Away Jobs, Culture," *The Washington Post,* December 6, 1997. Reprinted with permission; Page 294, from Craig Stori, "The Art of Coming Home." Copyright © 2001 *Nicholas Brealey Publishing and Intercultural Press, Inc.* Reprinted by permission of the publisher; Page 296, from "To Live in the Borderlands Means You," *Borderlands/La Frontera: The New Mestiza.* Copyright © 1987, 1999 by Gloria Anzaldúa. Reprinted by permission of Aunt Lute Books; **Chapter 9** Page 310, "Drawing of the Encoding/Decoding Model." Reprinted by permission of *Sage Publishing Ltd.* from Liesbet van

PHOTOS

Name Index

Subject Index